The Sociology of Elites
Volume II

Schools of Thought in Sociology

Series Editor: John Urry
Professor of Sociology
Lancaster University

Future titles will include:

Positivist Sociology
Peter Halfpenny

Psychoanalytic Sociology
M Rustin and J Praeger

For greater convenience, a cumulative index to all titles in this series will be published in a separate volume.

The Sociology of Elites Volume II

Critical Perspectives

Edited by

John Scott

Reader in Sociology
University of Leicester

An Elgar Reference Collection

Published by
Edward Elgar Publishing Limited
Gower House
Croft Road
Aldershot
Hants GU11 3HR
England

Edward Elgar Publishing Company
Old Post Road
Brookfield
Vermont 05036
USA

British Library Cataloguing in Publication Data
The sociology of elites. – (Schools of thought in
   sociology;1).
   1. Sociology
   I. Scott, John   II. Series
   301

   ISBN 1-85278-170-X (set of 3 volumes)
   ISBN 1-85278-390-7 v.1
   ISBN 1-85278-391-5 v.2
   ISBN 1-85278-392-3 v.3

Printed in Great Britain by Galliard (Printers) Ltd, Great Yarmouth

Contents

Acknowledgements

The editor and publishers wish to thank the following who have kindly given permission for the use of copyright material.

American Economic Association for article: R.J. Larner (1966), 'Ownership and Control in the 200 Largest Nonfinancial Corporations, 1929 and 1963', *American Economic Review*, **56**, 777–87.

Center for Social Research and Education for articles: R. Fitch and M. Oppenheimer (1970), 'Who Rules the Corporations?', *Socialist Revolution*, **1** (4), 73–108; (5), 61–114; (6), 33–94; J. O'Connor (1971), 'Question: Who Rules the Corporations? Answer: The Ruling Class', *Socialist Revolution*, **7**, 117–50; R. Fitch (1971), 'Reply to James O'Connor', *Socialist Revolution*, **7**, 150–70; P. Sweezy (1971), 'The Resurgence of Financial Control: Fact or Fancy?', *Socialist Revolution*, **2** (2), 157–90; R. Fitch (1972), 'Sweezy and Corporate Fetishism', *Socialist Revolution*, **3** (4), 93–127.

John Wiley & Sons, Inc. for articles: G.C. Means (1930), 'The Diffusion of Stock Ownership in the United States', *Quarterly Journal of Economics*, **44**, August, 561–600; R.A. Gordon (1936), 'Stockholdings of Officers and Directors in American Industrial Corporations', *Quarterly Journal of Economics*, **50**, 622–55; R.A. Gordon (1938), 'Ownership by Management and Control Groups in the Large Corporation', *Quarterly Journal of Economics*, **52**, August, 367–400.

British Sociological Association for articles: J. Scott and M. Hughes (1976), 'Ownership and Control in a Satellite Economy: A Discussion from Scottish Data', *Sociology*, **10** (1), 21–41; A. Francis (1980), 'Families, Firms and Finance Capital: The Development of UK Industrial Firms with Particular Reference to Their Ownership and Control', *Sociology*, **14** (1), 1–27.

Shoken Keizai for articles: H. Okumura (1984), 'Enterprise Groups in Japan', *Shoken Keizai*, **147**, 160–89; J. Scott (1987), 'Intercorporate Structure in Britain, the United States and Japan', *Shoken Keizai*, **160**, June, 51–64.

University of Chicago Press for articles: M. Zeitlin (1974), 'Corporate Ownership and Control: The Large Corporation and the Capitalist Class', *American Journal of Sociology*, **79** (5), 1073–119; M.P. Allen (1976), 'Management Control in the Large Corporation: Comment on Zeitlin', *American Journal of Sociology*, **81** (4), 885–94; M. Zeitlin (1976), 'On Class

Theory of the Large Corporation: Reply to Allen', *American Journal of Sociology*, **81**, 894–903.

Every effort has been made to trace all the copyright holders but if any have been inadvertently overlooked the publishers will be pleased to make the necessary arrangement at the first opportunity.

In addition the publishers wish to thank the Library of the London School of Economics and Political Science and the Librarian and Staff at the Alfred Marshall Library, Cambridge University for their assistance in obtaining these articles.

Introduction

The introduction to Volume I of this collection discussed the origins of modern studies of elites in the 'Machiavellian' tradition of elite analysis, the tradition of Pareto and Mosca.[1] The concept of 'elite' was formulated as the basis of a theoretical alternative to the conventional Marxian theory of class. Marx and orthodox Marxist writers saw class as an economic concept, rooted in the ownership and control of the means of production. Those who dominated the economy also dominate the cultural sphere and the exercise of political power. The Marxian concept of the ruling class expressed this fusion of economic, cultural and political power. The Machiavellian writers rejected what they saw as the economic determinism of this approach, seeking to stress the autonomy of political power through their usage of such terms as 'governing elite', (Pareto) and 'political class' (Mosca). This volume pursues these issues further by considering the implications of elite analysis for the study of the capitalist class and business power. The key figure in this area is, undoubtedly, James Burnham.

Burnham, who invented the term 'Machiavellian' to describe this tradition of thought, was also a major contributor to its development. A former Marxist, he sought to confront Marxism on its own heartland of the analysis of control over the means of production.[2] His aim was to show that the capitalist ruling class was but one of many elites – he used the term 'ruling classes' – which have achieved power in the course of human history. He traced the rise of the class of managers, which would struggle with and displace the capitalist elite and become the new ruling class of modern society. The circulation of elites described by Pareto was depicted in its contemporary manifestation as a 'managerial revolution'.

Burnham's position is a particularly sophisticated expression of the Machiavellian tradition of elite theory and, despite some of its more extravagant claims, it has had a considerable influence on theoretical and empirical analyses of business organization and class structure. Indeed, the central tenet of his position – that 'capitalists' are being replaced by 'managers' – has become part of the taken-for-granted orthodoxy of modern sociology, politics and economics. Burnham's work has, without exaggeration, set the research agenda for modern writing on economic elites and business power. Even those who reject his specific claims have pursued the same questions that motivated his work.

Burnham and the Managerial Revolution

Burnham's starting point is that 'control' is more fundamental than 'ownership': private property is only one possible basis for control over the means of production. Control in the economic sphere consists of the power to determine *access* to the means of production and the ability to secure an advantaged position in the *distribution* of the benefits from their use. This control is, in its turn, simply one facet of the total control over all aspects of a society's operations which the ruling classes of history have achieved. The ruling class is a truly controlling elite.

It is Burnham's specific views on the changes in patterns of control in the economy which have had the greatest influence on subsequent writers, and it is to these ideas that greatest attention must be given. Central to this aspect of Burnham's argument is the claim that *de facto* management of the instruments of production has got out of the hands of the controlling capitalists and into the hands of the technically qualified managers, who, alone, have the skills and knowledge necessary to operate them. It is the increasing technical complexity of the means of production which is the basis of managerial power. But the technical qualifications possessed by the top managers are not in science and engineering – though some may, of course, possess these – they are the skills of direction, organization and coordination described by such management analysts as Taylor and Fayol.[3]

Technical changes in industry, argues Burnham, have resulted in a process of role differentiation. The role of the capitalist entrepreneur of the nineteenth century combined three distinct elements, which have gradually become separated from one another. The entrepreneur combined *the provision of capital, planning for profitability*, and *technical coordination*. These three elements have increasingly been differentiated into the roles of, respectively, the *shareholder*, the *financial executive*, and the *manager*. These three players on the economic field have been joined, in the latest stage of capitalist development, by the *finance capitalists* whose role is to centralize the funds of individual shareholders and make them available to industry through the investment and banking system. It is the struggle for power between these groups, argues Burnham, which is central to the economic process, and it is, furthermore, a struggle which will be won by the managers.

Shareholders, even those who retain a majority of the shares in a particular enterprise, generally take a passive stance towards their businesses, and so are uninvolved in the technical process of production. Similarly, Burnham sees the finance capitalists, whose power depends on minority shareholdings, proxies, and loans, as marginal to actual production. While financial executives are more closely linked to the day-to-day production of goods, their concern is with the production of *profits*, and so their fate is linked to that of the shareholder and the finance capitalist. All four groups have common interests in the means of production, but there is a fundamental conflict of interest between managers and the others. Whereas shareholders, finance capitalists and finance executives are dependent on the maintenance of capitalist private property, managers are not. It is only the managers whose fate is allied with the inexorable increase in the complexity of the technology of production, all the other groups are tied to the framework of private property and profit-making which is passing away.

Managers find their control over access to the means of production constantly increasing, though the capitalists continue to monopolize the rewards generated by the system. There is, therefore, a partial separation of control over access to the means of production from preferential treatment in the distribution of the benefits of production. The position of managers will continue to improve, even within the framework of capitalist private property, as capitalists become increasingly superfluous and managers become increasingly indispensable.

Burnham draws on the earlier empirical work of Berle and Means[4] to substantiate this argument. These writers argued that the modern business enterprise operated on such a scale that it had to draw on ever larger pools of capital. No individual or family was in a position to meet the needs of such enterprises in full, and so more and more capital had to be subscribed by an anonymous mass of small shareholders mobilized through the stock exchange system. As a result, individual capitalists began to lose control of their enterprises: they simply held too small a proportion of the shares to have any significant impact on decision making. In the 'power vacuum' created, managers could grasp the control that formerly rested with private shareholders.[5] Burnham adds to this argument the claim that the rise of managers is reinforced by the voluntary withdrawal of capitalists. Finance capitalists and wealthy shareholders, he argues, have increasingly preferred a life of 'leisure' and participation in 'Society' to the daily grind of making money. The capitalist pursuit of leisure, therefore, enhances the power of managers.

The wider thesis of the managerial revolution, as formulated by Burnham, adds that the full flowering of managerial dominance will come only with the final abolition of private property and its replacement by state property, though this aspect of his argument has been far less influential than his narrower thesis. The managers are the agents of an evolving system of state ownership, which will form the basis of their dominance as a new 'ruling class'. Wherever state property predominates, individual shareholders and finance capitalists, together with their subordinate finance executives, are finally rendered redundant and the technically indispensable managers are able to consolidate their position. Writing in the 1940s, Burnham felt that this had been achieved only in the Soviet Union, Fascist Italy and Nazi Germany. In Britain and the United States, he argued, the finance capitalists and their associates remained the ultimate ruling class and could exercise 'veto rights' over management decisions on crucial occasions.[6] The managerial revolution will succeed in these countries, however, because the dislocations and inefficiencies of the stagnating capitalist system force governments to move from the 'limited state' to the more regulated economy of the 'unlimited managerial state'.

The core of Burnham's argument, which has set the agenda for research on business power, centres on the question of the changing social basis of an economic elite. The shift from capitalist to managerial dominance is seen as a circulation of elites, or of 'ruling classes', within the economy which has important implications for the overall distribution of power in society. This introduction will review the works of managerialist writers and of Marxist and radical writers who have, in varying ways, tried to confront Burnham's ideas.

Modern Managerialism

While the arguments of modern managerialist theory derive, ultimately, from the work of Burnham, they draw also on the contributions of such writers as Veblen and, above all, Berle and Means. As a result, there are a number of distinct strands of managerialist thought.[7] The mainstream of empirical research has remained close to the arguments of Berle and Means, though a number of more simplified accounts rely heavily on Burnham.[8]

What might be termed *classical managerialism* is that position which remains closest to Berle and Means. This position holds that the legal innovation of the joint stock company is of decisive significance in leading to the demise of the capitalist class and the rise of a new class of managers.[9] There is a 'dissolution' of the traditional rights of property, whereby the 'passive' rights of the investor to receive an income becomes separated from the 'active' rights of control which are vested in the company itself. Furthermore, the dispersal and dilution of shareholdings which occurs as enterprises increase in size effectively eliminates individual shareholders from any participation in this control. As their shareholding passes from complete ownership through a majority holding to a mere minority stake, so their power declines. Ultimately, when they hold no more than a few per cent, at most, they become completely powerless.

Recent strands within managerialist theory have departed from some aspects of this argument, recognizing certain crucial changes in the structure of shareholding which have occurred since the 1930s. Increasing numbers of shares have passed from the hands of individuals to those of financial institutions, such as banks, insurance companies, and pension funds. As a result there has been a reversal of the trend towards share dispersal, which was central to the argument of Berle and Means. Instead, shareholdings have become increasingly concentrated. This rise in 'institutional shareholding' was unforseen by Burnham, and barely recognized by Berle and Means, and its significance for power within business has been much disputed.

Modern managerialists such as Herman[10] have argued that the institutions have become an increasingly important constraint upon managerial autonomy. Managers are unable to completely ignore the interests of shareholders, as held by classical managerialism, as the leading shareholders are not isolated members of an anonymous mass of individuals, but are aggressive and powerful institutions. Herman, therefore, speaks of 'constrained management control', as characteristic of the modern economy. This position, therefore, advances beyond the earlier arguments in recognizing that the rise of a managerial 'elite' may not be quite the clear-cut process depicted by Burnham and classical managerialism. The managerial 'elite' may be constrained by the continuing impact of capitalist interests.

A third strand within managerialist theory, however, argues that the rise of the institutions is the basis of the final demise of the capitalist class. This theory of *pension fund socialism* or *post-capitalism* sees managers running large enterprises in the collective interest of the wider society. Peter Drucker,[11] for example, argues that the institutions are not capitalist enterprises but operate in the interests of the mass of the population who provide the capital for them: insurance companies operate in the interests of those they insure, and pension funds operate in the interests of their contributors and current pensioners. Far from being the agents of capitalist renewal, argues Drucker, the institutions are the instruments of popular control by managers. A related position has been put forward in Japan by Tadanori Nishiyama,[12] who holds that the growth of intercorporate shareholdings, and especially of the institutional holdings, has, in Japan, liberated enterprises from capitalist control and has resulted in the development of a non-socialist form of post-capitalism. Japan, he argues, no longer has any class divisions. It is a one-class society in which the managers run the economy in the interests of all, and all other capitalist societies will evolve in the same direction.

Marxist and Critical Theories

While the mainstream of Marxism has restated the claims of class analysis against the more extreme formulations of the thesis of the managerial revolution, a number of Marxists have attempted to confront Machiavellian and managerialist writers by refining and elaborating the concepts of Marxian theory. Some have accepted the thesis of the displacement of capitalist entrepreneurs by a managerial elite, but have argued that this, paradoxically, strengthens the dominance of capitalist relations of production. Others have argued, instead, that changes in the structure of the capitalist class have produced a small elite of finance capitalists which now dominates the economy.

The *Marxist managerialism* of Baran and Sweezy[13] has remained rather close to managerialist theory. This position holds that old-style family capitalists have, indeed, disappeared from the large business enterprises, for all the reasons identified by managerialists. But they hold that this serves only to integrate the modern enterprise even more fully into the constraints of the market and of profitability. The managers, that is to say, are constrained to use their power to make the capitalist system operate all the more effectively.[14] The rise of an elite of top managers is important in allowing large enterprises to operate effectively in the stage of monopoly capitalism. While a class of wealthy shareholders may still exist, they are not at all important as agents of the exercise of power in business.

Structural Marxism,[15] is a position which is close to Marxist managerialism in some respects, though it differs in its theoretical basis. The growth of institutional and other intercorporate shareholdings is seen as resulting in an increasingly impersonal system of capital ownership. Personal capitalists have disappeared in the face of this rise of the institutions. The enterprise is, as a result, freed from personal control and becomes, itself, the capitalist. Although managers may, in a purely nominal sense, acquire responsibility for business decision-making, they must obey the structurally determined dictates of this impersonal system of capital. Where Marxist managerialism takes over much of the managerialist theory of the market and pricing behaviour, structural Marxism sees these as secondary reflections of the determining role of capitalist relations of production. Each enterprise is a 'personification' of capital. If a capitalist class continues to exist, therefore, it is not a class of individuals but a class of enterprises. From this standpoint, the question of the identity of those who run large enterprises and of whether they form an elite are irrelevant. Such individuals, whether shareholders, bankers or managers are mere 'bearers' of the structural requirements of the capitalist system.

Theories of *finance capitalism* remain closer to the concerns of classical Marxism, and see modern business enterprises as embedded in a dense web of financial relations. Enterprises are not autonomous centres of market decision-making, as argued by the Marxist managerialists, but are mere units in a single system of 'finance capital'. According to Hilferding, both industry and banking have become increasingly monopolized, and the two sectors have been closely tied together into large financial groups.[16] The rivalry and conflict between these financial groups determines the overall pattern of economic development. The system of finance capital is headed by a financial oligarchy drawn from the rival groups, which is able to ensure some degree of coordination of group activity. This economic élite of financiers, an 'inner circle', of corporate controllers, runs the business system in the interests of the capitalist class as a whole.[17]

A further strand in these debates is the theory of *bank control*, a derivative from the framework of finance capital.[18] Bank control theorists argue that banks act as centres of control within the system of finance capital and that, therefore, banks control industry. The dominant force in the modern economy, therefore, is the small élite of bankers who control the affairs of all the major enterprises. This is often linked with the idea that the banks themselves remain subject to the control of individual capitalist families and that the mechanisms of family capitalism have been transformed rather than undermined.

The confrontation of Marxist and managerialist theories has, in recent years, generated a number of radical theories which cannot straightforwardly be allied with conventional Marxism. Three of these theories, taken together, provide the basis for a reconceptualization of business power which embodies many of the valid points raised in earlier approaches.

The first of these theories is that of *financial hegemony*, developed by Beth Mintz and

Michael Schwartz.[19] This approach recognizes the fusion of banking and industry into a system of finance capital, and it sees the centrality of banks in the flow of capital, but it departs from some of the central tenets of both the finance capital and the bank control theories. It holds that there is a strong element of intercorporate unity within the business system. Large financial institutions, and especially the big banks, dominate the flow of capital, but they do not exercise direct control over particular dependent enterprises. However, through their collective control over the availability of capital they have the power to determine the general conditions under which all other enterprises must formulate their corporate strategies. They can exercise power without direct intervention. Patterns of interlocking directorships can identify the existence of an 'inner circle', a 'corporate elite' of key directors, but they also disclose the continuity, unity and cohesion of the capitalist class from which they are recruited. Financial hegemony, therefore, is part and parcel of a class-based system of production.

The theory of *constellations of interests*, developed by John Scott,[20] shares many of the arguments of the theorists of financial hegemony, but it adds to this a concern for the control status of particular enterprises. This concern, of course, is shared with managerial theory, and the theory of constellations of interests has attempted to integrate some of the insights of modern managerialism with those of Marxism. The growth of intercorporate shareholdings which produced the unified system of finance capital, has also produced a dominant sector of enterprises whose ownership is now 'depersonalized' in form. Large enterprises are increasingly dominated by their leading institutional shareholders, including the big banks, rather than by personal propertied interests. This situation is described neither as 'bank control' nor as 'management control' but as 'control through a constellation of interests'. A small number of large institutional shareholders hold controlling blocks of shares in many of the largest enterprises, but they do not form a cohesive controlling group. They overlap with the controllers of other enterprises and form simply a diverse 'constellation' of financial interests with little capacity for concerted action, except in extreme circumstances. The major shareholders are able to cooperate to determine the composition of the board, but cooperation beyond this is difficult to achieve. In such a situation, the board of directors and top management of an enterprise are not the mere tools of dominant shareholding interests, but neither do they have the kind of autonomy from proprietary influence depicted in managerialist theory.

The substantial area of agreement between the theories of financial hegemony and constellations of interests can be seen as a reflection of the fruitful development in empirical research which followed from the confrontation of managerialist and Marxist theories. In Japan there has been a similar confrontation of these two traditions of theory, and researchers there have moved towards a conceptualization of business power which is more appropriate to the Japanese situation. The works previously considered focused their attention on Britain and the United States, but writers such as Hiroshi Okumura and Yusaku Futatsugi have formulated a distinctive theory of *financial groups*.[21] This theory is based on the distinctive features of intercorporate shareholdings in Japan, which do not take the form of 'institutional capital' but of 'corporate capital'. In the latter system, industrial companies as well as banks and insurance companies hold shares, and all tend to hold these shares on their own account rather than as institutional trustees for others. These shareholdings are, furthermore, formed into tightly structured interest groups within which industrial and financial interests are fused.[22]

Conclusion

The more sophisticated of the writers discussed above, in all the traditions considered, have abandoned the general idea of the 'ruling class' or 'elite with which Burnham worked. Instead, more specific terms have been used, and if the word appears at all – as it does in the works of many American writers – it is qualified as in the phrase 'corporate elite'. This latter term refers to the category of top directors and executives identified at the head of major business corporations. As such, it is a neutral, descriptive term, and the important questions raised concern the composition and the social basis of the corporate elite. One of the central techniques used in the study of such groups is social network analysis,[23] which allows patterns of interlocking directorships to be traced. In this way, it is possible not only to study the integration and recruitment of the corporate elite, but also to investigate its internal structure, its economic foundation and its connections with the wider class structure. Where the idea of a corporate elite figures more centrally in explanatory concerns, it has invariably been converted into more useful analytical concepts such as the 'inner circle'.[24]

The collection of papers reprinted in this volume represent the major contributions to the development of research on economic elites and business power since the original works of the early managerialist writers. For reasons of space, however, the selection concentrates on the work of American scholars, so allowing the theoretical debates to unroll through the consideration of a single economic system. Parts I and II introduce the leading writers in the managerialist and critical traditions. While much of the debate has centred on the United States, the articles in Part III draw on wider evidence from Britain and Japan. Part IV explores the central issue of bank control, as formulated in the enormously influential work of Fitch and Oppenheimer.

Notes

1. The term 'Machiavellian' to describe these writers was introduced by James Burnham (1943) in *The Machiavellians*, New York, John Day. The background to this position is reviewed in the introduction to Volume I of this collection.
2. J. Burnham (1941), *The Managerial Revolution*, New York, John Day.
3. See the classical statements of the principles of 'scientific management', in F. W. Taylor (1923), *The Principles of Scientific Management*, New York, Harper and Row, and H. Fayol (1949), *General and Industrial Management*, London, Pitman. An earlier, but less influential statement of the thesis of the decline of the capitalist, that of Thorstein Veblen, stressed scientific qualifications as the basis of the power of a new class, a position very different from that of Burnham. See T. Veblen (1921), *The Engineers and the Price System*, New York, Viking.
4. A. A. Berle and G. C. Means (1932), *The Modern Corporation and Private Property*, New York, Macmillan.
5. Berle and Means, however, were careful to leave the identity of the 'managers' as an open question. The managers were simply those who were able to run the enterprise without significant personal shareholdings. Investment bankers, for example, could be 'managers' in this sense. Subsequent writers, including Burnham, have tended to ignore this crucial element in the argument of Berle and Means. This is discussed further in J. Scott (1985), *Corporations, Classes and Capitalism*, 2nd edn, London, Hutchinson.
6. Burnham, *op.cit.*, 92–7.
7. See the review in Scott, *op.cit.*, Chapters 1 and 2.
8. See, for example, D. Bell (1961), *The End of Ideology*, New York, Collier Books, and J. K. Galbraith (1967), *The New Industrial State*, London, Hamish Hamilton.
9. In addition to the work of Berle and Means themselves, cited above, see the selection of papers reprinted in Part I of this collection.

10.   E. O. Herman (1981), *Corporate Control, Corporate Power*, Cambridge, Cambridge University Press. Herman's political stance is on the left, close to the Marxism of Paul Sweezy, but his analysis of business makes no reference to the framework of Marxist theory and so he is treated here as a managerialist writer rather than as an advocate of the 'Marxist managerialism' associated with Sweezy. The latter position is discussed later in this introduction.

11.   P. Drucker (1976), *The Unseen Revolution*, New York, Harper and Row. This position has been countered by the radical interpretation of pension funds in J. Rifkin and R. Barber (1978), *The North Will Rise Again*, Boston, Beacon Press.

12.   T. Nishiyama (1984), 'The Structure of Managerial Control', in K. Sato and Y. Hoshino (eds), *The Anatomy of Japanese Business*, London, Croom Helm. This is a translation of Chapter 1 of the author's *Shihai kozo ron*, Tokyo, Bunshindo, 1980. See also *idem.*, *Gendai kigyo no shihai kozo*, Tokyo, Yuhikaku, 1975.

13.   P. A. Baran and P. Sweezy (1966), *Monopoly Capital*, New York, Monthly Review Press.

14.   Compare, for example, the arguments of Sweezy and Herman reprinted in Part IV of this collection. Sweezy's earlier position, in a paper reprinted in Volume III, is significantly different from his later Marxist managerialism.

15.   A. Cutler, B. Hindess, P. Hirst and A. Hussain (1977), *Marx's Capital and Capital Today*, Vol. 1, London, Routledge and Kegan Paul, Chapters 10-12; P. Hirst (1979), *On Law and Ideology*, London, Macmillan; I. Kitahara (1980), 'Ownership and Control in the Large Corporation', *Keio Economic Studies*, **17** (2); *idem.* (1984), *Gendai shihonshugi ni okeru shoyu to kettei*, Tokyo, Iwanami Shoten.

16.   R. Hilferding (1910), *Das Finanzkapital*, translated as *Finance Capital*, London, Routledge and Kegan Paul, 1981.

17.   See, for example, the position of Kazuo Matsuin (1986), *Gendai Amerika kinyu shihon kenkyo josetsu*, Tokyo, Bunshindo. Matsui sees Useem's analysis of the 'inner circle' as central to his concerns. See M. Useem (1984), *The Inner Circle*, New York, Oxford University Press. See also the papers of Useem reprinted in Volumes I and III of this collection.

18.   See the papers of Fitch and Oppenheimer and of Zeitlin reprinted below. Other contributors to this theory are D. M. Kotz (1978), *Bank Control of Large Corporations in the United States*, Berkeley, University of California Press, and S. Aaronovitch (1955), *Monopoly: A Study of British Monopoly Capitalism*, London, Lawrence and Wishart.

19.   B. Mintz and M. Schwartz (1987), *The Power Structure of American Business*, Chicago, University of Chicago Press. See also the reprinted papers below.

20.   Scott, *op. cit.*; J. Scott (1986), *Capitalist Property and Financial Power*, Brighton, Wheatsheaf; J. Scott and C. Griff (1984), *Directors of Industry*, Cambridge, Polity Press.

21.   H. Okumura (1984), 'Enterprise Groups in Japan', *Shoken Keizai*, **147**; *idem.* (1983), *Nihon no rakudai kigyoshudan*, Tokyo, Daiyamondo Sha; *idem.* (1985), *Hojin shihonshugi*, Tokyo, Ochanomizu Shobo; Y. Futatsugi (1986), *Japanese Enterprise Groups*, Monograph No. 4, School of Business Administration, Kobe University [a partial translation of *Gendai Nihon no kigyoshudan*, Tokyo, Toyo Keizai Shinposha, 1976].

22.   Where writers on finance capital in Britain and the United States have tended to identify groups, somewhat questionably, on the basis of interlocking directorships alone, and have tended to identify this with bank control over groups, Okumura and Futatsugi are careful to define groups on the basis of high levels of mutual shareholding and are careful to distance themselves from the idea of bank control.

23.   See the reviews in J. Scott (1988), 'Social Network Analysis: Trend Report', *Sociology*, **22**(1); *idem.* (1988), 'Social Network Analysis and Intercorporate Relations', *Hitotsubashi Journal of Commerce and Management*, **23**, December. Many of the key texts in this area are reprinted in Volume III.

24.   See the especially important recent collection edited by M. Schwartz (1987), *The Power Structure in America: The Corporate Elite as a Ruling Class*, New York, Holmes and Meier.

Part I
Managerialist and
Mainstream Perspectives

[1]

THE

QUARTERLY JOURNAL

OF

ECONOMICS

AUGUST, 1930

THE DIFFUSION OF STOCK OWNERSHIP IN THE UNITED STATES

SUMMARY

Growth in number of book stockholders in recent years, 561. — More rapid growth in immediate post-war period, 566. — Customer and employee sales important only after 1920, 567.— Examination of income-tax data for possible shift in ownership, 570. — Large shift in ownership from rich to less rich apparent between 1916 and 1921, none thereafter, 574. — Check on validity of figures by examination of methods of manipulation, 575; by examination of income-tax data, particularly for tax evasion, 576; by discussion of possible explanations of shift, 585; by the evidence of growth in number of book stockholders, 591. — Conclusion, 591. — Statistical Appendix, Tables I–VIII, 593.

THE United States has been called "a nation of stockholders." [1] Exaggerated tho this statement is, it reflects the generally recognized fact that a great increase in the number of stockholders has occurred in this country in recent years.[2] It is the purpose of the

1. John H. Sears, The New Place of the Stockholder (New York, 1929), p. 35.
2. Joseph S. McCoy, "The United States Legion of Capitalists," American Bankers Association Journal, vol. xix, no. 8 (February, 1927), pp. 559–560 and 626–628; "Sources of Prosperity," American Bankers Association Journal, vol. xx, no. 7 (January, 1930), pp. 643–644, 702–703.
   National Industrial Conference Board, Employee Stock Purchase Plans in the United States, New York, 1928; The Conference Board Bulletin, October, 1927.
   National Bureau of Economic Research, Recent Economic Changes in the United States, New York, 1929.

present article to examine this increase in detail and, in particular, to indicate that while there has been a persistent tendency for the number of stockholders to increase, this has not involved a continuing shift in the ownership of industry from the rich to the less well-to-do. A sudden great diffusion of ownership occurred in the brief period from 1916 to 1921, but after that time no appreciable change. By 1921, the rich owned a very much smaller proportion of all corporate stocks than they had owned in 1916; from 1921 to 1927 their proportion remained fairly constant.

Before considering the growth in the number of stockholders, it must be recognized that there are two quite different connotations to the word stockholder: first, the individual who owns stock and, second, the name of an individual on the stock record books of a corporation. If a man owns stock in ten companies he is one stockholder by the first connotation and ten by the second. This double meaning forces us to consider the growth in the number of individuals who own stock and the growth in the number of book stockholders.

Because of the scanty information about the number of individuals who own stock, we shall consider primarily the increase in book stockholders. In 1924, H. T. Warshow [3] made a study of the increase in stockholders, obtaining figures for a large number of corporations either by direct correspondence or from their published statements. From this material, brought up to date and supplemented by the present author, three sets of figures have been compiled: first, the number of stock-

Proceedings of the Academy of Political Science, vol. xi, no. 3, pp. 355–552.

H. T. Warshow, "The Distribution of Corporate Ownership in the United States," Quarterly Journal of Economics (November, 1924), xxxix, 15–38.

Sears, op. cit.

3. Op. cit.

holders of three particularly important corporations; second, a similar figure for a sample group of large companies; and finally, an index reflecting the number of book stockholders of all corporations.

The three largest corporations in the country, the American Telephone and Telegraph Co., the Pennsylvania Railroad, and the United States Steel Corporation, all show a tremendous growth in their list of stockholders (Table I, page 593, and Chart I, 1, 2, 3). Of the three, the Telephone Company shows the most persistent upward trend, increasing steadily from 7,535 in 1900 to 454,596 at the beginning of 1929. The Pennsylvania Railroad shows a growth nearly as persistent tho not of such great proportions, increasing from 28,408 in 1902 to 157,650 in 1929. The growth in the stockholder list of the Steel Corporation is more fluctuating, but has increased from 15,887 in 1901 to 110,166 in 1929.

The experience of these three great companies is typical. Table II (page 594) gives the number of stockholders for thirty-one large corporations for which information was available from 1900 to 1928. The total number of book stockholders in this group (plotted on Chart I, 5) increased steadily from 226,543 in 1900 to 1,419,126 in 1928. An important proportion of the increase was due to the very great increase in the number of shareholders of the American Telephone and Telegraph Company, but even when this company is eliminated, the growth in the stockholders of the remaining companies is continuous, from 219,008 in 1900 to 964,530 in 1928 (plotted in Chart I, 6).

The indications of an increase in book stockholders shown in the preceding figures are amply sustained by material collected for a much larger number of corporations. This information, covering over 300 com-

564   *QUARTERLY JOURNAL OF ECONOMICS*

CHART I

RATE OF GROWTH IN NUMBER OF BOOK STOCKHOLDERS

1. Pennsylvania Railroad Co.
2. United States Steel Corp.
3. American Telephone and Telegraph Co.
4. Index of Total Book Stockholders.[1]
5. Book Stockholders of thirty-one representative companies.
6. Book Stockholders of thirty-one representative companies excluding American Telephone and Telegraph Co.

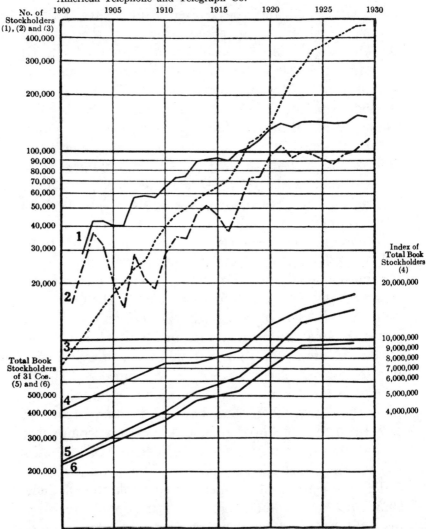

[1] For the index covering the book stockholders of all corporations, there is reason to question the rapidity of the growth shown between 1900 and 1910. The index is based on data for a very small number of companies in 1900, and is dominated by the American Telephone and Telegraph Company which increased very rapidly in number of stockholders.

panies, cannot be presented as a unit since it is incomplete for all but the thirty-one companies already cited. It can be used, however, as the basis for an index of growth. Such an index was constructed by Mr. Warshow covering the period from 1900 to 1923. It was obtained by dividing the estimated capital stock of all corporations by the average holding per stockholder in the sample companies. This method gave a figure for each year purporting to be the number of book stockholders of all corporations. Mr. Warshow made no pretence that the results were more than very rough approximations to the actual number of book stockholders. They are, however, most useful as an index of growth, particularly since he chose a method of estimating the capital stock of all corporations such as to minimize the change in number. The index has a bias which causes it to show a smaller growth throughout the whole period than probably occurred.

This index has been extended by the present author to cover 1928. The figure obtained is comparable to those of Mr. Warshow, but it is in no sense the author's estimate of the number of book stockholders in that year. It is an additional figure in an index of growth, and can be construed as only the most approximate measure of book stockholders. Above all, it must not be taken as the number of individuals who own stock.

As in the case of the large companies and the sample group of corporations, this index (Table III, **page 595**, and Chart I, 4) shows a persistent upward trend in the number of book stockholders, increasing from 4,400,000 in 1900 to 18,000,000 in 1928. One must conclude, therefore, that the trend toward an increase in the number of book stockholders which Mr. Warshow pointed out in 1924 has continued in the later period.

One fact stands out, however, which was not apparent

in 1924. A more detailed examination of Chart I shows that while there was an increase in book stockholders in every period since 1900, the rate of growth was much more rapid in the war and immediate post-war periods than either before or since. From 1917 to 1920 the annual rate of increase for the book stockholders of all corporations was 12 per cent and from 1920 to 1923, $6\frac{1}{4}$ per cent, while for the period before 1917 it was less than 4 per cent and after 1923 was less than $4\frac{1}{2}$ per cent. For the thirty-one large corporations, exclusive of the Telephone Company, the annual growth from 1917 to 1923 was 9 per cent, while in the earlier period it was under $5\frac{1}{2}$ per cent and subsequent to 1923 was less than $1\frac{1}{2}$ per cent. This same difference in rate of growth is shown in the case of the three big companies. The exact period of growth is more clearly defined, since the figures are annual rather than for three-year periods. Here the more rapid growth is shown to occur between 1916 and 1921. After 1921, the steel and railroad companies showed very little growth, while the Telephone Company continued to increase its stockholders, but at a slower rate.

It appears, then, that during the war and immediately thereafter the number of book stockholders was increasing rapidly and that after that time the growth was slow.

Considerable light is thrown on this difference in rate of growth when the railroads, industrials, and public utilities are grouped separately (Table IV, page 595). The three groups show a marked difference in the basic rate of increase, but in each case the same war acceleration and subsequent slowing up appears. The information covering all the companies is not easily placed in tabular form, but that for the thirty-one companies already considered is given below, since this small group

DIFFUSION OF STOCK OWNERSHIP   567

reflects so accurately the differences which are shown when the larger body of material is examined.[4] Both the rapid growth from 1917 to 1923 and the slower growth since 1923 are clearly marked. In each period, furthermore, the growth of the railroads was slowest and that for the utilities most rapid.

For the railroads, the lack of gain in stockholders from 1923 to 1928 was undoubtedly due in large part to the efforts of single interests to acquire control of certain roads. The number of stockholders of the Erie Railroad, for example, declined from 14,495 in 1923 to 3,491 in 1928, the period during which the Van Sweringens obtained control.

The specially rapid increase in the stockholders of public utilities must be attributed in part to the very rapid growth of the larger companies in this particular industry, both by merger — a particular company acquiring new stockholders at the expense of another company — and by the addition of new capital. The customer ownership campaigns which have received so much publicity do not appear to have been an important factor before 1921. According to a compilation made by the Customer Ownership Committee of the National Electric Light Association and reproduced in Table V, (page 596,) the number of separate sales of utility stocks directly to customers amounted to less than 100,000 up to the end of 1920. Part of these were undoubtedly additional sales to the same customers, involving no increase in the names on the company's books. It is

4. For instance, in the period 1923 to 1928, twenty-two railroads, covering half the mileage in the country, showed a decline of $\frac{7}{10}$ of 1 per cent in the number of stockholders, compared with no change in the less important sample. Thirteen large public utilities, controlling nearly a quarter of all utility property, showed an increase of $12\frac{1}{2}$ per cent, compared to the 9 per cent in the small sample. A less comprehensive group of eighteen large industrials showed a growth of $2\frac{3}{4}$ per cent, as against $2\frac{1}{4}$ per cent for the lesser sample.

therefore probable that considerably less than 100,000 book stockholders were added by customer ownership campaigns during the period when stockholders were increasing most rapidly.

In the period after 1921 customer sales became very popular and must account for an appreciable share of the increase in book stockholders. By the end of 1928 a total of 1,884,148 separate sales had been made. While part of these must have involved duplication,[5] and in many cases the purchasers must have disposed of their stock before 1928, it is probable that more than a million new book stockholders were added.

There are several indications that this form of selling was primarily a post-war product. Examination of Table V (page 596) shows that the peak in new companies adopting the plan was reached in 1922, when forty-nine companies were added to those already having such plans in operation. By 1928 the number of new recruits had declined to five. This would be less significant if it were not the forerunner of a decline in the number of actual sales. These reached a peak in 1924 and subsequently decreased. The total value of shares sold annually did not begin to decline until after 1925, but by 1928 it was less than three fifths of its maximum, while the proportion of new capital raised by light and power companies through sales to customers had declined from 23 per cent in 1925 to 10 per cent in 1928.[6]

A second important factor tending to increase the number of book stockholders was the sale of securities to employees, both in the utility and other fields. Its

5. The Electrical World reports that in one case of a sale to customers by a public utility in 1929 "out of a total of 5,344 sales, 2,541 were sales to new customer owners," that is, in only 48 per cent of the sales was the customer buying for the first time and, thereby, adding to the number of book stockholders. Electrical World, vol. xcv, no. 1 (Jan. 4, 1930), p. 75.

6. Electrical World, vol. xciii, no. 1 (January 5, 1929), p. 7.

history has been in many ways parallel to that of customer sales. The increase came mainly in the period after 1921, and, while still continuing to add new stockholders, its annual addition appears to be on the decline. No figures are available for the number of sales or stockholders added each year, but the National Industrial Conference Board, in an excellent study of employee stock purchase plans, reports the year of inauguration of such plans covering "the bulk of employee-owned stock." [7] The number of plans instituted each year is given in Table VI (page 597). The real popularity of such plans began in 1919 and reached its peak in 1923, only a year after the peak for the adoption of customer ownership plans. Thereafter the decline was marked. (The small figure for 1927 probably covers only part of the year.) It is impossible to say whether this decline in new plans adopted indicates a corresponding decline in the number of new stockholders. But it is certain that the major part of such addition to the number of stockholders as was due to such plans came after 1920. By 1928 there were more than 800,000 employee stockholders. [8] The growth in book stockholders from 1921 to 1928 must therefore be due to employee sales to an important extent, both in the public utility and industrial fields.

It is a striking fact that neither customer nor employee ownership was an important factor from 1916 to 1921, when the number of book stockholders was increasing most rapidly, yet after 1921, when over a million and a half names must have been added to the books of corporations through customer and employee sales, the rate of increase in book stockholders was very

7. National Industrial Conference Board, op. cit., p. 36.
8. Ibid., p. 35. The 806,068 employee stockholders was reported as covering the bulk of such individuals, including subscribers.

slow. This still further emphasizes the difference in rate of growth in the earlier and later periods.

From all the evidence thus adduced three conclusions can be drawn: first, the trend toward an increase in number of book stockholders shown by Mr. Warshow in 1924 has continued; second, the increase was very rapid in the war and immediate post-war periods, an increase which can be accounted for only in very slight measure by customer and employee stock ownership; and, finally, the increase after 1921–23 was much slower than in the preceding period, and can be accounted for to a very considerable extent by sales to customers and to employees.

So little information is available concerning the actual number of individuals who own stocks that it is impossible to indicate their increase. It is, however, fair to assume that the large growth in book stockholders involved a considerable addition to the number of individual owners. In part, however, the added book stockholders may have simply reflected the increased popularity of diversified investment and to that extent would mean, not more individuals holding stock, but rather a greater variety held by each. On the other hand, the evidence of an increase in the number of employee and customer owners points to a considerable addition to the group of individual holders. Our further investigation will give still more evidence of such increase.

It must not be lightly assumed that, because there was a very great increase in book stockholders and, unquestionably, a large increase in the number of individuals owning stock, there was also an appreciable shift in the ownership of industry. A tremendous growth in stockholders could take place and yet affect

DIFFUSION OF STOCK OWNERSHIP   571

only a very small proportion of corporate ownership. For example, the 800,000 employee stockholders reported by the Conference Board owned stocks having a market value of approximately $1,000,000,000 in 1928,[9] or less than one per cent of all corporate stocks outstanding.[1] The total sales by Public Utilities to their customers amounted to only $1,659,000,000 [2] to the end of 1928, or less than 1½ per cent of all stocks outstanding. Thus a shift in ownership of only 2½ per cent of all stocks could have added almost two million stockholders. This would be a very great increase in stockholders, by a negligible shift in ownership. The question, therefore, is raised: Has the increase in stockholders involved an appreciable change in the proportions of corporate industry owned by the rich on the one hand, and by the less well-to-do on the other?

The answer can be found in a study of the Statistics of Income compiled by the Treasury Department from income-tax returns. Tables showing the amount of dividends reported by different income groups classified by size of income have been published for each year from 1916 to 1927. The number of individuals in each group is also reported. The figures do not cover all dividends received by individuals, since persons with small incomes are not required to file returns. In addition, the different years are not immediately comparable since the exemption limits varied from year to year. However, dividends not reported have here been estimated and allocated to the proper groups so as to

9. National Industrial Conference Board, op. cit., pp. 35 and 36. This includes stocks subscribed for but not yet fully paid for.

1. The capital stocks and surplus of all corporations in 1927 amounted to more than $130,000,000,000. Statistics of Income, 1927, p. 373.

2. See Table V.

make the figures comparable from year to year. The original data from the Statistics of Income and the estimates for the lowest groups are printed in Table VII (page 598).

Assuming that individuals received dividends in the same proportion as they owned corporate stocks, Table VII may be regarded as a fair picture of the distribution of the ownership of the stocks of all corporations. A quick examination shows a marked decrease in dividends received by the three higher income brackets from 1916 to 1921, balanced by an increase in the four lower brackets. This would suggest a shift in ownership from rich to less rich during the period. After 1921, both groups increase, but with no positive indication of change in relationship. Table VII does not therefore lend itself to a comparison of the different years. It is rather raw material from which more revealing figures can be derived. A shift in ownership becomes more apparent when the dividend receivers are divided into groups containing equal numbers of individuals, rather than individuals of equal income. It is then possible to compare the proportion of all dividends received in a particular year by, say, the individuals reporting the 100,000 largest incomes, with the proportion reported by the 100,000 largest in other years.

In reorganizing the data in Table VII into groups of equal numbers the method of interpolation employed was as follows: each column was cumulated from above and the results for each year were then plotted on single logarithmic paper, the number of individuals being measured along the logarithmic scale and the amount of dividends along the natural scale. Through the various points obtained, a smooth curve was drawn; the amount of dividends received by each particular number of in-

DIFFUSION OF STOCK OWNERSHIP   573

dividuals reporting the largest incomes was then estimated by inspection.[3]

The results of this interpolation are given in Table
VIII (*a*) and (*b*) (page 600) and are converted into percentages in Table VIII (*c*). In Table VIII (*d*) the percentages have been combined into three groups: the first
containing the 25,000 largest incomes, all over $35,000 in
1916; an intermediate group containing the next largest
75,000 incomes; and a group containing the remainder,
individuals with less than $12,000 income in 1916.
The results are plotted in Chart II.

When cast in this form the figures show two striking
facts: first, a tremendous shift in ownership of corporate
shares appears to have taken place in the five-year
period from 1916 to 1921; second, no appreciable shift
appears to have taken place in the six-year period from
1921 to 1927. In 1916 the individuals reporting the
25,000 largest incomes appear to own 57.2 per cent of
all corporate shares. By 1921 this group appears to
own only 36.8 per cent. In the same period the proportion owned by individuals *other* than those reporting
the 100,000 largest incomes appears to have increased
from 22.0 per cent to 44.0 per cent of all corporate shares.
The proportion received by the intermediate group
(75,000 individuals) remained fairly constant. Taken
in terms of social groups this would mean that the
share of corporate stocks owned by the rich and very

3. This rough method of interpolation was tested for 1926 and 1927
by means of additional data supplied in the Statistics of Income, and
proved to be as accurate as the data warranted. The income-tax returns were reported by groups intermediate to those given in Table I.
The dividends received by these intermediate groups were estimated
from the logarithmic chart and the results compared with the actual
amount of dividends reported in Statistics of Income. The maximum
error found was 1.2 per cent and the mode was .4 per cent. This small
error also vindicated the assumption underlying this method of interpolation, viz., that the distribution of dividends could be represented
by a smooth curve.

rich, i.e. individuals with incomes of at least $35,000, declined from 58 to 36 per cent between 1917 and 1921 and remained constant thereafter, while the share owned by individuals with small to moderate incomes, i.e. under $12,000, increased from 21 to 44 per cent. At the beginning of the period half of all dividends were reported by 15,000 persons, while at the end of the period it required the combined dividends of the 75,000 largest incomes to cover half of all dividends received. This represents a shift of almost revolutionary proportions, and of great social significance.

Before examining this shift in greater detail we must raise and answer questions as to the validity of the figures themselves. Four questions present themselves. First, is the apparent shift in ownership due to the manipulation of the income-tax data, and in particular to the estimates made in the lower brackets, where complete figures were lacking? Second, even if complete figures had been supplied by the income-tax returns, could the apparent shift in ownership be due to changes in the methods of making returns in different years, rather than to an actual shift in ownership? Third, are there valid reasons why such a shift should have taken place in this five-year period and not in the period after 1921? Fourth, are there any supporting data derived from other sources which indicate such a shift in ownership?

The methods of manipulating the original data are not a serious cause of error. The one step subject to question, the method of interpolation, was checked and found to be reasonably accurate.[4] More subject to question are the methods employed in making estimates where the original data were lacking. To check the results, a second study was made similar to the first,

4. See n. 3, p. 573.

but confined to the upper income brackets for which
the original data was complete except in 1916 when it
was very nearly so. Such accurate original data for
income groups including the half million largest incomes are supplied in Table VII. For 1916 an estimate
had to be made for the dividends received by individuals
with incomes between $3,000 and $5,000, but this was
of small proportions. When this material was manipulated so as to show the dividends reported by the
largest half million incomes, divided among the different
income groups, the same shift in ownership was shown
which appeared in the more comprehensive but less
certainly accurate figures for all dividends. Thus, of
all dividends reported in the half million largest incomes,
63.4 per cent were received by the 25,000 largest incomes in 1916 and only 46.5 per cent in 1920. In the
same period the proportion received by the smallest
400,000 incomes in the group increased from 15.0 per
cent to 28.0 per cent. The proportion received by this
latter group is plotted in the dotted line of Chart II
and shows a shift almost step by step with the shift
shown where all dividends are included. It is therefore safe to say that the apparent shift in ownership
indicated in the general figures was not the result of
errors in the estimates made where original data were
lacking. Furthermore, the estimates were made throughout with a view to minimizing the shift in ownership,
particularly in the earlier years, and may for that reason
be disregarded as a misleading influence.

A more serious cause of possible error lies in the
changes in the reporting of incomes. These can be
taken up under the following heads: failure to report
dividends received; the withholding of dividends by
corporations in order to save income taxes on the part
of the recipient; the use of a personal holding corpora-

576　　　*QUARTERLY JOURNAL OF ECONOMICS*

tion to avoid taxes; the creation of trusts for the same
purpose; and the division of income among members
of the family.

Since this study deals with the proportion of dividends
received by different classes, a failure to report dividends
received would have no effect on the results, if all classes
failed to report in the same proportion. It is probable
that as the machinery of tax collection improved with
experience, there was less such failure. The individual
with a large income was under greater pressure to
avoid reporting, but at the same time he was under
greater surveillance by the revenue authorities and his
dividends could be more readily traced from the paying
corporation. On the other hand, mere carelessness on
the part of the small-income receiver, resulting in
failure to report part of his dividends, would assume
greater relative importance when his individual dividends were small. The only accurate data we have
on the amount of failure to report is in the years 1922
and 1923, years in which the exemption limits were at
their lowest and in which figures for the total dividends
paid by corporations and received by corporations were
published for the first time by the Treasury Department. Unfortunately the bookkeeping year for all
individuals and corporations was not the same, so that
a discrepancy in the amount of dividends reported by
individuals and reported as paid by corporations and
not received by other corporations would not necessarily indicate a failure to report on the part of individuals. However, the discrepancy in 1922 and 1923 is
small. In 1922, dividends reported as received by individuals exceeded the dividends reported as paid by
corporations by 28 million. In 1923 they fell short by
172 million.[5] The average for the two years indicates

5. Statistics of Income, 1922, pp. 9, 18, 19; Statistics of Income,
1923, pp. 8, 12, 13.

that of all dividends received 98 per cent were reported. Part of this failure to report must be attributed to holdings of American stocks by foreigners. According to a study of 4,367 representative corporations (reporting approximately one eighth of all corporate stocks) made by the Federal Trade Commission for 1922, 1.65 per cent of stocks were held by foreigners.[6]

Only in the early years could a failure to report have appreciably affected the figures. It is probable that in 1916 an important number of receivers of small incomes failed to file any income-tax returns, even when their income was above the exemption limits. This would cause a smaller proportion of dividends to be reported by the lower brackets than were actually received and would give a fictitious appearance of a shift in ownership, as in successive years a larger number of those previously failing actually made returns. This probability has been considered in making the estimates for 1916 and an adjustment made accordingly. An adjustment of smaller proportions was also made in subsequent years. On the whole it is probable that the failure to report dividends received has not caused an appreciable distortion of the figures.

The second possible cause of distortion is the withholding of dividends by corporations, i.e. the failure to pay out a fair proportion of earned income in the form of cash dividends. It might be expected that the large stockholders of a corporation would prevail upon the management to accumulate income instead of paying dividends upon which the recipients would incur heavy surtaxes. Where rich stockholders dominated the company, such action tended to reduce the dividends received by the large stockholders or individuals with

6. Compiled from National Wealth and Income, Federal Trade Commission, Table 82, p. 150.

large incomes more than it reduced the dividends of individuals with small incomes, giving the appearance of
a shift in ownership when none had taken place. However, a study of the income and dividends of 108 large
corporations, representing roughly 20 per cent of all
corporate wealth, shows no change in dividend policy
which could be attributed to this cause between 1910
and 1927. Only in the case of the railroads was any
change noticeable. After the railroads were returned
to private operation following the war, a larger proportion of each year's income was reinvested in the business
and a smaller proportion was paid out in dividends.
This change is easily explained by the credit difficulties
of the railroads, and their serious need for capital, and
cannot be construed as an effort to save the owners
from income taxes. Furthermore, as the ownership of
the railroads was very widespread, it is unlikely that a
withholding of part of the income would cause an apparent shift in ownership. It is therefore reasonable to
disregard the very slight effect which withholding of
dividends in a few cases might possibly have on the
apparent ownership of corporate shares.

The third possible cause of misleading appearances
is the organization of personal holding companies. By
placing his securities in a privately owned corporation
and allowing all income to accumulate, the rich stock
owner was sometimes able to avoid the surtax, since
he himself would receive no dividends. If this practice
had been extensive, it would distort the picture given
by the figures of dividends reported by individuals,
since some of the dividends formerly received by the
rich would subsequently be reported as received by corporations, giving a fictitious appearance of a shift in
ownership.

It is most difficult to estimate the extent of this

type of tax dodging. The income-tax law of 1916 and all subsequent acts contain a clause requiring the individual to report dividends received by such a holding company as if he, personally, had received them. A heavy penalty is placed on failure to so report them, and "the very fact that gains and profits are permitted to accumulate beyond the reasonable needs of the business shall be *prima facie* evidence of a fraudulent purpose to escape such tax."[7] The clause, however, has not been enforced and it is clear that an important amount of tax evasion has been accomplished by this means.

While a definite quantitative estimate of the distortion caused by this form of tax dodging cannot be made, an upper limit can easily be set. In 1923, the first year for which the information is available, the total dividends received by all, finance, banking, insurance, and holding companies, incorporated stockbrokers, etc., reporting a net income, amounted to only $126,700,000.[8] An important part of this must have been received by other than holding companies, particularly fire-insurance and finance companies; and some holding companies must have been active before 1916. Furthermore, some of the holding companies must have been used for other purposes than tax evasion, paying out again an important part of the dividends received. Even in the case of the companies contrived for dodging taxes, some of the dividends were probably paid out. In the case of some holding companies the dividends received may have been reported, in accordance with tax regulations, as if they had been received by the individual. It is unlikely therefore that a large part of the $126,700,000 dividends represents an effort to escape taxes. Even if rich in-

7. Federal Income Tax Law, Act of Sept. 8, 1916, 39 Stat. L. 756–777, C. 463, sec. 3.

8. Statistics of Income, 1923, p. 18.

dividuals had put stock yielding $100,000,000 of dividends into private corporations between 1916 and 1923, less than one twelfth of the shift indicated in Chart II would be accounted for. There is reason to think that even a smaller part was due to this device, probably not more than one twentieth.

In the years subsequent to 1923, the holding corporation was more extensively employed, but to what extent it is impossible to say. It is clear, however, that it could not have caused an important distortion in the figures of the latter period.

The fourth cause of distortion was the creation of private trusts. This was also done to avoid taxes. By creating a trust in favor of a relative a man could ensure a lower rate of tax or avoid tax altogether on the income of the securities placed therein. Such a trust could often be made revocable, so that virtual control of the securities could be maintained. An approximate idea of the volume of such trusts can be obtained from the Statistics of Income. Figures for trusts alone are not given, but in 1927 the net income of all estates and trusts reporting income over $5,000 amounted to only $299,000,000.[9] The income of estates can be estimated as follows. During the year 1927, to take an example, the total estates of resident decedents with a net estate of over $100,000 had an aggregate worth of $2,260,000,-000.[1] If the average estate had a life of one year, and if each estate settled was replaced by a new one which did not have a return filed during the year, the net income of all estates would amount at 5 per cent to $113,-000,000. This would leave $186,000,000 as the income of trusts in 1927. Only part of this would be dividends. For the estates filed during that year, 38 per cent was

9. Statistics of Income, 1927, p. 12.
1. Statistics of Income, 1926, p. 53.

CHART II

DISTRIBUTION IN OWNERSHIP OF CORPORATE STOCKS
AS REFLECTED IN DIVIDENDS RECEIVED BY DIFFERENT INCOME GROUPS

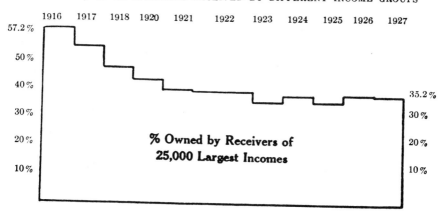

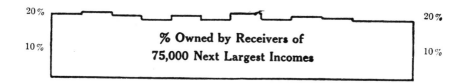

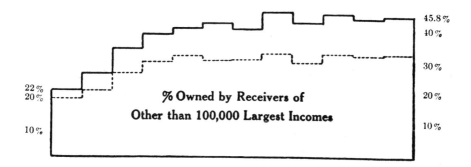

composed of stocks of domestic corporations.[2] Applying this ratio to the income of all trusts would give dividends of $70,000,000.

While this is a very rough figure, it does indicate the relative unimportance of such trusts. Since many trusts must have been in existence before 1916, the increase for the whole period would be less than $70,000,-000, and, even if it were that figure, it could account for less than one twentieth of the shift shown by Chart II.

All the factors so far considered which might lead to a fictitious appearance of a shift in ownership have on examination proved to be of relatively small significance. There remains one factor which is undoubtedly of considerable importance and whose influence it is very difficult to measure. This is the effort of the taxpayer to reduce his income taxes by distributing his wealth among members of his family, either by an actual distribution or merely for tax purposes. When the individual actually gives away property to avoid paying heavy surtaxes upon the income from it, we may regard the result as a shift in ownership, presumably involving a widening in the distribution of wealth. But when a parent, in order to avoid heavy surtaxes, gives property to his children at an earlier age than he otherwise would, there is a real question whether in the social sense a true increase in the distribution of wealth has taken place. While such a gift would cause the figures to show a shift in ownership, I am inclined to regard the shift as fictitious. It is certainly a fictitious shift when a husband gives property to his wife, so that they can save taxes by filing separate returns; or when husband and wife file a joint return in one year and subsequently file separate returns.

The cases of joint or separate returns by husband and

2. Statistics of Income, 1926, p. 52.

wife is the more simple and will be discussed first. In 1916 a couple with a taxable income of $35,000 could save $150 or approximately one fifth of their tax by dividing the income between them and filing separate returns. They could thereby avoid the surtax altogether. For individuals with larger incomes the saving would be more than proportionately greater. There was therefore considerable pressure among the rich and very rich for husband and wife to file separate returns, each accounting for part of their total income. By the Revenue Act of 1917 the surtaxes were very greatly increased, so that a couple with an income of $35,000 could save practically $1,000, or one third of their tax, if they filed separate returns. Of course not all income could be divided, and often it must have been impossible to save by filing separate returns. It is probable that in a large proportion of the cases where an appreciable saving could be made, separate returns were actually filed in 1916. Certainly this must have been true in 1917 with the greater opportunity to save.

Even tho a considerable splitting of returns did occur after 1916, it could not have caused more than a small part of the apparent shift in ownership. If we assumed that all husbands and wives in the upper brackets filed combined returns in 1916 and separate returns in 1921, it would mean that 16,000 wives [3] were included in the 25,000 largest incomes in 1916 and excluded in 1921. However, the total combined income of the 16,000 wives filing separately from their husbands and reporting the largest incomes amounted to only $314,000,000. [4] Assuming that 40 per cent of this income was received as dividends, the total dividends which might have been

3. Estimated on the basis of the proportion of all returns which involved married couples in 1921.

4. Statistics of Income, 1921, p. 51.

reported jointly in 1921 would amount to only $126,-
000,000. On the other hand, in 1916 the 25,000 largest
returns contained approximately 3,700 cases [5] in which
a husband's return did not include that of his wife.
The total income reported by the 3,700 wives amounted
to $156,000,000. Again assuming that 40 per cent was
received as dividends, the wives filing separate returns
would have reported $62,000,000 of dividends in 1916.
The amounts of dividends paid out in 1916 and 1921 were
approximately equal, and, therefore, if the dividends
received by the 16,000 wives in 1921 amounted to only
$126,000,000, the maximum dividends which could
have been shifted during the period would amount to
only $64,000,000 or less than one eighth of the shift in
ownership which is actually shown by the figures. [6] There
is ample reason to believe that the shift due to the filing
of separate returns was very much less than this, probably not accounting for more than one twentieth of the
total shift.

One further misleading factor remains to be considered. While the splitting of incomes between husband and wife cannot have been important, being so
largely accomplished by 1916, there is no reason to
believe that distribution of income among other members of the family did not continue over a considerable
period. No basis is available for measuring the amount
of such distribution which actually took place. However, it is apparent that it could not account for a very
large part of the shift. One person out of every five
could have given half of his or her estate to a relative
other than wife or husband and yet only one twentieth

5. Statistics of Income, 1916, p. 24.
6. This cause of error would be more than twice as effective, for a
given sum of dividends, as the two types previously considered, since
it would involve not only an addition to the dividends in the upper
brackets but also a reduction in those in the lower brackets.

of the shift between 1916 and 1921 would be explained. Such a gift would mean almost complete loss of legal control of the property involved. Furthermore, the recipient had to be of the immediate family, usually a son or daughter over twenty-one years of age and not already having an income sufficient to be included in the upper income brackets. Probably not more than a third of the individuals filing returns were in a position to make such a division, even if they had so desired, and the proportion actually doing so must have been even smaller.

In summary, then, only three of the factors which could give a misleading appearance of a shift in ownership seem likely to have had more than a negligible effect by themselves. Of these three factors the use of personal holding companies and of trusts may each explain as much as one twentieth of the shift in ownership, while the distribution of wealth among members of a family probably explains less than one tenth. Even when these various factors are taken in combination they do not account for more than a small part of the total shift, probably less than one fifth. The conclusion seems warranted, therefore, that the apparent shift in ownership shown by the income-tax figures reflects for the most part a real shift in the ownership of corporate shares.

This conclusion is strengthened when the possible causes of such a shift are considered. The most important single factor was the surtax itself. This, coupled with the increased income received by the lower brackets, might have been expected to cause a considerable shift in proportionate ownership. No doubt the Liberty Bond campaigns familiarized a large number of potential investors with securities and to this extent played a part. Much had been said of employee ownership and customer ownership campaigns, but we have seen that these did not assume important proportions before 1921.

The chief influence of the surtax was to make the rich man a poor market for corporate securities. By 1919 a man with a taxable income of $100,000 was required to pay $61,000 in taxes. Even the individual with a taxable income of only $35,000 had to pay over $6,000 to the government. Plainly after paying the tax the rich and particularly the very rich did not have as large an income as formerly with which to buy corporate securities,[7] and since there is no reason to think that their living expenses decreased in proportion to the drop in income, it is evident that their expenditure on new investments must have decreased in even greater proportion. Moreover, that portion of their income which they did invest would tend to be invested in the forms in which at least a part of the tax could be avoided, i.e. tax-exempt bonds, real estate, and insurance.

At the same time the man of moderate means became a potential market for securities of all sorts. According to figures compiled by the National Bureau of Economic Research, the *per capita* realized income in terms of the 1925 dollar averaged 5 per cent [8] higher from 1916 to 1919 than in the previous three-year period. Since the income of the rich man was reduced by his taxes, the bulk of the increase in income must have gone to those less well-to-do, giving to them additional income, part of which could have been invested.

This reduction of the market for securities among the rich and the increased market among people of moderate or small means would tend to shift the proportion-

7. This is equally true if they shifted into tax-exempt securities, since the income from such securities is, as a rule, very much smaller than from taxable securities of equal risk.

8. Recent Economic Changes, ii, 763.

ate ownership of the two groups, a shift which might be of very considerable size. If each person owning corporate shares in 1916 still held them in 1921, but all new issues (which we assume to amount to 3 per cent of all issues previously outstanding) were each year purchased by individuals with incomes under $12,000, one half of the shift in ownership actually shown by the figures would be accounted for. In practice it would not be necessary that the particular new issues should be purchased by the lower group, but only that the new funds invested in corporate shares should come from this source. If the rich bought some of the new issues and sold an equivalent amount of old stocks to the lower group, the resulting shift in proportionate ownership would be the same as if the lower group bought the new issues directly. No effort has been made to measure the exact significance of this combination of factors tending to shift the proportionate ownership of industry, but it is apparent that it must have been considerable.

The surtax not only made the rich man a poor market for securities but also put him under a heavy pressure to shift into tax-exempt or partially exempt investments. If the rich as a class sold stocks, they must have been purchased by the less well-to-do, since banks and life-insurance companies could not or did not buy an appreciable volume of stocks, and foreign demand was negligible. (The investment trust or trading company was not a factor in those days.) The importance of this shifting is apparent. If there had been no increase in stocks outstanding, but the individuals with the largest 25,000 incomes had sold one fifth of their holdings to individuals with small incomes, more than one half of the shift in proportionate ownership indicated in Chart II would be accounted for. Assuming

588   *QUARTERLY JOURNAL OF ECONOMICS*

that stocks yielded 6½ per cent in cash dividends in 1916, this would have required the selling of $4,370,-000,000 of stocks between 1916 and 1921.

It has often been stated that the shifting into tax-exempt securities was not in significant amounts.[9] While this is undoubtedly true, if importance is measured in terms of loss of revenue to the government, it is probably not true in respect to a shift in ownership of corporate shares. A government report gives $9,169,-000,000 as the total volume of tax-exempt securities outstanding on June 1, 1921.[1] Part of the amount was held by banks and the like, but a government actuary estimated that nearly $5,000,000,000 was in the hands of individuals.[2] If the whole of this amount had been purchased by the rich with the proceeds of stock sales almost three quarters of the shift in corporate ownership between 1916 and 1921 would be accounted for.

In addition to the wholly tax-exempt securities (chiefly state and local issues — the bulk of Liberty Bonds are subject to surtaxes) there were two types of investment whereby at least part of the surtaxes could be avoided. By purchasing life insurance, the individual could invest his money and postpone the time at which he received his income from it, thus escaping an immediate tax. If he died, the income tax would be avoided altogether since there would be none on the insurance payment to his estate. In the case of an endowment policy the odds were in his favor that the surtax rates would be lower when his time to be taxed arrived. There was thus a considerable tax-avoiding advantage in the purchase of life insurance.

9. See New Republic, vol. lvi, no. 572 (November 4, 1925), "Special Tax Section," pp. 24, 25.
1. Annual Report of the Secretary of the Treasury, on the State of the Finances, 1928, p. 567.
2. New Republic, op. cit., pp. 24, 25.

Real estate was the other type of investment by which the surtaxes could be partially avoided. To an important extent the return to the owner of certain types of real estate lies in the appreciation of his property rather than in an actual cash income. To the extent that the gain could be postponed to a time when surtax rates were likely to be lower, there was an inducement to invest in real estate rather than in corporate stocks.

One further influence is worth mentioning. To the individual paying 50 to 60 per cent of the final increment of his income to the government in taxes, the emphasis in valuing securities would shift from high return to safety of principal. Even tho he was not seeking tax-exempt investments, a safe but taxable government bond (of such there were $21,000,000,000 outstanding in June 1921 [3]) would be preferable to a high-yield but risk-bearing stock.

In the light of these influences, all tending to make the rich man not only a poor market for stocks but an actual seller of stocks and the man of moderate income an excellent buyer, it is not surprising to find the shift in ownership which is shown in Chart II. That the shift did not continue after 1921 is, however, surprising. The surtaxes were still heavy, tho less than in 1921, and the man of moderate means was receiving a fairly steadily increasing real income. True, the surtaxes showed a progressive drop between 1921 and 1927, as is shown by Chart III, and the expectation of such a lowering may have been sufficient to lead the rich stockholder to increase his holdings. There is no reason to believe that the figures in this later period are mis-

3. Annual Report of the Secretary of the Treasury on the State of the Finances, 1928, p. 569.

leading, since they are based not only on the reports of individuals but also on the reports of dividends paid out by corporations, and also since the various factors which would have given a false picture of shift must have run their course to such an extent before 1921 as to be negligible thereafter.

CHART III

THE WEIGHT OF SURTAXES UPON THE RICH AS MEASURED BY THE RATE OF TAX ON THE SECOND HUNDRED THOUSAND DOLLARS OF TAXABLE INCOME [1] 1913–1927

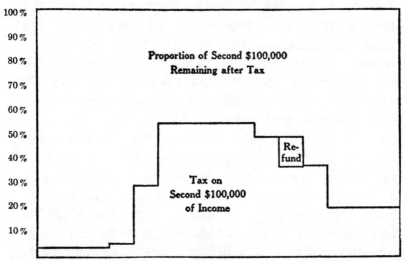

[1] Derived from Table B, Statistics of Income, 1927, pp. 35–37.

That there was a very marked shift in ownership between 1916 and 1921 and little shift subsequently is further substantiated by the figures of the growth in book stockholders which we have already examined. We saw that in the first period the number increased at a very much faster rate than in the second period, while in the latter period the growth in the popularity of stock sales to employees and customers may well account for much of the increase in book stockholders without having caused an appreciable shift in the proportions in which stocks were held by different income groups.

To conclude: This study indicates that a great distribution of stock ownership took place during the war and immediate post-war periods, increasing both the number of stockholders and the proportion of corporate industry owned by persons of moderate means; that this widespread ownership was a legacy of the war period, much as the increase in the number of small landholdings was a legacy of the French Revolution; and that thereafter, while the number of stockholders continued to increase, this involved no appreciable shift in the proportion of corporate industry owned by the different income groups.

In addition three tentative conclusions can be drawn, which, tho more open to question, are of greater social significance. First, the great popularity of customer and employee stock-selling plans was to a considerable extent due to the drying up of the market for corporate stock among the rich and the necessity of seeking new capital among individuals of moderate means. Second, the remarkable diffusion in ownership from 1917 to 1921 was primarily the result of the heavy surtaxes of the war period, a non-recurring phenomenon, not the result of a permanent trend. And third, the surtaxes have been reduced to a point where they no longer curb the purchase of corporate stocks by the rich.

Finally, it is worth suggesting that the surtax concentrated the attention of the former owners of industry

592   *QUARTERLY JOURNAL OF ECONOMICS*

on the possibility of retaining control without important
ownership, either through the wide diffusion of stock
or through various legal devices,[4] and thereby acceler-
ated that separation of ownership and control which
has become such a marked feature of our modern
economy.

4. Non-voting common stock, voting trusts, pyramided holding
companies, etc.

GARDINER C. MEANS

COLUMBIA UNIVERSITY

STATISTICAL APPENDIX

TABLE I

STOCKHOLDERS OF THE THREE LARGEST AMERICAN CORPORATIONS

	American Telephone and Telegraph Co.	Pennsylvania Railroad	United States Steel Corp.[7]
1929	469,801 [8]	156,601 [5d]	120,918 [10]
1928	454,596 [6]	157,650 [5a]	100,784
1927	423,580	143,249 [5b]	96,297
1926	399,121	142,257 [5c]	86,034
1925	362,179	140,578 [4]	90,576
1924	345,466	145,174	96,317
1923	281,149	144,228	99,779
1922	248,925	137,429	93,789
1921	186,342	141,699	107,439
1920	139,448	133,068	95,776
1919	120,460	117,725	74,318
1918	112,420	106,911	72,779
1917	87,000 [9]	100,038	51,689
1916	71,000	90,388	37,720
1915	66,000	93,768	45,767
1914	60,000	91,571	52,785
1913	57,000	88,586	46,460
1912	50,000	75,155 [3]	34,213
1911	48,000	73,165	35,011
1910	41,000	65,283	28,850
1909	37,000	56,809	18,615
1908	26,000	58,273	21,093
1907	23,000	57,226	28,435
1906	19,000	40,153 [2]	14,723
1905	18,000	40,385	20,075
1904	17,000	42,230	33,395
1903	16,000	42,437	37,237
1902	12,000	28,408	24,636
1901	10,000	....	15,887
1880		13,000 [1]	

[1] The Growth and Development of the Pennsylvania Railroad Co., H. W. Schotter (Philadelphia, 1927), p. 11.
[2] Ibid., p. 186.
[3] Ibid., p. 303.
[4] Ibid., p. 415.
[5] Standard Corporation Records, revised July 18, 1929, and Dec. 20, 1929.
    (a) As of May 1, 1929.
    (b) As of May 1, 1928.
    (c) As of Feb. 1, 1927.
    (d) As of Sept. 1, 1929.
[6] Standard Corporation Records, revised March 20, 1929.
[7] Wall Street Journal, October 26, 1929. (Common stock only.)
[8] Annual Report, 1929, p. 19.
[9] Bell Telephone Securities, 1929, issued by Bell Telephone Securities Co., New York, p. 10. (Derived from chart.)
[10] Standard Corporation Records, revised March 25, 1930. (Common stock only.)

594   *QUARTERLY JOURNAL OF ECONOMICS*

TABLE II

STOCKHOLDERS OF THIRTY-ONE LARGE CORPORATIONS [1]

Name of company	1900	1910	Number of shareholders 1913	1917	1920	1923	1928
Am. Car and Foundry	7,747	9,912	10,402	9,223	13,229	16,090	17,152
Am. Locomotive	1,700	8,198	8,578	8,490	9,957	10,596	19,359
Am. Smelt. and Refin.	3,398	9,464	10,459	12,244	15,237	18,583	15,040
Am. Sugar Refin..........	10,816	19,551	18,149	19,758	22.311	26,781	22,276
Du Pont Powder	809	2,050	2,697	6,592	11,624	14,141	21,248
Gen. Electric	2,900	9,486	12,271	12,950	17,338	36,008	51,882
General Asphalt	2,089	2,294	2,184	2,112	1,879	2,383	1,527
Gt. North. Iron Ore	3,762	4,419	4,685	4,855	6,747	9,313	7,456
International Paper........	2,245	4,096	3,929	4,509	3,903	4,522	23,767
Proctor and Gamble	1,098	1,606	1,881	2,448	9,157	11,392	37,000
Stand. Oil of N. J.	3,832	5,847	6,104	7,351	8,074	51,070	62,317
Swift and Co.............	3,400	18,000	20,000	20,000	35,000	46,000	47,000
Union Bag and Paper	1,950	2,250	2,800	1,592	1,856	2,263	1,278
United Fruit	971	6,181	7,641	9,653	11,849	20,469	26,219
United Shoe Machy........	4,500	7,400	8,366	6,547	8,762	10,935	18,051
U. S. Rubber	3,000	3,500	12,846	17,419	20,866	34,024	26,057
U. S. Steel Corp.	54,016	94,934	123,891	131,210	176,310	179,090	154,243
	108,233	209,188	256,883	276,953	374,099	493,660	551,872
Am. Tel. & Tel.	7,535	40,381	55,983	86,699	139,448	281,149	454,596
Brooklyn Union Gas	1,313	1,593	1,646	1,834	1,985	1,879	2,841
Commonwealth Edison.....	1,255	1,780	2,045	4,582	11,580	34,526	40,000
Western Union	9,134	12,731	12,790	20,434	23,911	26,276	26,234
	19,237	56,485	72,464	113,549	176,924	343,830	523,671
Atlantic Coast Line........	702	2,278	2,727	3,404	4,422	5,162	4,212
Chesapeake and Ohio	1,145	2,268	6,281	6,103	8,111	13,010	6,885
Chicago and Northwestern .	4,907	8,023	11,111	13,735	19,383	21,555	16,948
Del. Lack. and Western	1,896	1,699	1,959	2,615	3,276	6,650	7,957
Great Northern	1,690	16,298	19,540	26,716	40,195	44,523	43,741
Illinois Central	7,025	9,790	10,776	10,302	12,870	19,470	21,147
N. Y. N. H. & Hartford	9,521	17,573	26,240	25,343	25,272	24,983	27,267
Pennsylvania	51,543	65,283	88,586	100,038	133,068	144,228	157,650
Reading	6,388	5,781	6,624	8,397	9,701	11,687	9,844
Union Pacific	14,256	20,282	26,761	33,875	47,339	51,022	47,932
	99,073	149,275	200,605	230,528	303,637	342,290	343,583
	19,237	56,485	72,464	113,549	176,924	343,830	523,671
	108,233	209,188	256,883	276,953	374,099	493,660	551,872
Book Stockholders	226,543	414,948	529,952	621,030	854,660	1,179,780	1,419,126
Total Book Stockholders excl. Am. Tel. & Tel. Co.	219,008	374,567	473,969	534,331	715,212	898,631	964,530

[1] Data derived from Warshow for 1900–1923, op. cit., and from Annual Reports, Moody's Manuals, Standard Corporation Records and news clippings for 1928.

TABLE III

INDEX OF NUMBER OF BOOK STOCKHOLDERS [1] 1900–1928

Year	Total capital stock of all corporations in the United States	Average number of $100 par value shares per stockholder	Estimated number of stockholders in the United States	Annual rate of increase during preceding interval (Per cent compounded annually)
1900	$61,831,955,370	140.1	4,400,000	
1910	64,053,763,141	86.3	7,400,000	5¼
1913	65,038,309,611	87.0	7,500,000	½
1917	66,584,420,424	77.3	8,600,000	3½
1920	69,205,967,666	57.3	12,000,000	12
1923	71,479,464,925	49.7	14,400,000	6¼
1928	91,881,243,985 [2]	51.0 [3]	18,000,000	4½

[1] As compiled and computed by Warshow (op. cit. p. 28) for 1900–1923 and compiled by the present writer for 1928 on a comparable basis.
[2] Statistics of Income, 1927, p. 373.
[3] The wide use of no-par stock makes both the figure for total stock of all corporations and the estimate of the average shares per stockholder less reliable than in earlier years.

TABLE IV

RATE OF ANNUAL INCREASE IN NUMBER OF BOOK STOCKHOLDERS
OF SELECTED CORPORATIONS [1]

	1900–1917 Per cent	1917–1923 Per cent	1923–1928 Per cent	Entire period 1900–1928 Per cent
10 Railroads	5	7	0	4½
17 Industrials	5½	10	2¼	6
4 Public Utilities	11	20	9	12½
31 Companies	6	11¼	3¾	6¾

[1] Derived from Table II.

TABLE V

STOCK SALES MADE BY PUBLIC UTILITIES TO CUSTOMERS
1914–1929

Year	Number of additional companies adopting customer ownership plan [1]	Sales made [*][1]	Shares of stock sold [1]	Value of sales [2]
1914	7	4,044	92,310	. . . .
1915	3	4,357	57,130	. . . .
1916	4	3,681	38,183	. . . .
1917	8	8,242	82,007	. . . .
1918	7	5,186	42,388	. . . .
1919	12	19,872	194,021	. . . .
1920	34	53,063	454,139	$ 43,000,000
1921	37	118,544	830,222	80,000,000
1922	49	156,725	1,450,707	130,000,000
1923	24	279,186	1,806,300	175,000,000
1924	23	294,467	2,478,165	254,000,000
1925	18	236,043	2,926,271	297,000,000
1926	2	248,867	2,686,187	236,000,000
1927	18	249,491	3,581,206	263,000,000
1928	5	227,961 [3]	2,081,071	181,000,000 [3]
1929	..	230,000 [3]	. . . .	145,000,000 [3]

[*] In the compilation of these statistics, each separate purchase of stocks has been recorded by many of the reporting companies as being the acquisition of an additional "stockholder." There are possibilities of duplications, arising from:

    (a) Repeat purchases of stock of the same company by the same individual.
    (b) The purchase of stock in two or more companies by the same individual.
    (c) In addition, the situation is further complicated by the purchase of stocks by customers from other sources than through the company's office.

[1] National Electric Light Association, Serial Report of Customer Ownership Committee 1928–29, p. 4.

[2] Electrical World, vol. xciii, no. 1, p. 27.

[3] Ibid., vol. xcv, no. 1, p. 67. Figures for 1929 are preliminary estimates based upon figures for ten months.

DIFFUSION OF STOCK OWNERSHIP 597

TABLE VI

THE INCREASE OF EMPLOYEE STOCK PURCHASE PLANS IN
THE UNITED STATES

Year	No. of companies instituting stock purchase plans. [1]
1900 or earlier	5
1901–1905	13
1906–1910	14
1911	1
1912	7
1913	7
1914	6
1915	7
1916	10
1917	11
1918	8
1919	24
1920	46
1921	35
1922	17
1923	51
1924	29
1925	29
1926	13
1927	4
No information	49

[1] Compiled from appendix of National Industrial Conference Board, op. cit.

TABLE VII

DISTRIBUTION OF DIVIDENDS BY INCOME GROUPS[*]

Income group	Individuals	Dividends reported in million dollars	Individuals	Dividends reported in million dollars	Individuals	Dividends reported in million dollars
		1916		1917		1918
Over $500,000	582	413.9	456	384.5	245	193.2
300–500,000	714	127.3	559	119.9	382	76.6
150–300,000	2,437	244.5	2,347	266.7	1,514	162.6
100–150,000	2,900	156.8	3,302	213.0	2,358	141.9
50–100,000	10,452	323.7	12,439	447.9	9,996	355.8
25– 50,000	23,734	326.6	30,391	473.4	28,542	428.6
10– 25,000	80,880	359.2	112,502	464.2	116,569	454.4
5– 10,000	180,553[1]	194.3[1]	270,666	279.9	319,356	326.2
3– 5,000	440,000[1]	163.0[1]	560,763	163.0[2]	932,336	202.0
Total over $3,000		2,309.3		2,812.5		2,341.3
under 3,000		165.0[1]		218.2[3]		233.6[3]
Total Dividends[10]		2,474.3		3,030.7		2,574.9
		1919		1920		1921
Over $500,000	254	170.9	156	132.0	84	79.8
300–500,000	425	75.8	239	61.1	162	55.4
150–300,000	1,864	158.4	1,063	125.6	739	97.1
100–150,000	2,983	146.0	2,191	143.4	1,367	100.6
50–100,000	13,320	350.4	12,093	409.5	8,717	322.2
25– 50,000	37,477	426.7	38,548	525.5	28,946	425.7
10– 25,000	162,485	471.0	171,830	574.1	132,344	485.2
5– 10,000	438,851	322.0	455,442	386.0	353,247	349.2
3– 5,000	1,180,488	198.3	1,337,116	220.5	1,072,146	230.0
Total over $3,000		2,319.5		2,577.7		2,145.2
under 3,000		227.5[3]		251.8[3]		331.8
Total dividends		2,547.0		2,829.5		2,477.0
		1922		1923		1924
Over $500,000	228	138.0	215	143.6	317	187.1
300–500,000	309	64.3	327	72.2	457	92.0
150–300,000	1,323	134.0	1,301	145.4	1,876	183.3
100–150,000	2,171	126.2	2,339	153.8	3,065	181.7
50–100,000	12,000	352.0	12,452	398.6	15,816	468.7
25– 50,000	35,478	437.9	39,832	520.9	47,061	555.1
10– 25,000	151,329	562.8	170,095	662.0	191,216	657.7
5– 10,000	391,373	356.3	387,842	346.1	437,330	292.1
3– 5,000	1,190,115	227.3	1,719,625	421.3	1,800,900	380.8
Total over $3,000		2,398.8		2,868.9		2,998.5
under 3,000		263.4		362.5[4]		352.1[5]
Total dividends		2,662.2		3,226.4		3,350.6

DIFFUSION OF STOCK OWNERSHIP 599

TABLE VII (*Continued*)

Income group	Individuals 1925	Dividends reported in million dollars 1925	Individuals 1926	Dividends reported in million dollars 1926	Individuals 1927	Dividends reported in million dollars 1927
Over $500,000	686	264.0	699	361.6	847	406.7
300–500,000	892	119.1	892	151.0	1,141	171.7
150–300,000	3,223	252.3	3,267	301.5	3,873	331.1
100–150,000	4,759	225.9	4,724	271.1	5,261	276.5
50–100,000	20,958	512.5	20,520	578.8	22,573	623.8
25– 50,000	59,721	618.3	57,487	666.6	60,123	679.9
10– 25,000	236,779	731.9	246,730	815.4	252,079	834.5
5– 10,000	503,652	321.3	560,549	435.3	567,700	430.6
3– 5,000	1,880,000[9]	400.0[6]	1,880,000[9]	400.0[7]	2,120,000[9]	450.0[9]
Total over $3,000		3,445.3		3,981.3		4,204.8[9]
under 3,000		400.0[6]		400.0[7]		450.0[9]
Total dividends		3,845 3		4,381.3		4,654.8

* Figures for individuals by years taken from Statistics of Income, 1927, p. 25; figures for dividends by years derived from Statistics of Income for respective years.

[1] In 1916 the exemption limit was $3,000 for both married and unmarried, but it is apparent that the returns are not complete. Therefore $3,000–$5,000 dividends were assumed to be in the same ratio to $5,000 or over dividends as the average for 1917 and 1918 or 7.8 per cent. In the same way under $3,000 dividends were assumed to be in the same proportion to all dividends over $3,000 as the average of 1917 and 1918 or 7.3 per cent. The individuals in the $3,000–$5,000 group were assumed to be in the same proportion to individuals in the over $5,000 group as the average for 1917 and 1918 or 16.2 per cent. Also 50.0 million dollars and 30,000 individuals were arbitrarily added to the $5,000–$10,000 group to make up for possible failure to file returns.

[2] Dividends reported by the class $2,000–$5,000 in 1917 were prorated to the classes under $3,000 and $3,000–$5,000 in the same proportion as the average from 1918 to 1923 or 70 per cent to the $3,000–$5,000 group.

[3] For the group under $3,000 in 1917–1920 an adjustment was made by arbitrarily adding 100.0 million dollars to dividends to account for the dividends received by individuals not required to report.

[4] Of the total dividends reported as paid by corporations in 1923, all but $172.6 mil was reported as received by individuals or corporations. Of this remainder 100.0 million dollars was arbitrarily attributed to dividends received by the under $3,000 group. This seems reasonable, since the $1,000 to $3,000 group increased greatly over 1922 and the under $1,000 dropped over 75.0 million dollars.

[5] Of the total dividends reported as paid by corporations in 1924, all but $173.6 mil. was reported as received by individuals or corporations. Of this remainder 100.0 million dollars was arbitrarily attributed to dividends received by the under $3,000 group.

[6] Because of the raising of the exemption limits in 1925, $969.7 mil. of dividends reported as paid by corporations was not reported as received by corporations or by individuals with incomes over $5,000. Eight hundred million of this amount was attributed to the under $3,000 and the $3,000 to $5,000 groups in the same proportion as the average of the previous three years, or 50 per cent to each.

[7] In 1926, $857.9 million of dividends paid by corporations was not reported as received by corporations or by individuals with incomes over $5,000. $800 mil. of this amount was divided as in (6) between under $3,000 and $3,000 to $5,000.

[8] In 1927, $1,003.0 mil. of dividends was unaccounted for. $900 mil. of this was divided as in (6) and (7).

[9] Same ratio of individuals to dividends assumed as the average for the same income class from 1921–1924.

[10] The total dividends received by individuals as shown by this table differs very markedly in certain years from the estimate of dividends received by individuals recently published by the National Bureau of Economic Research in the National Income and its Purchasing Power (Willford I. King, New York, 1930).

The discrepancy seems to arise, in large part, from two facts. First, the figures that are given in the present table do not purport to be the same as those of Dr. King. The present figures do not include dividends paid by domestic corporations to foreigners; and, further, the assumption has been made that a considerable amount of failure to report dividends received occurred among all income classes in the earlier years, particularly in 1916. Therefore, the total dividends reported in income-tax returns, even if the lower brackets were included, would give a smaller figure than the total dividends paid to individuals by corporations.

A second cause of discrepancy between the two sets of estimates appears to be due to a weakness in the method employed by Dr. King in making certain of his estimates for the years before 1922.

For those years he assumed that the same rate of dividends was paid on all stocks as was paid on the outstanding stock of a sample group of corporations. Unfortunately, the stock of very large corporations composed the bulk of the sample. Since the large corporations are known to have been very much more prosperous than the average corporation, and presumably paid larger dividends, the sample is not representative. It would naturally lead to a very considerable overestimate in certain years. Dr. King has acknowledged the weakness in the method.

The difference between Dr. King's estimates and those used as the basis for the present discussion does not, therefore, impair the validity of the conclusions here drawn.

TABLE VIII

DIVIDENDS RECEIVED BY DIFFERENT INCOME GROUPS [1]

Total dividends in millions of dollars

(a)

Income groups		1916[2]	1917	1918	1919	1920	1921	1922	1923	1924	1925	1926	1927
Largest	1,000	475	505	310	290	275	225	260	290	305	320	420	445
Largest	5,000	825	895	605	540	540	460	520	555	605	645	825	860
Largest	25,000	1,385	1,550	1,140	1,035	1,055	910	980	1,075	1,190	1,280	1,575	1,635
Largest	100,000	1,890	2,195	1,660	1,520	1,635	1,385	1,545	1,695	1,875	2,045	2,410	2,520
Largest	500,000	2,240	2,675	2,150	2,045	2,270	1,890	2,125	2,370	2,525	2,890	3,340	3,500
Largest	1,000,000	2,350	2,805	2,280	2,215	2,450	2,030	2,280	2,575	2,720	3,095	3,630	3,800
Total		2,424	3,031	2,575	2,547	2,829	2,477	2,662	3,226	3,351	3,845	4,381	4,655

(b)

Income groups		1916[2]	1917	1918	1919	1920	1921	1922	1923	1924	1925	1926	1927
Largest	1,000	475	505	310	290	275	225	260	290	305	320	420	445
Next	4,000	350	390	295	250	265	235	260	265	300	325	405	415
Next	20,000	560	655	535	495	515	450	460	520	585	635	750	775
Next	75,000	505	645	520	485	580	475	565	620	685	765	835	885
Next	400,000	350	480	490	525	635	505	580	675	650	845	930	980
Next	500,000	110	130	130	170	180	140	155	205	195	205	290	300
Other than 1,000,000		74	226	295	332	379	443	382	651	631	750	751	855

Percentage of total dividends received by individuals

(c)

Income groups		1916[2]	1917	1918	1919	1920	1921	1922	1923	1924	1925	1926	1927
Largest	1,000	19.6	16.7	12.0	11.4	9.7	9.1	9.8	9.0	9.1	8.3	9.6	9.6
Next	4,000	14.5	12.9	11.5	9.8	9.4	9.5	9.8	8.2	9.0	8.5	9.2	8.9
Next	20,000	23.1	21.6	20.8	19.4	18.2	18.2	17.3	16.1	17.5	16.5	17.1	16.7
Next	75,000	20.8	21.3	20.2	19.0	20.5	19.2	21.1	19.3	20.4	19.9	19.1	19.0
Next	400,000	14.4	15.8	19.0	20.6	22.4	20.4	21.8	20.9	19.4	22.0	21.2	21.0
Next	500,000	4.5	4.3	5.0	6.7	6.4	5.7	5.8	6.4	5.8	5.3	6.6	6.4
Other than 1,000,000		3.1	7.4	11.5	13.1	13.4	17.9	14.4	20.1	18.8	19.5	17.2	18.4
		100.0	100.0	100.0	100.0	100.0	100.0	100.0	100.0	100.0	100.0	100.0	100.0

(d)

Income groups		1916[2]	1917	1918	1919	1920	1921	1922	1923	1924	1925	1926	1927
Largest	25,000	57.2	51.2	44.3	40.6	37.3	36.8	36.9	33.3	35.6	33.3	35.9	35.2
Next	75,000	20.8	21.3	20.2	19.0	20.5	19.2	21.1	19.3	20.4	19.9	19.1	19.0
Other than	100,000	22.0	27.5	35.5	40.4	42.2	44.0	42.0	47.4	44.0	46.8	45.0	45.8

[1] Derived by interpolation from Table VII; for method see text.
[2] In 1916, the returns of husband and wife filing separately were combined by the Treasury Department and reported as one individual. An adjustment was made for this, based on the number of wives filing separate returns. The figures given here are comparable for those of subsequent years when husband and wife, reporting separately, were compiled as two individuals.

[2]

STOCKHOLDINGS OF OFFICERS AND DIRECTORS IN AMERICAN INDUSTRIAL CORPORATIONS

SUMMARY

I. Nature of data and of sample: 1. The SEC data on stock ownership, 622; 2. Choice of companies in sample, 624; 3. Limitations of the data, 628. — II. Proportion of stock outstanding owned by management: 1. Percentage of stock owned by management groups, 631; 2. The relation between total percentage holdings and size of management groups, 633; 3. The relation between percentage holdings and size of company, 635. — III. The market value of stock owned by management: 1. Individual value-holdings of leading executives, 640; 2. Average value-holdings of management groups, 644; 3. The relation between average value-holdings and size of firm, 650. — IV. Summary and conclusions, 650.

I

Much has been said in recent years concerning the separation of control and ownership in the large American corporation.[1] In this connection, considerable emphasis has been placed upon the small degree of stock ownership by those who manage and direct our great corporate enterprises.[2] The present article represents an attempt to investigate this phenomenon in some detail for a small section of American industry — through a study of management stockholdings in a representative sample of the industrial companies listed on the New York Stock Exchange.

As a result of the regulatory activities of the Securities and Exchange Commission, much new information bearing on

1. The writer is indebted to the Harvard University Committee on Research in the Social Sciences for a grant of money to undertake the research embodied in this study. Thanks are also due to Mr. H. J. Borneman and Mr. R. L. Tebeau, of the New York Stock Exchange, for their courtesy and assistance in making available the SEC records on file there. Finally, acknowledgment is due to Mr. E. I. Epstein and Mr. Theodore Norman for their aid in compiling this material and in carrying through the necessary computations.

2. Cf., for example, A. A. Berle, Jr., and G. C. Means, The Modern Corporation and Private Property (New York, 1933), Bk. I, chs. IV–V. No attempt has been made in the present study to investigate the wide range of related topics which these authors discuss.

STOCKHOLDINGS OF OFFICERS AND DIRECTORS   623

many phases of corporate structure and corporate activity
is now being made available. Through the Commission's
Form 10 (application for registration on a national securities
exchange) and through Forms 4, 5, and 6 (reporting the
amount of and changes in the security holdings of corporate
executives), detailed stock ownership figures can now be
secured for all officers and directors of corporations whose
securities are listed on registered stock exchanges.[3] The full-
ness of the information presented in these forms makes
possible for the first time a really complete and detailed
analysis of the extent to which the officers and directors of
these registered companies actually own the corporations
which they manage and direct.[4]

3. Form 10 is not used by companies under the jurisdiction of the
I. C. C. or the Federal Communications Commission, by insurance
companies, banks, and investment trusts, or by companies going through
bankruptcy proceedings. Forms analogous to Form 10 are filed by such
companies, however, if their securities are registered or are not exempt;
and the officers and directors of all registered companies are required
to file stock-ownership data on one or more of Forms 4, 5, and 6.

Item 28 of Form 10 gives for each officer and director, as well as
for every person owning more than ten per cent of any class of equity
security, the amount of each of the company's stock issues owned on
some date within ninety days prior to the day of filing. Form 5 requires
the repeating of such information for the date on which registration
became effective, which was July 1, 1935, for the New York Stock
Exchange companies included in this study. Monthly reports of changes
in ownership must be reported by these individuals on Form 4, while
new officers and directors report their stockholdings on Form 6 immediately upon taking office. This study has been based primarily upon the
data available from Form 5, which gives the information as of the same
date for practically all companies listed on the New York Stock
Exchange.

4. One of the first investigations of the stockholdings of corporate
management was made by Taussig and Barker, in "American Corporations and Their Executives," this Journal, XL (1925), pp. 11–18.
About 400 companies, a good many quite small in size, were studied —
but only for a pre-war period. The Federal Trade Commission, in the
course of its study on National Wealth and Income (Washington,
1926), compiled data on percentage and par value stockholdings of
officers and directors in 1922 for a wide sample of 4,367 corporations
(see pp. 148, 158, 159). No detailed analysis, beyond a classification of
average holdings by industries, was attempted.

Berle and Means, of course, have much to say concerning the extent
of stock ownership among officers and directors (op. cit., Bk. I, chs.
IV–V), but they deal only with the 200 largest American corporations,

In making this analysis our attention will be confined to a selected group of companies, almost entirely in the manufacturing field, all of which are listed on the New York Stock Exchange. The sample to be studied was chosen in connection with a wider project involving a series of case studies of enterprise and profits in American industrial corporations. Two factors were kept in mind in making the choice: (1) the desire to limit the study to industrial corporations, and (2) the consideration that valuable information concerning executive compensation for a selected group of 120 companies in the industrial field was already accessible, through work previously done by Professor W. L. Crum and Mr. John C. Baker, of Harvard University.[5] In the light of these two factors it seemed advisable to take over essentially the sample selected by the above-mentioned writers.[6]

The population from which this sample was drawn was arbitrarily limited in two important respects: only companies with securities listed on the New York Stock Exchange and with assets over $1,000,000 were considered, and only industrial, for the most part only manufacturing, companies were included. The sample as finally chosen was in part random and partly selected by design in order to make the entire group more representative.[7]

nearly half of which are public utilities or railroads, a section of American industry in which absence of ownership among officers and directors is to be expected in large degree. Further, the authors had to rely on the stockholdings data then available, which were meagre and incomplete even for the large companies with which they dealt.

5. See their article, "Compensation of Corporation Executives — The 1928–1932 Record," Harvard Business Review, XIII (1935), pp. 321–333, based on material made available as a result of the 1933 Federal Trade Commission investigation of executive compensation.

6. For a description of their method of selecting the sample, see ibid., pp. 321–322, note.

7. Cf. ibid. Essentially their process of selection was this. From the industrial companies listed on the Stock Exchange which submitted data on executive compensation to the Federal Trade Commission they selected 100 at random. Twenty of these were omitted because of defective data, and an equal number were added by design, both to make the sample more representative and to bring the number up to 100. The present writer has taken over the entire group of 120 companies as his sample.

STOCKHOLDINGS OF OFFICERS AND DIRECTORS   625

Stock ownership data have been collected for these companies from the SEC material previously described. Of the 120 original companies, nine were dropped for lack of data,[8] and four were excluded because they were chiefly in the fields of mining or retail trade.[9] The final sample of 107 companies may be considered a fairly representative cross-section of the nearly 500 New York Stock Exchange companies which comprise the population from which it was drawn. No inferences based upon random sampling theory, however, can be drawn from any analysis applied to these companies; and the limited nature of the population from which the sample has been selected should be kept firmly in mind. A list of the 107 companies studied is given in an appendix.

Table I indicates the general nature of the sample, presenting for each industrial group the number of companies included in the sample and the total number of such companies listed on the New York Stock Exchange. It is to be noted that, among the so-called "industrials," amusement companies, as well as those in the fields of mining and retail trade, are excluded, while the broad fields of finance, railroads, and public utilities are also entirely unrepresented.

In size (see Table IV) the 107 companies range from one with total assets of slightly less than a million dollars on December 31, 1934, to two with total assets over one billion dollars. The sample seems to give fairly adequate representation to the moderately small industrial corporation as well as to the very large. The inclusion of both small and large companies should permit of conclusions broader in nature than those which would be possible were only the largest companies studied. As we shall see later, one fruitful result of the inclusion of companies varying widely as to size is that an interesting analysis of the relationship between the

8. Eight were in bankruptcy or receivership and filed no data with the SEC, while the information for the ninth, tho available, was obviously incomplete.

9. Adequate representation of these two fields would have involved the addition of a considerable number of companies. Further, it was felt that the sample would be rendered more homogeneous by the exclusion of these fields.

TABLE I. — DISTRIBUTION BY INDUSTRIAL CLASSES OF COMPANIES
LISTED ON NEW YORK STOCK EXCHANGE AND THOSE
INCLUDED IN SAMPLE[1]

Class	Number Listed on Stock Exchange (July 1, 1935)	Number in Sample
Automobile[2]	53	9
Aviation	10	3
Building[3]	22	4
Chemical[4]	55	16
Food and Tobacco	74	16
Iron and Steel[5]	36	11
Leather and Boots	9	1
Machinery and Metal Products[6]	81	20[7]
Paper and Publishing	19	1
Petroleum	42	6
Railroad Equipment	14	3
Rubber Goods and Tires	7	5
Shipbuilding and Operating	7	2
Textiles	31	8
Miscellaneous[8]	24	2
Total	484	107
Amusement	13	
Mining (excluding Iron)	42	
Retail Trade	61	
Total "Industrial"	600	
Finance	27	
Public Utilities	62	
Railroads	86	
Grand Total	775	

[1] Classification derived by combining industrial groups used by Stock Exchange. Cf. New York Stock Exchange Bulletin, July, 1935, pp. 122–123.
[2] Includes automobile accessories.
[3] Includes building materials.
[4] Includes glass manufactures.
[5] Includes iron mining and coke.
[6] Includes farm machinery and business and electrical equipment.
[7] Of two companies here included (as manufacturers of electrical equipment), the Stock Exchange classifies one under amusement companies and the other under public utilities. A third company here included is classified by the Stock Exchange under mining. Although partly engaged in mining, its activities are chiefly concerned with smelting and refining.
[8] Includes Stock Exchange miscellaneous, shipping services, and land-realty-hotels groups.

STOCKHOLDINGS OF OFFICERS AND DIRECTORS   627

extent of management ownership and size of company, for
the corporations here studied, is thus made possible. Finally,
something should be said as to the effect of the nature of the
sample upon the type of result to be expected. The inclusion
only of industrial companies and the fact that relatively
small companies play an important part in the sample should
lead to figures for the proportion of stock outstanding owned
by corporate executives larger on the whole than would have
been the case had the large companies in the public utliity,
banking, and transportation fields also been studied.

The procedure in compiling the data was as follows. A
complete list of all officers and directors for each of the 107
companies was first drawn up. From the SEC Form 5, which
gives stockholdings for each individual as of July 1, 1935,
the number of shares of each equity security owned by each
officer and director was then transcribed.[1] For some individuals data from Form 5 were not available, but in practically all such cases ownership figures were secured from
Forms 4, 6, or 10.[2] In those cases where Form 10 was used,
the figures were for a date other than July 1 (in every case
some date in the first six months of 1935). The number of
such cases was relatively small, and it is extreme unlikely
that the figures would have been significantly different had
data for July 1 been directly available.[3]

1. Both direct and indirect ownership are required to be reported:
Thus the data give not merely shares held directly, but also all stock
owned beneficially through holding companies, partnerships, trusts,
etc. Direct holdings include stock held on margin in brokerage accounts
as well as that owɛed outright. In a very few cases, Form 5 was for a
date slightly different from July 1.

2. For a description of these forms, see footnote 3, p. 623, above.
Duplicate copies of all these forms are on file at the New York Stock
Exchange.

3. For one thing, all changes in ownership after the date for which
stockholdings were given in Form 10 should have been reported on
Form 4. If neither Form 5 nor Form 4 was filed by an officer or director,
either no change in ownership took place after the date given in Form 10
or else there was direct evasion of the SEC regulation on this point.
Such cases of evasion were probably not numerous. Recourse was had
to Form 6 on a few occasions to secure data for executives taking office
after Form 10 was filed, in cases where such executives had not also
reported on Form 5.

It is important to bear in mind the fact that the stockholdings figures compiled for this study represent the extent of management ownership on a single day, July 1, 1935. A new study of such holdings on July 1, 1936, might give results somewhat different. One recent development in particular leads to a strong presumption that at least *large* management holdings are today somewhat smaller than they were last summer. To anticipate higher federal gift taxes which became effective this year, many corporate executives gave away substantial blocks of stock during the closing months of 1935.[4] The net effect has probably been to lower only slightly the general extent of management ownership among all companies, but without question some large individual stockholdings have been reduced substantially.

There are at least two serious imperfections in the SEC data which call for some caution in interpreting the results to follow. First, the information regarding executive stock ownership filed with the SEC is in many cases almost certainly incomplete. Even tho we assume that all officers and directors complied with the letter of the pertinent regulations and reported all their direct and beneficial holdings, many undoubtedly had given stock outright to members of their families or placed it in trusts in which legally they had no beneficial interest. In some cases, such stock was reported (usually accompanied by formal disclaimer of any beneficial ownership), and in such cases the stock has been included as a part of the reporting executive's ownership if it appeared that the latter in fact controlled the voting of these shares. It is apparent that there must be an unknown number of cases in which ownership, at least from the point of view of control and perhaps even as to the right to income, was in fact but not in law vested in officers and directors who made no report regarding such ownership.[5] Inclusion of such

4. These gifts can be traced through the monthly reports on Form 4 filed with the SEC.

5. Counsel of the SEC has ruled that an officer is the beneficial owner of securities in his wife's (or other relative's) name if for any reason "he has benefits substantially equivalent to those of ownership" or if he has the power to revest title in himself in exchange for no more

cases would undoubtedly raise the averages computed from these data, but by how much is conjectural. In the writer's opinion, it is unlikely that this fact would alter the general order of magnitude of the results.

A further difficulty arises out of the fact that in some cases stock is owned by individual executives not directly but indirectly through partnerships, personal holding and trading companies, etc., in which particular executives may have an ownership interest. In such cases the total stock owned by the holding company, etc. must be reported, but the individual need not divulge the exact extent of his interest therein.[6] The procedure here has been to attempt to allocate beneficial ownership to particular individuals on the basis of whatever information was available. In some cases, however, such allocation was impossible. As a result, the total beneficial ownership for certain individuals is undoubtedly understated.[7] In other cases, the attempted allocation may have resulted in some overstatement.

Here, as with the preceding difficulty, the writer has, in cases of doubt, tried to err in the direction of making the holdings large rather than small. Many of the errors arising from these two major defects in the data may, on balance, offset each other. On the whole, the probable net effect of these imperfections is that the computed averages are somewhat too small, but too small by an amount less than would have been the case had a less liberal attitude as to what constituted beneficial ownership been adopted.

For the purposes of this study, the officers and directors

than a nominal consideration. (Press Release No. 175 [Class A], April 16, 1935.) This ruling may have led to somewhat wider reporting of such holdings than would otherwise have been the case.

6. Or, as an alternative, he may indicate the extent of his beneficial interest in the stock held by the organization in question (in terms of number of shares) without revealing either the total amount of stock owned by the partnership, etc., or his proportionate ownership therein.

7. For one company, it was quite obvious that this sort of situation gave rise to considerable understatement. In this case, allocation of known holdings yielded a figure of 10 per cent for the proportion of stock owned by total management. The data indicated, however, that more complete information might have raised this figure to 20 or 30 per cent. The case was clearly exceptional.

of each corporation have been classified into the following groups.

A. OPERATING EXECUTIVES

Group I (narrowly selected). This group includes only the Chairman of the Board, the President, and, in some cases, men known to be of equal importance on the basis of compensation, responsibility, or some similar criterion. The total number of men in this group, for all 107 companies, was 181.

Group II (more widely selected). This group includes the men in Group I and other responsible, highly paid officials. In moderately large companies, the men in this group received during 1928–1932 annual salaries of $25,000 or more. Selection for this group was somewhat arbitrary. The purpose was to secure a group of important operating executives somewhat wider than that encompassed by Group I. The number of men included in Group II was 423.

All Officers. Here are included the men in Group II and all other operating executives except assistant secretaries, assistant treasurers, and other assistants, unless such men were unusually highly paid or on the Board of Directors. A total of 869 men is included in this "all officers" group.

B. NON-OFFICER DIRECTORS

Men listed only as directors who received substantial salaries in 1928–1932 or 1934 (years for which salary data were available) were considered as operating executives and included in the above officers groups.[8] The directors category here used includes men listed *only* as directors — or at most as members of executive or finance committees — who did not receive any compensation in excess of customary directors' fees or quite small salaries. No officers are included in this group, even tho such officers were also directors. The number of such non-officer directors was 660.

8. In all, about forty such men, listed only as directors, were included as officers.

STOCKHOLDINGS OF OFFICERS AND DIRECTORS   631

C. Total Management

This group is merely the result of combining the "all officers" and "non-officer directors" categories. "Total management," therefore, includes all directors and all operating executives, excluding only the minor functionaries previously mentioned. In all, 1,529 officers and directors are included.

II

Table II presents the basic figures for a study of the proportion of stock outstanding owned by total management and its various subgroups. No attempt is made here to study other than voting common stock. All preferred (voting and non-voting) and all non-voting common issues have been excluded.[9] The purpose has been to study at this point only the extent of control thru ownership of voting common stock. Voting control can be exercised through ownership of other voting issues,[1] but holdings of such securities by these officials were, on the whole, negligible. To test the effect of omitting other issues, a tabulation was made of the percentages of stock other than common owned by total management. The result was to indicate unmistakably that the proportion of these other issues held by management was considerably less than the percentage of voting common owned.[2] Clearly, therefore, the effect of including in each case only voting common stock was to overstate somewhat, rather than to understate, both the degree of voting control through stock ownership and the fraction of all stock outstanding owned by management.

Table II gives, for each of the management groups and for total management, the number of companies in which these groups owned the stated percentage of common stock

9. There were only six companies having two issues both of which could be called common stock. In each case, the leading voting issue was taken. In all other cases, stock excluded represented only preferred issues.

1. And, of course, control itself can be exercised without the benefit of voting power acquired through stock ownership.

2. The median percentage was less than half that obtained for the proportion of voting common owned by management.

TABLE II.— FREQUENCY DISTRIBUTION OF 107 INDUSTRIAL COMPANIES ACCORDING TO THE PROPORTION OF VOTING COMMON STOCK OUTSTANDING OWNED BY VARIOUS MANAGEMENT GROUPS, JULY 1, 1935[1]

(1) Actual Number of Companies
(2) Cumulative Number of Companies[4]

Proportion of Stock Outstanding[2] (per cent)	Number of Companies									
	Operating Officers				All Officers		Non-Officer Directors[3]		Total Management	
	Group I		Group II							
	(1)	(2)	(1)	(2)	(1)	(2)	(1)	(2)	(1)	(2)
0-1	37	37	27	27	23	23	42	42	13	13
1-2	11	48	17	44	16	39	12	54	9	22
2-3	9	57	6	50	11	50	13	67	6	28
3-4	8	65	5	55	3	53	11	78	4	32
4-5	8	73	9	64	6	59	3	81	8	40
5-10	15	88	14	78	15	74	13	94	19	59
10-15	7	95	13	91	12	86	5	99	18	77
15-20	4	99	4	95	2	88	5	104	6	83
20-25	2	101	5	100	10	98	...	...	7	90
25-30	1	102	1	101	2	100	...	...	6	96
30-35	0	102	0	101	0	100	...	...	3	99
35-40	1	103	2	103	2	102	...	...	2	101
40-45	1	104	0	103	0	102	...	...	1	102
45-50	1	105	2	105	3	105	...	...	1	103
Over 50	2	107	2	107	2	107	...	...	4	107
Median	2.33%		3.53%		4.11%		1.89%		8.10%	

[1] Stockholdings are based on SEC data (see text). Stock outstanding figures are from Standard Corporation Records and are for July 1, 1935 or the nearest available date.
[2] Lower limit of class interval inclusive.
[3] Three companies have no non-officer directors, all directors being treated as officers.
[4] These cumulative frequencies represent the total number of companies in which the groups own less than the proportion of stock corresponding to the upper limit of each class interval.

outstanding. The data refer to the *total* stockholdings of the various management groups and not to the average owner-ship per man in a given group. Thus — referring to Officers, Group I — in 37 of the 107 companies this group *as a whole* owned less than one per cent of the outstanding voting common stock, etc. Column (2) for each group presents the frequencies of column (1) in cumulative form.

The figures in Table II strongly suggest a widespread absence of substantial stock ownership among the manage-ments of these corporations.[3] Despite the inclusion of many relatively small corporations, in only four of the 107 com-panies did all officers and directors *together* own so much as a majority of the voting common stock outstanding.[4] In the great majority of cases, total ownership of management was much less. In as many as forty companies, total manage-ment holdings represent less than five per cent of the out-standing voting common. In over half of the companies, total management ownership amounts to less than ten per cent. The median company holding is 8.10 per cent.

The results for subgroups within management, of course, indicate the same absence of ownership in a much more marked degree. Most interesting is the contrast between officers and non-officer directors. It is clear that in most companies active operating executives hold the bulk of what-ever stock is owned by management, while the holdings of non-officer directors are very small indeed. In no less than forty-two companies, these directors as a whole owned less

3. We disregard for the moment the fact that a very small *propor-tionate* ownership, particularly in large companies, may represent a quite substantial investment in absolute money terms. On this point, see Section III, below.

4. In one of these four companies, voting power is restricted to a single issue of only 2,000 shares, all owned by one officer. There is also a non-voting participating common issue of nearly 200,000 shares, of which management owns less than one-tenth of one per cent. Of the other three companies, one represents a less pronounced case of a similar sort, while in the other two both management and majority ownership are in the hands of one man or a family group. All four are relatively small firms.

than one per cent of the voting common stock outstanding.[5] In over half (54) of the companies, the non-operating directors owned less than two per cent of the outstanding voting common. The median was precisely 1.89 per cent. In not a single company did all directors not serving also as active executives own together as much as twenty per cent of the voting common stock outstanding. Whatever may be the case with respect to the actual responsibility and active functions of non-officer directors in these companies, it is clear that they do not possess, on the whole, even a moderate minority interest in the stock of the companies whose broad policies they supposedly help shape.[6]

The officers group, as a whole and in its subdivisions, indicates the same absence of substantial stockholdings, but to a much less marked degree. In twenty-three companies, all operating officers together owned less than one per cent of the voting common stock outstanding.[7] In over half of the companies all officers owned less than five per cent of the outstanding voting common. The median percentage is 4.11 per cent, compared to 1.89 per cent for directors. On the average, it would seem, stockholdings of the officers group were more than twice as large as those of non-officer directors.[8]

5. In five of these forty-two companies, not a single non-officer director reported ownership of as much as one share of stock of any kind. In each of four of these five companies, however, no more than two men were treated as non-officer directors.

6. The significance of this absence of stock ownership among directors should be considered in connection with the extent to which such men act as the representatives of investment banks, large minority stockholders, or other outside control groups. In such capacity, they may conceivably represent a substantial stock ownership and may exercise considerable control. No attempt has been made to ascertain the extent to which this is actually the case among these companies.

7. In four companies, all officers together owned either no stock at all or at most a few shares. Two of these corporations are controlled by other concerns, and several of the officers of one of them own stock in the controlling company. No such outside control, at least through stock ownership, was apparent in the case of the other two companies.

8. This relation exists also between the arithmetic mean holdings, the figures being 9.71 per cent and 3.39 per cent, respectively. Medians rather than arithmetic means have been cited in the text because of the undue influence of extreme items on the latter type of average in cases of this sort.

STOCKHOLDINGS OF OFFICERS AND DIRECTORS   635

There were nineteen companies in which the operating executives owned more than twenty per cent of the outstanding common shares, a proportionate stock ownership achieved by not one directors group.

The picture is altered but little by setting aside the less important executives and considering only the men included in Group II. As is to be expected, the less important officers not in this group contribute but little to the total stockholdings of management. More significant is the proportion of total officers' holdings owned by the very few important executives in Group I. The average number of men per company in this group is only 1.7, whereas the average number of men per company in the "all officers" group is 8.1. Yet the few chief executives, representing in number not much over a fifth of all officers, owned, on the average, well over half of the stock held by all operating executives.[9] Further, these 181 most important officers owned more stock than did the total of 660 non-officer directors, to whom, in part, they are supposedly responsible.

A possible objection to the figures and analysis thus far presented may be that no allowance has been made for the fact that the number of men in each management subgroup is not the same for every company. It may be argued that the companies with relatively small management ownership may be simply those in which only a few executives are included. Similarly, the larger holdings of the officers group may be due only to the fact that there are many more operating executives than there are non-officer directors. Some light is thrown upon this point by Table III, which presents for each management group the average number of men owning the percentages of stock outstanding given in Table II.[1]

Except for non-officer directors, the correlation between number of men and total group holdings is certainly not

9. About 57 per cent, if the medians are compared; but about 71 per cent if arithmetic means are used.

1. For convenience, the intervals between zero and 5 per cent and over 25 per cent have been combined in Table III;

636   *QUARTERLY JOURNAL OF ECONOMICS*

TABLE III. — AVERAGE NUMBER OF MEN PER COMPANY
IN MANAGEMENT GROUPS, CLASSIFIED ACCORDING TO
PERCENTAGE STOCKHOLDINGS[1]

Proportion of Stock Outstanding[3] (per cent)	Average Number of Men Per Company				
	Operating Officers			Non-Officer Directors	Total Management
	Group I	Group II	All Officers		
0–5	1.67	4.06	8.46	6.09	15.65
5–10	1.73	4.21	9.53	6.69	16.58
10–15	1.71	3.54	6.58	7.40	12.56
15–20	1.50	4.50	6.50	8.60	13.83
20–25	3.00	4.00	8.50	...	14.00
Over 25	1.50	2.86	5.56	...	10.65
All companies	1.69	3.95	8.12	6.35[2]	14.29

[1] Derived primarily from company annual reports and SEC Form 10. The figures represent the average number of men per company on or about July 1, 1935. Averages are arithmetic means.
[2] Total number of non-officer directors divided by 104 companies, there being three companies in which all directors were treated as officers.
[3] Lower limit of class interval inclusive.

positive. No particular relation is to be expected in Group I of officers, since so few men are included. But for the other officers groups, as well as for management as a whole, the relation between the average size of each group and total proportionate stockholdings is, if anything, inverse. For the most part, the smaller management groups hold relatively more stock than do the larger groups. Clearly, then, the number of companies for which management ownership is small cannot be accounted for by the fact that fewer officers are included in these companies.

In the case of non-officer directors, however, part of the variation in total directors' holdings can be explained by a corresponding variation in number of men included. But the figures also indicate quite clearly that the extent of ownership increases much faster than does the number of men; that is to say, average proportionate ownership (per man) is by no means constant.

STOCKHOLDINGS OF OFFICERS AND DIRECTORS   637

Further, the larger total holdings of officers cannot be explained merely by the fact that these companies have on the average more officers than directors. The average number of operating executives per company is 8.12; the average number of directors is 6.35. The ratio between these two figures is much less than that between the typical total stockholdings of these two groups. (See Table II; cf., also, Table IV.)

The reason for the inverse relation between number of men and total stockholdings is fairly obvious. The larger management groups represent larger companies, and in these companies management may be expected to own a smaller proportion of the outstanding stock. It is far more difficult to own one per cent of the stock of a billion dollar corporation than it would be to acquire the same proportion of the stock of, say, a small company with assets of only a million dollars. Further, the diffusion of stock ownership in very large companies is by now a widely recognized fact upon which there has already been considerable comment,[2] and management holdings in these companies would naturally tend to be small.

Table IV indicates that the explanation here suggested is the correct one.[3] For all officers and for total management,

2. It is to be remembered that we are dealing exclusively with companies listed on the New York Stock Exchange. Hence we must expect some participation of the public in the ownership of even the smaller companies of our sample.

3. Table IV calls for some comment. For convenience, total assets have been taken as the criterion of size. Theoretically, perhaps, since we are studying *stock* ownership, net worth or aggregate market value should have been used. But use of either of these two latter measures (in view of the wide size groups used and the high degree of correlation between each of these two measures and total assets in the case of industrial companies) would not materially alter the nature of the relationship shown in Table IV. In addition, net worth computations are frequently none too accurate, while market values suffer the disadvantage of being relatively unstable.

Asset figures represent total stated assets, without any adjustment, for December 31, 1934, or the nearest available date. (Source: Poor's Manual of Industrial Companies.) The asset classes in Table IV have been made wide enough so that a reasonable number of companies could be included in each size group, but yet small enough so that the

TABLE IV. — PERCENTAGE STOCKHOLDINGS AND AVERAGE NUMBER OF MEN IN MANAGEMENT, BY ASSET GROUPS[1]

Assets[3] (Unit: $1,000,000)	No. of Companies	Officers		Non-Officer Directors		Total Management	
		Stock-holdings %	Average No. of Men per Company	Stock-holdings %	Average No. of Men per Company	Stock-holdings %	Average No. of Men per Company
0–5	14	14.86	5.8	1.62	4.1	16.48	9.9
5–10	20	17.58	6.3	4.07[2]	4.8[2]	21.45	10.9
10–25	16	12.33	6.9	4.55	5.4	16.88	12.4
25–50	19	7.18	8.2	3.99	7.3	11.17	15.5
50–100	14	4.55	8.2	4.63	8.5	9.18	16.7
100–250	16	3.83	10.8	1.99	6.9	5.83	17.8
250–500	3	3.12	12.7	1.30[2]	9.5[2]	3.99	19.0
500 and over	5	2.34	13.8	1.26[2]	9.3[2]	3.35	21.2

[1] Based upon the same data as those from which Tables II and III were derived For derivation of asset groupings, see text (page 637, note 3).
[2] In each of these groups, one company had no non-officer directors (all directors being treated as officers). These companies have been omitted in computing average percentage stockholdings and average number of men for non-officer directors.
[3] Lower limit of class interval inclusive.

the negative correlation between size of company and extent of ownership is unmistakable — altho somewhat exaggerated by use of the arithmetic mean as an average.[4] On the whole, the percentage of stock owned by all officers and by total management declines almost uninterruptedly as the size of company increases.[5] In the smallest companies, total man-

companies in any one interval are all of comparable size. Averages are unweighted arithmetic means of percentage stockholdings for the companies falling into each size group.

These averages conceal considerable variation among the percentage figures for the individual companies in each class interval, but in this case the nature of the variation was not considered sufficient to invalidate use of the mean. Nevertheless, the fact of such dispersion, as well as the effect of unusually large items upon the mean, should be kept in mind.

4. The few extremely large percentages occur chiefly in the smaller size groups, a fact which tends to exaggerate to some extent the average percentage stockholdings in these intervals. And even in these groups, there are some cases of small percentage stockholdings.

5. All three of the management groups show smaller proportionate holdings for the companies with assets under $5,000,000 than for those

agement owns on the average about fifteen or twenty per cent of the outstanding voting common. In companies with total assets between 25 and 100 millions, officers' and directors' holdings together average about ten per cent. In the largest companies, the proportion of stock owned by management as a whole falls well below five per cent.[6] The same consistently inverse relationship is also found between size of company and the stockholdings of officers alone.

In the case of directors' holdings, the declining tendency as the companies become larger is scarcely noticeable — at least not until the largest companies are reached. Even in companies of small size, directors' holdings are very small. One result is that the contrast between officers' and directors' holdings tends to diminish as the companies become larger; directors' holdings become a larger, and officers' holdings a smaller, proportion of total management stock ownership.

Table IV indicates clearly that the average number of men in management and in each of its subgroups tends to increase markedly with the size of company. This relation makes all the more noteworthy the negative correlation discovered between the percentage total stockholdings of the management and officers groups and size of firm. Proportionate ownership *per man*, apparently, declines even more pronouncedly than is indicated by the total stockholdings figures presented in Table IV.

The inverse relation between percentage stockholdings and size of firm suggests a further point. Since management holdings are relatively smallest in the largest companies, the proportion of total industrial wealth (in our sample) that is

with assets between five and ten millions. An examination of the individual percentages for each company yielded no obvious explanation that would account for this exception to the general tendency.

6. Subdivision of the asset groups into smaller intervals reveals that the declining tendency takes place by a few pronounced steps, rather than gradually. The breaks come for companies with assets of about 15 and 150 million dollars. Below $15,000,000, the percentages for management stockholdings average about 20 per cent; for the intervals between 15 and 50 millions, they are close to 10 per cent; for companies with assets above $150,000,000, the percentages fall to 5 per cent or less. The same tendency is apparent in officers' holdings.

affected by the separation of management and ownership should be much greater than that indicated by the distribution of companies in Table II. The following figures are of interest in this connection. Column (1) represents the percentage of total assets of all 107 companies owned by those companies in which total management held the stated proportion of voting common stock outstanding.

Total Stockholdings of Management (Per Cent)	(1) Proportion of Assets of All Companies (Per Cent)	(2) Number of Companies
0–5	66.3	40
5–10	21.8	19
10–25	9.0	31
25–50	2.7	13
50 and over	0.2	4
	100.0	107

The results are in line with what we should expect. While too much emphasis should not be placed on the actual size of the largest percentage in column (1), since this figure depends primarily on the assets of only a very few extremely large firms, there can be little doubt that a similar set of results would follow if the computations were repeated for a wider sample of Stock Exchange companies.

III

The implication of the figures thus far presented is that management, even in the smaller companies, tends to participate only to a minor extent in corporate ownership, and that in the larger companies particularly the holdings of officers and directors are very small indeed. If, instead of group totals, averages were computed — showing for all companies the average percentage ownership *per* officer or *per* director — the figures, of course, would be much smaller.

Percentage figures, however, give but an incomplete picture of the extent of management stock ownership. The absolute dollar amount of officers' and directors' stockholdings may be of as much or even more significance than

STOCKHOLDINGS OF OFFICERS AND DIRECTORS   641

their proportionate holdings in percentage terms. Whatever may be our conception of the entrepreneur of economic theory, it remains true that much of the responsibility, initiative, and active leadership in the successful conduct of the productive process must rest with just the men with whom this study deals — the officers and (to a less extent) the directors of publicly owned companies such as those here studied. What incentives exist, under our modern corporate system, to stimulate the efficient exercise of this initiative and leadership? Altho these men do not possess enough stock to control their companies, it is conceivable that the absolute value of their stockholdings may be sufficiently large to provide a real incentive through ownership alone. While there have been many and contradictory assumptions regarding the importance of this incentive in practice, little precise factual evidence on this point has heretofore been available.

In an attempt to shed some light upon this problem, actual market values have been computed as of July 1, 1935, for the shareholdings of the officers and directors here under study. It is to be noted that these market values are as of a given day, that for which figures on share-holdings were available, and hence must be considered with reference to the level of stock market prices then prevailing.[7] Frequency distributions and averages of these values are nevertheless important, both in showing the distribution and range of such dollar holdings among individuals and companies and in indicating the general order of magnitude of the amounts involved.[8]

7. Values computed by averaging prices over a longer period would suffer from the same defect, tho to a less extent, and would have added to a statistical burden already quite heavy.

8. A further limitation should be kept in mind in interpreting these value figures. When the original data were compiled, the criterion in determining ownership in doubtful cases was: Who controlled the voting of the stock? This criterion may not necessarily be the one proper to a study of the market value of stock owned — at least, if implications are to be drawn as to the financial gains and losses possible from such ownership. How serious an error is involved here is unknown. It seems safe to assume, however, that the error is not large enough to alter materially the general nature of the results obtained.

Of all the officers and directors making up total management, the most important are clearly the few leading executives included in Group I. It is particularly interesting to know, therefore, the nature of the economic incentives which motivate these men in their direction of the productive process. One such incentive is obviously the financial gain possible from ownership in the companies they manage.

Table V presents a frequency series of the 179 leading executives which make up Group I,[9] classified according to the market value of stock owned on July 1, 1935. The frequency distribution here presented, be it noted, is of individual executives, not companies — market values being computed for each man irrespective of the company to which he belonged. To facilitate the analysis, figures are given both for the value of common stock alone and for the value of all equity securities. It is in the ownership of common stock, of course, that the greatest possibilities of gain or loss arise.[1]

Both ends of the frequency distributions presented in Table V provide food for thought. Attention may be called first to the number of men the value of whose stockholdings (whether common alone or all equity securities) must be considered large by any reasonable standard. Considering common stock only, no less than 31 of the 179 men (about 17 per cent) each had an ownership interest in their companies the value of which exceeded $1,000,000. Each of 45 men (about 25 per cent) owned common stock valued at $500,000 or more. And 92 executives, or over half, held common stock with a value of at least $100,000. The corresponding figures for the total value of all stock held are somewhat higher.

9. One company, with two Group I officers, has been excluded from the market value computations in Tables V–VII. This is the company in which the small voting issue outstanding was all owned by one official (see p. 633, note 4, above). Naturally, no quotations were available for this stock.

1. In the figures on percentage ownership (Tables II and IV), only the voting common stock was considered. In the present section, however, all common issues were taken together in computing the value of common stock owned.

STOCKHOLDINGS OF OFFICERS AND DIRECTORS   643

TABLE V. — DISTRIBUTION OF 179 LEADING EXECUTIVES BY MARKET
VALUE OF STOCK OWNED ON JULY 1, 1935[1]

(1) Actual Number of Men
(2) Cumulative Number of Men[2]

Value-Holdings[3] (Unit: $1,000)	Number of Men			
	Common Stock		All Issues	
	(1)	(2)	(1)	(2)
0–25	50	179	42	179
25–50	13	129	10	137
50–75	15	116	20	127
75–100	9	101	8	107
100–200	19	92	18	99
200–300	14	73	17	81
300–400	6	59	6	64
400–500	8	53	6	58
500–750	9	45	13	52
750–1,000	5	36	6	39
1,000–5,000	24	31	26	33
5,000–10,000	4	7	4	7
10,000 and over	3	3	3	3
Median[4]	$113,600		$137,000	

[1] Covers 106 companies only, one company, with two selected officers, being omitted (see text, p. 642, note 9). Market values are based on New York Stock Exchange closing prices on July 1, 1935, where available, otherwise on bid quotations. In some cases, not all issues were listed on the Stock Exchange. For these, New York Curb or over-the-counter prices or bid quotations were used — for July 1, 1935, if available, otherwise for the nearest available date. See text (p. 642) for further discussion of the method of deriving this table.
[2] In this case, the cumulative frequencies represent the total number of men with value-holdings equal to or greater than the lower limit of each class interval.
[3] Lower limit of class interval inclusive.
[4] Medians computed from original arrays and rounded to nearest hundred dollars.

On the other hand, there were fifty executives (about 28 per cent) with common stockholdings of less than $25,000 (and of these 28 reported holdings valued at less than $5,000). If all issues are considered, the number of men with very small holdings in value terms is reduced somewhat.

The median holdings are: for common alone, $113,600; for all issues taken together, $137,000.[2] These averages, being

2. Medians were computed from the original arrays and are given to the nearest hundred dollars. In view of the extreme range of the

based merely on the middle item in each series, do not reflect the very high values in the upper ranges. Additional significance, therefore, attaches to the fact that the typical value-holdings are as large as those here cited.

Part of the variation in the value of stock held by these executives is undoubtedly related to the diversity in the size of companies included in the sample. The nature of this correlation in the case of all officers is indicated in Table VII below.

Before considering further the implications of these figures, it would be well to extend the analysis to management as a whole. To this end, series of *average* value-holdings per man have been computed. For each company, the market value of the stock owned by all officers was divided by the number of such executives, and similar computations were performed for non-officer directors and for management as a whole. The resulting figures give for each company the average value-holding per man in each of these three groups. These calculations were carried through both for common stock alone and for all stock issues together. The results are given in Table VI, which presents frequency distributions of the 106 companies according to the average value of stock owned per individual in each of the three groups.[3]

As is to be expected, the figures indicate that average value-holdings of all officers, as well as of non-officer directors and of all men in total management, tend to be smaller than the individual holdings of the important executives previously studied. The contrast is most marked in the upper ranges of the frequency distributions. It is perhaps worth

value holdings, arithmetic means are of even less use here than in the study of proportionate ownership.

3. Attention is called to the fact that the figures in Table VI (and Table VII) are average value-holdings *per individual*. Our interest here is in the dollar stake of the officers and directors individually — in the incentive and possibilities of gain or loss acting upon each man. In studying percentage ownership as an index of voting control, on the other hand, our chief interest lay in the total proportionate stockholdings of each management subgroup taken as a whole. Control can be exercised by a group of officers or directors working together; but the possibilities of gain or loss react chiefly upon these men as individuals.

TABLE VI. — DISTRIBUTION OF 106 INDUSTRIAL COMPANIES BY AVERAGE MARKET VALUE OF STOCK OWNED PER MAN IN VARIOUS MANAGEMENT GROUPS, JULY 1, 1935[1]

(1) Actual Number of Companies
(2) Cumulative Number of Companies[2]

Average Value-Holding[3] (Unit: $1,000)	All Officers				Non-Officer Directors[4]				Total Management			
	Common		All Issues		Common		All Issues		Common		All Issues	
	(1)	(2)	(1)	(2)	(1)	(2)	(1)	(2)	(1)	(2)	(1)	(2)
0–25	31	31	26	26	43	43	38	38	25	25	18	18
25–50	14	45	14	40	16	59	11	49	19	44	19	37
50–75	10	55	12	52	8	67	12	61	12	56	14	51
75–100	6	61	6	58	6	73	8	69	8	64	10	61
100–200	17	78	19	77	9	82	11	80	14	78	15	76
200–300	6	84	4	81	6	88	6	86	8	86	7	83
300–400	4	88	5	86	2	90	2	88	4	90	4	87
400–500	4	92	6	92	4	94	4	92	2	92	5	92
500–750	6	98	6	98	5	99	7	99	11	103	10	102
750–1,000	4	102	4	102	1	100	1	100	2	105	3	105
1,000 and over	4	106	4	106	3	103	3	103	1	106	1	106
Median[5]	$71,800		$80,100		$35,800		$53,900		$69,200		$81,300	

[1] See text (p. 644) and footnote 1 to Table V for method of deriving this table.
[2] Cumulative frequencies represent total number of companies in which group average value-holdings per man were less than the upper limit of each class interval.
[3] Lower limit of class interval inclusive.
[4] Includes only 103 companies, there being three with no non-officer directors.
[5] Computed from original arrays and rounded to nearest hundred dollars.

TABLE VII. — DISTRIBUTION OF 106 INDUSTRIAL COMPANIES BY AVERAGE VALUE OF ALL STOCKHOLDINGS PER OFFICER AND DIRECTOR AND BY SIZE OF COMPANY[1]

A. ALL OFFICERS

Total Assets[3] (Unit: $1,000,000)	Average Value-Holdings per Officer[2] (Unit: $1,000)						Total Number of Companies	Median Value-Holding	Mean Value-Holding[4]
	0–25	25–50	50–100	100–250	250–500	500 and Over			
0–5	5	3	2	3	..	..	13	32.5	46.8
5–10	8	3	4	3	..	2	20	33.5	127.1
10–25	3	1	6	5	1	..	16	78.3	94.7
25–50	3	3	1	6	4	2	19	147.8	222.6
50–100	3	1	2	1	5	2	14	248.0	272.0
100–250	4	3	..	2	2	5	16	116.1	376.6
250–500	..	..	1	1	..	1	3	101.6	478.6
500 and over	..	..	2	..	1	2	5	392.7	953.4
Total Number of Companies	26	14	18	21	13	14	106		

B. NON-OFFICER DIRECTORIES

Total Assets[2] (Unit: $1,000,000)	Average Value-Holdings per Director[2] (Unit: $1,000)						Total Number of Companies[4]	Median Value-Holding	Mean Value-Holding[3]
	0–25	25–50	50–100	100–250	250–500	£ 500 and Over			
0–5	11	..	2	..	..	..	13	5.5	17.8
5–10	10	2	5	1	1	..	19	20.0	57.5
10–25	6	4	2	3	1	..	16	38.3	70.2
25–50	5	1	5	3	3	2	19	90.6	278.3
50–100	2	2	2	3	1	4	14	172.8	282.6
100–250	3	2	3	2	3	3	16	112.0	286.1
250–500	1	..	..	..	..	1	2	296.9	296.9
500 and over	..	..	1	2	..	1	4	174.4	671.2
Total Number of Companies	38	11	20	14	9	11	103		

[1] Value-holdings cover all classes of stock and are the same as those used in the "All Issues" columns of Table VI. For derivation of asset groupings, see p. 637, note, above.

[2] Lower limit of class interval inclusive.

[3] These means are unweighted arithmetic averages of the mean value-holdings for the companies in each size group. Being unweighted, they take no account of the fact that not the same number of men is included in each company. Weighted means of average value-holdings would give results somewhat but not significantly different.

[4] Three companies in which all directors were treated as officers have been omitted in this tabulation of directors' holdings.

noting, however, that there were as many as 14 companies in which the average value-holdings of all officers were as large as $500,000. The size of these average holdings is due partly to the very large value-holdings of a few leading executives, but partly also to the fact that in some of these companies even the less important officials owned stock of substantial value (altho not necessarily a large fraction of the total stock outstanding). Further, in as many as eleven companies non-officer directors *on the average* owned as much as $500,000 in equity securities (nine companies if only common stock is considered).

In many companies, significantly, the average value-holdings of both officers and directors were fairly small. In over 40 per cent of the companies, all officers on the average owned less than $50,000 of common stock, and in over 50 per cent directors' holdings were less than this amount. The extent of small holdings is somewhat reduced if all stock issues are considered.[4]

The median value figures bring out clearly the contrast between officers' and directors' holdings, the average for the executives' group being twice that for non-officer directors. The median for the average value-holdings of common stock by all officers is $71,800, or somewhat less than two-thirds the typical value-holding for leading executives in Group I.

The figures for total management call for some comment. There were 31 companies in which the ownership of common stock by officers averaged less than $25,000, and in 43 companies average value-holdings of directors were less than this. Yet when officers' and directors' holdings are combined, we find that in only 25 companies is the average value-holding per individual in total management as low as $25,000. In a number of companies, it is evident, small officers' holdings must have been associated with relatively large directors' holdings; otherwise there could not have been so

4. In most cases, apparently, value-holdings are not significantly increased if all issues are taken, rather than common stock alone. In relation to ownership of common, holdings of preferred issues seem to be greatest among directors. For an indication of this, compare the medians in Table VI.

STOCKHOLDINGS OF OFFICERS AND DIRECTORS   649

few as only 25 companies in which the average for management as a whole was under $25,000.

The possibility of an inverse relationship between mean
value-holdings of officers and those of directors seems also
to be indicated if we refer to the medians for the various
groups, particularly in the case of all stock issues. Here the
median for the average value-holdings of total management
is *larger* than the medians for average holdings of either
officers or directors. Put in somewhat technical terms, the
median of a series made up by averaging the items in two
component series is larger than the median of either of these
two series. This result, in the case of our study, is surprising,
tho certainly not mathematically impossible. Actually (and
this is borne out by a detailed study of the original data) it
seems to arise not out of an inverse relation between officers'
and directors' holdings, but rather out of the absence of any
marked positive correlation. Thus, altho in a good many
companies small average holdings for officers go with small
directors' holdings, in many cases the relation is the inverse
of this. The net result of these conflicting tendencies is that
there are somewhat fewer companies with smaller average
holdings for total management, and hence there is a higher
median figure for the average holdings of this group than we
should at first thought expect.

More detailed analysis of the figures in Table VI must be
left to the reader. We now turn our attention to a final
point regarding these value-holdings; to wit, the relation
between the average value of stock owned by management
and size of company. The facts bearing upon this question
are presented in the two sections of Table VII. (Average
value-holdings are for all issues taken together, not merely
for common alone.)

In this case, it has been thought advisable to present
actual two-way frequency tables, rather than merely one
summary average for each asset group as was done in
Table IV.[5] In both sections of Table VII, the class intervals

5. Because of the extreme range of average value-holdings as among
companies, it was thought unwise to rely merely on arithmetic means

reading vertically represent size groups (by total assets); horizontally, the intervals indicate average value-holdings. Thus referring to Section A of the table, there were five companies with assets less than $5,000,000 in which officers' value-holdings were less than $25,000, three companies with assets between five and ten millions in which average value holdings were between $25,000 and $50,000, etc.

In both sections of Table VII there seems to be some positive correlation between average value-holdings and size of company — i.e. average value-holdings per man for both officers and directors tend, on the whole, to be larger, the larger the size of the company. In neither case, however, is the degree of correlation very high. In practically all asset intervals except the very lowest, the distribution of companies according to the average value-holdings of both management groups is wide.

The relatively large frequencies in the upper left corner of Section B of the table tend to create the impression that the correlation between directors' value-holdings and size of firm is somewhat higher than that existing in the case of officers' holdings. But if allowance is made for the fact that directors' holdings tend to be small in all companies and particularly so in the smaller firms, there is little to choose between the degree of correlation in either case. The rapidity with which either officers' or directors' holdings tend to increase with size of company is indicated by the averages appended to Table VII.[6]

IV

The results of the statistical analysis of the preceding pages tend to bear out the conclusions which have been

of the average value-holdings for the companies in each size group. Medians, when the number of items in each group is not large, are also unsatisfactory. (In Table IV, the range of the percentages in each size group was not deemed wide enough to invalidate the use of the arithmetic means there presented.) In order to present as complete a picture as possible, both medians and means are given as added data in Table VII, but the limitations of these averages in this case should be kept in mind.

6. As indicated above, these averages need to be interpreted with caution.

STOCKHOLDINGS OF OFFICERS AND DIRECTORS   651

reached by others concerning the separation of management and ownership in American industry, and in some respects to fill in gaps in our previous knowledge of this phenomenon. The present study indicates that the proportion of stock owned by management is small not only in the giant corporations in the public utility, railroad, and industrial fields, but also in a wide range of smaller industrial corporations. While all of these are publicly owned to a sufficient degree to be listed on the New York Stock Exchange, many are far from the "giant" class. These conclusions, however, cannot be extended to the large body of more closely held companies, the securities of which are listed merely on local exchanges or are not listed at all.

In most of the companies here studied, the total stock ownership of all operating executives taken together amounts to no more than a small minority interest, while holdings of directors are considerably less important than those of officers. Hence, even when officers and directors are taken together, the proportion of stock owned by management as a whole is found to be small. And what is true of these management groups, of course, is much more true of officers and directors as individuals.

The absence of substantial stock ownership by management becomes more pronounced if related to total assets rather than to number of companies. This fact, already commented on by others, is associated with an important, altho not unexpected, relation which has been brought out in the course of the preceding analysis. This is the negative correlation existing between the percentage of management stockholdings and size of company. The largest proportionate ownership naturally exists in the smaller companies, altho even here management stockholdings amount to no more on the average than an important minority interest. And even for these companies, the holdings of directors alone are surprisingly small: the relationship between total management ownership and size of firm arises primarily out of the variation in officers' holdings alone.

With respect to *value*-holdings, the observed relations

seem to be less clear-cut. The dollar value of stock owned by many executives is surprisingly large, especially among the officers in Group I. Yet by and large the extent of stock ownership even in this sense cannot be considered substantial for most operating executives; and this absence of substantial value-holdings, of course, is even more marked among directors. Nor is there any very marked degree of correlation between value-holdings and size of company, altho, as is clearly to be expected, the largest holdings are mainly to be found in the larger companies.

Not only is the statistical picture presented by these value-holding figures somewhat conflicting, but the economic significance of such tendencies as are apparent must be weighed with caution. To the extent that value-holdings are very large, particularly among leading executives, they indicate that the profit incentives of the individual proprietorship or close corporation exist even where control and ownership are to a large extent separated. But what constitutes a "substantial" value-holding is not easy to determine; primarily it depends on the income of the executive from all other sources. For example (and this is a consideration of considerable importance), seemingly large value-holdings may not in themselves supply an important incentive to entrepreneurial activity if dividends and possible capital increment from such holdings are small in comparison to salary and bonus receipts.

There has been much discussion in recent years concerning some of the social and legal implications of phenomena such as are brought to light by the preceding analysis. Yet there seems to have been but little recognition among economists of the need for revising the relevant parts of orthodox economic theory in the light of what we are learning about the facts of our modern corporate system. This is particularly true with respect to current theories of enterprise and profits.[7]

7. For some discussion touching on this problem, cf. Berle and Means, op. cit., Bk. IV; P. M. O'Leary, Corporate Enterprise in

The writer does not believe that any concept of the entrepreneurial function can be complete, or even very useful,
unless the definition of that function encompasses the active
decision making and responsibility for policy which is
involved in control over the allocation of the factors of
production and in the direction of the productive process.
This is what is usually meant by "entrepreneurial control,"
and it is this which is implied in our conception of responsible
business and financial leadership. Some such concept of
entrepreneurial control is held even by those who emphasize
the supposed risk bearing aspect of the entrepreneur's rôle.

A point which has been almost completely neglected in the
literature on enterprise and profits is that practically all
our profits theories assume, at least tacitly, an *association*
of entrepreneurial control and ownership such as is found
in the individual proprietorship. Only under such an assumption can the residual income of ownership, some part or all
of which is what is usually meant by "profits," [8] be said to
accrue to the "entrepreneurs"; i.e. to those in control of
industry. If this is not the case, entrepreneurial control may
be exercised by other than those who receive the residual
"profits" of ownership. In other words, where ownership is
dissociated from entrepreneurial control, "profits" in the
usual sense go to others than those who are the entrepreneurs.
What then happens to our concept of "profits" as the functional return to enterprise? [9] No more can be attempted
here than to indicate a few of the questions which must be
answered if an adequate solution to this problem is to be
found.

Modern Economic Life (New York, 1933), ch. III; C. O. Hardy, Risk
and Risk-Bearing (revised ed., Chicago, 1931), pp. 52–54. Cf. also
B. W. Lewis, in the Journal of Political Economy, XLIII (1935),
pp. 551–552.

8. The net income or "profit" of an enterprise accrues to those who
are the legal owners of the enterprise. It is in this sense that the term
"ownership income" is here used.

9. Cf. Berle and Means, op. cit., Bk. IV, ch. II. It may be added
here that it seems to have been the nature of "profits" as a residual,
fluctuating income (supposedly going to the entrepreneur but actually
accruing to him only in his capacity as owner) which has led to the

First of all, the question as to which individual or individuals actually do exercise the entrepreneurial function in the modern corporation needs to be reconsidered. It is clear that the great body of passive stockholders, the chief recipients of ownership income, have little to do with active control, and that we must look elsewhere for the true entrepreneur. It is the present writer's opinion — but proof must await more detailed analysis — that much of the entrepreneurial function in the 107 companies here studied is exercised by one or at most a few important executives.[1]

If this be true, is it these individuals who receive "profits," or do "profits" accrue to the owners, whose chief productive functions seem to be merely the supplying of capital and the assumption of a certain degree of risk?[2] An answer to the question can perhaps be found by starting with a redefinition of profits in a functional sense and in a frank admission that income to passive owners is not entrepreneurial income and may be to some extent functionless in nature. This solution would imply considering as functional profits part or all of the income of the entrepreneur derived from the concern regardless whether such income was received through ownership, salaries, financial manipulation, or in some other manner.[3] A further implication of this method of attack emphasis placed by some economists on the risk bearing nature of the entrepreneurial function. At the same time, the control aspect of enterprise has been so obvious it could not fail to have some recognition. Hence the association of control and risk-bearing in such theories as Professor Knight's. The latter does not seem fully to have faced the difficulty here outlined. Professor Hardy, in considering this problem, has attempted the negative solution of refusing to apply the entrepreneur concept where control and ownership have been separated. Cf. Risk and Risk-Bearing (revised ed.), p. 54, note. For a viewpoint akin to Professor Knight's and opposed to that adopted here, see B. W. Lewis, loc. cit.

1. This is not to deny that in some cases an outside "control group," entirely apart from management, may exercise a good part of the entrepreneurial function.

2. With regard to risk-bearing, it is to be remembered that bondholders also take risks, and that only a difference of degree distinguishes this risk-bearing from that assumed by stockholders.

3. In addition, of course, the entrepreneur may also secure for himself wholly unearned "gains of position."

STOCKHOLDINGS OF OFFICERS AND DIRECTORS　　655

would be that profits from many points of view must be considered in terms of individual men rather than in terms of whole enterprises. This sort of analysis may have considerable bearing on orthodox equilibrium theory. For example, where economic decisions depend on individual men whose "profits" are distinct from the net income of the enterprise, maximization of individual gain may frequently take precedence over maximization of the revenue of the firm.

An adequate answer to the questions here raised must wait upon a far more detailed analysis than we have yet had of all the ramifying aspects of modern business leadership. One final point, however, may be mentioned. It has been frequently alleged that profits in the sense of ownership income are necessary if we are to secure the industrial progress characteristic of the period since the Industrial Revolution. But to the extent that control of the productive process now rests with men whose value-holdings in their enterprises are relatively small, the initiation of economic change may have become divorced from those gains or losses accruing through ownership which arise from such change — a fact which may indicate that progress of a fairly rapid order is possible without the incentive of profits in the usual sense.

R. A. GORDON.

HARVARD UNIVERSITY

[3]

THE

QUARTERLY JOURNAL

OF

ECONOMICS

MAY, 1938

OWNERSHIP BY MANAGEMENT AND CONTROL GROUPS IN THE LARGE CORPORATION[1]

SUMMARY

I. Scope of the study and nature of the data, 367.—II. The extent of management ownership, 372.— Ownership by directors and operating executives, 376.—III. Ownership of the remaining voting stock, 379.— IV. Analysis of outside holdings separately, 383.— Problems of intercorporate ownership, 385.— V. Analysis of holdings by management and outside groups combined, 388.— VI. Proportion of all stock outstanding held by control groups, 390.— VII. Summary and conclusions, 396.

I

The modern large corporation has given rise to a wide variety of problems — social, legal, economic — of far-reaching importance. One such set of problems concerns the separation of active control from ownership and the effects of this separation upon the manner in which business leadership is exercised in the conduct of modern large-scale industry. In an earlier study, some attempt was made to throw light on the extent of stock ownership among the managements of our large corporations.[2] The sample then studied, however, was limited to industrial (chiefly manufacturing) companies, and many of the firms were of relatively small size.

1. I am indebted to the Harvard University Committee on Research in the Social Sciences for a grant of money to undertake the research embodied in this study. Thanks are also due to Mr. E. I. Epstein, who carried through a good part of the necessary computations.

2. R. A. Gordon, "Stockholdings of Officers and Directors in American Industrial Corporations," Quarterly Journal of Economics, L (1936), pp. 622–57.

The present article attempts to carry further the analysis of the institutional setting within which modern business leadership is exercised. Railway and public utility enterprises, as well as so-called "industrials," are now to be studied; and an attempt will be made to shed some statistical light on the extent of ownership by control groups other than management. Finally, the data now available will be utilized to estimate, albeit only roughly, for a selected group of very large corporations, the proportion of ownership which is in all likelihood fairly completely divorced from any measure of actual control.

Our concern here is only with the so-called "giant" corporations. The two hundred non-banking firms which Berle and Means found to be the largest in the United States in 1929 have therefore been chosen for analysis.[3] With some exceptions, these companies dominate the industrial scene in this country today. The relative importance of this group of companies has already been indicated by Berle and Means, and newly available data should throw further light upon the analysis and conclusions of their study, which has been widely quoted.

Only 155 of the original 200 companies are included in the present sample. Reasons for omitting the remaining 45 are given in Table I. In all except two cases, the exclusion of companies was due to the failure of these firms to file the pertinent data with the S. E. C. — chiefly because they either were in receivership or, not having securities listed on a national stock exchange, were not required to report to the Commission. To confine the study to the very large corporation, $50,000,000 in net assets (on December 31, 1935) was arbitrarily taken as the minimum size, and therefore two industrial companies whose assets had by 1935 fallen below this amount were also excluded.[4] No attempt has been made

3. A. A. Berle, Jr., and G. C. Means, The Modern Corporation and Private Property, Book I, Chap. III.

4. In a third case an operating company with assets of more than $50,000,000 was substituted for the holding company used by Berle and Means, since in 1935 the latter reported its assets as being less than $50,000,000.

MANAGEMENT AND CONTROL GROUPS 369

TABLE I.— REASONS FOR OMISSION OF COMPANIES IN ORIGINAL LIST

Reason for omission	NUMBER OF COMPANIES			
	Railroads	Public utilities	Industrials	Total
In receivership.........	1	5	9	15
Stock not listed on an exchange............	5	4	7	16
Dissolved or merged	0	2	4	6
Assets below $50,000,000.........	0	0	2	2
Data not available for miscellaneous reasons .	0	6	0	6
Total................	6	17	22	45
Total in the original list of 200..............	42	52	106	200
Number included in present sample..........	36	35	84	155

TABLE II.— DISTRIBUTION OF 155 COMPANIES CHOSEN FOR STUDY BY SIZE AND INDUSTRIAL CLASSIFICATION, DECEMBER 31, 1935[1]

Assets[2] (unit: $1,000,000)	NUMBER OF COMPANIES			
	Railroads	Public utilities	Industrials	Total
50–100..............	2	2	17	21
100–250..............	11	9	45	65
250–500..............	9	10	13	32
500–1,000............	8	10	6	24
1,000 and over	6	4	3	13

[1] Asset figures are based on consolidated balance sheets as given in Moody's Investment Manuals (1936) and are for December 31, 1935, or the nearest available date. Assets are after deducting depreciation and other offset reserves.
[2] Lower limit of class interval inclusive.

370   *QUARTERLY JOURNAL OF ECONOMICS*

to include companies not in the original list which at the end
of 1935 might have had total net assets of more than
$50,000,000. Table II presents some further details con-
cerning the nature of the group finally chosen.

The basic material for the present analysis comprises data
on stockholdings taken from a summary annual volume published by the S. E. C.[5] This summary lists for each reporting
officer and director of every corporation listed on a national
stock exchange the extent of his stockholdings in that company on December 31, 1935 (in a few cases, for some other
date near the end of the year). Similar data are also given
for non-management stockholders who owned ten per cent
or more of any equity security outstanding. The data refer
not only to stock held directly but also to shares owned
beneficially through holding companies, partnerships, trusts,
etc. Direct holdings include stock held on margin as well as
that owned outright. These stockholdings figures refer to a
single day. While it is doubtful whether the results would
be materially changed by using some later date, the limitations implied in the use of a single day as a reference point
should be remembered.[6]

Two more serious limitations are inherent in the data as
reported. First, it is almost certain that not all stock held
indirectly by officers and directors has been reported —
particularly in cases where nominal ownership has been transferred to relatives, directly or through trusts — even tho
the officials in question actually controlled the voting of
(and perhaps the income from) these shares. Where such
stock was reported, it has been included in the individual's
holdings, if he seemed actually to control the voting of such
shares. Secondly, in reporting beneficial ownership through
holding companies, etc., the stockholder may, but need not,
indicate his proportionate interest in the stock held by the

5. Securities and Exchange Commission, Official Summary of Holdings of Officers, Directors, and Principal Stockholders (Washington,
Government Printing Office, 1936). This volume is based upon individual reports filed with the Commission.

6. Cf. my earlier study, op. cit., p. 628, for mention of one change in
management holdings in the latter part of 1935.

MANAGEMENT AND CONTROL GROUPS 371

Table III.— Distribution of 155 Large Corporations According to the Proportion of Voting Stock Owned by Management, by Industrial Classes, December 31, 1935[1]

("Rr.," "P. U.," and "Ind." indicate, respectively, railroad, public utility, and industrial companies.)

Proportion of stock outstanding[2] (per cent)	NUMBER OF COMPANIES											
	All officers				Non-officer directors[3]				Total management			
	Rr.	P. U.	Ind.	Total	Rr.	P. U.	Ind.	Total	Rr.	P. U.	Ind.	Total
0–1	31	27	38	96	27	19	41	87	23	16	22	61
1–2	1	2	11	14	4	10	10	24	3	7	9	19
2–3	2	…	9	11	2	1	6	9	3	3	5	11
3–4	…	3	6	9	…	1	6	7	2	3	11	16
4–5	…	…	1	1	…	1	4	5	…	…	5	5
5–10	…	1	14	15	1	1	7	9	1	2	13	16
10–15	1	…	2	3	1	1	6	8	2	1	8	11
15–20	…	…	1	1	…	…	1	1	…	…	3	3
20–25	…	…	1	1	…	…	1	1	…	1	5	6
25–30	…	…	1	1	…	…	…	…	…	…	2	2
30–35	1	…	…	1	1	…	…	1	1	…	…	1
35–40	…	…	…	…	…	…	1	1	…	…	1	1
40–45	…	…	…	…	…	…	…	…	1	…	…	1
45–50	…	…	…	…	…	…	…	…	…	…	…	…
50 and over	…	2	…	2	…	…	…	…	…	2	…	2
Total no. of companies	36	35	84	155	36	34	83	153	36	35	84	155
Median	0.04	0.17	1.38	0.40	0.38	0.37	1.01	0.71	0.58	1.18	3.60	1.74
Arithmetic mean	1.47	3.91	3.05	2.88	2.18	1.48	3.37	2.67	3.64	5.35	6.40	5.52

[1] Stockholdings are based on S. E. C. data (see text, p. 370).
[2] Lower limit of class interval inclusive.
[3] Two companies (one utility and one industrial) had no non-officer directors.

holding company, as long as the total holdings of the latter are given. In such cases, I have attempted to allocate ownership to individuals on the basis of whatever information was available.[7]

With regard to both of these difficulties, I have tried to err in the direction of making the holdings large rather than small. The net result of these imperfections is that the computed averages for management holdings are probably too small, but that the error is less than would have been the case had not so liberal an attitude been taken toward what constituted beneficial ownership.

To facilitate analysis, management has been divided into (1) operating executives and (2) non-officer directors. Officers who are also directors are included in the first of these two groups.[8] An analysis will first be made of management stockholdings; thereafter data will be presented on the stockholdings of certain important groups outside of management.

II

Table III presents the basic figures for an investigation into the extent of management ownership in these corporations. For railroads, public utilities, and industrial companies, this table indicates the number of firms in which management and its two constituent groups owned stated percentages of the voting stock outstanding. Actually, the

7. For further discussion of the nature and limitations of the S. E. C. data, see the earlier study previously cited, pp. 623, 627-29. The limitations here mentioned affect primarily management holdings. For specific discussion of the data on outside holdings see pp. 380-83, below.

In addition to the other defects mentioned, a check-up revealed that apparently an occasional officer or director did not report at all to the S. E. C. There is no way of knowing whether these men held any stock or not. Such cases were few, however, and the possible error involved is much less serious than that arising from the fact that those who did report did not disclose all their indirect holdings.

8. In the earlier study, it was possible to treat as officers certain non-officer directors who received large salaries. In the present study, unfortunately, adoption of a similar procedure did not prove to be feasible.

percentages refer to the fraction of total voting control, rather than to the proportion of voting stock outstanding. All voting issues are included, and where two or more issues of a company participated unequally in the voting privilege, share holdings of each issue have been weighted by the number of votes to which that type of share was entitled.[9]

The figures confirm previous findings concerning the relatively small holdings of management. Considering first all companies, in 61 cases (about 40 per cent) all of management together owned less than one per cent of the total voting stock outstanding. In half the companies, management controlled through ownership no more than 1.74 per cent (the median) of the total number of votes outstanding.[1] Management holdings were less than five per cent in 112 companies, less than ten per cent in all but 27 cases. In only two companies did management have majority control.

Of the companies with management holdings of ten per cent or more, nineteen were industrials (23 per cent of the total number of industrials) and only eight were rails or public utilities (11 per cent of all companies in these two groups). The median holding for officers and directors together in the industrial companies was more than three times the median holding for total management in either of the two other fields. Clearly then, *as far as these companies are concerned,* management tends to own a smaller proportion of the total voting stock among the railroads and public

9. In general, the following types of stock were omitted: completely non-voting classes, issues entitled to elect only a minority of the directorate, and contingent voting preferred stocks (unless the contingency had eventuated sufficiently early so that the voting privilege had been exercised for a considerable period).

Test computations indicated that Table III would not have been greatly altered had only voting common stocks been taken, as was done in the earlier study.

1. The arithmetic mean was 5.52 per cent. Medians, rather than means, are cited in the text, because of the influence of extreme items on the latter type of average in these distributions. For example, the thirteen items over 20 per cent (about 8 per cent of the total) account for nearly half of the mean. To complete the picture, however, both means and medians are given at the bottom of Table III.

utilities than among the so-called industrial companies.[2]
The relatively larger holdings among the industrials, however, are still small in absolute terms. In general, in all three
fields, for these very large concerns management ownership
does not represent even a substantial minority of voting
stock outstanding. This finding is in accord with the conclusions of other studies bearing on this topic.[3]

The differences in the number of companies in each group
and the differences among the groups as to the extent to
which they represent all relatively large companies in their
respective fields require some caution in interpreting these
facts. On the whole, however, this contrast in the degree of
management ownership in the three fields does seem significant. It cannot be explained by arguing that, since the public
utilities and railroads are on the average larger companies
than the industrials, it is more difficult for executives and
directors to own a given proportion of the total stock outstanding. As may be seen by reference to Table IV (p. 378),
even among companies of roughly the same size (as to assets),
the contrast seems in general to hold. There is further evidence that management's larger proportionate ownership
among the industrials means not merely relatively more
voting control but also a significantly larger investment in
dollars. In more than twice as many industrials as rails and
utilities combined, management holdings were more than
ten per cent (cf. above, p. 373), yet the average market
value per company of voting stock outstanding (December
31, 1935, prices) was about ninety million dollars for the
industrial companies with these large management holdings,
and only about twenty-five millions for the rails and utilities

2. The two largest management holdings, it is true, were in public
utilities. In both these companies, however, only one class of stock
had the voting privilege. In both cases, management's proportionate
ownership of *all* stock outstanding was much smaller than its proportionate ownership of merely voting stock.

3. Of the original 200 companies, sixteen of the forty-five omitted
from the present sample are not listed on a stock exchange. It is possible,
if not probable, that management holdings in these sixteen companies
average appreciably higher than in the 155 firms whose securities are
listed.

MANAGEMENT AND CONTROL GROUPS   375

in this group.[4] We may conclude, therefore, that management holdings represented larger percentages of the voting stock among the industrials, even tho there was, on the average, more voting stock (in value terms) to own.[5]

The relatively small ownership by management in public utility and railroad enterprises is not surprising. In both fields, the nature of the business, at least on the operating side, is fairly routine; there has been an increasing tendency toward professionalization of management; participation of the public in ownership is widespread; and the tendency existing among many industrial companies for the founder of the firm (or his descendants) to continue in at least partial control is relatively absent. The first two of these tendencies exist among many industrial companies, but in general probably to a less extent. The way in which the third factor, widespread public ownership, is related to the particularly small management holdings in the railroad and utility fields is rather complex. Intercorporate stockholdings and the building up of loose "systems" are more prevalent among the rails and utilities than among the industrials; and consequently, as later sections will indicate, relatively less voting stock of the companies in these two fields is held by the general public than is the case among industrials. On the other hand, the prevalence of these intercorporate holdings among rails and utilities has led to considerable concentration of control; and this building up of loose systems with the probable greater influence of banker control almost certainly makes for smaller direct holdings by management, which in

4. In making these computations, one industrial (out of nineteen) and one public utility (out of eight rails and utilities) were omitted because, in each case, no price was available for one important issue. The contrast cited in the text would unquestionably still hold if data were available for these two cases.

5. The surprisingly small average value of the voting stock among the rails and utilities is to be explained not so much by smaller average assets as by (1) the fact that more of the assets are represented by bonds, and (2) the fact that market value typically bears a smaller ratio to book value than among industrials.

376   *QUARTERLY JOURNAL OF ECONOMICS*

such cases is likely to be under direct orders, or at least strong influence, from some outside group.[6]

From the point of view of the total ownership by those in control, management holdings alone are obviously much less significant than the total of the holdings of management and of such other groups — banks, individuals, and other corporations — as possess some measure of actual or potential control. Some attempt to shed further light on this matter of outside control will be made at a later point.

If we take all 155 firms together, there does not seem to be a clearly marked tendency for directors as a group to hold relatively more or less stock than operating executives.[7] Closer study of Table III, however, and resort to test computations not presented here (see note 8) suggest that among industrial companies officers' holdings do tend to run somewhat higher than those of directors, altho this difference is by no means either pronounced or uniform for all companies. Among railroads and public utilities there is some reason for believing that the opposite relationship tends to hold — again, however, only in somewhat irregular fashion.[8] This affords some confirmation of the statement made above that there is a more pronounced tendency toward professionali-

6. Another factor not mentioned in the text may also tend to make management holdings in industrial companies larger. Arrangements for the distribution of stock among officers (through the issuance of purchase warrants, bonuses in stock, etc.) are likely to be more common among industrial companies.

The relative attractiveness of securities in the three fields as investment and speculative media is another point which should not be neglected. This factor by itself would probably tend to produce the smallest management holdings in the railroads, the largest perhaps in the industrials, altho the speculative possibilities of utility holding companies should perhaps be mentioned. The attractiveness of holding company securities was undoubtedly a much stronger factor working toward large management holdings during the 1920's than it was in 1935, the year on which this study is based.

7. The average number of officers per company was approximately the same as the average number of directors.

8. The contrast stated in the text is more apparent if medians in Table III are compared, rather than arithmetic means. Extreme items distort the means, particularly in the case of the railroad and public utility figures.

The contrast between officers' and directors' holdings shows up fairly

MANAGEMENT AND CONTROL GROUPS   377

zation of management among public utility and railroad enterprises. At least, the operating executives seem to depart more from the owner-manager type of entrepreneur than they do in industrial concerns, altho among large companies the departure is extremely pronounced in all fields.[9] The figures here given provide no evidence concerning a further problem, namely, whether directors tend to have relatively more actual control over policy in the two fields in which they own somewhat more stock than executives. For a study of the actual conduct of business enterprise in modern industry, this problem is obviously an important one.

In the earlier study previously cited, which covered 107 companies, the median stock ownership for total management was found to be 8.10 per cent, compared with 1.74 per cent for the companies in the present sample.[1] It was found, however, that proportionate ownership by officers and by total management declined relatively rapidly as the companies increased in size. Average management holdings among the largest companies fell to well under five per cent.[2] A similar analysis by size for the large firms in the present sample yielded the results presented in Table IV.

For industrials, the inverse relation between percentage stockholdings and size of company seems to hold, tho some-

clearly if the companies are classified by assets (as is done in Table IV) and average holdings are computed for officers and directors separately for the companies in each asset group. In every asset group but one, median directors' holdings are larger than those of officers in the rails and utilities, while the reverse is uniformly true for industrials. Limitations of space make it impossible to present here the detailed figures for officers and directors separately by asset groups.

It should be added that tho the average number of directors per company is slightly higher than the number of officers in both the rails and utilities, these differences in themselves are not sufficiently great to account for the differences in stockholdings of the two groups.

9. In the earlier study of industrial companies alone, it was found that among relatively small firms officers owned considerably more stock than directors, but that this difference tended to become less pronounced as the firms increased in size.

1. Since the companies in the earlier study were all industrials, the more valid comparison is between the median for industrials in the present sample (3.60 per cent) and the corresponding figure in the earlier study (8.10 per cent).

2. Cf. R. A. Gordon, op. cit., pp. 638–39, especially Table IV.

TABLE IV.— AVERAGE PERCENTAGE STOCKHOLDINGS OF MANAGEMENT, BY ASSET GROUPS[1]

(Percentage figures not in parentheses are median holdings for companies in each asset group.[2] Figures in parentheses represent arithmetic mean holdings. "Rr.," "P. U.," and "Ind." indicate respectively railroad, public utility, and industrial companies.)

Assets[3] (Unit: $1,000,000)	NUMBER OF COMPANIES			PERCENTAGE STOCKHOLDINGS OF TOTAL MANAGEMENT (Unit: one per cent)		
	Rr.	P. U.	Ind.	Railroads	Public utilities	Industrials
50–100	2	2	17	6.89 (6.89)	0.85 (0.85)	3.27 (6.19)
100–250	11	9	45	0.82 (7.28)	1.03 (2.19)	4.57 (8.36)
250–500	9	10	13	0.52 (2.23)	3.16 (10.20)	2.00 (2.51)
500–1,000	8	10	6	0.48 (1.03)	0.92 (5.86)	1.54 (2.63)
1,000–2,000	6	3	3	0.88 (1.48)	1.74 (1.74)	2.71 (2.71)
2,000 and over	..	1	..	....	0.07 (0.07)	....

[1] Based on same data as those from which Table III was derived. Total assets are net of depreciation and other offset reserves, as given in consolidated balance sheets for December 31, 1935 (or nearest available date) and reported in Moody's Investment Manuals.
[2] Medians are averages of the central three or four items in each group (depending upon whether the number of items in each group was odd or even). If there were only two or three items in a group, all were averaged to secure both mean and median.
[3] Lower limit of class interval inclusive.

what roughly. For the other two groups, the tendency is less clear-cut — in part, because of the small number of firms in each size interval and the consequent unreliability of either mean or median as a typical figure. On the whole, some inverse relation is evident among the rails (particularly if means rather than medians are compared), but no clear-cut tendency toward either positive or negative correlation is apparent among the public utilities.[3] In the case of the latter, once a certain size has been achieved (apparently below 50 millions in assets), relative holdings of management do not continue to decline in any significant fashion as the companies increase further in size. In the case of the industrials, and probably also of the rails, the minimum size beyond which this inverse relation ceases to hold is much larger.[4]

III

Granted that ownership by management among these large corporations is as small as the above figures indicate, how is the ownership of the remaining voting stock distributed? In particular, are there large holdings in the hands of other individuals or groups, or perhaps in the possession of other corporations? To the extent that such is the case, the leading figures in management may act simply as representatives of outside interests; and the small degree of management ownership becomes less significant than it would

3. Curiously, several of the largest holdings in this group are concentrated in the same size interval (assets of 250–500 million), and this coincidence is reflected in the averages for that asset group.

4. A comparison of the averages for industrial companies in this and the former study may be of interest. The data refer only to total management.

Assets (in Millions)	Present Study		Former Study	
	No. of Cos.	Mean Holdings (per cent)	No. of Cos.	Mean Holdings (per cent)
50–100	17	6.19	14	9.18
100–250	45	8.36	16	5.83
250–500	13	2.51	3	3.99
500 and over	9	2.65	5	3.35

Limitations of space make it impossible to give in the present study separate figures for officers and directors, by asset groups, as was done in the earlier study.

380   *QUARTERLY JOURNAL OF ECONOMICS*

otherwise be. An investigation of these large outside holdings is clearly necessary, if we are ever to trace out the
various threads of power and control running through our
corporate structure and discover in whose hands responsible
business leadership ultimately rests and how it is exercised.

As already indicated, the work of the S. E. C. has now
made available data on holdings not merely of management
but also of every stockholder owning ten per cent or more of
any equity issue of a corporation listed on a national stock
exchange. This additional information has been compiled for
our 155 companies, with the results shown in Table V. The
first part of this table presents figures giving the number of
companies in which it was known that some individual,
corporation, or other stockholder outside of management
owned the stated percentages (given in the first column) of
the total voting stock outstanding. The last four columns
give the distribution of companies according to the holdings
of such outside groups and management *combined*.[5]

These data on outside stockholdings are at best unsatisfactory. There has probably been some failure to report.
Some owners of ten per cent or more of an issue may have
concealed their large holdings by nominal division among
several persons. More important, holdings of less than ten
per cent need not be reported, and yet important elements
of control may rest with occasional holders of a somewhat
smaller fraction, particularly if there are no other holdings
as large. Further, voting control may conceivably be exercised by a group of individuals whose combined holdings
exceed ten per cent of the voting stock, tho no one person's
ownership is large enough to require reporting. Despite
these weaknesses, which should be kept in mind, the data do
throw additional light on the distribution of ownership in
these large corporations.

The first row of Table V gives the number of companies
for which no data on outside holdings are available. For
these firms there were presumably no holdings large enough

5. Certain other, smaller, outside holdings are also included. See
p. 382, below.

TABLE V.— DISTRIBUTION OF 155 LARGE CORPORATIONS ACCORDING TO PROPORTION OF VOTING STOCK OWNED BY IMPORTANT OUTSIDE GROUPS AND BY SUCH GROUPS AND MANAGEMENT COMBINED, DECEMBER 31, 1935[1]

("Rr.", "P. U.", and "Ind." indicate, respectively, railroad, public utility, and industrial companies.)

Proportion of stock outstanding[2] (per cent)	Number of Companies							
	Important holdings outside of management				Combined outside and total management holdings			
	Rr.	P. U.	Ird.	Total	Rr.	P. U.	Ind.	Total
No data on outside holdings	14	18	54	86	...	...	...	...
0–5	3	2	9	14	15	16	42	73
5–10	0	1	3	4	1	1	11	13
10–15	2	1	6	9	1	2	8	11
15–20	3	1	2	6	3	1	4	8
20–25	0	3	2	5	0	4	4	8
25–30	2	1	3	6	2	2	1	5
30–35	1	1	1	3	1	1	4	6
35–40	1	1	0	2	0	1	5	6
40–45	3	1	0	4	4	1	0	5
45–50	2	1	2	5	3	1	1	5
50 and over	5	4	2	11	6	5	4	15
Total no. of companies	36	35	84	155	36	35	84	155
Median[3]	33.63	28.22	11.37	20.70	16.19	11.50	5.01	5.40
Arithmetic mean[3]	36.41	34.46	18.41	28.10	25.89	22.09	12.82	17.95

[1] For source and nature of data, see text pp. 370 and 380.
[2] Lower limit of class interval inclusive.
[3] Averages (medians and means) in the first four columns are based only on those companies with some outside holdings; the frequencies in the first row of the first four columns have been excluded from the averages. Averages of combined hodings in the last four columns are based on all firms.

to require reporting. The next two lines present frequencies corresponding to holdings of less than ten per cent of all voting stock. The sources of the data on outside holdings of less than ten per cent were twofold. First, a stockholder may have owned ten per cent or more of one issue, but such ownership represented less than ten per cent of all voting shares. More frequently, these smaller holdings arose as a by-product of the computation of management ownership. For example, in allocating to individuals included in management their proportionate interest in the stock owned by some trust, partnership, or personal holding company, there remained unallocated a block of stock indirectly belonging to others, usually amounting to less than ten per cent of all voting issues.[6] Such unallocated stock has been included as outside holdings. Undoubtedly there are many other outside holdings as large for which we have no data. Therefore these figures probably mean little, if taken by themselves. Their significance lies in the fact that they probably represent the ownership of individuals or groups closely associated with management, being usually parts of larger holdings in which the latter have an interest.[7] If they are combined with management holdings and those of ten per cent or more, as has been done in the last four columns of Table V, we then have information on the total holdings of three important stockholding groups: management, large outside holders, and a limited group of smaller holders probably associated with management.

Some stockholders with varying degrees of control are undoubtedly not covered by these figures; probably, also, some of the holdings included carry with them little control. Despite these limitations, the data summarized in Table V should help to throw light on three important questions: (1) the nature and extent of important outside stockholding

6. Cf. p. 370, above.

7. There are almost certainly a number of smaller unreported holdings also representing interests associated with management which these data do not cover, particularly the holdings of relatives and close friends who own stock directly and not through holding companies and other devices in which management also has an interest.

interests, (2) the order of magnitude of the proportion of ownership in the hands of those stockholders most probably exercising voting control, and (3), partly as a corollary from (2), the degree to which ownership has probably been separated from control. These three questions will be considered in turn. It should be emphasized that the conclusions reached apply only to the 155 corporations on which this study is based.

IV

Let us first consider outside holdings alone (first four columns of Table V). Important differences in the three industrial groups are immediately evident. Outside holdings of more than 10 per cent existed in nineteen (53 per cent) of the rails, in fourteen (40 per cent) of the utilities, and in eighteen (only 21 per cent) of the industrials. On the basis of both medians and means, average outside holdings were largest for the rails, somewhat smaller for the utilities, much the smallest for the industrials.[8] These large outside holdings are, however, significantly frequent in all three fields.

The order of magnitude of the computed averages is worth noting; but, because of limitations of the data and the inclusion of companies with outside holdings of less than 10 per cent, not too much significance should be attached to the exact figures given. If we take all companies for which we have data (69 firms out of the total of 155), average holdings were around 30 per cent or more for the rails and utilities, between 10 and 20 per cent for the industrials. If only outside holdings of 10 per cent or more are taken, the averages are of course somewhat larger. In eleven of these companies (five rails and four utilities, but only two industrials) outside holdings represented actual majority ownership of the *voting* stock.[9]

8. Averages are based on all firms with outside holdings, not merely on those with holdings above ten per cent. The same relations among the three fields hold, however, if averages are computed only for companies with holdings above ten per cent.

9. Of these eleven firms, seven also had non-voting issues outstanding. If voting and non-voting issues are taken together, in eight of these eleven cases majority voting control represented ownership of 50 per cent or more of the market value of all stock outstanding.

Who were these "outside" owners? Of the nineteen rail-roads in which 10 per cent or more of the voting stock was held by some individual, firm, or group outside of management, the dominant owner was, in all except three cases, another railroad or a holding company associated with a railroad.[1] In one of the three exceptional cases, the identity of the ultimate owner of the largest holding was unknown, but may have been another railroad; in the other two exceptional cases, the owners were apparently personal or family holding companies. Each of these last two holdings represented less than 20 per cent of voting control. In the case of the fourteen utilities with outside holdings of 10 per cent or more, the dominant holding was owned directly or indirectly, in all except two instances, by another public utility or an investment company interested in the public utility field. In both of the two exceptional cases, the outside holder was the same trust, and the beneficial owners of the latter were apparently two individuals closely related to one of the two companies.[2] Among the industrials we find relatively more cases in which the important outside stockholders are individuals or groups, but here again the majority of these outside holders are other corporations. Of the eighteen non-management holdings of 10 per cent or more, five represented the ownership of personal holding companies, estates or trusts; one was owned by a foundation bearing the name of the chief figure in management; and in twelve the outside owners were firms other than personal holding companies. Of these twelve, two seemed to be merely top holding or parent

1. The firms here mentioned are those in which combined outside holdings, compiled as explained in Section III, totaled 10 per cent or more of the voting stock. In some firms there was more than one outside holder. In classifying these the identity of the largest outside owner was uniformly taken as the basis of classification.

2. Part of the information concerning the ultimate ownership of the outside holdings of these last two companies refers to the situation as it apparently existed in 1933, as reported in Relation of Holding Companies to Operating Companies in Power and Gas Affecting Control, Report of the Committee on Interstate and Foreign Commerce, House of Representatives (73rd Congress, 2nd session, House Report No. 827).

companies, and six were investment or operating companies whose chief activities were in the same industry. The remaining four were firms in other industries.[3]

It is clear, then, that very substantial outside holdings exist in a significant number of these large corporations, and that these outside owners, especially among the railroads and utilities, are chiefly other corporations, not individuals or personal or family holding companies.[4] Two considerations should be kept in mind in weighing the significance of these facts. If a person owns as much as 10 per cent of the voting stock of a corporation, he is likely to be at least a director and, as such, would be included in our data on management holdings.[5] Secondly, in some cases where there was a large holding by another corporation, the controlling interest in the latter might have been owned, directly or through yet other companies, by individuals or groups.

The prevalence of intercorporate ownership presents a number of interesting problems. In both the railroad and public utility fields these corporate stockholders are almost uniformly firms in the same industry. We have here, in short, indications of the "system building" and concentration of control which have become highly significant developments in these two industries. Does this mean that we have taken too small a unit of measurement? Conceivably, this interlocking ownership may reflect merely a series of holding company situations in which we have been dealing in large part really with subsidiaries rather than with independent

3. This classification is at best rough; some outside owners classed in one group might have been listed in some other group. Three of the six firms operating in the same field, for example, seemed to be close corporations and might almost be called personal holding companies. One of these three might also be classed as a top holding company.

4. It is significant that there were practically no very large (10 per cent or more) holdings by banks (none by investment banks). This is not to say, of course, that banker control may not exist. Such control, insofar as it does exist, merely does not seem to need the reinforcing power of ownership.

5. In only twelve firms, however, out of 155 (three rails and utilities, nine industrials) did holdings of all directors *combined* amount to 10 per cent or more of the voting stock. Cf. Table III. Note that most of these large directors' holdings were among the industrial companies.

firms. Should we have dealt only with systems of companies or the firms in ultimate control of these systems?

It is difficult to draw a hard and fast distinction in all cases between firms which, as parts of closely knit systems, should be considered merely as subsidiary companies and those which seem to have sufficient importance in their own right to deserve separate treatment. No single criterion is of itself sufficient. It is clear that the various regional companies making up the Bell System do not belong in our list. They are subsidiaries of the American Telephone and Telegraph Company, which has been included; the management of the system seems to be in good part centralized; in all except a few minor cases there is majority ownership (usually considerably more) by the parent company. In such a case as this intercorporate ownership is indicative of the existence of a giant combination which would remain essentially unchanged if the various corporate boundary lines were abolished. Columbia Gas and Electric Corporation, on the other hand, is a member of the United Corporation "system" or "group," about 20 per cent of its voting stock being owned by the latter. Yet for most purposes Columbia Gas and Electric, the top holding company in an important system, is a significant economic entity in its own right, with widespread public ownership of a good part of its equity securities. Other utility companies and many railroads — such as the New Haven, in which the Pennsylvania has an important minority interest — represent similar cases.

In our sample most of the firms with substantial outside corporate ownership fall in varying degrees between these two extremes. The great majority of them probably lie closer to the latter than to the former, tho the exact results of any classification along these lines will naturally depend on the criteria used. Where they are parts of "systems," the latter are chiefly loose confederations rather than closely knit groups with centralized management and only incidental, relatively unimportant, minority ownership (in the subsidiaries) by the public. In these cases intercorporate ownership is not a sign of giant combinations which have

MANAGEMENT AND CONTROL GROUPS   387

taken the holding company form. The firms possess a certain degree of independence; the investing and risk-taking public has an important stake in them; and the intercorporate ownership is essentially only an indication of the burrowing into these firms by other companies in an attempt by individuals and groups to concentrate control over increasing sectors of the productive process.[6]

It is impossible to discuss here the various reasons for such interlocking ownership and to trace out the various threads of control running through our complex corporate structure,[7] but something more will be said about the phenomenon in the last section of this study, when the bearing of intercorporate stockholdings upon the separation of ownership and control will be briefly considered.

From the facts presented in the earlier part of this section we may conclude, therefore, that voting control in the large corporations in the present sample is most frequently in the possession either of another corporation (and those who control the latter) or, via the proxy machinery, of management with typically little ownership of its own.[8] The latter situation seems to be relatively more frequent among the industrials; the former, among the rails and utilities. Voting control owned directly by *individuals* outside of management and management control through relatively large ownership both seem to occur, but much less frequently than the two

6. Of the forty firms in which some other corporation owned 10 per cent or more of the voting stock, eight represented cases of majority ownership of the voting stock. In six of these eight firms other companies owned a majority of all stock, voting and non-voting, outstanding. It is doubtful whether in all of these six cases there was completely centralized management emanating from the stockholding companies.

7. Cf., however, the following: Regulation of Stock Ownership in Railroads (71st Congress, 3rd Session, House Report No. 2789 [1931]); Relation of Holding Companies to Operating Companies in Power and Gas Affecting Control, Report of the Committee on Interstate and Foreign Commerce, House of Representatives (73rd Congress, 2nd Session, House Report No. 827 [1935]); J. C. Bonbright and G. C. Means, The Holding Company (1932).

8. In some cases, of course, both types of situation might exist together.

388   *QUARTERLY JOURNAL OF ECONOMICS*

types just mentioned.[9] Unfortunately our data throw no
light on a further interesting problem — the extent of control by non-management groups with little ownership, such
as banks.

V

For many purposes data on the combined holdings of
management and of these outside groups are more significant
in studying the concentration or diffusion of voting control
than data on either type of holding taken separately. Management and an important minority group may occasionally
clash,[1] but in the typical case the two interests work harmoni-
ously. Figures on the combined holdings of these two groups
should therefore provide a valuable statistical indication of
the concentration of voting control in the very large American corporation. In considering this question, however, the
limitations of the data being used should be kept in mind.
In particular, some stockholders with significant elements
of control are probably not included, and some of the outside
holdings that are included may represent little actual control.[2]

The pertinent data are given in the last four columns of
Table V, which show the number of companies in which
management and important outside groups *combined* owned
stated percentages of the total voting stock outstanding.
Considering first all companies together, the median combined holding is 5.40 per cent, the mean, 17.95 per cent,
averages considerably in excess of those found for management holdings alone. In somewhat less than half the firms,
combined holdings were under 5 per cent; on the other hand,
such holdings were more than 10 per cent in almost as many

9. These conclusions are not altogether comparable with those of
Berle and Means (op. cit., Book I, Chap. 5), who were more interested
in the method of securing and maintaining control. Our results indicate
chiefly *where* the voting control apparently rests, rather than the means
whereby control is secured and maintained.

1. As J. D. Rockefeller, Jr., and the management of Standard Oil
of Indiana in 1929, or more recently Mr. J. P. Getty and the management of Tidewater Associated Oil. The former case has been frequently
cited; for details of the latter episode, cf. *Time*, November 30, 1936,
pp. 58–60.

2 Cf. pp. 380–82, above.

cases. In forty-two companies, or a little over a fourth of the total number, this combined ownership amounted to more than 25 per cent; in fifteen an actual majority of the voting stock outstanding was held.[3]

Examination of the data for the three groups separately yields results of considerable significance. Both the individual frequencies and the averages indicate that combined holdings are largest among the rails, much the smallest among the industrials. This is the same relation that was discovered for outside holdings taken separately, but the inverse of that found for management holdings alone. The size of the averages is also worth noting. Median combined holdings are about 16 per cent for the rails, 11.50 per cent for the utilities, and only about 5 per cent for the industrials. The means, of course, are larger. Combined holdings were under 10 per cent in less than half of the rails or utilities, but in some 63 per cent of the industrials. In more than a third of the rails, holdings were more than 40 per cent. Of the twenty-five largest percentage holdings, thirteen were in railroads, seven in public utilities, and only five in industrial companies; and yet there are more industrials in the sample as a whole than there are rails and utilities combined. As we have seen, by far the most important contribution to the relatively large combined holdings in the railroad and utility companies is made by outside groups, chiefly other corporations in the same field.

Tho the combined holdings of the groups in a position to exercise a substantial degree of voting control are, in a considerable number of these companies, of no insignificant amount, yet taking all companies together it is still true that in the great majority of cases these combined holdings amount to, at best, only a substantial minority interest.[4]

3. In only nine of these fifteen firms, however, did such ownership amount to 50 per cent or more of all stock outstanding, voting and non-voting.

4. It is to be remembered that only voting stock is taken into account here. The proportions of *total* ownership (including non-voting stock) held by the control groups are likely to run lower than percentages of voting stock alone.

Most of the very large combined holdings are in the railroad and public utility fields. Table V seems to indicate that there is less ownership (of voting stock) associated with control among the industrial companies than is the case in either of the other two fields.

This last conclusion leads us to a paradox. Extensive intercorporate ownership among railroad and public utility companies has undoubtedly tended to concentrate power in the hands of relatively few individuals, and this development has accentuated the tendency toward the separation of ownership and control in these two fields. Yet to the extent that these large intercorporate holdings exist, there is that much less direct ownership by the general public — and therefore that much less ownership presumably without control. Should we conclude, then, that the separation of ownership and control has, or has not, progressed further among the rails and utilities than among the industrial companies?

VI

Before we attempt to answer this question, it is necessary to estimate the proportion of *all* stock outstanding, not merely of voting shares, which is held by those presumably in control. Further, the averages cited thus far are unweighted, and can be interpreted only as representing percentage holdings in the "typical" large corporation. We seek now a summary figure, what might be called an "over-all" index, that will measure for all 155 corporations taken together the proportion of the *total* ownership of all stock outstanding which is held by the groups assumed to be in control.[5]

One measure which might be taken for this purpose is a weighted arithmetic mean of the proportions of the various issues (voting and non-voting) owned by the control groups, each proportion being weighted by the market value of the outstanding shares of that issue. This would indicate the

5. I am indebted to Prof. W. L. Crum for helpful advice in settling some of the rather difficult statistical questions that arose in carrying out the analysis of this section.

fraction of the market value of the total stock investment in all these firms taken together which is in the hands of those in control. The chief objection to an average computed in this fashion comes from the possibility that one or two exceptionally large firms may contribute disproportionately to the total market value of the stock of all companies, with the result that the control holdings in such companies (receiving relatively great weight) dominate the final average.[6]

Another possible "over-all" index might be computed by finding the proportion of the number of all shares outstanding of all companies which is owned by those in control. This, of course, is equivalent to taking a weighted average of the percentage holdings of each issue, each percentage holding being weighted by the number of shares of that issue outstanding (rather than by market values). This measure is also open to objections. If voting and non-voting stock are both included, no significant and precise meaning can be attached to the final average; it represents a proportion neither of voting power nor of total stock investment (in value terms). Further, weighting by the number of shares outstanding is to some extent haphazard weighting; a small firm may have issued more shares than a large firm, its stock merely selling at a much lower price per share. If, however, such an average is computed only for voting stock, there is one significant meaning which can be attached to the measure. It would represent the proportion of total voting power, in all of these firms taken together, which is in the possession of the control groups.

In short, there seems to be no single measure which can be taken as giving, without qualification, the proportion of total ownership held by selected stockholders. To throw as much light as possible, therefore, on the problem that we

6. This kind of situation raises a rather difficult statistical question. If an aggregate is dominated by a few extreme items, what meaning should be attached to the total (or to an average based on the total)? The aggregate is still the sum of the component items, and as such has a certain meaning. The chief difficulty lies in the fact that, in distributions including markedly extreme items, averages based on totals cannot be considered adequately representative of the bulk of the items, and therefore are likely to lead to misinterpretation.

are attempting to study, a number of averages have been presented in Table VI. Taken together, they may indicate, somewhat more clearly than did the unweighted averages previously presented, how far the separation of ownership and control has progressed in these very large firms.

TABLE VI.— AVERAGES INDICATING PROPORTION OF TOTAL OWNERSHIP IN 155 LARGE CORPORATIONS HELD BY "CONTROL GROUPS," BY INDUSTRIAL CLASSES, DECEMBER 31, 1935[1]

Industrial group	AVERAGES OF PERCENTAGE HOLDINGS BY CONTROL GROUPS (Unit: one per cent)		
	Unweighted: voting stock only[2]	Weighted by numbers of shares: voting stock only[3]	Weighted by market values of stock: *all* issues[4]
Railroads:			
All 36 cos..............	25.89	15.94	17.34
Three largest cos.......	15.37	4.51	13.64
All cos., excluding three largest..............	26.85	19.49	20.59
Public utilities:			
All 35 cos..............	22.09	13.17	6.94
Largest company.......	0.07	0.07	0.07
All cos., excluding largest	22.74	14.60	11.42
Industrials:			
All 84 cos..............	12.82	11.52	11.89
Five largest cos.........	13.71	15.45	17.99
All cos., excluding five largest..............	12.76	10.20	8.70
Total			
All 155 cos.............	17.95	12.39	11.14
Nine cos. excluded above	12.75	12.37	13.10
All cos., excluding above nine................	18.27	12.39	10.01

[1] These averages are weighted or unweighted arithmetic means of the individual percentage holdings in the various companies owned by the assumed control groups. For further discussion, see text, pp. 393–94. For assumptions concerning the identity of the various control groups, see pp. 380–82.

[2] These are unweighted means of the percentage holdings in the groups of companies specified. For all companies in each group, they are the means in the last four columns of Table V.

[3] Computed by adding, for the companies specified, all voting shares (each share multiplied by the number of votes to which it was entitled) owned by the control groups and dividing by the number of voting shares outstanding.

[4] Computed by adding, for the companies specified, the market value of the shares of each issue owned by the control groups and dividing this total by the market value of all stock outstanding.

Market values are based on closing prices for December 31, 1935, or the nearest available date. In some cases, where no actual prices were available, bid quotations were used. No quotations at all were available for a few issues. For these, book or stated values (as given in the balance sheets) were taken as an approximation to market values.

MANAGEMENT AND CONTROL GROUPS   393

The first column of figures in Table VI presents unweighted means of the percentage holdings of voting stock. The averages in this column for all companies are simply the means already presented in Table V. The second column gives averages, again of holdings of voting stock, in which each percentage holding is weighted by the number of outstanding shares of that issue. In the last column are averages based upon holdings of both voting and non-voting stock, the percentage holdings of each class of stock for each company being weighted by the market value of the shares of that issue outstanding.

In each of the three groups one or more companies dominate the averages based upon market values. In the utility group, for example, the stock of the American Telephone and Telegraph Company accounts for about 40 per cent of the market value of the stocks of the thirty-five companies in this group. The percentage of stock in this company held by the assumed control groups was extremely small; as a result the average weighted by market values is much less than the corresponding unweighted average or the one based on numbers of shares.[7] Both these latter averages, it is true, are based only on voting stock; but, altho non-voting shares are fairly common in the public utility field, the market value of such stock bears only a small ratio to the value of all stock outstanding. Hence the inclusion of non-voting stock would not in itself greatly change our averages. If American Telephone is included, the proportion of voting power held by the control groups in the utilities field falls from 14.60 per cent to 13.17 per cent, while the proportion of total market value falls from 11.42 per cent to 6.94 per cent. In the other two fields the presence of a few extremely large firms has a similar, tho much less marked, effect on the average holdings based on market values. Consequently, to present as much information as possible, three figures are given for each type of average for each industrial group: (1) the average for all firms in the group, (2) that for the

7. American Telephone accounted for only about 10 per cent of the total number of public utility shares outstanding.

extremely large firms, (3) the average for all companies, excluding the largest.[8]

If we are interested in the proportion of the total stock of all firms taken together which is held by the control groups, clearly the unweighted means give a much less accurate picture than averages in which weights based in some way on the relative importance of the various firms are used. As we should expect, the proportion of all stock held, taking either set of weighted means, is in general considerably less than the proportion of stock owned in the "typical" corporation as given by the unweighted means.[9] The use of weights seems to make least difference in the case of the industrials. For the 155 firms taken together the assumed control groups seem to hold about 12 per cent of the total voting power and only a slightly smaller percentage of the total value of all stock outstanding. When all the fields are taken together, much the same result is secured whether the very largest firms are included or not.

The largest proportion both of total voting power (about 16 per cent) and of total market value (about 17 per cent) is held by the control groups in the railroad field. These percentages are raised somewhat if the largest firms are omitted.[1] In the utility field those in control held about 13 per cent of the total voting power and about 7 per cent of total market value. The latter figure is considerably raised if the largest firm is excluded. In the case of the industrials the control groups held about 12 per cent of both total voting power and total market value; but if the five largest firms

8. The method used to exclude large companies was to array the firms according to market value of the outstanding stock and then take out the one or more firms whose stock had a market value greatly in excess of that of the remaining companies. This method resulted in the exclusion of one utility, three rails, and five industrials.

9. But greater (except for the public utility averages based on market values) than the unweighted medians of Table V, which are better typical figures than the means.

1. The wide discrepancy between the proportion of voting power and the fraction of market value held in the largest companies is easily explained. The largest control holding was in a company which had relatively few shares outstanding. The stock, however, sold at a very high price. Hence the large holding for this company got a small weight based on number of shares and a large weight based on market value.

MANAGEMENT AND CONTROL GROUPS   395

(which include two with very large outside holdings) are excluded, these percentages are reduced somewhat.[2]

The figures in Table VI have been presented in order to measure the total stockholdings of those in control and, inferentially, the ownership of the general investing public, which presumably possesses little actual control. In considering this question, it should be remembered that our data on "combined holdings" reflect but imperfectly the ownership of those in control. The chief defects of the data in this connection have already been mentioned.[3] On the whole, the net effect of these limitations is that our averages may understate somewhat the proportion of ownership in the hands of the groups actually in control, and overstate the proportion directly held by merely passive owners.

Even after making allowance for limitations in the data, it seems improbable that much more than 15 per cent of the total ownership of these 155 corporations can be said to be associated with control.[4] The figure is probably higher for the railroad group, and, if market values are used, may be smaller for the public utility group. This conclusion leads to the corollary that some 85 per cent of the total ownership in these firms is probably separated from all but restricted elements of potential control.[5] This holds, however, only for

2. In several cases in Table VI, the averages based on the market value of *all* issues are higher than those based on the number of *voting* shares. Non-voting issues were most numerous among the utilities, but had relatively the greatest market value among the industrials. In no field, however, did non-voting stock amount to 10 per cent of the value of all issues. What tendency there was for small holdings of non-voting stock to reduce averages based on all issues seems in the cases cited to have been more than counterbalanced by the fact that in some companies with large control holdings market values contributed relatively more weight to the final averages than did numbers of shares.

3. See pp. 380, 382, and 388, above. The fact that partial control may rest with non-owners (as banks) need not be considered a defect. It would still be true that stock not owned by the *stockholding* control groups represented ownership without control.

4. This is apparently true whether number of shares or market value is taken as the index of ownership (cf. Table VI).

5. This statement is subject to the limitations which the prevalence of intercorporate stockholdings imposes on conclusions concerning the ownership of the groups ultimately in control which may be drawn from our data. See pp. 398-99, below.

the large corporations here studied. In equally large corporations, none of whose stock is listed on a stock exchange, the situation is undoubtedly different. And for smaller corporations, with assets of less than $50,000,000, almost certainly those in control own relatively more stock than do the control groups in these large corporations.[6]

VII

To summarize our results thus far In these very large corporations the separation of both management and control from ownership has proceeded far; and the nature and the degree of separation show significant differences for the three groups. Management alone, on the average, tends to own but an extremely small proportion of the voting stock, the percentages owned being the smallest among the railroads, largest among the industrials. Among the industrials, officers apparently tend to own slightly more stock than directors; the reverse is the case, on the whole, albeit far

6. The S. E. C. has published a tabular analysis of these stockholdings for all corporations registered with the Commission (Summary of Reports of Holdings as of December 31, 1935, of Officers, Directors and Principal Shareholders Made to the Securities and Exchange Commission Pursuant to Section 16 (*a*) of the Securities Exchange Act of 1934 [multigraphed unbound pamphlet, 1936]). In all, reports were received for 1,736 companies, ranging in size from under one million to several billion dollars in assets and covering all industries. For all these companies taken together, the S. E. C. reports that 22.3 per cent of all shares outstanding was held by those reporting (officers, directors, and principal stockholders); for companies with assets above 50 million dollars, the figure would be 18.4 per cent.

These figures are somewhat difficult to interpret, nor is it easy to compare them with the results of the present study. First of all, both voting and non-voting shares are apparently taken. But the S. E. C. figure is based on the number of shares of the various issues; it is therefore a proportion neither of voting power nor of value of all stock. Consequently it is not directly comparable with any of the averages presented in the text. Further, the S. E. C. data seem to include holdings of parent companies in direct subsidiaries, if the latter are forced to register with the Commission — as they would presumably have to do, if they had one issue listed on a stock exchange. Inclusion of many such direct subsidiaries, which have for the most part been excluded from the present study, would, of course, yield higher proportionate holdings by "control groups" than would be the case if only the parent companies were included.

from uniformly, among the railroads and public utilities. While there is undoubtedly a tendency for management holdings (in percentage terms) to decrease as the firms become larger, this inverse relationship apparently ceases to hold once corporations achieve a certain size. This crucial size seems to be largest in the industrial field, smallest among the utilities.

Substantial holdings by groups other than management were found to exist in these firms. Such holdings were most important among the railroads, least important among the industrials. If these large outside holders and management are taken as together representing those stockholders in actual control, most of the ownership of those in control belongs to these outside holders in the case of the railroads and public utilities; among the industrial companies, however, management owns as much as, or more than, these outside groups. There is a marked absence of large outside holdings by individuals or families among the railroads and utilities; the outside holders are almost always other railroad and utility companies. Such intercorporate ownership is found also in the industrial field, but to a much less marked extent.

If we combine the holdings of these outside control groups with those of management, and include non-voting as well as voting stock, we find that probably not more than 15 per cent of the total ownership of our 155 corporations rests with those most probably in direct control of these companies. The ratio is highest for the rails, because of extensive intercorporate holdings. The proportion of total voting power held is smallest for the industrials. The situation with respect to the fraction of the total market value of all issues held by the control groups is somewhat obscured, particularly in the case of the utilities, by the influence of a few large firms on the final figures.

This estimate refers only to the proportion of stock ownership in the possession of those in control. It therefore connotes that a much smaller fraction of the total capital investment is owned by the control groups. This is particu-

398   *QUARTERLY JOURNAL OF ECONOMICS*

larly true among the rails and public utilities. In the first place, especially in these two fields, a portion of the total investment is represented by bonds; and, secondly, to the extent that there are subsidiary companies with minority interests outstanding, ownership of a given fraction of the parent company's stock represents ownership of less than that proportion of the companies dominated by the parent concern. This latter type of situation is most important in the public utility field. All in all, the stockholdings of our control groups probably represent 10 per cent or less of the *total* investment in these 155 firms and their immediate subsidiaries.[7]

One highly important problem remains to be considered. The extensive intercorporate ownership discovered among these companies requires a more refined interpretation of the results of the present study. Our results thus far indicate that, some 15 per cent of the ownership of the 155 companies being in the hands of the control groups, 85 per cent represented ownership immediately divorced from control. This gives one answer to the question how far the separation of ownership and control has proceeded in these companies, but it is not enough. The prevalence of intercorporate ownership indicates that actually the separation of ownership and control has gone further, probably much further, than these figures imply. Of the 15 per cent, a substantial part represents the holdings of other corporations, and these corporations are controlled, indirectly through other corporations or directly, by individuals whose ownership is almost always considerably less than complete. An extreme but by no means unusual case would be that in which working control, say a 20 per cent stock interest, in one of the 155 firms was owned by another corporation controlled by management

---

7. The above argument in reality is based on a comparison of *book* value of stock with total investment. Our general conclusion holds also for a comparison of *market* value of stock with total investment, except in the highly unlikely case in which total market value of the stock of all companies very greatly exceeds total book value. While such may have been the case for some industrial companies in 1935, it was hardly true of all companies in all three fields taken together.

with little ownership. The 20 per cent would be, in our study, counted as ownership by the control group; but the control group itself — here a corporation — is in turn controlled by certain *individuals*, with the result that the ownership by those in ultimate control of the first corporation is negligible. In proportion to the extent of intercorporate holdings, our figures exaggerate the actual ownership of those individuals really in control.

This fact accounts for the apparently strange result, implied by the figures in Table VI, that the control groups held a larger proportion of the outstanding stock in the railroad than in either of the other two fields. If we were able to trace back the large intercorporate holdings and the related threads of control in the railroad industry, we might very well find that the total holdings of those exercising ultimate control represented no larger proportion of the total ownership than did the holdings of corresponding groups in the other two fields. Indeed, the proportion is probably smaller than that in the industrial field. A cursory investigation indicates that the holdings of the individuals probably in control of the dominant stockholding railroads are not, in general, very large; and therefore the proportionate ownership of these persons in the companies controlled indirectly through intercorporate stockholdings would tend to be very small.

We have estimated that the 15 per cent of the total ownership in these companies held by the control groups, including corporations, probably represents 10 per cent or less of the *total* investment in these firms. If control were traced back in all cases to individuals and groups of persons in *ultimate* control, it is likely that we should find these persons holding less than 10 per cent of the total ownership of our 155 firms. It is doubtful, therefore, if the investment associated with control would amount to much more than 5 per cent of the total net assets (excluding duplications arising from intercorporate stockholdings). These estimates are little better than guesses, of course, but they probably indicate the general order of the magnitudes involved.

400   *QUARTERLY JOURNAL OF ECONOMICS*

The present study provides additional factual background for the growing literature on the separation of ownership and control and on the social and economic significance of this phenomenon. But only the surface, even of the available factual evidence, has been scratched. More remains to be done with the general statistical information available, particularly with respect to the great mass of smaller listed firms, and with respect to the effects of intercorporate ownership on the degree of concentration of control.

Statistical aggregates and averages, however, supply only a background for a more intensive type of analysis which needs to be made. The nature of the threads connecting firms with yet other firms and with dominant industrial and financial interests, the content of control and its division among groups and individuals connected with a given firm, the origins of control and of the ways in which it is exercised — these and many other important problems can be handled only by resort to case studies of individual firms and controlling groups. One question in particular presents a challenge to both the theorist and factual analyst. What is "control"? Is it a passive or an active force, and how is it related to the function which economists have assigned to the entrepreneur of theory? Further research into these problems is needed to improve our understanding of modern economic development and of the institutional framework within which our productive system operates.

R. A. GORDON.

HARVARD UNIVERSITY

[4]

OWNERSHIP AND CONTROL IN THE 200 LARGEST NONFINANCIAL CORPORATIONS, 1929 AND 1963

By ROBERT J. LARNER*

In 1932, Adolf Berle and Gardiner Means published their classic study, *The Modern Corporation and Private Property*, a major thesis of which was that "Ownership of wealth without appreciable control and control of wealth without appreciable ownership appear to be the logical outcome of corporate development" [4, p. 69]. Since then, the existence of management control among giant corporations and its increasing extent over time have been generally accepted in the literature as part of the "conventional wisdom" [2, pp. 70–74] [3, p. 30] [5] [7] [13, p. 53]. Yet, with the exception of the 1939 study which the Securities and Exchange Commission prepared for the Temporary National Economic Committee [18], no attempt seems to have been made to determine the extent of management control in the years since the Berle and Means study.

This article attempts to measure systematically the extent to which management control actually exists among the 200 largest nonfinancial corporations in the first half of the 1960's. The article is divided into two parts: the first part describes the method followed in the study, and the second summarizes the results of the study and compares them with the findings of the 1929 Berle and Means study.

I. *The Method of This Study*

To assure as direct a comparison as possible between the 1929 and the 1963 findings, this paper will follow very closely the definitions, procedures, and classifications used in the Berle and Means study. Since direction over the activities of a corporation is legally and theoretically exercised by its board of directors, Berle and Means defined control as the "... actual power to select the board of directors (or its majority)" [4, p. 69]. Although the power to control and the actual exercise of that power can conceivably reside in different individuals, there are nevertheless cogent reasons for accepting Berle and Means's definition of control. First, even if the owner of a majority or substantial minority of a corporation's voting stock were to surrender control to the manage-

* The author is a graduate student in economics at the University of Wisconsin. He wishes to thank Professor Leonard Weiss of that university for the encouragement, advice, and over-all supervision he has so kindly given in the preparation of this article, an earlier draft of which was written for his seminar in industrial organization. The author, however, is solely responsible for all errors. Part of the research was financed by the National Science Foundation.

ment, he would still retain the legal power to vote an unsatisfactory board of directors out of office, and even such a dormant power can be a strong influence. Secondly, to prevent biased results which are solely dependent on arbitrary judgements, it seems wise to use objective criteria which are easily observed and capable of precise measurement in determining the type of corporate control.

Berle and Means distinguished between "ultimate control" and "immediate control." This distinction occurred where one corporation controlled another through a dominant minority stock interest.[1] In this case, the controlled corporation was always classified as immediately controlled by either minority or joint-minority interests. If the controlling corporation itself was management-controlled, then the controlled corporation was also classified as ultimately controlled by management. If the controlling corporation was not management-controlled, then the controlled corporation was said to be ultimately controlled through pyramiding. The present study also uses this distinction.

Following Berle and Means, our list of the 200 largest nonfinancial corporations is composed of firms primarily engaged in manufacturing, mining, merchandising, transportation, and electric, gas, and pipeline utilities. Banks, insurance companies, and investment companies are excluded. Size is measured in terms of book assets, a procedure which overstates the size of the transportation and utility companies relative to the size of firms in other industries. The use of sales to measure size, however, would introduce an equally serious opposite bias.[2] Moreover, since Berle and Means, the SEC study [18], and R. A. Gordon [6] all used assets to measure size, this paper will follow the same procedure to maintain comparability.[3]

Berle and Means classified the firms in their study according to the following five types of corporate control: (1) privately owned, (2) con-

[1] In the Berle and Means study, a corporation which was majority-controlled by another corporation was classified as a subsidiary of the latter and was disregarded, except where an important element of pyramiding entered in. The present study follows the same procedure, except where the controlling corporation is a smaller firm not included among the "200 largest." In this case the controlled corporation is retained as if it were an independent company: e.g. Hughes' Tool Co. is ignored and TWA is treated as majority-controlled. If the controlling corporation is a foreign firm, no attempt is made to determine if the foreign firm is management-controlled, and the controlled corporation is assigned either to ultimate minority control or to ultimate control through pyramiding. This is the same procedure which Berle and Means followed.

[2] Perhaps the best measure of size is value added, since it compares the value of the factors of production controlled by each firm [1], but data on value added by firm are not generally available.

[3] The names and assets of the 200 largest nonfinancial corporations in 1963 appear in the appendix to this article, which may be obtained from the author on request. Requests can be addressed in care of the Department of Economics, University of Wisconsin, Madison, Wisconsin 53706.

trolled through the ownership of a majority of the voting stock, (3) controlled through the ownership of a dominant minority of the voting stock, (4) controlled by means of a legal device,[4] and (5) management-controlled.[5] This study uses the same categories.

A firm is considered to be privately owned if an individual, a family, or a group of business associates holds 80 per cent or more of its voting stock. For majority ownership, the individual, family, or group of business associates must own between 50 and 80 per cent of the voting stock. In the Berle and Means study, stock ownership of between 20 and 50 per cent was generally necessary for minority control, although in several specific instances a smaller holding was credited with the power of control. In view of the greater size of the 200 largest nonfinancial corporations in 1963 and the wider dispersion of their stock, this lower limit to minority control seems too high. In the present study a firm is classified as immediately controlled by minority stock ownership if 10 per cent or more of its voting stock is held by an individual, family, corporation, or group of business associates.[6]

Berle and Means assigned corporations in which no base of control in stock ownership could be found to management control on the belief that no group of stockholders would be able under ordinary circumstances to muster enough votes to challenge the rule of management. This study follows the same procedure.[7]

When all of the above criteria are applied to the 1963 data, it is generally not difficult to distinguish management control from the other types of control, but several errors or distortions occur when ownership control is further broken down into privately owned, majority-controlled, and minority-controlled corporations, and those controlled through a legal device.[8]

[4] Berle and Means recognized four kinds of legal devices by which corporate control might be obtained: (1) pyramiding, (2) nonvoting common stock, (3) stock with disproportionate voting power, and (4) the voting trust. Only the first and the fourth devices are found today.

[5] For a more detailed description of these five categories and of the criteria for each, see Chapter 5 in *The Modern Corporation and Private Property* [4].

[6] In two cases, this rule has been disregarded. The Transcontinental Gas Pipe Line Company is classified as management-controlled even though the Stone & Webster Company holds of record an 11 per cent stock interest, since the latter is not represented on Transcontinental's board of directors. On the other hand, May Department Stores Company is classified as minority-controlled even though the May family has only a 3.9 per cent stock interest, since members of the May family hold the offices of chairman, vice-chairman, and president. and occupy five seats on the board of directors.

[7] In addition, Berle and Means found 16 companies to be controlled jointly, either by two or more minority interests or by a minority interest and management. In the latter case, they divided the corporation into two "half companies," each possessing one-half of the assets of the original company. One of these "half companies" was then classified as management-controlled and the other as minority-controlled. This joint minority-management control category is not used in the present study.

II. *Summary and Comparison of the Results*

Each of the 200 largest nonfinancial corporations in 1963 is listed in the appendix, together with its size and rank in assets, its type of control, immediate and ultimate, in both 1963 and 1929, and the source and basis of its classification in 1963.[9]

Tables 1 and 2 provide a summary of the type of control, by number of corporations and by assets in 1963 and 1929, for the 200 corporations as a whole and for each of the three major industrial groups (industrials, public utilities, and transportation companies). A significant finding of this study is that management control[10] has substantially increased among the 200 largest nonfinancial corporations since 1929. As Table 1 illustrates, 44 per cent of the 200 largest nonfinancial corporations in 1929 and 58 per cent of their assets were management-controlled. In 1963, however, 84.5 per cent of the "200 largest" of that year and 85 per cent of their assets were so controlled. Management control increased substantially within each of the three industrial groups and became the overwhelmingly predominant type of control within each group.

As shown in Table 1, private ownership had *completely disappeared* among the 200 largest nonfinancial corporations by 1963. Of the 12 privately owned firms on the 1929 list, six had dropped out of the "200 largest" by 1963. Of the remainder, one (A & P) was majority-controlled, four (Alcoa, Ford, Gulf Oil, and National Steel) were minority-controlled, and one (Jones & Laughlin) was apparently management-controlled. Only five companies (A & P, Duke Power Co., Kaiser Industries, Sun Oil, and TWA) were found to be majority-controlled in 1963, and in the case of TWA actual control was, at least temporarily, in the hands of trustees.

---

[8] Following the Berle and Means definitions, the author classified Tidewater Oil, Shell Oil, and the Coca-Cola Company as ultimately controlled by pyramiding because of their peculiar organizational structures, even though the evidence suggests that Tidewater and Shell are effectively majority-controlled and Coca-Cola effectively management-controlled. The Berle and Means definitions were followed exactly in order to keep the two studies as comparable as possible. Similarly, although Trans World Airlines is classified as majority-controlled, an equally convincing argument might be made for classifying it as controlled by a legal device, since Howard Hughes's 78 per cent stock interest (through the Hughes Tool Company) in TWA was, at least temporarily, being held in trust by a group of insurance companies and banks in 1963. Hughes's stock was sold to the general public in May, 1966. The TWA management was reported to be "anxious that no one should gain effective control—which might be done with as little as 10 per cent of the stock" [19, p. 145].

[9] The principal sources used in determining type of corporate control were the definitive proxy statements filed with the SEC by all of the 200 corporations, the annual reports filed with the Interstate Commerce Commission by each railroad, and the annual reports filed with the Federal Power Commission by the utilities which it regulates. A more complete description of these sources and references to other sources used can be found in the appendix.

[10] "Management control" without qualification should be understood to mean *ultimate* control by management. The same applies, *mutatis mutandis*, to the other types of corporate control.

TABLE 1—SUMMARY ACCORDING TO THE TYPE OF ULTIMATE CONTROL OF THE 200 LARGEST NONFINANCIAL CORPORATIONS, 1963 AND 1929

Part 1: Number of Corporations

Type of Control	Number of Corporations				Proportion of Companies by Industrial Groups			
	Total	Industrials	Public Utilities	Transportation Cos.	Total	Industrials	Public Utilities	Transportation Cos.
1963					%	%	%	%
Private Ownership	0	0	0	0	0	0	0	0
Majority Ownership	5	3	1	1	2.5	3	2	4
Minority Control	18	18	0	0	9	15	0	0
Legal Device	8	5	0	3	4	4	0	13
Management Control	169	91	58	20	84.5	78	98	83
	200	117	59	24	100	100	100	100
1929								
Private Ownership	12	8	2	2	6	8	4	5
Majority Ownership	10	6	3	1	5	6	6	2
Minority Control	46½	34½	7½	4½	23	32	14	11
Legal Device	41	14½	19	7½	21	14	36	18
Management Control	88½	43	19½	26	44	40	38	62
In Receivership	2	—	1	1	1	0	2	2
Total	200	106	52	42	100	100	100	100

Sources: 1963—Appendix (see footnote 3); 1929—Berle and Means, *The Modern Corporation and Private Property* [4, p. 115].

TABLE 1—(*Continued*)

Part 2: Assets of Corporations

Type of Control	Assets (In Millions of Dollars)				Proportion of Assets by Industrial Groups			
	Total	Industrials	Public Utilities	Transportation Cos.	Total	Industrials	Public Utilities	Transportation Cos.
1963					%	%	%	%
Private Ownership	0	0	0	0	0	0	0	0
Majority Ownership	3,307	2,098	697	512	1	1	1	2
Minority Control	28,248	28,248	0	0	11	19	0	0
Legal Device	8,765	4,959	0	3,806	3	3	0	15
Management Control	224,377	117,732	85,300	21,345	85	77	99	83
Total	264,697	153,037	85,997	25,663	100	100	100	100
1929								
Private Ownership	3,366	2,869	221	276	4	9	1	1
Majority Ownership	1,542	779	480	283	2	3	2	1
Minority Control	11,223	9,258	1,261	704	14	31	5	3
Legal Device	17,565	4,307	9,406	3,852	22	14	37	15
Management Control	47,108	13,142	14,291	19,675	58	43	55	79
In Receivership	269	0	108	161	*	0	*	1
Total	81,073	30,355	25,767	24,951	100	100	100	100

* Less than 1 per cent.

Sources: 1963—Appendix (see footnote 3); 1929—Berle and Means, *The Modern Corporation and Private Property* [4, p. 115].

LARNER: 200 LARGEST CORPORATIONS 783

TABLE 2—SUMMARY ACCORDING TO THE TYPE OF IMMEDIATE CONTROL OF THE 200 LARGEST NONFINANCIAL CORPORATIONS, 1963 AND 1929

Part 1: 1963

Type of Control	Total		Industrials		Public Utilities		Transportation Cos.		Distribution of Total	
	Number of Companies	Assets ($000,000)	Number of Companies	Assets ($000,000)	Number of Companies	Assets ($000,000)	Number of Companies	Assets ($000,000)	By Company	By Assets
Private Ownership	0	0	0	0	0	0	0	0	0%	0%
Majority Ownership	9	8,387	5	5,218	2	1,480	2	1,689	4	3
Minority Control	28	37,252	23	31,641	0	0	5	5,611	14	14
Legal Device	0	0	0	0	0	0	0	0	0	0
Management Control	160	216,818	87	114,792	57	84,517	16	17,509	80	82
Joint Minority Control*	3	2,240	2	1,386	0	0	1	854	2	1
Total	200	264,697	117	153,037	59	85,997	24	25,663	100	100

* Includes corporations jointly controlled by two or more minority interests.

Source: Appendix (see footnote 3).

TABLE 2—(Continued)
Part 2: 1929

Type of Control	Total		Industrials		Public Utilities		Transportation Cos.		Distribution of Total	
	Number of Companies	Assets ($000,000)	Number of Companies	Assets ($000,000)	Number of Companies	Assets ($000,000)	Number of Companies	Assets ($000,000)	By Company	By Assets
Private Ownership	12	3,367	8	2,870	2	221	2	276	6%	4%
Majority Ownership	10	1,542	6	779	3	480	1	283	5	2
Minority Control	73	25,593	38	11,179	22	10,105	13	4,309	36.5	32
Legal Device	21	9,232	10	2,260	10	5,372	1	1,600	10.5	12
Management Control	65	35,802	41	12,736	10	8,040	14	15,026	32.5	44
Joint Control*	16	5,164	3	532	4	1,441	9	3,191	8	6
Special Situations	3	374	0	0	1	108	2	266	1.5	—
Total	200	81,074	106	30,356	52	25,767	42	24,951	100	100

* Includes corporations jointly controlled by two or more minority interests or jointly controlled by a minority interest and management.
Source: Berle and Means, The Modern Corporation and Private Property [4, p. 116].

Only 18 firms were found to be controlled by minority stockholders in 1963, roughly a third of the $46\frac{1}{2}$ firms which Berle and Means classified as minority-controlled in 1929. Control through legal devices decreased even more sharply—from 41 in 1929 to 8 in 1963. On the other hand, the number of management-controlled firms almost doubled, from $88\frac{1}{2}$ in 1929 to 169 in 1963.

Five companies on the 1963 list which are classified as management-controlled appear to be controlled, or at least very strongly influenced, by a single family within their management. Yet these families owned only a very small fraction of the outstanding voting stock. The five companies and their controlling families are: IBM (Watson), Inland Steel (Block), Weyerhaeuser (Weyerhaeuser), Federated Department Stores (Lazarus), and J. P. Stevens (Stevens). Federated Department Stores is the best illustration of this. In 1963 its chairman of the board, its president, and five of its 19 directors were members of the Lazarus family, even though the combined stock interest of the entire family was only 1.32 per cent. Since the present basis of control by these families appears to be their strategic position in management and the traditional identification of the corporation with the family rather than any appreciable amount of stock ownership, these companies are classified as management-controlled.

Management control was distributed rather evenly among the three industrial groups in 1963. Its highest incidence was among the utilities where it accounted for all but one of the 59 firms. Yet the public utilities had the lowest incidence of management-controlled firms in 1929 (38 per cent). This drastic change can be explained by the "death sentence" provision of the Public Utility Holding Company Act of 1935, which proscribes pyramiding beyond the second degree among public utility holding companies. Management control was the predominant type of control for the industrials and the transportation companies as well, accounting for 78 per cent of the former and 83 per cent of the latter.

A significant difference between 1963 and 1929 is that the proportion of the 200 largest nonfinancial corporations that were management-controlled in the later year was about the same as the proportion of assets so controlled, while in 1929 the proportion of assets that were management-controlled was a good deal larger than the proportion of companies so controlled. This indicates that management control, which was concentrated among the larger firms on the 1929 list, has since reached down to relatively smaller (though absolutely larger) firms than it touched in 1929 and has become rather evenly distributed among the "200 largest." This contrast is illustrated by Table 3, which divides the "200 largest" of each year by rank into five groups of 40 firms each and lists the number of management-controlled firms in each group.

TABLE 3—"200 LARGEST" DIVIDED BY RANK INTO 5 GROUPS AND NUMBER
OF MANAGEMENT-CONTROLLED FIRMS IN EACH GROUP

Firms Ranking	Number of Management-Controlled Firms	
	1963	1929
1 through 40	34	27
41 through 80	33	21
81 through 120	32	15¼
121 through 160	37	15¼
161 through 200	33	9½
Total	169	88¼

Source: Appendix (see footnote 3)

This evidence suggests that a firm may reach a size so great that, with
a few exceptions, its control is beyond the financial means of any individual or group. This point appears to have been reached only by the
larger firms on the 1929 list, but by all of the firms on the 1963 list. The
smallest corporation among the top 200 in 1963 had assets of 423 million
current dollars or, deflating by the GNP deflator, 204 million 1929
dollars. A corporation of this size would have ranked 111th on the Berle
and Means list. Of the 110 firms which would have ranked ahead of it,
55 per cent were management-controlled, compared with only 31 per
cent of the remaining 90 firms. Moreover, many of the remaining 45 per
cent of the top 110 firms in 1929 were either public utilities controlled by
a kind of pyramiding which is now illegal or industrial firms still owned
and controlled by their founder.

The present study may classify some firms incorrectly because of the
limited information available to outsiders about the control of the 200
largest nonfinancial corporations. Generally, such errors would involve
failure to locate an existing center of ownership (especially minority)
control, so that the company is mistakenly classified as management-
controlled. This would result, of course, in our overstating the extent of
management control in 1963. Berle and Means, however, would seem to
be in greater danger of overstating the extent of management control
because of the less authoritative and less systematic sources of data upon
which they had to rely and because of the larger minimum stockholding
which they required as sufficient evidence of minority control. It follows
that, even though the findings of the present study may overstate somewhat the *extent* of management control in 1963, they are also likely to
understate the *change* in the extent of management control from 1929 to
1963 when compared with the findings of the Berle and Means study.

In summary, it would appear that Berle and Means in 1929 were
observing a "managerial revolution" in process. Now, 30 years later,

that revolution seems close to complete, at least within the range of the 200 largest nonfinancial corporations.

REFERENCES

1. M. A. ADELMAN, "The Measurement of Industrial Concentration," *Rev. Econ. Stat.*, Nov. 1951, *33*, 269–96; reprinted in R. B. Heflebower and G. W. Stocking, eds., *Readings in Industrial Organization and Public Policy*, Homewood 1958, pp. 3–45.
2. A. A. BERLE, *Power Without Property*. New York 1959.
3. ———, *The 20th Century Capitalist Revolution*. New York 1954.
4. ——— and G. C. MEANS, *The Modern Corporation and Private Property*. New York 1932.
5. ———, *et al.*, "Symposium on the Impact of the Corporation on Classical Economic Theory," *Quart. Jour. Econ.*, Feb. 1965, *79*, 1–51.
6. R. A. GORDON, *Business Leadership in the Large Corporation*. Washington 1945.
7. R. J. MONSEN, JR. AND A. DOWNS, "A Theory of Large Managerial Firms," *Jour. Pol. Econ.*, June 1965, *73*, 221–36.
8. *Moody's Industrial Manual, 1964*. New York 1964.
9. *Moody's Public Utility Manual, 1964*. New York 1964.
10. *Moody's Transportation Manual, 1964*. New York 1964.
11. M. J. PECK, *Competition in the Aluminum Industry, 1945–1958*. Cambridge, Mass. 1961.
12. T. K. QUINN, *Giant Business: Threat to Democracy*. New York 1953.
13. E. V. ROSTOW, "To Whom and for What Ends Is Corporate Management Responsible?", in E. S. Mason, ed., *The Corporation in Modern Society*, Cambridge, Mass. 1959, pp. 46–71.
14. Standard and Poor's, *Standard Listed Stock Reports*. Ephrata, Pa.
15. R. B. TENNANT, *The American Cigarette Industry*. New Haven 1950.
16. "*Fortune*'s Directory of the 500 Largest Industrial Corporations," *Fortune*, July 1964, *70*, 179–98.
17. "*Fortune*'s Directory: Part II," *Fortune*, Aug. 1964, *70*, 151–62.
18. TEMPORARY NATIONAL ECONOMIC COMMITTEE, *Distribution of Ownership in the 200 Largest Nonfinancial Corporations*, "Monograph No. 29." Washington 1940.
19. "What's behind the Big TWA Sale?," *Business Week*, April 16, 1966, 145–50.

Part II
Critical Perspectives

[5]

USA: The economy

Stock ownership and the control of corporations

by Don Villarejo

Editors' comment: the editors of New University Thought *feel that a major function of the magazine is to publish original research on aspects of contemporary American society. The discussion of corporate owner- ship and control is felt to be particularly important because the large corporation is one of the primary influences in our society, and because the prevalent theories, which are only infrequently examined, color much contemporary social theory and have a heavy bearing on social policy. This article is the result of more than two years' research, most of it spent in extracting primary data from voluminous government reports and many scattered private sources. The tables present data unavailable elsewhere in this form. Don Villarejo, one of our editors, is a graduate student at the University of Chicago.*

This report constitutes the formal presentation of a portion of an ex- tensive research into the operation of the American economy. We have selected the 250 largest industrial corporations as our sample space and have attempted to gather information on the specific nature of con- trol in each case. In particular we seek to examine the various extant theories of control and weigh the evidence we have found with a view to determining a working theory of the "control of large corporations." Many views are well known in the academic and liberal community in- cluding Lundberg's *America's Sixty Families* (hardly a formal theory of control), Berle and Means' *The Modern Corporation and Private Property*, as well as the Madison Avenue "People's Capitalism" advanced by representatives of the New York Stock Exchange. While space does not permit a detailed examination of each of the many possible views, the more important will be considered in the light of our data.

In Part I we present data designed to shed some light on the general pattern of stock ownership in America and to equip the reader with the jargon of the field. In addition, Part I begins to enter into the general nature of the problem and the type of data involved. This section pro- vides the basic framework for our discussion. Part II deals more specifically with the question of control. Here we discuss the theory of control extensively and present our findings in condensed form. Finally, Part III discusses the problem of control in connection with the individuals enjoying a prominent position in the corporations studied. This is done by examining interlocking directorates, correlating informa- tion on personal holdings of these directors, and studying the identity of the individuals—how many are bankers, how many are large stock- holders, etc. This analysis leads logically to the presentation of a theory

33

of control which takes into account the relationship of the men enjoying power to the institutions they control.

Part I: Stock ownership

In the past few years more and more of the public's attention has been directed to the ownership and trading of stocks. There are many reasons for this development not the least important of which is the expansion of stock ownership during the great stock market boom of the late fifties. More recently, the detection of fraud on the market has led to a full scale investigation of the nation's major security markets by the Securities and Exchange Commission.

Throughout this period, however, there has been a remarkable absence of study of the means of controlling corporations and the relation of this to the fact of expanding stock ownership. There exist, however, a number of theories attempting to advance an understanding of the devices used to control corporations. Among these, the most prominent, in terms of general acceptance, is that of A.A. Berle, Jr.: "management control." This idea has been fully exploited from the time it was first introduced in 1932 up to Berle's recent work *Power Without Property*. Briefly, it is Berle's position that increasingly the largest corporations are under the control of management (by which we mean the individuals primarily responsible for the day to day operations of the corporation), a group without significant personal stockholdings. We shall consider this theory at a later point. Another view pushed before the public is the theory of "People's Capitalism," which in its most developed form, insists that the ordinary people of the country own, and therefore control, the great corporate enterprises. G.K. Funston, President of the New York Stock Exchange, primary proponent of this view, has said:

"As such, the gradual creation of a 'People's Capitalism' is an economic landmark without parallel. It has tremendous appeal to the uncommitted people of the world."[1]

We shall test this view as a part of this article. Yet another position is that of the economist Victor Perlo. Perlo asserts that economic institutions such as the major banks and brokerage firms have come to occupy a central position controlling the bulk of economic activity.[2] Finally, there is C. Wright Mills, who holds the position that a new level of development has been reached in modern times. His view is that the old propertied rich and the new privileged managerial class has evolved into a more compact group he calls the Corporate Rich.[3]

While all of these views express portions of the truth, none of them rely on a systematic study of the major corporations using recent data. For example, the TNEC data of 1940[4] provides much of Perlo's data. Berle has also not undertaken a full scale study to support his view; i.e., he has not studied the position of various stockholders in the corporations of interest in great enough detail. The New York Stock Exchange, while publishing data on the number of stockholders, has never studied even the fraction of stock owned by various income groupings. Mills relies on the sociologist's approach. He does not examine the mech-

34

anism of control in specific corporations. Another economist, R.A. Gordon, has explored this question in some detail but, again, relies heavily on the now outdated TNEC data. [5]

It seems appropriate, therefore, to re-examine the available data in order to obtain an understanding appropriate to the present time. But before turning to this question in detail, it is necessary to have a firm grasp of the general characteristics of stock ownership as well as the various devices used to hold stock.

The corporation

Corporations own roughly two-thirds of America's national wealth. The complete dominance of the corporate form is familiar to all of us. General Motors, U.S. Steel, General Electric, Standard Oil, and a whole host of other names are a part of our common understanding, yet they can not be found in the dictionary. A little less familiar is the extent of concentration of size among American corporations. In commenting on the fact that roughly 500 domestic corporations control about two-thirds of the non-farm economy, A.A. Berle, Jr. stated:

"This is, I think, the highest concentration of economic power in recorded history. Since the United States carries on not quite half of the manufacturing production of the entire world today, these 500 groupings—each with its own little dominating pyramid within it—represent a concentration of power over economics which makes the medieval feudal system look like a Sunday School party. In sheer economic power this has gone far beyond anything we have yet seen." [6]

It is our intention to examine some of these "little dominating pyramids" at a later point.

In theory, the corporate form is a device for pooling the resources of a large number of investors or, alternatively, it is a means of concentrating the ownership of property. Each of the many investors owns a portion of the enterprise and receives stock certificates as evidence of this fact. The *stockowner* enjoys the various rights accruing to investors including the right to participate in the election of directors. Stock certificates, or "stocks" as they are known, may be purchased or sold. Ordinarily, the market place for the sale of stocks is the stock exchange. The stock exchanges have grown at roughly the same pace as the corporate form. The New York Stock Exchange, for example, was founded in 1792.

In practice, the modern corporation rarely raises new funds by turning to the large number of small investors through the issuance of more stock. Consequently, the ownership and exchange of stocks has tended to become a more speculative activity. This type of activity, of course, attracts the crooks and fast buck operators as evidenced by the frenzy of speculative activity prior to the great stock market crash of 1929. The recent boom in the stock market has again brought the speculators to the fore. In fact, the large scale investigation of the stock markets to be undertaken by the SEC was triggered recently by the activity of some unscrupulous stockbrokers. This fact of growing speculative activity has had important effects on the various devices used to hold stock, as we shall see at a later point.

35

As a form of organization the corporate structure is quite simple. The stockholders, be they the original investors or others, elect a group of *directors* (usually numbering between ten to eighteen men). Each *share* is entitled to one vote, thus distinguishing corporate democracy from a political democracy in which each *citizen* has one vote. However, since the size of the investment determines the number of shares owned, the corporate form preserves (in the determination of directors at least) the relative weight or importance of each investor. Presumably the larger investor has more to lose and is therefore entitled to a larger voice in the determination of policy (albeit indirectly through the board of directors). In turn, the board of directors selects the management: a president, several vice-presidents, a secretary, a treasurer, etc. Thus, the line of responsibility is clearly laid out and, in one form or another, this structure is common to most modern corporations. It should be noted that Berle claims that in those corporations under management control it is actually the management and not the many thousands of stockholders who actually select the directors. We shall discuss this view at a later point.

While the structure described above seems to be relatively simple, the modern corporation is actually a bit more unwieldy than indicated. For example, the giant of them all—American Telephone and Telegraph—has nearly 2,000,000 stockholders of record. A stockholders' meeting of all holders is obviously not possible. Indeed, the most recent meeting of stockholders of A.T.&T. brought together the largest stockholders meeting in history, some 19,000 owners.

Shareowners and shareholdings

Various devices are used to hold stock in a corporation. Shown in Table I is a tabulation of *shareholdings* of record by category of *shareholder* in a large sample of domestic corporations. It is important to understand the distinction between shareholdings and shareowners. A *shareowner* is an individual who owns stock in one or more corporations. A *shareholding* is an entry in the records of the corporation indicating ownership of stock. A shareowner who owns stock in five corporations is represented by five shareholdings. On the other hand, one person may own stock in one corporation but may register the holding using several names, a portion of the total holding under each name. This single shareowner, then, would be represented by several shareholdings.

It is evident from Table I that the majority of corporate stock is owned directly by individuals. In fact, some 57.4 per cent of the common stock included in this study was owned directly by individuals. Equally important, 39.1 per cent of the stock was owned by one or another type of financial intermediary, institution, or corporation. For our purposes, a financial intermediary is a stockholder of record who holds stock for the benefit of others. For example, a brokerage firm may hold stock in its own name but the actual beneficiary may be one of the firm's clients. Let us now systematically investigate the various types of shareholders of record.

36

Table I: Shareholdings of record by class of shareholder; common stock of 6,679 issues: 1956

VILLAREJO:
Stock ownership
and the control
of corporations

Classification	Number of shareholder	Shares held	Average number shares per holding
Domestic individuals	26,030	4,250	163
Fiduciaries	1,297	549	423
Brokers & dealers	326	693	2,126
Nominees	213	732	3,437
Institutions & others	491	1,174	2,391
Foreign	752	265	352
Total	29,109	7,663	263

Note: Number of shareholdings in thousands; number of shares held in millions; average number of shares per holding in units.

Source: *Who Owns American Business*, 1956 Census of Shareowners, New York Stock Exchange, pp. 23-25.

Shareholdings of individuals

As we have seen, the most common device for holding stock is the direct ownership by an individual (we include joint ownership by a man and wife, commonly known as a joint account, as direct ownership by an individual). However, this method of holding stock has diminished in relative importance. The last one hundred years have seen the growth of various types of financial intermediaries as well as a growth of holdings by insurance companies, foundations, investment companies, and the like. As shown in Table I, the average holding of an individual is only 163 shares. Since the typical large corporation may have several million shares of stock outstanding, it is clear that the average individual holding is negligibly small. This one fact has been the starting point for many discussions of the wide diffusion of stock ownership. But a moment's thought shows that this figure of 163 shares per shareholding is almost devoid of meaning as it averages over millions of *shareholdings*.

A better measure, by contrast, of the holdings of individuals is the ownership of stock by families, distributed by the size of the holdings. About one-third of all families owning publicly traded common stock have investments of $5,000 or less. (See table VI.) In addition, roughly four-fifths if all shareowning families own less than $25,000 worth of publicly traded common stock. Also, only one-fifth of share-owning families own perhaps one-half or more of all common stock held directly by individuals.[7] We are led to the conclusion that the average shareholding appears small simply because the bulk of individuals have small holdings while a small minority of owners have moderate or very large holdings. (See also our later discussion of Table IX.)

Shareholdings of fiduciaries

A fiduciary is one who holds property in trust for another. Fiduciary shareholdings account for 4.6 per cent of all shareholdings and 9.4 per cent of common stock. The average holding of a fiduciary is about two and one-half times as large as the average holding of an individual. But these figures shed little light on the full importance of fiduciaries.

Since we have defined the term fiduciary in terms of another term not generally well known, the term "trust," it is appropriate for us to describe fiduciaries in greater detail. In order to fully appreciate this description it is necessary that the reader assume what is essentially a new view of property. This view requires that one regard property as of central importance and that one must plan in great detail to keep property intact. Thus, the death of a beneficiary does not mean distributing *property* to many beneficiaries but rather the redirection of *income* from the property to a new beneficiary. Changes in the tax laws require planning to lessen the impact on one's property. In the world of the propertied rich, the destruction of property via taxation or other means is regarded as a disaster. One of the most popular devices for maintaining property intact is the trust.

A trust may be defined as follows:

"A trust is a fiduciary relationship in which one person is the holder of the title to property, subject to an obligation imposed either expressly or by implication of law..." [8]

Within this general framework there are many types of trusts in actual use today. Historically, the first type of trust to gain widespread usage was the *testamentary trust* under which an estate was left to the management of trustees for the purpose of insuring proper management of the property in question. If, for example, a decedent left only a wife and minor children, the testamentary trust was the ideal means of insuring proper management of the family property. Beginning in 1850 numerous trust companies began a period of rapid growth and their functions were described as follows:

"They are the recipients and trustees of funds in large and small sums, held for account of widows, minors, and others; and are safe depositories for those who wish to avoid the risks arising from investments in the public securities of the times." [9]

By 1961, however, the *living trust* has assumed central importance. A living trust is a trust arrangement in which the individual places his property in trust while he is alive and continues to derive income from the trust. As we shall see, the living trust is a useful means of avoiding a large tax bite. In order to establish a trust, the individual gives property (no gift tax on gifts of this type) to the trust, appoints trustees, and sets up the terms of the trust. If an individual owns property directly and wishes to split up the income to several beneficiaries the trust is the perfect means of saving taxes. The income to the trust is not taxable to the trust if the income is distributed to beneficiaries. Thus, instead of paying one big tax bite on the direct income from the property, each beneficiary pays taxes only on the portion he receives at a much lower tax rate. In addition, one can direct that income from a trust be redirected at the death of a beneficiary to one or more other beneficiaries. Legally, the property does not change hands if a beneficiary should happen to die. Thus, there is no estate tax to pay since there has been no transfer of property. However, one cannot establish a perpetual trust,

38

so that after several generations estate taxes must be reckoned with.

As the tax structure has grown in complexity, the trust has assumed an even greater importance in the economy. To underscore this point, Table II shows the growth of large fiduciaries in the twenty-one year period from 1937 to 1958.[10] In this period the number of fiduciaries with incomes in excess of $5,000 more than tripled (it should be remembered that an income of $5,000 probably represents property value in excess of $100,000). In the same period, dividend income of these fiduciaries more than doubled.

Table II: Large income fiduciaries, selected income component: dividends, 1937 - 58

Income class	Number of tax returns		Dividend income	
	1937	1958	1937	1958
$5,000 to $10,000	25,143	84,899	93,915	293,783
$10,000 to $20,000	14,817	55,839	123,049	374,170
$20,000 to $25,000	3,056	11,660	42,880	118,138
$25,000 to $50,000	5,672	22,007	129,392	327,920
$50,000 to $100,000	2,269	9,456	108,716	273,919
$100,000 to $500,000	1,191	4,157	160,271	300,706
$500,000 to $1,000,000	73	304	45,719	62,893
$1,000,000 or more	29	185	44,287	123,216
	52,250	188,507	748,229	1,874,745

Note: Dividend income in thousands of dollars. The figures as presented are not strictly comparable. In 1937, the published figures were classified by Balance Income Class, i.e., total income less total deductions (but before distributions to beneficiaries and taxes). 1958 figures are classified by Total Income Class (before any deductions). Further, in 1937 12,247 returns were misfiled on improper returns. These returns have been distributed by the author on a proportional basis to the shown income classes. Finally, in 1937 the requirements for filing were less stringent than in 1958. Thus, it is possible that in the lower income classes especially the figures shown are actually underestimates.

Sources: *Statistics of Income for 1937, Part 1*, U.S. Treasury Department, Bureau of Internal Revenue, Washington, D.C. 1940, pp. 173-178. *Statistics of Income, 1958: Fiduciary, Gift and Estate Tax Returns*, U.S. Treasury Department, Internal Revenue Service, Washington, D.C., 1961, p. 15, Table 2.

Using these data, it is most difficult to estimate the number of individuals owning stock through fiduciaries. This is because a given person may derive income from several trusts or, alternatively, several individuals may derive income from a single trust. As an example of the former there is the case of Mrs. Marie Hartford Robertson who, with her children, derives income from no less than eighteen trusts holding about 745,785 shares of the Great Atlantic and Pacific Tea Company.[11] A typical case of the other kind is provided by the Stewart family trust, holding about 129,186 shares of Union Oil of California.[12] In this case A.C. Stewart benefits from about 24,029 shares, while W.L. Stewart, Jr. benefits from about 28,001 shares.[13] Both gentlemen are directors of Union Oil of California. The identity of the beneficiaries of the remaining 77,156 shares is not publicly known, but they are presumably other members of the Stewart family.

Paralleling the growth of the trust as a means of holding property has been the growth of the modern trust company, designed explicitly to provide fiduciary services for individuals and corporations. However, the major trust institutions do not use a separate fiduciary for each account. Rather, an elaborate system of *nominees* has been developed and, in most studies of share ownership, one makes a careful distinction between shares held by individual fiduciaries and trust institution fiduciaries or nominees. The main reason for this distinction is that the bulk of the trust institution fiduciary business is handled by a rather small number of banks, leading to a considerable concentration of shareholdings by the trust departments of the major banks. On the other hand, non-institution trusts are almost invariably managed by a beneficiary or an employee of the beneficiary, in which case the degree of concentration is not so great.

Shareholdings of nominees

To those not familiar with the nominee system, the complexity of this means of holding stock must appear enormous. Briefly, the system works as follows: a private citizen opens an account with a trust institution; once the account has been opened and shares purchased in various corporations, the registration of the name of the owner on the list of shareholders of record in these corporations is not that of the beneficial holder or even the title of the actual trustees. Instead, the shares will appear under one of several standard names used by the bank. For example, the following names are in current use by the giant Bankers Trust Co. of New York: Eddy and Co., Salkeld and Co., Boehm and Co. [14] To the uninitiated examining the list of stockholders of a large corporation, these names are somewhat mystifying. Yet they provide a simple, effective means of protecting the indentity of beneficiaries of large trust holdings. Furthermore, this system of nominees is an effective method of bookkeeping within the trust institution. Certain trust institutions use a separate nominee for all testamentary trusts, etc. Some trust institutions have as many as twelve nominee names in standard use.

In order to appreciate the nominee system we have reproduced in Table III a list of the thirty largest holders of one of the nation's large corporations, the Chesapeake and Ohio Railway Company. Perhaps the only shareholding familiar to most readers is that Cyrus S. Eaton, the Cleveland financier. Further down the list we find the name Milbank, & Co., a nominee for members of the Milbank family. These are the only shareholdings easily identifiable as to the actual beneficiaries. All the remaining twenty-eight holdings are nominees of various banks and institutions, and brokers and dealers. Thus, A.A. Welsh and Co. is a nominee for the Cleveland Trust Co.; Sigler and Co. is a nominee for the Hanover Bank; Shaw and Co. is a nominee for the Morgan-Guaranty Trust Co.; King and Co. is nominee for the First National City Bank trust affiliate; Atwell and Co. is a nominee for the United States Trust Co.; Salkeld and Co. is a nominee for the Bankers Trust Co.; and so on. The ultimate beneficiaries of these holdings and of the holdings of the various brokers listed are, of course, not revealed.

40

Table III: Thirty largest holdings of record in the Chesapeake and
Ohio Railway Company: 1959, common stock

VILLAREJO:
Stock ownership
and the control
of corporations

Name	Shares held	Per cent of Shares outstanding
Merrill Lynch (a)	331,954	4.03
O'Neill & Co.	136,900	1.66
Hanab Company	133,984	1.63
Cyrus S. Eaton	103,427	1.26
Croft and Co.	90,000	1.09
Carothers and Clark	80,000	0.97
Touchstone and Co.	75,000	0.91
Ferro and Co.	53,500	0.65
French and Co.	50,000	0.61
N.V. Algemeene Tr. Maatschappi	49,650	0.60
Sigler and Co.	46,652	0.57
Shaw and Co.	46,321	0.56
Jacquith and Co.	46,055	0.56
Char and Co.	45,000	0.55
King and Co.	34,656	0.42
A.A. Welsh and Co.	32,364	0.39
Saxon and Co.	31,440	0.38
Salkeld and Co.	30,484	0.37
Genoy and Co.	26,262	0.32
Bache and Co.	25,029	0.30
Edal and Co.	23,000	0.28
Lages and Co.	22,700	0.28
Milbank and Co.	22,500	0.27
Carson and Co.	21,182	0.26
Paine, Webber, Jackson & Curtis	20,016	0.24
Loriot and Co.	20,000	0.24
Atwell and Co.	19,551	0.24
Francis I. DuPont and Co.	18,825	0.23
John F. Frawley and Co.	18,300	0.22
Goodbody and Co.	18,257	0.22
Total	1,673,010	20.32

Note: (a) Merrill Lynch, Pierce, Fenner and Smith, Inc.

Source: Annual Report of The Chesapeake and Ohio Railway Company to the Interstate Commerce Commission for the year ended December 31, 1959, p. 108.

With this brief description in mind we turn to the holdings of nominees as shown in Table I. We observe that nominees account for only 0.8 per cent of all shareholdings but, surprisingly, about 9.9 per cent of common stock. Nominee holdings average about twenty times the average holding of an individual. Yet this is only the beginning. The typical trust institution holds stock in about 790 corporations.[15] Since many of the large institutions use several nominees, a single bank may be represented by 8,000 shareholdings in our figures. On the other hand, it is known that only 412 trust institutions had trust assets under administration amounting to $10 million or more.[16] Therefore, the 213,000 holdings attributed to nominees may only represent several hundred banks. By any measure, this certainly represents an enormous concentration of shares in so few shareholders. If we accept the figure of 790 as representative of the average number of corporations in which

41

the trust institutions hold stock, then the average number of shares per nominee is an enormous 2,714,000 shares. Since a typical institution uses more than one nominee, it is clear that a very large concentration of shares reside with the major trust institutions.

Table IV: Shares owned through banks, brokers, and dealers in sixteen large corporations: 1951

Corporation	Banks		Brokers & dealers	
	Number	Holding	Number	Holding
American Airlines	65	8.6%	307	24.7%
American Telephone & Telegraph	123	4.8	348	2.3
Celanese Corp.	85	14.0	258	9.1
Cities Service Co.	81	10.0	284	17.6
Consolidated Edison	108	10.0	293	5.5
E.I. du Pont de Nemours	125	12.4	310	1.7
Electric Bond and Share	62	12.6	268	27.0
General Electric Co.	125	20.2	327	3.2
General Motors Corp.	126	7.5	352	2.3
International Tel. & Tel.	41	3.0	296	41.2
Pacific Gas and Electric	102	7.7	272	4.1
Pennsylvania Railroad	93	5.4	325	13.0
Radio Corporation of America	96	5.2	338	20.0
Sears, Roebuck and Co.	119	14.7	266	1.8
Standard Oil Co. (New Jersey)	125	17.9	343	3.2
United States Steel Corp.	106	8.8	337	8.9

Note: Holding is the combined number of shares owned as a per cent of total outstanding stock (common stock only) in each company.

Source: *Share Ownership in the United States*, L.H. Kimmel, The Brookings Institution, Washington, D.C., 1952; pp. 50, 57. Moody's Corporation Manuals (for shares outstanding as of 12/31/51).

In order to grasp the full importance of nominee holdings in a specific corporation, Table IV gives the results of a survey of major trust institutions and their holdings in certain domestic corporations. Of greatest interest is the extent of nominee holdings in General Electric Co., a corporation generally believed to be widely held. Yet, a minimum of 20 per cent of the stock of G.E. is held by a mere 125 banks. While this is not the place for a full discussion of the various methods used to control corporations, it is important to realize that it is generally considered that a handful, possibly fifteen, New York banks dominate the personal trust business. The holding of 20 per cent by 125 banks fails to convey the full extent of concentration.

(An especially interesting account of the trust business and the importance of the major New York financial houses will be found in Perlo's book, Chapter IV--see footnote 2)

In spite of the great importance of personal trust holdings managed by the giant banks, there is very little public interest in or awareness of the booming trust business. There is all too little information publicly available concerning the relative importance of the major trust institutions and, equally important, very little is known of the holdings of specific institutions in specific corporations. This aura of secrecy is but another reflection of the common place attitude in the business world that a man's business transactions are his own private affair. Even government regulatory agencies have great difficulty in penetrating this great wall of secrecy. To this day there is virtually no information concerning the identity of most of the beneficiaries of these trusts.

Brokers and dealers

Stockbrokers play a role of considerable importance in the holding of stocks. Most people make stock transactions through a broker and, hence, the brokerage house enjoys a unique position as the "middle man." While certain firms are closely connected to one or more of the major banks, many of the very large firms are independent. One of the biggest, Merrill Lynch, Pierce, Fenner and Smith, recruits new business in somewhat the same spirit as vacuum cleaner salesmen. Merrill Lynch handles a very large number of small accounts. In terms of the average holding registered in the name of a broker, Table I shows that the average shareholding is only about two-thirds that of the average nominee. Table IV underscores the importance of the holdings of brokers and dealers in certain specific corporations. Of great interest is the better than 41 per cent of the stock of International Telephone and Telegraph registered in the names of only 296 brokers and dealers.

It must also be realized that since brokers are middle men, they carry the bulk of the active *trading accounts* (accounts which attempt to play the market and "make a killing"). Thus, in terms of long range interest in a given corporation, the holdings of brokers and dealers obviously rank below the nominees in overall importance.

Institutions and others

In this catchall category we find the holdings of the foundations, life insurance companies, investment companies, college and university endowments, mutual savings banks, and corporations. Unfortunately, the NYSE survey does not give a detailed breakdown of the relative importance of the various types of institutional investors. But it is clear that in terms of the size of average stockholding, they rank in importance on a par with the brokers and dealers. A more detailed consideration of these investors will be postponed to a later point.

Now that we have gained some idea of the relative importance of various classes of shareholders, we move to the pattern of stock ownership at the present time. We turn first to a discussion of the number and characteristics of shareowners.

Number and characteristics of shareowners

At the end of 1959 there were roughly 13.5 million individual shareowners in the United States. This compares with about 1.5 million shareowners in 1900.[17] The bulk of the rapid increase in the number of shareowners occurred in comparatively recent times. In 1952 only 6.5 million persons owned stock, while in 1937 perhaps 5 million individuals held shares.[18] Of greater interest than the number of owners is the pattern of ownership among income classes. In particular, we are concerned with the existence or absence of concentration of ownership. Table

43

V shows the distribution of ownership of common stocks as of the end of 1959. As noted earlier, about one-fifth of the shareowning families control nearly one-half of the stock owned directly by individuals.

Table V: Concentration of direct common stock ownership by income income class: 1959

Income class	Per cent of population in this class	Per cent in each class owning stock	Share in total value
Under $5,000	47	6	10
$5,000 - $9,999	39	16	26
$10,000 - $14,999	10	36	22
$15,000 and over	4	55	42
Total	100	14	100

Source: *1960 Survey of Consumer Finances*, Survey Research Center, Institute for Social Research, University of Michigan, Ann Arbor, 1961, p. 101, table 6-2.

In spite of the fact that more and more families own stock, there is overwhelming evidence to indicate that there has been little change in the historical pattern of marked concentration of ownership of stocks. As indicated in Table VI, the wealthiest one per cent of the population has maintained a tight grip on roughly two-thirds of outstanding beneficially held corporate securities.

On its face, Table VI appears to contradict the results shown in Table V. However, these results refer to different years and, in addition, use different measures—wealth vs. income. The reader should be cautioned that wealth and income are not interchangeable. Further, Table V uses data obtained from interviews and probably represents an understatement of the case.

Table VI: Percentage of corporate stock held by wealthiest one per cent of adults: selected years

Year	1922	1929	1939	1945	1949	1953
Amount	61.5	65.6	69.0	61.7	64.9	76.0

Note: Represented is fraction of stock beneficially owned by individuals based on market value.

Source: *Changes in the Share of Wealth Held by Top Wealth Holders, 1922-1956*, Robert J. Lampman, Occasional Paper 71, National Bureau of Economic Research, Inc., New York, 1960, p. 26, (Note that Lampman warns that these figures are very rough and should be used with caution.)

These facts seem to present us with a dilemma. If, on the one hand, stock ownership by families has expanded rapidly, and on the other hand, the very wealthy have maintained their position as regards the fraction of stock owned, hasn't stock ownership actually become more and more concentrated? A careful examination shows that this is not the case. Even though a fixed *percentage* of the total population may have actually increased their ownership of this vital asset, it is clear that the *number of persons* classified among the wealthiest one per cent has also increased at the same rate as the growth of the population. That is, while the top one per cent as a group has increased its concentration, its individual members have not necessarily done so.

Further, there is abundant evidence to show that more of the wealthy own stock than ever before. This last point deserves further amplification. One group of stockholders enjoying an especially rapid expansion of ownership has been the corporate executives or "top management." An extraordinarily well paid group—median income of 1,674 top executives of the 834 largest corporations is $73,584 [19]—these men have reached the top of the business world. Their major worry, of course, is taxation and the methods of avoidance. The general public is familiar with the fat expense account, but not as many are aware of the favorable stock deals now offered to most executives. This is the device of the stock option whereby an executive is offered the "option" of purchasing company shares at a pegged price, usually well below the market value. A favorable tax ruling in the late 1940's made the stock option gambit most lucrative and desirable. Today most major companies issue thousands of shares of stock yearly to officers of their organizations.

As an example of the gain to the buyer, consider the case of Air Reduction Co. During 1959 various officers exercised options on 22,643 shares at an aggregate option price of $704,627. [20] In December 31, 1959, the market price of Air Reduction Co. stock was $84 per share, so that the market value of the stock purchased by the Airco officers was $1,903,012. The rate of return to the executives in question was better than 150 per cent *computed annually*.

One effect of such deals has been the expansion of stock ownership among major executives. Back in 1939 only seven of the officers, excluding directors, of U.S. Steel Corp. owned common stock in their company. The aggregate holding of these seven was 3,660 shares, or 0.042 per cent of the outstanding common stock. [21] At the end of 1959, forty-eight major officers held 207,504 shares. [22] Similarly, in the giant Westinghouse Electric Corp., only three non-director officers held stock in 1939 (a total of 31 shares or 0.001 per cent of the total outstanding common stock) while in 1959 we find that thirty-five major officers held shares. [23] This pattern holds for many thousands of U.S. corporations in greater or lesser degree. The average holding of such officers is clearly moderate in size, although much larger than the typical holding of an individual.

Another group enjoying a rapid expansion of ownership has been the "professionals." Doctors, lawyers, engineers, and a whole host of others have enjoyed the fruits of stock ownership in increasing numbers. In fact, proportionately more families in which the family head is a professional own shares directly than in any other classification. [24] Only in the classification "managerial" do we find larger holdings on the average. Thus, while professionals tend to be stockholders, their holdings, on the average, are smaller than those of the managerial class. But of course the professionals do not enjoy the benefits of stock option plans.

Yet another aspect of this changing pattern is illustrated in Table VII, which shows the distribution of dividend income as revealed on income tax returns for the years 1928 and 1958. It is important to realize that dividend income from *all* sources is included in this tabulation, whether from trusts, holding companies, or direct holdings. It is clear that beneficial ownership of stock as exhibited in this table shows evidence of spreading to more of the moderate stockholders. On the other

45

Table VII: Distribution of dividend income by size of dividend
income: 1928 and 1958 (for large stockholders only)

Size of dividend income	Number		Dividends received	
	1928	1958	1928	1958
$5,000 - $10,000	70,513	172,887	493,457	1,216,728
$10,000 - $25,000	51,047	107,520	781,571	1,631,807
$25,000 - $50,000	17,510	30,207	603,569	952,890
$50,000 - $100,000	7,574	11,822	519,509	829,517
$100,000 or more	4,187	5,070	1,082,941	1,118,998
	150,831	327,506	3,481,047	5,749,940

Note: Number refers to number of tax returns of individuals reporting dividend
income in the indicated size classification. Amount received in thousand dollars.

Sources: 1928 figures: *Statistics of Income for 1928*, U.S. Treasury Dept., Bureau
of Internal Revenue, Washington, D.C., p. 13. 1958 figures: Based on *Statistics of
Income, 1958: Individual Income Tax Returns*, U.S. Treasury Department, Internal
Revenue Service, Washington, D.C., 1960, pp. 29, 44 (See Appendix I for a brief
description of the computational method used.)

hand, one must take into account the fact that a dividend income of
$5,000 represents property worth at least $100,000—certainly a sizable shareholding. The number of returns showing dividend income
between $5,000 and $10,000 more than doubled in the thirty-one
year period, while those showing dividend incomes greater than
$100,000 increased by only one-quarter in the same period. More im-
portant, those with smaller dividend incomes (between $5,000 and
$25,000) received a larger fraction of total dividends received in 1958
than in 1928 (49.5 per cent in 1958 and 36.6 per cent in 1928). At the
other extreme, those with dividend incomes greater than $100,000 re-
ceived about 31 per cent of dividends paid to these stockholders in 1928,
but only 19.5 per cent in 1958. By any measure, one finds that there
has been some broadening of ownership by the moderately rich.

At the lower end of the income spectrum there is a rapid decline in
the number of families owning stock. In particular, some 94 per cent
of families with incomes below $3,000 own no stock whatsoever; about
92 per cent of families with incomes between $3,000 and $4,999 do not
own stocks; 84 per cent of families with incomes between $7,500 and
$9,999 do not own stock. Further, the total market value of holdings
of these low income shareowners is about 36 per cent of the total value
of publicly traded common stocks held by individuals, even though more
than 60 per cent of all shareowning families are in this classification. [25]
Thus, while there has certainly been some expansion of stock ownership
by families with small incomes, the bulk of low income families do not
hold stock and those that do hold stock have rather small holdings.

In summary, we find that the number of shareowners has expanded
rather rapidly but that the distribution of ownership remains concentrated. Further, those enjoying a larger share of ownership, at least to
a significant degree, are those among top management of the great corporate enterprises and the ever-growing middle class.

Financial intermediaries and institutions

The ownership of common stocks by various financial intermediaries and institutions and corporations is summarized in Table VIII. The holdings of these financial intermediaries amounts to roughly one-third of outstanding common stock publicly traded (excluding foundations and colleges and universities). The most important of all of the financial intermediaries is revealed to be the trust institution whose holdings were discussed in earlier sections. The various insurance companies have relatively smaller holdings while the financial intermediaries not under trust company administration rank second only to the trust institutions (this includes non-bank administered trusts, personal holding companies, and investment trusts).

Table VIII: Stockholdings of principal financial intermediaries
and institutions: 1958

Classification of owner	Common stock holdings in billions at market value	Source
Trust Institutions	$66.2	a
Personal trust accounts	30.7	b
Trusteed corporate pension funds	9.5	c
Common trust funds	1.3	d
Estates and others '	24.7	e
Fire and casualty insurance companies	6.8	f
Life insurance companies	2.5	g
Investment trusts	13.2	h
Colleges and universities	2.0	i
Personal holding companies	3.1	j
Non-bank administered trusts	13.4	k
Foundations	1.2	m
Sub-total	108.4	
Non-financial corporations	37.2	n
Grand total	145.6	
All holders	$363.0	p

Sources: a) Based on 1957 figures quoted in *Trusts and Estates*, Vol. 98, No. 2, February, 1959. We have simply taken into account the increase in holdings of the Pension Funds and Common Trust Funds. No allowance has been made for the increase in holdings of personal trust accounts from 1957 to 1958. Thus, the figure is certainly on the small side. b) *The Trust Bulletin*, Vol. 39, No. 1, Sept. 1959, "Report of National Survey of Personal Trust Accounts," J.H. Wolfe, Table I. It is my belief that this figure is on the low side since many banks estimate the value of an account on a *book value* (cost when purchased or acquired) basis rather than on a current market value basis. c) *Securities and Exchange Commission Statistical Bulletin*, June 1960, p. 6, Table 3. d) *Federal Reserve Bulletin*, May 1959, p. 478. e) Line a less the sum of lines b, c and d. f) Compiled by the author from *Moody's Bank and Finance Manual, 1959*, Moody's Investor's Service, 99 Church St., New York. g) *Life Insurance Fact Book*, Institute of Life Insurance, p. 79. h) Author's estimate based on source cited in f (above). i) Author's estimate based on source cited in a (above). j) Computed by author from data in *Statistics of Income: Corporation Income Tax Returns: 1958-59*, U.S. Treasury Department, Internal Revenue Service, Washington, D.C., 1961, pp. 175-176. k) Computed by author from data in *Statistics of Income: Fiduciary, Gift and Estate Tax Returns*, U.S. Treasury Department, Internal Revenue Service, Washington, D.C., 1961, p. 23. m) Same as a (above). Since domestic foundations have total assets of roughly $11.5 billion, mostly in stocks, (see *New York*

47

Times. July 11, 1960, p. M1) it is clear that the estimate shown is much too small. However, the source cited has been used as a reference for other entries above and is used for the sake of consistency. See the discussion below. n) Computed by the author from the source cited in j (above). p) Computed by the author from *U.S. Securities and Exchange Commission*, 25th Annual Report, Washington, 1960, pp. 63, 67.

Comment: The figures cited above do not include the holdings of mutual savings banks, commercial bank direct holdings, holdings of brokers and dealers, holdings of law firms, and holdings of partnerships. In addition, the figure shown for personal trust accounts is believed to be on the liw side, as is the figure for foundations. Furthermore, those figures based on dividends received do not take into account shares held but not paying dividends. Clearly, the above estimate is well on the low side and, by my estimate is actually fifteen to twenty billion dollars larger than the figure shown. That is, the holdings of all but non-financial corporations should total in the neighborhood of $125 billion while the total holdings of non-financial corporations should be perhaps one or two billion dollars larger. Thus, the grand total should be in the neighborhood of $165 billion.

The investment trusts or investment companies are often referred to as mutual funds because they pool the resources of many individuals for common investment. These companies actively seek small accounts and have enjoyed a rapid growth in the recent boom period of the stock market. In terms of number of stockholders, the investment companies rank at the top of the list with such giants as General Electric and General Motors. It is presumed that each investor reaps the benefits of a balanced portfolio without having to pay the large outlay needed to obtain shares in perhaps a hundred different corporations. However, the service and sales charges are quite steep if one invests small sums. For the investment of large sums the charges are relatively smaller. In fact, a recent tax ruling permitted the exchange of investment company shares in return for shares of another corporation. Thus, the privilege accumulates to those owning property.

The shareholdings of certain insurance companies are limited by law to less than two per cent of the outstanding stock of the corporation in which the investment is made. However, most insurance companies have only recently begun to expand their investment activities in the common stock field. In fact, several of the larger insurance companies have announced their intention to buy the legal limit of stocks allowed. As we shall see, insurance companies number among the largest domestic industrial corporations. The full importance of such holdings has not been generally recognized by most students of share ownership.

While we have discussed the role of the trust institutions at an earlier point, it is fruitful to return for a few words concerning the trusteed corporate pension funds. These pension funds are currently the largest single net purchasers of stock on the open market. The rapid growth of these funds has been the subject of much comment by economists recently. [26] In the five year period from 1955 to 1959, the ownership of common stocks by trusteed pension funds increased from $4.8 billion to $12.3 billion. [27] For our purposes, it is important to realize that this is a field dominated by a relatively small number of financial institutions —again the handful of New York banks.

In conclusion, then, we find that the major financial intermediaries account directly for about one-third of publicly traded common stock and of this total, roughly half is held by the major trust institutions,

48

a field dominated by the major New York banks. One begins to appreciate the term "Wall Street" as a center of financial power.

Part II: control

While we have focused much of our attention on the general features of stock ownership, we have yet to address ourselves to the problem of greatest interest in this investigation. Namely, who in particular is in a position to exercise leadership in a giant corporation and how do such persons derive their power? In oversimplified terms, who *controls* the giant enterprise? Is it a ruthless robber baron still hanging around from the 19th century? Or is it a well bred and well mannered executive whose sound judgement is based on a thorough technical familiarity with his organization and products?

Before we can tackle these questions we need an understanding of the term "control." By control we mean the power, whether exercised or not, to make the major decisions demanded by the mere existence of the enterprise. More than this, we mean the power to direct the affairs of the corporation. It is most important to realize that the normal day-to-day decision-making involved in operating the firm is not what we are talking about. We refer to the fundamental decisions, including the selection of management. Our language suggests a single individual as a "controller" in a given corporation. Yet we must admit the possibility that several individuals might jointly share such a position of power.

Methods of determining control

On the basis of our earlier discussion we can conclude that there are several possible measures for determining the individual or group enjoying a controlling position in a corporation. We need to know who are the directors and officers of the corporations of interest. We also need to know the extent of their stockholdings as well as the identity of the largest stockholders; and, finally, we need some information as to who, among all the persons referred to, makes the kind of decisions in which we are interested. Of the four pieces of data required, only the first two can be obtained from publicly accessible sources. Data on the largest stockholders is all too often scanty or badly out of date. Finally, systematic information on just who makes what decisions in specific corporations is available in only a few cases.

Other writers have used additional data also. Most prominently one finds the use of information on the identity of the stock transfer agent and the stock registrar in a corporation of interest Another type of data used is the identity of the banking houses which head bond issues in securing new capital for a given corporation. Such facts, while certainly of interest, are generally conceded to be of secondary importance as compared with data on stock ownership. Therefore, we shall turn our primary attention to the identification of officers, directors, and large stockholders.

But why do we use the somewhat vague term "large stockholders?" Shouldn't we seek the identity of those stockholders who command a clear majority of the stock, even though they are, by definition, in the category "large?" Shown in Table IX is the distribution of shareholdings by size of shareholding, measured in terms of number of shares held as of late 1951. More recent data is not available. The table indicates the distribution in some 1,411 common stock issues of manufacturing corporations. Included are the common stock issues of many small as well as many very large corporations. Thus, we indicate numerical averages even though this is hardly representative of a specific corporation of interest. We find that, on the average, only 118 shareholdings account for about 57 per cent of the outstanding stock. These 118 holdings average nearly 5,000 shares each and represent only a little more than 2 per cent of all shareholdings. The heavy imbalance noted in Part I of the study is again evident: a small minority of holdings account for the bulk of corporate shares.

Table IX: Distribution of shareholdings by size of holding in manufacturing corporations

In the total survey:			
Size of holding	Number of holdings	Number of shares	Average holding
1 - 99 shares	4,742,366	147,294	31.1
100 - 999 shares	2,475,497	481,453	194.5
Above 1,000 shares	166,150	825,572	4,968.8
Total	7,384,013	1,454,319	197.1
In the average corporation:			
Size of holding	Number of holdings	Average number of shares	Per cent of stock held
1 - 99 shares	3,360	31.1	10.1
100 - 999 shares	1,755	194.5	33.1
Above 1,000 shares	118	4,968.8	56.8
Total	5,233	197.1	100.0

Note: Shown in the first part of this table is a survey of shareholdings in 1,411 common stock issues of manufacturing corporations. Number of shares held in thousands; number of shareholdings and average holding in each size class in units. In the second part of the table we have attempted to indicate how this pattern might look in an average corporation. Thus we have formed averages by dividing by 1,411 (the number of issues covered) to find an average of 5,233 shareholdings in our mythical average corporation. Also shown is the fraction of stock represented by holdings in each size class. For example, shareholdings of 1,000 shares or more account for nearly 57% of the outstanding stock in the sample corporations.

Source: L.H. Kimmel, *Share Ownership in the United States,* The Brookings Institution, Washington, D.C., 1952. Figures are for the end of 1951.

We would like, then, to obtain lists, on a corporation by corporation basis, of, say, the largest 150 shareholdings. Unfortunately, no modern corporation will part with such a list unless required to do so by law. However, in the late 1930's a government agency, the Temporary National Economic Committee, did collect data of this sort. The TNEC compiled lists of the 20 largest shareholdings in each of the 200 largest non-financial corporations in the land. In addition, the TNEC compiled

VILLAREJO:
Stock ownership
and the control
of corporations

a list of the beneficial holdings of officers and directors of these corporations. In sum, this volume of material represents the most comprehensive and systematic collection of data of this type currently available. Unfortunately, the data is now more than 20 years out of date. Substantial changes have occurred rendering much of the material useless. For example, many of the persons listed have disposed of all or a portion of their holdings while others have died passing only a fraction of their holdings on to descendents. On the other hand, many individuals have actually increased their holdings over the years. Therefore, TNEC data must be avoided or at least used with considerable caution.

Even though lists of the largest stockholdings in specific corporations are not available, it is possible to collect certain facts. In the case of corporations with securities listed on stock exchanges one can collect data on the holdings of officers and directors. In addition, one can collect data on the holdings of insurance companies and investment companies. Finally, by scouring the financial pages of many periodicals one can determine some information not officially available. While the systematic information we would like to have cannot be obtained at present, the situation is far from hopeless.

Holdings of directors and "community of interest"

As a first step in trying to obtain a currently valid picture of control we have selected the 250 largest industrial corporations for intensive study. The list of the 250 largest, as ranked by total assets, appeared in the July, 1960, issue of *Fortune*. In addition, data on securities owned was requested from 16 of the largest insurance companies in the United States. Only Metropolitan Life Insurance Co. refused to supply the requested data stating that it is not the policy of Metropolitan to reveal lists of securities owned. Data on the holdings of the 18 largest investment companies in the corporations of interest was also collected. The method of tabulating the holdings of directors is fully explained in Appendix II of this article. It was found that useable data could be obtained in the case of 232 of the corporations studied.

Table X: Distribution of directors' holdings by size of holding in each of 232 large industrial corporations

Size class	Total	Number of corps. in which directors' holdings are in the indicated size class				
		I	II	III	IV	V
0.00 - 0.99	68	27	22	5	7	7
1.00 - 1.99	45	8	9	13	6	9
2.00 - 2.99	14	1	5	2	1	5
3.00 - 3.99	17	3	1	5	6	2
4.00 - 4.99	12	3	2	5	2	0
5.00 - 9.99	39	3	3	10	14	9
Above 10.00	37	3	5	8	7	14
Total	232	48	47	48	43	46
Median holding	2.20%	0.72%	1.12%	3.66%	4.73%	4.36%

Note: Size class refers to the total per cent of stock held by all directors in a corporation of interest. Thus, in 37 corporations the aggregate holding of directors ex-

51

ceeded 10 per cent. The roman numerals I, etc. refer to a ranking of the 250 largest industrial corporations by size of total assets. We have arbitrarily divided these 250 corporations into five groups according to size of total assets. For example, in quintile I we include the 50 largest corporations among the 250 chosen for study. Of these 50, data was available for 48. And so on for the other four quintiles. For purposes of tabulation we have included among holdings all shares listed in the indicated sources even though the director may not benefit from the ownership of all such shares. This point is explained in Appendix II. A special note is required in the case of Ford Motor Co. In this company directors held only 2.30 per cent of the common stock. However, three members of the Ford family held 44.8 per cent of class B common stock, which, as a class, has 40 per cent of the voting power. Based on the number of shares of each class of common stock outstanding we have assigned 1.7475 vote per class B share and 1 vote per common share. Using this technique, directors of Ford hold 19.01 per cent of the voting power.

Shares outstanding, *Moody's Industrial Manual, 1960.*

Medians computed by the author from the original arrays.

Sources: See table of "Large stockholdings and directors holdings in major industrial corporations" and Appendix II for the holdings of directors and the sources used.

A considerably compressed view of the results is shown in Table X which presents the distribution of the aggregate holdings of directors in the 232 sample corporations expressed as a fraction of the total shares outstanding. The median holding of directors is 2.20 per cent of the outstanding stock. In other words in half the corporations studied the aggregate directors holding is greater than 2.20 per cent of the outstanding stock. Also clearly observed is the well known fact that directors tend to hold proportionately less stock in the very largest corporations than in the moderate size corporations. Thus, the median holding in quintile I is 0.72 per cent and in quintile V is 4.36 per cent. Even though the median directors holding is small, in no less than 76 corporations the directors alone hold more than 5.00 per cent of the outstanding stock. Furthermore, we must realize that the directors holding, taken alone, is not a valid indicator of concentration. For example, in Tidewater Oil the directors hold only 0.16 per cent of the outstanding stock while 65.55 per cent of the stock is held by Mission Corp., Mission Development Co. and Getty Oil Co., all under the solid control of the Getty family. Also, in most cases only a fraction of a family's total holdings are actually included in the total shown for directors. As a case in point consider Firestone Tire and Rubber. Four Firestone family members are directors of the company accounting for 4.43 per cent of the outstanding stock. Yet, the total holding of the Firestone family is authoritatively put at 25 per cent of the stock. (The reader should refer to our table of large stockholdings for verification of these statements.) Similarly, in Swift and Co. we find that H.H. Swift and T.P. Swift held 1.19 per cent of the stock while a private communication to R.A. Gordon indicated that total Swift family holdings is about 7 per cent. (Again see our table.) It should be ovbious that data of this type is fully necessary when we discuss the holdings of directors.

In order to better appreciate the significance of the data we have shown in Table XI the holdings we presume are represented on the board of directors of Phelps Dodge Corp. Phelps Dodge ranks 89th on our list of 250 largest industrials placing it in the second quintile of Table X. The *direct* holdings of the 17 directors totals 85,324 shares

52

VILLAREJO:
Stock ownership
and the control
of corporations

Table XI: Holdings represented on the board of Phelps Dodge
Corporation: 1959

Officer-Directors	Holding	Reference
R.G. Page, Pres. of Phelps Dodge, D	1,400	5/52; a
C.E. Dodge, V.P. of Phelps Dodge, D	62,206	9/56; b
W.C. Lawson, V.P. of Phelps Dodge, D	500	(1/58)
H.T. Brinton, Pres. of subsidiary, D	358	10/59
Directors (former officers)		
P.G. Beckett, formerly a V.P., D	200	7/50
C.R. Kuzell, formerly a V.P., D	300	6/57
Non-officer Directors		
P.L. Douglas (V.P., Otis Elevator), D	100	4/57
W.S. Gray (Chmn., The Hanover Bank), D	200	12/43
Continental Insurance Co. (director)	107,000	c
R.L. Ireland (Off., Consolidation Coal), D	0	(2/53)
M.A. Hanna Co. (director)	80,000	d
K.L. Isaacs, D	200	2/49
Mass. Investors Trust (vice-chmn.)	250,000	e
T.S. Lamont (V.-Chmn., Morgan-Guaranty), D	4,356	5/57
W.D. Manice (Dir., Southern Pacific), D	8,100	3/59
R.S. Perkins (Off., First Nat'l. City Bank), D	200	9/58
New York Life Ins. Co. (director)	25,200	f
J.C. Rea, D	2,956	12/48
Franz Schneider, D	0	(3/54)
Mutual Life Ins. Co. of N.Y. (director)	4,900	g
H.D. Smith, D.	600	4/58
Newmont Mining Co. (director)	296,238	d
A.C. Tener, D	3,448	8/49
Grand Total	848,462	
Total (directors only)	85,324	
Shares outstanding	10,142,520	

References: *Poor's Register of Directors and Officers, 1960.* Dates such as 10/59 refer to monthly report in which holding was found as described in App. II. Those in parentheses refer to unpublished reports found in Securities and Exchange Commission files. a) Also a director of the Hanover Bank; b) Also a director of the First National City Bank; c) *Annual Report, 1960;* d) *Moody's Industrial Manual, 1960;* e) *Moody's Bank and Finance Manual, 1960;* f) *Schedule of Securities, 1960;* g) *Schedule of Securities, 1960.*

Note: Of the seventeen directors listed, six (Dodge, Lamont, Manice, Rea, Smith, Tener) were directors on Sept. 30, 1939 date of the TNEC study. Rea and Dodge family holdings in excess of holdings shown above are believed to total 7.98 as shown in the TNEC study. See footnote 4.

D refers to direct holdings.

or 0.84 per cent of the outstanding stock placing it slightly below the median for corporations in this quintile. In addition, the holding is well below the median for all 232 corporations. As can be seen we have indicated holdings of several companies in which the Phelps Dodge directors are prominently involved. Using publicly accessible sources we are easily able to identify the basis of representation of directors whose aggregate indirect holdings are in excess of 7.50 per cent. Furthermore, there is a strong possibility that at least another 7.98 per cent of the stock is also represented on the board. The holdings which are represented are held by three insurance companies, two investment companies, and one industrial company (which has large holdings in several major

53

industrial corporations). In each case the representation is direct in that a single man is both a director of Phelps Dodge and of the company holding the shares. It is less obvious that other stockholdings are indirectly represented, i.e., shares held by some insurance companies are also actually represented but in this case the holding company and Phelps Dodge do not have directors in common. For example, the Insurance Co. of North America holds 20,000 shares and is not directly represented. Yet, Morgan Guaranty Trust Co. shares a director with Insurance Co. of North America and does have a representative on the Phelps Dodge board. [28] This kind of "indirect representation" is actually quite extensive in the large corporations and certainly reveals the community of interest concept to be of central importance in understanding the control of large corporations. While this discussion of Phelps Dodge Corp. is hardly exhaustive, it is evident that a full understanding of stock ownership in a given corporation demands that we identify the holdings of various insurance companies, investment companies, and other large holders as well as the holdings of directors.

The holding necessary for control

Let us now turn to the problem of just how much stock is required to control a corporation. Berle and Means assert that control by a minority interest is obtained only when 15 per cent of the stock (or more) is held by the group in question [29] Yet, financial analysts and observers, perhaps closer to the problem than the academic community, assert that a controlling interest can actually be obtained with a much smaller interest. For example, we find the comment about the Prince family holding in Armour and Co.:

"In the Prince trust today there are still 320,900 shares out of 5,158,305 outstanding, ample for control in a situation where the rest of the stock is well dispersed." [30]

Thus, in the case of Armour and Co., a holding of a little better than 6 per cent is viewed by responsible observers as being ample for control. And this situation is stated to obtain precisely when most of the holdings are small which Table X demonstrated was the case in most manufacturing corporations with publicly held stock. It should also be pointed out that the initiative for making decisions in Armour and Co. rests squarely with W.W. Prince, currently scion of the Prince family fortune. Can we regard, therefore, a holding of 6 per cent as the minimum necessary for control? Hardly, for this conclusion may only be valid in the case of Armour and Co. and, on the other hand, the Prince family may need only a portion of this 6 per cent holding to retain control.

At this point it is useful to consider a concept mentioned in the discussion of Phelps Dodge Corp., namely the idea of "community of interest." As we have seen many different holdings are often represented on the board of directors of a given corporation. Representation, whether direct or indirect, is obviously accorded to groups whose ownership position demands some attention. In discussing the fraction of stock needed for control one financial writer states: "... control on a very slim margin

54

VILLAREJO:
Stock ownership
and the control
of corporations

can be held *through friendship with large stockholders outside the holding company group* [31] confirming the conclusion reached in our examination of Phelps Dodge Corp. As C. Wright Mills' brilliant work pointed out, we must think of those in a power position as part of a general framework of interdependent interests: what he prefers to call an elite. We shall see in Part III that interlocking directorates among the various corporations studied form an extraordinarily complex network, the full tabulation of which would fill the pages of a large volume. It seems obvious that the community of interest concept provides the key to understanding how a compact minority may enjoy a commanding position in a corporation with thousands of shareholdings. It should be noted in this context that the median holding of the twenty largest owners of record as a group, in the 92 industrial corporations studied by the TNEC and included in our study, was 31.86 per cent of the outstanding common stock. [32]

One final bit of evidence regarding the fraction of stock needed for control should also be mentioned. In discussing the large holdings of the trust departments of the major banks, through the nominee system, the financial writer A.L. Kraus states:

"*At the same time the larger an institutional investor becomes the greater risk it runs that it will assume a controlling position in individual companies...To avoid such a situation* some banks now place a limitation on their holdings of a single company's shares at 5 per cent of the total outstanding." [33]

Implicit in this statement is the fact that a holding of five per cent or more may give a *single interest* working control irrespective of other interests in the large corporation in question (providing, of course, that the 5 per cent position is the largest single interest). Naturally, we do not contend that the 5 per cent figure is in any sense the "magic number." The fraction actually necessary in a specific corporation may well be larger or smaller depending on circumstances. Nonetheless, the figure does provide a useful yardstick in our study.

The theory of management control

Let us now examine another, wholly different, theory of control: the Berle theory of management control. In essence this theory rests on the fact that most large corporations actually have many thousands of shareholdings representing ownership. Because their holdings are tiny (refer to Table IX), the smaller stockholders rarely attempt to seek representation on the board of directors of a large corporation. Indeed, it would require the cooperation of many thousands of such small owners to obtain a sizable "collective vote" in the selection of directors. Furthermore, the small sums represented in these investments make it unlikely that the owners will spend the money and the time to attend the annual shareowners meeting. For example, we find that only 125 stockholders attended the March 16, 1960 annual meeting of International Harvester Co. [34] International Harvester had at the end of 1959 about 102,000 shareholdings of record. [35] An article in a leading business periodical bemoans such attendence records and cites further examples:

> "The 1960 figures for some other leading annual meetings were: General Electric, 2,114 stockholders present out of 417,053; General Motors, just over 3,000 out of 781,970; RCA, 1,600 out of 164,000; Standard Oil of New Jersey, some 4,500 out of 607,627. There were many more annual meetings at which scarcely any stockholders turned out at all."[36]

Therefore, the mass of small stockholders who do not attend the annual meetings have to submit their votes to a proxy committee if they wish to have their shares voted. And—this is the key point—the proxy committee, in almost all cases, is selected by management (by which we mean the executives of the corporation in question). Since the proxy committee may vote the shares as it sees fit, Berle suggests that this represents a considerable concentration of power in the hands of management. Now, most officers of the major corporations do not hold much stock (in a relative sense) and, thus, if management wishes to stay in power, may do so by merely selecting directors through the proxy machinery who will heed their wishes. Therefore, in Berle's view, ownership has been effectively separated from control. Tending to confirm Berle's view is the fact, as we have noted, that in many corporations the personal holdings of the directors are quite small (Table X showed that the median holding of directors was only 2.20 per cent). In conclusion, then, Berle describes a mechanism which places power not in the hands of the directors, but in the hands of management alone. Because this view is widely accepted in academic circles we shall consider it carefully.

To bolster his position, Berle's initial work in this field classified 200 corporations as to the character of control. Unfortunately, Berle did not have the useful TNEC data at his disposal and relied heavily on sources then publicly accessible. In fact, Berle's work was completed before it was possible to learn the precise holdings of even the directors of the corporations studied. Therefore, it is not surprising to find that Berle classifies corporations as under management control whenever his sources did not supply information to the contrary. For example, Firestone Tire and Rubber was classified as under management control though, as we have noted, the Firestone family even today holds 25 per cent of the stock. More important, Berle failed to recognize the fact, as we have noted, that many directors only *represent* large holdings (recall the case of Phelps Dodge Corp.). Therefore the TNEC data helped to overcome the failures of Berle's work. It is our opinion that this issue can only be settled today if lists of, say, the largest 150 shareholdings in each corporation of interest became available to the public. Clearly, one must regard the theory of management control with some suspicion until all the evidence is available. However, we do find some cases in which the management appears to enjoy a dominant position. For example, G.W. Romney is generally conceded to be in command of American Motors Corp. and, incidentally, may well emerge as one of the dominant stockholders in that company by virtue of lucrative stock options.

A final word on the theory of management control. One of the most celebrated examples of this type of control is the case of Chrysler Corp. in which the directors hold only 0.47 per cent of the stock. L.L. Colbert is usually cited as the management representative who dominates the Chrysler Corp. pyramid of power. Yet recent events have shattered this illusory view. Following conflict of interest scandals in the company W.C. Newberg, Chrysler president, was unceremoniously dumped and replaced by a new man. But, in addition, Colbert himself, though chairman of the board of directors, was later removed. Outside interests named G.H. Love, of M.A. Hanna Co. and Consolidation Coal, as board chairman. We see that *outside directors*, representing a variety of interests, easily unseated the men supposedly maintaining power through the mechanism of management control. The basis of power of these interests is not, all too unfortunately, well known.

The tabulation of large holdings

Now that we have examined the more important formal theories of control in some detail it is appropriate to discuss our data. At the outset it must be stated that our list of large stockholdings relies completely on publicly accessible sources and, therefore, is somewhat incomplete. Moreover, we have listed large stockholdings even when those interests are not directly represented on the board of directors. This is done in the spirit of illustrating the large position of some of the institutional investors in the corporations under study. Also, it was not possible to find the holdings of 73 directors of the 3,190 sought. This was because no data was on file in the SEC office for these directorships. It is likely that reports either have not been filed or are being used by members of that agency and are not available. In any case, every effort to secure these missing reports has been to no avail. The absence of these reports, however, does not significantly affect our tabulation. The grounds for this assertion lies in the fact that most of these directors are officers of the corporations of interest and, in general, we find that most officer-directors have rather small relative holdings. We believe that the reader will agree that the absence of this data does not justify withholding the data we have collected. In any case, our list of director's holdings is therefore an underestimate in a number of corporations.

Another technical point deserves some mention. A number of the corporations studied have preferred stock with regular voting privileges. Data on holdings of these preferred shares has been collected in the same way as data on common stockholdings. But space does not permit the publication of this data at present time. Equally important from our point of view is the fact that even in such cases the preferred stock usually represents only a small fraction of voting power (almost invariably less than 5 per cent of the overall voting power). But in some cases the holdings of voting preferred stock are quite important. This is because voting preferred stock enjoys a privileged position often with six or eight votes per share as contrasted with the one vote per share allotted to common stock. A case in point serves to illustrate. New York Life Insurance Co. holds 99,650 shares of American Can Co., 7 per cent cumulative preferred stock with each share enjoying six votes. In addition, New York Life holds 67,400 common shares of American Can.[37] The total voting power represented is 665,300 votes or 2.60 per cent of the overall number of votes. While this example represents a case of rather extreme concentration as compared with most cases, it is clear that a refined treatment must take such cases into account.

An examination of our tabulation of holdings shows that many wealthy individuals are active on the boards of a number of the corporations studied. Furthermore, it is apparent that considerable wealth is concentrated in the hands of a few of the propertied rich. One of the most striking cases is that of Richard K. Mellon whose extensive holdings in the five corporations of the sample in which he is a director are listed below.

Holdings of Richard K. Mellon as revealed in five major corporations

Company	Shares held	Market value
Aluminum Co. of America	1,587,476	$169,066,194
General Motors Corp.	240,000	13,080,000
Gulf Oil Corp.	6,362,319	233,815,223
Koppers Co.	115,732	5,265,806
Pittsburgh Plate Glass	108,500	8,639,312
		$429,866,535

Market value based on closing price per share as of Dec. 31, 1959. As breathtaking as this great wealth is we must realize that additional holdings in corporations in which he is not a director have not been taken into account. Nor for that matter have his holdings in several corporations not studied. Certainly, Mr. Mellon's vast wealth, all inherited, reveals that the very rich have not disappeared from the American scene.

Perhaps the most obvious revelation contained in our table of large holdings is the fact that the propertied rich control a rather large number of corporations through extensive stockholdings. The Mellon family, the Dorrance family, the Thomson family, du Ponts and Woodruffs, Cannons and Cones, Houghtons and Deeres, Dows and Firestones, Motts and Pratts, Heinzes and O'Neils, Phipps' and Watsons, Blocks and Kaisers, Reynolds' and Meads, Ordways and Rockefellers, and a whole host of others represent concentrations of wealth and power which are, to say the least, awe-inspiring. That the oridinary small stockholder shares in a "people's capitalism" is a notion that borders on absurdity in the face of such facts. One can not but wonder what a full scale tabulation of large holdings, as we have proposed in suggesting the compilation of the 150 largest owners in each corporation, would reveal. In addition, the tabulation proposed would certainly allow an objective evaluation of the currently accepted theory of "management control" as opposed to our hypothesis of control within the framework of the concept of community of interest.

The exercise of control

With our data in mind, we turn, finally, to a question of considerable importance, namely, what are the fruits of control? C. Wright Mills has

VILLAREJO:
Stock ownership
and the control
of corporations

presented a concise evaluation of one aspect of the answer to this question in his theory of "accumulation of advantage." The privileges which accumulate to those in a position of power, including liberal expense accounts, profitable stock options, tax advantages to those who own property (as contrasted with the tax position of those not owning property), and the like are obvious advantages accruing to the "elite." But of equal importance are those business deals, often extremely lucrative, open only to those enjoying a measure of control in a corporation. As an example of some interest, there is the case of Carroll M. Shanks, now the deposed president of Prudential Life. Mr. Shanks is also a director of Georgia-Pacific Corp., an important company in the lumber business. While still president of Prudential, Mr. Shanks engineered a deal involving Georgia-Pacific which, had it not come to light, would have resulted in a most lucrative personal return. It is somewhat amusing that the unfavorable publicity directed against Mr. Shanks in this particular deal resulted directly in his resignation from Prudential. Briefly, the transaction was the following: Mr. Shanks put up $100,000 of his own money and borrowed $3,900,000 toward the purchase price of Timber Conservation Co. The remaining $4,400,000 was advanced by Georgia-Pacific in which, as we have noted, Mr. Shanks was a director and in which Prudential holds 89,107 shares or 1.64 per cent of the stock. While the Prudential holding certainly does not represent control, under the community of interest concept we must view this holding as significant and as representing a measure of influence. Of great interest is the fact that Georgia-Pacific purchased the Shanks interest in Timber Conservation Co. the very day of the initial purchase and, in return, gave Mr. Shanks a cutting contract. Reportedly, the transaction would have resulted in a tax saving of $400,000 to Mr. Shanks yielding a full return on his investment plus a handsome profit.[38] Clearly, the position of Prudential in Georgia-Pacific had considerable influence in the decision to purchase Timber Conservation Co. While the violent reaction to this transaction resulted in Mr. Shanks' demise from Prudential, as well as the necessity to dispose of the cutting contract, the advantage of an important investment position in a specific corporation is clear.

More often, control means the ability to redirect a company's policies in case the company should cease to be a profitable object of investment. As a case in point let us consider a recent event involving a corporation we have not studied. Commercial Solvents Corp. was, for many years, under the management of J.A. Woods, the firm's president. To the investor interested in Commercial Solvents it was apparent by late 1958 that the company was not flourishing under Woods' leadership. Whereupon, the Milbank family, the dominant interest took steps to replace Woods with another man. These steps merely involved informing Woods, through H.H. Helm a director of Commercial Solvents and Chairman of Chemical Bank New York Trust Co., that his term was up. Woods, underestimating the shares the Milburns represented, was reluctant to surrender without a fight. Upon learning that the Milbanks spoke for 30 per cent of the stock, representing personal holdings as well as some holdings of friends and business associates, Woods expressed some surprise and quickly resigned. Though Woods wanted to fight to retain his position, another view won the day: "... Woods was a hired hand who had been well paid. Now a group of owners simply wanted to dismiss him."[39]

It is evident that control, in this case passive until management proved to be incompetent, is often mainly concerned with the proper operation of the firm. It is for this reason that management often appears to be in a controlling position in so many of the more successful firms. Why exercise a controlling position when management is doing a good job? The fruits of a large investment are such that a threat to the investment is often the only motivation for those enjoying the dominant position to exercise leadership.

In this section of our report we have presented some of our data in an effort to underscore the hypothesis of control we think is demanded by the facts. In Part III we shall consider the holdings of directors and the identity of the individuals in greater detail with an eye to correlating the fact of extensive interlocking directorships with the findings summarized in our table of large stockholdings. In addition we shall attempt to specify precisely the controlling group in each corporation.

1 "America Embraces a Peoples Capitalism", G.K. Funston, New York Stock Exchange, Oct. 25, 1956, p. 2.

2 *The Empire of High Finance*, Victor Perlo, International Publishers, New York, 1957.

3 *The Power Elite*, C. Wright Mills, Oxford University Press, 1957.

4 *Investigation of Concentration of Economic Power*, Monograph No. 29, "The Distribution of Ownership in the 200 Largest Non-Financial Corporations", U.S. Government Printing Office, Washington, D.C., 1940.

5 *Business Leadership in the Large Corporation*, R.A. Gordon, The Brookings Institution, Washington, D.C., 1945.

6 "Economic Power and the Free Society", A.A. Berle, Jr., Fund for the Republic, December, 1957, p. 14.

7 See *1960 Survey of Consumer Finances*, Survey Research Center, Institute for Social Research, The University of Michigan, pp. 100-101. This data represents only direct personal holdings in publicly traded common stocks. Data based entirely on responses to questionnaires and is subject to reporting errors by respondents.

8 *The Development of Trust Companies in the United States*, James G. Smith, Henry Holt and Co., New York, 1928, p. 45.

9 "The Trust Companies of New York", Bankers Magazine, Vol. 4, 1854, pp. 321-5. Cited in J.G. Smith, *The Development of Trust* ..., op. cit., p. 289.

10 . Unfortunately, 1937 was the first year in which income tax data on non-taxable fiduciaries became available. Thus, we cannot make precise comparisons with earlier years.

11 *New York Times*, March 5, 1959.

12 *Official Summary of Security Transactions and Holdings*, Vol. 27, No. 5, U.S. Securities and Exchange Commission, May 1961. Note that we have taken into account stock dividends subsequent to Dec. 31, 1959 but prior to report date to give holdings as of Dec. 31, 1959.

13 Ibid, Vol. 26, Nos. 1 & 9. Corrected to give holdings as of Dec. 31, 1959.

14 *Directory of Trust Institutions of the United States and Canada*, Fiduciary Publishers, Inc., 50 E. 42nd St., New York, 1959 revised edition.

15 *Share Ownership in the United States*, The Brookings Institution, Washington, D.C., 1952, p. 49, L.A. Kimmel.

16 *The Trust Bulletin*, Vol. 39, No. 1, Sept. 1959, "Report of National Survey of Personal Trust Accounts", J.H. Wolfe, p. 5.

17 Figure for 1900 - author's estimate; Figure for 1959 - New York Stock Exchange estimate.

18 Figure for 1952 - L.A. Kimmel, *Share Ownership* ..., op. cit.; Figure for 1927 - A.A. Berle, Jr. and G.C. Means, *The Modern Corporation and Private Property*, 1932

19 *Fortune*, Nov. 1959, p. 138.

20 Annual Report, 1959.

21 TNEC, op. cit.

22 Compiled from *Official Summary* ..., op. cit., various reports.

23 TNEC, op. cit. and *Official Summary* ..., op. cit.

24 *Survey of Consumer Finances*, op. cit., p. 104, Table 6-5.

25 *Survey of Consumer Finances*, op. cit., pp. 101-102, Tables 6-1, 6-2.

26 *Pension Funds and Economic Power*, P.P. Harbrecht et al., Twentieth Century Fund, New York, 1959.

27 Securities and Exchange Commission,"Statistical Bulletin", June, 1960, p. 6.

28 Annual Reports, 1959.

29 See *The Modern Corporation and Private Property*, A.A. Berle, Jr. & G.C. Means, The Macmillan Co., New York, 1932, pp. 83-84.

30 *Fortune*, Oct. 1959, p. 122.

31 *New York Times*, Nov. 11, 1958, p. Fl.

32 See TNEC, op. cit. We have omitted from this computation such corporations as Climax Molybenum subsequently merged with American Metal Co.

33 *New York Times*, Sept. 30, 1959, p. Fl.

34 *New York Times*, March 17, 1960, p. 45.

35 See *Moody's Industrial Manual*, Moody's Investor's Service, 1960.

36 *Dun's Review and Modern Industry*, August 1960, p. 65.

37 New York Life Insurance Co., Schedule of Securities, 1960.

38 *New York Times*, Sept. 14, 1960, p. 61,

39 "How Well-Bred Investors Overthrow a Management", *Fortune*, May 1959, pp. 134 ff.

VILLAREJO:
Stock ownership
and the control
of corporations

Large stockholdings and directors holdings in major industrial corporations: Part I*

Relevant stockholder	No. of shares outstanding	Per cent of shares outstanding	References
Air Reduction Co.			
Directors	32,476	0.83	
Southern Natural Gas Co.	172,600	4.41	a
Prudential Insurance Co.	54,500	1.39	b
Allegheny Ludlum Steel			
Directors	155,340	4.01	
R.M. Arnold	51,299	1.33	3/56
L.W. Hicks	54,980	1.42	2/56
W.C. Kirkpatrick (ex)	57,218	1.48	9/55
Allied Chemical Corp.			
Directors	110,385	1.17	
C.W. Nichols	86,736	0.92	1/52
Bank of New York	1,209,626	12.80	c
Aluminum Co. of America			
Directors	2,664,081	12.64	
R.K. Mellon	1,587,476	7.54	1/52
R.A. Hunt	857,796	4.07	5/52
A.V. Davis (hon. chrmn)	936,824	4.45	3/57
Sarah M. Scaife (est.)	1,542,540	7.33	d
Paul Mellon (est.)	1,230,000	5.85	d
Ailsa M. Bruce (est.)	600,000	2.85	d
Amerada Petroleum			
Directors	98,300	1.56	0
Alfred Jacobsen	72,000	1.14	6/51
Corey and Co. (nominee)	681,912	10.80	e
Phelps Dodge Corp	200,000	3.17	f
U.S. & Foreign Securities	160,000	2.53	g
Mass. Investors Trust	200,000	3.17	h
Continental Insurance Co.	147,100	2.33	i
American Home Products Corp.			
Directors	273,075	3.54	
A.H. Diebold	130,000	1.69	5/53
H.S. Marston	48,000	0.62	3/59
American Machine & Foundry			
Directors	318,822	4.29	
Morehead Patterson	158,120	2.13	9/59
George Arents	100,960	1.36	7/52
H.P. Patterson	22,652	0.30	(11/59)
J.P. Beaird (ex.)	54,234	0.73	11/58
American Metal Climax			
Directors	892,707	6.29	0

* See explanatory note at end of this part.

H.K. Hochschild........	601,658	4.25	1/58
Walter Hochschild......	122,683	0.86	11/58
Selection Trust Co., Ltd. ...	1,751,797	12.35	k
Phelps Dodge Corp........	712,161	5.02	f

American Sugar Refining

Directors	169,590	9.42	0
M.J. Ossorio	152,400	8.47	1/58
F.E. Ossorio (Became director after 1960)	47,760	2.65	1/61

American Viscose

Directors	70,352	1.37	
Allied Chemical Corp......	395,264	7.72	f
Courtaulds, Ltd. (England)	85,417	1.67	f

Armour and Co.

Directors	235,590	4.56	
M.R. Bauer	110,000	2.13	3/59
Milton Steinbach.......	67,100	1.30	12/59
Prince family trust .... (W.W. Prince is President of Armour and Co.)	293,370	5.69	10/58

Ashland Oil and Refining

Directors	483,203	7.98	
W.W. Vandeveer.......	117,659	1.94	2/55
F.R. Newman..........	82,241	1.36	4/55
R.D. Gordon..........	67,286	1.11	2/52
P.G. Blazer...........	55,952	0.92	6/59
W.G. Bechman.........	38,674	0.64	7/52
J.F. Breuil	35,429	0.58	7/57

Babcock and Wilcox

Directors	110,143	1.78	
C.W. Middleton	70,528	1.14	4/55
A.G. Pratt	30,612	0.50	5/57
E.G. Bailey (ex.)	115,514	1.86	7/52
Continental Insurance Co. (A.G. Pratt is listed as a director of one of the affiliates of Cont. Ins.)	152,400	2.47	j

Baldwin-Lima-Hamilton

Directors	272,538	6.42	
McClure Kelley	170,928	4.02	4/51
G.A. Rentschler.......	73,000	1.72	2/59

Brunswick Corp.

Directors	575,717	7.36	
R.F. Bensinger........	226,140	2.89	1/60
B.E. Bensinger........	188,322	2.41	11/59
H.P. Cowen	39,429	0.50	11/59

Burlington Industries

Directors	587,704	6.06	
J.S. Love	209,717	2.16	1/60
M.G. Lowenstein	122,728	1.27	(4/57)
H.M. Kaiser...........	69,425	0.72	12/59
J.L. Eastwick.......... (became vice-chmn. in 1960)	207,463	2.14	11/60

Burroughs Corp.

Directors	175,639	2.65	
G.L. Todd.............	91,690	1.38	1/60
H.S. Chase...........	67,600	1.02	7/49
Descendants of J. Boyer(est)	789,765	11.93	m
Consol. Electrodynamics ...	144,878	2.19	n

Campbell Soup

Directors	140,817	1.31	
W.C. Swanson	118,932	1.11	(1/59)
Dorrance family	8,709,649	81.18	f

Cannon Mills

Directors	190,085	18.32	
C.A. Cannon..........	163,155	15.72	f
W.C. Cannon..........	13,609	1.31	2/60
Cannon Foundation.......	103,140	9.93	5/60

J.I. Case

Directors	171,448	5.99	
M.B. Rojtman	155,000	5.42	6/58

Celanese Corp.

Directors	107,979	1.47	
A.R. Balsam...........	73,206	1.00	5/59
Dreyfus family and Foundation	734,471	10.01	2/56;p

Cerro de Pasco Corp.

Directors	75,541	3.03	
R.H. Lewin............	32,260	1.26	(7/59)
R.P. Koenig...........	22,443	0.90	1/60
Wellington Fund (Invest.Co.)	78,750	3.16	h

Champion Paper and Fiber

Directors	315,198	7.15	
D.J. Thomson..........	100,000	2.27	7/58
L.C. Thomson..........	63,390	1.44	12/59
H.T. Randall..........	50,300	1.14	11/57
R.B. Robertson, Jr.	48,550	1.10	6/58
R.B. Robertson........	27,650	0.63	4/59
H.W. Suter............	23,808	0.54	8/58
Thomson family (total hold.)	1,763,200	40.00	q
Mass. Investors Trust.....	165,000	3.74	h
John Hancock Mutual Life Ins...............	50,000	1.13	r

Cities Service Co.

Directors	448,938	4.18	
W.A. Jones	260,800	2.42	7/57
Stanhope Foster........	133,648	1.24	8/53
Investors Mutual (Invest.Co.)	151,808	1.41	h

Clark Equipment

Directors	122,195	5.14	
Frank Habicht	50,911	2.48	4/58
D.H. Ross	41,000	1.72	10/58
Clark family (est.)........	65,120	2.74	s
One William Street Fund...	55,600	2.34	h

Cleveland Cliffs Iron Co.

Directors	135,552	5.98	
J.H. Wade	40,650	1.79	(12/57)
George Gund	35,912	1.58	8/47
P.R. Mather...........	30,000	1.32	9/54
Portsmouth Corp.	388,672	17.15	8/59
S.L. Mather (ex.)........	11,875	0.49	8/47

Coca Cola Co.

Directors	150,478	3.53	
R.W. Woodruff.........	76,135	1.78	1/60
Winship Nunnally	22,666	0.53	12/59
Coca Cola Int'l.Corp.......	1,164,016	27.27	1/60

Colgate Palmolive

Directors	415,815	5.18	
J.K. Colgate..........	158,958	1.98	2/59
E.H. Little............	109,260	1.36	11/59
C.S. Pearce	60,739	0.76	1/60
S.B. Colgate (ex.)	25,200	0.31	1/58
H.A. Colgate (ex.)	63,093	0.79	11/56

Combustion Engineering

Directors	198,787	5.99	
C.M.F. Coffin	117,144	3.53	5/56
J.V. Santry............	19,300	0.58	1/60
W.H. Zinn	17,500	0.53	(2/59)
United Funds, Inc.........	67,700	2.04	h

Cone Mills

Directors	807,766	23.45	
Caeser Cone..........	288,866	8.38	10/53
Benjamin Cone........	254,433	7.38	11/51
Herman Cone, Jr.......	201,356	6.11	10/58
C.N. Cone............	23,175	0.67	4/59
M.H. Cone Memorial Hosp..	492,025	14.28	12/51

Consolidation Coal

Directors	417,423	4.54	
G.H. Love	104,900	1.14	1/60
R.L. Ireland	83,700	0.91	8/59
H.E. Davenport........	78,520	0.85	9/58
A.R. Matthews.........	59,675	0.65	10/58

G.M. Humphrey	55,000	0.60	10/58
M.A. Hanna Co.	2,310,000	25.11	1/60
Mellon family (est.)	1,299,321	14.12	†
Incorporated Investors,Inc.	121,400	1.32	h

Container Corp. of America

Directors	360,266	3.41	
R.G. Ivey	319,500	3.03	7/58
Container Corp. Bonus Plan	487,093	4.61	u
Owens Illinois Glass Co.	180,000	1.71	f
Insurance Co. of N. America	150,000	1.42	u
United Funds, Inc.	161,500	1.53	h
Fundamental Investors	150,000	1.42	h
Investors Mutual	143,000	1.36	h
Investors Stock Fund	116,000	1.10	h

Continental Oil

Directors	167,967	0.79	
L.F. McCollum	104,367	0.68	11/59
Newmont Mining Co.	973,440	4.61	f
Rockefeller Foundation	300,000	1.41	u
Cont. Oil Thrift Plan Trustee	268,753	1.27	u
Mass. Investors Trust	380,000	1.80	h

Corning Glass Works

Directors	3,675,016	54.41	
A.A. Houghton, Jr.	1,930,170	28.54	5/55
Amory Houghton	1,632,730	24.18	7/58
Continental Insurance Co.	76,250	1.13	i

Crane Co.

Directors	171,933	11.34	
T.M. Evans	163,500	10.79	1/60
Mrs.Emily Crane Chadbourne	121,000	7.99	w
E.L. Cord	47,500	3.14	x

Dan River Mills

Directors	787,320	17.56	
F.W. Jefferson, Jr.	286,665	6.40	12/59,y
F.W. Jefferson	230,820	5.15	(12/59,y)
J.W. Abernathy	106,700	2.38	7/57
A.A. Shuford, Jr.	71,650	1.60	9/59
Moses Richter	38,270	0.85	1/58
Oliver Iselin (ex.)	27,417	0.61	2/59

Dana Corp.

Directors	1,091,220	21.16	
C.A. Dana	1,050,000	20.34	4/55
Insurance Co. of N. Amer.	137,844	2.75	u

Deere and Co.

Directors	75,076	1.12	
B.F. Peek	35,834	0.54	2/59
Deere family trusts	997,051	14.87	f
Affiliated Fund	200,000	2.99	h

Diamond Alkali

Directors	297,425	10.23	
R.F. Evans	171,740	5.90	3/52
W.H. Evans	113,267	3.91	2/59
United Funds, Inc.	31,000	1.07	h

Diamond National

Directors	699,619	15.69	
R.G. Fairburn	301,330	6.76	1/60
B.W. Martin	212,262	4.76	8/55
E.T. Gardner	95,608	2.14	10/58
E.T. Gardner, Jr.	31,064	0.70	3/59
W.H. Walters	28,067	0.63	3/60

Dow Chemical

Directors	1,832,036	6.95	
A.B. Dow	745,380	2.94	11/54
H.H. Dow	296,266	1.12	12/57
H.D. Doan	205,643	0.78	12/57
C.J. Strosacker	201,027	0.76	9/57
Dow family (est.)	3,830,000	14.52	xx

E.I. du Pont de Nemours

Directors	2,001,760	4.37	
William du Pont, Jr.	1,269,488	2.77	3/59
L. du Pont Copeland	197,924	0.43	3/57
Bernard Peyton	153,704	0.34	4/59
Christiana Securities Corp.	12,199,200	26.63	4/58
Delaware Realty & Invest. Co.	1,217,920	2.66	4/58

Eastern Gas and Fuel

Directors	105,450	3.77	
Halfdan Lee	19,625	0.70	12/56
C.B. Houston	18,673	0.67	2/51
E.M. Farnsworth	18,039	0.64	7/54
Int. Utilities Corp.	71,500	2.55	1/60

Electric Auto-Lite

Directors	24,490	1.56	
C.R. Feldmann	16,200	1.03	11/57
Mergenthaler Linotype Corp.	378,950	24.20	1/60

Firestone Tire and Rubber

Directors	496,886	5.65	
R.C. Firestone	128,718	1.46	10/53
L.K. Firestone	101,181	1.15	8/59
R.S. Firestone	90,429	1.03	10/58
H.S. Firestone, Jr.	69,181	0.79	11/58
Harbel Corp.	979,379	11.13	7/58
(Firestone family holding co.)			
Firestone family (total)	2,198,500	25.00	f
Mass. Invest. Trust	235,000	2.67	h

Flintkote

Directors	415,239	8.20	
G.K. McKenzie	290,142	5.73	2/59
(As voting trustee)			

Ford Motor Co.

Directors	379,795	2.30	
Savings & Investment Program	1,269,207	7.70	5/59

Class B stock with 40% of total voting power is held by
members of the Ford Family and the Edison Institute.
Shares of class B stock shown below: f

Benson Ford	1,025,916	16.3	9/56
W.C. Ford	979,308	15.5	7/56
Henry Ford II	819,185	13.0	3/59

Foremost Dairies

Directors	827,131	10.64	
P.E. Reinhold	263,571	3.39	7/56
J.C. Penney	231,377	2.98	7/59
G.D. Turnbow	208,798	2.68	12/57

Fruehauf Trailer

Directors	314,370	4.73	
Roy Fruehauf	171,502	2.54	1/60
J.M. Robbins	50,030	0.74	8/59
Fruehauf family (total hold.)	473,000	7.00	z
Bernstein family	49,544	0.72	2/60
Fidelity Fund	148,500	2.20	h

General Mills

Directors	342,505	4.81	
J.F. Bell	213,606	3.00	11/52
P.D. McMillan	47,493	0.67	12/58
Continental Insurance Co.	75,000	1.06	i
Television Electronics Fund.	100,000	1.41	h

General Motors Corp.

Directors	5,139,742	1.83	
C.S. Mott	2,460,000	0.88	2/53
A.P. Sloan	1,185,156	0.42	5/59
J.L. Pratt	672,324	0.24	7/52
E.I. du Pont de Nemours	63,000,000	22.42	3/55
Christiana Securities Corp.	535,500	0.19	h
Donaldson Brown (ex.)	421,431	0.15	1/57

General Precision Equipment

Directors	108,084	9.60	
E.A. Link	39,101	3.47	2/59
G.C. Whitaker	20,881	1.85	12/59
H.G. Place	20,000	1.77	8/57
F.D. Herbert, Jr.	19,602	1.74	8/55

The Martin Co.	184,000	16.33	1/60
W.A. Reichel (ex.)	11,844	1.05	5/57
Television Electronics Fund.	25,000	2.22	h
General Telephone and Electronics Corp.			
Directors	337,995	1.54	
T.S. Gary	290,522	1.32	8/59
Voting trust	1,601,295	7.28	f
General Tire and Rubber			
Directors	345,956	6.57	
John O'Neil	118,086	2.24	8/59
T.F.M. O'Neil	106,442	2.02	3/54
R. Iredall	55,137	1.05	12/59
O'Neil family (total hold.)	1,125,090	21.33	aa
Georgia Pacific Corp.			
Directors	464,587	8.53	
O.R. Cheatham	193,534	3.55	1/54
J.N. Cheatham	59,130	1.09	3/59
J.L. Buckley	50,521	0.93	1/59
R.F. Johnson	39,016	0.72	2/59
C.E. Daniel	34,000	0.62	1/60
R.B. Pamplin	30,403	0.56	5/59
E.M. Howerdd (ex.)	143,835	2.64	5/54
Prudential Insurance Co.	89,107	1.64	i
W.R. Grace and Co.			
Directors	302,567	6.50	
J.H. & M.G. Phipps	185,837	3.98	9/58; 6/59
J.P. Grace	71,193	1.53	12/58
Gulf Oil Corp.			
Directors	6,731,142	6.72	
R.K. Mellon	6,362,319	6.35	1/56
W.K. Warren	318,270	0.32	3/59
Donaldson Brown (ex.)	598,797	0.60	7/51
Paul Mellon (est.)	9,206,553	9.19	d
Ailsa Mellon Bruce (est.)	7,970,766	7.96	d
Sarah Mellon Scaife (est.)	7,372,512	7.36	2/48
Phipps family holding co.(est.)	804,255	0.79	bb
H.J. Heinz			
Directors	369,490	21.88	0
H.J. Heinz II	368,659	21.83	1/60
Howard Heinz Endowment	242,155	14.34	1/52
Vera I. Heinz	52,129	3.09	9/56
Charles Heinz (officer)	11,803	0.70	3/47
Heinz family (total-est.)	1,284,000	76.00	z
Hooker Chemical Corp.			
Directors	419,383	5.72	
H.M. Dent	206,520	2.82	4/59
J.C. Cassidy	69,000	0.94	9/58
V.H. Shea	54,923	0.75	3/59; 4/59
Hooker family	458,000	6.24	f
Tri-Continental Corp.	110,000	1.50	h
Chemical Fund, Inc.	82,000	1.12	h
Hunt Foods and Industries			
Directors	602,397	21.04	0
Norton Simon	415,764	14.52	1/60
F.R. Weisman	69,960	2.44	8/59
Hart Isaacs	61,308	2.14	1/60
R.J. Miedel	30,526	1.06	1/60
J.R. Clumeck	18,350	0.64	2/59
R.E. Simon	349,567	12.21	1/60
Ideal Cement			
Directors	1,961,230	17.48	
Charles Boettcher II	1,265,841	11.28	8/57
Albert Coors	395,640	3.52	(2/59)
A.E. Humphreys	122,022	1.09	(8/57)
Wellington Fund	138,300	1.23	h
Investors Stock Fund	125,000	1.11	h
Ingersoll-Rand			
Directors	473,732	7.86	
J.H. Phipps	244,299	4.05	6/58
J.P. Grace	141,012	2.34	12/54
D.C. Keefe	35,670	0.59	7/48
Doubleday family holding Co.	187,884	3.12	7/48
Continental Insurance Co.	75,000	1.24	i
Inland Steel Corp.			
Directors	627,354	3.59	
J.L. Block	190,626	1.09	9/58
P.D. Block, Jr.	163,194	0.94	2/60
L.B. Block	139,734	0.80	5/58
A.M. Ryerson	68,850	0.39	4/50
E.L. Ryerson (hon. director).	148,482	0.85	7/54
Cleveland Cliffs Iron Co.	759,000	4.35	f
Interlake Iron Co.			
Directors	41,337	1.84	
E.A. Jones	25,400	1.13	3/59
P.R. Mather (ex.)	75,200	3.35	1/48
Mather Iron Co.	357,041	15.90	8/56
International Business Machines Corp.			
Directors	339,078	1.86	
E.E. Ford	113,412	0.62	1/60
S.M. Fairchild	99,866	0.55	12/59
T.J. Watson, Jr.	60,472	0.33	8/59
J.K. Watson	33,757	0.18	3/58
A.K. Watson (officer)	64,460	0.35	3/61
Watson family (total)	548,000	3.00	cc
Mass. Investors Trust*	180,288	0.99	h
Continental Insurance Co.	127,884	0.70	i
International Packers			
Directors	38,466	1.38	
First National City Bank	885,000	31.75	f
(As voting trustee for Armour & Co.)			
International Paper			
Directors	454,815	3.41	
Ogden Phipps	329,722	2.47	10/58
L. Dalsemer	53,760	0.40	(12/59)
Long family	144,388	1.08	dd
Chase Manhattan Bank (est.)	474,906	3.56	ee
Rockefeller Foundation	72,800	0.55	r
Mass. Investors Trust	311,472	2.34	h
International Shoe			
Directors	291,656	8.59	
A.W. Johnson	69,088	2.03	3/52
O.F. Peters	58,561	1.72	3/52
N.H. Rand	56,980	1.68	3/60
J.L. Johnson	49,045	1.44	4/51
H.H. Rand	40,037	1.18	1/52
Johnson and Johnson			
Directors	2,950,360	49.80	
R.W. Johnson	1,447,110	24.43	2/54
J.S. Johnson	596,003	10.06	3/59
R.W. Johnson, Jr.	439,390	7.42	4/59
H.S. McNeil	190,194	3.21	(9/59)
R.L. McNeil	148,210	2.50	(9/59)
Kaiser Aluminum and Chemical			
Directors	28,098	0.19	
Kaiser Industries Corp.	6,581,079	43.84	1/60
Kennecott Copper Corp.	1,925,000	12.82	f
Kaiser Industries Corp.			
Directors	10,934,702	47.78	
H.J. Kaiser, Jr.	4,273,452	18.67	2/59
H.J. Kaiser	3,170,766	13.85	2/59
E.F. Kaiser	1,957,770	8.54	2/59
D.V. McEachern	637,221	2.78	2/59
E.E. Trefethen, Jr.	512,529	2.24	4/56
A.B. Ordway	382,939	1.67	2/59
H.J. Kaiser Foundation	3,546,188	15.50	1/59
Sue Mead Kaiser	1,954,549	8.54	2/59
J.F. Reis (officer)	441,614	1.93	2/59
C.P. Bedford (officer)	412,789	1.80	2/59

Kerr-McGee Oil Industries

Directors	534,864	22.33	
R.S. Kerr	240,813	10.05	11/59
D.A. McGee	144,000	6.00	ff
J.B. Saunders	46,120	1.92	5/61
T.M. Kerr	25,326	1.06	9/58
F.W. Strauss	19,075	0.80	11/59
F.C. Love	19,069	0.80	9/58
Dean Terrill	12,633	0.53	5/59
R.S. Kerr, Jr.	12,170	0.51	10/58
Grace B. Kerr	183,596	7.66	2/57
Mass. Investors Growth Fund	88,900	3.67	h
Wellington Fund	50,000	2.09	h
Lehman Corp.	50,000	2.09	h
Investors Stock Fund	47,700	1.99	h

Kimberly Clark

Directors	606,845	6.95	
W.P. Schweitzer	235,231	2.69	9/58
J.S. Sensenbrenner	168,835	1.93	5/59
Ernst Mahler	110,518	1.26	1/60
J.R. Kimberly	73,904	0.85	8/59
J.L. Sensenbrenner (ex.)	126,997	1.45	2/56
S.F. Shattuck (ex.)	73,232	0.84	5/56
Investors Mutual	130,000	1.49	h
Mass. Investors Trust	118,800	1.36	h

Koppers Co.

Directors	134,663	5.87	
R.K. Mellon	115,732	5.05	3/56
Investors Mutual	70,000	3.05	h
Investors Stock Fund	40,000	1.74	h

Lehigh Portland Cement

Directors	244,227	5.81	
J.S. Young	100,120	2.31	9/58
R.A. Young	86,219	2.05	10/57
R.R. Bear	31,200	0.74	6/51
J.M. Huebner	23,573	0.56	12/59
Insurance Co. of N. America	49,000	1.16	u

M. Lowenstein

Directors	652,079	22.96	
Leon Lowenstein	446,700	15.72	9/57
Robert Bendheim	83,792	2.95	2/56
J.M. Bendheim	64,260	2.26	5/52
L.S. Gilmour	16,116	0.57	12/54
A.L. Lowenstein Estate	733,125	25.81	f

Mack Trucks

Directors	143,291	5.24	
H.L. Fierman	65,625	2.40	11/59
C.A. Johnson	38,850	1.42	2/60
W.R. Kaelin	31,156	1.14	11/59
Central Securities Corp.	197,000	7.20	h
(Controlled by C.A. Johnson)			

Martin Co.

Directors	100,819	3.44	
G.M. Bunker	73,741	2.52	1/60
J.B. Wharton, Jr. (ex.)	18,522	0.63	10/56
United Funds, Inc.	97,300	3.32	h
Wellington Fund	84,000	2.87	h
Investors Stock Fund	80,900	2.76	h
Fidelity Fund, Inc.	58,800	2.01	h
G.L. Martin estate (est.)	295,684	10.09	3/55; gg

McDonnell Aircraft

Directors	392,987	23.87	
J.S. McDonnell	355,706	21.61	4/59
W.R. Orthwein, Jr.	12,196	0.74	11/57
C.W. Drake	10,326	0.63	3/55

McGraw-Edison

Directors	631,114	11.26	
Charles Edison	145,840	2.60	2/60
M.M. McGraw	120,656	2.15	10/56

A. Bersted	92,312	1.65	5/52
D.S. Elrod	90,774	1.62	(1/59)
W.E. Kerr	74,567	1.33	(7/59)
J.W. Overstreet	69,872	1.25	(2/59)
Profit Sharing Trust	392,000	7.00	u
W.D. Kyle, Jr. (ex.)	29,308	0.52	10/55
Fundamental Investors	115,000	2.09	h
United Funds, Inc.	112,500	2.01	h
Investors Mutual	104,700	1.87	h
Affiliated Fund	79,000	1.41	h
Investors Stock Fund	60,000	1.07	h

Mead Corp.

Directors	400,756	7.90	
G.H. & H.T. & N.S. Mead	334,638	6.61	hh
A.L. Harris	39,768	0.78	12/57
R.J. Blum (officer)	52,382	1.03	3/58
Fundamental Investors	110,000	2.17	h
Investors Stock Fund	63,144	1.25	h
Incorporated Investors	54,600	1.08	h
Insurance Co. of N. America	57,694	1.15	u

Merck and Co.

Directors	350,802	3.30	
A.G. Rosengarten, Jr.	189,080	1.78	11/59
G.W. Perkins	113,885	1.07	12/59
Merck family trusts	350,184	3.30	8/57
Merck family (direct)	389,952	3.67	ii
Mass. Investors Trust	125,225	1.08	h

Merritt-Chapman and Scott

Directors	241,571	4.15	
L.E. Wolfson	166,100	2.85	7/59
P.H. Hershey	40,000	0.69	2/59

Minneapolis-Honeywell Regulator

Directors	338,880	4.77	
H.W. Sweatt	84,415	1.21	5/59
C.B. Sweatt	64,810	0.93	5/59
R.P. Brown	62,503	0.90	1/59
M.C. Honeywell	41,120	0.59	11/52
J.J. Wilson	40,660	0.58	12/58
Tri-Continental Corp.	125,500	1.79	h

Minnesota Mining and Manufacturing

Directors	3,650,965	21.46	
J.G. Ordway	1,625,068	9.56	12/59
W.L. McKnight	927,854	5.46	2/60
A.G. Bush	619,935	3.65	6/59
R.H. Dwan	321,400	1.89	(12/59)
G.H. Halpin (officer)	125,820	0.74	8/59
R.P. Carleton (ex.)	192,240	1.12	1/51

Monsanto Chemical

Directors	550,335	2.38	
Edgar Monsanto Queeny	319,386	1.38	11/55
C.A. Thomas	92,805	0.40	1/60
Queeny family trust (est.)	542,183	2.34	ii
Owens Illinois Glass Co.	338,130	1.46	f
T.H. Barton (ex.)	96,486	0.42	1/59

Motorola

Directors	384,945	19.48	
R.W. Galvin	356,295	18.04	f
E.H. Wavering	10,450	0.53	2/51
P.V. Galvin estate	97,403	4.93	f
Galvin family (total hold.)	646,000	32.70	z
Investors Mutual	55,000	2.78	h
Prudential Insurance Co.	35,250	1.79	j
Investors Stock Fund	30,900	1.56	h
Television Electronics Fund	23,400	1.18	h

National Cash Register

Directors	173,913	2.30	
S.C. Allyn	103,598	1.37	11/58
E.A. Deeds (hon. Chmn.)	175,877	2.32	1/52

National Distillers and Chemical

Directors	37,266	0.36

Panhandle Eastern			
Pipeline Co.	1,500,000	14.44	f
National Gypsum			
Directors	179,546	3.26	
C.F. Favrot	50,894	0.93	7/59
M.H. Baker	49,551	0.90	1/60
Investors Stock Fund	80,000	1.45	h
One William Street Fund . . .	61,200	1.11	h
National Steel			
Directors	239,357	3.18	c
Leon Falk, Jr.	117,746	1.56	1/60
T.E. Millsop	46,460	0.62	9/57
L.S. Mudge.	44,720	0.59	9/58
Descendants of E.T. Weir . . .	158,000	2.10	8/55
G.R. Fink (ex.)	64,270	0.85	4/55
M.A. Hanna Co.	2,001,390	26.65	f
Mass. Investors Trust	165,000	2.19	h
Continental Insurance Co.	147,500	1.96	j
Ohio Oil			
Directors	83,470	0.60	
J.R. Donnell	40,220	0.29	2/50
J.C. Donnell II.	33,430	0.25	2/52
Rockefeller Foundation	200,000	1.43	r
Mrs. Alta Rockefeller			
Prentice.	154,344	1.10	d
David Rockefeller (est.)	101,000	0.72	d
L.S. Rockefeller (est.)	101,000	0.72	d
Winthrop Rockefeller (est.)	101,000	0.72	d
Other Rockefeller			
holdings (est.)	793,000	5.67	kk
Investors Mutual	278,144	1.99	h
Olin Mathieson Chemical			
Directors	2,409,575	18.04	
J.M. Olin	888,673	6.65	1/59; mm
S.T. Olin.	811,434	6.07	4/58; mm
Edward Block.	184,913	1.38	mm
C.H. Palmer	146,626	1.10	4/58 3/59
R.G. Stone	101,150	0.76	1/52; nn
E.F. Williams, Jr.	96,700	0.72	(1/55)
Voting Trusts.	1,018,230	7.62	f, pp
Owens-Corning Fiberglass			
Directors	177,330	2.67	
Harold Boeschenstein . . .	132,430	1.99	6/59
James Slayter (officer).	80,195	1.21	7/59
J.M. Briley (officer)	48,000	0.72	7/59
Corning Glass Works	2,115,000	31.81	f
Owens-Illinois Glass Co.	2,100,000	31.58	f
Owens-Illinois Glass Co.			
Directors	179,504	2.49	
W.E. Levis	67,412	0.93	2/59
J.P. Levis	29,100	0.40	7/59
Allied Chemical Corp.	400,000	5.54	f
Affiliated Fund	100,000	1.39	h
Parke, Davis and Co.			
Directors	60,990	0.41	
Buhl family (est.)	999,258	6.74	qq
Investors Mutual	225,000	1.52	h
Affiliated Fund	165,000	1.11	h
Mass. Investors Trust	150,000	1.01	h
Peabody Coal			
Directors	1,005,589	10.39	
M.C. Kelce	836,095	8.64	2/60
T.L. Kelce	120,880	1.25	9/60
C.P. Arnold (officer)	175,873	1.82	7/56
R.O. Park (officer)	102,000	1.05	8/58
Donald Johnston (officer). . .	71,105	0.73	8/58
R.F. Barrow (officer)	63,917	0.66	6/58
C.M. Guthrie (officer).	83,224	0.86	1/61
United Funds, Inc.	200,000	2.06	h
Tri-Continental Corp.	100,000	1.03	h
Chas. Pfizer and Co.			
Directors	622,865	3.80	
G.A. Anderson	322,350	1.97	11/58
J.E. McKeen	130,500	0.80	9/59
Fundamental Investors	300,000	1.84	h
Investors Mutual	251,400	1.54	h
Mass. Investors Trust	230,000	1.40	h
Phelps Dodge Corp.			
Directors	85,324	0.84	
C.E. Dodge	62,206	0.61	9/56
Newmont Mining Co.	296,238	2.92	f
M.A. Hanna Co.	80,000	0.79	f
Mass. Investors Trust	250,000	2.46	h
Continental Insurance Co.	107,000	1.05	j
Philco Corp.			
Directors	85,745	2.10	
R.F. Herr	24,953	0.61	1/59
Profit Sharing & Savings Plan	449,270	11.02	11/59
Investors Mutual	80,356	1.97	h
Affiliated Fund	67,000	1.64	h
Pittsburgh Plate Glass			
Directors	3,204,505	31.59	
Pitcairn family (3 dir)	3,075,356	30.31	1/46; (12/59)
R.K. Mellon	108,500	1.07	6/47
Pittsburgh Steel			
Directors	9,764	0.62	
J.H. Hillman and Sons	401,124	25.28	1/60
(Holding co. for			
Hillman family)			
Quaker Oats			
Directors	196,090	5.32	
John Stuart	67,150	1.82	11/52
R.D. Stuart	52,418	1.42	4/52
R.D. Stuart, Jr.	18,179	0.49	2/54
Ralston Purina			
Directors	465,395	7.17	
Donald Danforth	424,515	6.39	11/52
W.H. Danforth family (est.)	104,075	1.60	1/54
Rayonier, Inc.			
Directors	182,413	3.21	
C.B. Morgan.	90,600	1.60	1/60
R.M. Pickens (officer)	64,993	1.14	5/57
Hammermill Paper Co.	366,868	6.47	f
Incorporated Investors	412,000	7.26	h
United Funds, Inc.	163,450	2.88	h
Affiliated Fund.	105,060	1.85	h
Fundamental Investors	103,000	1.81	h
Investors Stock Fund	103,000	1.81	h
Investors Mutual	91,150	1.61	h
Revere Copper and Brass			
Directors	10,012	0.38	
American Smelting & Refining	938,148	35.15	f
Investors Stock Fund	60,000	2.24	h
Fidelity Fund, Inc.	32,000	1.20	h
Wellington Fund	29,500	1.10	h
Rexall Drug and Chemical			
Directors	365,353	9.53	
J.W. Dart	210,120	5.48	9/55
V.F. Taylor.	32,548	0.85	8/56
W.T. Lillie.	23,072	0.60	8/52
John Bowles.	22,524	0.60	12/60
P.A. Draper	20,600	0.54	7/54
United Funds, Inc.	55,000	1.43	h
Reynolds Metals			
Directors	391,903	2.31	
J.L. Reynolds	106,049	0.63	10/59
D.P. Reynolds	96,310	0.57	10/59
W.G. Reynolds	69,709	0.41	10/59

R.S. Reynolds, Jr.	58,876	0.35	6/59
U.S. Foil Co.	8,014,055	47.36	f
Reynolds Corp.	501,380	2.96	f
(Voting stock in U.S. Foil is owned by Reynolds family)			
Incorporated Investors	420,700	2.49	h
Richfield Oil			
Directors	23,500	0.58	
Cities Service Co.	1,257,977	31.15	f
Sinclair Oil Corp.	1,223,581	30.29	f
Stock Purchase Plan	97,123	2.41	u
Rockwell-Standard			
Directors	309,694	5.75	
G.T. Pew	105,566	2.15	1/60
Willard F. Rockwell	65,616	1.22	7/59
A.G. Wallerstadt	45,569	0.85	11/52
W.R. Timken (est.)	105,758	1.96	7/51;rr
H.H. Timken (est.)	31,246	0.58	7/51;rr
Rohm and Haas			
Directors	506,829	45.37	
Otto Haas	287,571	25.75	11/52
Trust for F.O. & J.C. Haas	184,309	16.50	2/60
E.C.B. Kirsopp	10,517	0.94	8/59
Louis Klein	7,067	0.63	12/53
Haas Foundation (est.)	110,000	9.80	f
Haas family (total hold.)	692,500	62.00	z
Mass. Investors Trust	17,293	1.55	h
Lehman Corp.	12,581	1.13	h
St. Regis Paper			
Directors	451,861	4.82	
L.S. Pollack	128,366	1.37	(4/59)
J.B. LeClere	94,406	1.01	(4/59)
J.C. Pace	93,180	1.00	5/52
R.K. Ferguson	33,150	0.35	5/57
Eastern States Corp.	800,700	8.55	h
(controlled by R.K. Ferguson)			
Incorporated Investors	114,100	1.22	h
Schenley Industries			
Directors	1,075,471	18.26	
L.S. Rosensteil	918,800	15.60	7/60
T.C. Wiehe	100,353	1.70	10/58
Scott Paper			
Directors	416,013	5.26	
T.B. McCabe	298,055	3.76	12/59
R.H. Rausch	35,955	0.45	5/58
Signal Oil and Gas (class 3 voting stock)			
Directors	554,851	62.84	
S.B. Mosher	469,830	53.20	12/59
J.W. Hancock	49,850	5.65	5/60
R.H. Green, Jr.	25,038	2.84	1/50
Skelly Oil			
Directors	3,819	0.07	
Mission Corp.	3,412,280	59.38	f
(Controlled by Getty family)			
Investors Mutual	90,000	1.56	h
Mass. Investors Trust	71,000	1.23	h
Tri-Continental Corp.	65,000	1.13	h
A.O. Smith			
Directors	166,073	8.06	
L.B. Smith	164,022	7.96	12/50
Smith Investment Co.	1,096,000	53.14	f
(Holding co. for the Smith family-includes holdings listed under L.B. Smith)			
United Funds, Inc.	25,700	1.26	h
Socony Mobil Oil			
Directors	15,132	0.03	
Rockefeller Foundation	300,000	0.62	r
David Rockefeller (est)	901,466	1.85	kk
Winthrop Rockefeller (est)	901,332	1.85	kk
L.S. Rockefeller (est)	872,389	1.80	kk
Abby Rockefeller Mauze (est)	204,000	0.42	kk
J.D. Rockefeller 3rd (est)	191,250	0.39	kk
Other Rockefeller (est.)	3,037,648	6.25	kk
Standard Oil of California			
Directors	134,133	0.21	
Rockefeller Foundation	200,000	0.32	r
Abby Rockefeller Mauze (est)	632,062	1.00	kk
J.D. Rockefeller 3rd (est)	632,062	1.00	kk
N.A. Rockefeller (est.)	587,086	0.93	kk
Rockefeller family (total)	3,162,000	5.00	ss
Standard Oil Co. (Indiana)			
Directors	1,475,979	4.13	
Jacob Blaustein	1,407,714	3.94	(4/57)
Rockefeller Foundation	1,000,000	2.80	r
Alta Rockefeller Prentice	710,700	1.99	kk
Other Rockefeller (est.)	746,568	2.08	kk
Standard Oil Co. (New Jersey)			
Directors	224,617	0.10	
Rockefeller Foundation	6,000,000	2.77	r
Standard Oil Co. (Ind.)	2,883,519	1.33	f
N.A. Rockefeller (est.)	988,140	0.46	kk
J.D. Rockefeller 3rd (est)	988,140	0.46	kk
Abby Rockefeller Mauze (est)	988,140	0.46	kk
Other Rockefeller (est.)	12,284,723	56.67	kk
Stauffer Chemical			
Directors	1,746,745	19.14	
John Stauffer	729,185	7.99	12/55
Christian de Guigne	340,494	3.73	1/59
August Kochs	213,577	2.34	6/60
R.C. Wheeler	133,232	1.46	12/59
Christian de Dampierre	132,257	1.45	4/59
G.C. Ellis	104,452	1.15	5/59
Hans Stauffer	78,870	0.86	6/59
Mitzi S. Briggs	675,956	7.41	9/56
Chemical Fund	130,600	1.43	h
J.P. Stevens			
Directors	420,060	10.14	
R.T. & J.P. Stevens, Jr.	260,008	6.27	8/56; 2/58
W.J. Carter	29,451	0.71	6/59
K.W. Fraser	29,209	0.70	10/48
Sun Oil			
Directors	1,841,556	14.94	
J.H. Pew	710,939	5.76	2/60
J.N. Pew, Jr.	640,624	5.20	8/57
W.C. Pew	334,026	2.71	4/58
Glenmede Trust (Pew fam.)	3,387,443	27.48	f
Pew Memorial Foundation	2,610,968	21.18	1/55
Ins. Co. of N. America	148,963	1.22	h
Superior Oil			
Directors	131,019	31.03	
W.M. Keck	103,296	24.46	2/60
H.B. Keck	26,146	6.19	1/52
W.M. Keck, Jr. (ex.)	26,759	6.31	7/52
Keck family (total hold.)	216,600	51.30	z
Lehman Corp.	8,500	2.01	h
Incorporated Investors	5,000	1.18	h
Swift and Co.			
Directors	80,603	1.35	
H.H. Swift	50,025	0.84	2/49
Swift family (total)	403,000	7.00	tt
Affiliated Fund	125,000	2.10	h
Textron, Inc.			
Directors	280,520	5.87	
Royal Little	160,242	3.35	10/58
H.E. Goodman	51,001	1.07	12/59
K.L. Lindsey	35,750	0.75	9/59
Thompson Ramo Wooldridge			
Directors	228,438	7.32	
Simon Ramo	49,589	1.59	11/58
D.E. Wooldridge	45,335	1.45	11/58

F.C. Crawford	38,484	1.23	5/56
H.L. George	35,885	1.15	11/59
S.L. Mather (ex.)	24,488	0.78	3/55
Ins. Co. of N. America	52,000	1.67	u
Television Electronics Fund	48,500	1.53	h
Tidewater Oil			
Directors	22,301	0.16	
Mission Development Co.	6,612,339	47.73	f
Getty Corp.	1,987,448	14.35	f
Mission Corp.	458,886	3.47	f
(All controlled by Getty family)			
Timken Roller Bearing			
Directors	632,319	11.87	
H.H. Timken, Jr.	214,745	4.03	7/57
W.R. Timken	197,399	3.71	7/57
J.M. Timken	185,785	3.49	7/57
Joint trust for the above	24,200	0.45	7/57
A.A. Welsh and Co.	694,328	13.04	f
(Nominee for Cleveland Trust Co.)			
Fundamental Investors	125,000	2.35	h
United Funds, Inc.	75,000	1.41	h
Union Bag-Camp Paper			
Directors	409,467	5.55	
J.L. Camp, Jr.	101,175	1.37	7/57
H.D. Camp	88,189	1.19	5/59
W.M. Camp	85,006	1.15	1/60
J.M. Camp	67,734	0.92	(7/58)
Alexander Calder	45,137	0.61	8/59
Other Calder family (est)	509,100	6.90	s
Fundamental Investors	125,000	1.70	h
Wellington Fund	83,000	1.12	h
One William Street Fund	76,000	1.03	h
Continental Insurance Co.	85,500	1.16	i
United Merchants and Manufacturers			
Directors	329,299	5.49	
Lawrence Marx, Jr.	189,349	3.16	11/59
M.J. Schwab	48,895	0.82	(12/59)
J.W. Schwab	45,980	0.77	5/58
Fidelity Fund, Inc.	187,000	3.03	h
Affiliated Fund	100,000	1.67	h
U.S. Gypsum			
Directors	149,615	1.86	
S.L. Avery	117,350	1.46	12/51
Descendants of W.A. Avery	278,575	3.47	uu
Mass. Investors Trust	200,000	2.49	h
Fundamental Investors	100,000	1.24	h
Continental Insurance Co.	135,000	1.68	i
U.S. Plywood			
Directors	86,757	3.58	
Simon Ottinger	48,043	1.98	9/59
Louise Ottinger	127,504	5.26	8/52
Descendants of			
Lawrence Ottinger	144,750	5.97	11/54
Affiliated Fund	90,000	3.71	h
United Funds, Inc.	27,000	1.11	h
Upjohn			
Directors	3,223,890	22.94	
D.U. Dalton	667,090	4.75	(2/59)
W.J. Upjohn	579,928	4.13	11/60
R.A. Light	433,937	3.09	9/59
D.G. Gilmore	415,975	2.96	9/61
R.H Light	403,808	2.88	8/59
P.S. Parish	190,844	1.36	(10/59)
M.U. Light	136,712	0.97	4/59
E.G. Upjohn	85,906	0.61	11/59
Upjohn family (total)	8,434,000	60.00	vv
West Virginia Pulp & Paper			
Directors	524,399	10.20	
Sidney Frohman	204,217	3.97	(1/59)
D.L. Hopkins	79,436	1.54	7/52
C.E. Frohman	73,109	1.42	1/60

D.L. Luke	64,587	1.26	1/59
W.G. Luke	59,000	1.15	10/53
D.L. Luke III	15,292	0.30	11/57
Wheeling Steel			
Directors	27,304	1.30	
Cleveland Cliffs Iron Co.	102,432	4.89	
Stock Thrift Plan	9,500	0.45	u
Whirlpool Corp.			
Directors	667,064	10.74	
M.H. Murch	275,772	4.44	(3/58)
F.S. Upton	180,308	2.90	2/55
Elisha Gray II	76,400	1.23	3/59
W.G. Seeger	59,590	0.96	1/52; ww
J.S. Hall	56,321	0.91	1/52; ww
Radio Corp. of America	1,158,563	18.65	h
Sears, Roebuck and Co.	1,027,013	16.64	f
One William Street Fund	70,400	1.13	h
Worthington Corp.			
Directors	98,871	5.91	
H.P. Meuller, Sr.	58,415	3.49	9/58
Howard Bruce	18,738	1.12	10/54
H.H. Ramsey	10,903	0.65	11/58
One William Street Fund	51.300	3.07	h
United Funds, Inc.	46,000	2.75	h
Prudential Insurance Co.	40,600	2.43	i
Youngstown Sheet and Tube			
Directors	85,464	2.46	
S.L. Mather	25,224	0.72	9/56
Fred Tod, Jr.	24,500	0.70	7/52
Cleveland Cliffs Iron Co.	176,500	5.07	f
Mass. Investors Trust	125,000	3.60	h
Incorporated Investors	49,400	1.42	h
Fundamental Investors	45,000	1.29	h
Singer Manufacturing (first listed in 1960)			
Directors	597,303	13.38	
S.C. Clark	574,188	12.86	(8/60)
F. Ambrose Clark	533,387	11.94	1/61

Explanatory Note:

The 141 corporations included in part I are selected from a total of 232 included in the overall study. The basis of selection was the existence of concentrated ownership to the extent of securing potential working control in the corporation in question. This point has been discussed in the text of the article. It is, of course, possible to question the listing in this category of about 14 or 15 of those actually included. Nonetheless, at least 126 corporations must be so classified.

The organization of the table is alphabetical by name of corporation. In the first column the name of the relevant stockholder is listed, in the second column the number of shares held as of Dec. 31,1959, and in the third column the per cent of shares outstanding represented by the indicated holder. Finally, the last column gives the reference enabling the determination of the listed holding. Immediately under the name of each listed corporation the total holding of all directors of the corporation is listed. In the case of almost all of the listed corporations, we have indicated as a sub-heading the few largest holders among the directors. In all cases we have listed director's shareholdings which exceed 0.50% of the total stock outstanding. To illustrate, refer to the Aluminum Co. of America. The directors of Alcoa hold 2,664,081 shares representing 12.64% of the outstanding stock as of Dec. 31, 1959. The largest holders among the directors are R.K. Mellon and R.A. Hunt.

In the reference column we have indicated the reference by the following technique: if a date is given, e.g., 8/54, it is the date of the published monthly report of the Securities and Exchange Commission. This reference is formally as follows: *Official Summary of Securities Transactions of Officers and Directors of Listed Companies*, Securities and Exchange Commission, Washington. Thus, in the case of Alcoa, we have used the report published in the March, 1957 issue of *Official...* for the holding of A.V. Davis. As discussed in Appendix II, we have always used the most recent (prior to 1/60) published report of the individual in question. In some cases, however, there does not exist a published report of a person's holdings. In these cases it has been necessary to examine the SEC files directly and, when these reports are used, we have so indicated by placing parentheses about the *report date*. For example, the holding of H.P. Patterson in American Machine and Foundry was found in SEC files and was for the report date November, 1959. This is indicated in our notations as (11/59). The remaining references use the alphabet symbols a, b, ... thru vv, ww, xx. The list of references of this type follows this note.

Finally, we note that holdings of investment companies in excess of 1.60% of the outstanding stock of a given corporation are listed as are similar holdings of insurance companies. This refers only to investment companies and insurance companies in the sample group as indicated in the text. In certain cases, respect for the truth demands that we include certain other holdings even though such holdings are not by officers or directors. If the individual in question is a former director, now retired, then we have used the notation (ex.) to indicate ex-director. In some cases, as that of A.V. Davis in Alcoa, the individual has been given a title even though he is no longer on the board. Typical is the title Honorary Chairman or Honorary Director. In a few cases it has proved necessary to use old data, such as TNEC data, in the absence of more recent information. Such cases are denoted by the notation (est.) for estimate. The data shown in these few cases should be used with care as it is probably subject to some error.

Finally, Appendix III lists the many holding companies (as distinct from investment companies) appearing on the list of prominent

holders and attempts to show who controls them. Thus, one has ability to track down the ultimate source of power in the few cases where holding companies provide the basis for ultimate control.

The list of references for Part I follows—
a) *Moody's Public Utility Manual*, Moody's Investors Service, 1960. b) Schedule of Securities Owned, 1960. c) *Moody's Industrial Manual*, Moody's Investors Service, 1960. Held under trust agreement between North American Solvay, Inc. (American branch of the Belgian company, Solvay and Cie) and First National City Bank. d) *The Distribution of Ownership in the 200 Largest Nonfinancial Corporations*, Monograph No. 29, Temporary National Economic Committee, Investigation of Concentration of Economic Power, Washington, 1940. Estimate based on number of shares held as reported in this monograph taking into account subsequent stock splits and stock dividends only. e) *Moody's Industrial Manual*, 1960. Nominee for unknown investor. Possibly the investment banking house of Dillon, Read and Co. f) *Moody's Industrial Manual*, 1960. g) *Moody's Bank and Finance Manual*, 1960. Controlled by Dillon family of Dillon, Read and Co. h) *Moody's Bank and Finance Manual*, 1960. j) Annual Report, 1960 or Schedule of Securities, 1960. k) *Moody's Industrial Manual*, 1960. Selection Trust, Ltd. is an English corporation with extensive influence in South Africa, the Rhodesias and elsewhere. m) *Official Summary of Transactions of Officers and Directors*, Securities and Exchange Commission, October, 1938. Distribution from trust created under the will of Joseph Boyer, one of the founders of Burroughs Corp. n) Based on Dec. 31, 1958 holdings, at market value, of $5,940,000 in common stock. Consolidated Electrodynamics has been subsequently brought into Bell and Howell as an operating division. It is of some interest to note that C.H. Percy, President of Bell and Howell, is a director of Burroughs. See *Moody's Industrial Manual*, 1959 for holdings of Consolidated Electrodynamics. p) Indicated is the source giving the holdings of Camille Dreyfus who died on September 9, 1956. It is presumed that his widow, brother and the Dreyfus Foundation benefited from the bulk of the indicated holding. q) *Fortune*, May, 1960, p. 81. Includes holdings of D.J. Thomson, L.C. Thomson, R.B. Robertson, R.B. Robertson, Jr., H.T. Randall listed above. r) Annual Report, 1959. s) *Official Summary ...*, Securities and Exchange Commission, December 31, 1935. t) TNEC, Mono. No. 29 (see ref. d above). Based on holdings in Pittsburgh Coal Co. and terms of subsequent merger with the Consolidated Coal Co. u) Annual Report, 1959. w) *Fortune*, May, 1960,

p. 228. x) *New York Times*, May 12, 1958,
y) Both share in 375,250 shares held by family
holding companies. Half of this total has been
assigned to each. z) *Moody's Handbook of
Widely Held Common Stocks*, First 1x99
Edition, Moody's Investors Service. aa) *Fortune*, December 1957. bb) *Fortune*, November
1960. cc) *Fortune*, September 1956. dd) Based
on holdings in Long Bell Lumber and terms of
merger with Int. Paper (see Long Bell Lumber,
3/52 and *Moody's Industrial Manual*). Does
not include holdings of R.A.L. Ellis, the family
representative on the International Paper
board of directors. ee) Extimate based on report
in 4/42. Use with caution. ff) *Fortune*, March
1959. gg) Based on holdings of G.L. Martin before his death. Disposal of the shares is not clear.
hh) Combined holdings including holding of
Mead Investment Co. in which they all share.
See 1/51; 2/51; 4/51; (6/59). jj) See 8/57;
New York Times, Jan. 18, 1959; *SEC Statistical
Bulletin*, May 1958 (secondary distributions).
kk) See note on Rockefeller family holdings at
end of table. mm) Includes shares held in voting
trust. nn) Based on holdings in Mathieson Chemical and terms of subsequent merger with Olin
Industries. pp) Exclusive of holdings of directors
of shares held in these voting trusts. qq) Based on
holdings of L.D. Buhl, A.H. Buhl (see 6/51;
12/35). A.H. Buhl, Jr. is currently the largest
stockholder among the directors. rr) Based on
holdings in Timken Detroit Axle. Subsequently
merged with Standard Steel Spring to form Rock-
well-Standard. Holding shown based on terms of
merger and subsequent stock div. ss) *Fortune*,
November 1958. tt) R.A. Gordon, *Business
Leadership in the Large Corporation*, University
of California Press, 1961. uu) *New York Times*,
Feb. 4, 1959; see also 12/49. vv) *Fortune*, July
1959. ww) Based on holdings in Seeger Refrig-
erator and terms of subsequent merger to form
Whirlpool-Seeger (name finally changed to the
present Whirlpool Corp.). xx) *Fortune*, May
1952, p. 109. Includes reported Doan family.
Estimate is based on reported 18% holding
in 1952.

**A note on the treatment of the Rockefeller fam-
ily holdings.**—No member of the Rockefeller
clan (current generation) is either a director or
officer of the various Standard Oil companies.
Thus, a search of the SEC *Official Summary*... is
fruitless. In addition, the secretiveness of major
stockholders, like the various members of the
Rockefeller family. prevents a detailed accounting
of the holdings of the six elders of the clan. However, we need not give up hope for it is possible
to track down some information, though admittedly incomplete, and try to piece together a

consistent picture. Therefore, we have listed
holdings of various Rockefeller family members
in each of the oil companies where holdings are
of importance. The source is the TNEC report as
previously indicated. In addition, we have listed
holdings of the Rockefeller Foundation as of
Dec. 31, 1959. Finally, we lump under the
vague category "Other Rockefeller holdings"
the shares owned by John D. Rockefeller, Jr.
and his wife, both since deceased. However, his
second wife is alive and, as we shall see, received
a portion of his holdings. This last procedure will
now be justified.

When John D. Rockefeller, Sr. died his estate
was appraised at only $25,000,000, only a small
fraction of the value of the securities he once
owned. What had happened to his vast holdings?
A newspaper report provides the answer:

*"Before the elder Rockefeller died in 1937
at the age of 97, he had transferred most of his
vast estate to his son and to the philanthropic
interests in which both were engaged." (New
York Times, May 12, 1960, p. 27)*

Thus, he managed to escape the estate taxes by
means of gifts before his death. His son, John D.
Rockefeller, Jr. held the vast blocks of stock in
the Standard Oil companies until late 1934 when
he began establishing trusts for his children.
It is of more than passing interest that he reduced his holdings at a time when it would have
been necessary for him to report his holdings
under the Securities Exchange Act had he retained ownership of the shares. However, he
retained direct ownership of the bulk of the
shares. In 1940 he established the Rockefeller
Bros. Fund through the gift of securities then
valued at $59,000,000. Many years later, in
1957, his fortune was estimated at between $400
million and $700 million. When he died in 1960
his fortune was appraised at roughly $150 mil-
lion. Again, a newspaper report provides an explanation:

*"John D., Jr. had further reduced the size of
his estate by setting up trust funds long before his
death for his six children and twenty-two grand-
children. The children receive the income from
the trusts, and at their deaths, the principal
will go to their children." (New York Times,
May 20, 1960, p. 1)*

Furthermore, the estate which John D., Jr. left
was equally divided between the Rockefeller
Bros. Fund and his widow. The property held
for his widow in trust will be distributed to his
five sons at her death.

Hence, John D. Rockefeller, Jr. had followed
the clever example of his father and had disposed of the largest fraction of his estate before

70

his death and avoided confiscatory estate taxes. Since the precise terms of the various trusts are not public property we cannot make any estimate of the distribution of holdings among the surviving members of the clan aside from the information revealed in the TNEC report. Hence, these holdings are clearly held for the benefit of Rockefeller family members and are grouped under the heading "Other Rockefeller family holdings." It is also clear, though, that almost all shares indicated in the TNEC report remain under the control of the family, though a large portion of the shares provide income for various philanthropic activities and do not provide income for the use of family members.

Large stockholdings and directors holdings in major industrial corporations: Part II*

Corporation & largest shareholding	Number of shares	Per cent of out- standing shares	Ref- erence
ACF Industries	4,337	0.31	
Television Electronics Fund	50,000	3.52	a
Acme Steel	44,528	1.60	
C.D. Norton (D)	22,543	0.81	9/59
Allis Chalmers Mfg.	28,592	0.31	
Television Elect. Fund	85,000	0.94	a
American Can Co.	117,722	0.75	
Estate of Paul Moore	264,000	1.68	11/55; b
American Cyanimid	66,648	0.31	
Wellington Fund	77,800	0.37	a
American Motors	63,457	1.07	
G.W. Romney (D)	24,685	0.42	8/59
American Radiator and Std. San.	23,288	0.22	
Sharon Steel Corp.	96,632	0.83	c
American Smelting & Refining	16,219	0.30	
Mass. Investors Trust	155,000	2.85	a
American Tobacco Co.	16,062	0.25	
Affiliated Fund	75,000	1.15	a
Anaconda Co.	15,474	0.14	
Tri-Continental Corp.	50,000	0.48	a
Armstrong Cork Co.	53,065	1.05	
Wellington Fund	107,000	2.11	a
Atlantic Refining	28,315	0.31	
Mass. Investors Trust	135,000	1.49	a
Avco Corp.	136,714	1.33	
Victor Emanuel (D)	51,033	0.50	10/59
Bendix Corp.	76,786	1.50	
Investor's Mutual	96,150	1.89	a
Bethlehem Steel	32,693	0.07	
Mass. Investors Trust	720,000	1.58	a
Boeing Airplane	64,493	0.86	
Television Elect. Fund	44,370	0.59	a
Borden Co.	84,111	1.72	
Investor's Mutual	34,424	0.70	a
Borg-Warner Corp.	121,873	1.36	
Television Elect. Fund	45,000	0.50	a
Budd Co.	82,028	1.89	
Grascom Bettle (D)	33,500	0.77	8/59
California Packing	83,429	1.70	
Investor's Mutual	152,808	3.11	a
Carrier Corp.	28,582	1.40	
Affiliated Fund	62,000	3.04	a
Caterpillar Tractor	185,187	0.68	
Mass. Investors Trust	330,000	1.21	a
Chrysler Corp.	41,524	0.47	
Fundamental Investors	90,000	1.03	a
Colorado Fuel and Iron	44,483	1.19	
Charles Allen, Jr. (D)	27,194	0.73	11/57
Continental Can Co.	63,505	0.52	
Owens-Illinois Glass Co.	334,813	2.72	c
Corn Products Refining Co.	52,905	0.49	
Continental Insurance Co.	111,700	1.02	d
Crown Zellerbach	368,511	2.67	
J.D. Zellerbach (D)	107,862	0.78	10/59
Crucible Steel	24,732	0.64	
United Funds, Inc.	30,007	0.78	a
Curtiss-Wright	31,000	0.40	
Television Electronics Fund	50,000	0.65	a
Douglas Aircraft	32,543	0.85	
United Funds, Inc.	71,600	1.88	a
Dresser Industries	37,074	0.79	
Fundamental Investors	78,000	1.66	a
Eastman Kodak	185,172	0.48	
Mass. Investors Trust	222,000	0.58	a
Eaton Mfg.	161,521	3.36	
Television Electronics Fund	80,000	1.67	a
Fairbanks Whitney	97,614	1.31	
Theodore Blumberg (D)	60,012	0.81	3/59
Fiberboard Paper Products	34,922	2.00	
Affiliated Fund	49,000	2.80	a
Food Machinery and Chemical	135,698	1.95	
Wellington Fund	120,000	1.73	a
General American Trans.	48,823	0.89	
Investor's Mutual	60,000	1.09	a
General Dynamics	127,732	1.28	
Television Electronics Fund	45,000	0.45	a
General Electric	76,937	0.09	
Mass. Investors Trust	350,000	0.40	a
General Foods Corp.	103,026	0.84	
Marjorie M. Post	290,270	2.37	7/58
Gillette Safety Razor	150,068	1.61	
Mass. Investors Trust	230,000	2.47	a
Glidden Co.	27,818	1.20	
Investor's Mutual	35,000	1.52	a
B.F. Goodrich	113,079	1.26	
Mass. Investors Trust	165,000	1.83	a
Goodyear Tire and Rubber	200,650	0.61	
Mass. Investors Trust	988,380	2.98	a
Granite City Steel	26,123	1.22	
Tri-Continental Corp.	50,000	2.34	a
Hercules Powder	45,352	0.54	
Chemical Fund, Inc.	116,600	1.38	a
International Harvester	30,249	0.22	
Cyrus McCormick	223,069	1.61	12/50
International Tel. and Tel.	162,603	1.05	
Affiliated Fund	142,000	0.91	a
Johns Manville	30,954	0.37	
Company Stock Purchase Plan	140,711	1.66	e

* See explanatory note at end of this part.

71

Jones and Laughlin Steel. . . .	96,182	1.23	
Cleveland Cliffs Iron Co.	170,719	2.18	c
Kennecott Copper	33,264	0.30	
American Smelting & Ref. . .	100,481	0.91	c
Libby-Owens-Ford Glass	194,260	1.85	
Mass. Investors Trust	190,000	1.81	a
Libby, McNeill and Libby	27,243	0.64	
A.J. Hoefer (D)	12,167	0.28	1/57
Liggett and Myers Tobacco . . .	11,395	0.29	
Affiliated Fund	72,000	1.83	a
Lockheed Aircraft	221,428	3.08	
R.E. Gross (D).	144,272	2.00	9/57
Lone Star Cement	105,196	1.35	
Mass. Investors Trust	149,200	1.92	a
P. Lorillard	107,128	1.63	
United Funds, Inc.	120,000	1.83	a
National Biscuit Co.	12,340	0.19	
Estate of Paul Moore	167,300	2.62	f; b
National Dairy Products Corp. .	172,244	1.23	
H.W. Breyer, Jr. (D)	86,157	0.61	9/57
National Lead	103,441	0.89	
Continental Insurance Co.	76,300	0.65	d
North American Aviation.	33,933	0.42	
Investor's Stock Fund.	150,000	1.85	a
Otis Elevator	117,715	2.85	
Television Electronics Fund	71,600	1.73	a
Philip Morris	101,231	3.07	
H.S. Cullman &	69,430	2.11	12/59;
J.F. Cullman, 3rd			10/59
Phillips Petroleum	177,896	0.52	
Phillips Investment Co.	560,000	1.63	1/48
Procter and Gamble.	125,439	0.61	
Chemical Fund, Inc.	72,300	0.35	a
Pullman, Inc.	17,758	0.77	
Mass. Investors Trust	105,000	4.55	a
Pure Oil	76,635	0.88	
Investor's Mutual	116,000	1.33	a
Radio Corp. of America	72,648	0.52	
Investor's Mutual	167,800	1.20	a
Raytheon Co.	59,373	1.73	
C.F. Adams (D)	32,644	0.95	7/58
Republic Steel Corp.	65,704	0.42	
Cleveland Cliffs Iron Co.	486,228	3.09	c
R.J. Reynolds Tobacco	147,882	0.74	
Affiliated Fund	260,000	1.30	a
Sinclair Oil	30,793	0.20	
Mass. Investors Trust	125,000	0.81	a
Sperry Rand	215,877	0.76	
H.F. Vickers (D)	158,491	0.56	1/58
Standard Brands.	61,420	0.93	
Mass. Mutual Life Ins. Co. . .	20,000	0.30	g
Standard Oil Co. (Ohio)	17,077	0.35	
One William Street Fund . . .	40,000	0.82	a
Sterling Drug.	23,864	0.30	
Chemical Fund, Inc.	27,000	0.34	a
Studebaker-Packard	18,262	0.27	
H.E. Churchill (D)	8,512	0.13	1/60
Sunray Mid-Continent Oil	187,479	1.05	
Fundamental Investors	200,000	1.12	a
Texaco, Inc.	692,226	1.14	
Mass. Investors Trust	537,642	0.89	a
Union Carbide	125,291	0.42	
Continental Insurance Co.	172,400	0.57	d
Union Oil of Cal.	205,123	2.50	
Stewart family trust.	129,186	1.58	5/61
Union Tank Car	8,463	0.24	
Rockefeller Foundation	100,000	2.84	h
United Aircraft	33,934	0.53	
Fundamental Investors	75,000	1.17	a
United Shoe Machinery	46,414	2.00	
S.W. Winslow, Jr. (D)	20,828	0.90	4/60
U.S. Rubber.	77,672	1.36	
United Funds, Inc.	109,800	1.92	a
U.S. Steel.	126,457	0.23	
Mass. Investors Trust	560,000	1.04	a
Westinghouse Air Brake	13,160	0.31	
Television Electronics Fund .	35,000	0.83	a
Westinghouse Electric	30,127	0.17	
Mass. Investors Trust	110,000	0.63	a
White Motor Co.	57,290	2.86	
R.F. Black (D).	17,950	0.90	12/59
Wilson and Co.	31,836	1.41	
United Funds, Inc.	48,000	2.13	a

Explanatory note

Listed in part II are 91 corporations in which the evidence did not indicate highly concentrated holdings by directors or other large stockholders. This does not imply that centers of control do not exist in these corporations but rather that the data collected was inconclusive. However, in the case of certain of the corporations centers of control are already apparent. For example, the Zellerbach family appears to exercise leadership in Crown Zellerbach Corp. even though the holdings of J.D. Zellerbach and H.L. Zellerbach account for less than 2.00% of the stock in this company. The dominance of the Zellerbach family was firmly established in the TNEC report. Similarly, in Union Oil of Cal. the Stewart family appears to dominate. Again, the Gross family of Lockheed Aircraft holds a little better than 2.00% of the stock of that company, at least in so far as the two Gross family members on the board are concerned. Several other cases of this type will also be noted by the reader. It was felt that for the sake of completeness a separate appendix listing corporations in which a lesser degree of concentration was noted should be added.

Listed above is the name of each corporation together with the holdings of directors (both number of shares held and shares held as a fraction of the outstanding stock). In addition, the identity of the largest shareholding is listed beneath the name of the corporation with shares held, etc. The pattern for listing references is the same as used in Appendix II. It should also be noted that the largest shareholding is almost invariably an investment company or insurance company. This largest shareholding may not, in fact, be the largest holding but rather is the largest holding that could be determined from publicly available materials.

References for part II — a) *Moody's Bank and Finance Manual, 1960.* b) Paul Moore died on Dec. 19, 1959 so that his holdings are not included in our tabulation of director's holdings. The shares which he held were subsequently sold in a secondary offering. c) *Moody's Industrial Manual, 1960;* d) *Annual Report, 1960.* e) *Annual Report, 1959;* f) Temporary National Economic Committee, Monograph No. 29, *The Distribution of Ownership in the 200 Largest* *Non-financial Corporations,* U.S. Government Printing Office, Washington, 1940. g) *Schedule of Securities, 1959.* h) *Annual Report, 1959.* *Note:* (D) indicates director of the corporation of interest.

Appendix I: Discussion of table VIII and computational method

The raw data for 1928 was available in the indicated source book and is reproduced intact. The 1958 data however, presented numerous difficulties. In the first place, the indicated source book contained only the *number of returns* in each dividend income size category and did not contain data on the fraction of total dividend income received by all members of each dividend income class. Fortunately, the data was presented in a manner which lent itself to a ready computation. That is, the number of returns in each dividend income class were distributed according to *gross income class.* In addition, data was also available yielding the total dividend income by all returns in each gross income class receiving dividends. The model chart below (copied directly from the indicated source book) shows the raw data as available:

	Size of Dividend Income	
Gross Income Class	Under $100	$100 under $200
$600 under $1,000	31,060	16,709
$1,000 under $1,500	42,434	22,919
$1,500 under $2,000	33,498	25,931

Naturally, this is only a small portion of the chart in the source book but it does convey the nature of the available data, e.g., 31,060 returns showed dividend income of less than $100 (but larger than zero dividend income) in the gross income class $600 to $1,000. Using the given data (including the amount of dividend income received by all dividend receiving returns in each gross income class) it is possible to compute an *average* dividend income for each entry of the chart and then form a sum according to size of dividend income to obtain the results under discussion. Since it seems likely to the author that the assumed averages for the larger income classes might be more in dispute than say the lower income classes (especially in view of the exhibited degree of concentration), reproduced below are the computed average dividend incomes for the dividend income class $100,000 or more and for gross income classes in excess of $100,000.

Gross Income Class	Assumed Average Dividend Income
$100,000 under $150,000	$119,485
$150,000 under $200,000	150,249
$200,000 under $500,000	174,741
$500,000 under $1,000,000	513,934
Above $1,000,000	1,618,223

It is my firm belief that these figures are conservative if at all in error. This opinion is based on the fact that the computation was performed in several different ways yielding results varying only slightly. The totals used are the set indicating the smallest extent of concentration. In conclusion, it should be noted that data of the sort discussed in this appendix were, at one time, normally published in the Treasury Department's *Statistics of Income* but have not been published in recent years. One wonders what information might be revealed if the Treasury Department were to resume publication of these data.

Appendix II: The compilation of directors holdings

The major source for the holdings of the more than 3,000 directorships in the sample corporations has been the *Official Summary of Securities Transactions of Officers and Directors,* Securities and Exchange Commission, published monthly since December, 1935. The method is actually very simple: one compiles a list of directors (in our case from *Poor's Register of Officers and Directors, 1960*) and searches back through old monthly SEC reports to find the most recent transaction (in our case prior to December 31, 1959). Unfortunately, the SEC has changed its publication policy over the years so that in recent times one is not always guaranteed the existence of a published report on each individual. More precisely, the SEC no longer publishes so-called "initial reports" (required when an individual becomes an officer or director for the first time). Thus, we were unable to find about 450 shareholdings in the published reports. Fortunately, one has recourse to the SEC files where almost all the missing reports were found.

While we have mentioned the reports we have not indicated how they are so useful. The report contains, under present law, a complete list of securities owned by the officer or director in the corporation in question. If the individual sells or buys shares he must report the transaction to the SEC together with his holdings following the transaction. Thus, by diligent labor it is possible to piece together the holdings of all of the directors in a given corporation as of a known date. And this is most important, that our data be entirely comparable from corporation to corporation. For this reason, December 31, 1959 was chosen as our target date. Since a few reports date back as far as the early 1950's and 1940's it has been necessary to take careful account of stock dividends and stock splits. Even for the more recent report dates such splits must be taken into account. Thus, all stock splits and stock dividends subsequent to a given report date but prior to Dec. 31, 1959 have been taken into account. In the few cases where it has been necessary to use 1960 reports we have taken into account

such events during that year and have, of course, adjusted the shareholdings appropriately.

It should be noted that the report date and the publication date are quite distinct. That is, an individual may report holdings as of, say, May 1957 during early 1958. His published report may then appear in the March 1958 issue of *Official Summary...* for a transaction which took place ten months earlier. Most often a given monthly issue will contain reports concerning transactions during the previous month. Thus, we find the largest number of reports for a given month in the Jan. 1960 issue but valid as of Dec. 1959. The source for stock splits and stock dividends has been *Moody's Dividend Record,* Cumulative Edition.

Shortcomings of the data

The major shortcoming of this type of data, of course, is that one has no guarantee of finding either the largest holding in a given corporation or the control block of stock. This is because the officers and directors need not report holdings of all relatives. Further, in those cases where the controlling group is indirectly represented on the board there is no available information on the overall holding of the group. Given the aura of secrecy surrounding the identity of stockholders, this comes as no surprise. However, it is particularly annoying to find that trust holdings of banks in a corporation need not be reported if a director of the bank is a director of the corporation in question. A strict interpretation of the law, it would seem, would require the disclosure of this information. As a case of some interest concerning the existence of large blocks of stock, consider the revelations after the death of Howard Gould: it became known that his estate contained, among other things, some 300,000 shares of U.S. Steel—certainly one of the largest blocks of stock in that giant corporation. Yet, one wonders how many other blocks of this size exist. The publicly available data is too scanty to permit a full scale attack on this problem.

The other major shortcoming of the data is the possibility of errors. For example, the burden of the reporting responsibility lies with the reporting individual and not the SEC which merely publishes data. Thus, errors do appear and are subsequently corrected in later volumes of the *Official Summary* ... Of much greater importance, though, is the recent policy of the SEC to withhold publication of certain types of reports. Thus, if we rely entirely on published reports it is almost certain that errors will appear. However, it is important to have a measure of the magnitude of most errors. A careful check of widely separated (timewise) reports revealed no substantial errors. In fact the only errors amounted to less than one per cent in the number of shares held and would certainly not effect our figures on the fraction of outstanding shares owned. In summary, all of the major errors appear to yield estimates of shares held on the low side, even though when trust holdings are listed we do include holdings of this type under the individual's name. This, in spite of the fact that several persons may benefit from the trust. But because we approach the problem of control we need to know overall holdings of a family or group potentially in control of a corporation. Even in such cases there is no guarantee that all holdings are listed. Therefore the holdings shown in our tabulation are surely not all beneficial holdings but rather give some idea of the relative investment position of various individuals, families or groups.

Appendix III

We list here some eighteen corporations which must be regarded as "special cases". That is, systematic information of the type shown in our table of large stockholdings was not obtained. The reasons together with some information, are given below.

Domestic Subsidiaries of Foreign Corporations

It was felt that these corporations should be excluded from study because we are concerned primarily with the domestic pattern of ownership and control: *Shell Oil* (majority of stock owned by the Royal-Dutch Shell group of companies); *Lever Bros.* (sub. of Unilever, the giant British-Dutch chemical concern); *J. Seagram and Sons* (sub. of Distillers Corp.-Seagrams, Ltd.)

Stock Controlled by the Attorney General

General Aniline and Film (stock seized by the Alien Property custodian at the beginning of World War II as a result of the fact that I.G. Farben, the giant German cartel, owned the bulk of the stock).

The four corporations listed above have been excluded from the overall study entirely. That is, our examination of interlocking directorates and the like will not take into account these four corporations. The remaining fourteen, however, will be considered on an equal footing with the 232 corporations in which it was possible to collect data on the directors' holdings.

Corporations Controlled by Domestic Corporations

Substantially all of the stock of these two corporations is owned by only three domestic corporations with whom these corporations have an especially close relationship. For all practical purposes they may be regarded as operating subsidiaries of the parent concern: *Chemstrand* (Jointly owned by Monsanto Chemical and American Viscose); *Western Electric* (99.82% of the stock owned by American Telephone and Telegraph).

Privately Held

In these corporations no stock is publicly held. All stock is privately owned and no other individual may purchase shares in the open market: *Norton Co.*

(Stock held by descendents of the founding families including Jeppson and Higgins families); *Springs Cotton Mills* (Owned by E.W. Springs family.)

Others

In these ten corporations all or a portion of the stock is publicly held but are not listed on an exchange. Thus, the shares are traded over-the-counter usually indicating the fact that much of the stock is "closely held." Where information is available we have indicated the controlling group. Since shares in these corporations are not listed it is not possible to compile lists of the holdings of directors.

American-Marietta—Hermann family owns all class B stock equivalent to 21.8% of the voting power. See *Moody's Industrials,* 1960; *Anheuser-Busch*—Busch family holds 65% of the outstanding stock and is clearly in control. See *Life,* May 2, 1955; *Carnation Co.*—More than 50% of the stock held by E.H. Stuart family, founders of the company. See *Business Week,* Oct. 4, 1947, pp. 96ff.; *Kaiser Steel*—Kaiser Industries holds 79.97% of the stock. See *Moody's Industrials, 1960.* A majority of the stock of Kaiser Industries is held by the H.J. Kaiser family. See our table of large stockholdings; *Eli Lilly*—Non-voting class B stock is publicly held. However, the common stock, with sole voting power, is privately held by the Lilly family among others; *Lone Star Steel*— Little precise data is known. But E.B. Germany, president of Lone Star, holds about 1.50% of the stock personally and numbers among the five largest holders. See *Business Week,* March 29, 1952, p. 66. Among the institutional investors, United Funds, Inc. hold 1.30%. See *Moody's Bank and Finance Manual,* 1960; *McLouth Steel*—Until his death, D.B. McLouth was the largest holder with 12% (possibly more). Little is now known; *Sherwin Williams*—Largest holder is Cyrus S. Eaton. Other large holders are not known; *Time, Inc.*—See Nov. 1960 issue of *Fortune* for listing of all holders of more than one per cent of the stock. Included are the Luce family, Larsen family, and H.P. Davison. *Weyerhaeuser Co.*—TNEC data revealed that the Clapp, Weyerhaeuser, McCormick and Bell families held the controlling stock. The same individuals, in several cases, remain in the leadership of this company. It may be presumed that their position in the company has not substantially changed. However, the Kieckhefer family has a large holding resulting from the merger of Eddy Paper Co. and Kieckhefer Container Co. into Weyerhaeuser. The Kieckhefers have representation on the board of directors.

Appendix IV

Listed below are 21 holding companies which play an important role in the control of some of the corporations under study. In each case we attempt to identify the largest stockholding interests. We have also indicated the corporations in which the company in question holds important blocs of stock. The pattern used in this listing is the same as used in the table of large holdings in the sample corporations. Namely, where a date is indicated we refer to the published monthly reports of the *Official Summary* ... mentioned previously. Other references are noted by letters of the alphabet with a complete list of these references given at the end of this appendix. Finally, we indicate the per cent of voting common stock held as of Dec. 31, 1959 as well as the number of shares held by each of the presumably important stockholders.

American Manufacturing Co. (owns 18.25% of Mergan-thaler Linotype, see below)

Webster Investors	161,234	34.46%	a
Century Investors	59,320	12.68	a
G.W. Wattles	53,800	11.50	b

Central Securities Corp. (owns 7.20% of Mack Trucks)

C.A. Johnson	269,511	31.90%	1/60

Century Investors (owns 37.8% of Webster Investors, see below; 12.68% of American Mfg. Co., see above; 1.05% of Merganthaler Linotype, see below)

G.W. Wattles	88,930	59.27%	2/51
Robert Pulleyn	4,500	3.00	10/49
W.W. Cohu	2,000	1.33	9/51

ᵇ Christiana Securities Corp. (owns 26.63% of E.I. du Pont de Nemours)

Delaware Realty & Invest	49,000	32.67%	10/52
Irenee du Pont	7,301	4.87	1/51
W.S. Carpenter, Jr.	1,643	1.10	1/52
6 other directors	2,483	1.65	c

Coca Cola Int'l. Corp. (owns 27.27% of Coca Cola Co.)

Woodruff Foundation	21,558	14.53%	9/59
Piedmont Securities Co.	14,344	9.67	4/51; d
Winship Nunnally	2,580	1.74	12/59; e

Delaware Realty & Investment (owns 2.66% of Du Pont and 32.67% of Christiana Securities Corp., see above)

H.B. du Pont	72,300	10.62%	12/50; f
Lammot du Pont Copeland	52,299	7.69	1/60; f
S. Hallock du Pont	23,482	3.45	2/58; f
W.W. Laird	17,737	2.61	5/58; f
W.K. Carpenter	16,250	2.39	2/51; f
Irenee du Pont, Jr.	14,887	2.19	1/57; f
Pierre S. du Pont, 3rd	5,095	0.75	8/59; f
Sharp family trust	85,000	12.50	12/50; f

Eastern States Corp. (owns 8.55% of St. Regis Paper)

R.K. Ferguson	164,621	28.78%	9/59; f

Getty Oil Co. (owns 14.35% of Tidewater Oil; 58.55% of Mission Development Co., see below; 49.54% of Mission Corp., see below)

J. Paul Getty	—	79.05%	a

Hammermill Paper Co. (owns 6.4% of Rayonier, Inc.)

D.S. Leslie	32,158	2.60%	1/56
N.W. Wilson	30,576	2.48	10/58
10 other directors	29,604	2.41	c

M.A. Hanna Co. (owns 25.11% of Consolidation Coal; 26.65% of National Steel Corp.)

Class B (voting stock)

G.H. Love	23,871	2.32%	10/51
G.M. Humphrey	23,000	2.23	9/52
R.L. Ireland	11,445	1.11	10/51
10 other directors	10,060	0.98	c
Hanna family (min. est.)	40,000	3.88	g

Mather Iron Co. (owns 15.90% of Interlake Iron Co.)
Privately held, probably by members of Mather family, among others.

Merganthaler Linotype (owns 24.20% of Electric Auto-Lite)

American Manufacturing Co.	106,420	18.25%	12/59
Webster Investors	68,125	11.65	12/59
Century Investors	6,137	1.05	12/59

Mission Corp. (owns 59.38% of Skelly Oil; 3.47% of Tidewater Oil)

Getty Oil Co.	—	49.54%	a

Mission Development Co. (owns 47.73% of Tidewater Oil)

Getty Oil Co.	—	58.55%	a

Missouri-Kansas Pipe Line Co. (owns 12.96% of Panhandle Eastern Pipe Line Co., see below)

Common (elects, as a class, four of seven directors)

W.G. Maguire	74,134	18.22%	10/51
SOFINA (Belgium)	73,794	18.13	11/51
A.G. Logan	8,470	2.08	5/54

Class B (elects, as a class, three of seven directors)

W.G. Maguire	146,037	36.49%	10/52

Newmont Mining Co. (owns 4.61% of Continental Oil; 2.92% of Phelps Dodge Corp.)

Boyce Downey	51,025	1.80%	11/59
Theodore Schulze	41,764	1.48	10/60
11 other directors	21,538	0.76	c
Margaret Thompson Biddle	288,744	10.22	6/56
Mass. Investors Trust	138,000	4.89	h
Continental Insurance Co.	80,000	2.83	i

Panhandle Eastern Pipeline (owns 14.44% of National Distillers and Chemical Corp.)

Missouri-Kansas Pipe Line Co.	819,040	12.96%	I

Portsmouth Corp. (owns 17.15% of Cleveland-Cliffs Iron Co.)

C.S. Eaton	82,377	7.59%	2/58
D.G. Baird	28,233	2.60	2/59
W.R. Daley	27,117	2.50	3/58
M.J. Zivian	21,000	1.93	10/59
F.A. LeFevre	10,000	0.92	8/59
Eaton-LeFevre holding cos.	35,400	3.26	2/58

Reynolds Corp. (owns 2.96% of Reynolds Metals)

U.S. Foil Co.	—	53.50%	a

U.S. Foil Co. (owns 47.36% of Reynolds Metals; 53.50% of Reynolds Corp.)
Reynolds family owns all outstanding voting stock. However, non-voting class B stock is publicly held.

Webster Investors (owns 11.65% of Merganthaler Linotype and 34.46% of American Manufacturing, see above)

Century Investors	100,900	37.79%	10/58
G.W. Wattles	76,330	28.60	10/58
Everett Meyer	10,000	3.75	10/58

References a) *Moody's Industrials,* 1960. b) *Fortune,* May 1960, p. 226. c) Various reports in *Official Summary* ... d) Piedmont Securities Co. is believed to have been dissolved. The fate of these shares is not at all clear. However, this holding company is known to be the property of the Woodruff family which is obviously the important family in Coca Cola Co. e) Based on reported proportionate ownership of Coca Cola Co. shares through Coca Cola Int'l. Corp. f) Based on estimate of 680,000 outstanding shares. g) Based on reported holding of L.C. Hanna, Jr. in 1/49. h) Includes holding of Mass. Investors Trust and Mass. Investors Growth Stock Fund. See *Moody's Bank and Finance Manual,* 1960. i) *Annual Report,* 1960. j) *Moody's Public Utilities,* 1960. It is stated in this reference that this holding represents control.

USA: The economy

Stock ownership and the control of corporations: part III

by Don Villarejo

Editors' comment: We here present part three of a New University Thought *research project by one of the editors of the magazine. Parts one and two of this study, which appeared in the previous issue, discussed stock ownership in general and the problem of control. This material is presented with the view that an analysis of the large corporations and the individuals prominent in them is necessary for an understanding of contemporary American society. Don Villarejo, author of "American investment in Cuba" which appeared in the first issue of* New University Thought, *is a graduate student in physics.*

In Parts I and II of this study we placed heavy emphasis on the identification of large stockholdings in a group of major corporations. We were interested in the distribution of stock ownership in general as well as in the 232 industrial corporations chosen for detailed study. The major results were summarized in tabular form and presented together with the body of our report. In Part III of this study we shall be concerned with the individuals who hold these shares as well as with certain key figures in the economic power structure. More precisely we shall study the characteristics of the directors of these corporations. In addition, we shall expand the concept of "community of interest" as first stated in Part II of this study to include phenomena other than mere *individual* pecuniary interests.

At the outset certain technical points need mention. First, we shall refer to the 232 corporations chosen for study as the *sample* corporations. The interested reader is referred to Appendices I and II of Part II of this article.[1] Second, an individual has been regarded as a director of a sample corporation if he was a director on December 31, 1959.[2] Thus, in keeping with the method of Parts I and II of this article we seek data valid as of a known date for each of the sample corporations. This is especially important when dealing with individuals serving as directors of corporations because of the rather large turnover of directors (due primarily to deaths, retirements and the like). Third, when we refer to an individual's shareholding or the market value of his holding we mean data valid as of December 31, 1959.

The board of directors

As we have indicated in Part I of this study, the corporate board is elected by the shareowners of the corporation. In theory, the board selects the management which in turn operates the company. Thus, the corporate board is the key instrument of the corporate power structure, for it is the board that bridges the gap between those who own property and those who operate it. As such, it is hardly surprising to find many substantial property holders serving on the corporate board. But are property owners the only ones who serve as directors? Actually not, as we shall see. In addition to property owners, we find lawyers, commercial bankers, investment bankers, insurance company executives, educators, corporate executives and many others serving on the boards of the sample corporations (we even find a sprinkling of retired generals and admirals as well as the former president of the Farm Bureau Federation). In order to grasp the complexities of the corporate power structure let us turn to an examination of these various types.

1. *Propertied Rich:* In this category we find those directors with a large and continuing stockholding in one or more of the sample corporations. By "large and continuing" we mean inherited or otherwise acquired holdings which grant the owner a measure of control. Specifically excluded are persons employed by the corporation in executive capacities who have acquired large holdings during the period of their employment. In Part II we encountered an example *par excellence* of what we mean by "propertied rich," namely Richard K. Mellon, whose holdings in the sample corporations exceeds $425 million. Another example is William du Pont, Jr. who owns 1,269,488 shares of E.I. du Pont de Nemours and Co. with a market value of $335 million.[3] We also include as propertied rich those members of wealthy families serving as directors though their personal holdings may be comparatively small. A good example is provided by P. S. du Pont, III, whose holdings in du Pont amount to only 3,864 shares (market value of a little over $1 million). [4]

A second category of propertied rich is that of directors without enormous holdings in the sample corporations but who have large holdings in other corporations. An example of this type is furnished by Allan P. Kirby who is a director of International Telephone and Telegraph Corp. and who owns 38,783 shares of IT&T (market value $1.5 million). However, Mr. Kirby also owns 300,100 shares of the New York Central Railroad Co., some 363,185 shares of F.W. Woolworth Co. and more than 1,000,000 shares of the Allegheny Corp. In sum his holdings are worth nearly $300 million.[5] Clearly, such persons number among the propertied rich though the bulk of their holdings are not in the sample corporations.

It is evident that those who enjoy a position among the propertied rich serve as directors in the sample corporations as a direct consequence of their ownership of property. In fact, many of these directors are decendents of the persons who launched these great enterprises and they continue, as a result of their inherited wealth, to represent their families' interests. It is no surprise, therefore, to find Firestones, Fords, Mellons, du Ponts, Rockefellers, Dows, Heinzes and the like in this group.

2. *Investment Bankers:* The individuals termed investment bankers are those directors who are partners in one or another of many investment banking houses which raise new capital for the giant enterprises. We include brokers and dealers in this category as well. A typical case of an investment banker is provided by C.B. Harding, a senior partner in the

well known firm Smith, Barney and Co. Mr. Harding is also a director of both Cerro de Pasco Corp. and Scott Paper Co.

An investment banker may serve as a corporate director in one of several capacities. First, he may represent substantial holdings by the banking firm itself, by one of the firm's other partners, or by clients. Second, and more often, he represents the firm's connection to the money market. That is, the banker may represent a firm that handles all stock and bond offerings when the corporation in question needs new capital. A third, and much less obvious function is closely related to the first: a banker may represent financial interests with important stakes in the corporation which he serves as a director. An example of this type follows. In discussing the recent management changes at Studebaker-Packard Corp., *Fortune* magazine commented in passing:

> "*In the reorganization, Harold Churchill, a long-time Studebaker engineer who had been president under Hurley, became chief executive,* though the real control was now in the hands of the New York bankers."[6]

If we examine the board of directors of Studebaker-Packard we find that J. R. Forgan of Glore, Forgan and Co. and F.J. Manheim of Lehman Bros. serve as representatives of these controlling interests.

3. Commercial Bankers: In this category we find officers of the nation's great commercial banking houses. Commercial bankers are found on corporate boards less frequently than are investment bankers. A case of this type is provided by H.C. Alexander, Chairman of the Board of Morgan Guaranty Trust Co. and a director of the following corporations in the sample group: American Viscose, General Motors, Johns-Manville, Standard Brands.

While commercial bankers are often preoccupied with deposits (note that a giant industrial corporation means millions of dollars in deposits for some commercial bank), many commercial bankers serve as corporate directors in their role as fiduciaries. That is, since the trust departments of these giant banks act as trustees for $66 billion worth of common stock, the banker actually represents a large stockholding over which he is bound to be concerned.[7]

4. Lawyers: In this category we find the partners of the handful of law firms which handle the legal matters of many of the large corporations. Also we find more "independent" lawyers, i.e., those not connected to one of the large law firms. Deliberately excluded are "inside" lawyers, i.e., those who are essentially employees of the corporation. An example of the first type is provided by D.B. Steimle, a partner in the law firm Shearman and Sterling and Wright. Mr. Steimle is a director of Air Reduction Co. and his firm is general counsel for that corporation. Thus, the corporation lawyer brings his special skills to the corporate board just as the investment banker brings his.

Another category of lawyers is provided by those who serve as trustees of large estates. Thus, C.M. Robertson, a director of J.I. Case (and also a member of the Case board's executive committee) serves as trustee for several estates, among them the following: Estate of Charles L. McIntosh, Estate of Anne Hamilton McIntosh, Estate of H.A.J. Upham, and others.

VILLAREJO:
Stock owner-
ship and the
control of
corporations

49

In this capacity, the lawyer is representing property.

5. *Insurance Company Executives:* These are officers of the major life and property insurance companies. Since the giant insurance companies not only hold common and preferred stock of many of the sample corporations, but· also hold large portions of the bond issues of these same enterprises, it is hardly a surprise to find their executive officers among the directors. Furthermore, it appears as though insurance companies (with millions to invest every week of the year) are rapidly increasing their holdings of common stock in many corporations.

To grasp the indebtedness of certain corporations to the giant insurance companies we may take the example of the Prudential Insurance Company of America which holds, among its more than $5 billion in industrial bonds, notes for $126 million and $150 million from the Olin Mathieson Chemical Corp. and Union Carbide Corp. respectively. Simultaneously, we note that C.M. Shanks, President of the Prudential, holds a directorship in Union Carbide. The presence of insurance company executives on the boards of the sample corporations is a reflection of the growing role of insurance companies as a source of capital.

6. *Local Businessmen:* These directors are important businessmen in communities where their corporations have major plants. Thus, J.T. Wilson, Chairman of the Board of the First National Bank of Kenosha, Wisconsin, is a director of the American Motors Corp. which has its giant Rambler plant in Kenosha.

Evidently, such directors serve more as a matter of what we might call prestige, than in a functional capacity. But, quite often, the local businessman is an important link to the community in which the corporation operates, serving some purpose in this way.

7. *Corporation Executives (corporations in sample, CS):* In this category we find the many executives of the sample corporations who also serve as directors of the corporation which employs them. Most often, these persons have been employed by "their companies" for the bulk of their business careers. In some cases, they may actually have built up sizable shareholdings in the corporations. However, such persons, even though they are now wealthy, began their careers without the advantage of large property holdings. These persons are the true members of the so-called managerial class. Their median income is probably in excess of $70,000 annually and though they are building up big holdings they are by and large dependent on a salary income.

8. *Corporation Executives (corporations not in sample, CNS):* In this category we have those professional executives who, while directors of one or more of the sample corporations, are also executive officers of one of the major non-financial corporations not included in our sample. Thus, F.C. Brown, President of Schering Corp., is a director of ACF Industries. The function of such executives on the boards of sample corporations is not at all clear. It is significant, however, that we find cases of important suppliers having representation on the boards of their purchasers and vice versa.

Again, certain executives represent large holdings of stock in the sample corporations while others provide counsel on special matters of current interest to the corporation.

9. *Former Officers:* Included are retired executives of the sample corporations as well as a handful of persons from non-sample corporations. Often, their directorships are a kind of token honor for concluded careers with the company. In other cases they undoubtedly provide counsel either to management or to the board.

10. *Miscellaneous:* We find here all those who cannot be placed in any of the preceding categories. In particular, we find educators such as F.L. Hovde, President of Purdue University and a director of both General Electric and Inland Steel; we find retired army officers such as General Douglas MacArthur who is Chairman of the Board of Sperry Rand; we find public relations experts such as Stanley Resor who is a director of Scott Paper and also chairman of J. Walter Thompson. While certain of these types have special functions in respect to the ordinary activities of the corporation, some are simply directors because of their contacts (Who in the Pentagon would turn away from a retired general who comes to promote the latest in military hardware?) or because of their prestige value.

However, a separate group deserves special mention and attention. These are the persons who while not large property owners themselves, merely represent the holdings of certain individuals or families. An example is in order: J.M. Kingsley is the president of Bessemer Securities Corp. To the ordinary citizen, this organization might appear to be some kind of corporation specializing in investments. He is quite correct, but he is off target. In fact this company is the literal nerve center of one of this nation's major family fortunes: Bessemer Securities Corp. is a private holding company for the Phipps fortune. Owning property worth $300 million, the company is popularly known as the "office" among members of the clan. The "office" handles *all* family finances for the seventeen separate families of the current Phipps generation. If a family member wants to buy a yacht, he has the office write out a check and handle the details. More important, the office is actually a network of more than seventy-five enterprises designed to take advantage of every possible tax loophole. Moreover, the stock of Bessemer Securities is held in trust by another Phipps family agency, the Bessemer Trust Co. In the words of *Fortune:*

"*The corporate structure of Bessemer Securities was complicated in the extreme, embracing seventy-six or more subsidiary enterprises organized for tax purposes or special projects, but in essence it was the money machine for Bessemer Trust Co., the family trust.*"[8]

Such are the measures taken to preserve property intact through the generations of propertied rich.

Analysis of directors

Now that we have a firm idea of the types of individuals serving as directors of the sample corporations as well as an understanding of their functions on the board, we turn to an analysis of the 2,784 individuals who occupy directorships in these companies. Presented in Table I is the distribution of these individuals according to the categories outlined above.

Table I: Distribution of directors in sample corporations

Category	Number of Individuals
Propertied Rich	520
Investment Bankers	134
Commercial Bankers	100
Lawyers	118
Insurance Company Executives	24
Local Businessmen	78
Corporation Executive (CS)	1,240
Corporation Executive (CNS)	149
Former Officer	246
Miscellaneous	75
Undertermined	100

Explanatory note: As previously indicated we have included only individuals who were directors of the sample corporations on December 31, 1959. In making the classification indicated we have used the annual reports of the corporations as well as Standard and Poor's *Register of Officers and Directors*, 1960 and *Who's Who in Commerce and Industry*, various years. The last category, "undertermined", represents the 100 persons for whom it was impossible to find sufficient biographical data to permit classification. Also, if there seemed to be any ambiguity of classification we placed the individual in this category.

Perhaps the most obvious feature of this distribution is the rather large number of active and retired executives. Indeed more than one-half of all persons were of one of these two types. This is a reflection of the professionalization of management, a subject which has been the topic of much discussion in recent years. As industrial corporations grew and developed in complexity, more skilled persons were required to keep affairs running smoothly. Moreover, the rapid technological developments of this century have placed greater demands on the management of large concerns. Decisions based on technical understanding became more frequent and the demands on management increased in direct proportion. Thus, a very large fraction of these executives rose through the ranks as specialists of one sort or another. Of course, there are quite a few old-fashioned bureaucrats in this group as well. Nonetheless, it seems apparent, to the author at least, that this trend to professionalization will continue, particularly as automation takes hold.

No less important than the executives, and perhaps more important, we find that nearly one-fifth of the sample group are members of the propertied rich. That is, those who hold large blocks of stock in many of the sample corporations participate actively in the formulation of basic policy. Of the 520 in this category, no less than 197 *also* serve as executives of the corporations in which their interests are located (we include chairman of the board in this category). Thus, in our sample, roughly two-fifths of the propertied rich participate as management in

addition to being directors of the given corporation. At this point we
should also note that exactly 50 of this group are persons whose property
holdings are in corporations not in the sample group. Thus, the fraction
of propertied rich who actively participate in management is actually
somewhat larger than 40 percent.

A fact of equal interest is that 376 directors are genuine "outsiders"
in that they represent established centers of interest outside the sample
group. We refer to various bankers, lawyers and insurance company executives who bring special skills to the board or represent large investments. At this juncture we also note that 21 persons in the
miscellaneous category are simply representatives of large individual
property holders. With this in mind let us turn to an examination of the
market value of holdings of the directors. The basic data is summarized
in Table II.

Table II: Distribution of directors' holdings by market value

Size Class	Category of Director									
	I	II	III	IV	V	VI	VII	VIII	IX	X
$10,000,000 and above	99	0	0	0	0	0	0	1	0	3
$5,000,000-10,000,000	68	0	0	0	0	0	0	5	0	13
$1,000,000-5,000,000	198	3	8	2	0	2	3	37	1	110
$500,000-1,000,000	52	10	16	6	0	1	5	25	2	152
$100,000-500,000	50	33	33	18	5	17	12	78	27	445
Under $100,000	45	72	74	69	19	56	55	96	113	487
Unknown	8	0	3	5	0	2	0	4	6	30

Note: Shown are the number of persons with reported holdings in the indicated
market value size class distributed by the category in which we have classified the
director. No usable market value data could be found for 58 individuals of the sample
group. Further, we have not shown the 100 persons not classified in the indicated
categories (called "undetermined" in Table I). The key to the category symbols
follows: 1 - Propertied Rich; 2 - Lawyers; 3 - Investment Bankers; 4 - Commercial
Bankers; 5 - Insurance Co. Executives; 6 - Local Businessmen; 7 - Miscellaneous; -
8 - Former Officers; 9 - Corporation Executives (CS); 10 - Corporation Executives
(CNS).

From the table we immediately see certain facts. First, 99 of the 103
persons with holdings in excess of $10 million in the corporations in
which they are directors, are in the category propertied rich. This statement is nothing more than an expression of the fact that the propertied
·rich are rich indeed. Further, we observe that in all categories other
than propertied rich, the distribution of holdings is sharply peaked at
the lower end of the market value spectrum, that is, in these other categories the individuals have rather small holdings (though a holding of
$100,000 must be considered large by any measure). Further, we find
that these 99 propertied rich, each with holdings in excess of $10 mil-
lion, own $5,173 billion worth of stock as compared with $7,128 billion
for *all 2,784 directors.*[9] Thus, *these 99 hold 72.56% of the total value
of stock held by all directors.* That this represents an enormous concentration of holdings should be obvious to all. But, further, if we take into

account the holdings identified in Part II of this study which include shares owned by other non-director family members, trusts not included in the directors' totals and stock held by these directors in sample corporations in which they are not directors, then we find an additional $7,309 billion held by the propertied rich. In sum, this total of $14,437 billion for all directors represents 6.11'ι of all the outstanding common stock of all 232 sample corporations. Of this total a little over $13 billion represents holdings of the propertied rich alone. Moreover, if we now take into account the enormous amount of stock in certain holding companies, as well as stock held in bank-administered trusts that we were able to identify and, finally, stock held by sample corporations where the controlling interest is apparent, the sum reaches nearly 12'ι of the outstanding market value of common stock in our sample. This excludes the holdings of the insurance companies, investment companies (open-end), and the great bulk of the shares in bank-administered trusts and estates. The total figure is of course one of the great "unknowable" statistics in this field of inquiry. But the fact that such a large fraction of stock is so readily identifiable forces one to wonder just how much other stock is in the hands of the propertied rich, or controlled by them.

Because of the importance of the 99 very rich, we have included an appendix listing the holdings of these persons at the end of the body of this article.

In conclusion, then, we find various types of directors holding positions on the boards of the sample corporations. The majority of these persons are professional executives, but the propertied rich control the bulk of stock held by directors. Further, we find that a rather large fraction of the outstanding common stock of these corporations is controlled by those we term propertied rich.

Interlocking directorates

In Part II of this study we mentioned the phenomenon of interlocking directorates but postponed discussion of this important aspect of the inquiry. It is appropriate to take up this subject here.

"Interlocking directors" simply means that a single person holds directorships in two or more of the sample corporations. We must also take into account the presence of bankers and insurance company executives on the boards of the sample corporations, but for the present we shall limit ourselves to interlocks among the sample corporations and between sample corporations and financial corporations. This material could be presented in several ways. First, we might simply enumerate the various interlocks we find. However, the mere enumeration of this data would certainly fill the pages of this magazine, and then some. As a workable, and certainly more interesting alternative we shall confine ourselves to comments on some general features of interlocking directorates and then study a few simple cases in some detail.

First, we observe that the 3,196 directorships in the sample corporations are held by only 2,784 persons. Hence, a number of persons hold two or more seats in the sample corporations. More precisely, 303 individuals so interlocked hold 712 seats on these corporate boards. Of these, 221 hold two seats, 56 hold three seats and the remaining 23 hold four or more seats. But the really interesting result is that 65 of the interlocked persons are among the propertied rich, 79 among the corporate executives (CS) and 53 are among the groups of investment and commercial bankers and insurance company executives. Together, the propertied rich and financial interests account for more than one-third of interlocked individuals. A result of even greater importance is the fact that 31.86% of the individuals considered (we now refer to all 2,784 directors) are somehow interlocked with one or more banks, insurance companies, investment companies (both closed and open-end variety). In other words, nearly one-third of the total number of individuals serving as directors in the sample corporations are in personal contact either with banking interests or with those interests representing large holdings.

Let us now consider a few examples in some greater detail and attempt to shed further light on why interlocks occur. A first example is that of J.H. Phipps who holds directorships in W.R. Grace and Co. and Ingersoll-Rand Corp. In this case, Mr. Phipps is representing large family holdings in both corporations. Moreover, the Phipps family is intermarried with the Grace family so that we find J.P. Grace, a director and president of W.R. Grace and Co., on the board of Ingersoll-Rand and, in fact holding a large bloc of stock in both corporations. While intermarriage brings a new dimension to the discussion, we observe that these persons represent overlapping family financial interests, and this is the basis on which they hold several directorships in the sample corporations.

An equally significant example is provided by William Ewing, a general partner of the investment banking firm Morgan, Stanley and Co. Mr. Ewing is a director of American Can Co., American Viscose Co. and J. I. Case Co. All three companies are generally regarded as being allied with the so-called Morgan interests (a group centered about the financial and industrial enterprises built by J.P. Morgan). Morgan, Stanley and Co. was created in the early 1930's representing the Morgan solution to the new laws divorcing investment banking from commercial banking. This divorcement decree was pushed through by the new deal as a direct consequence of the great market crash of 1929. The Morgans' response was to divide their forces between J.P. Morgan and Co., the commercial bank (since merged with Guaranty Trust Co., another commercial bank in the Morgan group), and Morgan, Stanley which was to be the investment bank. H.S. Morgan is a general partner in Morgan, Stanley and Co. while the other descendent in this generation, J.S. Morgan serves as a director of Morgan Guaranty Trust Co. The presence of Mr. Ewing on the boards of American Can, Viscose, and Case is a reflection of the continuing Morgan interest in these enterprises. At this point we note with some interest that J.S. Morgan serves as a director of American Can's major rival, the Continental Can Co.

Let us now consider the connections of a specific corporation in detail. In particular we study the giant General Electric Co.'s relationship to major financial institutions. In Table III are listed the directors of GE together with some of their directorships in financial corporations.

55

Table III: Financial interlocks of directors of General Electric

Name	Company
S.S. Colt	Bankers Trust Co. Mutual Life Ins. Co. of New York
D.K. David	Ford Foundation, Vice-Chmn.
C.D. Dickey	Morgan Guaranty Trust Co. New York Life Ins. Co.
John Holmes	Continental Ill. Bank & Trust Co.
G.W. Humphrey	National City Bank of Cleveland M.A. Hanna Co.
J.E. Lawrence	State Street Investment Co.
G.H. Love	Mellon National Bank and Trust Co. M.A. Hanna Co.
G.G. Montgomery	Bankers Trust Co. American Trust Co.
H.S. Morgan	Morgan, Stanley and Co.
R.T. Stevens	Mutual Life Ins. Co. of New York
R.W. Woodruff	Morgan Guaranty Trust Co. Metropolitan Life Ins. Co.
Remaining directors (without major financial interlocks)	
Henry Ford II	Ford Motor Co. (Pres.)
F.L. Hovde	Purdue University, Pres.
T.B. McCabe	Scott Paper Co., Pres.
N.H. McElroy	Procter and Gamble, Chmn.
R.J. Cordiner	Chmn. of GE
Robert Paxton	Pres. of GE.

Aside from the fact that the GE board of directors is graced by two former secretaries of major government bureaucracies (McElroy is a former Secretary of Defense, Stevens a former Secretary of the Army), we see that certain financial interests have considerable representation on the top levels. Two directors of Morgan Guaranty Trust, two directors of Bankers Trust Co., a partner in the firm Morgan, Stanley and Co., give the Morgan interests five seats. If we also recognize the fact that the Stevens family of J.P. Stevens and Co. is closely allied with the Morgan group, then the Morgan group enjoys one-third of GE seats. Since this giant corporation was launched by J.P. Morgan himself, it is not surprising to find that his interests still have considerable representation.

In addition, investment companies, other banks and life insurance companies are interlocked with the GE board. If we recall from Part I of this study that more than 20% of GE common stock is held in the trust departments of major banks, then the fact that so many directors of that corporation are connected with these financial institutions comes as no real surprise.[11]

Let us now turn to a case that seems to be quite different. As we have noted, the Rockefeller family continues to hold large blocs of stock in the Standard Oil companies. But no member of the family serves as a director of any of these companies. However, David Rockefeller serves as vice-chairman of the giant Chase Manhattan Bank (in which the Rockefeller family holds roughly 5% of the outstanding stock, David himself holding 135,756 shares of Chase Manhattan).[12] It is therefore of more than passing interest that Eugene Holman, Chairman of the Executive Committee of Standard Oil Co. (New Jersey) and F.O. Prior, Chairman of the Board of Standard Oil Co. (Indiana) are also Chase Manhattan directors. In this case, unlike the GE situation, the executives operating the oil companies sit as directors of Chase Manhattan at the nerve center of an important and wealthy family's operations.

At this point we can begin to see a pattern in the network of interlocking directorates. That is, alliances among the various corporations considered (both sample corporations and financial corporations) fall into a definite pattern based on *financial* connections. One also begins to see that certain groups or centers of interests appear. Rockefellers, Morgans, Mellons, du Ponts and the like each have little empires that close among themselves. On the other hand, this is by no means always the rule. It is equally clear that a large fraction of the companies considered may well be loosely allied to an existing power center and yet each of these enterprises has a power structure of its own. Consider the example of H.J. Heinz Co. which has been shown to be under the control of the Heinz family (recall that the Heinz family holds roughly 76% of Heinz stock), and yet H.J. Heinz II is a director of Mellon National Bank and Trust Co. (center of the Mellon power structure). Furthermore, J.A. Mayer, President of Mellon National is also a director of H.J. Heinz. Thus, the Heinz family is allied with the Mellon interests. But the power in H.J. Heinz is the Heinz family and not the Mellon family.

As our final example, let us try to get some feel for what is meant by a center of power by examining an outstanding instance in detail: the Mellon "group" of companies. This great fortune was founded by Thomas Mellon, a banker who made his money through shrewd and often ruthless dealings. Thomas Mellon was the father of Andrew W. Mellon and Richard B. Mellon. The four elders of the present Mellon clan are Richard K. Mellon, Paul Mellon, Mrs. Allan Mellon Scaife and Mrs. Ailsa Mellon Bruce. R.K. Mellon and Mrs. Scaife are the children of Richard B. Mellon while Paul Mellon and Mrs. Bruce are descendants of Andrew W. Mellon (Richard B. Mellon's brother). A *Fortune* survey of large American fortunes in 1957 indicated that all four of the current Mellon elders had personal fortunes in the range of $400 million to $700 million.[13] Our research indicates that this estimate is valid. In addition to these holdings, the children of these four persons have extensive holdings of their own (usually in the same companies: Gulf, Alcoa, etc.) In sum, the holdings of all family members is probably in the range of $3.5 billion.[14]

The major financial centers of Mellon power are two: Mellon National Bank and Trust Co. (eleventh largest commercial bank in the country), and T. Mellon and Sons (an investment management firm). Both Paul Mellon and Richard K. Mellon are directors of both concerns (Richard K. Mellon is chairman of Mellon National Bank and president of T. Mellon and Sons). In addition, Richard Mellon Scaife is a director of

Mellon National Bank (the Scaife family controls Scaife Co., a privately held, Pittsburgh-based industrial concern).

Thus, Mellon National and T. Mellon and Sons, is the core of the Mellons' power. Let us see the extent of Mellon influence. On the board of Mellon National we find directors of the following corporations in the Mellon group (the number in parentheses indicates the number of common directors):

Allegheny Ludlum Steel	(1)
Aluminum Co. of America	(4)
Consolidation Coal	(3)
Crucible Steel	(1)
Diamond Alkali	(2)
H. J. Heinz	(2)
Gulf Oil	(4)
Jones & Laughlin Steel	(4)
Koppers Co.	(3)
Pittsburgh Plate Glass	(3)
Pullman, Inc.	(1)
Westinghouse Air Brake	(4)
Westinghouse Electric	(5)

In addition, A.B. Bowden (Vice-President of Mellon National) is a director of Allegheny Ludlum Steel, I.N. Land (Senior Vice-President of Mellon National) is a director of Crucible Steel, A.V. Davis (director emeritus of Mellon National) is honorary chairman of Alcoa, and W.C. Robinson (also director emeritus of Mellon National) is a director of Westinghouse Electric.

Of equal importance, we find that these interlocked directors have themselves or represent large holdings in their respective industrial corporations. Thus a Mellon National director, R.F. Evans, chairman and president of Diamond Alkali, holds 171,740 shares in that company (equivalent to 5.90% of the outstanding common stock).[15] His brother, not a director of Mellon National, holds 113,267 shares of Diamond Alkali (3.91%).[16] H.J. Heinz II holds the position of chairman of H.J. Heinz Co. and holds 21.83% of the stock of Heinz.[17] Also, B.F. Jones III holds 40,750 shares of Jones and Laughlin Steel and, like H.J. Heinz, is a director of Mellon National.[18] Overall, the related Jones and Laughlin families hold roughly 14.15% of their namesake company.[19] Again, R.A. Hunt, chairman of the executive committee of Alcoa, holds 857,796 shares in that company (4.07%) and serves on the Mellon National board of directors.[20] Finally, W.P. Snyder, Jr. serves as a director of Crucible Steel (he is a member of the executive committee of the board of directors) and is also a Mellon National director. The importance of this relationship is seen when we realize that Shenango Furnace Co. (of which Mr. Snyder is chairman and which is controlled by the Snyder family) holds an estimated 132,000 shares of Crucible.[21] Thus, the propertied families allied with the Mellon interests have representation on the big bank.

If we examine the fiduciary services provided by Mellon National for this group of companies, we find that only Westinghouse Electric does not have its fiduciary services performed by the big bank. This is because the giant electric equipment firm is thought to be under the joint control of several "groups" and the Mellons are only partners in sharing control with others. In addition, First Boston Corp. (in which R.K. Mellon and Mrs. Scaife hold 112,500 shares) [22] underwrites the bond issues or stock issues of Jones and Laughlin Steel, Alcoa, and Gulf Oil.

It is, of course, difficult to convey the full extent of the power represented in the control of these corporations. But their combined assets total in the billions of dollars, they employ hundreds of thousands of persons and are key companies in oil, steel, aluminum, coal, glass, chemicals as well as electrical machinery.

One step away from the Mellon group itself, we find connections to other industrial corporations in our sample. In addition to the Mellons, the second important interest group in Consolidation Coal is the Hanna group which controls some 28'; of this largest coal company in the United States. [23] Now Hanna also controls National Steel and has important investments in Texaco and Phelps Dodge. Moreover, G.H. Love, Chairman of both M.A. Hanna Co. and Consolidation Coal is a director of both National Steel and Mellon National. B.F. Fairless, former chairman of U.S. Steel is also on the Mellon board of directors. Thus, the nation's giant steel companies have representatives on the Mellon National board.

Finally, we are able to discern relations with other major centers of power. We observe that the Phipps family has a holding of 156,000 shares in Mellon National itself and a holding of roughly 800,000 shares of Gulf Oil. [24] Again, Remington Arms (a majority of this company's stock is held by E.I. duPont de Nemours) [25] holds 150,000 shares of Crucible Steel [26] Another important interest in Remington Arms is M.H. Dodge who owns 674,074 shares of that company and who married Geraldine Rockefeller, daughter of William Rockefeller (brother of John D. Rockefeller). [27] The descendents of William Rockefeller are believed to hold controlling shares in the First National City Bank of New York (indeed, J. Stillman Rockefeller is Chairman of the Board of First National City).

The giant Cleveland-Cliffs Iron Co. holds 170,719 shares of Jones and Laughlin Steel (H.S. Harrison, a V.P. and director of Cleveland-Cliffs holds a directorship in Jones and Laughlin Steel to represent this holding). [28] Since Cleveland-Cliffs holds large blocs of stock in Inland Steel, Youngstown Sheet and Tube, and Republic Steel, this means that continuous relationships exist between Mellon National and all of the major steel companies except Bethlehem Steel. It is clear that if one digs deeply into the facts of the situation, one finds relationships to many other interests (in the case of Cleveland-Cliffs it is the Eaton-Mather Wade families who have connections to the Mellon group). In summary then, we find definite connections of the Mellon group not only among companies within their immediate sphere of influence, but also to other major financial and industrial interests.

In this brief sketch of the problem of interlocking directorates we have tried to give a general characterization by example rather than a thorough and formal analysis. Our conclusions, however, are based upon much more data than has been presented here; the author can make a detailed statistical analysis available to interested persons. To conclude: we find extensive interlocking directorates between sample corporations and various financial corporations. These interlocks often indicate a pattern of connection through financial entities to certain centers of power.

The community of interest

The power structure we have observed in the sample corporations leads us to postulate the existence of working relationships among the corporations considered as well as among the individuals who dominate these enterprises. It is in this sense that we mean a "community of interest" has grown. Many of the corporations here considered were launched by a single family, and yet, over the years through mergers and acquisitions these enterprises have had to reach an understanding with other enterprises, as well as with financial interests controlling the lifeblood of capitalism, namely capital. An even more recent phenomonon has been the growth of new relationships among major previously separate interests. A good illustration of this point is shown in the merger of the Mellon Securities Corp. into the First Boston Corp. (First Boston is an investment banking firm formed from the investment banking departments of the old Chase National Bank and the First National Bank of Boston). Now First Boston is closely aligned with the Rockefeller interests and Mellon Securities was jointly owned by Richard K. Mellon and Sarah Mellon Scaife. Thus, an alliance was formed between two of the most powerful families in the economic elite of this country. Now the Gulf Oil Corp., controlled by the Mellon family, and the Rockefeller oil companies have several working relationships in operation. For instance, Gulf and Standard Oil (N.J.) share in the ownership of the Venezuela Gulf Refining Co. In addition, Gulf participates along with the Rockefeller companies in a number of other operations forming an important cornerstone of the international petroleum cartel.

Approaching the concept of "community of interest" from another point of view, the recent price-fixing scandals are another reflection of the growing "cooperation" among major corporations. It appears that administered prices may prove to be the rule rather than the exception among industrial corporations. As one steel executive defined competition: when prices of identical products are the same there is competition for quality! One wonders what happened to the old-fashioned (and strangely magical) "market" of classical economic theory.

What are the consequences of this growing community of interest? The first is the rather remarkable trend to mergers among so many of the giant industrial firms. Olin Mathieson Chemical was the result of a merger of Olin Industries, Mathieson Chemical and the later absorption of E.R. Squibb and Sons and Blockson Chemical Corp. General Dynamics resulted from the merger of the Electric Boat Co., Consolidated Vultee Aircraft (itself the result of a merger of Consolidated Aircraft and Vultee Aircraft and the later acquisition of Stromberg-Carlson and Liquid Carbonic Corp. Another consequence of the community of interest is the growth of jointly-owned subsidiaries of the giants. Dow-Corning is jointly owned by Dow Chemical and Corning Glass; Ormet is jointly held by Olin Mathieson and Revere Copper and Brass. These joint ventures even jump oceans to bring in European partners. Armco and Thyssen Steel of West Germany have jointly launched a subsidiary. An exhaustive enumeration of such ventures, however, would take many pages.

Corporate cooperation has also begun to function on a different level. A consciousness has developed among the economic power elite of the public image of big business. Industry associations spend large sums creating what they call "confidence" in the free enterprise system. Millions more are spent to get the public to accept and understand the "business point of view." Again, as in the drug industry, a united front is formed to defend the industry as a whole from "government attack," the term the drug industry uses in referring to the investigation of the industry by the Kefauver anti-monopoly sub-committee.

One begins to wonder, in view of these facts, just how far this trend of cooperation will continue. There are hopeful signs that the Justice Department may prosecute a number of anti-trust and price fixing cases. These cases may show whether or not the trend can be stopped.

Concluding remarks

Before concluding a few points concerning the general scope and approach of this study are necessary. The first point relates to how much of the domestic economy is represented here: we have treated the 250 largest industrial corporations; these corporations account for 58.4% of the profits of all industrial corporations.   To complete a truly encyclopedic investigation of this character, it would be necessary to treat transportation, utility, merchandising and financial firms in addition. We have deliberately chosen industrial corporations for a number of reasons. First, due to government regulations requiring railroads and utilities to report on large stockholders, much information concerning them is already easily available. On the other hand, merchandising and financial companies are relatively more concentrated in ownership than industrial corporations so that a study of them would tend to give a greater indication of concentration than is perhaps justified for the total economy.

A similar cautionary note should, perhaps, be made with respect to our list of the 99 propertied rich as a pinpointing of the economic "power elite." It should be remembered both that we have not included all kinds of companies nor the holdings of directors in companies of which they are not directors. In some cases, such as that of Allan P. Kirby, these other holdings can be quite extensive. Thus our figures for the directors will be on the low side, and the listing does not necessarily encompass all the wealthiest persons in the sample corporations.

Of course the problem of finding who are the real top "controllers" and decision-makers, or if in fact they operate as such, remains one of the key unknowns in this field. Unfortunately, although certain facts are generally acknowledged, this is a topic which at this stage must rely entirely upon inferences from incomplete data, "insider" rumors and the like, and therefore has no place in a study of this type.

Finally, it is very important for the reader to realize that our method has been a very cautious one. We have relied entirely upon data which are known with certainty. Guesswork is often necessary in this field due to the efforts made to keep many of the facts from public view, but we have avoided it, and with it that crutch of much work in economics, the "guesstimate." Therefore, our data must be regarded as a conservative estimate of the situation, even to the point of distorting the truth somewhat.

In this study we have attempted to show what seems to the author to be a rather simple fact: namely, in a free enterprise system, the means of production are privately owned, i.e., the great mass of the populace neither owns nor controls corporate stock but rather a relatively small group of persons, the propertied rich, both own and, substantially, control the giant enterprises of the nation. While the study has been hampered by the absence of publicly accessible source materials, it is clear that it is possible to make considerable headway in understanding that this is indeed true. On the other hand, many points will only become clarified with the revelation of information now withheld. That so much can be found on the basis of publicly available information provokes a strong desire to examine information hidden, and deliberately so, from public view.

1 *New University Thought*, Vol. II, No. 1, Autumn 1961, pp. 61ff.

2 We have used the following sources in compiling our list of directors: Annual Reports for all corporations, 1959; *Who's Who in Commerce and Industry,* various years; Standard and Poor's *Register of Officers and Directors*, 1960.

3 *New University Thought*, op. cit.

4 *Official Summary of Securities Transactions of Officers and Directors of Listed Corporations*, U.S. Securities and Exchange Commission, April, 1958.

5 *Time*, Vol. LXXVI, No. 24, Dec. 12, 1960.

6 *Fortune*, December, 1961, p. 158.

7 R.A. Gordon, *Business Leadership in the Large Corporation*, The Brookings Institution, Washington, D.C., 1945, p. 158. Gordon states: "One important fact about the representatives of commercial banks needs to be stressed. A good many of them serve on boards not because they are bankers but because their institutions represent trusts or estates holding large blocks of stock in the companies."

8 *Fortune*, October, 1960, p. 175.

9 Computed by the author from data presented in *New University Thought*, op. cit.

10 Based on data presented in *New University Thought*, op. cit. We have simply taken into account the holdings of corporations such as Christiana Securities an enterprise under the solid stock control of the du Pont family.

11 *New University Thought*, Vol. II, No. 1, Autumn 1961, p. 42, Table IV.

12 *New York Times*, July 6, 1960.

13 *Fortune*, November, 1957.

14 Estimated by the author. Using our data and TNEC data we arrive at a fair guess of $3.5 billion. For example, we estimate the total Mellon holding in Gulf Oil to be 42.60% as of December 31, 1959 and the Mellon holding in Koppers Co. to be 17.80%.

15 *New University Thought*, op. cit., p. 63.

16 Ibid.

17 Ibid, p. 64.

18 *Security Transactions* ..., January, 1959.

19 Based on data from TNEC and terms of the reorganization of the capital structure of Jones and Laughlin Steel in 1941.

20 *New University Thought*, op. cit., p. 61.

21 Based on data from TNEC.

22 See *Moody's Bank and Finance Manual*, 1960.

23 *New University Thought*, op. cit., p. 63.

24 Based on information contained in *Fortune*, November, 1960, p. 163.

25 See *Moody's Industrial Manual*, 1960.

26 Ibid.

27 See *Wall Street Journal*, July 31, 1961.

28 *New University Thought*, op. cit., p. 72.

The propertied rich: 99 directors with holding of more than $10 million in their companies

Appendix I

This appendix contains a listing of the 99 individuals who are directors of the sample corporations and who have holdings of $10,000,000 in the firms in which they are directors. We list the person's name, the name of the corporations in which the individual is a director, the number of shares held in each corporation and the total market value of the holdings as of December 31, 1959.

Director & corporations	No. of Shares	Market Value
Richard K. Mellon		$429,866,534
Aluminum Co. of America	1,587,476	
General Motors	240,000	
Gulf Oil	6,362,319	
Koppers Co.	115,732	
Pittsburgh Plate Glass	108,500	
William du Pont, Jr.		$335,144,832
E.I. du Pont de Nemours & Co.	1,269,488	
J.G. Ordway		$286,011,968
Minnesota Mining & Manufact.	1,625,068	
A.A. Houghton, Jr.		$235,451,870
Corning Glass Works	1,623,806	
U.S. Steel	NA	
Otto Haas		$209,926,830
Rohm and Haas	287,571	
Amory Houghton		$193,336,910
Corning Glass Works	1,333,358	
W.L. McKnight		$163,302,304
Minnesota Mining & Mfg.	927,854	
W.M. Keck		$136,454,016
Superior Oil	103,296	
Charles S. Mott		$134,070,000
General Motors	2,460,000	
A.G. Bush		$109,108,560
Minnesota Mining & Mfg.	619,935	
Benson Ford		$93,101,877
Ford Motor (Class B stock)	1,025,916	
R.A. Hunt		$91,335,274
Aluminum Co. of America	857,796	
W.C. Ford		$88,872,201
Ford Motor (Class B stock)	979,308	
R.W. Johnson		$87,550,155
Johnson and Johnson	1,447,110	
Nathan Pitcairn		$81,629,480
Pittsburgh Plate Glass	1,025,174	
H.F. Pitcairn		$81,623,030
Pittsburgh Plate Glass	1,025,093	
Raymond Pitcairn		$81,622,712
Pittsburgh Plate Glass	1,025,089	
Henry Ford II		$80,875,876
Ford Motor (Common)	71,900	
Ford Motor (Class B stock)	819,185	
General Electric	100	
A.B. Dow		$73,606,275
Dow Chemical	745,380	
J.C. Haas		$70,368,350
Rohm and Haas	96,395	
H.J. Kaiser, Jr.		$69,443,595
Kaiser Industries	4,273,452	
F.O. Haas		$69,400,370
Rohm and Haas	95,070	
A.P. Sloan, Jr.		$64,793,002
General Motors	1,185,156	
Jacob Blaustein		$62,115,380
Standard Oil Co. (Indiana)	1,407,714	
R.W. Galvin		$61,282,740
Motorola	356,295	
R.H. Dwan		$56,566,400
Minnesota Mining & Mfg.	321,400	
Lamont du Pont		$52,351,936
E.I. du Pont de Nemours & Co.	197,924	
H.J. Kaiser		$51,524,948
Kaiser Alum. & Chemical	0	
Kaiser Industries	3,170,766	
E.E. Ford		$49,702,809
International Business Mach.	113,412	
J.M. Olin		$47,655,090
Olin Mathieson Chemical	888,673	

John Stauffer		$47,123,581
Stauffer Chemical	729,185	
C.A. Dana		$45,809,300
Dana Corp.	1,050,000	
Curtiss-Wright	100	
Ogden Phipps		$44,759,762
International Paper	329,722	
Texaco	NA	
S.M. Fairchild		$43,766,774
International Business Mach.	99,866	
S.T. Olin		$43,534,098
Olin Mathieson Chemical	811,434	
Owens-Illinois Glass	200	
Bernard Peyton		$40,577,856
E.I. du Pont de Nemours & Co.	153,704	
C.L. McCune		$39,835,526
Texaco	456,193	
Armstrong Cork	18,000	
Charles Boettcher II		$39,715,761
Ideal Cement	1,256,841	
J.H. Pew		$38,390,706
Sun Oil	710,939	
J.L. Pratt		$36,641,658
General Motors	672,324	
J.S. Johnson		$36,058,182
Johnson and Johnson	596,003	
J.G. Pew		$34,593,696
Sun Oil	640,624	
H.B. Keck		$34,538,866
Superior Oil	26,146	
H.J. Heinz II		$33,455,804
H.J. Heinz Co.	368,659	
L.S. Rosensteil		$32,961,950
Schenley Industries	918,800	
S.C. Clark		$32,154,528
Singer Manufacturing	574,188	
E.F. Kaiser		$31,813,762
Kaiser Alum. and Chemical	0	
Kaiser Industries	1,957,770	
H.H. Dow		$29,256,268
Dow Chemical	296,266	
Arthur K. Watson		$28,249,595
International Business Machines	64,460	
D.U. Dalton		$27,767,621
Upjohn	667,090	
R.W. Johnson, Jr.		$26,583,095
Johnson and Johnson	439,390	
T.J. Watson, Jr.		$26,501,854
International Business Machines	60,472	
H.F. du Pont		$24,711,720
E.I. du Pont de Nemours & Co.	93,605	
T.S. Gary		$24,440,163
General Telephone & Electronics	290,522	
W.J. Upjohn		$24,139,503
Upjohn	579,928	
J.H. Phipps		$24,132,931
W.R. Crane & Co.	93,780	
Ingersoll-Rand	244,299	
T.B. McCabe		$24,055,755
Scott Paper	298,055	
Campbell Soup	7,500	
General Electric	2,500	
A.H. Diebold		$22,295,000
American Home Products	130,000	
Christian de Guigne		$22,004,425
Stauffer Chemical	340,494	
H.D. Doan		$20,307,246
Dow Chemical	205,643	
C.J. Strosacker		$19,851,416
Dow Chemical	201,027	
R.A. Light		$18,062,628
Upjohn	433,937	
W.C. Pew		$18,037,404
Sun Oil	334,026	
Donald Danforth		$17,829,630
Ralston Purina	424,515	
R.C. Firestone		$17,765,084
Firestone Tire and Rubber	128,718	
Edgar Monsanto Quenny		$17,725,923
Monsanto Chemical	319,386	
D.S. Gilmore		$17,314,959
Upjohn	415,975	
R.U. Light		$16,808,508
Upjohn	403,808	
W.P. Schweitzer		$16,701,401
Kimberly Clark	235,231	
A.G. Rosengarten, Jr.		$15,220,940
Merck and Co.	189,080	
J.P. Grace		$14,696,382
Ingersoll-Rand	141,012	
W.R. Grace & Co.	71,193	
Kennecott Copper	100	
M.C. Kelce		$14,631,662
Peabody Coal	836,095	
H.H. Timken, Jr.		$14,595,164
Timken Roller Bearing	222,811	
H.K. Hochschild		$14,590,206
Americal Metal Climax	601,658	
S.B. Mosher		$14,329,815
Signal Oil and Gas (Class B)	469,830	
L.K. Firestone		$14,017,902
Firestone Tire and Rubber	101,579	
August Kochs		$13,802,414
Stauffer Chemical	213,577	

W.R. Timken...............		$13,458,000
Timken Roller		
Bearing.....................	205,465	
J.M. Timken		$12,697,285
Timken Roller		
Bearing....................	193,852	
W.A. Jones		$12,693,400
Cities Service.............	260,800	
Chrysler.....................	2,000	
Richfield Oil...............	500	
R.S. Firestone...............		$12,479,207
Firestone Tire and		
and Rubber	90,429	
J.S. McDonnell.............		$12,449,710
McDonnell Aircraft.....	355,706	
P.S. Achilles..................		$12,448,285
Eastman Kodak	115,798	
A. Coors........................		$12,413,205
Ideal Cement	395,640	
R.S. Kerr		$12,100,853
Kerr-McGee Oil	240,813	
J.S. Sensenbrenner.......		$11,987,285
Kimberly Clark	168,835	
Norton Simon...............		$11,953,215
Hunt Foods and		
Industries	415,764	
H.W. Sweatt		$11,936,976
Minneapolis-		
Honeywell................	84,415	
General Mills.............	1,800	

W.K. Warren...............		$11,696,422
Gulf Oil	318,270	
Sidney Frohman............		$11,598,315
West Virginia Pulp		
and Paper................	204,217	
R.W. Woodruff.............		$11,520,250
Coca Cola Co..............	76,135	
General Electric	1,500	
H.S. McNeil..................		$11,506,737
Johnson and Johnson .	190,194	
Leon Falk, Jr................		$11,185,870
National Steel............	117,746	
S.L. Avery		$11,051,238
U.S. Gypsum	117,350	
R.G. Fairburn		$10,923,212
Diamond National.......	301,330	
R.F. Evans.....................		$10,776,685
Diamond Alkali..........	171,740	
T.M. Evans		$10,668,375
Crane Co....................	163,500	
G.A. Anderson		$10,637,550
Chas. Pfizer & Co.	322,350	
L.I. Doan		$10,170,460
Dow Chemical............	102,992	

Note: The symbol NA refers to holdings undetermined and not available. The reader is referred to Part II, App. I of this article for source references.

[6]

Corporate Ownership and Control: The Large Corporation and the Capitalist Class[1]

Maurice Zeitlin
University of Wisconsin

An "astonishing consensus" exists among academic social scientists concerning the impact of the alleged separation of ownership and control in large corporations on the class structures and political economies of the United States and similar countries. The question is whether this separation is a "pseudofact," which has, therefore, inspired incorrect "explanations," "inferences," and "theories," namely, that the presumed separation has either transformed or eliminated the former "capitalist class" and therefore rendered inapplicable a class theory of the division of the social product, class conflict, social domination, political processes, and historical change. If the separation of ownership and control has not occurred, then "managerial" theories are without foundation. The discrepant findings of numerous studies are reviewed and problems of method and measurement discussed, concluding that the empirical question is quite open. Critical questions are posed for research into the internal differentiation and integration of the dominant ("upper") class in the United States.

The originating question of this article is, how has the ascendance of the large corporation as the decisive unit of production affected the class structures and political economies of the United States, Great Britain, and other "highly concentrated capitalist" countries?[2] In particular, our concern is with the alleged "separation of ownership and control" of the large corporation and the presumed impact of this separation on the internal structures, if not actual social existence, of the "dominant" or "upper" classes in these countries. This article does not provide any answers to this difficult issue; rather it questions the evidence for the

[1] I have benefited from the critical comments on an earlier draft of this article by many colleagues of diverse and often opposing theoretical persuasions, all of whom are absolved of any responsibilities for what follows. Thanks are due Michael Aiken, Robert Alford, Daniel Bell, G. W. Domhoff, Lynda Ewen, Robert Larner, Ferdinand Lundberg, Harry Magdoff, Robert K. Merton, Barrington Moore, Jr., Harvey Molotch, Willard F. Mueller, James O'Connor, Victor Perlo, and Paul M. Sweezy. The comments of the anonymous referees for the *AJS* were also useful. I am particularly grateful to the editors of the *Journal*, especially to Florence Levinsohn, for their careful reading and cogent criticisms.

[2] Bain (1966, p. 102) refers here to the United States, England, Japan, Sweden, France, Italy, and Canada, which were included in his study.

American Journal of Sociology

accepted ones, which underlie what Ralf Dahrendorf (1959), a leading proponent of the prevailing view, has called the "astonishing degree of consensus among sociologists on the implications of joint-stock companies . . . for the wider structure of society" (p. 42). This consensus extends, it should be emphasized, to other social science disciplines. E. S. Mason, though himself dissatisfied with economic theories derived from the prevalent view, wrote recently (1967): "Almost everyone now agrees that in the large corporation, the owner is, in general, a passive recipient; that, typically, control is in the hands of management; and that management normally selects its own replacements" (p. 4). Peter Drucker (1971), himself an early managerial theorist, writes that ideas concerning the separation of ownership and control represent "the most conventional and most widely accepted theses regarding American economic structure" as expressed in "the prevailing and generally accepted doctrine of 'managerialism'" (pp. 50–51). For Robert A. Dahl (1970), the facts are "resounding"; indeed, it is "incontrovertible" that ownership and control have been "split apart." In his view, "the question that was not asked during the great debate over socialism *versus* capitalism has now been answered: ownership has been split off *de facto* from internal control" (p. 125).

The question is whether this "astonishing consensus" derives from the findings of appropriate social research or from an unwitting acceptance of what Robert K. Merton has termed "the socially plausible, in which appearances persuade though they may deceive."

Thus, this article poses a type of question which, however simple, "is often undervalued in sociology"—a question which "calls," in Merton's words (1959), "for discovering a particular body of social fact. It might at first seem needless to say that before social facts can be 'explained,' it is advisable to ensure that they actually are facts. Yet, in science as in everyday life, explanations are sometimes provided for things that never were. . . . In sociology as in other disciplines, pseudofacts have a way of inducing pseudoproblems, which cannot be solved because matters are not as they purport to be" (pp. xiii–xv). Such pseudofacts may, of course, also serve to deflect attention from critical aspects of social structure, determinant social relations, and basic social processes, They may inspire not merely "explanations," but "inferences" and "theories" as well, which further confuse and obscure social reality. The methodological premise of this article, then, as well as its irreducibly minimal rationale, is the "obvious and compelling truth that 'if the facts used as a basis for reasoning are ill-established or erroneous, everything will crumble or be falsified; and it is thus that errors in scientific theories most often originate in errors of fact.' "[3]

[3] Merton 1959, p. xiii. The internal quote is from Claude Bernard.

Corporate Ownership and Control

THE "THEORY"

The prevailing view is that the diffusion of ownership in the large corporation among numerous stock owners has resulted in the separation of ownership and control, and, by severing the connection between the family and private property in the means of production, has torn up the roots of the old class structure and political economy of capitalism. A new class of functionaries of capital, or a congeries of economic "elites," in control of the new forms of productive property, appear: nonowning corporate managers displace their capitalist predecessors. "The capitalist class," as Pitirim Sorokin (1953) put it, is "transformed into the managerial class" (p. 90). In Talcott Parsons's view (1953), "The *basic phenomenon* seems to have been the shift in control of enterprise from the property interests of founding families to managerial and technical personnel who as such have not had a comparable vested interest in ownership" (pp. 122–23; italics added).

In the view of these writers, a class theory of contemporary industrial society, based on the relationship between the owners of capital and formally free wage workers, "loses its analytical value as soon as legal ownership and factual control are separated" (Dahrendorf 1959, p. 136). This class theory is, therefore, inapplicable to the United States, England, and other countries in which ownership and control have been severed: it cannot explain, nor serve as a fruitful source of hypotheses concerning the division of the social product, class conflict, social domination, political processes, or historic change in these countries. Thus, Parsons and Smelser (1957) refer to the separation of ownership and control as "one particular change in the American economic structure which has been virtually completed within the last half century"—a "structural change in business organization [that] has been associated with changes in the stratification of the society." The families that once "controlled through ownership most of the big businesses . . . by and large failed to consolidate their positions as *the dominant class* in the society" (p. 254; italics added).

This "shift in *control* of enterprise from the property interests of founding families to managerial and technical personnel," according to Parsons (1953), is the "critical fact" underlying his interpretation that "the 'family elite' elements of the class structure (the Warnerian 'upper uppers') hold a secondary rather than a primary position in the overall stratification system" (p. 123). The shift in control, "high progressive taxation," and other "changes in the structure of the economy, have 'lopped off' the previous top stratum," leaving instead "a broad and diffuse one with several loosely integrated components. *Undoubtedly* its main focus is now on occupational status and occupational earnings. Seen in historical as well as comparative perspective this is a notable *fact*, for the entrepre-

American Journal of Sociology

neurial fortunes of the period of economic development of the nineteenth century, especially after the Civil War, notably failed to produce *a set of ruling families on a national scale* who as family entities on a Japanese or even a French pattern have tended to keep control of the basic corporate entities in the economy" (p. 123; italics added). Thus, in Parsons's view, a " 'ruling class' does not have a paramount position in American society" (p. 119).

Similarly, Daniel Bell (1958) has argued that a "silent revolution" has subverted the former "relations between power and class position in modern society." In his view, "The *singular fact* is that in the last seventy-five years the established relations between the systems of property and family . . . have broken down," resulting in "the breakup of 'family capitalism,' which has been the social cement of the bourgeois class system" (italics added). If, in general, "property, sanctioned by law and reinforced by the coercive power of the State" means power, and if a class system is maintained by the "fusion" of the institutions of the family and private property, economic development in the United States has "effected a radical separation of property and family." Therefore, in his view, if "family capitalism meant social and political, as well as economic, dominance," that is no longer the situation in the United States. "The chief consequence, politically, is the breakup of the 'ruling class' "—"a power-holding group which has both an established *community* of interest and a *continuity* of interest" no longer exists in the United States (pp. 246–49).

The profound implications of the acceptance of the separation of ownership and control as a social fact are, according to Parsons, that the former relations between classes have been replaced by an occupational system based on individual achievement, in which "status groups" are ordered hierarchically in accordance with their functional importance. Further, as Dahrendorf has put it (1959), the basic social conflict is no longer between capital and labor because "in post-capitalist society the ruling and the subjected classes of industry and of the political society are no longer identical; . . . there are, in other words, in principle [*sic*], two independent conflict fronts. . . . This holds increasingly as within industry the separation of ownership and control increases and as the more universal capitalists are replaced by managers" (pp. 275–76). The political economy of capitalism and the class interests which it once served have been replaced by a sort of capitalism without capitalists (Berle 1954)—if not post-capitalist society—shorn of the contradictions and class conflicts that once rent the social fabric of "classical capitalism." The basis of social domination in such societies, as these theorists would have it, is no longer class ownership of the means of production, and such a class clearly does not "rule" in any sense, economically, socially, or politically. "The decisive power in modern industrial society," in Galbraith's (1971)

Corporate Ownership and Control

representative formulation, "is exercised not by capital but by organization, not by the capitalist but by the industrial bureaucrat" (p. xix).

Assuredly, the answer to this "theory"—particularly the propositions concerning the separation of ownership and control—rests on empirical grounds (Bell 1958, p. 246). However, logic, concepts, and methodology are certainly intertwined and inseparable aspects of the same intellectual process of discovering the "facts."

One common source of conceptual and analytic confusion in the writings on the issue of ownership and control derives from a teleology of bureaucratic imperatives. Bureaucratization is implicitly assumed to be an inexorable historic process, so that even the propertied classes and their power have fallen before its advance. Parsons and Smelser (1957) have written, for example, that the "kinship-property combination typical of classical capitalism was *destined*, unless social differentiation stopped altogether, to proceed toward 'bureaucratization,' towards differentiation between economy and polity, and between ownership and control" (p. 289; italics added).

The tendency toward the bureaucratization of enterprise, and of management in particular, is taken as an index of the appropriation of the powers of the propertied class by the managers. This confuses the (*a*) existence of an extensive administrative apparatus in the large corporation, in which the proportion of management positions held by members of the proprietary family may be negligible; and (*b*) the locus of control over this apparatus. Dahrendorf (1959) for instance, noting that the managers of large enterprises generally have neither inherited nor founded them, concludes from this that these new managers, "utterly different than their capitalist predecessors," have taken control for themselves. In place of of the "classical" or "full capitalist," there stands the bureaucratic manager and "organization man" (pp. 42, 46). From the observation that in the large corporation, functions that (allegedly) were fulfilled in the past by a single owner-manager are now institutionalized and split up among differing roles in the bureaucratic administrative organizations, it is concluded that bureaucratic management (if such it is) means bureaucratic control. However, there is nothing in bureaucratic management itself that indicates the bureaucracy's relationship to extrabureaucratic centers of control at the apex or outside of the bureaucracy proper, such as large shareowners or bankers, to whom it may be responsible.

Max Weber (1965) clearly conceptualized this relationship, referring to the "appropriation of control over the persons exercising managerial authority by the interests of ownership." If "the immediate appropriation of managerial functions" is no longer in the hands of the owners, this does not mean the separation of *control* from ownership, but rather "the separation of the managerial *function*" from ownership. "By virtue of their

1077

American Journal of Sociology

ownership," Weber saw, "control over managerial positions may rest in the hands of property interests *outside the organization as such*" (pp. 248–49; italics added).

It is precisely this relationship between propertied interests and the bureaucracy, and between "capitalists" and "managers," which has received at best inadequate and usually no attention among those who report that they have seen a "corporate revolution" silently abolish private ownership in the means of production. Thus, Daniel Bell (1961) can write that "private productive property, especially in the United States, is largely a fiction" (p. 44), and Dahrendorf (1959) can claim: "Capital—and thereby *capitalism*—has *dissolved* and given way in the economic sphere, to a plurality of partly agreed, partly competing, and partly simply different groups" (p. 47; italics added).

Two issues, then, have to be separated: (1) whether the large corporations continue to be controlled by ownership interests, despite their management by functionaries who may themselves be propertyless; (2) whether the undisputed rise of managerial functions means the rise of the functionaries themselves. Do they constitute a separate and cohesive stratum, with identifiable interests, ideas, and policies, which are opposed to those of the extant owning families? Are the consequences of their actions, whatever their intentions, to bring into being social relationships which undermine capitalism? How, with their "rise," is "the incidence of economic power" changed? (Bendix 1952, p. 119).

These are not merely analytically distinguishable issues, A number of social scientists, "plain marxists" preeminent among them,[4] concede the reality of the split between ownership and control in most large corporations. However, they reject the implication that this renders inapplicable to the United States and other developed capitalist countries a theory which roots classes in the concrete economic order and historically given system of property relations, and which focuses, in particular, on the relationship between the direct producers and the owners of the means of production. In their view, whatever the situation within the corporation as the predominant legal unit of ownership of large-scale productive property, the "owners" and "managers" of the large corporations, taken as a whole, constitute different strata or segments—when they are not merely agents—of the same more or less unified social class. They reject the notion, as Reinhard Bendix has observed (1952), "that people in the productive system constitute a separate social group because they serve

---

[4] "Plain marxists" (uncapitalized) was C. Wright Mills's (1962) phrase to characterize thinkers to whom Marx's "general model and . . . ways of thinking are central to their own intellectual history and remain relevant to their attempts to grasp present-day social worlds" (p. 98). He listed such varied thinkers as Joan Robinson, Jean Paul Sartre, and Paul M. Sweezy, as well as himself, as plain marxists.

Corporate Ownership and Control

similar functions and that they are powerful because they are indispensable" (p. 119). Rather, the corporations are units in a class-controlled apparatus of appropriation; and the whole gamut of functionaries and owners of capital participate in varying degrees, and as members of the same social class, in its direction (cf. Baran and Sweezy 1966, chap. 2; Miliband 1969, chap. 2; W. A. T. Nichols 1969, pp. 140–41; Playford 1972, pp. 116–18). This class theory, as we discuss below in detail, demands research concerning the ensemble of social relations, concrete interests, and overriding commitments of the officers, directors, and principal shareowners of the large corporations in general. Rather than limiting analysis to the relationship between the "management" and principal shareowners of a given corporation, the analysis must focus on the multiplicity of their interconnections with other "managements" and principal shareowners in other large corporations, as well as the owners of other forms of large-scale income-bearing property.[5] Were research to show that the putative separation of ownership and control within the large corporation is a "pseudofact" and that identifiable families and other cohesive ownership interests continue to control them, this might surprise certain "plain marxists," but it would, of course, be quite consistent with their general class theory.[6] Most important, were "managers" and "owners"

[5] Domhoff (1967, pp. 47–62) and Kolko (1962, pp. 60–69), who may also be considered "plain marxists," reject as incorrect both the separation of ownership and control within the large corporation and argue that "managers" belong to the same social class as the "owners." Their books contain brief empirical studies of the ownership of stock (Kolko) and "upper-class membership" (Domhoff) of large corporate directors. This is also the view of Ferdinand Lundberg (1946, 1968), who, in particular, lays stress on the need to study the kinship relationships among the owners and executives—a point we discuss in some detail below.

[6] Though it might not accord with their "economic" theory. As we discuss briefly below, Baran and Sweezy (1966, chap. 2) discard the concept of "interest groups" or "communities of interest" binding together a number of corporations into a common system. They argue "that an appropriate model of the economy no longer needs to take account of them" (p. 18). Further, they also assert, without evidence, that they "abstract from whatever elements of outside control may still exist in the world of giant corporations because they are in *no sense essential* to the way it works" (p. 20; italics added). Unfortunately the issue is one which would require a new article, if not full-length monograph, to grapple with, and extended discussion here is impossible. However, I have not yet seen an explanation of why Baran and Sweezy have concluded that the question of "outside" or familial control is irrelevant to understanding the American political economy, nor why they should be so insistent on this point. They have not explained how the continuation of communities of interest and familial control groups would alter the ability of the system to face the problem of what they term "the tendency of surplus to rise," which is the central issue of their essay and cornerstone of their neo-marxian theory of "monopoly capitalism." If, as they argue, (*a*) the large corporations tend, in their interaction, to produce a "surplus" of investment funds in excess of private investment outlets; and (*b*) this disparity between a rising surplus and available investment outlets is a chronic threat of crisis in our political economy, how would this tendency be affected by the existence of controlling ownership interests in the "giant corporations"? How would this tendency

American Journal of Sociology

to be found to occupy a common "class situation" (Weber 1968, p. 927), the theory that ownership and control of the large corporations reside in the same social class would be confirmed. In contrast, either set of findings would tend to invalidate the essential assumptions, propositions, and inferences of managerial theory. In any event, each alleged implication requires careful analysis and empirical testing on its own.

MANAGERS AND CAPITALISTS: THE HISTORIC CONTROVERSY

The theory of managerial capitalism has hoary antecedents. Not only did Marx himself make rather confusing Hegelian comments about the emergence of the corporation, but the theory of a society in which the capitalist class is gradually replaced by an administrative stratum no longer devoted to the interests of property was being enunciated even while the epoch of "finance capital" and the large corporation was dawning in late 19th- and 20th-century Germany. Eduard Bernstein and Konrad Schmidt, Social Democratic theoreticians of what came to be known as "revisionism," argued that the property form of the corporation presaged and was part of a gradual alteration in the essence of capitalism. The splitting up of property into shares brought with it "armies of share-holders" representing a new "power over the economic life of society. The shareholder," wrote Bernstein (1961), "takes the graded place in the social scale which the captains of industry used to occupy before the concentration of businesses" (p. 54). The capitalist class, said Schmidt, was undergoing a process of "expropriation by stages." The "decomposition of

---

be affected by "interest groups" able to coordinate the prices, production, sales, and investment policies of ostensibly independent corporations? Would not such groups, rather than the individual corporation, constitute the "basic unit of capital"? An original thinker like Paul M. Sweezy might be expected to grapple with this question, rather than merely asserting its irrelevance. When he authored the NRC report on interest groups in 1939, he wrote: "This study should be regarded as doing no more than posing the problem of the larger significance of the facts which it seeks to portray" (Sweezy 1953, p. 184). He ended his essay by a couple of questions concerning their significance to which, to my knowledge, he has yet to speak: "What is the significance of the existence of more or less closely integrated interest groups for the pricing process? What are its implications for the relation between economic and political activity?" These questions seem to me to be quite as relevant today as when Sweezy first asked them. Indeed, when he republished this study in 1953, nearly two decades after its original appearance, he wrote: "No . . . study [of interest groups] . . . has been made in recent years, though there is an *obvious need* for one. I hope that the republication of this earlier attempt to deal with what was and *remains one of the crucial aspects of our whole social system* will stimulate the interest of younger social scientists and provide them with both a starting point and some useful methodological pointers" (pp. 158–59; italics added). Perhaps I may immodestly hope that this article by a "younger social scientist" will stimulate the interest of Paul M. Sweezy to explicitly deal with the issues he has so far avoided, but which he once thought of paramount importance!

Corporate Ownership and Control

capital" was leading to the gradual extension of the rights of "sovereignty" over property to society as a whole. The capitalist was being transformed "from a proprietor to a simple administrator."[7]

This was substantially the same thesis of a work which appeared three decades later in 1932, in the United States and which has been the most enduring source of the theory of managerial capitalism: *The Modern Corporation and Private Property*, by Adolph Berle, Jr., and Gardiner C. Means. "The dissolution of the atom of property," they wrote (1967), "destroys the very foundation on which the economic order of the past three centuries has rested" (p. 8). They reported that 65% of the 200 largest corporations appear to be "controlled either by the management or by a legal device involving a small proportion of ownership" (p. 110). The latter category, "control through a legal device," such as pyramiding, is clearly a form of ownership control, as Larner (1970) points out, "since it is based on stock ownership and not on a strategic position in management. The legal device simply reduces the share of stock ownership required for control" (p. 132). Berle and Means classified 44% of the top 200 corporations as actually under management control. However, they claimed to have "reasonably definite and reliable information" on at most two-thirds of the companies (Berle and Means 1967, p. 84). Indeed, they cited, in a detailed and extended table covering 20 pages of their book (pp. 86–105), the source of their information on each corporation and, most important, noted those corporations about whose locus of control they were merely surmising. Thus, they listed 73 corporations under the heading "majority of stock *believed to be widely distributed* and working control held either by a large minority interest or by the management" (italics added). Of these, 29 were considered *"presumably"* under the control of a minority interest, while 44 were *"presumably"* under management control. Indeed, of a total of 88½ corporations which they classified under management control,[8] they provided *no* information on 44, which they could only consider "presumably" management controlled. Among industrials, they classified fully 39 of the 43 management-controlled corporations as only "presumably" under management control. Thus, they had information which permitted them to classify as definitely under manage-

[7] For a contemporary polemic against these views, written in 1899, see Luxemburg (1970), pp. 16–20. Several colleagues, including Professors Merton and Bell, who read this article in an earlier draft, urged me to discuss "Marx's confusing Hegelian comments." Those who are interested in this discussion will find it in the Appendix.

[8] If one corporation was controlled by another through ownership, but the latter itself was found to be under management control, it was classified by Berle and Means as "ultimately management controlled." If it was ultimately under the "joint control" of a minority interest and management, or other combinations, they counted the corporation as one-half in each of the categories. Thus, the figure 88½ corporations under management control.

American Journal of Sociology

ment control only 22% of the 200 largest corporations, and of the 106 industrials, only 3.8%! Yet numerous scholars over the years have cited the work by Berle and Means (when giving citations at all) as the main or only source of their own assertions that ownership and control were split apart in the large corporations. In part, this may be explained by the fact that Berle and Means presented their summary table and conclusions (pp. 109–10) without any mention of their earlier qualifications concerning the adequacy and validity of their information. If we take the information contained in parts J and K of their table 12 on pages 103–5, a correct summary of their findings, with the necessary qualifications made explicit, would be as shown in table 1.

TABLE 1

TYPE OF CONTROL OF THE 200 LARGEST CORPORATIONS, 1929, ACCORDING TO
BERLE AND MEANS

TYPE OF CONTROL	RR		PU		IND.		TOTALS	
	N	%	N	%	N	%	N	%
Private ownership ..	2	4.8	2	3.8	8	7.5	12	6.0
Majority ownership	1	2.4	3	5.8	6	5.7	10	5.0
Minority control:								
"Presumed"	0	0	5	9.6	24	22.6	29	14.5
Others	4½	10.7	2½	4.8	10½	9.9	17½	8.7
Legal device	7½	17.8	19	36.5	14½	13.7	41	20.5
Management control:								
"Presumed"	0	0	5	9.6	39	36.8	44	22.0
Others	26	61.9	14½	27.9	4	3.8	44½	22.3
In receivership	1	2.4	1	1.9	0	0	2	1.0
Total	42	100	52	100	106	100	200	100

NOTE.—RR = railroads; PU = public utilities; Ind. = industrials; "minority control" was assumed to be present when a single individual or cohesive group was found to own at least 20% of the corporation's stock; "presumed" refers to Berle and Means's classification of firms believed to be widely distributed and presumably under specified type of control.

In 1945, R. A. Gordon published a study, based in part on a secondary analysis of the Temporary National Economic Committee (TNEC) data, which came to conclusions much like those of Berle and Means. He wrote that "the real revolution [in property rights] has already largely taken place; the great majority of stockholders have been deprived of control of their property through the diffusion of ownership and the growth in the power of management" (1966, p. 350).

Quite recently, Robert J. Larner duplicated the Berle-Means methods in his own study of the 500 largest nonfinancial corporations in the

Corporate Ownership and Control

United States and concluded that the "managerial revolution" in process in 1929 was now "close to complete." Corporations in which the largest individual stockholder or members of a single family or a group of business associates were found *not* to own 10% or more of the voting stock were classified by Larner as under "management control." By this criterion, he classified 84% of the top 200 and 70% of the next 300 largest nonfinancial corporations in 1963 in the United States as "management controlled."[9] John Kenneth Galbraith (1968), who had relied on Berle and Means's and Gordon's studies to advance his own interpretation of the loss of stockholder control in the "new industrial state" not merely to management, but to the new "technocracy," found that Larner's findings, some of which appeared as Galbraith's book was going to press, "explicitly confirmed" his view of the process (p. 90).

In contrast to these studies and others following similar methods of analysis and classification are several studies by analysts taking a quite different approach. These researchers have argued that without an investigation of the specific situation in a given corporation, and of the interconnections between the principal shareholders, officers, and directors, and other corporations, the actual control group is unlikely to be identified.

Thus, studies which appeared at virtually the same time as that of Berle and Means, by Anna Rochester (1936) and Ferdinand Lundberg (1937), respectively, concluded, as Lundberg put it, that "a very small group of families," through their ownership interests and control of the major banks, were still in control of the "industrial system" (1946, pp. 506–8). Analyzing the same corporations that Berle and Means claimed were under management control, Lundberg found that "in most cases [the largest stockholding] families had themselves installed the management control or were among the directors," while several others were "authoritatively regarded in Wall Street as actually under the rule of J. P. Morgan and Company." "Exclusion of stockholders from control, within the context as revealed by Berle-Means," Lundberg concluded (pp. 506–8), "does not mean that large stockholders are excluded from a decisive voice in the management. It means, only, that small stockholders have been [excluded]." The National Resources Committee (NRC) also conducted a study of the control of the largest U.S. corporations during the same period. Unlike either Berle and Means or Gordon,

---

[9] Larner 1970, p. 21. Berle and Means had used 20% as the minimum necessary for minority ownership interests to maintain control. In a note to a new edition of their work, Berle and Means (1967), refer to Larner's original article in the September 1966 *American Economic Review* as "a study [which] has duplicated the 1929 analysis for 1963, making only one significant change in concept" (p. 358), the reduced amount (10%) necessary for ownership control.

American Journal of Sociology

the NRC study included not only the 200 largest nonfinancial corporations but also the 50 largest banks, which permitted its author (Paul M. Sweezy) to discover centers of "outside" control or abiding influence which were missed by the former studies. The NRC study also took account of corporation histories and information on the careers of key officers and directors, as well as of information on primary interlocks between corporations. Almost half of the top 200 corporations and 16 of the banks were found to belong to eight different "interest groups" binding their constituent corporations together under a significant element of common control by wealthy families and/or financial associates and investment bankers (NRC 1939, pp. 100–103; 306–17; Sweezy 1953).

Of 43 industrial corporations which Berle and Means categorized under "management control," 36 appeared on the lists of top corporations studied by the TNEC (Goldsmith and Parmelee 1940) and NRC in the late thirties. Victor Perlo compared their findings concerning these particular corporations and found that of these 36, the TNEC located "definite centers of control" for 15 and the NRC for 11; in addition, Perlo's own research (1957) revealed that another seven were under the control of identifiable ownership interests, leaving only three industrial corporations on the original Berle and Means list for which other investigators did not locate definite control centers (p. 49).

Differences in the findings of recent studies also indicate the wisdom of considering the empirical question as open: Don Villarejo studied the locus of control in 250 of the largest industrial corporations (though not other types of nonfinancial corporations) on the 1960 *Fortune* list. He concluded (1961/62) that, of the 232 corporations on which he obtained usable data, "at least 126 corporations," or 54%, and perhaps as many as 141, or 61%, were controlled by ownership interests, that is, he found "the existence of concentrated ownership to the extent of securing potential working control of the corporation in question" (p. 68). His findings were criticized by Larner (1970) "as open to challenge because he aggregated the stockholdings of directors, investment companies and insurance companies in each corporation without providing specific evidence, such as family or business relationships, to suggest a community of interests or to indicate the likelihood of either intragroup or intergroup cooperation" (p. 22). This criticism of Villarejo's work may or may not be correct, but it is remarkable that Larner should make it, since it is at least as applicable—if not more so—not only to Berle and Mean's original study, which Larner chose to emulate procedurally, but also to Larner's own findings. Larner certainly does not present systematic evidence of the kind he requires of Villarejo, yet he concluded that most large corporations were under "management control." It is relevant, therefore, that *Fortune*, using essentially the same definitions

Corporate Ownership and Control

and procedures as Larner, and taking 10% as the minimum necessary for proprietary control, found in 1967 that 147 corporations of the top 500 were controlled through ownership interests, or over half again as many of Larner's 95 (Sheehan 1967).

PROBLEMS OF METHOD AND MEASUREMENT

Further brief review of recent contradictory findings concerning the control of the largest corporations in the United States highlights the most significant problem faced by investigators of this subject: the data needed for adequate measurement are, in the first place, often inaccessible. As Joseph Kahl (1957) points out, power, "because it is potential, . . . is usually impossible to see. Furthermore, where it exists it tends to be deliberately hidden; those who sit among the mighty do not invite sociologists to watch them make their decisions about how to control the behavior of others" (p. 10). Two separate problems of "inaccessibility of the data," the relative importance of which cannot be settled a priori, require investigation so that we can assess the limitations to our understanding: first, there is no official list of the largest corporations, ranked by assets, sales, or profits. Investigators must have access to the sources of information that will allow them to compile such a list or even make reasonable guesses. Studies in recent years have relied largely on *Fortune's* 500 as their primary source of a list of which corporations to investigate. Thus, even the Patman Committee on Banking and Currency of the House of Representatives used that list in its analysis of interlocking relationships between large commercial banks and the largest corporations (Patman Report 1968, p. 91). In 1966 *Fortune* plainly disclosed that over the years since it had been publishing its list it had been omitting "privately owned or closely held companies that do not publish certified statements of their financial results." On the basis of *Fortune's* knowledge, it now named 26 companies which it believed "had sufficient sales in 1965 to qualify for the 500 list" (Sheehan 1966). (Because of a high ratio of sales to assets, some of these firms might not rank among the top 500 if we knew their assets.) Obviously, any adequate generalization about the ability of families to maintain control through ownership, indeed private ownership, of very large firms would have to take account of such previously ignored privately owned firms. Were these added to the "list," there would be not merely five privately owned firms as found by Larner, but 31, over six times as many as previously counted among the 500 largest. Whether other such large privately owned firms have still escaped notice is an important question to which there is no presently reliable answer.

Perhaps of greater importance as a source of inaccessibility of the

American Journal of Sociology

relevant information is the fact that new methods of control, some of which rely on secrecy, have been devised by the principal shareowning families. The extent (though not the fact) of this secrecy is, once again, unknown. The problem, put most simply, is to discover who are the actual "beneficial owners" of the shareholdings held by the "shareholders of record." Shareholdings may appear in the name of voting trusts, foundations, holding companies, and other related operating corporations in which the given family has a dominant interest. "Use of nominees [brokers, dealers, bank trust departments], also known in the securities trade as 'street names' or 'straws' [usually nonfinancial firms listed as record shareholders but whose control is not publicly known] to hide beneficial ownership of stock is a common corporate practice today," as Senator Lee Metcalf recently noted (1971). Corporations *"habitually list nominees rather than beneficial owners,"* whatever the supposed formal reporting requirements (Metcalf and Reinemer 1971). In this way, the presence of principal proprietary families may be hidden or rendered scarcely noticeable among the reports of stock ownership filed with the Securities and Exchange Commission, which are required by law to list the stockholdings of each director of the firm and of the beneficial owners of 10% or more of the outstanding amount of its stock.

Even the presence of large bank holdings may be hidden in this way—not to speak of the proprietary controlling interests of the bank itself. Thus, in addition to the discrepancy between *Fortune's* findings and Larner's, the Patman Committee's unprecedented studies (1968) suggest that three dozen corporations classified as "management-controlled" by Larner are really under the control of very large banks (pp. 13–15). Larner has rejected the Patman Committee's conclusions on the grounds that the banks do not hold at least 10% of the voting stock in most of the corporations named by the committee. There are six, however, in which more than 10% of the common stock is held by a single bank, and another in which 9.5% is held by a single bank. To Larner's 95 corporations controlled through ownership interests, then, we may add the 17 privately owned firms which the *Fortune* lists have excluded,[10] the 52 discovered by *Fortune* among the 500 to be be under proprietary control through at least 10% minority holdings by an individual or family, and at least the six found by the Patman Committee to be under "bank minority control" by 10% or more stock ownership. This is a total

---

[10] I do not include all 26 privately owned firms named by *Fortune* (Sheehan 1966) because when the estimated sales of these firms are taken into account and they are ranked (and the others on the original 500 list reranked) by sales, only 17 belong in the top 500. If all 26 were included, and the number of "proprietary" firms (179) figured among the 526, the proportion would be the same: 34%. By sales, the 26 privately owned firms are ranked as follows: top 100, none; 101–50, 3; 151–200, 1; 201–50, 2; 251–300, 1; 301–50, 3; 351–400, 1; 401–50, 3; 451–500, 3; 501–26, 9.

Corporate Ownership and Control

of 170 firms, or 34% of the 500 largest nonfinancial firms which are controlled through ownership interests. Further, Larner (1970) correctly argues, as we noted earlier, that "control through a legal device" such as pyramiding, contrary to Berle and Mean's view, is "more realistically seen . . . as a form of ownership control" (p. 132). He found 26 corporations in this category. Larner also classified two corporations as under "unknown" control; however, he believes "it is likely" that these are, in fact, privately owned. Adding these 28, we have a total of 198, or 39.6% of the top 500 firms controlled through a minimum of 10% ownership interest—a figure more than double Larner's original 95, or 19%.

It should be emphasized that we have so far used the criterion of 10% as the minimum proportion of the outstanding stock which an individual or cohesive group must have to exert minority control through ownership. This is the standard employed by Larner and other recent authorities (e.g., Monsen et al. 1968, 1969; Hindley 1970; Sheehan 1967; Vernon 1970), in place of the original 20% cutoff point used by Berle and Means, on the assumption that stock is now even more widely dispersed and that, therefore, a bloc of 10% should assure working control. However, on the basis of its investigations, the Patman Committee concluded that effective control could be assured with even *less* than a 5% holding, "especially in very large corporations whose stock is widely held" (1968, p. 91). Were this assumption correct, then another 14 corporations in which the Patman investigators found a single bank holding *more* than 5% but less than 10% of the voting stock would also clearly belong under proprietary rather than management control—bringing the total so far to 211, or 42.2% of the top 500 firms controlled by identifiable ownership interests.[11]

---

[11] Larner (1970) also apparently has some doubts concerning the adequacy of the residual definition of management control, using the less than 10% ownership criterion. He names five firms among the top 200 (and refers to "several others among the top 500") which, though he classified them as management controlled, "appear to be controlled, or at least strongly influenced, by a single family within their management. Yet these families owned only a very small fraction of the outstanding voting stock" (p. 19). With these included, there are 216 (not counting the unenumerated "several others"), or 43.2%, of the top 500 firms in the United States which are visibly controlled by identifiable individuals, families, or banks. We might note, also, that there are 335 industrial corporations among the top 500 nonfinancials. Of these, Larner found 89, or 27%, controlled through ownership; 19, or 6%, through ownership via a legal device; and another 2, or 1%, "unknown" which he believes likely to be privately owned. Fourteen of the "bank-controlled" corporations found by Patman among Larner's management-controlled corporations are industrials. Three of Larner's firms that he classified under management control but thinks are family controlled are also industrials. All 17 of the *Fortune* (Sheehan 1966) privately owned firms are industrials. This makes 144. We do not know (nor would *Fortune* provide the information when asked) the industrial classification of the 52 corporations *Fortune* (Sheehan 1967) found under proprietary control. Were they all industrials, 196, or 59% of the 335 top industrial corporations in the United States would be classified as controlled by identifiable individuals, families, or banks.

American Journal of Sociology

Moreover, these findings do not consider "any of the various coalitions that may indeed assure working control for small groups in many companies" (Sheehan 1967). (For example, another six corporations which Larner classified under "management control" were found by the Patman investigators to have a group of two or three banks holding 10% or more of the common stock between them.) Indeed, the official sources of information ordinarily relied on in such investigations are highly unlikely to permit discovery of such coalitions. These coalitions, moreover, can scarcely be revealed by residual definitional modes of analysis which merely classify by exclusion those corporations as management controlled in which no specified minimum proportion of shares has been found in the hands of a single individual or cohesive group. Genuine disclosure would require an investigation into the recent history of the corporation, and, perhaps, "inside information" which is not immediately accessible. At the least, information on critical phases of the founding, promotion, and expansion (or mergers) of the corporation—and the place in the present structure of control of individuals and families that played important roles during these phases—is needed to identify the implications of given shareholdings (Sweezy 1953, p. 160). Not since the NRC investigation of "interest groups in the American economy" has such a study been done in the United States.

However, most recently a very important study has been done which attempted—paradoxically—to systematically mine the publicly available "inside information" on the controlling interests in America's largest industrial corporations. Our own reference to *Fortune* and the *New York Times* (Sheehan 1966, 1967; Murphy 1967; Jensen 1971) has already indicated their possible value as sources of "publicly available inside information." Thus, Philip Burch "searched carefully" through *Fortune, Time, Business Week, Forbes* and the business section of the *New York Times* over the period dating roughly from 1950 to 1971 in order to collect the information these business media contained on any of the 300 largest manufacturing and mining corporations (plus the next 200 largest less intensively) as well as the top 50 merchandising and transportation companies. He supplemented this information by *Moody's* manuals and Standard and Poor's *Corporation Records,* as well as SEC reports, though he found these of less use. "The results of this research and analysis," according to Burch (1972), "show a marked difference in stock ownership totals as contrasted with those arrived at through examination" of the SEC's *Official Summary of Securities Transactions and Holdings.* He found "disparities of very sizeable proportions" and is "of the firm opinion that the higher figures [using his business sources] are the more accurate ones" (pp. 25–27). He did a "company-by-company analysis of the control status of most [300] of America's large corpora-

Corporate Ownership and Control

tions . . . as of the mid 1960's" (p. 29); classified the corporations, ranked by *Fortune*'s figures on sales, into three categories, "probably management control," "possibly family control," and "probably family control"; and he found that only among the 50 largest industrial corporations did his category of "probably management control" bulk largest, with 58% of them falling in that category. Of the total top 300, he found that 40% probably were under management control, 45% were probably under family control, and 15% *possibly* under family control (p. 70). Burch considers these "conservative figures," and it is his opinion that "they represent the most reliable findings that can be assembled on this difficult and important subject without resort to governmental subpoena and investigatory powers," and notes further that his study took no account of "vast blocks of corporate stock held by the big institutional investors, particularly the top 50 commercial banks and trust companies" (p. 17).

These findings obviously contradict the received view that the largest corporations are virtually all under management control—and which Larner purportedly showed in his own recent study. One question, then, aside from Burch's use of business sources not utilized systematically before, is by what criteria Burch classified the corporations under probable family control. Two conditions had to be met: (1) "that approximately 4%–5% or more of the voting stock was held by a family, group of families, or some affluent individual" according to one or more of his sources; and (2) that he found representation "on the part of a family on the board of directors of a company, generally over an extended period of time" (Burch 1972, pp. 29–30). Whether this is a more or less valid index of proprietary control than using 10% as the required minimum (and using predominately official sources whose reliability has been shown to be questionable) cannot be determined in any simple manner—precisely because we have no independent criteria by which to measure "control" other than by the whole variety of hints, clues, and solid information we can get on the actual proprietary interests in a given corporation.

THE CONCEPT OF CONTROL

In short, how "control" is conceptualized is a critical question—apart from the problem of obtaining reliable and valid information. Following Berle and Means, "control" has generally been defined to refer to the "actual power to select the board of directors (or its majority)," although control may also "be exercised *not* through the *selection* of directors, but through *dictation* to the management, as where a bank determines the policy of a corporation seriously indebted to it" (Berle and Means 1967, p. 66; italics added). Thus control refers to the "*power* of determining

American Journal of Sociology

the broad policies guiding a corporation and not to . . . the actual influence on the day to day affairs of an enterprise" (Goldsmith and Parmelee
1940, pp. 99–100; italics added). Control is not business management,
or what Gordon (1966) has termed "business leadership" (p. 150). This
would seem to be clear conceptually. However, in practice Berle and
Means and their followers have simply assumed away the analytical issues
by their operational definitions. They have merely assumed, rather than
demonstrated, that once a cohesive ownership interest having at least
a minimum specified proportion of the stock (whether 20% as in the
original Berle and Means work or the current 10% criterion) disappears,
the corporation slips imperceptibly and inevitably under "management
control." At this point, presumably, the top officers, given the wide dispersion of stock among small shareowners and the officers' control of the
proxy machinery, become capable of nominating and electing a compliant
and subservient board of directors, of perpetuating themselves in office,
and of abrogating, thereby, the control of proprietary interests (Gordon
1966, pp. 121–22; Larner 1970, p. 3; *Business Week*, May 22, 1971,
p. 54). "In the mature corporation," as Galbraith (1968) sums it up,
"the stockholders are without power; the Board of Directors is normally
the passive instrument of the management" (pp. 59, 90–95).

However, as I have emphasized repeatedly, it is necessary to study
the concrete situation within the corporation and the constellation of
intercorporate relationships in which it is involved before one can begin
to understand where control is actually located. The Berle and Means
method of investigation, the definitions and procedures utilized, do not,
in fact, even begin to accord with the actual content of their own concept. For this reason, it seems advisable to conceptualize control in such
a way as to link it inextricably with a method that is not reducible to a
single criterion, such as a minimum percentage of stock held by a single
minority bloc, but which requires instead a variety of interrelated yet
independent indicators. The modalities of corporate control utilized by
specific individuals and/or families and/or groups of associates differ
considerably, vary in complexity, and are not easily categorized. Our
concept of control must, therefore, compel attention to essential relationships. No less than the generic sociological concept of power, the concept
of control, as Berle and Means (1967) themselves put it, is elusive, "for
power can rarely be sharply segregated or clearly defined" (p. 66). The
relationship between the actual locus of control, formal authority (bureaucratic executive posts), and legal rights (shareownership) is problematic. If control refers to the capacity to determine the broad policies of
a corporation, then it refers to a social relationship, not an attribute.
Control (or power) is essentially relative and relational: how much
power, with respect to whom? (cf. Wrong 1968, p. 679; Etzioni 1968,

Corporate Ownership and Control

pp. 314–15). Therefore, control is conceptualized here as follows: when the concrete structure of ownership and of intercorporate relationships makes it probable that an identifiable group of proprietary interests will be able to realize their corporate objectives over time, despite resistance, then we may say that they have "control" of the corporation (cf. Weber 1968, p. 926). To estimate the probability that a given individual or group controls a corporation, then, we must know who the rivals or potential rivals for control are and what assets they can bring to the struggle.

This has two obvious implications concerning the study of corporate control: it means that a specific minority percentage of ownership in itself can tell us little about the potential for control that it represents. We can discover this only by a case study of the pattern of ownership within the given corporation. However, it also means that confining our attention to the single corporation may, in fact, limit our ability to see the pattern of power relationships of which this corporation is merely one element; and it may restrict our understanding of the potential for control represented by a specific bloc of shares in a particular corporation. An individual or group's capacity for control increases correspondingly, depending upon how many other large corporations (including banks and other financial institutions) in which it has a dominant, if not controlling, position. The very same quantitative proportion of stock may have a qualitatively different significance, depending on the system of intercorporate relationships in which the corporation is implicated.

Of course, our reference here is to "structural" analysis rather than "behavioral" analysis of actual "struggles for control." Even such struggles, however, can rarely provide real insight concerning the question of control without the type of analysis emphasized here. Otherwise, one cannot know who the contending powers actually are—what may look like a "proxy fight" between "management" and certain shareowners, may, in fact, be a struggle between contending proprietary interests. The latter type of research, therefore, also requires the former, if it is to provide valid and reliable findings.

There remains the question as to what "broad corporate policies or objectives" are—over which control is to be exercised. I have found no usable definition in my studies of the writings on this question. Nor am I convinced it is amenable to definition apart from a specific theoretical framework in which it is conceptualized. We must have a theory of the objective necessities of corporate conduct and the imperatives of the political economy—and to attempt to outline such a theory here would take us rather far afield from the focus of this article. However, such questions as the following would be essential: what relationships must the corporations in an oligopolistic economy establish with each other?

American Journal of Sociology

with the state? with foreign governments? with the workers? with sources of raw materials and markets? What common problems, which their very interaction creates, must they resolve? Then we may ask whether the individuals who actually decide among proposed long-range strategies and determine the "broad policies and objectives" of the corporations are merely members of "management."

We know, for instance, that the largest corporations in the United States are now typically "multinational" or "transnational" in the sense that the "sheer size of their foreign commitment," as *Fortune* puts it (Rose 1968, p. 101), and the "extent of their involvements is such that, to some degree, these companies now regard the world rather than the nation state as their natural and logical operating area." Is it the "managements" of these corporations that determine their broad policies? Or do the individuals, families, and other principal proprietary interests with the greatest material stake in these corporations impose their conceptions of the issues and demand that their objectives are pursued in order to maintain the "world . . . as their natural and logical operating area"? Here, clearly, we verge, once again, on the class questions raised at the outset of this article. To take a more limited issue, however: many of the multinational corporations face increasing risk of nationalization of their foreign properties. "Management" may plan for such contingencies, exercise their "discretion," and decide on the tactics to be adopted. When their planning goes awry or proves ineffective, however, must the management answer to their corporation's principal shareowners and other proprietary interests (such as banks) or not? Having left management in charge of the everyday operations of the corporations abroad, with little or no interference, do the principal proprietary interests have the power to interfere when deemed necessary? Without an analysis of concrete situations and the specific control structure of the corporations involved, we cannot answer such questions—though occasionally particular events momentarily illuminate the actual relationships involved (though they may still remain largely in the shadows). Thus, for example, the Chilean properties of Kennecott Copper Corporation and Anaconda Company were recently (1971) nationalized in Chile. These two corporations, which owned the major copper mines of Chile, had adopted different long-range strategies to deal with the rising probability of nationalization. We cannot explore the details here, but suffice it to say that Kennecott's strategy was reportedly aimed at insuring, as Robert Haldeman, executive vice-president of Kennecott's Chilean operations explained, "that nobody expropriates Kennecott without upsetting customers, creditors, and governments on three continents" (Moran 1973, pp. 279–80). Kennecott was able to "expand very profitably in the late 1960's with no

Corporate Ownership and Control

new risk to itself and to leave, after the nationalization in 1971, with compensation greater than the net worth of its holdings had been in 1964. In contrast, Anaconda, which had not spread its risk or protected itself through a strategy of building transnational alliances, lost its old holdings, lost the new capital it committed during the Frei regime [preceding Allende's socialist administration], and was nationalized in 1971 without any hope of compensation" (Moran 1973, pp. 280–81).[12]

Now, according to Berle and Means (1967, p. 104) and Larner (1970, pp. 74–79), both Kennecott and Anaconda have long been under "management control." In Kennecott's case, there is relatively persuasive evidence that it is, in fact, probably controlled by the Guggenheim family and associated interests rather than by "management."[13] Whether this is

[12] The destruction of the constitutional government and parliamentary democracy of Chile, and the death of her Marxist president, Dr. Salvador Allende, at the hands of the armed forces on September 11, 1973, has once again given Anaconda (and other foreign corporations) "hope of compensation." The military regime's foreign minister, Adm. Ismael Huerta, announced within a week of the coup, that the " 'door was open' for resumption of negotiations on compensation for United States copper holdings nationalized by President Allende" (*New York Times,* September 30, 1973, p. 14).

[13] Kennecott illustrates well our insistence on the importance of knowledge of a corporation's critical historic phases in disclosing the actual locus of control. The Guggenheim interests bought control of the El Teniente copper mine from the Braden Copper Company in 1908; in 1915 they sold it to the Kennecott Copper Corporation, in which Guggenheim Brothers was the controlling stockholder. In 1923, Utah Copper, in which the Guggenheims had a minority interest, also purchased a large bloc of Kennecott's shares (Hoyt 1967, p. 263). Yet for Berle and Means (1967) only six years later (their data were for 1929) Kennecott was "presumably under management control" (p. 104). When World War II began, as a historian close to the Guggenheim family has written, "the Guggenheims created a new Kennecott Copper Corporation, which would have three million shares. This corporation bought up the Guggenheim copper holdings," including 25% of Utah Copper Company's stock, and controlling interests in Copper River Railroad and other "Alaska syndicate holdings" (Hoyt 1967, p. 263). The Guggenheim Brothers also had (until purchased recently by the Allende government) the controlling interest in Chile's Anglo-Lautaro Nitrate Company, organized in 1931 out of previous nitrate holdings controlled by the Guggenheims (Lomask 1964, p. 281) and reorganized in 1951 by Harry Guggenheim (a senior partner of Guggenheim Brothers), to bring in two other smaller Guggenheim-controlled firms. Guggenheim presided as board chairman and chief executive officer of Anglo-Lautaro until his retirement in 1962. Previously, he had been "absent from the family business for a quarter of a century," until in 1949 his uncle enjoined him to reorganize Guggenheim Brothers (Lomask 1964, p. 65). In 1959 the Guggenheim Exploration Company, one of whose partners was a director of Kennecott Copper Corporation in which "the Guggenheim foundations" now also held large holdings, was also revived (Lomask 1964, p. 281). The son of one of the original Guggenheim brothers (Edmond A., son of Murry) "maintained an active interest in Kennecott Corporation" as a director (Lomask 1964, p. 295), while Peter Lawson-Johnston, a grandson of Solomon Guggenheim, was, as of 1966, a partner in Guggenheim Brothers, a director of the advisory board of Anglo-Lautaro, a director of Kennecott, a director of Minerec Corporation, the vice-president of Elgerbar Cor-

American Journal of Sociology

so or not, Kennecott's "successful tactics" in Chile did not test the reality
of its alleged control by management. However, Anaconda's "management" was submitted to a rather clear test of the extent to which it had
control. Within two months after the Chilean government "intervened"
in Anaconda's properties and a month after it took over Anaconda Sales
Corporation's control of copper sales, it was announced in the *New York
Times* (May 14, 1971, p. 55) that Mr. John B. Place, a director of
Anaconda, and a vice-chairman of the Chase Manhattan Bank (one of
its four top officers, along with David Rockefeller, chairman, and the
president and another vice-chairman) was to become the new chief
executive officer of the Anaconda Company. (Other Anaconda directors
who were bankers included James D. Farley, an executive vice-president
of First National City Bank, and Robert V. Roosa, a partner in Brown
Brothers, Harriman and Company.) As the *New York Times* reporter
(Walker 1971) explained, Mr. Place had no mining expertise ("it is
assumed he would not know a head frame from a drag line"), and though
he had been an Anaconda director since 1969, he "lives in the East and
has never attended the annual [stockholders] meeting held regularly in
Butte, Montana," where Anaconda's most important American copper
mines are located. In the wake of this Chase Manhattan officer's installation as Anaconda's chief executive officer, "at least 50% of the corporate
staff," including John G. Hall, Anaconda's former president, "were fired.
Chairman [C. Jay] Parkinson took early retirement" (*Business Week*,
February 19, 1972, p. 55). The decimation of Anaconda's allegedly controlling management illustrates the general proposition that those who
really have control can decide when, where, and with respect to what
issues and corporate policies they will intervene to exercise their power.

PROFIT MAXIMIZATION?

Fortunately, some issues to which the question of control is relevant are
somewhat more amenable to systematic, even quantitative, analysis than
the ones just posed. Chief among these, which has occupied considerable
theoretical, but little empirical, attention, is the proposition concerning
"managerial discretion" (see and cf. Baumol 1959; Kaysen 1957, 1965;
Marris 1963, 1964; Gordon 1966; Galbraith 1968; Simon 1957; Williamson 1963, 1970). It posits different motives and conduct for managers
than owners, and, thereby, differences in the profit orientations of owner-

poration, and the trustee of three Guggenheim foundations (Hoyt 1967, p. 348). In
the period from roughly 1955 to 1965, Burch (1972, p. 48) found Kennecott had
"significant family representation as outside members of the board of directors," and
concluded it was under "possibly" Guggenheim family control. This is certainly a
cautious understatement, given the historic evidence presented here, drawn from
works by two writers close to the Guggenheim family.

Corporate Ownership and Control

controlled versus management-controlled corporations. "The development of the large corporation," as Gordon puts it (1966), "has obviously affected the goals of business decision-making. . . . It clearly leads to greater emphasis on the non-profit goals of interest groups other than the stockholders," such as the management. The executives "do not receive the profits which may result from taking a chance, while their position in the firm may be jeopardized in the event of serious loss" (pp. xii, 324). Dahrendorf has stated the proposition succinctly. In his view (1959), the separation of ownership and control "produces two sets of roles the incumbents of which *increasingly move apart* in their outlooks on and attitudes toward society in general and toward the enterprise in particular. . . . Never has the imputation of a profit motive been further from the real motives of men than it is for modern bureaucratic managers. Economically, managers are interested in such things as rentability, efficiency and productivity" (p. 46; italics added). This is an oft-asserted but rarely investigated proposition, on which Larner has recently provided systematic negative evidence. Drawing on his study of the separation of ownership and control, he found the following: using multiple-regression analysis and taking into account assets, industrial concentration, Federal Reserve Board indices of economywide growth and fluctuation of profit rates, and equity-asset ratios, Larner found that the rate of profit earned by "management" and "owner"-controlled firms was about the same; both were equally profit oriented. Second, the evidence on fluctuations in profit rates suggested no support for the view that allegedly nonowning managements avoid risk taking more than owners do. Third, Larner found that the corporation's dollar profit and rate of return on equity were the major determinants of the level of "executive compensation." Compensation of executives, he concluded, has been "effectively harnessed" to the stockholders' interests in profits. In Larner's words, "Although control is separated from ownership in most of America's largest corporation, the effects on the profit orientations of firms, and on stockholders' welfare have been minor. The magnitude of the effects," he concluded (1970), "appears to be too small to justify the considerable attention they have received in the literature of the past thirty-eight years" (p. 66).[14]

[14] Similar findings are reported in Kamerschen (1968, 1969), Hindley (1970), and Lewellen and Huntsman (1970). Contrary findings, which show small but statistically significant differences in profit rates between allegedly owner-controlled and allegedly management-controlled corporations, appear in Monsen, Chiu, and Cooley (1968). The study by Lewellen and Huntsman (1970) differed from the others cited here, since no attempt was made to contrast performance by owner versus management-controlled corporations. Their focus was on the specific question of whether a corporation's profitability or its sales revenue more strongly determined the rewards of its senior officers. By means of a multivariate analysis, they found that "both reported profits and equity market values are substantially more important in the determination of executive compensation than are sales—indeed, sales seem to be quite

American Journal of Sociology

Larner's findings contradict managerial theory, but are consistent both with neoclassical and neo-Marxian reasoning concerning corporate conduct: even where management is, in fact, in control, it is compelled to engage in a "systematic temporal search for highest practicable profits" (Earley 1957, p. 333). The conduct of the large corporation, in this view, whether under management control or ownership control, is largely determined by the market structure—the nature of competition, products produced, and the constraints of the capital markets (Peterson 1965, pp. 9–14; O'Connor 1971, p. 145). Growth, sales, technical efficiency, a strong competitive position are at once inseparable managerial goals and the determinants of high corporate profits—which, in turn, are the prerequisites of high managerial income and status (Earley 1956, 1957; Alchian 1968, p. 186; Sheehan 1967, p. 242; Baran and Sweezy 1966, pp. 33–34). Management need not spend "much of its time contemplating profits as such" (Peterson 1965, p. 9), so long as its decisions on pricing and sales and on the planning and organization of production must be measured against and not imperil corporate profitability. "This," argues Peterson, "is the essence of profit-seeking and of capitalist behavior in employing resources." Significant deviation from profit-maximizing behavior also

---

irrelevant—[and] the clear inference is that there is a greater incentive for management to shape its decision rules in a manner consonant with shareholder interests than to seek the alternative goal of revenue maximization" (pp. 718–19). The use of multiple-regression analysis (Larner) or analysis of variance (Monsen) does not resolve the problem of causation (time-order). It merely shows, at one point in time, how corporations classified under different types of control differ on selected variables. It might plausibly be argued that a control group, whether an individual, family, or coalition of business associates, might gradually dispose of its holdings in a corporation precisely because its profit performance was not satisfactory over a period of time—for reasons not connected to how it was managed. This might be particularly the case for small control groups, to whom not the corporation's profits as such but the dividend yield and price appreciation of their stockholdings ("combined return") is primary. Thus, a finding that owner-controlled corporations were more profitable than management-controlled corporations (assuming the latter exist) might simply mean that control groups do their best to retain control of the more profitable corporations and get out of those that are less profitable. A genuine causal study requires information on changes over time in types of control and in corporate performance. Unfortunately, the nature of the data available probably precludes such a study. Are the same corporations that were once owner controlled, more or less profitable once they come under management control? Take an extreme example. In 1923, Guggenheim Brothers sold control of Chile Copper Company, whose major asset was the Chuquicamata mine in Chile, to the Anaconda Copper Company, headed by John D. Ryan. The family was split over this issue: some of them thought that this would become an extraordinary profit-yielding asset—as it did; others were for accepting the immediate profits to be made by Ryan's offering price of $70 million for the controlling interest. The result was that, although they sold the controlling interest, the family retained a large block of stock as an investment (Hoyt 1967, pp. 258, 263). Did the loss of "family control" and its acquisition by Anaconda result in lessening effort at profit maximization in the Chile Copper Company? Posed in this way, the question appears (at least to me) to be rhetorical, though, of course, it is empirical.

Corporate Ownership and Control

would lead to the lowering of the market price of the corporation's stock and make it an attractive and vulnerable target for takeover—and the displacement of the incumbent management (Manne 1965; *Business Week,* May 22, 1971, p. 55). Furthermore, some economists have suggested that professional management, particularly the use of "scientific budgetary planning" and the emphasis on the "time-value of money" (Earley 1956; Earley and Carleton 1962; Tanzer 1969, pp. 32–34), strengthens, rather than weakens, the drive toward profit maximization. Whether or not managers are actuated by the "profit motive," as a subjective value commitment, "profit maximization" is an objective requirement, since profits constitute both the only unambiguous criterion of successful managerial performance and an irreducible necessity for corporate survival (Peterson 1965; Tanzer 1969, pp. 30–32). In the words of Robin Williams, Jr. (1959), "the separation of ownership and control shows that the 'profit motive' is not a *motive* at all . . . ; it is not a psychological state but a social condition" (p. 184).

This reasoning is persuasive and consistent with the findings that purportedly management-controlled and owner-controlled corporations are similarly profit oriented, and that profits and stock market values determine executive compensation. However, once again the difficulty is that since independent investigations concerning the control of the large corporations, including the two most recent and exhaustive studies by Larner and Burch, have come to very different conclusions, we cannot know if the "independent variable" has even been adequately measured. In reality, the allegedly management-controlled corporations may—appearances aside—continue to be subject to control by minority ownership interests and/or "outside" centers of control.

ENTANGLING KINSHIP RELATIONS AND SPHERES OF INFLUENCE

The problem is further complicated if, in fact, a number of seemingly independent corporations are under common control. Few today consider the concept of the "interest group" or "financial group" or "family sphere of influence" relevant to the workings of the large corporations. Indeed, Paul M. Sweezy (Baran and Sweezy 1966, pp. 17–20) has discarded the concept also, as noted earlier, although he was the principal author of the investigation for the NRC (1939) which provided one of the *two* most authoritative studies (the other by the TNEC) of the question to date (Goldsmith and Parmelee 1940, chap. 7). However, we know that the very object of such groups, as they were relatively well documented in the past, "is to combine the constituent companies into a system in such a way as to maximize the profits of the entire system irrespective of the profits of each separate unit," as Gardiner Means himself long ago pointed

American Journal of Sociology

out (Bonbright and Means 1932, pp. 45–46). Much as in the multi-national corporation's relations with its affiliates and subsidiaries, the constituent corporations in a group may adjust intercorporate dealings in such a way as to raise or diminish the profit rates of the different ostensibly independent corporations (cf. Rose 1968, p. 101; Tanzer 1969, pp. 14 ff.). Under such circumstances, studies attempting to compare the conduct of corporations, several of which may in fact be involved in different groups to which their policies are subordinated, cannot provide valid or reliable results. We cannot be certain what is being measured.

In the United States today, the Mellons and DuPonts are among the most publicized instances of enduring "family spheres of influence." The TNEC found the Mellon "family . . . to have considerable shareholdings in 17 of the 200 corporations, 7 of which they controlled directly or indirectly" (Goldsmith and Parmelee 1940, p. 123). Today, according to *Fortune* (Murphy 1967; see also Jensen 1971) the Mellons, utilizing "various connections, and through a complicated structure of family and charitable trusts and foundations" and other "eleemosynary arrangements," have known controlling interests in at least four of the 500 largest nonfinancial corporations (Gulf Oil, Alcoa, Koppers Company, and Carborundum Company), as well as the First Boston Corporation, the General Reinsurance Corporation, and the Mellon National Bank and Trust Company (the fifteenth largest United States bank by deposits [Patman Report 1968, p. 79]). In turn (according to the Patman Report [1968], p. 14), Mellon National Bank holds 6.9% of the common stock in Jones and Laughlin Steel, another of the top 500.[15] It seems as reasonable to hypothesize that the Mellons are only instances of a less visible but prevalent situation among principal proprietary families as to assume they are "deviant cases" or historical vestiges. Morever, given such family "spheres of influence" which radiate out among several large corporations, it should be understood that the same small proportion of the stock in the hands of such a family in a specific corporation carries different implications and potential for control than when held by a

---

[15] Jones and Laughlin Steel was classified under "management control" by Larner. Aside from the 6.9% Mellon National Bank holding, the Bank also has two directors on the Company's Board. Koppers Company, in which *Fortune* (Murphy 1967) claims the Mellons held at least 20%, was also classified as under "management control" by Larner, indicating the difficulty of locating "control" without access to "street knowledge" or insiders. This emphasizes again the secrecy in which holdings are shrouded and the fact that insufficient account of this is taken when considering "findings" about control centers. Larner himself notes, though without considering its possible general significance, that the Alcoa mandatory 10-K report filed with the SEC in 1963 states that no shareholder has more than 10% of the outstanding common shares, although from the proxy report and other sources he concluded that Alcoa was under Mellon control. *Fortune* (Murphy 1967) and the *New York Times* (Jensen 1971) estimate Mellon interests in Alcoa at 30%.

Corporate Ownership and Control

single individual with no other major resources and institutions to buttress his position. It is known that a great number of related individuals may participate in the ownership of a family bloc, utilizing a complex holding pattern to keep control concentrated, despite the diffusion of ownership. If control is exercised through entangling interests in several interrelated corporations, rather than limited to one, then such kinship information is vital to an understanding of the control structure. Indeed, the kinship relations between the top officers, directors, and principal shareholders of the large corporations (and banks) are the least studied but may be the most crucial aspect of the control structure.[16]

BANK CONTROL?

The banks are major institutional bases of economic power and corporate control which the managerialists, from Berle and Means to John Kenneth Galbraith, either have ignored or considered unimportant. Offering no substantial evidence to support his assertion, Gordon (1966) recently restated (in a new preface to his original study of the situation as of the 1930s) the accepted view that "large-scale industry is much less dependent on the banking community than it was a half-century ago, and such power as bankers have is less likely to be translated into corporate control than was true then" (p. ix). Noting the extensive interlocking between the largest banks and corporations, he simply claims that this is a "far cry from what was once meant by 'financial control' " (p. x). What implications such interlocking might have, Gordon fails to suggest. Galbraith's (1968) "commonplace observation" is that "the social magnetism of the banker" is "dwindling," and that the largest corporations are emancipated from reliance on bankers and outside sources of financing because they now have a source of their own capital, derived from their earnings, and "wholly under [their] own control" (pp. 68, 92).

   Contrary to Galbraith's commonplace observations, however, uncommon but systematic research on the question does not seem to indicate

[16] Larner's own statements in his notes on sources occasionally suggest how important, if not vital, is such kinship information if we are successfully to locate the actual centers of corporate control. Thus, for instance, Larner (1970) refers to *Moody's Industrials* as the source of his information that in the Dow Chemical Company, which he classified under "minority control," there were "78 dependents (plus spouses) of H. W. Dow [who] owned 12.6% of [the] outstanding common stock" (p. 75). Similar references were made to the Newberry Company, Cabot Corporation, and R. R. Donnelly & Sons Company, in which the descendants and kindred through marriage of the original founder are taken into account in establishing the share of these families in ownership. Clearly, systematic independent research of this type into the kinship interconnections of the principal shareowners, officers, and directors of the 500 largest corporations has not yet been done by anyone purporting to locate their centers of control. The outstanding recent unsystematic attempt to do this is, once again, the work of Ferdinand Lundberg (1968, chaps. 4–6).

American Journal of Sociology

decreased corporate dependence on external funds. For all U.S. firms
whose assets exceed $5 million, John Lintner (1967) reports that "the
dependence on outside liabilities for financing is about the same regardless of the size of the firm" and that the "relative shifts in the reliance on
internal or external funds . . . have been remarkably stable over a full
half century" (pp. 179, 184). The Federal Reserve Bank of San Francisco
reports a sharp increase in the past decade in reliance on external funds
for financing, and if the bank's data is reanalyzed to exclude depreciation
allowances—on the premise that only profits can be used to finance net
investments to increase the firm's capital stock—the reported trend is
even more clearly toward dependence on external financing. Most important, the largest corporations are found to be least self-financing (cited in
Fitch and Oppenheimer 1970, no. 1, pp. 68 ff.).

If, contrary to managerialist assumptions, the large corporations must
continue to rely on the capital market no less than in the past, this is
of critical importance: since the distribution of banking assets and deposits is highly skewed, this means that "reliance on external financing" is,
in fact, dependence on a small number of very large financial corporations.
As of 1964, the 100 largest commercial banks in the United States held
46% of all the deposits of the 13,775 commercial banks in the country.
The 14 largest alone, representing one-tenth of 1% of all commercial
banks, held 24% of all commercial bank deposits (Patman Report 1966,
p. 804). Thus, the relationships between the large banks and corporations
are essential to our understanding of the locus of corporate control.
Where it might otherwise appear as if, lacking a visible controlling ownership interest, a corporation is under "management control," it may, on the
contrary, be under the control of one or more banks and other financial
institutions. Even in corporations in which a substantial minority of the
stock (or even majority) is held by an identifiable ownership interest,
this may not assure control: if the corporation has a long-term debt to
a given bank or insurance company, has that institution's representatives
on its board, and must receive prior approval of significant financial and
investment decisions, then control of that corporation may be exerted
from the "outside"; and this may be accentuated if several related financial institutions have a similar interest in that corporation. (The dismissal under the "prodding" of its bankers of Anaconda's chief executive
officer and other top officers—discussed earlier—when their performance
in Chile turned out to be inferior to Kennecott's and had led, in any case,
to the company's deteriorating situation, seems to be a case in point [see
Business Week, February 19, 1972, pp. 54–55]).

Whatever the dwindling "social magnetism" of the banker divined by
Galbraith, this may be a questionable indicator of his economic power.
Indeed, the Patman Committee, which gathered unprecedented informa-

Corporate Ownership and Control

tion on the stockownership of large commercial banks, believes the power of the banks is growing. The committee found a ". . . pattern of control whereby large blocks of stock in the largest *non*financial corporations in the country are becoming controlled by some of the largest financial corporations in the country. "This," the Patman Committee concludes, "is shifting economic power back to a small group, repeating in somewhat different manner the pattern of the trusts of the late nineteenth and early twentieth centuries." This "emerging situation" appears to the committee to be one involving increasing "bank minority control." The committee found that the largest banks surveyed in 10 major cities, not including the West Coast, hold 5% or more of the common stock in 147 (29%) of the 500 largest industrial corporations. At least 5% of the common stock of 17 of the 50 largest merchandising companies and the same number of transportation companies is held by one or more of the 49 banks. These 49 banks are also represented on the boards of directors of 286 of the 500 largest industrial corporations. The same pattern appears among the 50 largest merchandising, utilities, transportation, and insurance companies (Patman Report 1968, p. 13). Whether or not, and to what extent, such fusion of financial and industrial capital indicates "financial" or "bank control" is an open question. However, it cannot be ignored if we want to understand its implications. Thus, Peter C. Dooley (1969) found that precisely those corporations—the largest ones—which the managerialists claim to be most independent of the banks, are in fact, most closely interlocked with large banks and other financial corporations. Among the 200 largest nonfinancial corporations, the greater the assets of the nonfinancial corporation, the greater the incidence of interlocks between them and the 50 largest financial corporations (32 banks and 18 insurance companies) (p. 318).

This may mean that the conceptualization of the largest corporations, banks, and insurance companies as independent institutions may obscure the actual coalescence of financial and industrial capital which has occurred. On the one hand, as noted above, large banks and insurance companies frequently are themselves principal shareholders in the large corporations. On the other, the very same individuals and families may be principal shareowners in large banks and large corporations, even when these do not have institutional holdings in one another. Aside from the Mellons, with controlling interests in at least four of the 500 largest nonfinancial corporations and in an investment bank, insurance company, and the fifteenth largest commercial bank, whom we noted above, other well-known industrialist families in the United States may be cited who also have dominant and/or controlling interests in the largest banks. For example, there are both branches of the Rockefeller families, as well as other principal families in the Standard Oil corporations. The Rockefel-

American Journal of Sociology

lers and associates reportedly (*Time,* September 7, 1962; Abels 1965, p. 358) held over 5% of the stock in the Chase Manhattan Bank (ranking second by deposits of all banks in 1963),[17] whose chairman of the board is David Rockefeller; the Stillman-Rockefeller families and associates are said to be dominant in the First National City Bank (ranking third in 1963) (*Fortune,* September 1965, p. 138). The Fisher and Mott families, among the principal shareowning families in General Motors, reportedly held over 5% of the stock of the National Bank of Detroit (U.S. Congress, 1963, pp. 227, 416), the country's sixteenth largest bank in 1963. The Henry Ford family owns 4% of the thirtieth ranking Manufacturer's National which, in turn, owns 7% of Ford Motor Company common stock (Patman Report 1968, p. 664). The M. A. Hanna family that controls at least two the 500 largest corporations, National Steel and Consolidation Coal (Larner 1970, p. 120; Burch 1972, p. 58), has a dominant minority interest of at least 3% in the thirty-fourth ranking National City Bank of Cleveland (U.S. Congress 1963, p. 165), which, in turn, holds 11% of the stock of Hanna Mining Company. These are, of course, merely instances, as I said, of prominent families whose interests overlap banking and industry. They illustrate the general theoretical issue, however, of the extent to which it is valid to speak at all of "bank control" of "industry"—as does the Patman Report, for instance, or other recent writers (Fitch and Oppenheimer 1970). Rather, these families' interests transcend the banks and corporations in which they have principal or controlling interests; and the banks may merely be units in, and instrumentalities of, the whole system of propertied interests controlled by these major capitalist families.

There appears, in fact, to be a special segment of the corporate world which represents the fusion of financial and industrial capital, to which Rudolf Hilferding (1910, chap. 23) long ago called attention, and whom he termed "finance capitalists" (cf. also Schumpeter 1955*b*, pp. 80–81; Lenin 1967, chap. 3; Sweezy 1942, pp. 261, 266). Hilferding was referring to "a circle of persons who, thanks to their own possession of capital or as representatives of concentrated power over other people's capital (bank directors), sit upon the governing boards of a large number of corporations. Thus, there arises a kind of personal union, on the one hand, between the different corporations themselves, [and,] on the other, between the latter and the banks, a circumstance which must be of the greatest importance for the policy of these institutions since a community

[17] The 1963 rankings are given since this was the year of the House Select Committee's study. The source of the rankings is the *Fortune Directory for 1963.* The latest rankings by *Fortune* (July 1973) for 1972 are Mellon, 15; Chase, 3; First National City, 2; National Bank of Detroit, 18; National City Bank of Cleveland, 49.

Corporate Ownership and Control

of interests has arisen among them" (Hilferding [1910], as slightly reworded from the translation by Sweezy [1956], p. 261).

Do such "finance capitalists" or representatives of banks who sit on the boards of the large American corporations today, have a special role in coordinating the interests of these corporations? Do they differ, for example, from other outside directors that interlock the largest corporations between themselves, as well as with other firms? These are critical questions, which no single indicator can suffice to answer. We would need information concerning their own propertied interests, their relative wealth, their kinship relations, before being able to ascertain whether the "finance capitalist" represents a special social type in contrast to other officers and directors of the largest corporations and banks. One relevant issue, however, on which we do have some information, is the extent to which they are likely to sit on a number of large nonfinancial corporation boards, compared with "outside directors" (i.e., those who do not actually hold posts as officers in the corporate management) who are not bankers. I have analyzed raw data presented elesewhere (Smith and Desfosses 1972) on interlocking directorates among the 500 largest

TABLE 2

PRINCIPAL EMPLOYER OF OUTSIDE DIRECTORS OF THE 500 LARGEST INDUSTRIAL
CORPORATIONS IN THE UNITED STATES IN 1968
(%)

TYPE OF PRINCIPAL EMPLOYER	NUMBER OF SEATS OCCUPIED						TOTAL
	1	2	3	4	5	6 plus	
Other top 500 firm	13.9	25.9	15.7	12.9	18.2	0	15.4
Law firm	14.1	10.3	3.4	3.2	9.1	0	13.0
Bank	18.5	25.8	41.6	45.1	45.5	80.0	20.9
Commercial	10.8	14.5	19.1	29.0	36.4	40.0	12.0
Investment	7.7	11.3	22.5	16.1	9.1	40.0	8.9
Consulting firm	6.3	6.0	1.1	6.5	0	0	6.0
Other*	47.3	32.0	38.2	32.3	27.2	20.0	44.7
Total %	100	100	100	100	100	100	100
Total N	1,932	282	89	31	11	5	2,350

SOURCES. Calculated from raw data given in Smith and Desfosses (1972, table 4, p. 65), on the composition of the outside directorships of the 500 largest industrials listed in *Fortune*, May 15, 1969, ranked by 1968 sales. Principal employer was obtained from information in the proxy statements of 460 corporations and from Standard and Poor's *Register of Corporations, Directors, and Executives*, 1970, for 35 corporations. Smith and Desfosses did not obtain information on five corporations.
* Types of employers which did not employ more than 5% of the total number of outside directors in the 500 largest industrials, including utilities; merchandising, insurance, real estate, railroad firms, as well as educational institutions, foundations, government agencies, plus "unlisted companies."

American Journal of Sociology

industrial corporations, ranked by sales, in 1968. What we find is that
commercial and investment bankers are disproportionately over represented among the occupants of multiple corporate directorships (table
2). Bankers constituted 21% of all outside directors in the 500 largest
industrials, but well over twice that proportion among the outside directors with seats on three or more corporate boards. Indeed, the proportion
of bankers who are outside directors rises directly with the number of
corporate posts held. And among the select few ($N = 16$) outside directors having five or more posts, 56% were bankers; of the five outside
directors with six or seven posts, four were bankers. Viewing the same
relationship differently (table 3), commercial and investment bankers

TABLE 3

NUMBER OF THE 500 LARGEST U.S. INDUSTRIAL CORPORATIONS ON WHOSE BOARDS
OUTSIDE DIRECTORS ARE REPRESENTED, BY TYPE OF PRINCIPAL EMPLOYER, 1968
(%)

	NUMBER OF SEATS OCCUPIED				
TYPE OF PRINCIPAL EMPLOYER	1	2	3	4 plus	(N)
Other top 500 firm	74	20	4	2	(361)
Law firm	89	9	1	1	(306)
Bank					
Commercial	75	15	6	5	(283)
Investment	71	15	10	4	(208)
Consulting firm	86	12	1	1	(141)
Other*	87	9	3	11	(1,051)
All outside directors	82	12	4	2	(2,350)

SOURCES.—See table 2.
* See table 2.

stand out in marked contrast to other outside directors in the top 500
corporations: a far higher proportion of them have multiple corporation
posts than do outside directors from other top 500 corporations, law firms,
consulting firms, or other types of companies and institutions. Outside
directors from other top 500 corporations are second only to the bankers
in the proportion with multiple directorships. But well over twice the
proportion of bankers occupy multiple posts: 11% of the commercial
bankers and 15% of the investment bankers have seats on three or more
top 500 corporate boards compared with 6% of the directors from other
top 500 firms.

WHO CONTROLS THE BANKS?

Who the controlling interests are in the largest banks is not publicly
known. The Select House Committee report on chain banking (1963) and

Corporate Ownership and Control

the Patman Reports (1964, 1966, 1967) for the first time provided an authoritative glance—however limited—inside. The 1963 and 1964 reports listed the 20 largest shareholdings of record (and the percentage of stock held) in each of the 200 largest commercial bank members of the Federal Reserve System in recent years. The 1966 Patman Report focused on commercial banks' holdings of their own shares and also listed the total market values (though without calculating the percentages) of the outstanding stock held by all financial institutions in the 300 largest commercial banks in 1966; and the 1967 Patman Report also focused on holdings in the banks by other financial institutions, particularly the major commercial banks in 10 metropolitan areas. The lists of the reported "beneficial owners" of the banks' shares obtained by the Patman Committee have not been released to date. With only the shareholdings of record available so far, the same difficulties arise here as has already been discussed earlier in detail. Any attempt to locate the actual ownership interests by identifying recognizable surnames alone, without knowledge of kinship relations, nominees, etc., cannot provide reliable and valid information. A recent study of this type, based on the 1963 Select Committee report, and utilizing the 10% minimum to define an ownership-controlled bank, came to the predictable conclusion that "management control had become the dominant form of control among the large member banks by 1962," accounting for 75% of the banks (Vernon 1970, p. 654). In contrast, Burch (1972) utilized other business sources of information cited earlier, as well as the 1963 Select Committee report, investigated representation on boards of directors, and consulted several family histories. However, like Vernon, he did not attempt any systematic investigation of kinship ties, so, once again, his are absolutely minimum estimates of control of these banks by ownership interests. He studied only the 50 largest, and concluded that 30% were probably under family control, another 22% possibly under family control, and 48% probably under management control (pp. 89–96). Vernon (1970) broke down his analysis into categories by total bank assets, rather than ranks, so no direct comparison is possible from their published reports. However, of the 27 largest banks having $1 billion in assets or more, he classified only two under "owner control," with the possible addition of another three in which he identified an interest greater than 5% but less than 10% (p. 655). Of the 27 largest banks listed by Burch, however, he classified eight as probably family controlled and four more as possibly family controlled. Once again the disparities in results by two different methods are striking. Other close students of the banks (aside from the Patman investigators [1968, p. 91] already cited) object to the ownership level of 10% as "arbitrary." Thus, Eisenbeis and McCall (1972), financial economists at the Federal Deposit Insurance Corporation, state that " 'minority con-

American Journal of Sociology

trol' can be achieved . . . through ownership of a much smaller proportion of stock than the arbitrary 10% levels" (p. 876).

In any event, the theoretical significance of such an alleged split between ownership and control in large banks was not suggested by Vernon, nor, to my knowledge, has any managerial theorist yet to suggest that the banks might somehow or other become non-profit-maximizing institutions, were they no longer under the control of specific ownership interests. Furthermore, neither Vernon nor Burch took account in their studies of the extent to which the banks themselves are interlocked and, most important, hold significant amounts of stock in each other. The Patman Committee (1966) did a survey, whose results have only been partially reported, which found that 57% of the 210 largest commercial banks hold more than 5% of their own shares and 29% hold more than 10% of their own shares. The banks (and other types of corporations) buy their own stock—sometimes termed "defensive buying" on Wall Street—to keep their shares out of the "unfriendly hands" of potential rivals for control.[18] If other financial institutions, including commercial banks, mutual savings banks, and insurance companies in which the same owning families appear among the principal shareholders, or which have long-standing business associations and common interests (including interlocks between banks and insurance companies), also hold the bank's stock, this further decreases the amount of stock which the principal individual and familial shareholders must own to maintain control. Nearly a third (30%) of the 275 large banks reported on by the Patman Committee had more than 10% of their shares which could be voted exclusively by other financial institutions. Nearly half (47%) had more than 5% of their shares similarly held (Patman Report 1966, p. 832). In addition, the extent and pattern of interlocking bank stockownership by the same principal shareowners is not known. Very preliminary data received by the Patman Committee found several "situations where the beneficial owners of large blocs of commercial bank stock are in fact holdings by a few families who have management connections with competitor banks in the same geographic area." Though banks may not legally interlock, officers and directors (and their families) of one bank may have principal shareholdings in other banks, and the preliminary data of the Patman Committee also revealed such situations (Patman Report 1966, pp. 878–79).

[18] Corporations may purchase their own shares for other reasons: (1) to maintain the price of their stock, (2) to prepare for possible mergers and acquisitions, (3) to allow them to convert bonds to shares, etc. Whatever the reasons, such holdings are of use in control, when necessary.

Corporate Ownership and Control

CONCLUSION

Our review of discrepant findings on the alleged separation of ownership and control in the large corporation in the United States,[19] and of the problems entailed in obtaining reliable and valid evidence on the actual ownership interests involved in a given corporation, should make it clear that the absence of control by proprietary interests in the largest corporations is by no means an "unquestionable," "incontrovertible," "singular," or "critical" social "fact." Nor can one any longer have confidence in such assurances as the following by Robert A. Dahl (1970): "Every *literate* person now *rightly takes for granted* what Berle and Means *established* four decades ago in their famous study, *The Modern Corporation and Private Property*" (p. 125; italics added). On the contrary, I believe that the "separation of ownership and control" may well be one of those rather critical, widely accepted, pseudofacts with which all sciences occasionally have found themselves burdened and bedeviled.[20]

News of the demise of capitalist classes, particularly in the United States, is, I suspect, somewhat premature. In place of such generalizations, extrapolated from an insufficiently examined American experience or deduced from abstract ahistorical theoretical premises, detailed empirical studies are necessary.

The methods and procedures, and the basic concepts and units of analysis, in such research will have to be quite different than those which have been most commonly employed in the past. Most important, such research must focus at the outset on the complex relationships in which

---

[19] We have, of course, not reviewed empirical studies of the question in other countries. The principal study in England is by Florence (1961). The only other such systematic study of which I am aware is by Wheelwright (1957) on Australia, as well as my own forthcoming collaborative volume with Ewen and Ratcliff on Chile.

[20] An example of a critical unwitting pseudofact appears in two articles by Daniel Bell (1958, 1961). In both articles, Bell refers to the "X" family of "Middletown" as an instance of the end of family control. "[B]y and large," Bell wrote (1958, p. 248; and similarly, 1961, p. 45), "the system of family control is finished. So much so that a classic study of American life like Robert Lynd's *Middletown in Transition,* with its picture of the 'X' family dominating the town, has in less than twenty years become history rather than contemporary life. (Interestingly enough, in 1957, the Ball family, Lynd's 'X' family, took in professional management of its enterprises, since the family lineage was becoming exhausted.)" Perhaps Bell really knows who now dominates Muncie, Indiana, and what role the Ball family plays there, but as an instance of "the breakup of family capitalism" and the end of family control, this is a singularly poor choice. Given the context in which Bell refers to the "X" family, his statement is quite misleading, since Ball Brothers, Inc., which is, according to *Fortune,* probably among the 500 largest corporations, ranked by sales, in the country today, continues to be privately owned. "Edmund F. Ball, a founder's son, is chairman of the company, but he has employed plenty of non-family talent. . . . 'Ours is still,' says Edmund Ball, 'essentially a closely held, privately owned business' " (Sheehan 1966, p. 343).

American Journal of Sociology

the single corporation is itself involved: the particular pattern of holdings and their evolution within the corporation; and the relationships
between it and other corporations; the forms of personal union or interlocking between corporate directorates and between the officers and directors and principal shareholding families; the connections with banks,
both as "financial institutions" and the agents of specified propertied
interests, including those who control the banks themselves; the network
of intercorporate and principal common shareholdings. In a word, it will
be necessary to explore in detail the institutional and class structure in
which the individual large corporations are situated.

For these purposes, sociologists must reclaim the concept of class from
the disuse and misuse into which it has fallen. Classes, as Dahrendorf
(1959) rightly states, "are clearly not layers in a hierarchical system of
strata differentiated by gradual distinctions. Rather, 'the analysis of
social class is concerned with an assessment of the chances that common
economic conditions and common experiences of a group will lead to organized action.' . . . *Class* is always a category for purposes of the analysis
of the dynamics of social conflict and its structural roots, and as such it has
to be separated strictly from *stratum* as a category for describing hierarchical systems at a given point in time" (p. 76).[21] If, as I think Daniel
Bell (1958) argues correctly, a class system is maintained through the
fusion of the family as an institution and extant property relations, and
"capitalism . . . is a social system, wherein power has been transmitted
through the family," then we must make that an important focus of our
empirical investigations (pp. 246–47). We should pursue Bell's (1961)
own analytical starting point and original (though subsequently ignored)
sociological emphasis on the relationship between "the peculiar cohesiveness of dominant economic classes" and "the linkage of the family and
property system" (pp. 39–40). For this reason, it will also be necessary
to focus, to use Parsons' term (1953) on the "members of the most
effective kinship unit" (p. 120). This, in turn, means investigating the
intricate network not only of general social interaction and shared concrete interests, but also the actual kinship relations between officers, directors, and principal shareholders, within the same and different
corporations.

This point is worth underlining, for it has been essential to our argument. If we are to locate the actual centers of corporate control, we must
discover "the most effective kinship unit." Without research into the
web of kinship relations binding apparently unrelated individuals into a
cohesive owning unit for purposes of control, analysis of the locus of control of the large corporation is hobbled at the outset. Furthermore, by pro-

[21] The phrase in single quotes is from Lipset and Bendix (1951), p. 248.

Corporate Ownership and Control

ceeding from such an analysis it will become possible to answer, on the most unambiguous empirical grounds, whether or not a capitalist "class" exists in the United States or similar countries and to what extent and in what ways that class has really been "decomposed" as the managerial theorists have assumed. Joseph Schumpeter (1955a) rightly argued that "the family, not the physical person, is the true unit of class theory" (p. 113). Classes are constituted of freely intermarrying families variously located in the social process of production and system of property relations. People similarly located economically are more likely to associate with each other freely than with others, and, therefore, to freely intermarry. Particularly among the wealthy, a variety of specific institutions, from debutante balls to select social clubs, resorts, and assorted watering places, as well as the "proper" schools, colleges (fraternities, sororities, and "living groups"), assure their commingling and psychological compatibility—and, therefore, differential propensity to intermarry. Protection of the family's property (and "good name"), which injects a further note of caution in the selection of proper marriage partners, merely increases this "natural" social tendency (cf. Domhoff 1967, 1970, 1972; Mills 1957; Baltzell 1966a, 1966b). Our empirical investigations of the separation of ownership and control must lead us, therefore, to investigate the extent to which the families of the officers, directors, and principal shareowners of the large corporations are bound by interwoven kinship ties—the extent to which, in other words, those who own and control the decisive units of production freely intermarry to form a social class.[22] Particularly relevant here is Baltzell's conclusion (1966a): "One of the functions of upper class solidarity is the retention, *within a primary group of families*, of the final decision-making positions within the social structure. As of the first half of the twentieth century in America, the final decisions affecting the goals of the social structure have been made primarily by members of the financial and business community" (pp. 183, 275; italics added).

Studies of the internal structure of capitalist classes will have to answer questions that include the following: what is the relationship between the

---

[22] Diverse authorities on kinship have noted that the "upper" classes everywhere, the United States included, tend to be characterized by an extended and tightly organized network of kin relations (see Goode 1964; Cavan 1963; Goode, Hobbins and McClure 1971). Yet such findings have been ignored by sociologists in their discussions of the alleged "breakup of family capitalism" and the separation of ownership and control. Bert Adams (1970) is one of the few sociologists specializing in kinship relations to call specific attention to the interrelationship between kinship and "the entire debate regarding who rules or controls the U.S. economic system," stating that "the evidence points unquestionably to strong kin links among the extremely wealthy in the society." He suggests that "much exciting research lies ahead for those who would pursue the links between kinship and economics, not only in the middle and working classes, but among the wealthy or upper classes as well" (pp. 591–92).

American Journal of Sociology

"new group of managers who are utterly different from their capitalist predecessors" and the old owning families—from whom they are said (Dahrendorf 1959, p. 46) to be increasingly moving apart? How are the different strata and segments of this class, and the incumbents of the new roles brought about by the "decomposition of capital" and the growth of managerial functions, related? What role do the overlapping and inter-related interests of principal shareowning families in the large corporations play in class integration and corporate control? What is the relationship between formal authority in the bureaucratic administrative apparatus, ownership interests, and kinship status? What role do the banks, as institutions, play in the control structure of the class? By whom are the banks owned and controlled? Do those who sit at the center of the web of interlocking directorates between corporations, or in the decisive posts which unite the banks and nonfinancial corporations, have a special position in the class? How, in sum, is the class internally differentiated and integrated?

To none of these questions do we have anything like adequate answers. There have been significant contributions to our understanding of the formation of earlier historically dominant classes. Studies of existing ones, however, are rare, and are usually limited to quantitative measurement of their social composition and to counting the social mobility of individuals. These studies have not explored the relationships within the class, between individuals, families, "elites," strata, and segments of that class. They have—with few exceptions—ignored the structure of dominant classes.[23]

Such studies are necessary, among other reasons, if we are not to "read politics in an extraordinarily abstract fashion," bereft of the knowledge of the interaction and relationships between "concrete interest groups, or classes." I think it is correct, as Bell (1958) argues, that, "if the important considerations of power are *what people do with that power*, then we have to have more *particularized ways of identifying the groupings* than 'institutionalized orders,' 'domains,' 'circles,' etc." (p. 240; former italics in original; latter added). And this requires analysis of the internal relationships within the "dominant" or "upper" class—of the modes of articulation and association, as well as differentiation be-

[23] Aside from the works cited already by Domhoff, Mills, and Baltzell, Hunter's work (1959)—although not using the concept of class—contributes important information on interaction between corporate executives on a national level. Studies by Perlo (1957), Rochester (1936), and Lundberg (1946), as well as Lundberg's latest relevant work (1968), which is a mine of excellent ideas worth researching, are important non-academic contributions. Barber and Barber (1965) contains excellent short historical studies. Other notable historical studies of dominant classes are by Bailyn (1955), Barber (1955), Ford (1953), Forster (1960; 1963), Edwards Vives (1927), Heise Gonzales (1950), and Rabb (1967).

Corporate Ownership and Control

tween given interest groups, class segments, etc.—so that we may be alert to possible internal structural sources of class cohesion and conflict. "Power," as William Kornhauser has put it (1966), "tends to be patterned according to the structure of interests in a society. Power is shared among those whose interests converge, and divided along lines where interests diverge," and this applies within a dominant class as it does in the society at large, though to what extent we can scarcely say, lacking such information as we are (p. 213).

The separation of ownership and control has meant at the least, its proponents argue, that whatever the capacity for organized action of the "full-blown capitalists" who constituted "a homogeneous capitalist class" in the past, this situation has been superseded by the "decomposition of capital" into a rather loose aggregate of fragmented groups having fundamentally different, often opposing, values and interests. "This is a peculiar state of affairs," in Dahrendorf's view (1959) "in which it is indeed virtually impossible to locate the ruling class" (p. 305). Once America had a "ruling class of businessmen [who] could relatively easily (though perhaps mistakenly) decide where their interests lay and what editors, lawyers and legislators might be paid to advance them," as David Riesman has put the syllogism, but "the captain of industry *no longer runs business,* no longer runs politics," and that class has been replaced by "an amorphous power structure." Power in America has become "situational and mercurial; *it* [*sic*] resists attempts to locate *it* (Reisman et al. 1953, pp. 247, 242, 257; italics added). Certainly these are no more than statements of the merely plausible; they are alleged social facts.

A contrary, and at least equally plausible, argument may be made that precisely because the individual capitalists of an earlier competitive era were compelled to struggle among themselves for economic survival, this also inhibited their acting in common, in comparison with the present, relatively unified power and capacity for action possessed by those who own the principal portions and control the large corporations. Thus, for instance, Joseph Schumpeter (1955b) attempted to explain in political economic terms what he considered the artificial conjuncture of capitalism and imperialism, as the result of the emergence of "monopoly capitalism" and the merger of formerly antagonistic "capitalists and entrepreneurs." In place of a "mass of capitalists competing with one another," there appeared what he termed "organized capital": the structural integration of large industrial enterprises and the "close alliance" of bankers and industrialists, "often going as far as personal identity. . . . Here capitalism has found a central organ that supplants its automatism by conscious decisions" (pp. 80–81). Therefore, it may be hypothesized that the social and economic interweaving of once opposed financial and industrial in-

American Journal of Sociology

terests, increased economic concentration, the fusion of formerly separate large capitals, and the establishment of an effective organizational apparatus of interlocking directorates, heightens the cohesiveness of the capitalist class and its capacity for common action and unified policies (see and cf. Hilferding 1910, chap. 23). Whether, as Riesman might claim, such a theory applied to contemporary America is a spectral survival of an earlier time, is an empirical question.

We cannot know what "the capabilities and opportunities for cooperation among those who have similar interests, and for confrontation among those with opposing interests" (Kornhauser 1966, p. 213) are at the national level within the dominant class unless we investigate the internal differentiation and integration of that class through the best available techniques of empirical inquiry. The fact is that there is far more systematic information available on the poor, on farmers, workers, and black Americans, than on the men and women of the rich and the well-born, on those who make up the "upper strata"—if not the "capitalist class"—of our society. Yet by now it ought to be apparent, if only from our most recent past, that we must discover as much as we can about those who occupy the upper reaches of American society if we are to understand—and act effectively in—the present as history.[24]

Studies of contemporary dominant classes elsewhere, including not only "advanced" but less developed and misdeveloped countries, are also essential. Such studies, aside from their intrinsic importance, may help reveal theoretical gaps and errors, as well as inadequate methodologies, in the present body of research and writing and allow us to clarify, elaborate, and specify given generalizations. These studies may provide the basis for a comparative theory of capitalist classes that is more comprehensive and valid than the extant one embodied in the "astonishing consensus" among social scientists. In place of abstract models based on ostensible "universal" elements in social structures, we need analyses of the structures of specific capitalist classes, related to the actual historic processes within which they have been formed.

---

[24] Several years ago I wrote that "just as a society's class structure is a major basis of its political diversity and cleavage, so too is *intra*class social differentiation politically significant, and by exploring the structure of the working class it will be possible to locate fundamental sources of its political behavior. This does not mean that *inter*class differences, or conflicting class interests, are in any way secondary to the internal structure of the working class as the source of its politics. Quite the contrary. Any conflict between classes tends to erase or minimize the significance of *intra*class differences and to maximize *inter*class differences" (Zeitlin 1967, pp. 8–9). I take it as a working hypothesis that this statement applies equally well to a society's *dominant* class. A fine recent work which is replete with historical sociological interpretations that rest on, or require, analysis of the internal differentiation and integration of specific dominant classes is that by Moore (1966, e.g., pp. 36–39 on England; pp. 162–65, 192, on Imperial China; pp. 237 ff. on Japan).

Corporate Ownership and Control

APPENDIX

Dahrendorf has taken Marx's writings in volume 3 of *Capital* to support his own theses concerning the dissolution of capitalism as the result of the separation of ownership and control. Not only does Dahrendorf (1959) explicitly reject what I have termed the "plain marxist" proposition that the functionaries of capital and the owners of capital (when they are not identical individuals) belong to the same social class, but he also asserts that this "view is *clearly contrary* to Marx's own analysis" (p. 43; italics added). In volume 3 of *Capital*, Marx wrote briefly on the "credit system" (stock market) and "joint-stock companies," whose economic importance in England was increasingly evident. He noted that (1) they involved "an enormous expansion of the scale of production and of enterprises, that was impossible for individual capitals" and that (2) capital is "here directly endowed with the form of social capital [capital of directly associated individuals] as distinct from private capital." However, it is two additional propositions, which anticipated the debate about the separation of ownership and control, that Dahrendorf and others consider supportive of their own managerial theory. Marx also wrote that (3) the corporations, being "social undertakings as distinct from private undertakings" mean "the abolition of capital as private property within the framework of capitalist production itself." (4) This means also the "transformation of the actually functioning capitalist into a mere manager, administrator of other people's capital, and of the owner of capital into a mere owner, a mere money-capitalist" (3:436).

Now, as to the first two propositions there can be no debate. Few would disagree that Marx correctly anticipated the profound significance of the corporation for large-scale production and rapid economic development. And the second point is an unexceptionable description of the obvious fact that pooling individual capital allows "undertakings" which smaller individual capitalists could not undertake separately. As to the third proposition, it is what I mean by "confusing Hegelian comments." For myself, its meaning is clear; for others it has been confusing (e.g., Bernstein, Schmidt, Bell, Dahrendorf, etc.). Marx had a penchant for Hegel's language and often used it precisely because he wished to honor that "mighty thinker" when others were currently treating him as a "dead dog." Therefore, he "coquetted with the modes of expression peculiar to him" (*Capital*, 1:19–20). One of Marx's oft-used Hegelian concepts was *"aufgehoben,"* or *"aufhebung."* In the volumes of *Capital* translated into English, this has usually been rendered "abolition." Yet this is clearly not its Hegelian meaning, nor the meaning Marx intended. As Ivan Soll (1969) explains, for Hegel, "the understanding's finite categories must be both preserved and negated—or to use a term favored

American Journal of Sociology

by Hegel just because it possesses this double meaning, *aufgehoben*" (p. 134). Or in Hegel's own words "*Aufheben* exhibits its true double meaning . . . it negates and preserves at the same time" (cited from his *Logic* by Soll 1969, p. 134). Reinhard Bendix has written me in a private communication: "The implication [of *aufheben*] is to *re-create* in the process of *abolishing*—which is one of those conundrums Hegelians thrive on and the rest of us mortals despair over." The corporation, as a new form of "social capital" negates "private capital" while preserving it. That this is Marx's likely meaning must be concluded. For, in even greater exaggeration, he goes on to say, "This is the abolition of the capitalist *mode of production* within the capitalist mode of production itself" (3:438). This can only be jibberish in English (or at best "confusing") unless it is understood in its Hegelian sense of negating while preserving, re-creating while abolishing. In fact, Marx makes this clear in another passage: "However, this expropriation appears within the capitalist system in a contradictory form, as *appropriation of social property by a few*. . . . There is antagonism against the old form in the stock companies, in which the social means of production appear as private property; but the conversion to the form of stock still remains ensnared in the trammels of capitalism; hence, *instead of overcoming* the antithesis between the character of wealth as social and as private wealth, the stock companies merely *develop it in a new form*" (3: 440; italics added).

Further, it is in this context that Marx refers to the development which Hilferding was later to elaborate, as were many others, including Lundberg, Bonbright and Means, and then (though secondarily) Berle and Means. The latter authors laid out several types of control other than private ownership and management control. In these types, "the separation of ownership and control" meant that the large property owners, those who owned the majority, or predominant minority of shares in a corporation, directly or indirectly ('pyramiding'), appropriated control from the small shareowners. This was Marx's point when he stated that the form of the stock company and of credit offers the capitalist "absolute control within certain limits over the capital and property of others, and thereby over the labor of others" (3:439).

As to the fourth proposition, it, too, is quite consistent with the "plain marxist" class analysis. For Marx, in elaborating this point, states: "profit is henceforth received . . . as compensation for *owning capital* that now is entirely divorced from the *function* in the actual process of reproduction, just as this *function* in the person of the manager is divorced from ownership of capital" (3:436–37; italics added). This, of course, is also the view I cited above from Weber. Further, from the standpoint of the analysis of social domination, class conflict, and surplus appropriation (exploitation), Marx's view, as already quoted here and as in

Corporate Ownership and Control

the following passage, is directly opposed to the managerialist doctrine of "satisficing," "corporate conscience," "post-capitalist society," or "new industrial state." The role of the emerging corporation and stock market system, Marx wrote, was "to develop the incentive of capitalist production, enrichment through exploitation of the labor of others, to the purest and most colossal form of gambling and swindling, and to reduce more and more the number of the few who exploit the social wealth" (3:441).

REFERENCES

Abels, Jules. 1965. *The Rockefeller Billions*. New York: Macmillan.
Adams, Bert. 1970. "Isolation, Function, and Beyond: American Kinship in the 1960's." *Journal of Marriage and the Family* 32 (November): 575–97.
Alchian, Armen. 1968. "Corporate Management and Property Rights." In *Economic Policy and the Regulation of Securities*. Washington, D.C.: American Enterprise Institute.
Bailyn, Bernard. 1955. *The New England Merchants in the Seventeenth Century*. Cambridge, Mass.: Harvard University Press.
Bain, Joe S. 1966. *International Differences in Industrial Structure: Eight Nations in the 1950's*. New Haven, Conn.: Yale University Press.
Baltzell, E. Digby. 1966a. " 'Who's Who in America' and 'The Social Register': Elite and Upper Class Indexes in Metropolitan America." In *Class, Status, and Power*, edited by Reinhard Bendix and S. M. Lipset. 2d ed. New York: Collier-Macmillan.
———. 1966b. *Philadelphia Gentlemen: The Making of a National Upper Class*. New York: Macmillan.
Baran, Paul A., and Paul M. Sweezy. 1966. *Monopoly Capital*. New York: Monthly Review Press.
Barber, Eleanor G. 1955. *The Bourgeoisie in Eighteenth-Century France*. Princeton, N.J.: Princeton University Press.
Barber, Eleanor G., and Bernard Barber, eds. 1965. *European Social Class: Stability and Change*. New York: Macmillan.
Baumol, William J. 1959. *Business, Behavior, Value, and Growth*. New York: Macmillan.
Bell, Daniel. 1958. "The Power Elite—Reconsidered." *American Journal of Sociology* 64 (November): 238–50.
———. 1961. "The Breakup of Family Capitalism." In *The End of Ideology*. New York: Collier.
Bendix, Reinhard. 1952. "Bureaucracy and the Problem of Power." In *Reader in Bureaucracy*, edited by R. K. Merton, Ailsa P. Gray, Barbara Hockey, and Hanan C. Selvin. Glencoe, Ill.: Free Press.
Berle, Adolph, Jr. 1954. *The 20th Century Capitalist Revolution*. New York: Harcourt, Brace.
Berle, Adolph, Jr., and Gardiner C. Means. 1967. *The Modern Corporation and Private Property*. New York: Harcourt, Brace & World (originally published in 1932 by Macmillan).
Bernstein, Eduard. 1961. *Evolutionary Socialism*. New York: Schocken (originally published in Germany in 1899).
Bonbright, James C., and Gardiner C. Means. 1932. *The Holding Company*. New York: McGraw-Hill.
Burch, Philip H., Jr. 1972. *The Managerial Revolution Reassessed*. Lexington, Mass.: Heath.
Business Week (no author given). 1971. "The Board: It's Obsolete Unless Overhauled." May 22, pp. 50–58.
———. 1972. "An Ex-Banker Treats Copper's Sickest Giant." February 19, pp. 52–55.
Cavan, Ruth. 1963. *The American Family*. New York: Crowell.

American Journal of Sociology

Dahl, Robert A. 1970. *After the Revolution?* New Haven, Conn.: Yale University Press.

Dahrendorf, Ralf. 1959. *Class and Class Conflict in Industrial Society.* Stanford, Calif.: Stanford University Press.

Domhoff, G. William. 1967. *Who Rules America?* Englewood Cliffs, N.J.: Prentice-Hall.

———. 1970. *The Higher Circles: The Governing Class in America.* New York: Random House.

———. 1972. *Fat Cats and Democrats.* Englewood Cliffs, N.J.: Prentice-Hall.

Dooley, Peter C. 1969. "The Interlocking Directorate." *American Economic Review* 59 (June): 314–23.

Drucker, Peter F. 1971. "The New Markets and the New Capitalism." In *Capitalism Today,* edited by Daniel Bell and Irving Kristol. New York: Basic.

Earley, James S. 1956. "Marginal Policies of Excellently Managed Companies." *American Economic Review* 46 (March): 44–70.

———. 1957. "Comment." *American Economic Review. Papers and Proceedings* 47 (May): 333–35.

Earley, James S., and W. T. Carleton. 1962. "Budgeting and the Theory of the Firm." *Journal of Industrial Economics* 10 (July): 165–73.

Edwards Vives, Alberto. 1927. *La fronda aristocratica.* Santiago: Editorial del Pacifico.

Eisenbeis, Robert A., and Alan S. McCall. 1972. "Some Effects of Affiliations among Savings and Commercial Banks." *Journal of Finance* 27 (September): 865–77.

Etzioni, Amitai. 1968. *The Active Society.* New York: Free Press.

Fitch, Robert, and Mary Oppenheimer. 1970. "Who Rules the Corporations?" *Socialist Revolution* 1 (1): 73–107; also 1 (5): 61–114; 1 (6): 33–94.

Florence, P. Sargant. 1961. *Ownership, Control and Success of Large Companies: An Analysis of English Industrial Structure and Policy, 1936–1951.* London: Sweet & Maxwell.

Ford, Franklin L. 1953. *Robe and Sword: The Regrouping of the French Aristocracy after Louis XIV.* Cambridge, Mass.: Harvard University Press.

Forster, Robert. 1960. *The Nobility of Toulouse in the Eighteenth Century.* Baltimore: John Hopkins Press.

———. 1963. "The Provincial Noble: A Reappraisal." *American Historical Review* 68 (April): 681–91.

Galbraith, John K. 1968. *The New Industrial State.* New York: New American Library (also, "Introduction," 2d ed. 1971). New York: Houghton Mifflin.

Goldsmith, Raymond W., and Rexford C. Parmelee. 1940. *The Distribution of Ownership in the 200 Largest Nonfinancial Corporations.* In *Investigations of Concentration of Economic Power.* Monographs of the Temporary National Economic Committee, no. 29. Washington, D.C.: Government Printing Office.

Goode, William J. 1963. *The Family.* Englewood Cliffs, N.J.: Prentice-Hall.

Goode, William J., Elizabeth Hobbins, and Helen M. McClure, eds. 1971. *Social Systems and Family Patterns: A Propositional Inventory.* Indianapolis: Bobbs-Merrill.

Gordon, Robert A. 1966. *Business Leadership in the Large Corporation.* Berkeley: University of California Press (originally published in 1945 under the auspices of the Brookings Institution).

Heise, Gonzales, Julio. 1950. "La constitucion de 1925 y las neuvas tendencias politico-sociales." *Anales de la Universidad de Chile* 108 (80; 4th trimester): 95–234.

Hilferding, Rudolph. 1910. *Das Finanzkapital.* Munich: Literarische Agentur Willi Weisman.

Hindley, Brian V. 1970. "Separation of Ownership and Control in the Modern Corporation." *Journal of Law and Economics* 13 (April): 185–221.

Hoyt, Edwin P. 1967. *The Guggenheims and the American Dream.* New York: Funk & Wagnalls.

Hunter, Floyd. 1959. *Top Leadership, U.S.A.* Chapel Hill: University of North Carolina Press.

Corporate Ownership and Control

Jensen, Michael C. 1971. "A New Generation Comes of Age." *New York Times.* May 2, sec. 3, pp. 1, 5.

Kahl, Joseph. 1957. *The American Class Structure.* New York: Rinehart.

Kamerschen, David R. 1968. "The Influence of Ownership and Control on Profit Rates." *American Economic Review* 58 (June): 432–47.

———. 1969. "The Effect of Separation of Ownership and Control on the Performance of the Large Firm in the U.S. Economy." *Rivista internazaionale di scienze economiche e commerciali* 16 (5): 489–93.

Kaysen, Carl. 1957. "The Social Significance of the Modern Corporation." *American Economic Review* 47 (May): 311–19.

———. 1965. "Another View of Corporate Capitalism." *Quarterly Journal of Economics* 79 (February): 41–51.

Kolko, Gabriel. 1962. *Wealth and Power in America.* New York: Praeger.

Kornhauser, William. 1966. " 'Power Elite' or 'Veto Groups'?" In *Class, Status, and Power,* edited by Reinhard Bendix and S. M. Lipset. 2d ed. New York: Collier-Macmillan.

Larner, Robert J. 1970. *Management Control and the Large Corporation.* Cambridge, Mass.: University Press, Dunellen.

Lenin, Nikolai. 1967. "Imperialism." In *Lenin: Selected Works.* New York: International Publishers (originally published in Petrograd in 1917).

Lewellen, Wilbur G., and Blaine Huntsman. 1970. "Managerial Pay and Corporate Performance." *American Economic Review* 60 (September): 710–20.

Lintner, John. 1967. "The Financing of Corporations." In *The Corporation and Modern Society,* edited by E. S. Mason. New York: Atheneum.

Lipset, S. M., and Reinhard Bendix. 1951. "Social Status and Social Structure: A Re-Examination of Data and Interpretations." Part 1. *British Journal of Sociology* 2 (September): 150–68.

Lomask, Milton. 1964. *Seed Money: The Guggenheim Story.* New York: Farrar, Straus.

Lundberg, Ferdinand. 1946. *America's Sixty Families.* New York: Citadel (originally published by Vanguard in 1937).

———. 1968. *The Rich and the Super-Rich.* New York: Bantam.

Luxemburg, Rosa. 1970. *Reform or Revolution.* New York: Pathfinder (originally published in Berlin in 1899).

Manne, Henry. 1965. "Mergers and the Market for Corporate Control." *Journal of Political Economy* 72 (April): 110–20.

Marris, Robin. 1963. "A Model of 'Managerial' Enterprise." *Quarterly Journal of Economics* 77 (May): 185–209.

———. 1964. *The Economic Theory of "Managerial" Capitalism.* London: Macmillan.

Marx, Karl. 1967. *Capital.* Vols. 1–3. New York: International (originally published in German in 1867, 1885, 1894).

Mason, E. S. 1967. "Introduction." In *The Corporation in Modern Society,* edited by E. S. Mason. New York: Atheneum.

Merton, Robert K. 1959. "Notes on Problem-Finding in Sociology." In *Sociology Today,* edited by R. K. Merton, Leonard Broom, and Leonard S. Cottrell, Jr. New York: Basic.

Metcalf, Lee. 1971. *Congressional Record* 117, pt. 17:22141.

Metcalf, Lee, and Vic Reinemer. 1971. "Unmasking Corporate Ownership." *Nation.* July 19, pp. 38–40.

Miliband, Ralph. 1969. *The State in Capitalist Society.* New York: Basic.

Mills, C. Wright. 1957. *The Power Elite.* New York: Oxford University Press.

———. 1962. *The Marxists.* New York: Dell.

Monsen, R. Joseph, Jr., J. S. Chiu, and D. E. Cooley. 1968. "The Effect of Separation of Ownership and Control on the Performance of the Large Firm." *Quarterly Journal of Economics* 82 (August): 435–51.

———. 1969. "Ownership and Management." *Business Horizons* 12 (August): 45–52.

American Journal of Sociology

Moore, Barrington. 1966. *Social Origins of Dictatorship and Democracy.* Boston: Beacon.

Moran, Theodore H. 1973. "Transnational Strategies of Protection and Defense by Multinational Corporations." *International Organization* 27 (Spring): 273–87.

Murphy, Charles J. V. 1967. "The Mellons of Pittsburgh." Part 1. *Fortune* 75 (October): 120 ff.

National Resources Committee (NRC). 1939. *The Structure of the American Economy.* Washington, D.C.: Government Printing Office. Reprinted in Paul M. Sweezy. 1953. *The Present as History.* New York: Monthly Review Press.

Nichols, W. A. T. 1969. *Ownership, Control, and Ideology.* London: Allen & Unwin.

O'Connor, James. 1971. "Who Rules the Corporation?" *Socialist Revolution* 2 (January/February): 117–50.

Parsons, Talcott. 1953. "A Revised Analytical Approach to the Theory of Social Stratification." In *Class, Status, and Power,* edited by Reinhard Bendix and S. M. Lipset. Glencoe, Ill.: Free Press.

Parsons, Talcott, and Neil Smelser. 1957. *Economy and Society.* London: Routledge & Kegan-Paul.

[Patman] Staff Report. 1964. *Twenty Largest Stockholders of Record in Member Banks of the Federal Reserve System.* 5 vols. U.S. Congress, House, Committee on Banking and Currency, Domestic Finance Committee. 88th Cong., 2d sess. Washington, D.C.: Government Printing Office (cited as Patman Report).

———. 1966. "Bank Stock Ownership and Control" (reprinted in Patman Report 1968, vol. 1).

———. 1967. "Control of Commercial Banks and Interlocks among Financial Institutions" (reprinted in Patman Report 1968, vol. 1).

———. 1968. *Commercial Banks and Their Trust Activities: Emerging Influence on the American Economy.* U.S. Congress, House, Committee on Banking and Currency, Domestic Finance Committee. 90th Cong., 2d sess. Washington, D.C.: Government Printing Office (cited as Patman Report).

Perlo, Victor. 1957. *The Empire of High Finance.* New York. International.

Peterson, Shorey. 1965. "Corporate Control and Capitalism." *Quarterly Journal of Economics* 79 (February): 1–23.

Playford, John. 1972. "Who Rules Australia?" In *Australian Capitalism,* edited by Playford and Douglas Kirsner. Harmondsworth: Penguin.

Rabb, Theodore K. 1967. *Enterprise and Empire: Merchant and Gentry Investment in the Expansion of England, 1575–1630.* Cambridge, Mass.: Harvard University Press.

Riesman, David, et al. 1953. *The Lonely Crowd.* Garden City, N.J.: Anchor.

Rochester, Anna. 1936. *Rulers of America.* New York: International.

Rose, Sanford. 1968. "The Rewarding Strategies of Multinationalism." *Fortune,* September 15, pp. 101–5, 180, 182.

Schumpeter, Joseph. 1955a. "Social Classes in an Ethnically Homogeneous Environment." In *Imperialism and Social Classes.* New York: Meridian (originally published in German in 1923).

———. 1955b. "The Sociology of Imperialism[s]." *Imperialism and Social Classes* (originally published in German in 1919).

Sheehan, Robert. 1966. "There's Plenty of Privacy Left in Private Enterprise." *Fortune,* July 15, pp. 224 ff.

———. 1967. "Proprietors in the World of Big Business." *Fortune,* June 15, pp. 178–83, 242.

Simon, Herbert A. 1957. *Administrative Behavior.* 2d ed. New York. Macmillan.

Smith, Ephraim P., and Louis R. Desfosses. 1972. "Interlocking Directorates: A Study of Influence." *Mississippi Valley Journal of Business and Economics* 7 (Spring): 57–69.

Soll, Ivan. 1969. *Introduction to Hegel's Metaphysics.* Chicago: University of Chicago Press.

Corporate Ownership and Control

Sorokin, Pitirim. 1953. "What Is a Social Class?" In *Class, Status, and Power,* edited by Reinhard Bendix and S. M. Lipset. Glencoe, Ill.: Free Press.

Sweezy, Paul M. 1953. "Interest Groups in the American Economy." In *The Present as History.* New York: Monthly Review Press.

———. 1956. *Theory of Capitalist Development.* New York: Monthly Review Press (originally published in 1942).

Tanzer, Michael. 1969. *The Political Economy of International Oil and the Underdeveloped Countries.* Boston: Beacon.

U.S., Congress, House, Select Committee on Small Business. 1963. *Chain Banking: Stockholder and Loan Links of 200 Largest Member Banks.* Washington, D.C.: Government Printing Office.

Vernon, Jack R. 1970. "Ownership and Control among Large Member Banks." *Journal of Finance* 25 (3): 651–57.

Villarejo, Don. 1961/62. *Stock Ownership and the Control of Corporations.* Radical Education Project. Ann Arbor, Mich. Reprint of articles in *New University Thought* (Autumn 1961 and Winter 1962).

Walker, Robert. 1971. "A Banker for Anaconda." *New York Times,* May 23, sec. 3, pp. 3, 11.

Weber, Max. 1965. *Theory of Social and Economic Organization.* Edited by Talcott Parsons. New York: Free Press (originally published in German in 1925).

———. 1968. *Economy and Society.* Edited by G. Roth and C. Wittich. New York: Bedminster (originally published in German in 1921).

Wheelwright, E. L. 1957. *Ownership and Control of Australian Companies.* Sydney: Law Book.

Williams, Robin, Jr. 1959. *American Society.* New York: Knopf.

Williamson, Oliver E. 1963. "Managerial Discretion and Business Behavior." *American Economic Review* 53 (December): 1032–57.

———. 1970. *Corporate Control and Business Behavior.* Englewood Cliffs, N.J.: Prentice-Hall.

Wrong, Dennis. 1968. "Some Problems in Defining Social Power." *American Journal of Sociology* 73 (May): 673–81.

Zeitlin, Maurice. 1967. *Revolutionary Politics and the Cuban Working Class.* Princeton, N.J., Princeton University Press.

[7]

Commentary and Debate

MANAGEMENT CONTROL IN THE LARGE CORPORATION:
COMMENT ON ZEITLIN

As demonstrated recently by his article "Corporate Ownership and Control:
The Large Corporation and the Capitalist Class" (*AJS* 79 [March 1974]:
1073–1119), Zeitlin is an able theorist as well as a competent researcher.
By any standards, his systematic critique of the conventional sociological
wisdom concerning the relationship of the capitalist class to the large
corporation is most profound. Although I am sympathetic with his concern
for the issue of control in the large corporation and concur with many
of his conclusions, I must take exception to his discussion at several points.
For the most part, my comments are restricted to the issue of management
control in the large corporation.

Separation of Ownership and Control

Certainly the most important problem involves Zeitlin's interpretation of
the theory of the "separation of ownership and control." Indeed, he does
not seem to appreciate fully some of the central components of that theory.
He is quite correct in his criticism of the "teleology of bureaucratic imperatives" espoused by several sociological theorists. However, it must be
noted that this teleology is not to be found in the original theory proposed
by Berle and Means (1932). To the contrary, they assert that the separation of ownership and control occurs only as a result of the capital requirements of the large corporation. As they put it, "In general the larger the
company, the more likely is its ownership to be diffused among a multitude
of individuals" (p. 53). In short, large corporations tend to be management
controlled simply because their capital requirements have resulted in a
dispersion of stock ownership. Also, Berle and Means clearly consider the
separation of ownership and control to be more of an emergent historical
process than an accomplished historical fact. For example, they declare
that "the dispersion of ownership has gone to tremendous lengths among
the largest companies and has progressed to a considerable extent among
the medium sized" (p. 53).

   After reviewing the results of the recent studies of corporate control,
Zeitlin concludes that their findings are "discrepant" and that the separation of ownership and control may well be a "pseudofact." Zeitlin may
have overstated his case in this regard. Although the studies he cites arrive
at somewhat different results, that fact is almost entirely attributable to
the different samples and criteria for management control employed by

American Journal of Sociology

TABLE 1

TYPE OF CONTROL BY SIZE RANK OF CORPORATIONS FOR 500 LARGEST CORPORATIONS

	1–100	101–200	201–300	301–400	401–500	Total
Larner study:						
Minority	22	17	22	34	38	133
Management	78	83	78	66	62	367
Burch study:						
Family	36	43	49	58	50	236
Management	64	57	51	42	50	264
Sheehan study:						
Family	10	23	39	38	37	147
Management	90	77	61	62	63	353

NOTE.—The original control categories have been collapsed, whenever necessary, to ensure the comparability of results. In the Larner study, minority control includes all forms of control other than management control. In the Burch study, management control includes all forms of control other than family control.

each researcher. In table 1 I present a summary of the results of the three major studies of corporate control by the size rank of the corporations. Although Larner (1970) and Burch (1972) study the same sample of the 500 largest nonfinancial corporations as ranked by their assets in 1963, Larner uses 10% stock ownership as the minimum criterion for minority control, whereas Burch uses 4% stock ownership and representation on the board of directors as the minimum criteria for family control. Sheehan (1966) studies the 500 largest industrial corporations as ranked by their sales in 1966, using 10% stock ownership as the minimum criterion for family control. Given these differences in samples and criteria, the minor inconsistencies in results are hardly surprising. Nevertheless, each of the three researchers finds that a majority of the 500 largest corporations are subject to management control. More important, these empirical results consistently confirm the theory of the separation of ownership and control inasmuch as management control is positively associated with the size of the corporations. Among the 100 largest corporations, the proportion that are management controlled is between 64% and 90%, while among the 100 smallest in the samples of the 500 largest, the proportion is between 50% and 63%. It is apparent that the original theory of the separation of ownership and control advanced by Berle and Means is generally substantiated by these results. Although management control among the large corporations may not warrant the status of an incontrovertible social "fact," management control does appear to be the predominant form of control among large corporations.

Unfortunately, in his attempt to document the extent of private ownership and family control among the large corporations, Zeitlin largely neglects the empirical adequacy of the theory of the separation of ownership and control. For example, he notes that the use of the *Fortune* directory

Commentary and Debate

of the 500 largest industrial corporations as the sample for studies of corporate control entails an inherent bias, since privately owned corporations are excluded from the directory unless they publish annual financial statements. Citing the Sheehan study (1967) which lists 26 privately owned corporations that would otherwise qualify for inclusion among the 500 largest industrial corporations as ranked by sales, Zeitlin concludes that the addition of these corporations to those studied by Larner (1970) raises the number of privately controlled corporations among the 500 largest from five to 31, or sixfold. This methodological point is well taken. Nevertheless, these data are entirely consistent with the theory of the separation of ownership and control in the large corporation. Specifically, none of Sheehan's 26 privately owned corporations would rank among the 100 largest industrial corporations in 1966; and well over half, 15 to be exact, would rank among the smallest 100 of the 500 largest in terms of sales.

Corporate Interlocks and Corporate Control

At one point, Zeitlin implies that director representation, through interlocking directorates, constitutes an alternative form of corporate control to direct stock ownership (p. 1101). He notes astutely that it is the large corporations, those most likely to be management controlled in terms of the dispersion of stock ownership, which maintain the greatest number of interlocks with financial institutions and nonfinancial corporations. Unfortunately, none of the studies of corporate interlocks or corporate control have examined directly the relationship between stock ownership and interlocking directorates. However, it is possible to examine that relationship among the 200 largest nonfinancial corporations in 1970 (Allen 1974). Table 2 presents the average number of interlocks with the 50 largest financial corporations and the 200 largest nonfinancial corporations, as well as the proportion of directors drawn from management, by

TABLE 2

Average Number of Financial and Nonfinancial Interlocks and Proportion of Management Directors for 200 Largest Nonfinancial Corporations in 1970 by Degree of Management Control

Type of Control	Financial	Nonfinancial	Directors from Management (%)
Probable management (135)	3.6	5.9	31.8
Possible family (33)	3.1	5.0	38.0
Probable family (32)	2.6	3.9	44.5

Note.—*N*'s in parentheses.

American Journal of Sociology

the degree of management control among the 200 largest nonfinancial corporations. If any individual or family held more than 10% of the common stock, the corporation was classified as being under probable family control. If any individual or family represented on the board of directors held less than 10% but more than 1% of the common stock, the corporation was classified as being under possible family control. All other corporations were classified as being under probable management control. Information on stock ownership was drawn from earlier studies of corporate control (Larner 1970; Burch 1972) and from reports filed with the Securities and Exchange Commission. It is evident from these data that family control is associated with fewer interlocks with financial and nonfinancial corporations and with a larger proportion of directors drawn from management. This pattern can be attributed, in large part, to the fact that family-controlled corporations often have members of the family as directors. For example, family members serve as chairmen of the boards of such family-controlled corporations as Ford Motor, W. R. Grace, Getty Oil, Weyerhaeuser, North American Rockwell, Reynolds Metals, Loews, McDonnell Douglas, Lykes Youngstown, and Amerada Hess.

Financial Control of Nonfinancial Corporations

Certainly one of the most important issues raised by Zeitlin is the extent to which financial corporations control nonfinancial ones through a combination of stock ownership and director representation. To support his argument that large commercial banks control many nonfinancial corporations, Zeitlin presents a secondary analysis of data demonstrating that bankers occupy a disproportionate share of the multiple directorships held by interlocking directors. It is possible to demonstrate the influence of bankers even more clearly through a comparison of the average number of interlocks held by directors who are management officials of different types of corporations. Table 3 presents original data on the average number of directorships held by chairmen and other management directors among 800 major corporations in 1970 by type of corporation. This sample of 800 corporations includes the 550 largest industrial corporations and the 50 largest commercial banks, life insurance companies, public utilities, transportation companies, and retailing companies as ranked by either sales or assets in 1970 (*Fortune* 1971a; 1971b). In general, these data confirm the results presented by Zeitlin, but with one important qualification: position within a corporation is as important as the type of corporation in determining the number of directorships held by a management official. Chairmen of the boards, typically the chief executive officers of their corporations, are far more influential in terms of the number of

TABLE 3

AVERAGE NUMBER OF INTERLOCKS FOR MANAGEMENT DIRECTORS AMONG
800 MAJOR CORPORATIONS IN 1970 BY TYPE OF CORPORATION

Type of Corporation	Chairmen	Other Directors
Bank (50)	3.20 (50)	1.50 (126)
Life insurance (50)	1.84 (50)	1.14 (148)
Large industrial (50)	2.50 (50)	1.29 (268)
Other industrial (500)	1.88 (500)	1.16 (1,952)
Utility (50)	1.98 (50)	1.38 (98)
Retailing (50)	1.90 (50)	1.20 (264)
Transportation (50)	1.68 (50)	1.17 (121)

NOTE.—*N*'s in parentheses.

directorships held than are other management officials. Also, the chairmen
of the large commercial banks are more influential than chairmen of other
types of corporations, although the chairmen of the large industrial
corporations also appear to be quite influential in terms of the number of
directorships held.

Further evidence as to the dominant position of financial institutions
among the large corporations is to be found in the reports of recent congressional investigations (U.S. Congress 1967; 1968; 1973). These reports
disclose that large commercial banks, particularly the major ones in
New York, are often principal stockholders in many large corporations.
The stock in question is generally held by the trust departments, much of
it on behalf of employee-benefit plans. In 1973, approximately $400
billion were held in trust accounts administered by the 3,800 commercial
banks with trust departments; approximately $114 billion, over 25% of
the total, were administered by 10 large New York banks. Such funds are
typically invested in the common stock of large corporations. A recent
congressional investigation of the 30 principal stockholders of the largest
American corporations disclosed that seven large New York banks combined held an average of 11.1% of the common stock in 25 of the 99
largest industrial corporations (U.S. Congress 1973, p. 26). The remaining
74 industrial corporations failed to disclose voluntarily the identities and
holdings of their principal stockholders. Similarly, the same seven New
York banks combined held an average of 14.6% of the common stock in
15 of the 19 largest railroads and 8.4% of the common stock in 20 of the
51 largest public utilities. Consequently, commercial banks are often the
single largest stockholders in large corporations. For example, the seven
large New York banks were the single largest stockholders in 15 of the 25
industrial corporations which disclosed their principal stockholders.

The existing evidence on director representation and stock ownership
among major nonfinancial corporations by large commercial banks leaves
little doubt as to the influential position of these banks with respect to

American Journal of Sociology

nonfinancial corporations. However, it does not necessarily follow that banks represent an institutional mechanism for the indirect control of nonfinancial corporations by principal stockholders. The critical issue is the extent of management control among the large commercial banks. Although some very large banks are controlled by particular families, such as the Mellons and Rockefellers, minority or family control does not appear to be any more prevalent among commercial banks than among nonfinancial corporations. As Zeitlin acknowledges, approximately 75% of the 200 largest commercial banks are management controlled, if 10% stock ownership is used as the minimum criterion for family or minority control (Vernon 1970). It might also be noted that 25 of the 27 largest banks are management controlled. As in the case of nonfinancial corporations, management control seems to be associated with larger size among commercial banks. Indeed, congressional investigations have disclosed that the principal stockholders of most large commercial banks are other large commercial banks. For example, the six largest banks in New York combined held an average of 15.7% of each other's common stock. Moreover, the major New York banks are often their own principal stockholders. For example, the six largest banks held an average of 5.9% of their own common stock (U.S. Congress 1967, pp. 82–83).

Corporate Elites and the Capitalist Class

The distinction between managers and principal stockholders is not always easy to establish or maintain in practice. Certainly the senior management officials of the large corporations do not fit the stereotype of the bureaucratic manager suggested by sociological theory. It is not unusual for senior management officials, particularly chief executive officers, to receive extremely large salaries and bonuses from their corporations. The only source of accurate information on the remuneration of chief executive officers is the Form 10-K annual report filed with the Securities and Exchange Commission. According to these reports, the chief executive officers of the 200 largest industrial corporations received an average of $307,170 in total remuneration in 1973. This figure includes salary, bonus, director fee, and deferred compensation. It does not include capital gains from stock options or dividends from company stock owned by the chief executive officer. These salaries frequently reach almost astronomical levels. Among the chief executive officers of the 200 largest industrial corporations in 1973, 35 received more than $400,000, and six of the 35 received more than $600,000, in total remuneration for that year.

It is also not unusual for senior management officials to own considerable amounts of stock in the corporations they manage, owing in large part to their participation in stock-option plans. According to the official data on

Commentary and Debate

the 200 largest industrial corporations, the chief executive officers owned
common stock in their corporations worth an average of $22,611,915 as of
the end of 1973. However, this aggregate figure is somewhat misleading
inasmuch as it includes the stockholdings of several multimillionaire entrepreneurs or their descendants. Such entrepreneurs include Edwin H.
Land, J. Paul Getty, Sanford N. McDonnell, Charles Revson, and William
R. Hewlett. The descendants of entrepreneurs include Richard S. Reynolds,
Jr., George H. Weyerhaeuser, J. Peter Grace, Amory Houghton, and
Henry Ford II. If the 28 chief executive officers with more than $10,000,000
in corporation stock are excluded from the analysis, the average value of
the common stock held by the remaining 172 drops to a more modest
$1,531,331.

The fact that senior management officials receive large salaries and
own considerable stock in their corporations does not necessarily imply
that these managers constitute an autonomous class or that they have
been incorporated into the capitalist class. If the family is the basic unit
of social class, as Zeitlin maintains, it is far more accurate to speak of a
managerial elite rather than a class as such. Managerial positions are
transmitted on the basis of familial relationships only when a family is
also a principal stockholder in a corporation. In sociological parlance,
managerial position is usually an achieved status, whereas the position of
principal stockholder is typically an ascribed one. The senior management
officials of the large corporations may become relatively wealthy as a result
of their direct remuneration and their participation in stock-option plans,
but their wealth is rarely of the same magnitude as that of principal
stockholders. More important, management officials often have socio-
economic backgrounds very different from those of the principal stockholders. This differentiation between the managerial elite and the capitalist
class of principal stockholders is viewed by some with no little apprehen-
sion. Baltzell, for one, suggests that "a powerful, wealthy, yet declassed
elite may be one of the greatest threats to freedom in modern American
society" (1971, p. 215).

Profit Maximization and Management Control

Zeitlin devotes considerable attention to the notion of "managerial discretion" in the large corporation. On the basis of a review of the literature
on profit maximization and management control, he concludes that "purportedly management-controlled and owner-controlled corporations are
similarly profit oriented" (p. 1097). However, it is equally possible to
draw the opposite conclusion from the empirical research on profit maximization and management control because of the largely inconclusive results
of this research. For example, Larner does not find "systematic negative

American Journal of Sociology

evidence" concerning the hypotheses of managerial discretion, as Zeitlin asserts (p. 1095). Instead, Larner finds that "this evidence, though by no means conclusive, provides some support for hypotheses of managerial discretion, but suggests that the magnitude of this discretion is not as large as it is often implied" (1970, p. 29). Two other studies of managerial discretion (Kamerschen 1968; Hindley 1970) cited by Zeitlin report similar differences in the profit rates of management-controlled and owner-controlled corporations but conclude that the differences are not statistically significant. Finally, the original study of profit maximization and management control found that "the owner controlled group of firms outperformed the management controlled firms by a considerable margin" (Monsen, Chiu, and Cooley 1968, p. 442).

Despite his conclusions, Zeitlin is well aware of these inconsistencies and cogently identifies one of the major sources of the problem. Given the different criteria employed to classify particular corporations as either management controlled or owner controlled, it is difficult to put much store in the results of studies using this imperfectly measured variable of "corporate control" as the primary independent variable. Indeed, the fact that different classifications result from different criteria of management control is one of the major points offered by Zeitlin. Specifically, he argues that the lack of accurate information on the proportion of common stock held by principal stockholders leads to the misclassification of many owner-controlled corporations as management controlled. This possible source of bias could well account for the inconclusive findings on profit maximization and management control. If there is a significant relationship between owner control and profitability, it would be greatly attenuated by the misclassification of several owner-controlled corporations as management controlled. This interpretation is consistent with the literature in this area, inasmuch as the only study to have found a significant relationship between owner control and profitability also employed the most stringent criteria for management control (Monsen et al. 1968, pp. 438–39).

Conclusions

As I stated at the outset, my comments pertain chiefly to the issue of management control in the large corporation. I have sought to demonstrate not only the empirical adequacy of the theory of the separation of ownership and control proposed by Berle and Means but also some of the institutional developments associated with management control among the large corporations. I do not wish to imply that the owners of capital have been expropriated by the managers of capital; however, I do suggest that members of the managerial elite are far more influential in relation to the capitalist class of principal stockholders than many social scientists are

Commentary and Debate

prepared to admit. Furthermore, I contend that the theoretical aggregation of managers and principal stockholders into an amorphous capitalist class may obscure many issues of profound theoretical and substantive significance. By resurrecting the theory of the separation of ownership and control, I hope to redirect attention to the fundamental issue of cohesion and integration among the members of the economic elite. Even on the core issue of profit maximization, it is by no means clear that the problem of divergent economic interests between managers and owners has been effectively resolved by the incentive system of the large corporation. Moreover, the unification of the social and political interests of managers and principal stockholders is far more tenuous and problematic. The critical issue in this regard is the degree to which quantitative differences in the wealth and qualitative differences in the social origins of management officials and principal stockholders serve as barriers to the complete integration of the managerial elite into the capitalist class of principal stockholders. Unfortunately, this issue remains largely unresolved. Despite our differences with respect to the extent of management control among the large corporations and some of its consequences, Zeitlin and I agree on the importance of examining the often subtle processes of differentiation and integration among management officials and principal stockholders.

MICHAEL PATRICK ALLEN

Washington State University

REFERENCES

Allen, Michael Patrick. 1974. "The Structure of Interorganizational Elite Cooptation: Interlocking Corporate Directorates." *American Sociological Review* 39 (June): 393–406.
Baltzell, E. Digby. 1971. *Philadelphia Gentlemen: The Making of a National Upper Class.* Chicago: Quadrangle.
Berle, Adolph A., and Gardiner C. Means. 1932. *The Modern Corporation and Private Property.* New York: Macmillan.
Burch, Philip H., Jr. 1972. *The Managerial Revolution Reassessed.* Lexington, Mass.: Heath.
Fortune. 1971a. "The Fortune Directory of Large Corporations." 83 (May): 172–201.
———. 1971b. "The Fortune Directory of Large Corporations." 83 (June): 100–118.
Hindley, Brian. 1970. "Separation of Ownership and Control in the Modern Corporation." *Journal of Law and Economics* 13 (April): 185–221.
Kamerschen, David R. 1968. "The Influence of Ownership and Control on Profit Rates." *American Economic Review* 58 (June): 432–47.
Larner, Robert J. 1970. *Management Control in the Large Corporation.* Cambridge, Mass.: Dunellen.
Monsen, R. Joseph, John S. Chiu, and David E. Cooley. 1968. "The Effect of Separation of Ownership and Control on the Performance of the Large Firm." *Quarterly Journal of Economics* 82 (August): 435–51.
Sheehan, Robert. 1966. "There's Plenty of Privacy Left in Private Enterprise." *Fortune* 78 (July): 224 ff.
———. 1967. "Proprietors in the World of Big Business." *Fortune* 79 (June): 178–83, 242.

American Journal of Sociology

U.S. Congress, House. Subcommittee on Domestic Finance of the Committee on Banking and Currency. 1967. *Control of Commercial Banks and Interlocks among Financial Institutions*. 90th Cong., 1st sess. Washington, D.C.: Government Printing Office.
————. 1968. *Commercial Banks and Their Trust Activities: Emerging Influence on the American Economy*. 90th Cong., 2d sess. Washington, D.C.: Government Printing Office.
U.S. Congress, Senate. Subcommittees on Intergovernmental Relations, and on Budgeting, Management, and Expenditures of the Committee on Government Operations. 1973. *Disclosure of Corporate Ownership*. 93d Cong., 1st sess. Washington, D.C.: Government Printing Office.
Vernon, Jack R. 1970. "Ownership and Control among Large Member Banks." *Journal of Finance* 25 (3): 651–57.

[8]

ON CLASS THEORY OF THE LARGE CORPORATION: RESPONSE TO ALLEN[1]

Allen's note raises several interrelated issues (and a few quibbles) none of which can be dealt with fully here because of space limitations: my response is much shorter than I could wish.

"Management Control": Fact or Pseudofact?

To begin with, the three recent studies Allen cites do *not* "consistently confirm the theory of the separation of ownership and control." I presented an extensive analysis of the problems entailed in obtaining reliable and valid evidence on the actual ownership interests involved in a given corporation and concluded that the separation of ownership and control is probably a pseudofact. Allen presents no evidence or reasoning to alter that conclusion or to substantiate Larner's or Sheehan's findings. Further, Allen's assertion that "each of the three researchers concludes that a majority of the 500 largest corporations are subject to management control" is not correct. In fact, Burch (1972) classified only 124 of the top 300 under "probably management control" (PM), whereas he put 48 under "possibly family control" (F?) and 128 under "probably family control" (PF) (pp. 36 ff.). Employing "less intensive study" of the firms ranked by sales from 301 to 500, Burch classified them as follows: PM, 76; F?, 16; PF, 108 (pp. 160 ff.), yielding a total for the 500 of PM, 200 (40%); F?, 64

---

[1] I wish to call attention to an error in the original article (*AJS* [March 1974]). In table 3, p. 1104, under Other, the percentage in the column headed 4 plus should read 1, not 11.

Commentary and Debate

(12.8%); and PF, 236 (47.2%)—an estimate that Burch thinks *exaggerates* the extent of management control. With exemplary scholarly caution, he classifies firms under F? when the evidence is not conclusive enough to classify them as PF but when "one or more families have been identified as being prominently associated with the company in question" (p. 34). Without explanation, Allen has simply recategorized Burch's 64 "possibly family controlled" firms under "management" control, thereby creating a "majority" in the latter category.[2]

Management Control and Corporate Size

If we take the 500 industrial corporations studied by Burch and retain his classification, we find only a modest relationship between size rank and type of control ($C = 0.169$) (table 1). The relationship between size and

TABLE 1

Type of Control of 500 Largest Industrial Corporations, 1964, Burch Classification, by Sales Rank of Corporation

	Type of Control (%)					
Sales Rank of Corporation	PM		F?		PF	
1–50	58	} 44	20	} 20	20	} 36
51–100	30		18		52	
101–50	44	} 42	18	} 15	38	} 43
151–200	40		12		48	
201–50	36	} 38	12	} 13	52	} 49
251–300	40		14		46	
301–50	34	} 34	8	} 8	58	} 58
351–400	34		8		58	
401–50	40	} 42	8	} 8	52	} 50
451–500	44		8		48	
Total N	200		64		236	
Total %	40.0		12.8		47.2	

Sources.—Distribution calculated from Burch (1972, table 3-1, pp. 36 ff. and table C-1, pp. 160 ff.); rank from *The Fortune Directory for 1964*.
Note.— PM = probably management; F? = possibly family; and PF = probably family.

$$C = \sqrt{\frac{\chi^2}{N + \chi^2}} = 0.169.$$

[2] Chevalier's (1969) findings were inadvertently omitted from my article. With 5% as the management control threshold, and dominant influence (DI) referring to probable minority control, using public and numerous private sources, he classified the control of the 200 largest industrials as follows: management, 80; individuals (including directors) and families, 81 (plus 4 under DI); majority owned, 4; financial, 19 (plus 12 under DI). Chevalier considers this an *over*estimate of the number under management control.

American Journal of Sociology

management control is particularly weak. Within deciles, the relationship is anything but consistent. Moreover, of the three types of control, F? is most clearly associated positively with size rank, which probably means only that the *visibility* of controlling proprietary interests is negatively associated with size: the larger the corporation, *ceteris paribus*, the more difficult it is to discover the locus of control.

Otherwise, a finding that size and management control are positively associated is meaningless, since there are cogent reasons to doubt that the methods of analysis and data utilized by Larner (1970) and Sheehan (1966) provide valid and reliable evidence on the locus of control, and Burch's, while unquestionably superior, are also inadequate. After all, Larner (1970) himself presented a table that showed fewer management-controlled firms in the lowest assets ‚roups (301–500); and he tabulated Berle and Means's classifications and found "that management control . . . was concentrated among the larger firms" (pp. 18–19). Would that not mean, by Allen's logic, that the "theory" had already been confirmed by Berle and Means over three decades ago?

Three aspects of the "dispersion of ownership" are often confused: as the size of a corporation increases, there tend to be (1) an increasing number of shareholdings, (2) a decreasing proportion of shares held by management, and (3) a decreasing proportion of shares held by principal share-owners. Assuming their empirical validity, none of these developments necessarily means that proprietary interests are shorn of control of the large corporation. In fact, dispersion among a multitude of shareholders, or a slight ownership interest by management, may be precisely the basis for proprietary control. As Berle and Means (1967) themselves noted: "The larger the company and the wider the distribution of its stock, the more difficult it appears to be to dislodge a controlling minority" (p. 75). Therefore, as I argued in my article, the potential for control represented by a specific proportion of shares held cannot be discovered without a "case study of the pattern of ownership within the given corporation [and] . . . the system of intercorporate relationships in which the corporation is implicated" (p. 1091). I have since sought to demonstrate this in a study of the large corporation in Chile (Zeitlin, Ewen, and Ratcliff 1974). Much as in the United States and England, the largest corporations were most likely to be classified under management control using Berle and Means's methods and procedures. Rather than take appearances for reality, however, employing a method of analysis focusing on intercorporate relationships and the web of kinship revealed the actual controlling proprietary families and associates in 14 of the 15 firms originally classified under management control. A causal interpretation of the association between size and management control is spurious.

Commentary and Debate

Management Control and the Interlocking Directorate

Allen's evidence concerning the association between the frequency of corporate and financial interlocking and types of corporate control is consistent with what I suggested in my article, namely, that the corporations classified under management control interlock more frequently than others with the 50 largest banks and insurance companies, as well as with other top 200 corporations. Of course, since the largest corporations interlock more frequently, and also tend to be classified under management control more frequently than others, the effect of corporate size on the association between type of control and interlocking has to be investigated. Assuming that the type of control, even taking size into account, is associated with a greater frequency of interlocks, the question is: What relevance does this have for the managerial versus the class theory of the large corporation? On this, Allen is silent. Yet he has shown that one of the basic assumptions of managerial theory is false. In managerialist imagery, the large management-controlled corporation exists in a state of splendid autonomy, each one's management independent of the other, impregnable, and invulnerable to "external authority." Indeed, nary a word is uttered by managerialists about interlocking directorates. "Management," it is said, simply "selects itself and its successors as an autonomous and self-perpetuating oligarchy" (Galbraith 1967, pp. 88, 409). The managerialists also argue that, because of the "changed origin of finance capital" (*sic*)[3] the large corporation is emancipated from control by principal owners of capital and that the corporation's management, therefore, gains "complete decision-making power" over its capital. The large corporation, in Berle's words (Berle and Means 1967), "runs on its own economic steam. . . . Management thus becomes, in an odd sort of way, the uncontrolled administrator of a kind of trust, having the privilege of perpetual accumulation" (pp. xiv–xv). If corporate managements were really "uncontrolled administrators," because of decreased and decreasing dependence on outside liabilities for financing (itself an assumption contradicted by the evidence [Lintner 1967, pp. 179–84; Payne 1961, pp. 130–39; Kuznets 1961, pp. 248, 264, 268]) we should certainly not expect to find, as Allen has, that "management-controlled" corporations interlock more frequently than the family controlled with the largest financial institutions, as well as with other large corporations. These findings are contrary to the implicit hypotheses of managerial theory. (Elsewhere, Allen [1974] also concluded that the implicit managerial hypothesis that the frequency of interlocks between large corporations and banks has

---

[3] Berle, of course, is using the term "finance capital" merely as a synonym for "loan capital" and not in the specific sense in which, following but departing slightly from Hilferding (1910), I have defined it. See below.

897

American Journal of Sociology

"declined through time, . . . because these corporations have attained an increased capacity to generate capital internally . . . ," was *"disconfirmed"* [pp. 402–3; italics added].)

Though contrary to managerial theory, Allen's findings are quite consistent with the class theory of corporate control elaborated in my article. In reality, "management-controlled" corporations are not shorn of proprietary control; their ownership is merely relatively dispersed in comparison with other corporations. Put with desperate brevity, they tend to interlock more frequently with other large corporations and the largest financial firms for the following reasons: The corporate form multiplies the potential for control inherent in every unit of capital by permitting several corporations to have common principal shareowners as well as to own shares in each other. The interlocking directorate is one formal method of corporate combination that enhances the ability of owners of large blocks of stock in several corporations to assure that these corporations' actions do not adversely affect each other—or the common principal shareowners' investments in them. Further, the consolidation of small minority control may be enhanced by formal representation in management. Therefore, the tendency for common principal shareowners in several corporations (even if those corporations are not under their control), as well as corporations that have intercorporate holdings, to attempt to place themselves or their representatives in those corporations' managements, is reflected in a pattern in which the putatively "management-controlled" corporations are more tightly interlocked than others with other large corporations.

This hypothesis, *mutatis mutandis,* also applies to Allen's finding that the "management-controlled" corporations interlock more frequently than others with the largest banks and to his other finding that bank directors, particularly board chairmen, have a higher average number of directorships than other directors. (The latter data, as Allen notes, "confirm the results presented by Zeitlin.") A large bank typically has principal interests in several large corporations, and usually plays a critical role in mergers, acquisitions, and reorganization. It will, therefore, strive to prevent those corporations from taking actions that might be adverse to the others' (and, thereby, its own) interests. Diversification and conglomeration increase the extent to which the largest corporations are actual or potential competitors throughout the economy; and a bank that has common dealings with several such corporations, therefore, finds it even more essential to attempt to coordinate their policies in the common corporate interest. The same bank may interlock several corporations in which it has interests (and which are prohibited from direct interlocks with each other) by placing a different representative in each. If several large banks form a lending syndicate for a given corporation, or if the banks interpenetrate in

Commentary and Debate

their ownership (see U.S. Congress 1974, p. 7), the necessity for them to coordinate their policies and reconcile their interests is even more imperative. The large corporation's "vulnerability to external authority" is greater if its stock is scattered among a multiplicity of small shareowners. Therefore, we should expect, as Allen finds, that ostensibly management-controlled corporations are more likely than others to have representatives of the largest banks on their boards. This permits, as J. P. Morgan once explained, "a certain number of men owning property . . . [to] do what they like with it . . . and act toward mutual harmony" (*New York Tribune*, March 27, 1902).

Who Controls the Banks?

Although Allen also emphasizes the "dominant position of financial institutions among the large corporations," he doubts my hypothesis that the large banks are units in, and instrumentalities of, the system of propertied interests controlled by principal capitalist families. For him, the "critical issue . . . is the extent of management control among the large commercial banks," and he refers to Vernon's (1970) finding (which I discussed) that 75% of the 200 largest commercial banks are under management control. However, Allen ignores Burch's (1972) finding (which I also discussed) that, at most, only 24 of the 50 largest commercial banks were management controlled. I suggest that studies with appropriate data would reveal that the other largest banks, behind the managerial veil protecting their proprietary modesty, are also controlled by principal owners of capital. But what if this were not so? What if, as Allen avers, the largest banks were management controlled? What implications would this have for the hegemony of the capitalist class and for the political economy? Allen states none. No longer under the control of specific owners, would the banks forsake the maximization of profit for "satisficing" (*sic*) (Simon 1962) conduct? Would the executives of such management-controlled banks be transformed, as was hoped (Berle and Means 1967) of their corporate counterparts, into a "purely neutral technocracy" allocating "the income stream on the basis of public policy rather than private cupidity" (p. 313)?

The startling fact is that bank trust departments "manage assets substantially exceeding the assets of the 100 largest corporations in the United States" and have "larger securities portfolios than all other institutional investors combined" (Lybecker 1973, p. 997). Whose investments are managed by the largest bank trust departments? Generally, they will not administer personal capital of less than $100,000. Morgan Guaranty, for instance, has a $200,000 minimum. Thus, these trust departments probably serve fewer than 1% of Americans (see Projector and Weiss

American Journal of Sociology

1966). What might these principal owners of capital do if the management-controlled banks pursued anything but profit-maximizing investment policies? Would these banks be long permitted to retain their trust (*sic!*)? Allen accepts Vernon's finding that most of the largest banks are management controlled. What investment policies have their trust departments pursued? Those "on which they have leaned very heavily in the last few years" have been to trade in the "market of a select few securities, usually with high price-earning ratios, so-called glamour stocks, . . . to the virtual exclusion of the other market" of less favored stocks (Loomis 1973, p. 83; U.S. Congress 1974, p. 16). Apparently the glamor has not gone out of the pursuit of profit, even for the management-controlled banks. Certainly, there would be far-reaching reverberations for a bank's survival if the principal owners of capital (whose trusts and investment portfolios constitute one of its prime sources of capital) found that the bank was giving them, on the average, a lower rate of return than other banks and, therefore, shifted their trusts elsewhere. It would set in motion a rapid succession of similar and related moves by major corporate clients, other large banks, and large depositors such that a general "loss of confidence" would drain the bank's funds, render it incapable of honoring its contractual obligations, and drive it into collapse. Thus the "discipline of the market," which reflects the investment decisions of principal individual and institutional owners of capital, requires the banks not to deviate significantly from profit-maximizing policies. To the extent, therefore, that the management-controlled banks are both the creditors and principal shareholders of the largest management-controlled corporations, and interlock tightly with them, these banks will, in turn, impose their own profit-maximizing requirements on them.

The "Inner Group" and "Finance Capitalists"

With this coalescence of financial and industrial capital, as I argued in my article, there also tends to emerge a new social type, the "finance capitalist." Neither "financiers" extracting interest at the expense of industrial profits nor "bankers" controlling corporations, but finance capitalists on the boards of the largest banks *and* corporations preside over the banks' investments as creditors *and* shareholders, organizing production, sales, and financing, and appropriating the profits of their integrated activities. Thus, even were certain banks and corporations to become so large that they were not ordinarily under the control of specific minority ownership interests, it would not mean that power had passed to the "new princes" of the managerial realm (Berle and Means 1967, p. 116; and see Zeitlin, Ewen, and Ratcliff 1974, pp. 113–17). Although the largest banks and

Commentary and Debate

corporations might conceivably develop a relative autonomy from *particular* proprietary interests, it would be limited by the *general* proprietary interests of the principal owners of capital. To the extent that the largest banks and corporations constitute a new form of class property—of social ownership of the means of production by a single social class—the "inner group" (U.S. Congress 1965, p. 4 and passim) of interlocking officers and directors, and particularly the finance capitalists, become the leading organizers of this system of classwide property. That is why I hypothesize that they "represent a special social type in contrast to other officers and directors of the largest corporations and banks" (Zeitlin 1974, p. 1103; also see p. 1110). They should be far more likely than ordinary corporate executives to be drawn from the "upper" or "dominant" or "capitalist" class—the social class formed around the core of interrelated principal owners of capital.[4] Since Allen has already provided supporting evidence for other hypotheses suggested in my article, I hope he will also carry out research on this particularly critical hypothesis concerning the internal differentiation of the capitalist class.

Profit Maximization and Management Control

Here Allen raises mainly quibbles. He forgets that Larner tested not one but three interrelated propositions: on *level* of profit rates, on *variability* of profit rates (to measure "risk taking"), and on executive compensation. That is why I summarized Larner's (1970) findings as providing "systematic negative evidence" concerning the main managerial propositions. Immediately after the words Allen quotes from him, Larner continues: "It appears that proponents of theories of managerial discretion have expended much time and effort in describing a phenomenon of relatively minor importance. Management-controlled corporations seem to be just about as profit oriented as are owner-controlled corporations" (p. 29). Larner's conclusion states: "No fundamental differences in the level or stability of profit rates which might be attributed to management control were found" (p. 63). Also, although I noted the opposite finding on

[4] Michael Soref, a graduate student in sociology at the University of Wisconsin, has found a pattern of upper-class membership via clubs, Social Register listings, and preparatory-school attendance among directors of large U.S. corporations consistent with this hypothesis. Recent findings in England are also consistent with it. Whitley (1974), in his analysis of the directors of "very large industrial companies" and "large financial institutions," has found that not only are "the 'City' and 'industry' . . . remarkably closely linked," but also "while aristocratic kinship links do not appear to be particularly relevant for the industrial companies considered alone, they are important in connecting these companies to financial institutions and in producing a large, integrated network of the two groups combined. The directorship connections between industry and financial institutions, that is, are reinforced by, or alternatively can be seen as reflections of, kinship ties" (p. 77; see also Zeitlin, Ratcliff, and Ewen 1974).

American Journal of Sociology

relative profit rates by Monsen, Chiu, and Cooley (1968), I stressed
Larner's work because of its greater sophistication and reliability: it took
account of critical variables and interrelations that Monsen et al. ignored,
as readers can verify. It also should be noted that while Monsen et al.
stressed the large differences found between the mean ratio of net income
to net worth of 12.8% for "owner-controlled" versus 7.3% for "manager-
controlled" firms, over 12 years, they also presented an appendix of
findings on other ratios they thought "less interesting for our purposes,"
which they did not discuss. They found small differences between owner-
and manager-controlled firms on the mean ratio of net income to total
assets, 7.65% versus 6.09%, and the mean ratio of net income to sales,
5.86% versus 5.29%.

Econometric studies have in common the attempt to test theories of
managerial discretion by comparing the reported differences in profit
performance of putatively management- versus owner-controlled firms.
However, managerial theory rests on a theory of managerial motivation,
as I noted, and posits different motives for managers than for owners.
"Never," as Dahrendorf has put it, "has the imputation of a profit motive
been further from the real motives of men than it is for modern bureaucratic managers" (1959, p. 46). Recently, two British sociologists (Pahl
and Winkler 1974) investigated this proposition. They carried out systematic in-depth interviews with directors, examined their daily work diaries,
held short discussion groups with selected directors and unobtrusively
observed each director of 19 firms (a "rough quota sample of British
industry") for a full day of his working life in order to discover how
"directors perceived and negotiated their role" (p. 102). Pahl and Winkler's
findings were quite contrary to the managerial proposition. They found
that "the argument that managers still operate in a capitalist market and
hence must be just as oriented to the traditional capitalist goal, profit, as
owners . . . was completely confirmed by our observations. . . . The professionals saw their *purpose* and their *legitimation* in improving profitability markedly compared with the last years of the family owners'
management. In *all* cases we encountered, they were successful. Not only
were they more *oriented* to profit, they were more capable of obtaining it"
(p. 118; italics added).

Maurice Zeitlin

University of Wisconsin—Madison

REFERENCES

Allen, Michael P. 1974. "The Structure of Interorganizational Elite Cooptation: Inter-
    locking Corporate Directorates." *American Sociological Review* 39 (June): 393–406.
Berle, Adolph, Jr., and Gardiner C. Means. 1967. *The Modern Corporation and
    Private Property*. New York: Harcourt, Brace & World (originally published in
    1932 by Macmillan).

Commentary and Debate

Burch, Philip, Jr. 1972. *The Managerial Revolution Reassessed*. Lexington, Mass.: Heath.

Chevalier, Jean-Marie. 1969. "The Problem of Control in Large American Corporations." *Antitrust Bulletin* 14 (Spring): 163–80.

Dahrendorf, Ralf. 1959. *Class and Class Conflict in Industrial Society*. Stanford, Calif.: Stanford University Press.

Galbraith, John K. 1967. *The New Industrial Estate*. New York: New American Library.

Hilferding, Rudolph. 1910. *Das Finanzkapital*. Munich: Literarische Agentur Willi Weisman.

Kuznets, Simon. 1961. *Capital in the American Economy*. Princeton, N.J.: Princeton University Press.

Larner, Robert. 1970. *Management Control and the Large Corporation*. New York: Dunellen.

Lintner, John. 1967. "The Financing of Corporations." Pp. 166–201 in *The Corporation and Modern Society*, edited by E. S. Mason. New York: Atheneum.

Loomis, Carol J. 1973. "How the Terrible Two-Tier Market Came to Wall Street." *Fortune* 88 (July): 2–88, 186.

Lybecker, Martin E. 1973. "Regulation of Bank Trust Department Investment Activities." *Yale Law Journal* 82 (April): 977–1002.

Monsen, R. Joseph, Jr., J. S. Chiu, and D. E. Cooley. 1968. "The Effect of Separation of Ownership and Control on the Performance of the Large Firm." *Quarterly Journal of Economics* 82 (August): 435–51.

Pahl, R. E., and J. T. Winkler. 1974. "The Economic Elite: Theory and Practice." Pp. 102–22 in *Elites and Power in British Society*, edited by Philip Stanworth and Anthony Giddens. London: Cambridge University Press.

Payne, W. F. 1961. *Industrial Demands upon the Money Market, 1919–1957*. New York: National Bureau of Economic Research.

Projector, Dorothy, and Gertrude Weiss. 1966. "The Distribution of Wealth in 1962." Pp. 33–36 and 98–99 in *Survey of Financial Characteristics of Consumers*, Federal Reserve System, as reprinted in *American Society, Inc.*, edited by Maurice Zeitlin. Chicago: Markham, 1970, pp. 105–12.

Sheehan, Robert. 1966. "There's Plenty of Privacy Left in Private Enterprise." *Fortune* (July 15), pp. 224 ff.

Simon, Herbert. 1962. "New Developments in the Theory of the Firm." *American Economic Review* 52 (1): 1–15.

U.S. Congress, House. Antitrust Subcommittee of the Committee on the Judiciary. 89th Cong., 1st sess. 1965. *Interlocks in Corporate Management*. Washington, D.C.: Government Printing Office.

U.S. Congress, Senate. Subcommittee on Intergovernmental Relations, and Budgeting, Management, and Expenditures of the Committee on Government Operations. 1974. *Disclosure of Corporate Ownership*. 93d Cong., 2nd sess. Washington, D.C.: Government Printing Office.

Vernon, Jack R. 1970. "Ownership and Control among Large Member Banks." *Journal of Finance* 25 (3): 651–57.

Whitley, Richard. 1974. "The City and Industry: The Directors of Large Companies, Their Characteristics and Connections." Pp. 65–80 in *Elites and Power in British Society*, edited by Philip Stanworth and Anthony Giddens. London: Cambridge University Press.

Zeitlin, Maurice, Lynda Ann Ewen, and Richard Earl Ratcliff. 1974. " 'New Princes' for Old? The Large Corporation and the Capitalist Class in Chile." *American Journal of Sociology* 80 (July): 87–123.

Zeitlin, Maurice, Richard Earl Ratcliff, and Lynda Ann Ewen. 1974. "The 'Inner Group': Interlocking Directorates and the Internal Differentiation of the Capitalist Class in Chile." Paper presented at the annual meetings of the American Sociological Association, August 27, at Montreal.

Part III
Comparative Perspectives

[9]

FAMILIES, FIRMS AND FINANCE CAPITAL: THE DEVELOPMENT OF UK INDUSTRIAL FIRMS WITH PARTICULAR REFERENCE TO THEIR OWNERSHIP AND CONTROL

Arthur Francis

Abstract This paper reports findings from the Oxford Growth of Firms project on the ownership and control position of the largest 250 UK companies and, in more detail, that of a sample of 21 of these large firms. An analysis is made of the social and economic historical context in which most of today's large firms grew up. A theoretical model is developed of the stages of control through which firms are likely to pass. It is suggested that most firms are unlikely ever to become controlled by their own professional managers and that there is a trend towards firms being controlled by financial institutions. Evidence is then put forward, from an analysis of the current control position of the 'top 250' UK firms and from brief histories of the 21 sample large firms, which supports the previously outlined theory.

1. Introduction

THERE has in recent years been a new wave of interest by economists and sociologists in the question of the ownership, control and behaviour of the modern large corporation. A considerable amount of new data has been produced which indicates that the managerial revolution heralded by Berle and Means in 1932 has probably not yet happened. Owners have not yet ceded control over their corporations to the professional managers who are paid to run them. For example Zeitlin (1974) has shown, using evidence made available to the Patman committee, that it is likely that a majority of large US corporations are still controlled by ownership interests, and that Berle and Means (1932) and Larner (1966) seriously underestimated the extent of ownership control in their studies. More recently Scott and Hughes (1976) have shown that the proportion of Scottish registered businesses having the potential for control by one shareholder is even higher than Zeitlin's figure for the US of 60%. Our Oxford Growth of Firms study[1] has revealed a similarly high figure for English registered companies, as reported in Nyman and Silberston (1978) who report over 55% of the largest 250 UK industrial companies under owner control. Also recent work on the pattern of interlocking directorships by Levine (1972) in the USA, Scott and Hughes (1980), in Scotland, Stanworth and Giddens (1975) in England, and Whitley (1973) also in England, indicates more structural possibilities for groups of institutions to exercise control than those who argue for managerial control have previously acknowledged.

Perhaps the most interesting recent study has been that by Fitch and Oppenheimer (1970) who showed that in the US there has been an increase in the involvement of financial institutions in the exercise of control over corporations.

2   ARTHUR FRANCIS

Moreover they suggest a divergence of objectives between the interests of these financial institutions and those of industry, irrespective of whether the industrial firms are controlled by either owners or managers.

Questions about the ownership and control of firms are only important, though, if there is a relationship between who controls the firm and its behaviour. This is a question that has traditionally been tackled only by economists who, with Fitch and Oppenheimer being a notable exception, have usually adopted an econometric approach. Moreover they have usually merely dichotomized the sample into owner-controlled and management-controlled firms. Studies of this nature are reviewed in Nyman and Silberston (1978) who conclude that from these studies it appears that the impact of control on corporate behaviour is neither very strong, nor conclusively proven. They argue that this is because of two fundamental shortcomings in these studies – they are cross-sectional and have a very narrow conception of the nature of ownership.

In this paper an attempt is made to suggest a more elaborate set of categories of control positions a firm might be in, and to set the discussion of who controls into a longer term historical perspective.

Set out below is an attempt to construct a model of the stages of corporate control of British firms, taking into account the historical development of capitalism in the UK. The historical context of the first stage, that of the founding of the firm, is described in some detail because it is argued that this has had a powerful influence on the shape of industrial development in the UK, and that current corporate control and behaviour cannot be fully understood without this background knowledge. Stage 2 describes the transition of the business from control by the original founder to one of a variety of possible controlling groups, and suggests that control is unlikely to fall into the hands of professional management at this stage. The third, more speculative, stage suggests that there is a tendency for most large firms eventually to fall into the control of financial interests.

Having set out the model, data are then presented about the stages of control which firms in the Oxford Growth of Firms project have passed through. Within the scope of this paper it is not possible to discuss fully the effect of control type on behaviour but we are able to show, using carefully collated case study material, that our sample contains an even higher percentage of firms with some degree of ownership control than might have been expected on the basis of figures for the top 250 taking conventional criteria of ownership control. Moreover, paralleling Fitch and Oppenheimer's finding for the US, we show that there appears to be a strong tendency in the UK for the financial institutions to become more involved in the exercise of control over the large corporations. We are also able to document apparent changes in the strategic behaviour of many of the firms in our sample which are associated with a change in the control of those firms.

2.   The Stages of Control and Growth

2.1   Stage 1 – The Beginnings

A notable feature of the development of UK industry has been the extent to which currently large successful firms were founded by men from minority groups.

FAMILIES, FIRMS AND FINANCE CAPITAL 3

Hagen (1962), for example, shows that in the late eighteenth century Nonconformists contributed about nine times as many entrepreneurs, relative to their total number in the population, as did the Anglicans (Hagen, 1962: 297).

This remarkable statistic serves as the starting point for the analysis developed here, for whereas Hagen attempts to explain the Nonconformist entrepreneur phenomenon in psychologistic terms, positing high need achievement and need autonomy in this group, an attempt is made here to set UK industrial entrepreneurial activity in its social and economic context.

The argument is that the particular way in which capitalism has developed in Britain has not been conducive to the growth of domestic industry. Only those blocked from more desirable pursuits have engaged in industrial entrepreneurial activity. Thus the high proportion of Nonconformist entrepreneurs is a product of their blocked mobility and the structure of the wider society rather than their particular cultural/psychological characteristics.

The principle features of the development of capitalism in Britain germane to this argument are the absence of a bourgeois revolution and the dominance of mercantile activity.

Anderson (1965), and later and more extensively Stone (1972) have argued that capitalism first emerged in Britain in an agrarian form long before the Industrial Revolution. The success of agrarian capitalism, based on capital released by the dissolution of the monasteries, allowed landowners to put up substantial capital sums in trading ventures and thus begin to participate in the emerging mercantile capitalism. Unlike other European countries there was thus, claims Anderson, no bourgeois revolution in Britain. The original landed class transformed itself into a capitalist class but still with the old values and institutions of land rather than capital associated with it.[2]

However, though there was considerable openness in the social structure between the landowning and merchant classes (Wilson, 1965: 9), there was a striking lack of interest shown by either landowners or merchants in *industrial* activities when eventually the industrial revolution gained momentum.[3]

As Gould (1972) points out 'there is a dramatic contrast between the desperate activity to which Matthew Boulton was reduced in an effort to raise the four thousand pounds needed to keep the engine-making partnership of Boulton and Watt solvent, and the ease with which eighty years earlier a two million pound loan to the new East India Company had been over-subscribed in three days'.

Hobsbawm (1968: 75) makes a similar point. 'The wealthiest classes and greatest potential investors in this period – the great landlords, mercantile and financial interests – did not invest to any substantial extent in the new industries. Cotton-masters and other budding industrialists were therefore left to scrape together a little initial capital and expand it by ploughing back their profits, not because there was an absolute capital shortage, but simply because they had little access to the big money.'

Mercantile capital did flow into industry but as loan capital not as equity. Mathias (1969: 150) describes how the factory owners put together their fixed capital by raising mortgages on their houses or land, and borrowing from relations. Merchants

4   ARTHUR FRANCIS

who were suppliers and customers provided most of the working capital. (Over six-sevenths of the total capital required by the early factories was tied up in work-in-progress (Mathias, 1969: 145) in the form of trade credit.) Banks only became heavily involved in 'fairly isolated instances' (*Ibid.*: 176) and then only as *rentiers*. Crouzet's study (1962) of the growth of the capital of a number of eighteenth and early nineteenth-century firms reveals that in most cases the firms expanded chiefly by self-financing.

Given this high level of self-financing by in the main family-owned firms, and taking Cairncross' (1953) estimate that 60-65% of all British capital investment, other than that used to replace depreciating assets and to keep domestic capital per head constant, was invested abroad, it appears that a very large proportion indeed of landowners' and merchants' capital was being used in foreign investment and mercantile activities and not in domestic industry.

At the same time the values of the landowners remained dominant, though apparently influenced by the need to govern the rapidly expanding Empire.

For example Wilson (1965: 123) notes that from the earliest days of mercantile activity 'the most affluent members of the London community . . . did not stay in the metropolis to form an urban patriciate, as their Dutch rivals had in Amsterdam. They had become country landowners, squires, even peers, and Anderson (1965), focussing on the imperialistic aspects of mercantile and overseas investment activities, observes that 'Imperialism automatically sets a premium on a patrician political style . . . the aristocrat is defined not by acts which denote skills but by gestures which reveal quintessences: a specific training or aptitude would be a derogation of the impalpable essence of nobility . . . the famous *amateurism* of the English 'upper class' has its direct source in this ideal'.

In this light one can understand the durability of the sponsored mobility system of English education (Turner 1960) with its output of quintessential patricians armed by their élitist classics-dominated public school education with an unassailable sense of their right to govern the Empire. This should be compared with the greater emphasis placed on numeracy, science and technology in the contest mobility system played out in America. It is noteworthy that in France, too, the more technical demands of industry (and also of the military) were recognized by Napoleon in his creation of the Grandes Ecoles to produce an élite of administrators and engineers and in Germany the Technische Hochschulen have had, at least until recently, a higher status than the universities. In Britain, by contrast, the Mechanics Institutes and Colleges of Commerce had to wait until the early part of the twentieth century, and in many cases the 1960s, before being accorded the status of universities.[4] Even now their status is perceived to be inferior to Oxbridge by many sixth-formers seeking university entrance.

The dominance of empire and trade has thus had two important results. Firstly, the institutions concerned with flows of capital had been concerned with trading and foreign investment. Indeed, the merchant banks of today grew out of trading houses. The aristocrats, who had previously obtained their wealth from their position as feudal landowners and were now gaining it from the investment of capital, were investing not in industrial undertakings at home but in trading

FAMILIES, FIRMS AND FINANCE CAPITAL   5

ventures and industrial undertakings abroad. The institutions of finance capital which handled this business were therefore concerned with mercantile and imperial affairs and not with domestic industry.

By contrast in other countries the financial and industrial sectors grew up together and symbiotically. In the US for example the railways were precursors, chronologically, if not necessarily the cause, of large scale industry in the United States, and much of the original capital for the early major railway lines came from London (Chandler, 1962). But the railway owners then set up the US money market in New York on the basis of revenue from their operations. Hence the financial institutions were establishing themselves at the same time as, and with the purpose of funding, the founding of many of the current large US companies whose massive organic growth put them in the top 100 by 1914.

Secondly, with surplus value coming into the country as profits from mercantile activities, the traditional hierarchy of status was maintained. The landowning élite maintained their position and many of the owners of domestic industry played a traditional craft, subservient, role. To the extent that industrial capitalists, i.e. owners of business enterprises, enjoyed status and power it was probably in the context of a 'two nations' split. Only in the 'second nation' of the North of England did the iron, coal, and textile masters dominate and this domination seems largely limited only to the local society of the towns and cities where the factories, mines and mills were situated. They appeared to have little influence in the metropolis. Industry appears to have been seen by the rich and powerful, as well as by the poor, as a provider merely of artefacts, and not of profits crucial to the maintenance of the élite's position. It was not an activity, therefore, in which the élite engaged. Those institutions which the élite controlled, or which served the élite, particularly those institutions concerned with education and the professions were in the service of imperialism, trade and foreign investment, not of industry. This was, and is, not a social matrix conducive to the growth of industrial enterprises. How, then, did UK firms develop?

The hypothesis here is that there have been two types of industrial entrepreneur each with their characteristic objectives for their enterprise, and each associated with a particular growth pattern for the firm. The first is the 'marginal man' entrepreneur, the phenomenon identified but, we believe, inadequately explained by Hagen. The second type is more inclusive, covering non-marginal men of both craft and middle/upper class background who in the former case may have been in business simply because it was a job, and in the latter case entered business often as a hobby or interest, particularly where new technologies were concerned.

In Britain it was expected, for the reasons already spelled out, that offspring of upper and middle class families not engaged full-time in managing their inherited wealth would have a career in the military, the professions, the City, the merchanting companies, or the Home or Colonial Civil Service. Rewards in terms of social prestige, wealth and the ability to exercise power were associated with careers in these areas. Only those in a socially marginal position might have been expected to want (or, rather, need) to engage in industrial entrepreneurial behaviour. Specifically, we hypothesize that the structural postion tending towards

6   ARTHUR FRANCIS

industrial entrepreneurial behaviour is membership of a social group which in the past was located in the middle or ruling class but for particular reasons then became barred either from a conventional middle class career or from getting income from inherited wealth. Such a structural position has been the lot of minority religious groups, e.g. Quakers and emigrés, particularly Jews, and now, possibly, Asians. The Quakers, for example, were originally blocked from professional careers because of the Test Acts and in many cases could not continue farming because their religious convictions prevented them paying tithes to the Church landowners. Thus it was their structural position that forced them into having to make do with the 'second best', in terms of English values and reward, of going into business. Once in a business their education, and aspiration for their families, enabled and motivated them to achieve a high rate of growth and profit for their business through methods probably similar to those used by the American entrepreneurs described by Chandler.[5] The competition they had to face was probably 1.ot great (Franko 1974).

The second type of entrepreneur, the non-marginal man, appears to have founded businesses which had a quite different pattern of growth. Some of these non-marginals were tradespeople or craftsmen who took up the new technologies in a small way, and others were more typical of the English amateur gentlemen. For example, the foundation of Vickers Limited appears to have had its roots in both these sources, Scott (1962). In each case there appears not to have been a strongly held growth objective. The trades and craftsmen appear to have had a 'minding the business' orientation. Many of the gentry had more of an intrinsic interest in the engineering or metallurgy, for example, than a concern with the possibilities of the wealth or power that a fast growth rate of the business could yield. To the extent that businesses founded by these non-marginals grew into today's large corporations, this appears to have happened by the defensive merger of a number of small businesses, rather than by fast organic growth. A structural explanation in terms of the particular development of capitalism in the UK is thus suggested here for the difference in entrepreneurial objective between marginal and non-marginal men. Individual profit-maximizing behaviour is accounted for here by reference not to some overall emergence of a Protestant ethic nor to the cultural characteristics of a specific minority group. There is no need to postulate that guild craftsmen or members of the gentry desired anything other than to maintain their own position in society. One would not expect them, therefore, to exploit the new technologies with the same intensity as, for example, the 'captains of industry' in America or the blocked socially marginal groups in Britain.

2.2   Stage 2 – The Transition

It has usually been assumed[6] that when firms move out of the control of the founding family they pass into the control of management. Both empirically and theoretically this seems unlikely. Some empirical evidence is presented later. In this section a variety of control positions are suggested and it is argued that the most likely transition is from founding family control to control by other industrial owners or by financial institutions.

Diagram I depicts a variety of different paths which the control of the company may follow. The founding individual, or group, is denoted Type I ('marginal' founder) or Type II ('non-marginal') control. From this control position the most likely transition seems to be from the original founder to his heir(s). In Diagram I this is characterized as Type III control.

DIAGRAM I: *Stages in Corporate Control*

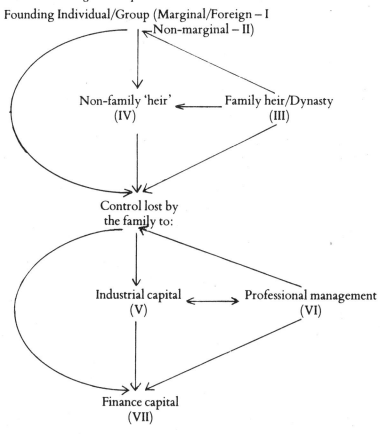

Founding Individual/Group (Marginal/Foreign – I
Non-marginal – II)

Non-family 'heir'
(IV)   ←   Family heir/Dynasty
(III)

Control lost by
the family to:

Industrial capital   ←→   Professional management
(V)   (VI)

Finance capital
(VII)

The evidence in general seems to be that the second or third generation of the founding family, particularly if it was from a marginal group, used the business as a means of getting into established society, through the acquisition of landed estates. Once in the gentry the dominant value system appears, in many cases, to have choked further entrepreneurial aspirations.[7] Nevertheless it was unlikely that the heirs to the business would have actually released control of it, because of the imperfect capital market then operating. In such a market a family may have been able to expropriate more surplus by owning a firm than from selling up and investing the capital elsewhere. High salaries, fringe benefits, use of company employees and materials for private work all add to the effective income the family

8   ARTHUR FRANCIS

enjoys from its ownership of the company. These are benefits which would not be available if the company were sold, control lost, and the capital reinvested in a diversified portfolio of stocks and securities. This particular reason for retaining control was probably more important in the early part of this century. Recent legislation on company accounting practices, information disclosure and on stock exchange regulation may have significantly reduced capital market imperfections and thus enabled owners to sell out without losing many of their 'rights' on surplus accruing from their capital. The recent behaviour of the founding families associated with Tesco and Mothercare, for example, who have significantly reduced their shareholdings in their respective companies in order to spread their assets more widely seems to be a modern phenomenon. It is not found in the history of the families owning, for example, J. Lyons or G.E.C. at a similar stage in their companies' development.

Thus in the past, and to a lesser extent now, families attempted to keep ownership *and* control for as long as possible. Moreover it can be argued that there are common interests between industrial capitalists, which at a number of points are different from, and even in conflict with, the interests of the financial institutions. Structurally, leaving aside any emotional commitment to a business he may have founded, or that has been in the family for generations, the owner of an industrial undertaking whose life-long experience has been within a particular industry and whose network of business contacts relates to that industry, is effectively locked into it. To sell out and reinvest elsewhere would be very difficult. Not so for the financier whose precise business it may be to switch resources from one company or industrial sector to another. It is in the interest of the industrial capitalist to stick by his business and of the finance capitalist to be looking for opportunities to release capital from ailing industries and relocate it elsewhere. From this basis of conflicting interests there is likely to emerge mutual hostility between industrial and finance capitalists.

A second major structural source of conflict is that created by the various sources of profit. Fitch, for example, suggests that in situations where financial institutions have control over industrial companies new investments are sometimes made and financed in ways that favour the financial institution at the expense of the other shareholders (Fitch 1970). Investments are funded by loans given by the finance house, and this may result in profits being diverted from shareholders' dividends towards interest paid financiers' loans. Thus the industrial capitalist holding only shares becomes worse off at the expense of the bank which holds both shares and the loan. Fitch cites Nader's finding that some American airlines overpurchased aircraft because financial institutions, which dominated the airlines' boards, gave loans for such purchases, the interest on which was greater than the reduced dividends which would result from the induced over-capacity.

Perrow (1970) has a different example of the conflict between industrialists and financiers in the story he quotes of the takeover of the Chicago Long Shore railroad by a financial conglomerate. Within a few years the conglomerate had bled the railroad white, realizing a large number of property assets held by the railroad but not using any of this to replace obsolete railroad stock and operating equipment.

FAMILIES, FIRMS AND FINANCE CAPITAL   9

The railroad couldn't break even on this basis and eventually the conglomerate got permission from the regulating authorities to close it down.

If we assume that industrial capitalists do perceive they have interests in common, and different from those of the financial institutions, and if partly for this reason and partly through being in the business a long time there is some network of relationships between industrial capitalists it is reasonable to expect that they will be reluctant to let control of their firms out of the control of industrial capital. If the founder cannot set up a dynasty, or if there are no suitable individual heirs to inherit, or when the line of succession fails, it seems common practice for the owning family to try to place the company in the hands of another *industrial* capitalist, either by selling it to him or, if the shareholding is already widely dispersed, inviting someone of high standing in the industrial (as opposed to the financial) world to take on the Chairmanship.

Alternatively there are a number of cases where the owning family has invited to become Chairman someone known to them in Establishment circles other than in industry, e.g. in the professions or the Civil Service. Such people are likely to pursue objectives for the firm in line with industrial rather than financial capital interests. Thus we have categorized all the above cases as Type V control (see Diagram 1).

Only very rarely is the Chairmanship given to a professional manager from within the company (Type VI control). We have come across only one case in our study (Unilever – see below) where the Board appears to have adopted a meritocratic approach to the appointment of a new Chairman. Here the Board effectively ran a selection procedure to appoint to the Chairmanship the internal career manager who in their view, at the time of the appointment being made, was the best one available.

Although one's reading of the literature on the managerial revolution would lead one to suppose it to be the norm that professional managers eventually replace family owners as controllers of the business, empirically it appears to be the exception. Theoretically one would suggest that this is because the two main contenders for control over the corporations are the owning families and the financial institutions and their power bases are, *pace* Galbraith (1967), much larger than that of internal management, at least so far as formal control is concerned.

A slightly less rare phenomenon appears to be the passing of the Chairmanship from family to what we have termed a 'non-family heir', (Type IV control). This is the situation in which an internal manager is singled out at a relatively early stage in his career and groomed to succeed the owner. With the degree of socialization this process involves it is likely that such an heir will adopt objectives for the firm similar to those of a family heir. However, such a shift in control involves considerable risk to the family (who for example will succeed the non-family heir?) and this control transition seems less favoured than the move to Type V control.

2.3   Stage 3– The Emergent Exercise of Control by Finance Capital.

We have argued that there has often been no pressure from, and indeed a reluctance by, industrial capital to create links with the financial institutions and to involve them in domestic industrial affairs. Similarly there has until recently been little pressure from the financial institutions to develop an interest in industrial capital. However, there are now a number of reasons why institutions appear to have been forced to concern themselves with industrial companies.

Firstly there has been the loss of Empire with its protected trading relationships, and the subsequent nationalization of many UK-owned companies in the ex-colonies. This, among other things, has led to a massive reduction in the relative size of UK physical assets held overseas, from a peak of 39% of all UK physical assets in 1910 (Halsey 1972) to under 8% by 1961 (Revell 1967). There has thus been a much greater reliance by domestic wealth-holders on UK based industrial companies for the creation of their profits.

Secondly there has been a significant increase in wealth-holding by white-collar and manual workers particularly in the form of rights on pension funds and insurance policies and this has provided additional capital to be invested by financial institutions, a number of which were set up by the established merchant banks to exploit this kind of business.

Two manifestations of this greater involvement by the institutions in domestic industry in the post-war period are the fast-rising number of quoted ordinary shares held by institutional investors and the increase in the percentage of new investment taking place through loans rather than new equity. In 1973 about 42% of all equity was held by financial institutions and some authorities assess this figure to have risen to about 60% by 1977. There has been a similar rise in the percentage of new funds coming from direct loans to companies from the financial institutions. In the early 1950s such sources of funds were only 2% of total sources of investment funds for industry, but had risen to 32% by the early 1970s. As the NEDO report (1975) from which these last figures were taken comments, 'the striking feature is the shrinkage of the capital market as a source of finance coincident with increased bank borrowing'.

During the same period as financial institutions appeared to become more reliant on domestic industry as a location for their capital, UK industry has itself been squeezed, partly due to the loss of protected markets in the Empire and to increased competition in home markets from foreign multinationals. This appears to have meant that the institutions have not been able merely to have an arms length relationship with all the companies in which they have invested but have had to take an active part both in the restructuring of industries and in the control of individual companies. Financial institutions were deeply involved, for example, in the Labour Government's Industrial Reorganization Corporation in the mid-sixties when large sections of British industry were restructured, and the ex-deputy Chairman of a large merchant bank is currently Chairman of the National Enterprise Board. Since the early 1960's there has been increasing influence exerted over individual companies by the institutions, notable examples being GEC in 1960 and Vickers and Debenhams in 1970. There seems no reason to suppose that the exercise of such control is not likely to continue. Control by financial institutions we have designated as Type VII in Diagram I.

In general we would expect at least three things to follow from the above analysis of the stages of control and growth of firms. Firstly a large number of firms will still be in family control even though the family shareholding in them is very small, because the financial institutions are still only beginning to move into the industrial arena and there may still be good reasons for families to hold tenaciously to their prime sources of wealth. Secondly, that when firms do move out of family control the families will prefer to pass control to other industrial capitalists, but thirdly, that increasingly control will be taken by financial institutions. We would expect only rarely to find control taken by professional career managers, as their power base for gaining control in the face of the other two competing interest groups is so slight. We now turn to the evidence.

3. The Assessment of Control

The first and crucial question is how one is to assess who controls a firm. By control we mean the exercise of power over strategic decisions relating to the firm. Zeitlin (1974) offers a list of these decisions, suggesting that strategic decisions are about relations with other companies, the state, foreign Governments, the workers, sources of raw materials and markets. But to discover how power is distributed amongst the many groups who participate in making decisions is immensely difficult and as yet there is no adequate sociology of the distribution of power over strategic decisions in large corporations. Most work up to the present has concentrated on two major competing groups, shareholders and professional managers. Economists have usually taken the rather mechanistic and hierarchical view that shareholders control the Board of Directors which controls the firm provided that shareholdings are concentrated enough for one particular group to vote together to remove an unsatisfactory Board. Thus their measures of owner-control have been in terms of a minimum percentage of the total voting shares held by one known individual, institution, or cohesive group, a figure of 5% or 10% usually being taken.[8] When all individual shareholdings have dropped below this figure shareholders are deemed in this view to have lost control over the Board and the Board itself, usually composed largely of professional employee managers in the company, now has full control over the firm. There are two other well-canvassed views of who controls the firm. The first, popularized by Galbraith (1967), argues that modern technology is so complex that strategic decisions can only be understood and taken by committees of expert technocrats and so control is exercised no longer by either shareholders or the Board but by what he terms the 'technostructure' – these lower level technical experts – irrespective of how concentrated the shareholding is. The second view, in direct contrast to this, argues that the level of concentration of shareholding has little or no effect on business behaviour. One strand of this argument focusses on the class background of senior management and prevailing dominant ideology, suggesting that even if managers are free to make a choice between, say, profit-maximizing and other objectives they will choose the former because of their ideology and class position (see for example Nicholls 1969). A second strand suggests that the pressures of the market, both for getting capital for investment and for products, are so tight that managers effectively have no choice but to take profit-maximizing strategic decisions (see for example Blackburn 1972).

A rather different view is presented here, though argued in more detail elsewhere (Francis, forthcoming). We suggest that firms are not so tightly constrained by product and capital markets that those who control them have no discretion. Also our Growth of Firms research indicates that hierarchy is still very important in firms. From observation, from interviewing and from administering a questionnaire in the companies in our study it was clear that the Chairman of the company was in a very dominant position. The role was viewed, both by the incumbent and by senior managers, as the peak of the firms' organizational hierarchy and not merely as *primus inter pares* at Board meetings. His influence in decision-making was acknowledged by all to be powerful.[9]

From this we argue that the ability to appoint and remove the Chairman is the crucial way in which groups can exercise control over a company, but that this ability may in some instances be exercised without a large shareholding and in some instances can not be exercised with such a shareholding. We found, for example, even in our rather small sample, a number of firms in which the family still exercised control over their companies, in the sense that they retained the Chairmanship and appeared to hold rather paternalistic third-generation family type objectives for the firm, even when their family shareholding had dropped below 5%. In two of these cases the family had continued to maintain the high degree of control even though outside interests had built up substantial (over 5%) holdings in the companies. It appears that families can still exercise control in such circumstances because the mechanisms by which shareholders in general, and financial institutions in particular, can replace Chairmen and/or chief executives is *are* at present still so ill-developed that it can usually only operate when the firm is willing to co-operate. Unless the firm is in severe need of large injections of capital or there is a potential buyer for the firm, the Board of the firm can strongly oppose proposals from outside interests that the Chairman should be replaced. The institutional shareholders would then have to engage in a proxy battle and might have to vote on a majority of new Board members in order to gain control.

We are thus arguing that an analysis of the shareholdings of a firm is a first approximation in answering the question of who controls it, but a better second approximation requires a detailed examination of who the Chairman is and how he came to be appointed. This in turn often requires a longitudinal examination of the history of the firm in terms of the changing composition of the Board of Directors and turning points in the firm's strategic behaviour and economic performance. In some instances for example the Chairman may be controlled by the Board. If, for example, the rest of the Board genuinely feel they represent financial interests then the Chairman, even though perhaps a third or fourth generation member of the founding family, and having paternalistic *status quo* type of objectives, may well have to fall in with the Board's objectives. The advantage to a financial institution of having representatives on the Board is that such representatives may successfully advocate an acceptance of objectives in line with the institution's interests. A longitudinal analysis may, for example, reveal this. A situation in which a firm is apparently family controlled (in that the Chairman is a member of the family or nominated by the family) but has actually been captured by finance capital interests, might be revealed by a discontinuity in the firm's behaviour, associated with a change in Chairmanship.[10]

4. *The Control Position of the 'Top 250' Firms**

A full analysis of who controls the biggest 250 corporations following the procedure outlined above is beyond the scope of one paper. What is presented here, therefore, is 'first approximation' analysis of the current control position of the top 250 firms, and in the following section is a 'second approximation' analysis of the stages of control through which the seventeen UK companies in our sample have passed.

TABLE I: *Ownership control of the U.K. 'Top 250'[11] in 1975*

% of voting shares held by a single institution or by the board of directors and their families	Type of holder								
	I	F	D	C	G	M	O	N	Total
Unquoted company	3	—	8	1	1	—	—	3	16
Over 50%	4	—	15	1	1	—	1	—	22
40%–50%	1	—	5	1	—	—	1	—	8
30%–40%	1	—	8	1	1	—	—	—	11
20%–30%	8	1	2	—	—	—	—	1	12
10%–20%	5	4	17	—	—	—	—	—	26
Other holdings greater than 10%	—	—	2	—	—	4	—	—	6
5%–10%	1	4	5	—	—	—	—	—	10
Total	23	9	62	4	3	4	2	4	111

Family Chairman or M.D. (but less than 5% shareholding by individual or group)	15
Total owner-controlled	126
No known control	98
Total firms	224
% owner-controlled	56.25

NOTES:

Types of Holder I = Another industrial company.
  F = Financial institution.
  D = Directors and their families.
  C = Charitable trust.
  G = Government or quasi-Government agency.
  M = Mixed control type.
  O = Other control type.
  N = Not classifiable due to lack of information.

*This section relies heavily on Nyman and Silberston (1978).

So far as shareholding is concerned we have identified over half of the top 250 UK firms as being at least minority controlled. This is in line with the very high percentage of owner controlled firms identified by Zeitlin (1970) in the US and by Scott and Hughes (1976) in Scotland. Excluding all those companies wholly owned by foreign firms an examination of the shareholding pattern of the *Times* 1000 (1975/76) 'top 250' companies revealed that 110 of the 227 UK companies listed had at least 5% of their shares held by one known individual, institution or cohesive group, see Table 1. The criterion of 5% is that used by the US Patman Staff Report (1968) who judged this figure to be enough to exercise control of a corporation. Even using Larner's (1966) less inclusive criterion of a minimum of 10% of the shareholding held by one group the number of firms which could be classified as at least minority owner controlled was still 101 (44.5%). If one were to add to the list those companies which had a descendant of the founding family as Chairman or Managing Director, though less than 5% shareholding by any individual or group, the number of owner controlled firms would rise to 127, 56% of the total.

Even this is likely to be an underestimate of the extent of ownership control because it took no account of large privately-owned companies, e.g. Littlewoods and the Vestey organization, some of whose sales and assets figures were not available. Nor did it take account of data recently made available under the 1976 Companies Act whereby nominee shareholders may have to declare themselves, and it did not, unlike the Scott and Hughes study, take account of control via interlocking directorships or by family chairmen who did not bear the name of the firm (except in a few instances where we had local knowledge).

Moreover of the owner-controlled firms we were able to identify 70 (31%) which could be classified as family controlled (Types I-III in Figure 1), another 24 (11%) controlled by industrial interests (Type V) and 10 (4.4%) controlled by financial institutions (Type VII). A further 10% had at least 10% of their shares held by an individual or group, but the interests of this controlling group could not be classified as family, industrial or financial.[11]

5. *How Control Changed Hands in the Growth of Firms Sample*[12]

It was not possible within the Growth of Firms research project to undertake the kind of 'second approximation' longitudinal analysis of changes in ownership, control and behaviour for each of the 227 companies for which we have data on their current control position. This would be immensely time consuming, and in many cases would have required cooperation of individual companies in order to get data on how and why significant changes took place. As a second best, we present here a summary of the ownership and control histories of the 17 large UK firms which made up the sample in the Oxford Growth of Firms project. So far as we are aware these represent, so far as ownership and control are concerned, a random sample of the Top 250 firms in the UK.[13]

For these firms we were able to undertake a longitudinal analysis along the lines outlined earlier of turning points in the companies' histories, and changes in Chairmen and in the composition of their Boards of Directors. The results are summarized in Table 2, where the seven stages of control are those laid out in

Diagram I. Three of the firms in our sample, Cadbury-Schweppes, GEC, and ICI, resulted from mergers between more-or-less equal partners and in these cases the merging firms are listed. Thus the number of firms listed in Table 2 totals 21 though only 17 separate firms were extant in 1976.

TABLE 2: *History of the Stages of Control of Firms in the Growth of Firms Sample*

FIRM	I	II	III	IV	V	VI	VII
				STAGE OF CONTROL			
Albright & Wilson	1855		1903	1957	1972	1967	
Assoc. Biscuit Manu.	1822		1857				
Baker-Perkins	1876		1918				1975
Cadbury (merged with Schweppes in 1969)	1831		*				1969
Schweppes	1790		*				1940 or earlier
Debenhams		1813	1863	1928		1950	1970
Dixon Photographic	1945						
E.M.I.	1898						1931
A.E.I. taken over by G.E.C. 1967	1894						1967
English Electric, merged with G.E.C. 1968		1919		1933			1968
G.E.C.	1889						1960
Nobel merged in 1926	1871				1877	1919	
Brunner Mond to form	1872		1918				
I.C.I.			1926		1938	1930	
J. Lyons	1887		*				
Mothercare	1962						
Sears Holdings							
W. H. Smith & Son		1792	early (19				
Stone-Platt (formed by merger of several small companies)		(18- (19	early (19			1 9 6 7?	
Tesco	1919		1968				
Unilever		1885	1929			1970	1925
Vickers		1829	1873				1926

* Date not known

The first major finding to note is that two thirds of the firms in our sample were founded by 'marginal' men. Four of the companies (Albright and Wilson, Associated Biscuits, Baker-Perkins and Cadburys) were founded by Quakers, two and a half companies (Schweppes, Nobel and Brunner of Brunner-Mond) were founded by foreign born emigrés, one (AEI) was originally a US subsidiary, and the rest had founders of Jewish origin. It is interesting to note that it is the earlier foundations that had Quaker origins and the later ones that had Jewish origins. This is further evidence for a 'structuralist' rather than 'cultural traits' explanation of entrepreneurial behaviour. Quaker foundations came into being at a time when

Quakers were being discriminated against, and as discrimination against them became less, their propensity to engage in entrepreneurial activity appeared to diminish.

The second major finding resulting from a detailed examination of the control position of these firms is the massive extent of owner involvement. Seven of the seventeen firms are still in family control, three of these still being run by the founder, and seven appear to be controlled now in some measure by the financial institutions. Just one can be categorized as under industrial capital control, and only two seem to be controlled by their own professional management. One of these (Stone Platt) may not be free from the financial institutions, as we discuss below.

In the following four sections we trace the paths taken by each of our firms to their current control positions.

5.1   *Firms still in family control*

Four of the seven firms in the sample which are still apparently under family control have only come into prominence in the post-war period and are still in, or have only just completed, their first stage of growth. Two of these, Dixons Photographic and Mothercare, are still run by their founders. The third, Tesco, has the founder as Life President and his son-in-law as Chairman. The fourth, Sears Holdings, a conglomerate built up by Sir Charles Clore, also has its founder as Life President but the Chairmanship has recently been given to Leonard Sainer. Nevertheless, Sir Charles Clore alone still holds 1.5% of the equity. All four founders were of Jewish origin, and it is worth noting that the four firms are either totally, or have strong interests, in retailing. This is an industry that has been revolutionized in the post-war period by massively increased consumer demand and the new computing technology, thus allowing Chandler-type economies of speed in distribution to be realized (Chandler 1977), and hence openings for new firms.

The three other firms still family controlled at the time of the study (1977) were Associated Biscuit Manufacturers (ABM), J. Lyons, and W. H. Smith.

ABM was formed as a holding company in 1921 as a result of the merger of Huntley and Palmer and Peek Frean – two of the largest UK biscuit firms which both had Quaker origins, in 1826 and 1857 respectively. In 1960 they were joined by another old established Quaker biscuit company – Jacobs of Liverpool. ABM has always been controlled by family interests (the Palmers and the Carrs of Peek Frean) who have supplied almost all the most senior executives until very recently. The various families still have a substantial shareholding (20% in 1974) though from the beginning of 1972 Rowntree Mackintosh began to build up a substantial stake in the Company, and it is likely that a takeover was only prevented, or perhaps merely postponed, by Rowntree making substantial losses on cocoa buying. It was not until 1977 that the dynastically controlled company had a group chief executive. Until that time, when an outsider was brought into the company to fill that position, the heads of the various divisions or functions, many of whom were family, reported direct to the company Chairman, who has always been a member of the family.

J. Lyons has also been run by a dynasty in the past. It was founded in 1887 by the

FAMILIES, FIRMS AND FINANCE CAPITAL   17

Salmon and Gluckstein families – Jewish immigrants who had previously run a small tobacco company in London – and has always had a family Chairman. Until recently the Board has been dominated by family members and family have held a majority of the voting equity. In the early 1970's the firm made a number of large overseas acquisitions, overstretched itself financially, had to sell off a number of UK assets and was left in a very vulnerable position, a situation it handled by agreeing in 1978 to a merger with another family-based firm, Allied Breweries.

W. H. Smith is an untypical case. It is a company which had very rapid growth to become a household name under the hand of the son of its founder, without there being any evidence of Nonconformist or foreign origins. The company was founded in 1792 by H. W. Smith. The son, W. H. Smith, built the company up. The family moved into establishment circles, were immortalised by Gilbert and Sullivan (their Admiral of the Fleet who had never been to sea was an early Smith), and still control the business. They own 11% of the shares (in 1975), have 30% of the votes and although the last two Chairmen have not been Smiths by name, they are related by marriage both to each other and to the Smith family.

5.2 *Firms controlled by professional management*

The firm most clearly to have escaped from the control of both the founding families and the financial institutions is Unilever, and even this has not been a straightforward progression from family to professional management control. For the founding Lever family things went wrong in 1920 when the founder, William Lever, over-extended the company with a large but misguided acquisition. The company began to run out of cash, the bankers were bearing in heavily and an accountant, Francis D'Arcy Cooper of the firm of accountants of Cooper Brothers, was called in. He pulled things round and in 1925 on the death of the first Lord Leverhulme he became Chairman of the company. This was against the original wish and expectation of Leverhulme who had been grooming his son for the job. Nevertheless, the financial institutions made no attempt to consolidate what control they had over the firm, perhaps because as suggested earlier in this paper such institutions had no desire or need in this case to get involved in domestic companies. The firm appears to have subsequently fallen back into family control. In 1929 it merged with the Dutch company, Margarine Unie, which was family owned and the Board of the new company then had a substantial number of family directors on it. Subsequently one of the three Heyworth brothers, who all came into Unilever 'through a family connection' (Wilson 1977) and all reached Board level, took over as Chairman in 1942. He was followed by George Cole who had come into the firm through personal contact with a friend of Lord Leverhulme (Cole, 1963) and the first totally 'unconnected' professional manager to become Chairman of Unilever Ltd. was Ernest Woodroofe in 1970.

Unilever is also noteworthy in having a Main Board comprised wholly of full-time executive directors. The only direct ownership control that can be exercised over Unilever, it would appear, comes from the Leverhulme Trust which owns 18% of Unilever's shares. Lord Leverhulme is one of the trustees but so are the present Chairman and one Vice-Chairman, and two previous Chairmen of Unilever, so this can hardly be counted as family control.

It is likely that Unilever had managed to escape any control from the financial institutions for two main reasons; it has always been in a very powerful product market position in most of its areas of business, and can by virtue of this more easily retain good-enough profits; it also has a depth of competent management due partly to a very sophisticated system of graduate recruitment, a system set up, perhaps significantly, by D'Arcy Cooper in the 1920's. It is also possible that graduate recruitment was less difficult than it might have been because of the nature of the Unilever business. Much of it was conducted in the colonies and may have seemed more like the kind of thing middle class young men would have done anyway. Thus it may have appealed to many who would not have been attracted to conventional UK based manufacturing industry.

The only other management controlled firm appears to be Stone-Platt, a large mechanical engineering company, but it is doubtful if it is correct to characterize it as such, even though the current Chairman is a professional manager with no known family or financial connections. Stone-Platt Industries was formed in 1958 as the result of a merger between J. Stone and Co. and Platt Bros. Ltd. The latter firm was itself the result of a merger in the 1930's of seven spinning machinery companies (mainly in Lancashire), a merger undertaken at the behest of the Midland Bank, to whom the largest of the seven firms owed a lot of money. The person handling this merger for the bank was Sir Walter Preston, Chairman of J. Stone in which company his family had a substantial shareholding. Immediately prior to the Stone-Platt merger Sir Kenneth Preston, Sir Walter's son, was Chairman of both companies and became Chairman of Stone-Platt on its formation. He remained its Chairman until his retirement in 1967 and thus the firm is characterized in Table 2 as being under family control to this point. He was succeeded by an employee of the firm with 40 years' service, and then by the current Chairman, who had previously been the company's first chief executive. This phase we have characterized as being under professional management control but it should be noted that in the year prior to Preston's retirement, a director of Hill Samuel, H. R. Moore, joined the Board. Moore has held the Chairmanship of at least two other major engineering companies, while holding his directorship of Hill Samuel, and it is likely that he was placed on the Stone-Platt Board by his merchant bank to oversee the succession of the Chairmanship. This procedure is not unknown, and it is fairly clear from the Company Report of that year that it was not on the initiative of Stone-Platt that he joined their Board.

5.3 Firms under industrial capital control

The two companies categorized as currently under industrial capital control are Albright and Wilson, and ICI. Both have an interesting history in control terms. Albright and Wilson remained under family control until 1957. Until 1955 a third generation Wilson (Kenneth H.) was Chairman and a third generation Albright (W. B.) was Managing Director. In that year Sir Sydney Barrett became Chairman. He had been recruited into the company at a high level from a

Readership in Chemistry at University College, London, some years earlier by the family who could see they were not going to be able to keep up the succession, although family members remained on the Board for at least another 20 years. Subsequently another distinguished scientist, this time from Cambridge via the post of Chief Scientist at the Ministry of Supply, Sir Owen Wansborough-Jones, was brought in and he took over as Chairman in 1967. Next, in 1969, as Chairman was a retired Permanent Secretary to the Board of Trade, recruited to the Board in 1967, but then the company got into severe difficulties with a large new venture in Newfoundland and had to be bailed out with a £17.5m loan from a US conglomerate, Tenneco. Part of the price for this was that one of their men, Sydney Ellis, took over the chair. Shortly afterwards Tenneco bought 49% of the equity, and in 1978 bought out the company entirely.

ICI too has had a turbulent past. It came into being in 1926 as the result of a merger between two large companies, Nobel Industries and Brunner-Mond, and two smaller ones, United Alkali and British Dyestuffs. The first Chairman of the new ICI was a second generation Mond (Alfred) and Managing Director was a career manager named McGowan, who had worked his way up through Nobel with no known family connections. On Alfred Mond's death McGowan, who according to Reader (1975) had a taste for power and an ability to wield it, took over the Chairmanship and also retained his role as sole Managing Director. He exercised almost despotic power for seven years. But the ICI Board, unlike that of Unilever, has always had a substantial number of non-executive outside Directors and four of these (Solway and Lord Weir, each of whom headed their own large family companies, another industrialist, Lord Colwyn, and a politician-banker Sir Christopher Clayton) organized a revolt. They originally planned to instal a third generation Mond (Lord Melchett) into the chair but he suffered a severe heart attack at the crucial moment. Instead the post of M.D. was abolished (it has never been reinstated), McGowan was stripped of his executive powers and a Management Committee was set up. McGowan was Chairman of this but the Committee also had to include two outside directors.

Quite unlike Unilever there has always been a strong representation of outside directors on the Board of ICI, and they do seem to have been influential. At present ICI has eight outside directors, whose other involvements cover a variety of interests, including banking, insurance, accountancy and a number of other major industrial companies.

It is for this reason, despite the fact that five of the last Chairmen since McGowan's retirement in 1950 have been professional managers with a lifetime career in the company, that the company is categorized as under industrial capital control.

5.4 *Firms controlled by finance capital*

Of particular relevance to the thesis being propounded here – that there is a steady trend towards firms becoming controlled by the financial institutions – is the finding that six of our 17 firms, 35%, are now apparently controlled by these interests. It is instructive to examine the process by which this appears to have occurred.

20   ARTHUR FRANCIS

In three of the six cases, Debenhams, GEC and Vickers the record is clear. Debenhams appears to have gone through most of the stages of control, eventually getting into professional management control in 1950 but then going through a period of such poor performance that eventually the institutional shareholders got together and demanded a change in the top personnel. As a result, a City accountant, Sir Anthony Burney, was appointed Chairman in 1970.

Vickers have had a more complex history. The founding Vickers family first lost control temporarily from 1867-1873 and then again permanently in 1926. This followed a financial crisis in 1925 when the company was under the Chairmanship of a third generation Vickers. A team of financiers were called in to advise. They restructured the finances of the company and left behind a new Chairman ideally qualified to run the armaments dominated company, General Sir Herbert Lawrence. Described as a soldier by birth and a banker by marriage (Scott, 1962), after leaving the Army he became a partner in his wife's family merchant bank. He was succeeded in 1937 by another finance capitalist, Si. Archibàld Jamieson, a partner in Flemings, another merchant bank.

As with Unilever, the financial institutions did not appear at this stage to be particularly careful to keep control and in 1949 an ex-soldier with no financial connections (though some family connections) took over the chair. He was followed by a series of Establishment figures until 1970 when a few months before the similar Debenham's case, the institutions intervened because of very poor economic performance. Arguably it was this curious history of control that made it easy for the institutions to make their intervention, the first time they had ever done so without some kind of triggering action from a company in trouble, e.g. a loan needing renegotiation. This resulted in (now Sir) Peter Matthews, a career manager who had become a British Steel Director, becoming Managing Director, and later in the year Lord Robens became Chairman.

GEC came into the hands of the financial institutions through the triggering action of a loan needing renewing. The General Electric Company Ltd. now comprises three merged giant electrical firms, AEI, English Electric and the original GEC. GEC, which took over AEI in 1967 and then merged with English Electric a year later, was founded in 1886 by Hugo Hirst. Hirst emigrated to England in 1880 because of Prussian anti-semitism in his native Bavaria, and the firm continued in family control until 1960. On Hirst's death his brother-in-law and then his son-in-law became Chairmen, following a line of succession laid down by Hirst himself. But by the third generation the business was failing badly and, when the need arose in 1960 to make a rights issue to repay some loan stock due for redemption, the financial institutions stepped in. The Prudential refused to take its share of the new issue without changes being made and a professional engineer within GEC, Arnold Lindley, took over as Chairman and Chief Executive. He bought Radio and Allied Industries for its management skills, a deal which brought into GEC Arnold Weinstock, the son-in-law of Radio and Allied's Chairman. By 1963 Weinstock had taken over from Lindley as Managing Director of GEC, and Lindley only retained the chair for another fourteen months. He was replaced by Lord Aldington, sometime Chairman of Sun Alliance and director of two banks who had

FAMILIES, FIRMS AND FINANCE CAPITAL   21

joined the Board in 1962 and Aldington became Chairman both of GEC and of a major merchant bank, Grindlays, in 1964. Aldington remained Chairman during the takeover of AEI, but stepped down to become Deputy Chairman when GEC merged with English Electric. Weinstock became Managing Director of the merged company and Lord Nelson, previously Chairman of English Electric, took the chair. English Electric, and the Nelson family, had a peculiar history. The company came into being as a result of mergers between no less than seven different companies in the 1910's, did not rationalize the resulting enterprise, got into financial difficulties and was secretly bought up by Westinghouse of America. Westinghouse did not exercise its control openly in order to maintain the illusion that English Electric was still a British Company, an image thought to be important for its trading position. So the company asked George Nelson and Sir Holbery Mensforth, both former trusted employees of British Westinghouse in the days when it had been controlled by American Westinghouse (Jones and Marriott, 1970: 132), to be Managing Director and Chairman respectively. By 1933 Nelson had proved his complete dedication to the company and was given the Chairmanship in addition to continuing as Managing Director. With Westinghouse having to maintain a low profile because of the total secrecy surrounding their ownership of the company Nelson was now in a powerful position. Although holding a negligible number of shares in the business he kept close and sole control over it both by his management style and by the device of not allowing company executives on to the main board. All board members were nominees and were culled from Cambridge dons and retired civil servants. There was thus no alternative power base in the firm or on the Board. He maintained this autocracy until his death in 1962 and even at that point exercised his influence to the extent that his son, the second Lord Nelson, succeeded him to the Chairmanship, thus achieving a lifelong ambition of the first Lord's . The second Lord Nelson is clearly an acceptable person in the City, currently holding a directorship of the Bank of England and another major bank. He was made Chairman of the combined GEC and English Electric after the merger. It should also be noted that the Board of the newly merged company contained no less than five non-executive directors who had strong City connections, and at least six members of the Board in 1977, including the Chairman, had directorships in major financial institutions. It is thus fairly clear that the financial institutions are not divorced from the control of GEC.

For the three other firms classified as finance capital controlled, Baker Perkins, Cadbury-Schweppes and EMI, the evidence is more circumstantial.

Baker Perkins appears to have moved from family to finance capital control fairly recently. Allan Ivor Baker, the fourth generation of the founding owner, took over the Chairmanship of the company in 1944 and held it until 1975 when he retired, aged 67, and the Chairmanship passed out of the family for the first time in the company's history. Family shareholding had dropped to a low level some time before this. The company went public in 1957 and in 1967, the first time the data were publicly available, the family had only a 3% shareholding. Hints of intervention from the financial institutions came in 1963. For the two previous years the company's profitability had declined rapidly, return on assets had halved in the three years 1961 to 1963 and, more importantly for shareholders, return on equity dropped by nearly 70% to 2.2%. Within months of the 1963 accounts being published a Managing Director of Morgan Grenfell, the company's financial advisors, had been appointed to the Board. In fairness it must be pointed out that he replaced another non-executive Consultant Director on financial affairs who retired through ill-health, but this latter financial advisor had no institutional connections and had been recruited to the Board when the company went public in 1957. It is tempting to infer that the Morgan Grenfell man represented the interests of non-family shareholders. The company's fortunes improved rapidly in the next two years but sank back to a rather low performance level and in 1971 another profits (and turnover) crisis hit the firm. On this occasion an industrialist, I. H. G. Gilbert, Chairman of British Match, joined the Board and the Chairman announced a policy of appointing a small number of non-executive directors with wide outside experience. In 1974 I. H. G. Gilbert was given the newly created title of Deputy Chairman and the next year succeeded Sir (Allan) Ivor Baker to the Chairmanship. This was despite the fact that J. F. M. Braithwaite, Managing Director (and Sir Ivor's younger cousin), had been Vice-Chairman of the company since 1956.

It is possible, of course, that Braithwaite chose to stay as full-time Chief Executive Director rather than become Chairman and it will be interesting to see who will be the Chairman by the time this paper is published. Gilbert in 1978 is 67 and Braithwaite only 61. If Braithwaite does succeed Gilbert on the latter's retirement this in itself will not refute the suggestion that the financial institutions are exercising control. Braithwaite himself has strong family connections with the City – his father was a stockbroker and Chairman of the Stock Exchange for ten years.

Cadbury-Schweppes came into being in 1969 when the two separate eponymous firms merged. Cadbury's origins date back to its Quaker foundation in 1831 and the company remained in the hands of the family until the merger. Schweppes was founded in Bristol in 1790 by Jacob Schweppes, a mineral water manufacturer from Geneva, but at some point in the nineteenth century ownership and control passed to the Kemp-Welch family. Though the company went public in 1897, a line of Kemp-Welchs were Managing Directors until 1941, and the family was represented on the Board until 1949. The Board in the immediate post-war period was rather illustrious, including two Barons, two Honourables and a Baronet. The Chairman from 1940 to 1968, the Hon. R. Hanning Philipps, was a member of the London Stock Exchange, a director of two other City institutions, had a brother who was a member of Lloyds and Chairman of an insurance company, and was related to the Kindersley banking family. Of the two directorial Barons, Lord Rockley was an ex-Government Minister, peer, and director of a bank and several trusts, and became Vice-Chairman. The other, Lord Milford, was a member of the Philipps family. On this evidence it seems reasonable to categorize Schweppes at this time as being under finance capital control.

On Hanning Philipps' retirement in 1968, Lord Watkinson, one-time Conservative Cabinet Minister, was appointed Chairman of Schweppes. The next year Cadbury and Schweppes merged and Watkinson became Chairman of the new company. The Chairman of Cadbury's at the time of the merger, GAH (now Sir Adrian) Cadbury, became Managing Director of the merged enterprise and then succeeded Lord Watkinson to the chairmanship on the latter's retirement at the end of 1974.

It is difficult to know to what extent Cadbury-Schweppes can still be thought to be controlled by finance capital interests as opposed to having reverted to family control. We have assigned it here to the former category on the following, admittedly rather slim, argument. Schweppes appeared fairly clearly to be controlled by finance capital interests. The merger was technically a takeover of Cadbury by Schweppes and the Chairman of the latter company remained Chairman of the merged enterprise. The Board after the merger contained two non-executive directors who were directors (one a Vice-Chairman) of merchant banks and it is likely that they would have been able to exercise some considerable influence if Watkinson's suggested successor was not acceptable to the merchant banking interests.

EMI has had a chequered history.[14] It was formed by the merger of the Gramophone Co. (better known by its brand name 'His Masters Voice') and Columbia. The marriage was arranged by an American company, RCA, and a merchant bank, Morgan Grenfell, who had a controlling interest in HMV and Columbia respectively. From the earliest days, therefore, finance capital has had an involvement in EMI. The first Chairman of EMI was an internal appointment – Sir Alfred Clark, formerly managing director of HMV but he was known to be pro RCA and its policies. All three subsequent chairmen have been appointed from outside the company and in the one appointment about which we have some detailed knowledge there was direct involvement by financial interests in the decision. This was the appointment of (now Sir) Joseph Lockwood, who was brought into the firm in 1954 as Deputy Chairman when it was performing badly, and then, after 15 months, was made Chairman. His recruitment was at the instigation of Sir Edward de Stein's merchant bank. de Stein at that time had a substantial holding in the company and a partner of that company has always had a seat on the Board from the inception of EMI.

The structure of the Board of EMI has a striking history in general. Not until Sir Joseph Lockwood was made Chairman in 1955 were any executives of the company (other than the Managing Director) members of the Board. Only after ten years with a minority of executive directors on the Board was a decision made to have more executive directors and so increase the maximum permissible size of the Board from 12 to 16. From this point non-executive directors have been in the minority but there has always been, and continues to be, a strong line-up of such people on the Board representing considerable experience (and connections and interests?) in merchant banking, government and industry. We have thus, cautiously, categorized EMI as under Type VII, finance capital control.

6. *Conclusions*

In this paper we have attempted to show that most of the growth of large-scale corporations in the UK has taken place outside the mainstream of élite English society, under the direction of men from marginal social groups, and without the direct involvement of finance capital. We have also argued that finance capital is now becoming much more involved in the control of domestic corporations. The history of the growth of the modern corporation is still of consequence today in that a surprisingly large number of the largest UK companies appear still to be under the control of descendants of their founding families. In addition many of those companies who are not controlled by such interests appear nevertheless to be controlled by ownership interests of one kind or another. Even a rather cursory inspection of the shareholding position of the largest 250 companies reveals a very high percentage still under ownership control. A more detailed analysis of a sample of these companies suggests that simple shareholding figures substantially understate the extent of ownership control. In particular it reveals the rarity with which firms operate as a meritocracy in the sense of appointing to the top position, the chairmanship, one of the more able internal career managers.

Of particular interest is the apparent secular trend whereby control passes eventually from industrial to finance capital interests. There are sound theoretical reasons why this should be a characteristic of the British economy in the last two decades. We have presented some tentative empirical evidence, and have suggested this is likely to be a growing phenomenon.

Three caveats must be entered. The first relates to the question of control. In Section 3 there is a brief discussion of this concept where it is suggested that the sociology of control over the large corporations is very under-developed. In this paper we have not sought to fill this theoretical lacuna and we have in the main adopted the common usage of control being an either-or concept, in the sense, for example, that either industrial or financial interests have control over a firm. This is clearly a gross simplification and in fact in any situation a plurality of interests will be exercising some power and influence over the direction any firm is taking. What we have tried to do in this paper is sketch out in a shorthand way who we feel has the ability to exercise a significant amount of control over a given firm, and to show, for example, that the financial institutions have this ability to a considerable extent more than is commonly suggested.

Secondly, there are only occasional references to the impact different control positions are likely to have on a firm's behaviour. Again, it was not felt to be within the scope of the paper to discuss this relationship. It was felt that so many studies in this area have foundered because too simple a notion was used of the possible types of control, that there was a need for an extended discussion of the complexity of the phenomenon, and that the shifts in control had to be set into a historical context. Once this has been done the ground is clear for a more sophisticated analysis of the relation between type of control and behaviour, and this analysis is currently under way for the firms in the Oxford Growth of Firms sample.

Thirdly, there is need for more debate about the current interests of the financial institutions. Much more work needs to be done in this area. It is almost certainly misleading to lump together into one category, as has been done in this paper, the merchant banks, clearing banks, pension funds and life and non-life insurance companies. In particular the difference in interest between those investing in equity and those investing in loan stock, as identified by Fitch (1970), is clouded by treating all these institutions in the same way. Nevertheless the treatment in this paper is at least one step forward from handling the ownership and control question in terms of the simple dichotomy of a competition for control between shareholders and professional managers. [15]

Notes

1. The Growth of Firms research is funded by the Social Science Research Council in the UK and by the Deutschen Forschungagemeinschaft in West Germany. The author acknowledges his indebtedness to the ideas and work of his colleagues on this project, John Child, Alfred Kieser, Steven Nyman and Aubrey Silberston, and to comments made on an earlier draft of this paper by Howard Aldrich, Colin Fletcher, Erhard Friedberg, Jane Marceau, Roderick Martin, Steve Nyman, W. J. Reader, Richard Scase, Aubrey Silberston and Dorothy Wedderburn.

2. This argument is developed both by Perry Anderson (1965) and E. J. Hobsbawm (1968: 31-2).

3. There were a number of partnerships between landowners and manufacturers in the very early days of industrialization e.g. in South Wales (Wilson, 1965: 305) but this type of arrangement did not appear to continue, presumably as better investment opportunities presented themselves as the Empire developed. Cairncross's data (1953) support this view.

4. Imperial college of Science and Technology was not formed until 1907, and the Colleges of Advanced Technology were not upgraded to technological universities until 1964.

5. A variant of the case of an enterprise being founded by a socially marginal person is that of businesses founded by foreigners coming to the country for various reasons, seeing the business opportunities, and staying. In many cases these people were Americans whose families had originally migrated from Britain. Baker Perkins Ltd., described later in the paper, has some of its origins in this type of foundation.

6. For a review of such studies see Nyman and Silberston (1978).

7. Although he was referring to Elizabethan peers, who were probably more active in business than their descendants, Stone's description of the objectives of the aristocracy are illuminating in this context. He suggests that 'though they needed the money, some of them desperately, the lives of few social groups have ever been less dominated by the profit motive. It was the various ways of conspicuous consumption, the maintenance of 'port' and hospitality, that was their main economic concern' (Stone, L. 'The Nobility in Business', *The Entrepreneur*).

8. For full details of their studies see Nyman and Silberston (1978).

9. This finding derives from interviews with 134 senior executives and directors in the 17 firms in the Growth of Firms study and is reported in detail in Francis (forthcoming).

10. The notable examples of institutional shareholders successfully bringing about a change in Chairmanship of a Company are all cases where either the company was willing – Vickers (1970), Debenhams (1970) or when the company needed the help of the financial institutions – Lever Brothers (1922), GEC (1960).

11. For full details of these results see Nyman and Silberston (1978) from which this Table is taken.

12. Although interviews were held with executives in all the firms comprising our sample, and our grateful thanks to them for all their help, all the data used in this section of the paper is from public sources, mainly company reports and the *Financial Times*. In some cases company histories were available, viz. for Albright and Wilson, Threlfall (1951); Associated Biscuit Manufactures, Corley (1972); Baker-Perkins, Muir (1968); EMI, Gelatt (undated but *c.* 1974); GEC, Jones and Marriott (1970); ICI, W. J. Reader (1975); Unilever, Wilson (1954); Vickers, Scott (1965).

13. Our sample was selected on criteria that so far as we are aware have nothing to do with type of ownership. Our strategy was to select five industries in which there were at least six companies in the top 250 and approach the two highest and two lowest performers in terms of return on capital and growth. In fact, as only 50% agreed to participate we had also to approach those of medium performance, but a check showed that of those originally approached, an even higher proportion were owner controlled than those eventually agreeing to respond.

14. For some of the detailed history of EMI we are indebted to their company historian Mr. L. Petts. The interpretations of the facts he made available is of course our own.

15. Accepted, 23.2.79.

References

ANDERSON, P. (1965). 'Origins of the Present Crisis'. in Anderson, P. and Blackburn, R. (eds.), *Towards Socialism*, London: Fontana, 11-52.

BERLE, A. A. and MEANS, G. C. (1932). *The Modern Corporation and Private Property*, New York: Macmillan.

BLACKBURN, R. (1972). 'The New Capitalism' in Blackburn, R. (ed.), *Ideology in Social Science*, Fontana.

CAIRNCROSS, A. K. (1953). *Home and Foreign Investment 1870-1913*, Cambridge University Press.

CHANDLER, A. D. (1962). *Strategy and Structure*, M.I.T. Press.

CHANDLER, A. D. (1977). *The Visible Hand*, Harvard.

COLE, G., Chairman of Unilever, in an interview with Kenneth Harris, *The Observer*, 6 and 13 January 1963.

CORLEY, T. A. B. (1972). *Quaker Enterprise in Biscuits: Huntley and Palmers of Reading 1822-1972*, London: Hutchinson.

CROUZET, F. (1962). 'La formation du capital en Grande Bretagne pendant la revolution industrielle', quoted in Gould, 1972: 164.

FITCH, R. and OPPENHEIMER, M. (1970). 'Who Rules the Corporation' (in 3 parts), *Socialist Revolution*, 1, nos. 4, 5, 6.

FITCH, R. (1970). 'Reply to O'Connor', *Socialist Revolution*, 150-70.

FRANCIS, A. Forthcoming. *Company Objectives, Managerial Motivations and the Behaviour of Large Firms: an empirical test of the theory of 'Managerial Capitalism'*.

FRANKO, L. G. (1974). 'The Move Toward a Multidivisional Structure in European Organisations', *Admin. Sci. Qtly.*, 19, 4, 493-506.

GALBRAITH, J. K. (1967). *The New Industrial State*, London.

GELATT, R. Undated. *A Voice to Remember: the Sounds of 75 years on EMI Records, 1898-1973*, EMI.

FAMILIES, FIRMS AND FINANCE CAPITAL   27

GOULD, J. D. (1972). *Economic Growth in History*, London: Methuen.

HAGEN, E. E. (1962). *On the Theory of Social Change*, Dorsey Press, Illinois.

HALSEY, A. H. (ed.) (1972). *Trends in British Society since 1900*, Macmillan.

HOBSBAWM, E. J. (1968). *Industry and Empire*, Harmondsworth: Penguin.

JONES, R. and MARRIOTT, O. (1970). *Anatomy of a Merger*, London: Jonathan Cape.

LARNER, R. J. (1966). 'Ownership and control in the Largest Non-Financial Corporations, 1929 and 1963', *Amer. Econ. Review*, LVI: 777-87.

LEVINE, J. H. (1972). 'The Sphere of Influence, *Amer. Soc. Rev.*, 37, 14-27.

MATHIAS, P. (1969). *The First Industrial Nation: an economic history of Britain 1700-1914*, London: Methuen.

MUIR, A. (1968). *The History of Baker Perkins*, Cambridge: W. Heffer.

N.E.D.O. (1975). *Finance for Investment: A study of mechanisms available for financing industrial investment.* HMSO.

NICHOLS, T. (1969). *Ownership, Control and Ideology.* Allen and Unwin.

NYMAN, S. and SILBERSTON, A. (1978). 'The Ownership and Control of Industry', *Oxford Economic Papers*, 30, 1, 74-103.

(PATMAN) STAFF REPORT. (1968). *Commercial Banks and their Trust Activities: Emerging Influence on the American Economy*, Washington D.C.: Government Printing Office.

PERROW, C. (1970). *Organisational Analysis*, Tavistock.

READER, W. J. (1975). *ICI: A History*, Vol. 2, 'The First Quarter Century, 1926-1952'. Oxford University Press.

REVELL, J. R. (1967). *The Wealth of the Nation: The National Balance Sheet of the UK, 1957-1961.* Cambridge University Press.

SCOTT, J. D. (1962). *Vickers: A history.* Weidenfeld and Nicolson.

SCOTT, J. and HUGHES, M. (1976). 'Ownership and Control in a Satellite Economy: A Discussion from Scottish Data', *Sociology*, 10.1.

SCOTT, J. and HUGHES, M. (1980). 'Capital and Communication in Scottish Business', *Sociology*, 14.1.

STANWORTH, P. and GIDDENS, A. (1975). 'The Modern Corporate Economy: Interlocking Directorships in Britain, 1906-1970, *Soc. Review*, 23, 5-28.

STONE, L. (1972). *The Causes of the English Revolution 1529-1642.* London.

THRELFALL, R. E. (1951). *The Story of 100 Years of Phosphorus Making, 1851-1951*, Oldbury: Albright and Wilson.

TURNER, R. (1960). Modes of Social Ascent Through Education: Sponsored and Contest Mobility. *Amer Soc. Rev.*, XXV, 5.

WHITLEY, R. (1973). 'Commonalities and Connections among directors of large financial institutions', *Soc. Review*, 21, 613-32.

WILSON, C. *The History of Unilever*, in 3 vols., London: Cassel 1954; vols. 1-2; 1958, vol. 3.

WILSON, C. H. (1965). *England's Apprenticeships: 1603-1763*, London: Longmans.

WILSON, C. (1977). 'Management and Policy in Large-Scale Enterprise: Lever Brothers and Unilever, 1918-1938', in Barry Supple (ed.), *Essays in British Business*, Clarendon Press, Oxford.

ZEITLIN, M. (1974). 'Corporate Ownership and Control: The large corporations and the capitalist class, *Amer. Jl. Soc.*, 79, 5, 1073-1119.

Biographical Note: ARTHUR FRANCIS is lecturer in Industrial Sociology at the Department of Social and Economic Studies, Imperial College, London. He was formerly Research Officer at Nuffield College, Oxford where the research reported here was undertaken.

[10]

OWNERSHIP AND CONTROL IN A SATELLITE ECONOMY: A DISCUSSION FROM SCOTTISH DATA*

JOHN SCOTT and MICHAEL HUGHES

Abstract This paper discusses various concepts and ideas concerned with patterns of ownership and control in industry. It is concluded that Maurice Zeitlin's discussion is the most sophisticated and the most useful for empirical research. Some of Zeitlin's ideas are related to the structure of ownership and control in Scotland. It is argued that sociologists, unlike economists and political scientists, have paid insufficient attention to the relative autonomy of Scotland as a region within British society. The 248 Scottish registered public companies are analysed and it is concluded that there is strong evidence in favour of the view that companies can be seen as units in a class-controlled system. Considerable doubt is thrown upon the 'managerial' view of the corporation. It is argued that a particularly important role is played by groups of investment trusts in controlling the network of Scottish companies—the ownership of Burmah Oil and other Scottish companies is discussed to illustrate this. Finally it is argued that further research must construct a typology of directors and relate this to the position of Scotland in the international economic system.

MOST discussions of 'industrialism' in British sociology start out from the published papers of the 1964 British Sociological Association annual conference on the theme of 'The Development of Industrial Societies' (Halmos, 1964). Most of the papers printed there clearly exhibit the confrontation between 'liberal' and 'Marxist' trends in sociology recently documented by Goldthorpe (1972). In particular, the papers by Worsley, Lockwood, and Banks point to the rise of bureaucratization and professionalism within the management of the industrial corporation, yet argue that this is occurring in the context of the persisting fusion of kinship and private property, family capitalism. For example, Banks, following the arguments of Florence (1961) and others, argues that the ideal type of the 'achievement oriented enterprise' is becoming the dominant force in the industrial economy—there is a trend towards the recruitment of managers from outside the firm, with an emphasis upon formal qualifications—nevertheless, this occurs within the context of ascriptive family relationships and family control over industrial property (Banks, 1964: 50, 53). It is necessary to examine whether this trend leads to the managerial corporation, or whether the continued presence of proprietary controllers can be documented. Our aim in this paper is to discuss the question

* A paper delivered to the Annual Conference of the British Sociological Association, University of Kent at Canterbury, 1975. Earlier versions of this paper have been read to seminars at the universities of Aberdeen and Strathclyde.

of ownership and control in the context of Scotland as a particular industrial society.

Scottish Society

Scotland is, in may respects, not merely a geographical region of the United Kingdom but also a distinct society—a fact perhaps not realized by people who have not lived or worked in Scotland. In terms of the distinctiveness and relative autonomy of its key social institutions—law, education, religion, etc.,—and its culture, it must be regarded as such. Aspects of, for example, its educational system cannot be adequately translated into unproblematic English equivalents. It is true to say, however, that this distinctiveness has rarely been the focus of attention of sociologists.

Very little work has been carried out on British regionalism, and Scotland in particular has received far less than its fair share of the research effort of British sociologists (Eldridge, 1974; but see Hechter, 1973, 1974, 1975). This creates considerable problems for sociologists attempting to rectify this situation. Political scientists have increasingly recognized the relative autonomy of the Scottish political system (Kellas, 1973). Equally, economists have attempted to construct models of the Scottish economy as a distinct unit (Johnson *et al.*, 1971)[1]. Our aim, as sociologists, is to approach Scotland as we would approach any society. In studying ownership and control in Scottish industry we focus on Scottish registered companies—those incorporated under Scottish law—and we treat English registered companies as 'foreign' multinationals. We do this *not* in order to make a pro-Nationalist political point—a political doctrine which we would reject—but in order to recognize the central elements of the social structure and political economy of Scotland.

The perspective which we employ recognizes that no society is totally self-sufficient; we live in a world in which various national and sub-national societies coexist in relations of dependence and interdependence. Owing to Scotland's distinctive culture and institutions, we may fairly see it as a distinct, though 'sub-national' society. In examining ownership and control we focus on Scottish registered companies, since they may rightly be regarded as the core of the Scottish economy. Most data on Scotland takes as the unit of analysis the concretely defined geographical region of Scotland and all economic activities which take place within those territorial boundaries.[2] However, should moves towards political devolution and national autonomy progress further, as they undoubtedly will, those companies which operate in Scotland but which are registered in England will increasingly come to resemble 'foreign' multinational firms. The major problems of Scottish society revolve around this fact, and from the fact that Scotland is doubly dependent on the English economy: dependent upon England as a market for produced goods and raw materials, and dependent on the high degree of external ownership and control. Crucial questions to ask are: how significant is the distinctively 'Scottish' sector of the economy in relation to the 'foreign' sector, who owns and controls the Scottish sector, and what are their connections with 'foreign' capital?

The concepts of ownership and control

By far the most sophisticated discussion of the concepts of ownership and control is that of Maurice Zeitlin (1974), which combines a comprehensive theoretical framework with a detailed empirical analysis. Zeitlin is specifically concerned with the same issue as the contributors to 'The Development of Industrial Societies': the interpretation of the separation of ownership and control. He argues that the dominant interpretation is a 'pseudofact'. His own view is that the relationship between the capitalist (kinship and property) complex and the managerial (bureaucratic and professional) complex must be regarded as empirically problematic; there may be a separation of the managerial *function*—what Pahl and Winkler (1973) call 'operational control'—from ownership, but not necessarily a separation of control *as such* from ownership (Zeitlin, 1974: 1078). Zeitlin wishes, in particular, to move away from the atomistic model of the corporation used by writers as diverse as Sweezy and Berle and argues that sociologists should investigate the interconnections between corporations: corporations may be 'units in a class-controlled apparatus of appropriation; and the whole gamut of functionaries and owners of capital participate in varying degrees, and as members of the same social class, in its direction' (*ibid*: 1079). The task of the sociologist is to discover whether identifiable families and other cohesive ownership interests continue to control the major corporations.

Atomistic studies which fail to identify a dominant ownership group within the corporation tend to define such corporations as 'managerial': but Zeitlin claims that over and above the owners and managers of the particular corporation, there are external groups, such as bankers, which may be able to exercise control. Of those studies which have analysed outside control or influence, many have identified various 'interest groups' which bind together their constituent corporations under the common control of wealthy families, financial associates and investment bankers.

The aim of research into the corporate world, according to Zeitlin, should be to try to identify the various spheres of influence: he points to the importance of the spheres of the Rockefeller, Mellon, du Pont, Ford, Fisher, Mott, and Hanna families in the USA (see also Levine, 1973). A great number of individuals may participate in the ownership of a family block, utilizing a complex holding pattern in order to keep control concentrated, despite the diffusion of ownership. Control may also be exercised through entangling interests in several interrelated corporations: it is necessary to investigate the interaction of proprietary and kinship relations in complex networks.[3] According to Zeitlin, banks are of crucial importance in this network, although their significance has been neglected by writers such as Berle and Means. The largest corporations tend to be the least self-financing and are, therefore, dependent upon bank funds—and this means reliance upon a small number of very large financial corporations. Banks may share control with proprietary interests or may have more or less full control in ostensibly 'managerial' corporations. It is this situation which gives considerable significance to the high degree of interlocking between banks and industrial corporations. The larger the corporation, the more heavily is it interlocked with financial firms; the larger the assets, the more banking interlocks. Banks themselves tend to be units in the whole system of propertied interests controlled by the major capitalist families.

Zeitlin also discusses the problem of operationalizing 'control' and points to the limitations of defining control in terms of the ownership of a particular percentage of the voting stock—the significance of a particular percentage block of shares will vary according to the overall distribution of the corporation's shares, the particular situation of the firm and the identity of the holder. Control, as a form of power, is a relationship, not an attribute; confining our attention to the single corporation and an arbitrary percentage of stock may limit our ability to see the pattern of power relationships of which this corporation is merely one element (*ibid*: 1091, 1108).[4] Zeitlin criticizes Berle and Means (1932), Gordon (1945) and Larner (1970) for basing their conclusions on inadequate information and for failing to see that control through a 'legal device' (pyramiding, voting trusts, etc.) is a form of ownership control (*ibid*: 1081). He follows Rochester (1936) and Lundberg (1937) and argues that the actual control group in any corporation can only be adequately identified if we investigate the specific situation of each corporation. Most studies have identified controlling groups by their holding of a particular percentage of the voting stock, the more recent writers tending to suggest that a lower percentage is necessary as share ownership becomes more and more diffused. The following cut-off points have been suggested:

50% and over — Berle and Means' 'majority control' situation.
20–50%   — Berle and Means' 'minority control' situation.
10–50%   — Larner's 'minority control' situation.
5–50%   — The Patman Committee 'minority control' situation, although they argue that less than 5% may give control in the very large corporations.

The problem is, however, that whichever cut-off point is used, it is necessary to look for coalitions and alliances among groups and corporations which may, individually, have less than the minimum, but who collectively exercise control. Equally, the significance of a particular percentage holding will vary from corporation to corporation. Zeitlin concludes that a particular percentage minority ownership constitutes a *potential* for control; *actual* control depends upon the specific context. Proprietary control is defined as the situation where 'the concrete structure of ownership and of intercorporate relationships makes it probable that an identifiable group of proprietary interests will be able to realize their corporate objectives over time, despite resistance (*ibid*: 1091).

An investigation of the question of ownership and control in Scotland should attempt to match the framework presented by Zeitlin. We must aim to identify the various proprietary interests which are active in Scottish business and must try to identify the extent of solidarity and conflict between these interests. Such an analysis would identify those interests which are dominant and the institutional structures through which they exercise this dominance.

In our analysis of corporate ownership and control in Scotland we shall focus primarily on the 10 per cent cut-off point and are, therefore, analysing potential proprietary allocative control. However, in so far as it is possible to obtain information on smaller blocks of shares to supplement our analysis of interlocking directorships we shall attempt to identify the controlling interests in the larger corporations.[5]

Ownership and Control in the Scottish Economy

Two recent studies of Scottish manufacturing industry provide some initial data for our study. John Firn, in his study of 'ultimate control' in manufacturing plants in Scotland, (Firn, 1973) shows that the percentage of Scottish manufacturing employment in non-UK firms rose from 7·2 per cent in 1963 to 17·1 per cent in 1973 and points out that there may have been similar increases in the percentage of employment in English firms operating in Scotland. Almost 46 per cent of Scotland's total manufacturing employment is in the 110 plants employing more than 1,000 people each: thus, the manufacturing sector of the Scottish economy is effectively dependent upon the decisions of the relatively small number of controllers of these plants.

Of the 110 large plants, only 28 are Scottish owned—accounting for only 12 per cent of manufacturing employment. 53 plants are English-owned, accounting for 22 per cent of manufacturing employment, and 23 plants are American-owned, accounting for 10 per cent of employment. Considering only the 14 largest plants which together account for 44 per cent of manufacturing employment, Firn found that a half (seven) were English-owned, four were US-owned, and only three were Scottish-owned.[6]

Additionally, Firn discovered that whilst 70 per cent of all manufacturing plants are Scottish-owned, such plants tend to be small and, therefore, account for only 40 per cent of manufacturing employment. English-owned plants account for a similar percentage of employment, but tended to be larger than the Scottish-owned plants. These findings would suggest that Scottish ownership is concentrated in small manufacturing plants and is of fairly small significance in comparison with US and English-owned firms. Thus, control over the fate of the Scottish economy would seem to be in non-Scottish hands. The importance of this satellite position of the Scottish economy is further exhibited in the fact that external ownership

26   JOHN SCOTT AND MICHAEL HUGHES

is highest in the industrial sectors with the fastest rate of growth, i.e. those which can be seen as high technology industries. This is clearly apparent from Forsyth's study of US firms in Scotland (Forsyth, 1974) and is of particular importance in the context of North Sea oil developments.

Forsyth focuses on *companies* rather than *plants* and found that in 1969 about 12·3 per cent of manufacturing employment was in US firms. A total of 124 US companies were operating in Scotland in 1969, but only 21 employed more than 1,000 people—together accounting for nearly three-quarters of all US manufacturing employment in Scotland. These 21 firms accounted for nearly nine per cent of Scottish manufacturing employment and the six largest US firms—Rootes, Singer, Burroughs, Honeywell, NCR, and Timex—account for about six per cent of total Scottish manufacturing employment.

Table 1 shows that the majority of the 124 US-owned firms are wholly-owned subsidiaries (or branch plants)—American firms tend to prefer this to either majority or minority control.

Table 1 .
American Ownership of Scottish Manufacturing Industry (1969)

% of voting equity in American hands	Number of Companies
100	105
51–99	11
50	3
25–49	3
Not known	2
	124

Source: Forsyth, 1974: 37.

Thus, the studies carried out by both Firn and Forsyth show the significance of external ownership and control in the manufacturing sector of the Scottish economy. It is impossible to assess, on the basis of their figures, the extent to which the Scottish registered sector of the economy is either Scottish-owned or externally-owned. This question is of central importance. Moves towards political devolution or national autonomy will highlight the position of the Scottish registered companies: they are likely to receive preferential treatment from and have privileged access to the Scottish polity. The orientation of these companies to the Scottish political system is, of course, likely to depend upon the extent of Scottish control. But equally important, if not more important, is the issue, which goes beyond mere 'nationality', concerning the interconnections and interests of the controllers of the Scottish registered sector of the economy. It is to this question that we now turn.[7]

In 1973 there were 248 Scottish registered corporations which received a stock exchange quotation, and of these 11 were wholly-owned subsidiaries of other

Scottish quoted companies: a net total of 237 Scottish companies could be analysed. Of these 237 companies, two were in liquidation or had their quotation suspended and we were unable to obtain any ownership information on seven. Of the remaining 228, eight were mutual or friendly societies and 220 were true proprietary companies.[8]

A first step in analysing the question of any separation of ownership and control must be to investigate the percentage of a company's shares held by its board of directors. Table 2 gives the figures on directors' shareholdings for the 198 companies on which it was possible to obtain information.

Thus, it can be seen that in about one-eighth of the companies the directors held at least half of the ordinary shares and in just over a quarter the directors held 30 per cent or more. Over half the companies were, according to Larner's criterion (Larner, 1970) in a situation of minority control by the board of directors—although the number of companies actually classed as in minority control is greater than this when account is taken of large block holdings by holders other than directors. In only a quarter of companies did the board of directors hold less than one per cent of the shares.

Table 3 gives figures, based primarily on annual reports, for companies in which large blocks of 10 per cent or more of the ordinary shares are held by an individual, group, or company other than the directors of the company itself. The table shows the percentage of ordinary shares held by large block holders and the number of companies falling into each category.

Table 2
Directors' Shareholdings (1973–4)

% of ordinary shares owned or controlled by board of directors	Number of Companies	% of Companies
Less than 1%	51	26
1%–5%	33	17
5%–10%	13	7
10%–20%	23	12
20%–30%	25	13
30%–40%	11	5
40%–50%	18	9
50%–60%	11	5
60%–70%	6	3
70%–80%	2	1
80%–90%	2	1
More than 90%	3	1
	198	100%
Unknown	4	
	202	

28   JOHN SCOTT AND MICHAEL HUGHES

Table 3
Percentage of shares held in large holdings (1973–4)

% held by large holders	Number of companies
10–20	26
20–30	13
30–40	12
40–50	6
50–60	4
60–70	3
70–80	5
80–90	3
90–100	4
Wholly-owned subsidiaries[9]	18
Total	94

Combining the figures of tables 2 and 3, it is possible to estimate the number of companies with identifiable proprietary interests. Table 4 gives these figures.

Thus, a third of Scottish registered companies can be seen as majority controlled by clearly recognizable propertied groups, and more than three-quarters are controlled by either majority or minority interests. In fact, the influence of propertied interests may be considerably greater than this since only large holdings which are, individually, in excess of 10 per cent (except those by directors) have been analysed. Two conclusions may be drawn: firstly, where there are no 'significant' block holdings there may still be a potential for control by groups holding five per cent, one per cent or less, particularly where the spread of share ownership is wide; and secondly, the aggregation of associated holdings of less than 10 per cent may push a number of companies into the category of minority control. As an example of the first case we would instance Burmah Oil, and as an example of the second case the Scottish and Continental Investment Company—both of

Table 4
Majority and Minority Control (1973–4)

Control category		Number of companies	% of companies
1. Majority control		74	33·6
(a) Wholly-owned subsidiaries	18		
(b) Other majority control	56		
2. Minority control[10]		96	43·6
(a) 20–50%	69		
(b) 10–20%	19		
(c) 5–10%	8		
3. No identifiable control		50	22·7
		220	

OWNERSHIP AND CONTROL IN A SATELLITE ECONOMY   29

which we discuss below. Figures on the spread of companies by industrial sector amongst the various control types show little relationship between industry and type of control. The only discernible relationship is that the majority of companies with no identifiable control are financial companies, particularly investment trusts. Table 5 gives comparative figures.

Another plausible relationship to be investigated, which is of considerable significance to the managerial debate, is that between size and control type. Table 6 gives figures on the control patterns of the twenty largest industrial and commercial companies. There is very little tendency for the larger companies to lack a controlling proprietary interest, and as Table 6 shows, a number of the giants have clearly recognizable controlling interests.

Table 5
Industrial Sector and Control Type (1973–4)[11]

Standard Industrial Classification	Wholly-owned subsidiaries	Other majority	Minority	No iden- tifiable interest	Total Sample
I Agriculture, Forestry, Fishing		7	7	1	15
II Mining, Quarrying			1		1
III Food, Drink, Tobacco	1	6	10	5	23
IV & V Coal, Petroleum, Chemicals		1	2	1	4
VI Metal manufacturing	2	4	6	2	15
VII–XII Misc. Engineering	2	6	5		13
XIII Textiles	2	3	6	1	12
XIV & XV Leather, Clothing, Footwear		4	1		5
XVI Bricks, Pottery, Glass, Cement			1		1
XVII Timber, Furniture		4			4
XVIII Paper, Printing, Publishing	1	1	6	1	9
XIX Industrial holding companies			6	3	9
XX Construction	1	4	6		11
XXII Transport, Communication	1		3		4
XXIII Distribution	2	5	10		18
XXIV Finance	5	10	12	36	74
XXVI Misc. Services	1	5	9		17
Unknown			1		2
Totals	18	56	96	50	237

30   JOHN SCOTT AND MICHAEL HUGHES

Table 6
Ownership and Control in the Top 20 Industrial and Commercial Companies (1973–4)[12]

	Top 20 by funds employed	Directors' holdings (%)	Block holdings (%)	Control category
1.	Burmah Oil	0·09		
2.	Distillers Company	0·34		
3.	Coats Patons	0·20		
4.	House of Fraser	2·16	25·03	Minority
5.	Scottish & Newcastle Breweries	2·40		
6.	United Biscuits	22·88		Minority
7.	Weir Group	10·86		Minority
8.	Scottish & Universal Investments	47·74		Minority
9.	Uniroyal		100	Wholly-owned
10.	Lindustries	0·84		
11.	Metal Industries		100	Wholly-owned
12.	William Baird	0·92		
13.	Howden Group	2·02		
14.	James Finlay & Co.	4·28	22·65	Minority
15.	William Collins	23·92		Minority
16.	Scottish Agricultural Industries	0·21	62·40	Majority
17.	Stenhouse Holdings	40·72	31·30	Majority
18.	Argyle Securities	13·73	39·66	Majority
19.	Consolidated Tea and Lands Co.	0·33	42·84	Minority
20.	Anderson Strathclyde	7·73		Minority

It can be seen that the distribution of control types within the top twenty non-financial corporations is remarkably similar to that for all companies (Table 4): a quarter (five) are majority controlled and two-thirds are either majority or minority controlled.

A major problem is to discover whether those companies labelled as having 'no identifiable control' are in fact subject to the influence of significant proprietary interests. An attempt can be made to discover this by examining the sparse evidence which is available on certain of the companies in Table 5. We propose to discuss ownership and control in the Murray Johnstone group[13] of investment trusts—six of which are amongst the twenty companies with the lowest degree of proprietary control—and in Burmah Oil and certain other large industrial companies. Table 7 gives the distribution of share ownership in the Murray Johnstone trusts.

The Scottish and Continental Investment Trust is the Scottish quoted company with the smallest share holding by directors, yet the 15 largest holders hold 42

OWNERSHIP AND CONTROL IN A SATELLITE ECONOMY   31

Table 7
Ownership of Murray Johnstone Trusts (1973–4)

Trust company	Directors' holdings (%)	Holdings over 10,000 shares No. of holders	% held
Scottish & Continental	0·01	15	42
Second Gt. Northern	0·06	16	50
Glendevon Inv. Trust	0·20	7	17
Scottish Western Inv. Co.	0·21	47	44
Clydesdale Inv. Company	0·21	47	54
Caledonian Trust Company	0·33	44	43

per cent of the ordinary shares, and 13 of these hold more than 40 per cent. Furthermore, evidence from various Company Reports shows that the five other Murray Johnstone trusts collectively hold 19·8 per cent of Continental's shares: the apparently most 'managerial' Scottish company is, in fact, minority controlled by a cohesive group of five commonly managed associates.[14] The Glendevon and the Second Great Northern Investment trusts both show a high degree of concentration: the Glendevon is minority controlled by seven holders and the Second Great Northern is majority controlled by 16 holders—in fact, 12 holders have 46 per cent. Even in the three remaining trusts, less than 50 holders have between 43 per cent and 54 per cent. These facts, although based on only limited data, suggest a high degree of concentration of share ownership amongst the largest holders and, therefore, a high potential for proprietary control. However, as Zeitlin emphasizes, a considerable amount depends upon the identity of the holders and the connections between them. The case of Burmah Oil illustrates this well.

As a result of the partial collapse of Burmah in January 1975 it is possible to make some assessment of the interconnections amongst large shareholders in a large and important corporation. According to the latest Annual Report, Burmah has 162,377 shareholders, most of whom hold less than £1,000 of ordinary stock; 285 holders with more than £50,000 each held, in total, over 40 per cent of the company's stock. However, a considerable amount depends upon how the stock is distributed amongst these 285. It has proved possible to use the techniques recommended by Zeitlin to obtain an unsystematic list of some of the largest shareholders in Burmah Oil. From various financial reports in the press the following list has been constructed:

Large shareholders in Burmah Oil

Scottish Widows Fund and Life Assurance Society
Murray Johnstone managed investment trusts
Robert Fleming managed investment trusts
Ivory and Sime managed investment trusts
Save and Prosper unit trusts
Scotbits Securities unit trusts

32   JOHN SCOTT AND MICHAEL HUGHES

Scotbits Securities is a Scottish-based subsidiary of Save and Prosper, the latter being jointly owned by Burmah's two merchant bankers—Robert Fleming's and Barings—and by the Bank of Scotland and Atlantic Assets Trust, the latter being managed by Ivory and Sime. The Murray Johnstone trusts have had a long association with Burmah—the company was founded by David Cargill and developed under the chairmanship of his son, Sir John Cargill, who was a chairman during the inter-war years of a number of trusts managed by Brown, Fleming and Murray (the forerunner of the Murray Johnstone group). The chairman of Burmah until 1974, now deputy chairman, is also chairman of all the Murray Johnstone trusts. Fleming's Bank has long been associated with these same trusts through the Fleming family's[15] association with the Murray family and the large Scottish accountancy firm of Whinney, Murray, and the legal firm of Maclay, Murray and Spens. Ivory and Sime manage the Scotbits unit trusts, and, through Atlantic Assets, have a large stake in Save and Prosper. Scottish Widows Fund is interlocked through directorships with the Murray Johnstone group (twice), the Fleming trusts (twice), Save and Prosper (once) and Ivory and Sime (once). The Save and Prosper/Scotbits group are additionally interlocked with Barings, Flemings, the Fleming trusts, the Bank of Scotland (twice), and Ivory and Sime (twice). Finally, and strongest argument of all, Burmah's board consists of seven executive and six non-executive directors; of the latter, three directors are also on Fleming trusts, one is on Flemings bank, one is on various Murray Johnstone trusts, one is on Scottish Widows, and one is on the Bank of Scotland. Thus, the dominant proprietary interests in Burmah are heavily interconnected through shareholdings, directorships, management, and other associations. The conclusion must be that these groups *do* exercise influence over Burmah's operations: an ostensibly 'managerial' corporation is enmeshed in a network of allocative controllers; it only appears to have no identifiable ownership interest.

It is worthwhile considering two further large companies in order to document more fully our contention that apparently 'managerial' companies are, in fact, proprietary. We look here at the Distillers Company and Coats Patons. In the case of Coats Patons, the third largest industrial corporation in Scotland and concerned with the manufacture of woollen and nylon yarn, the directors hold a mere 0·2 per cent of the ordinary capital. The latest Annual Report shows that 251 insurance companies hold 16·8 per cent of the shares, which would indicate a fairly wide spread of ownership; however, nearly half of this total is owned by only two companies—the Prudential and the Legal and General. These latter, together with the Church Commissioners for England, hold over nine per cent of Coats' shares—a situation of minority control.[16] In the Distillers case, the directors hold 0·34 per cent but the two largest holders—the Prudential and the Brittanic Assurance companies—hold 3·93 per cent, which is probably sufficient to give control in a company with as wide a spread of share ownership as the Distillers.

We have shown, for some of the largest Scottish companies, the identities of certain block holdings. In order to fully assess the potential for control it is necessary for us to discover this for the quoted companies as a whole. Table 8 gives the categories of holders, except directors, possessing more than 10 per cent of the ordinary capital of any Scottish quoted company.

It can be seen that the investment and industrial sectors account for most of the controlling interests in Scottish industry: the various investment trust companies, secondary and merchant banks together exercise control, with or without the directors, in about a third of the 94 companies concerned, whilst industrial and commercial companies exercise control in just over a third. The interests of industrial and commercial companies tend to be wholly-owned subsidiaries—12 of the 18 wholly-owned subsidiaries are subsidiaries of industrial or commercial companies. The influence of individual and private family trust holdings is significant, particularly if taken in conjunction with the data on directors' holdings, and indicate that much capital is still *private* property. As Zeitlin argues, control is exercised through a system in which individual and institutional holdings interlock in such a way that separate corporations become units in a class-controlled system.

When speaking of 'control', it is important to realize that we are not necessarily implying that control is exercised in a positive and direct way; allocative controllers may operate through negative control mechanisms—adopting a supervisory 'watching-brief'. So long as the operational controllers act in the interests of the allocaters, the latter are happy not to intervene. This is particularly true of the investment trusts and insurance companies—although, as we have shown with Burmah, this need not restrain them from providing non-executive board members.

Table 8
Institutional and Individual Block holdings (1973–4)

Type of Controller[17]	Number of companies in which interest is held
Individuals and groups of individuals	10
Private trusts	4
Investment companies and secondary banks	17
Merchant banks	4
Commercial banks	5
Insurance companies and pension funds	3
Investment trusts	10
Industrial and commercial companies	35
Bank nominees	2
Jointly:	
Individual and investment company	1
Merchant bank and pension fund	1
Private trust and industrial company	1
Other	1
	94

34   JOHN SCOTT AND MICHAEL HUGHES

This fact is apparent from our study of interlocking directorships amongst Scottish financial companies.[18]

In Scottish quoted companies there is, as compared with the UK as a whole, a much lower figure for share ownership by insurance companies and pension funds; a correspondingly higher figure is found in Scotland for ownership by investment trusts (Moyle, 1972). Given the central importance of the Scottish investment trusts in integrating the Scottish economy—documented below—it is interesting to note that there are known to be high figures for insurance company ownership of investment trust shares. Corner and Burton have shown (1968) that three of the largest trusts—Scottish United Investors, Scottish National Trust, and Securites Trust of Scotland—had, in 1964, more than 20 per cent of their shares held by insurance companies. This suggests that perhaps English insurance companies have an indirect hold over Scottish industry through the medium of their holdings in investment trusts.

Analysing interlocking directorships amongst the 13 top financial companies (five largest investment trusts, five largest insurance companies, and the three banking groups) we found evidence that banks and life insurance companies seemed central to the network—the National and Commercial Banking Group had 14 interlocks with seven other top financials, Scottish Widows had eight interlocks with four top financials and the Bank of Scotland had seven interlocks with three top financials. However, if we analyse the overall network of most interlocked financials, the investment trusts become dominant, in particular, three of the Murray Johnstone trusts and the Edinburgh-based Scottish Eastern Investment Company.

The Scottish investment trusts are formed into 13 groups, totalling 36 trusts, and 13 independent trusts. Of the 26 groups and independent trusts, 17 were interlocked into an investment trust network in which the group structure was particularly important. There were three 'central' groups in this network—Martin, Currie & Co., Chiene & Tait, and Baillie, Gifford & Co., together managing 10 trusts with total assets of about £430 m. Ivory and Sime and Murray Johnstone together managed 10 trusts and seemed to be more interlocked with other financial companies than with other investment trusts; these latter groups seemed to be the most 'corporate-minded' groups and appeared to coordinate their investments centrally.

Turning to the 68 top industrial and financial companies[19] it is possible to analyse the interlocking directorships with one another and with 'foreign' firms. A total of 477 men held 579 directorships. An elite of 69 multiple directors held 170 directorships, i.e. 14 per cent of directors held 29 per cent of directorships. About a third of the multiple directors held three or more directorships. Of the total of 68 companies, 49 were interlocked with one another. All the financial firms were interlocked into this network and tended to be more heavily interlocked than the industrials. Thus, the top Scottish companies appear to form a tightly integrated network of financial companies with a number of tentacles reaching out into industry. The Scottish registered sector of the economy is a proprietary controlled

OWNERSHIP AND CONTROL IN A SATELLITE ECONOMY   35

system of tightly integrated financial and industrial interests. It remains to investigate the various connections and dependencies between the proprietory interests
controlling the Scottish economy and 'foreign' capital.

The allocative controllers of the City of London are clearly of importance as sources of external finance and as owners and controllers of Scotland's satellite economy.
We would suggest that there are considerable constraints upon the formation of
an autonomous Scottish 'national' economic policy—the owners and controllers
of Scottish industry are essentially the same people who participate in the control
of British finance and industry as a whole. Table 9 gives an overall view of
interlocking directorships between top Scottish companies and non-Scottish
companies.

The external connections of top Scottish firms can clearly be seen from this
table. More than two thirds of the companies are externally interlocked and
although the proportion is higher for financial companies, half of the industrials
have such connections. More than half of the external interlocks of top Scottish
financials are with London financial companies, and the London connections of
these firms account for 41 per cent of the external interlocks of all top Scottish
companies. It can clearly be seen that, for both industrial and financial companies,
the majority of external interlocks are with London companies (more than three-
quarters of all external interlocks) and that, of these, the majority are with London
financials (nearly two-thirds of all external interlocks). Top Scottish industrials
and financials are both more likely to be interlocked with non-British companies
than they are with English companies based outside London, and, in both cases,
interlocks with non-London companies are evenly split between financial and
industrial companies, whilst interlocks with non-British companies tend to be
primarily with industrial companies. Thus, an analysis of externally interlocking
directorships of the top Scottish companies shows a high degree of integration
between the Scottish and 'foreign' sectors with most interlocks occurring with
London financial companies and foreign industrials.

Table 9
External Interlocks of Top Scottish Companies (1973–4)

| | Number of Companies | | Number of external interlocks | | | |
| | | | With all external | | With London companies | |
	Total	With external interlocks	Finan-cial	Indus-trial	Financial	Industrial
Scottish financial Companies	34	30	144	79	127	46
Scottish industrial Companies	34	17	51	37	46	21
Total	68	47	195	116	173	67

36   JOHN SCOTT AND MICHAEL HUGHES

It is possible to make some estimate of the 'direction' of these interlocks by examining the differences between multiple and single directors and by analysing primary directorships[20] within the top Scottish companies. Table 10 gives some data on directors and directorships.

Table 10

Directors and Directorships in Externally Interlocked Top Scottish Companies (1973–4)

| | (a) Directorships | | (b) Directors | | |
	Interlocking	Non-interlocking	Primary interest	Multiple directors	Single directors
Financial	28	47	Scottish Finance	10	6
			Scottish Industry	4	14
Industrial	12	23	Scottish Profession	8	8
			London Finance	3	15
Overall	28*	70	Other	3	27
			Total	28	70

* *Note*: the data in this column refer to interlocking directorships and, therefore, involve some double counting of individual directors. The figures for primary directorships refer to individuals and involve no double counting. The basic data for the whole table are the 98 directors of top Scottish companies who have non-Scottish directorships.

It can be seen from Table 10 that the majority of the multiple directors have primarily Scottish based interests, more than half of the latter being directorships in Scottish financial companies or partnerships in Scottish legal or accountancy firms involved in fund management. The evidence suggests that the 'foreign' directorships of these men are primarily areas where they represent Scottish interests. A large number of those externally connected directors who have only one directorship in the top Scottish companies are London based, suggesting that such men are 'received' into Scottish company boards as representatives of outside interests. The main type of outside interests represented on top Scottish industrial boards are London financial interests. Our evidence suggests that the industrial sector of the Scottish economy is dominated by both London and Scottish financial interests. It is also interesting to note that of the 16 financial interlocking directors with no top Scottish industrial connections, nine have primary interests in Scottish financial and professional firms similar to those of men with industrial connections, two have primary interests in large Scottish private companies, and one has a primary interest in an ostensibly 'London' based industrial company which is in reality a large, well-established Dundee firm with a London registration for its holding company and which would otherwise have appeared in our list of top Scottish companies.

Conclusions and Implications for Future Research

Our model of the Scottish economy is that its core consists of a tightly integrated network of companies held together by proprietary interests and interlocking directorships. Little evidence has been found of any trend towards managerialism, even amongst the largest industrial and financial corporations. The rise of technical and specialist directors has occurred, to the extent that it has occurred at all, within the context of persisting proprietary interests. The controllers of the Scottish-registered sector of the Scottish economy have multiple connections with 'foreign' companies, particularly the financial companies of the City of London. Thus, in terms of shareholdings and in terms of the interests of the controllers there is considerable evidence that the Scottish economy is heavily dependent upon and integrated with the rest of the British economy. This is not to deny the distinctiveness of Scottish society and of the directors of Scottish companies— the latter do tend to be Scotsmen[21] or to have Scottish connections. This suggests that the interests of the allocative controllers of Scottish business are more likely to be related to the position of the Scottish economy in its international context than they are to be involved with the autonomous political development of Scotland.

Some implications for the future development of our project have been suggested by the data presented above:

   1. *A typology of directors.* It has become increasingly obvious to us that a particularly important role in controlling the Scottish economy is played by the partners of large Scottish accountancy and legal firms who provide a 'pool' of potential directors. Such men are drawn upon not for their technical legal and accountancy knowledge, but for their broad financial experience. They are generally partners of those firms which act as fund managers for investment and unit trusts. We would tentatively suggest the following typology of directors:

     (a) *Professional directors*—those men discussed above whose real 'profession' is that of being a multiple company director.

     (b) *Specialist directors*—the expert employees of the company who provide day-to-day operational control in the spheres of management and technology. Such men tend to be directors in one company only.

     (c) *Representative directors*—those men who sit on company boards as representatives of proprietary or other financial interests, whether as direct representatives of particular companies or as representatives of specific sectors—e.g. the insurance sector. There is considerable overlap with the professional directors.

   2. *A typology of interlocks.* As we mentioned in connection with representative directors, a multiple director may be the representative of a particular company or of a specific sector. Our data suggests that even where minority control in a company is held by, for example, one or two insurance companies they may not be directly represented on its board; but it is invariably the case that one of the directors of the company will have some insurance connections. This further emphasizes that corporations are units in a system

rather than isolated atoms. Thus we would suggest an initial typology of 'direct' and 'indirect' interlocks.

3. *The flow of directorships.* Further information is required on the flow of directorships: which companies 'give' directorships and which 'receive' them. We have briefly discussed this in connection with prime directorships of externally interlocked directors and we conclude that: men who are multiple directors within the top Scottish companies have primarily Scottish-based financial interests and represent these interests on 'foreign' company boards; men who are single directors within the top Scottish companies are received onto Scottish boards as representatives of 'foreign' financial interests.

Appendix: Problems of Method

On 31st December 1973 the total number of companies registered under Scottish law was 27,886 (4·5 per cent of the British total), of which 26,582 were private companies and 1,304 were public companies (*Companies in 1973*, Department of Trade, HMSO). According to the *Stock Exchange Official Year Book* for 1973, there were 248 Scottish registered quoted companies. Thus, after allowing for the existence of mutual and friendly societies, etc., the Scottish registered quoted companies account for approximately 15–20 per cent of all Scottish public companies, the majority of the remainder being wholly-owned subsidiaries of Scottish quoted companies and of English and foreign companies. These figures are comparable with Britain as a whole, where in 1973 there were 15,576 public companies of which just over 3,000 (about 20 per cent) were quoted. Thus, the Scottish quoted sector is of comparable significance in the Scottish economy as the British quoted sector is to the British economy as a whole. It is, therefore, legitimate to sample from quoted companies in Scotland in the same way as one might sample from British quoted companies—e.g. as in the *Times 1,000*. We use the following 'samples':[22]

1. *Top Companies*—All Scottish registered companies listed in the relevant sections of the *Times 1,000*. N = 68.
2. *Quoted Companies*—All Scottish registered companies which have a Stock Exchange quotation. N = 248.
3. *Financial Companies*—All Scottish registered companies listed in the *Directory of Financial Institutions*, excluding unit trust management companies—i.e. banks, insurance companies and investment trusts. The majority of these companies, but not all of them, are quoted public companies. N = 73.

Any attempt to assess shareholdings must be based on examination of the official share registers kept at Companies House in Edinburgh—though even here there is the problem of nominee registrations, fragmentation of family and group holdings, etc. We have not, so far, been able to consult the company files and have

OWNERSHIP AND CONTROL IN A SATELLITE ECONOMY   39

therefore based our evidence on Annual Reports, in which all holdings of 10 per cent or more must be disclosed. The problems of disclosure and accuracy are even greater with this source of data. Our data refer entirely to ownership of ordinary shares except where it is clear that 'preference' or 'management' shares rank equally with ordinary shares for voting rights under all circumstances.

Notes

1. The Fraser of Allander Institute for Research on the Scottish Economy has been set up at Strathclyde University, directed by Dr. David Simpson, the aim of which is to collect and model basic data on the Scottish economy.
2. For example: *Scottish Abstract of Statistics*; *Scottish Economic Bulletin*; Firn (1973); and data collected by the Scottish Council (Development and Industry).
3. Various techniques have been suggested for analysing such networks; see the review given in Scott (1975).
4. Such an analysis requires considerable amounts of data which is often not readily available. For this reason in our own study we have not been able to meet all of Zeitlin's criteria. See Appendix.
5. In our own study we have not been able to meet all of Zeitlin's criteria. See the Appendix for a discussion of this.
6. In this paper we are employing two definitions of a 'Scottish' firm: Scottish registered and Scottish owned. Without resorting to an essentialist argument it is probably impossible to give an ultimate definition of when a firm or person is 'Scottish'.
7. Earlier reports are contained in Scott and Hughes (1975, 1976).
8. More detail on the various samples employed can be found in the Appendix.
9. The category of 'wholly-owned subsidiary' includes only those companies where 100 per cent of the shares are held by *one* other company. All companies which are wholly owned by more than one company or by a group of individuals are included in the 90–100 per cent category.
10. The 5–10 per cent category includes only directors' holdings and *not* blocks of shares in excess of five per cent held by people other than directors.
11. Figures for the total sample include mutual companies and those in liquidation or in which there is no ownership information. The eight mutual companies are all insurance companies.
12. The 'top 20' list was drawn up from *Business Scotland*, July 1974.
13. Investment trust companies, like unit trusts, are formed into groups of commonly managed funds with common secretarial services. Murray Johnstone & Co., a private company owned by a firm of accountants, is one of Scotland's largest fund managers.
14. We use the term 'associate' to refer to a meaningful economic relationship; we are not using the narrow definition embodied in the Companies Acts of 1948 and 1967.
15. The original Robert Fleming made his fortune by setting up investment trusts to invest the surplus created by the Dundee jute industry in the middle of the last century in American railroads. The family moved to the South and are still dominant in the bank. One brother of the present chairman did not go into banking, preferring to make his fortune by writing the 'James Bond' novels.
16. Evidence on this is drawn from *Times 1,000*, 1973.
17. These categories are not hard-and-fast divisions. Such is the nature of finance today that it is often difficult to categorize a particular company. Some 'nominee' entries have been allocated to the appropriate category when it is known who is the beneficial holder.
18. See Scott and Hughes (1975).

40   JOHN SCOTT AND MICHAEL HUGHES

19. See Appendix. Strictly speaking, our category of 'industrial' refers to all non-financial companies.
20. Multiple directors are those who have more than one directorship amongst the 68 top Scottish companies, a total of 69 men; single directors are those who have only one such directorship, a total of 409 men. A primary directorship is operationally defined in terms of that given in *Directory of Directors* as a person's main directorship. In what follows it is important to distinguish between: \
    (a) *Directors*—actual individuals who sit on company boards and may be multiple or single directors.
    (b) *Directorships*—the number of board seats, which may be greater than the number of Directors. Directorships occupied by multiple directors are termed interlocking directorships.
21. As pointed out in note six, it is difficult to give a satisfactory definition of who is a Scotsman.
22. Strictly speaking these are not samples, since we are taking all companies in the relevant category.

Bibliography

BANKS, J. 1964. 'The Business Enterprise in Industrial Society', in P. Halmos (ed), 1964.
BERLE, A. A. and MEANS, G. C. 1932. *The Modern Corporation and Private Property.* New York: Harcourt Brace and World, (1967 edition).
BROWN, G. (ed). 1975. *The Red Paper on Scotland.* Edinburgh University Student Publications Board.
CORNER, D. C. and BURTON, H. 1968. *Investment and Unit Trusts in Britain and America.* London: Elek Books.
ELDRIDGE, J. E. T. 1974. 'Sociology in Scotland: What Needs to be Done?'. Paper delivered to the Annual Meeting of the *British Association for the Advancement of Science*, Section N, Stirling 1974.
FIRN, J. 1973. Series of articles in *The Scotsman*, October 30th, 31st and November 1st, 1973.
FLORENCE, P. S. 1961. *Ownership, Control and Success of Large Companies.* London: Sweet and Maxwell.
FORSYTH, D. J. C. 1973. *American Investment in Scotland.* London: Praeger Publishers.
GOLDTHORPE, J. H. 1972. 'Class Status and Party in Modern Britain', in *European Journal of Sociology*, XIII, 342–372.
GORDON, R. A. 1945. *Leadership in the Large Corporation.* Berkeley: University of California Press, (1966 edition).
HALMOS, P. (ed). 1964. 'The Development of Industrial Societies', *Sociological Review Monograph*, No. 8.
HECHTER, M. 1973. 'The Persistence of Regionalism in the British Isles, 1885–1966', in *American Journal of Sociology*, 79, 2, 319–342.
HECHTER, M. 1974. 'The Political Economy of Ethnic Change', in *American Journal of Sociology*, 79, 5, 1151–1178.
HECHTER, M. 1975. *Internal Colonialism: The Celtic Fringe in British Political Development.* London: Routledge and Kegan Paul.
JOHNSTON, T. *et al.* 1971. *The Structure and Growth of the Scottish Economy*, Glasgow: Collins.
KELLAS, J. 1973. *The Scottish Political System.* Cambridge: Cambridge University Press.
LARNER, R. J. 1970. *Management, Control and the Large Corporation.* Cambridge, Mass: Dunellen University Press.
LUNDBERG, F. 1937. *America's Sixty Families.* New York: Citadel (1946 edition).
MACLAREN, A. A. (ed). 1976. *Social Class in Scotland: Past and Present* Edinburgh: John Donald.

OWNERSHIP AND CONTROL IN A SATELLITE ECONOMY   41

MOYLE, J. 1971. *The Pattern of Ordinary Share Ownership*. Cambridge: Cambridge University Press.
PAHL, R. and WINKLER, J. 1973. 'The Economic Elite: Theory and Practice', in Stanworth and Giddens (eds), 1973.
ROCHESTER, A. 1936. *Rulers of America*. New York: International Publishers.
SCOTT, J. 1975. 'The Mathematical Analysis of Interlocking Directorships: A Report', in *Quantitative Sociology Newsletter*, 15.
SCOTT, J. and HUGHES, M. 1975. 'Finance Capital and the Upper Class' in G. Brown (ed), 1975.
SCOTT, J. and HUGHES, M. 1976. 'The Scottish Ruling Class: Problems of Analysis and Data', in A. A. MacLaren (ed), 1976.
STANWORTH, P. and GIDDENS, A. C. (eds), 1974. *Elites and Power in British Society*. Cambridge: Cambridge University Press.
ZEITLIN, M. 1974. 'Corporate Ownership and Control: The Large Corporation and the Capitalist Class', in *American Journal of Sociology*, 79, 5, 1073–1119.

Biographical note: JOHN SCOTT, B.Sc.(Soc.) (London), at Kingston Polytechnic, 1971. Research student, London School of Economics, 1971–2. Lecturer in Sociology, University of Strathclyde, 1972 to present.
MICHAEL HUGHES, B.Tech. (Brunel), 1970. Tutorial Assistant, University of Lancaster, 1970–71 and Research Student, 1971–72. Lecturer in Sociology, University of Strathclyde, 1973–75. Lecturer in Administration, University of Strathclyde, 1975 to present.

[11]

INTERCORPORATE STRUCTURE IN BRITAIN, THE UNITED STATES AND JAPAN

John Scott

The research on which I shall report in this paper began in 1974 with a study of ownership, control, and interlocking directorships in Scotland. When it was planned to extend this research into a study of corporate control in Britain as a whole, contact was made with researchers in a number of countries. This led to a fundamental change in the research design. It was decided to collect information on interlocking directorships on a comparative basis in ten countries, and I was responsible for the British part of the research. This was to be supplemented, wherever possible, with information on ownership and share participations. For Britain, I decided to collect full information from the share registers of the companies, and I added to this some similar data for the United States and Japan. This research is now entering a new stage, with a proposed investigation of actual decision-making in a number of countries. In this latest phase of the research, the views and opinions of directors will be studied through questionnaires and interviews. In this paper I will demonstrate the relevance of this research for current debates in economics and sociology, and I will suggest some areas for further investigation.

Debates on Ownership and Control

For many years, the prevailing view on control in the modern corporation derived from the work of Berle and Means.[1] These writers argued that the growth in the scale of production since the nineteenth century had resulted in the dissolution of traditional property rights. A separation had arisen between the nominal ownership of company shares, involving merely an interest in the income which could be earned through dividends and capital gains, and the effective control over corporate assets. Shareholders no longer participated in the control of corporate assets, and it was possible for a small group of big shareholders or the company's directors to run the company without a significant ownership base. This idea was formalised

Shoken Keizai Jun. 1987 No. 160

in the construction of a typology of control, ranging from complete private ownership, through majority ownership and minority control, to management control.

This latter concept of 'management control' became fundamental to Berle and Mean's argument. Berle and Means defined the managers of a company as those who actually sat on the board of directors, whether they were career executives, bankers, or family shareholders. The dissolution of property rights which resulted from the dispersal of shareholdings created a 'power vacuum' in the large corporation, and allowed whoever sat on the board to exercise all the effective powers of control. Many later writers, however, took 'management' in the much narrower sense of the internal career executives of the company, and this has led to much confusion. Berle and Means' careful and considered conclusions were transformed into the simplistic idea that career managers had displaced shareholders in the modern corporation. It was this 'managerialist' theory which dominated British and American economic thought in the post-war period, and it was hardly questioned, outside Marxist circles, until the important paper of Maurice Zeitlin.[2]

Zeitlin argued that the managerialist theory was based on a 'pseudo-fact'. A close examination of the evidence simply did not support the idea of a separation of ownership from control. Instead, he proposed that there had been a strengthening of the link between the two as banks and other 'institutions' became large shareholders in the 1950s and 1960s. The drift towards institutional shareholding, therefore, resulted in the dominance of financial control in large enterprises. Banks and insurance companies with large minority blocks were able to dominate the boards of directors, and Zeitlin saw this as evidence for the Marxist concept of 'finance capital'.[3]

An important recent study by Edward Herman sought to reinstate Berle and Means' original thesis in the light of a sophisticated understanding of contemporary trends in share ownership.[4] Herman argued that neither the conventional view of management control nor the concept of finance capital were adequate accounts of the reality in large corporations. The rise of the financial institutions, he argued, reduced the autonomy of the managers, and so the form of control should be described as 'constrained management control'.

This idea is similar to that which I had been developing in my own work, though I aimed to recognise the fact that shareholdings by financial institutions can be the bases of direct intervention and control rather than simply of constraint. I introduced the concept of 'control through a constellation of interests' to reconcile the sophisticated managerialism of writers such as Herman with the Marxism of Zeitlin.[5] This concept was used to describe the situation in enterprises where financial intermediaries are the dominant shareholders but none is able, individually, to exercise majority or minority control. The largest shareholding interests comprise a diverse constellation of competing capitalist interests and no stable coalition can exercise the full powers of control; and the fact that these interests come into conflict with one another means that the board of directors represents the balance of power among them. Each enterprise, therefore, is embedded in its particular constellation of shareholding interests, and these have the ultimate powers of control over corporate affairs.[6]

This concept of 'control through a constellation of interests' involves a move away from the atomistic approach of much economic and sociological analysis. Managerialist writers, in particular, adopted an 'organisational' perspective rather than an 'interorganizational' perspective.[7] While the former is concerned with patterns of ownership and control within particular enterprises, treated largely in isolation from one another, the latter is concerned with the way in which bonds of ownership and control tie enterprises together into larger systems of relations. An interorganizational perspective is compatible with much work in the Marxist tradition, but is not tied to specifically Marxist concepts and conclusions. The research programme which evolves from adopting an interorganizational perspective, therefore, involves a move away from some of the more limited concerns of the traditional debate on ownership and control, and is reflected in three interdependent avenues of inquiry:

1. **Intercorporate Shareholdings.** The foundation of the modern capitalist economy is the interweaving pattern of shareholdings through which the exercise of control is constrained. Though this is of fundamental importance, its significance has, until now, been little recognised. Only in Japan has it been given serious attention.

2. **Interlocking Directorships.** One way in which the intercorporate shareholdings influence control is through the establishment of board-level connections between and among shareholders and the enterprises in which they invest. Interlocking directorships, however, have a relative autonomy from intercorporate shareholdings. This phe-

Shoken Keizai Jun. 1987 No. 160

nomenon has been much more widely studied, especially in the United
States.

3. **Corporate Decision-making.**   The actions and attitudes of directors
    must be seen as significantly shaped by their position in the structures
    of shareholding and interlocking.   It is important to investigate the
    implications of this influence for corporate decision-making, and to
    examine the extent to which directors are aware of the forces which
    shape their actions.

My own research began with a series of studies of interlocking directorships, which became part of a large international project.[8] This research led
to a systematic comparison of intercorporate shareholdings in Britain, Japan,
and the United States,[9] and is now leading on to an international investigation of corporate decision-making.   In this paper I shall report some of the
results of my investigations into intercorporate shareholdings and interlocking directorships.

Theories and Methods

The research technique employed to study intercorporate shareholdings
and interlocking directorships is that of social network analysis.   This
approach is concerned with the structural properties of social relations, and
has drawn on the mathematical framework of graph theory to evolve
concepts for studying these relations.[10] At its simplest, the idea of a
network involves a set of points (enterprises) connected by lines (shareholding or director relations); and it is possible to investigate the density,
fragmentation, and centralisation of the network.   In the present paper I
shall be concerned mainly with the existence of 'cliques' and 'components'
in a network, and with the relative centrality of different enterprises.

The main data sources employed for studying British companies are the
annual returns (including the Annual Report) made to the Companies
Registration Offices in London and Cardiff, and business directories, such as
Directory of Directors and the *Stock Exchange Official Yearbook*, which
collate and summarise some of the information from these sources.   Once
the names of all directors of the companies to be studied have been
collected, it is possible to examine the interlocking directorships among the
companies.   An investigation of intercorporate shareholdings is more
difficult, as names of shareholders must be extracted from the share

registers maintained by each company, and these are rarely in a form which can be directly used by researchers. Many shareholders divide their holding into a number of separately listed accounts, which it is necessary to identify in the register and to combine into a single total. This task is made difficult by the widespread practice of 'nominee' share accounts. Information from banks and other financial institutions made it possible to identify the beneficiaries and voting managers for the majority of the nominee accounts discovered, and it eventually proved possible to produce a definitive list of large shareholders for each company studied. The basic data used in the research were lists of the twenty largest shareholders in each company, except for those companies in which a single majority or minority controlling block could be identified. Shareholding data was collected for 1976, and directorship information for 1904, 1938 and 1976. In each case the 200 largest non-financial and the 50 largest financial enterprises were studied.

The Pattern of Impersonal Possession in Britain

In all the major capitalist economies, personal patterns of ownership have gradually given way to more impersonal forms of possession, though the form of impersonal possession varies and personal forms of ownership have by no means disappeared. It is my argument that the move to impersonal possession in Britain has led not to 'management control' but to 'control through a constellation of interests'. In the nineteenth century, and prior to the 1914–18 war, most firms were family-owned. Those large enterprises (such as banks, insurance companies, and railways) which were not family-owned tended to be owned by syndicates of family-owned firms or by coalitions of large shareholding families. A gradual dispersal of shareholdings took place as these families reduced or diversified their holdings, but the shares which were sold, together with many newly-issued shares, came increasingly into the hands of insurance companies and other financial institutions. By the 1950s the latter were the dominant force in the stock market and held a large proportion of all company shares. This resulted in the growth of a network of intercorporate shareholdings, in which the remaining family enterprises become increasingly entwined.

The consequences of these processes can be seen in Table 1, which shows that 100 of the 250 largest enterprises showed a dispersed pattern of shareholding. The remaining enterprises had dominant controllers; about one third each being controlled by enterpreneurs and foreign interests, and about

Shoken Keizai Jun. 1987 No. 160

Table 1. Share Dispersal in Large Enterprises

Number of Enterprises

	Britain 1976	USA 1980	Japan 1980
Dominant Interest	142	61	74
Dispersed Ownership	100	154	159
Other/No Information	8	37	17
TOTALS	250	252	250

Source: J. Scott, *Capitalist Property and Financial Power*, Tables 4.1, 6.1, 7.1.

one fifth by the state.[11] This appears to give considerable support to Berle and Means' idea of management control, as there were 100 enterprises in which no dominant shareholding interest could be identified. The data in Table 2, however, show that this conclusion must be resisted. It can be seen that in none of the 100 enterprises with dispersed ownership did the twenty largest shareholders control less than 10 per cent of the capital; in most cases they held, in aggregate, between 20 per cent and 29 per cent. In all of these companies, therefore, the largest shareholders had a clear base for 'minority control', as conventionally defined: there was no evidence for the high degree of dispersal required by the concept of management control. On the other hand, the largest shareholders did not comprise cohesive blocks of allied interests and so were unable to exercise the powers of minority control. The evidence clearly supports the idea of control though a constellation of interests: 'In such a situation, no one of the largest share-holders has sufficient shares to exercise minority control on its own, and any coalition of a subset of the major holders is likely to be countered by a coalition based on a different subset. Any coalition will be unstable since there is no community of interest among the large holders over and above certain minimal shareholder interests which are, in any case, shared with owners outside the group of major shareholders... The largest shareholders may, collectively, hold a block of shares which is large enough to give minority... control to a cohesive group, yet they lack the basis for a collective organisation which would enable them to act as a controlling group.'[12] In a company with this form of ownership, the internal management may achieve an autonomy from any *particular* ownership interest, but not from

INTERCORPORATE STRUCTURE IN BRITAIN, THE UNITED STATES AND JAPAN

all ownership interests. The composition of its board of directors, therefore, will tend to reflect the relations and accommodations established within its constellation of dominant shareholding interests.

Table 2. Concentration of Holdings in Large Enterprises

	Number of Enterprises		
% of Shares Held by top 20 holders	Britain 1976	USA 1980	Japan 1980
More than 50	0	0	1
40–49	4	8	25
30–39	13	43	68
20–29	61	61	59
10–19	22	9	6
Less than 10	0	0	0
TOTALS	100	121	159

Source: J. Scott, *Capitalist Property and Financial Power* Tables 5.2, 6.3, 7.6.
The Japanese data relate to the 10 largest shareholders only.

The transformation of ownership — from predominantly personal to predominantly impersonal possession — has taken place alongside a transformation of the banking system. Until the end of the nineteenth century the British banking system had a strongly regional and provincial character, the local banks often having locally-based insurance and investment companies allied with them. This decentralised financial system was the basis for local capital mobilisation and for the recruitment of directors to local companies. The City of London, predominant in overseas trade and government finance, gradually extended its influence over the domestic banking system at the same time as the large financial institutions were becoming major shareholders in British companies. By the 1950s a largely London-based 'national' financial system existed. At the same time that control through a constellation of interests was becoming widespread, a national financial system was consolidated.

These changes in ownership and finance had a great impact on patterns of interlocking directorships. Table 3 shows that the number of 'components' in the network — the number of separate connected pieces — fell from nine

Shoken Keizai Jun. 1987 No. 160

Table 3. Network Components: Interlocks and Shareholdings

| | Interlocking Directorships | | | Intercorporate Shareholdings |
	1904	1938	1976	1976
No. of components	9	4	3	2
No. in large component	177	194	185	137
Density of large component	0.025	0.031	0.032	0.035

Source:　J. Scott and C. Griff, *Directors of Industry* Table 2.5; project data. The information on intercorporate shareholdings relates to the results of the QCOMP procedure. See J. Scott, *Capitalist Property and Financial Power*, Appendix II.

in 1904 to three in 1976, and that the largest component came to include a larger number of enterprises.[13] By 1976, the enterprises outside the large component were predominantly isolated financial and public sector enterprises which had been established or expanded in the post-war period. The network of interlocks and the network of shareholdings in 1976 each showed a remarkably similar structure and cohesiveness.[14] In the period after 1904 the core of London banks became allied at board level with those enterprises which formerly recruited directors from regional financials, and so the enterprises became incorporated into the emergent London-based system.

There was not, however, a one-to-one relationship between interlocks and shareholdings. Table 4 shows some of the quantitative features of this non-correspondence, and Table 5 shows the major enterprises involved in each network. 'Centrality' in a network is measured by the 'adjacency' of the enterprises — the number of interlocks which it has, or the number of enterprises in which it invests.[15] It can be seen from Table 4 that the scale of linkage in the two networks differs significantly. Only three enterprises had twenty one or more interlocks within the top 250 of 1976, while thirty one enterprises had substantial shareholdings in twenty one or more enterprises. The largest number of participations (by Prudential Assurance) was ninety three, while the largest number of interlocks (by Lloyds Bank) was twenty eight. The bulk of the participations of these enterprises were,

INTERCORPORATE STRUCTURE IN BRITAIN, THE UNITED STATES AND JAPAN

obviously among the companies subject to control through a constellation of interests: the middle column in Table 4 shows the distribution within these 100 enterprises alone. Thus, eighty eight of the Prudential's ninety three participations were within the 100 enterprises with dispersed ownership.[16]

Table 4. Network Centrality: Interlocks and Shareholding 1976

| | | Number of Enterprises | |
| Centrality (adjacency) | Interlocking Directorships | Intercorporate Shareholdings | |
		In 100 cos.	In 250 cos.
91 – 100			1
81 – 90		1	0
71 – 80		1	1
61 – 70		4	3
51 – 60		3	3
41 – 50		6	6
31 – 40		6	8
21 – 30	3	7	9
16 – 20	7	8	3
11 – 15	13	1	2
6 – 10	54	4	3
1 – 5	112	21	30
0	61	190	181
TOTALS	250	250	250

Source: J. Scott and C. Griff, *Directors of Industry*, Table 6.3; project data. In the network of shareholdings, companies are listed by their 'outdegree' only.

Only nine enterprises appear in both lists in Table 5, indicating a low correspondence between centrality in the two networks. Commercial banks were especially prominent in the network of interlocking directorships, yet were less prominent among the largest investors. Conversely, Prudential Assurance's dominance in shareholding was not reflected in interlocking. Prudential interlocked with none of the enterprises in which it was a large shareholder. The large shareholders – the most important participants in the controlling constellations – were insurance companies, investment funds, and merchant banks involved in the management of pensions funds.[17] The

Shoken Keizai Jun. 1987 No. 160

Table 5. The Most Central Enterprises (1976)

Interlocking Directorships		*Intercorporate Shareholdings*	
Enterprise	*adjacency*	*Enterprise*	*adjacency*
Lloyds Bank	28	Prudential Assurance	93
Bank of England	26	National Coal Board	79
Midland Bank	21	Barclays Bank	69
British Petroleum	19	Legal & General Ass.	69
Barclays Bank	18	Pearl Assurance	67
Commercial Union	18	Hill Samuel	58
National Westminster Bank	18	Robert Fleming	56
Finance for Industry	17	Mercury Securities	53
Delta Metal	16	Electricity Council	49
Hill Samuel	16	Shell Transp. & Trading	49
Tube Investments	15	National Westminster Bank	48
Imperial Chemical	15	Royal Insurance	48
Eagle Star Insurance	14	Midland Bank	45
Standard Chartered Bank	14	Commerical Union	40
Shell Transp. & Trading	14	General Accident	40
Rank Organisation	14	Imperial Chemical	40
Guardian Royal Exchange	13	Save and Prosper	39
Royal Insurance	13	M. & G. Group	36
P & O Steam Nagivation	12	Schroders	36
Dunlop Holdings	11	Standard Life	33
General Accident	11		
Lucas Industries	11		
Lazard	11		

Source:　Project data. See note to tables 3 and 4.

financial institutions are dominant in the mobilisation of capital, but they do not, in general, control *particular* dependent enterprises. They occupy a position of hegemony — collective dominance — which enables them to constrain the opportunities available to all the enterprises in which they invest. It is for this reason that the network of shareholdings comprises a seamless web of participations with no real sign of internal divisions.

Yet the network of interlocking directorships *did* show signs of division. Not only did the banks occupy a prominent role in this network — disproportionate to the scale of their shareholdings — but they also stood at

INTERCORPORATE STRUCTURE IN BRITAIN, THE UNITED STATES AND JAPAN

the centres of loose 'cliques' of enterprises. When interlocking directorships established by executives were considered in isolation from those established by non-executives, it was apparent that the 'big four' commerical banks were pivotal points in loose groupings of industrial, trading and financial enterprises which have been termed 'bank-centred spheres of influence'. Banks play a key role in the structure of financial hegemony because of their role in corporate advice: in addition to whatever funds they can make available themselves, they are able to advise their clients on additional sources of finance and can use their contacts to make these funds available. Bank boards, therefore, are the arenas in which the major suppliers of credit come together with the major recipients of credit. Banks recruit their directors from their clients and associates, and the large industrials recruit directors from their primary bank. For this reason, banks appear as centres of large (but unstable and overlapping) spheres of influence. The banks act, in effect, as proxies for the wider financial community; they act as the guardians of the interests of the hegemonic financials.

Impersonal Possession in the United States and Japan

In Britain there was little support for either the theory of management control or the Marxist theory of bank control. Although banks stood at the centres of spheres of influence, these did not constitute tightly structured groups under bank control. In my research I was able to explore this further through a comparison of Britain with the United States and Japan. For the United States, data for the 252 largest enterprises of 1980 were taken from the directories produced by the Corporate Data Exchange, and it was possible to compile data analogous to that for Britain. The 250 largest enterprises in Japan were studied for the same year, using published sources, though only the ten largest shareholders in each company were investigated.[18]

Table 1 shows that the USA and Japan had very similar numbers of enterprises with dispersed ownership, both differing from Britain. The main source of difference was, in both cases, the low level of foreign and state enterprise compared with Britain. Levels of family control, however, were comparable in Britain and the United States, Japan showing a lower level. Forty nine British enterprises had some degree of family control, compared with thirty five in the United States and just twelve in Japan. Families in Japan were also of small significance as participants in the capital of

Shoken Keizai Jun. 1987 No. 160

companies with dispersed ownership: twenty six of these enterprises had family participants, compared with thirty six in Britain. The United States, on the other hand, showed a very high level of such family participation, and it seems clear that family shareholdings remain a potent force in both Britain and the United States. In Britain, families have concentrated their holdings in particular enterprises and have sought, wherever possible, to attain or retain a majority shareholding. In the United States, families have diluted and diversified their holdings and are content to act as minority controllers or as participants in controlling constellations. Only in Japan had family capitalism become an insignificant element in big business.

Table 2 brings out further similarities between Britain and the United States. The proportion of shares held by participants in the companies with dispersed ownership was such that control through a constellation of interests predominanted in both economies.[19] This was reflected in the discovery of a similar pattern of 'hegemony' in the network of inter-corporate shareholdings. As in Britain, the American insurance companies and pension funds played a key role, though commercial banks were relatively more important. In the network of interlocking directorships, there was a similar pattern of spheres of influence, though with a relatively strong regional character. These findings led me to conclude that the characteristic pattern of capitalist development in Britain and the United States involved a transition from the personal forms of majority and minority control to the impersonal form of control through a constellation of interests. The system of finance capital which evolved, centres around hegemonic financial institutions structured through bank-centred spheres of influences.

In Japan, as is well known, capitalist development differed. Although Tables 1 and 2 show that Japan has experienced a transition towards impersonal possession, this has not involved the dominance of financial institutions. Instead, Okumura has described Japan as a system of 'corporate capitalism':[20] shares in the companies with dispersed ownership are held not by financial enterprises in their capacity as fiduciary institutions, but by corporate interests in their own right. This is part of the group structuring of the Japanese economy, whereby such groups as Mitsui, Mitsubishi, Sumitomo, Fuyo, DKB, and Sanwa each control large numbers of enterprises. The interweaving of shareholdings in Japan involves not 'constellations' of interests but tight 'coalitions' of aligned shareholding interests. As a result, Japan shows much more evidence in support of the Marxist model

INTERCORPORATE STRUCTURE IN BRITAIN. THE UNITED STATES AND JAPAN

of financial 'interest groups', except that the *Kigyoshudan* are not to be seen as subject to bank control.

The group structure of the Japanese economy has been documented in numerous other surveys, and will not be further reviewed here. What can be pointed out, however, is the power of network analysis to disclose some of the key features of this structure. My own research brought out very clearly the differences between the Japanese and the Anglo-American networks, and made it possible to map in considerable detail the contours of financial power in Japan.[21]

Conclusion: Further Problems for Research

While the managerial thesis remains an important aspect of business ideology, research has firmly demonstrated its empirical inadequacy. Yet much remains to be done in elaborating the alternative account of business structure which I have outlined here. The research in which I am currently involved with colleagues, investigating corporate decision-making will do much to elucidate the impact of intercorporate structure on the behaviour of directors and enterprises, but also points towards broader issues of the position of business leaders in the class structure. Research on the role of property ownership in the formation of an upper class is rather sparse,[22] and little work has been done to explore the survival of a capitalist class in a framework of impersonal possession. Our conventional understanding of a capitalist class as based on direct family control is in need of considerable modification, it must not be assumed that the decline of personal possession leads inexorably to the demise of the capitalist class. In Japan, where business and political leadership are so closely entwined with the circles of the wealthy, this is an especially important issue which has received almost no attention by economists, sociologists, or political scientists. My own research on ownership and control has, I hope, provided some provisional evidence for an examination of these questions. Future research must push the frontiers of knowledge further forward.[23]

NOTES

(1)   A. Berle and G.C. Means, *The Modern Corporation and Private Property*.

(2)   M. Zeitlin, 'Corporate Ownership and Control: The Large Corporation and the Capitalist Class' *American Journal of Sociology*, Volume 79, 1974.

(3)   A similar argument can be found in D.M. Kotz, *Bank Control of Large Corporations in the United States*, Berkeley, University of California Press, 1978.

Shoken Keizai Jun. 1987 No. 160

(4) E.S. Herman, *Corporate Control, Corporate Power*, Cambridge, Cambridge University Press 1981.

(5) J. Scott, *Corporations, Classes, and Capitalism*, Second Edition, London, Hutchinson, 1985 (originally published in 1979).

(6) The concept was first outlined in preliminary research on the Scottish economy, and this research was reported in J. Scott and M. Hughes, *The Anatomy of Scottish Capital*, London, Croom Helm, 1980.

(7) Figure 1.1 in F. Stokman, R. Ziegler and J. Scott eds., *Networks of Corporate Power*, Cambridge, Polity Press, 1985 (Japanese translation in press). The figure is reprinted in Y. Ueda's article in *Report of Research on Securities (Shoken Report)* no. 1255, page 8.

(8) See Stokman *et. al., op. cit.*, and J. Scott and C. Griff, *Directors of Industry* Cambridge, Polity Press 1984 (Japanese translation in press).

(9) See J. Scott, *Capitalist Property and Financial Power*, Brighton, Weatsheaf Books, 1986 (Japanese translation in progress).

(10) A fuller discussion of this technique can be found in J. Scott, 'Social Network Analysis', Sociology, Volume 21, 1987, forth-coming, and in Scott and Griff *op. cit.*

(11) This figure includes public corporations with no share capital which were directly controlled by government ministries.

(12) J. Scott, *Corporations, Classes and Capitalism* p. 49.

(13) It can be seen from Table 3 that this was not a smooth, continuous trend. This is discussed further in Scott and Griff, *op. cit.* p. 45.

(14) As noted in Table 3, the measures of the intercorporate shareholding network derive from the QCOMP procedure, which looks at the links between enterprises which result from their having a shareholder in common. A related procedure, EBLOC, which looked at the actual chains of shareholding connections disclosed the existence of four components, the largest containing 159 enterprises. These procedures are discussed in J. Scott, *Capitalist Property, op. cit.,* Appendix II.

(15) In the network of shareholdings, adjacency comprises 'outdegree' and 'indegree', where the latter is the number of shareholders included for each enterprise. In the present research this was limited, by definition, to twenty. The data in Tables 4 and 5 refer only to outdegree, the number of other companies in which an enterprise invests.

(16) Table 5 ranks enterprises by their outdegree in all 250 enterprises. An analogous Table for participations in the 100 enterprises with dispersed capital can be found in J. Scott, *Capitalist Property*, Table 5.3.

(17) The non-financials which were involved in the network did so almost exclusively through their pension departments. Few non-financials invest directly in other enterprises.

(18) The full methods and results are discussed in J. Scott *Capitalist Property op. cit.*

(19) The total of 121 enterprises shown for the United States in Table 2 reflects the fact that satisfactory information was not available for all 154 enterprises shown in Table 1.

(20) H. Okumura, 'Enterprise Groups in Japan', *Shoken Keizai*, 147 1984.

(21) See J. Scott, *Capitalist Property op. cit.*, Chapter 7.

(22) J. Scott, *The Upper Classes*, London, Macmillan, 1982.

(23) This is a revised version of a paper delivered to the XI World Congress of Sociology in New Delhi, August 1986. The author is lecturer in sociology at the University of Leicester. Address for correspondence: Dr. J.P. Scott, Department of Sociology, University of Leicester, Leicester, LE1 7RH, United Kindgom.

[12]
Enterprise Groups in Japan

Hiroshi Okumura

Contents

1. The System of Monopoly Capitalism in Japan
2. Enterprise Alignments and Enterprise Groups
3. Control Structure of Enterprise Groups
4. The Corporate Capitalism and Enterprise Groups
5. Future Problems

1. The System of Monopoly Capitalism in Japan

The main characteristic of the contemporary Japanese economy is the
concentration of wealth within the incorporated enterprise sector.
As can be seen from Table One, which charts the change in ownership patterns
of the total assets of national economy during a period of 15 years, from
1955 through 1970, the share of assets held by the incorporated enterprise sector showed a considerable increase of from 31.0 % to 37.3 %.
This contrasted with a marked decline from 42.6 % to 34.6% in the
share held by individuals including households and non-incorporated

enterprises, and with the negligible increase from 22.4 % to 23.3 %
in the share held by the public sector including governments enterprises.
Furthermore, as shown by Table Two, which charts the change of asset
ownership by industrial groups within the enterprise sector including
both private and government enterprises from 1955 through 1970, the
manufacturing industry held the highest percentage of 37.7 in 1970,
and the substantial part of this percentage was due to the considerable
increase which occurred during the period from 1955 to 1970. This
considerable increase in the share of the manufacturing industry can be
explained mainly by the increased share of the so-called heavy and
chemical industries such as metal and metal products, machinery including
automobiles, ships, and other transport machines, and other manufacturing
industries. Therefore, the period of high growth of Japanses capitalism
after 1955 is also a period, during which national wealth has been
increasiugly concentrated into the hands of the private incorporated
enterprise sector, especially those enterprises which belong to the so-
called heavy and chemical industries. The national statistics which cover
more recent periods are not available at present. But it is safe to say
that this tendency toward the concentration of wealth in the private
incorporated enterprise sector is still at work, with service industries
magnifying their importance relative to the so-called heavy and cheimcal
industries.

The concentratoin of wealth in the private incorporated enterprise sector

証券経済147号1984年3月

means the concentration of wealth in large corporations. According to the

national statistics cited above, at the end of 1970, the number of

incorporated enterprises in Japan was about 703 thousand. Among these

enterprises, those enterprises who's equity capital exceeded one billion

yen, owned 55.5 % of the total assets owned by all these incorporated

enterprises, notwithstanding that the number of these corporations accounted

for only 0.2 % of the total of incorporated enterprises. According to the

"Statistical Yearbook of Incorporated Enterprises", at the end of the

1981 fiscal year, the number of incorporated profit-making enterprises

Table One. Change of Sectoral Composition of the Total

Assets of the National Economy. net.

(unit : %)

sector	1 9 5 5	1 9 7 0	change from 1955 to 1970
public sector excluding government enterprises	15.0	14.1	−0.9
central government	4.5	1.9	−2.6
local governments	5.3	3.9	−1.4
others	5.2	8.3	3.1
enterprise sector	50.8	54.0	3.2
government enterprises	7.4	9.2	1.8
central government	6.4	6.2	−0.2
local governments	1.0	3.0	2.0
private enterprises	43.4	44.8	1.4
incorporated	31.0	37.3	6.3
non-incorporated	12.4	7.5	−4.9
non-profit making oraganizations	4.0	4.8	0.8
households	30.2	27.1	−3.1
total	100.0	100.0	0

Source : Economic Planning Agency : "Comprehensive Report on
National Wealth " (in Japanese) ,vol.1,1975,p.65

excluding financial and insurance institutions, was 1,714,885. Among these

enterprises, the value of assets owned by enterprises with equity capital

of more than one billion yen, constituted 41.42 % of the total value of

all the incorporated enterprises, notwithstanding that the number of these

enterprises was 2,088.

Table Twe. Change of Industrial Composition of the Total
Assets of the Enterprise Sector. net.

(unit : %)

sector	1 9 5 5	1 9 7 0	change from 1955 to 1970
agriculture and forestry	11.1	7.3	−3.8
mining	1.9	0.7	−1.2
construction	1.7	6.4	4.7
manufacturing	29.9	37.7	7.8
food	2.9	3.1	0.2
textile and clothes	5.8	3.0	−2.8
wood and furniture	1.8	1.1	−0.7
metal and metal products	5.1	8.6	3.5
machinery including automobiles, ships and other transport machines	5.6	10.9	5.3
other manufacturing	8.7	11.0	2.3
wholesale and retail trade	18.8	14.8	−4.0
finance, insurance and real property transaction	6.0	6.0	0
communication	15.9	13.8	−2.1
electricty, gas and water	11.2	9.3	−1.9
others	3.5	4.0	0.5
total	100.0	100.0	0

Source : ibidem, p.65.

証券経済147号1984年3月

In addition to benefitting from this concentration of wealth, large
corporations further organize many firms into integral parts of their
business activities, and form enterprise groups with other large corporations, uniting themselves horizontally. At this stage of monopoly
capitalism, the concentration of assets and sales in large corporations,
that is, a high degree of concentration in general is observed everywhere
in the world. The outstanding characteristic of Japan is that concentration
of this kiñd has been achieved through vaious all pervasive bonds among
business enterprises. To create these bonds, equity participation,
concurrent appointment of board members of separate enterprises, the appointment of employees of another firms as board members, loans, and other
methods have been used. These methods foster long-term and stable business
ralationships among enterprises. Regarding equity participation,
more than 60 % of the stocks quoted on stock exchanges in Japan are owned
by financial institutions such as banks and other private corporations,
mainly for the purpose of forming bonds among enterprises. The concurrent
appointment of board members is not so common as in the United States and
West Germany. Nonetheless, it still plays its part in commercial life.
The appointment of employees of another firms as board members is much more
important than concurrent appointment of board members. In Japan, many
employees are sent by banks to business corporations and, by parents
companies to subsidiary companies and minor customer companies, to take
posts as directors of these enterprises. The importance of preferential bank
loans to foster the integration of many minor firms into the business

activities of one major corporation, is steadily declining. Nonetheless,
even today every enterprise is dependent on preferential bank loans of this
kind obtained from its principal bank. This fact is expressed by the Japanese cliche, " mein banku naki kigyo nashi " - there is no enterprise which
does not have its principal bank. Furthermore, the enormous size of inter-
firm credit is said to be one distingushing characteristic of the Japanese
financial system. Credit exteneded by " sogo shosha " - large trading
corporations - which forms a substantial part of inter-firm credit has been
instrumental in forming strong bonds among enterprises. Recently, as a result of the progress of computerized communication, the advantage imparted
to these corporations in collecting information is going a long way toward
strengthening their capability to create bonds among enterprises.

" Transactions among enterprises " are carried out among enterprises which
are knitted together by bonds of business intererest. If we take these enterprises as one entity, we can distinguish other entities such as individual
consumers , non-profit-making organizations including the government, and
foreign countries. One feature peculiar to Japan is said to be the large
volume of intra-enterprise transactions as a percentage of all the transactions within and among these entitities. For instance, in Japan, in 1976,
the value of wholesale trade, which roughly represents intra-enterprise
transactions, was four times that of retail trade, which roughly represents
transactions between enterprises and individual consumers. This figure is
obtained from Commerce Statisitics of Japan published by the government,

証券経済147号1984年3月

and it is incredibly high in comparison with the U.S.figure of 1.6 for
1972, the West German figure of 1.7 for 1975 and the British figure of
1.9 for 1974. Furthermore, the ratio of added value in parent companies
to the total value of production in the automobile industry is 30-40 % for
Toyota and Nissan in Japan, whereas the comparable figure for the big three
in the U.S.is said to be 60-70 %. This low ratio means a correspondingly
high ratio of parent companies' purchase of parts of products to the total
value of production,   that is , a high degree of dependence by parent
companies on transactions with other enterprises.
The enormous size of transactions among enterprises in Japan
is a reflection of tight existing bonds among enterprises all over the
country. At the same time, existing bonds among enterprises tend to become
further strengthened in order for these transactions to acquire a long-term
and stable character. Transactions among enterprises intrinsically tend to
be based on face to face negotiations between buyers and sellers rather than
on open transactions in the market place or on competitive bidding.
The market place can consist of many possible participants who are often
close to anonymous. But, in the case of face to fase negotiations, buyers
and sellers know each other from the beginning. In the United Ststess and
Europe, most transactions among enterprises are carried out through face to
face negotiations. However, these transactions often bear the character of
a once and for all transaction in an existing spot commodity at a given
time. In Japan, transactions among enterprises are characterized not only
by their size, but also by their long-term, continuous stability.

Notwithstanding these strong ties and long-term stable relationships among enterprises, there is also keen competition among enterprises in the market place. Such ties and competition among enterprises would seem to be contradictory concepts. Nonetheless, in Japanese reality, the two concepts have materialized fully side by side. Concretely, at the intermediate stage, transactions are carried out among enterprises knitted together by the bonds of business interst. But, at the final stage of retail marketing of consumer goods, enterprises are actively competing with one another for their increased share of the market for which they are producing. Even at the intermediate stage, if new customers appear, enterprises will compete with one another in order to get orders from these new customers, while maintaining long-term stable trasactions with their old customers. Such competition is usually carried out in a particular market area dominated by a few corporations,and keen competition often forces these enterprises to sell their products under their production costs in order to get orders from these new customers. The so-called "kato kyoso" - overcompetition will be a special case which can be explained by this same logic of competition peculiar to Japan.

2.Enterprise Alignments and Enterprise Groups

Bonds among enterprises in Japan are created by the integration of enter-

証券経済147号1984年3月

prises into "vertical" alignments or "horizontal" enterprise groups.
To begin with, let us examine enterprise alignments.

The term, enterprise alignments is a literal translation of Japanese "kigyo
keiretsu". The term in original Japanese began to be used during World War
Two and it is not easily translated into foreign languages. The term includes
not only subsidiary and affiliated enterprises, but also other enterprises of various kinds. Usually in Japan, subsidiary enterprises mean enterprises, more than 50 % of who's equity capital is owned by their parent
companies. Affiliated enterpeises mean enterprises, more than 20 % of who's
equity capital, or, in some cases, more than 10 % of who's equity capital is
owned by their parent companies. But enterprise alignments often include
enterprises, who's equity capital is not owned by their parent or dominating
enterprises. There are no comprehensive statistics on enterprise alignments.
According to an investigation of the 100 largest non-financial corporations
conducted by Japan's Fair Trade Commission in 1982, these corporations separately have obtained more than 10 % of the equity capital of 8,529 enterprises. Further, these corporations have obtained more than 50 % of the
equity capital of 2,995 out of these 8,529 enterprises. The corporations
which are most active in this kind of equity participation are said to be
"sogo shosha" - large trading corporations and large corporations in the
fields of electornics, automobiles and steel.

More important than the existence of a huge number of subsidiary and affiliated enterprises is the fact that these subsidiary and affiliated

enterprises also separately maintain a huge number of subcontractors, which

are organized in the pyramidal structure. These subcontractors are usually

divided into primary, secondary and tertiary subcontractors. This is the

typically Japanese phenomenon. According to "White Paper on Small and

Medium-Sized enterprises for the 1982 Fiscal Year ", an annual government

publication, "65.5 % of all small and medium-sized enterprises are subcon-

tractors and this figure is said to be increasing annually.

Within "vertically" organized alignments, enterprises in an alignment are

not all equal partners of the parent company. The various relations among

enterprises in the alignments are quite different from those in the U.S. and

Europe, which are sometimes described as a "horizontal" inter-firm

division of labor. Recently, an increasing numeber of Westewn writers are

paying attention to the alignments of enterprises in Japan as a source of

the strong international competitiveness of Japanese corporations.

They are surely correct in identifying this as one of the real sources of

the strength of the Japanese managerial system.

Among the many reasons for large corporations' active integration of many

enterprises into their alignments, the following deserve special mention :

The first is profitable utilization of the disproportionate wage structure

in the national economy. As was mentioned above , the organization of

証券経済147号1984年3月

alignments started during World War Two. After the war, 1950, that is, the

year in which the Korean War broke out, seems to have been the crucial year.

Since then, alignments have been one of the chief instruments of business

expansion in the hands of large corporations in Japan. At that time, there

was a wide difference in wage rates between large corporations, on the one

hand, and small and medium-sized enterprises, on the other.

The controversial issue of the "dual structure" of the Japanese economy

is closely related to the assessment of this kind of wage situation.

The benefits which accrued to large corporations from strengthened

alignments, were mainly derived from the utilization of low paid labour in

small and medium-sized enterprises. Since 1955, as a result of the shortage

of young workers caused by the rapidly growing economy, this difference in

wage rates has tended to decline. Nonetheless, even today, as regards middle-

aged or older workers, there is a wide difference in the wages of workers

employed by large corporations and those employed by small and medium-sized

enterprises. Therefore, it is difficult to deny that the benefits which are

to be gained by the utilization of lower paid workers in small and medium-

sized enterprises, constitute the main motivation for large corporations

to maintain their alignments.

The second is the avoidance of risk which can be achieved by large corpo-

rations throuth the use of enterprises in their alignments. For example,

large corporations usually enter new risky industrial fields through

enterprises in their alignments. They also engage in business activities

which might cause trouble with environmentalists through enterprises in
their alignments.

The third is the prevention of hypertrophied expansion of large corporations.
Recently, such corporations have often established new subsidiary enterprises
by making their existing departments legally independent. This practice
is called "kogaisha bunri hoshiki" - making parts of an organization
independent subsidiary conpanies. The practice is worth mentioning because
it represents an extension of "jigyobu sei " - the divisional system -
employed in order to make devolution of the power of central executive
offices more certain.

Many small and medium-sized enterprises organized into alignments, have
shown noticiable growth. Nonetheless, it is hard to deny that relationships
between parent companies and enterprises in their alignments are long-term
and stable ones which restrict freedom of transaction of the latter.
In any case, it is the old truth that, in times of depression, some enterprises in alignments will make sacrifices for large corporations and their
alignments as a whole.

The term, "enterprise group", means large coroporations combined together
by "horizontal" bonds, in contrast with the alignment of enterprises
"vertically" organized by one large corporation. Every large corporation
organizes many enterprises in its alignment. An enterprise group is composed

証券経済147号1984年3月

of these large corporations.

What, then, are the main characteristics of the enterprise groups ? The first

is the mutual ownership of capital stock within one enterprise group.

As the result of this joint ownership, the fact that every corporation

owns only 1- 2 % of equity capital of other corporations of the same group,

makes it possible for the group as a whole, to own 20 - 30 % of the equity

capital of every corporation in the same group.　This is a phenomenon

peculiar to post-war Japan. The second is the organization of " shacho-kai "

- the regular meetings of the presidents of member corporations.

What is discussed at these meetings is strictly confidential.

Nonetheless, it is rather easy to deduce that what is discussed is not far

removed from what will be discussed at the meetings of the shareholders who

as a whole own the controlling interest in the corporations. Although the

presidents do not own a large number of shares, as the chairmen of their

respective boards of directors, they exercise the rights acquired through

shares held by their corporations. Therefore, the meeting of the presidents,

de facto, becomes a meeting of shareholders who control these corporations

by virtue of the mutual ownership of equity capital of member corporations.

The meeting of the Mitsubishi group is called "kinyo kai " - Friday's meet-

ing, that of the Mitsui group,　"ni moku kai " - the second Thursday's

meeting, that of the Sumitomo group, "hakusui kai ", that of the Fuyo group,

" fuyo kai ", that of the Sanwa group, "sansui kai " - the third Wednesday

meeting, and that of the Daiichi Kangyo Bank group,　"sankin kai " - the third Friday meeting. The third characteristic is the establishment of

joint enterprises by member corporations. In the 1950's, these corporations

were established in the fields of atomic power and petro-chemical indust-

ries. In the 1970's, they have been established in the fields of urban

development, as in the case of the so-called " deberopaa ", a kind of

construction company with consulting functions on urban planning.

They have also been established in the fields of prospecting of oil

deposits, ocean development, the information industry, etc. These joint

enterprises have gone a long way toward strengthening the community of

common interest of the member corporations. The fourth characteristic is

the preferential loans granted to the enterprises in the alignments of the

group's corporations from the bank which forms the core of the group.

These loans are called " keiretsu yushi " -alignment loan. This bank will

also act as the principal bank to these enterprises. These loans are

supplemented by financial aid from the trust bank, the life insurance

company, the casualty insurance company and other financial institutions

of the same group. The fifth characteristic is the existence of the

" sogo shosha " - the large trading corporation in the group.

Besides the bank mentioned above, the large trading corporation forms

another core of the group. It not only mediates transactions among corpo-

rations within the group, but also actively endeavors to increase trans-

actions among these corporations. It also co-ordinates the activities of

member corporations in order to participate in large foreign development

projects. Furthermore, it serves as the bridge between corporations of its

証券経済147号1984年3月

group and other corporations. The sixth characteristic is the complex,all-
round industrial unity brought about by the co-operation among member
corporations. It occurs in all fields of the national economy, but its
center is the so-called heavy and chemical industries. Important member
corporations are located in these areas.

The enterprise group which bear the six characteristics just mentioned are
Mitsubishi,Mitsui, Sumitomo, Fuyo, Dai-ichi Kangin, and Sanwa. The degree to
which these characteristics are exhibited, differs among these six groups.
The Fuyo, Dai-ichi Kangin and Sanwa groups lack the strong cohesion which is
observed in the case of the Mitsubishi, Mitsui, Sumitomo groups. Besides
these groups, there are some groups of corporations which have been recently
organized by the Industrial Bank of Japan, the Tokai Bank and others. But,
as they lack some of the characteristics above mentioned, they ought not to
be considered as enterprise groups in the strict sense.

Table Three shows the extent of the power these six huge enterprise groups
exercise in the Japanese economy. It goes without saying that there are
large corporations other than member corporations of these six groups.
They are either so-called independent corporations, or corporations in the
alignments of the enterprise groups that are not admitted as members of these
groups.

Table Three. Six Enterprise Groups' Share

in the National Economy. 1981 fiscal year.

(unit : %)

	total assets	net assets	equity capital	sales	profit	profit accruing from business activities	employ-ees
six groups combined together	25.94	18.08	16.46	15.78	19.23	25.31	5.11
three groups, successors to per-war "zaibatsu"	12.42	8.23	7.53	7.38	8.49	11.71	2.03
three others	13.53	9.85	8.93	8.40	10.74	13.61	3.08
total incorporated enterprises	100.00	100.00	100.00	100.00	100.00	100.00	100.00

Source : Fair Trade Commission : "Actual Circumstances of Enterprise Groups" (in Japanese) ,1983, p. 22.

Note : 1. Equity capital does not include that of life insurance companies. Sales do not include that of financial institutions. Profit does not include that of casualty insurances companies. Employees do not include these of both life and casualty insurance companies.

2. Figures for two groups are obtained through some adjustment made for the figures for corporations which participate in more than two groups.

証券経済147号1984年3月

Enterprise groups are the consequences of historical development of " zaibatsu " - the pre-war organization of Japanese monopoly capital. There are
some differences between pre and post-war groups however. First, current
enterprise groups are coalitions of large corporations, each of which
organizes many enterprises in its alignments, whereas " zaibatsu " were
pyramidal organizations organized by their head company called " zaibatsu
honsha " , which was a kind of holding company. Second, enterprise groups are
not controlled by individual capitalists or families, whereas " zaibatsu "
were controlled by sush families as the holders of the controlling interest
in the " zaibatsu honsha " . Historical development of business organizations from " zaibatsu " to enterprise groups clearly shows the transformation of Japanese capitalism from capitalism with individual capitalists
to capitalism without individual capitalists, that is, from individual
capitalism to corporate capitalism.

So-called " modern economists " - post-war Japanese, non-Marxian, mainstream
economists, recently have emphasized risk aversion , information gathering
and other incentives as the motivation for the formation of enterprise
groups. These arguments are not convincing. Enterprise groups are not the
products of the rational calculation of merits and demerits of the functions
which are to be performed by these groups. Rather, they are the products of
the historical evolution of the pre-war " zaibatsu " , many functions of

which, some inherited and some newly invented, have been exercised in the
corporate interest as a whole. Furthermore, these groups are not closed, and
not self-sufficient. They are related to corporations outside the groups
through sizable transactions, which constitute an additional source of their
strength. In a word, the demarcation between insiders and outsiders in a
group can not be clearly defined, in the meaningfull way, by the application
of a set of pre-determined managerial functions which are available to the
members of these groups.

3. The Control Structure of Enterprise Groups

The argument for "managerial control" - control of big corporations by
their management, is drawn from the fact that corporate equity is distributed
among numerous stockholders. Such distribution of ownership of equity is
very hard to find in Japan. On the contraty, the equity of large corporations
is concentrated in the hands of corporations themselves, or, to be more
exact, in the hands of large corporations. Therefore, the classical thesis
of "managerial control" or "control without ownership" expounded by
A.A.Berle & G.C.Means and their followers, does not apply to post-war
Japan. Since the 1950's, in the United States, the "institutionalization"
of ownership of capital stocks has been in progress. It has meant an
increase in the value of stocks owned by pension funds, mutual funds, life
insurance companies, foundations, and trust departments of banks and other

証券経済147号1984年 3 月

financial institutions. Of course, trust departments of banks are in charge

of pension funds and other personal funds. The Patman and Metcalf Committees

of the U.S.Congress have called public attention to the possible domination

of corporations by these institutional investors, especially, the trust

departments of banks. But, in as far as these institutional investors are

in charge of assets management for their client-beneficiaries, they cannot

afford to remain long-term stable stockholders of some corporations only to

retain corporate control. This might prove to be detrimental to their

performance as managers of assets.

On the contrary, in Japan, owners of the greater part of capital stock are

banks and large corporations. In the U.S., commercial banks are not allowed

to own equity capital in business corporations. In Japan, from the time of

first purchase, banks and large corporations aim at control over business

corporations through the purchase of corporate stock. Therefore,

"institutionalization" of ownership in the U.S. and Britain is entirely

different from "corporatization " of ownership in Japan. In Japan,

"control without ownership " dose not exist, because those who control

corporations also own the controlling interest in these corporations.

Regarding the mutual ownership of corporations' stock within the enterprise

groups mentioned before, some important points require mentioning.

The first point is the fact that ownership of stock in corporations by

the group as a whole, always reaches 20 - 30 % of the total stock of these

corporations, although individual member corporations of the group own only
small quantities of stock. Some writers argue that these corporations do
not aim at control of other corporations by the negligible ownership of
1 - 2 % of the stock of these corporations. If so, what do these
corporations aim at by the purchase of the stocks of other corporations ?
It is quite clear that these corporations do not aim at gains which will
be received by dividends from or sales of these stocks in the future. Thus,
other writers argue that the purchases of other corporations' stocks by some
corporations are token acknowledgments of the former's courtesy by the
latter. It is said to resemble an exchange of "meishi" - Japanese business
visiting cards, and that it is just a business custom and bears no special
meaning. Or, in a more sophisticated interpretation, it is a courtesy
necessary before the start of new transactions between strangers.
These arguments notwithstanding, it is clear that the ownership of stock is
instrumental in securing control over corporations in the broad sense,
because the ownership enables the group as a whole to exercise control over
these corporations. This is impossible to achieve for member corporations
separately. Here, each corporation in a group is controlled by other
corporations of the same group, and, at the same time, each corporation
participates in the control of the other corporations. The situation
furnishes an example of a "constellation of interests" described by John
Scott in his book, "Corporations, Classes and Capitalism"
The second point is the fact that the leading directors in the group trust
in each other's abilities as businessmen. They represent their corporations

証券経済147号1984年3月

as major stockholders, and participate personally in the network of mutual
control over these corporations. This would be impossible without the
element of personal trust among them. If any one president does not trust
in the ability of the president of another corporation of the same group,
it shoud be natural that the latter feels the same way toward the former.
The personal strife between them usually ends in the exclusion of both from
membership as leading directors of the same group. Management of enterprise
groups is based on this kind of personal trust among the presidents as long
as something dangerous to the group does not happen. If a corporation in
the group registers an unredeemable deficit or harms the image of the
corporation by some scandal, presidents of member corporations replace the
president of the troubled corporation by someone else, in order to
reconstruct that corporation. Thus, leading directors of enterprise groups
as a whole control the corporations in their groups, deriving their power
from ownership of the controlling interst in the member corporations,
although they are not personnally stockholders in these corporations.
Therefore, those who control enterprise groups are leading directors or
presidents of member corporations in these groups. It is not "control
without ownership ", but "managerial control based on ownership by the
corporations". The power of these directors is solely derived from their
positions in the corporations, which participate in the collective control
of the enterprise groups. These directors, no matter how influential they
are in the management of the group, become powerless after retirement from
their corporation. "Rogai " - disadvantages caused by older working people

- in the business community often absorbs public attention. But, in practice,

many presidents, after leaving their posts, still want to remain in the same

corporations as " sodanyaku " - advisor - , " komon " - consultant - or in some

other capacity. The reason why they are so eager to remain in the same corpo-

ration is their fear of becoming forgotten, powerless men. What we find here

in Japanese business is not the dictatorship of executive directors, but

" corporate absolutism "

4. Corporate Capitalism and Enterprise Groups

Who rules Japan ? A union of politicians, bureaucrats and businessmen is

said to rule Japan. But, who are these businessmen? What does their community

look like ? Some writers take it for granted that Japan is ruled by monopoly

capitalists. But, who are these monopoly capitalists? We need a more

concrete, first-hand knowledge of them. In common usage, the word " capitalist "

implies an individual. In the case of both enterprise groups and independent

large corporations, it is hard to find individuals who are both owners of

large amounts of stock and also members of the board of directors of the same

corporation. There are some exceptions. For instance, Konosuke Matushita,

the founder of Matsushita Electric Indutries, Inc. is legendary controlling

stockholder of that corporation. Nonetheless, he owns less than 3 % of the

equity captal of that corporation. This figure is much lower than the

証券経済147号1984年3月

comparable figure for Sumitomo Insurance or Sumitomo Bank. It goes without

saying that the majority of small and medium-sized enterprises are controlled

by the owners of these enterprises. Their properties are enormous.

In contrast, the leading directors of large corporations who control these

corporations, have a firm grip on the whole business community of Japan, and

exercise a great deal of power over Japanese politics, are personally much

poorer than the owners of small and medium-sized enterprises, or the post-

war nouveaux riches who have made money out of the great appreciation in

land values. These leading directors are poorer than these owners or these

nouveaux riches not only in their property, but also in their income. Thus,

the contemporary Japanese scene clearly shows a division of businessmen into

two classes, that is, the personally wealthy people, on the one hand, and

those who control large corporations without personal wealth, exercising

influence over Japanese politics, on the other. In pre-war Japan, the propertied

class supplied business corporations with their senior managerial staff.

The same is still true even today in the U.S. and Europe. In contemporary

Japan, the propertied class is no longer the supplier of senior officials to

the major corporations. The two are now separated from each other. Before

answering the question "who rules Japan ? ", we must recognize the fact

that the businessmen who constitute a part of the ruling elite, are not the

owners of enterprises of modest size, but the leading directors of large

corporations. This is the main reason why the Japanese economy should be viewed

as a corporate capitalism. Businessmen form the core of the ruling complex

of politicians, bureaucrats and businessmen. These businessmen, that is,

the leading directors of enterprise groups and the big independent corporations,
have a firm grip on the whole community of businessmen all over the
country. In order to understand this point, the method of selection of the
senior officials of "keidanren",an organization of business corporations,
the otherwise known as "sohonzan"-the head temple - of the "zaikai" - economic
world - is illuminating. The chairman, Yoshihiro Inayama,ex-president of
Shin Nihon Steel Inc.represents independent business corporations whereas
several deputy chairmen are chosen from representatives of the Mitsubishi
group, the Mitsui group, the Sumitomo group, the Foyo group, the Tokyo Electric
Company, and other large corporations such as Idemitsu Kosan Corporation.
Representatives of enterprise groups have not been elected chairmen.
But, they are always elected deputy chairmen, because of their power in the
Japanese economy. According to Table Three compiled by Japan's Fair Trade
Commission, in fiscal year 1981, member corporations of six "shacho kai"-
regular meeting of presidents of member corporations of enterprise groups -
combined together, ownered 25.94 % of the total assets. of all
incorporated enterprises in Japan. Taking into account the fact that
the figure does not include the assets of enterprises in their
alignments and those of member corporations which do not participate in
these regular meetings openly, but do in effect, I am sure that these six
enterprise groups own a far greater percentage of the total assets of
incorporated enterprises. Being backed by the enormous economic power of
these groups, the directors of such enterprise groups are wielding enormous
power over the economic affairs of the country.

From the viewpoint that the socio-economic system of Japan ought to be characterized as corporate capitalism, the enterprise groups are the representative organizations of Japan's corporate capitalism. First, enterprise groups are corporate captalism itself, because they are not controlled by large stockholders. Second, enterprise groups succeed in retaining the loyalty of their workers, because mutual ownership of stock works against foreign takeover of member corporations and is instrumental in enlisting the support of workers on behalf of their corporations. Third, enterprise groups combined together by " horizontal " bonds, make it possible for corporate capitalism, that is, the " kaisha hon'i " - a system putting corporations' interests before their workers' - to work. In this sense, they are typical organizations within the corporate capitalist structure.

Enterprise groups are the bearers of the logic of corporate capitalism. Big independent corporations sometimes constitute incomplete parts of enterprise groups, and sometimes organize their own groups. Therefore, the logic behind the management of these big corporations is not far from that behind the management of enterprise groups. Independent corporations are not opposed in their character to enterprise groups.

Japanese corporate capitalism, the basic structure of which was erected just after " zaibatsu " dissolution, rapidly developed in the period of high economic growth beginning in 1955. The same is true of enterprise groups. Their basic structure was erected just after " zaibatsu " dissolution.

The period in which they developed rapidly, coincides with that of the high
economic growth of post-war Japan.

5.Future Problems

As noted before, important member corporations of enterprise groups in Japan
are located in the fields of so-called heavy and chemical industries. They
form the core of the Japanese monopoly system. The heavy and chemical
industries are congenial to the development of enterprise groups for two
reasons. The first is the methods of production with long gestation period used
in these industries. This means that more inter-enterprise trasactions need to
be carried out in these industries than in other industries. The second is
the enormous economy of scale in production in these industries. This means
that preferential loans to enterprises in groups are very instrumental in
giving a sharp competitive edge to these enterprises compared with the enterprises outside of these groups. Therefore, the secret of development
of enterprise groups can be found in an increasing share of so-called heavy
and chemical industries in the Japanese economy brought about by its high
growth. But, since the outbreak of the first oil crisis of 1973, these industries have experienced numerous, as yet unsolved problems. Enterprise groups
also face many difficulties. In order to overcome these difficulties, enterprise
groups are groping for new directions. Three alternatives exist at present.

証券経済147号1984年3月

They are the development of new technology and new industries, expansion
into overseas countries, and militalization of the economy. The first
alternative is most desired by these groups, but the prospects for this
alternative are rather gloomy. The second alternative is a very risky one as
shown by the recent failure of the Mitsui group's project of building
a petro-chemical complex in Iran. The third alternative is the most probable,
and the most alarming possibility.

The most grave concern to enterprise groups is the so-called " trade
frictin " with Western countries. The U.S. and the European Community are
officially accusing Japapese enterprise groups of piling up barriers to
imports from abroad, thus creating a trade conflict between Japan and
the other developed countries. The Japanese Ministry of Foreign Affairs and
the Fair Trade Commission are trying to deny this accusation, but their
arguments are not convincing. It is an irony of history that the U.S.,
which dissolved the Japanese " zaibatsu " , the pre-war organization of
Japanese monopoly capital, is now attacking enterprise groups, the successors
to the " zaibatsu " . At a time when public hostility against enterprise
groups is coming to an end in Japan, the U.S. and the European Community
have become severly critical of Japanese enterprise groups. The contrast is
a little amusing. There are two reasons for their accusations. One is the
obstruction of the importation of foreign commodities caused by enterprise
groups. The other is the obstruction to direct investment in Japan by the
foreign corporations   caused by enterprise groups' desire to prevent

takeover of Japanese enterprises by foreign corporations. This desire is
easily attained by the mutual ownership of stock within enterprise groups.
Japan has ostensibly liberalized capital transactions with other countries, but,
in practice, has also emasculated the liberalization of capital transactions
by " antei kabunushi kosaku " - clandestine collusion to support existing
management by manipulating stock exchanges. In fact, untill now, there is
no single case, in which foreign corporations have succeeded in any takeover
of a Japanese enterprise.

Thus, the most serious danger to enterprise groups in the future, is the
worsening relationships between Japan and Western countries.
Japan is politically dependent on the U.S., but is economically quite
vehemently hostille to her. This hostility will produce a dangreous
situation for major enterprise groups.

As mentioned above, corporate capitalism is " kaisha hon'i " - a system
putting corporations' interests before workers'. It " naibuka suru " - inter-
nalizes labor-managemoent relations and trade unions, resulting in " kigyo
ikka shugi " - family-stye relations within corporations. These relations
have been driving forces in Japanese corporations. At the same time, it
" gaibuka suru " - alienates a part of the work force which takes the form
of " rinjiko " - temporalily employed workers - , or " shagaiko " - workers
employed by sub-contractors - and part-time employees. Sub-contractors are
also the result of this " gaibuka " - alienation. Socially, older people,

証券経済147号1984年3月

housewives and children are " gaibuka sareru " - alienated from the benefits

of corporate capitalism. They are all victims of so-called " shiwayose "

- unjust shift of burdons to the weak. They " naiko suru " - introvert their

dissatisfaction into themselves and find vent for their dissatisfaction in

trifling displays as in the case of low teenagers' hooliganism.

Japanese corporate captalism seems to be victorious. But the victory is not

conclusive, because it faces challenges from formidable opponents overseas

in the U.S.and the European Community. In this sense, the so-called " trade

friction " is a serious menace to Japanese corporate capitalism and its

enterprise groups, which will prove hard to remove in the short run.

Japan's future depends on the way in which she deals with this danger, or,

to be exact, how she resolves the contradiction between her political

dependence on, and, economic hostility to Western countries.

N. B   Readers who like to know my views in more detail, are invited

to refer to my book, " Six Major Business Groups in Japan : new edition "

(in Japanese) published by Daiyamondo-sha in 1983. The following articles

written by me in English might alse be useful.

1. 'Interfirm Relations in an Enterprise Group : The Case of Mitsubishi',

   in " Japanese Economic Studies ", Summer, 1982.

2. 'Closed Nature of Japanses Intercorporate Relations' in " Japan Echo ",

   No.3, 1982.

3. 'Japanese Busines Grouping Face World Criticism' in " Oriental

Economist", December, 1982.

Part IV
Financiers and Corporate Rule

[13]

WHO RULES
THE CORPORATIONS?
PART 1

ROBERT FITCH AND
MARY OPPENHEIMER

The inability of various "Marxist" parties and sects to develop beyond trade unionist politics has been reflected in their failure to move beyond Marx's competitive model of capitalism and to analyze and understand large-scale corporate capitalism. An important step in the development of a new theory of advanced corporate capitalism was made by Paul Baran and Paul Sweezy in their Monopoly Capital *(1966). According to Baran and Sweezy, the modern corporation is far more stable than its predecessors largely because of the changed role of the state in regulating the economy and in absorbing the rising "surplus" (especially through military spending).*

During the era of competitive capitalism industrial corporations became increasingly dependent—especially in times of depression—on a small centralized group of banks that were alone capable of financing industrial growth. Hence, financial control of industry—"finance capital"—characterized the end of the era of competitive capital in the United States at the end of the nineteenth century.

During the 1930s and 1940s many on the left believed that "finance capitalism" still existed and that it would be the last phase of capitalism. In this view the irrationality of competition would usher in a final crisis. The split within corporations between "financiers"—whose main interest lay in speculation—and "managers" seeking to protect and develop the corporation itself was a major manifestation of that irrationality. In contrast Baran and Sweezy argue that in advanced capitalism the corporation is no longer controlled by banks but is self-financing. Thus they see the managers of the modern corporations as responsible to themselves rather than being under the control of any outside financial or "interest" group.

Robert Fitch and Mary Oppenheimer's "Who Rules the Corporations? The Resurgence of Finance Capital," examines the question of control and of corporate independence and challenges Baran and Sweezy's conclusions. Their study does not attempt a final judgment on the stability of corporate capitalism, since they do not examine the relationship of the corporations to the state or the ability of the state to continue to stabilize the economy. But their findings of increased "outside" control of corporations by various financial institutions does partially alter the conclusions of Baran and Sweezy in Monopoly Capital.

Fitch and Oppenheimer's article will appear in SR in three parts. The first section explores the concept of managerial control of corporations and presents empirical findings from the House Subcommittee on Banking and Currency Report on Commercial Banks and Their Trust Activities (the Patman Report).

TWO WEEKS BEFORE the Penn Central filed for bankruptcy, thirteen of its directors gathered in Philadelphia for the most important meeting in the company's 135-year history. A series of corporate disasters competed for their attention. Since the merger of the rival New York Central and Pennsylvania railroads, the new corporation had undertaken a real estate acquisition program costing hundreds of millions of dollars. Meanwhile, the 21,000-mile railroad system degenerated into a mass of confusion. Month-long shipment delays were commonplace. Fully loaded freight cars turned up at the shipper's factory instead of their destination. Some cars disappeared. "A massive case of constipation," was the diagnosis of one railroad man. "You can feed stuff into it, but nothing comes out."

These operating problems, however, were not high up on the directors' agenda. What preoccupied them were the company's financial problems. Several acquisitions had soured, and now the company could not meet the payments either on its short-term obligations or on its $2.6 billion long-term external debt. To meet loan deadlines, the directors authorized a $100 million bond issue at 11½ per cent interest. Even at this record rate, investors refused to buy Penn Central bonds. The corporation was stuck without cash.

Perhaps the most striking characteristic the thirteen directors shared was their unfamiliarity with railroad operations. None had ever worked for a railroad in any capacity. They were "outside" directors, people who devoted only part of their business careers to the supervision of the Penn Central. Most heavily represented on the board were directors of financial institutions. As of April 1970, eleven of the board members had fourteen interlocks involving twelve commercial banks. The bank with the largest number of representatives—the Morgan Guarantee Trust—also happened to be the Penn Central's largest stockholder and the corporation's largest holder of commercial paper. Unanimously, the thirteen outside directors fired the absent "inside" directors—the railroad men who managed the corporation. Unanimously, they appointed a new Chief Executive Officer responsible to a special committee of the board set up to "oversee his daily performance." Unanimously, the outside directors voted to seek government relief for the company's stockholders and creditors, i.e., the giant financial institutions they represented.

Their attempt to get the Department of the Navy to save the seven billion dollar rail dinosaur has failed, at least temporarily, and the liquidity crisis (cash shortage) has spread to the company's creditors. Shock waves were felt in the commercial paper market, the stock market, and the real estate market, suggesting that the system is far more fragile than its spokesmen allowed.

To conventional critics, e.g., John Kenneth Galbraith, the Penn Central case must seem like a gigantic conspiracy to undermine their theories in the most dramatic way possible. Nothing about the Penn Central fits their model of the corporation. The top people at corporate headquarters are supposed to be the managers, the insiders. Bank control of corporations supposedly went out with running boards and Rudy Vallee. Corporations are supposed to finance themselves from their retained earnings. Whereas for the Penn Central, not even $2.6 billion in external finance was sufficient. Management is supposed to be "self-perpetuating," yet in the case of the Penn Central, the entire "inside" management was thrown out by the outsiders with apparent ease.

The implication of their conventional analysis was that corporations run by a new kind of professional managers, people who avoided reliance on external funds for expansion, would be more stable than corporations run by entrepreneurs or representatives of banks. Freed from the pressure of the capital market, and free from large personal stock holdings, the managers could behave like good corporate citizens, aiming at reasonable rather than maximum profits. Monopoly capitalism could be socially beneficial. If it wasn't, it was because managers still worked toward the conventional goal of maximizing profits. But education and prodding from the government could set them straight.

But what about the Penn Central? Conventional corporate critics might counter that the Penn Central is an anomaly—a throwback to a vanished era. But this would only confirm that part of their convention depends upon maintaining a state of ignorance. Several corporations with assets larger than the Penn Central's have come close to playing out the same drama, with only a few of the lines changed.[1]

Unfortunately, radical economists have been unable to provide

---

1. Chrysler, the nation's sixth largest corporation, with four directors representing Manufacturers Hanover, has gone through a protracted crisis brought on by a profit decline. The various stages of the crisis have been marked by a purge of inside management by outside directors, a liquidity crisis, and a rescue operation led by Manufacturers Hanover. Ling-Temco-Vought, number eighteen in the Fortune 500, began to experience its profit squeeze after an aggressive corporate acquisition program financed by commercial and investment banks. External debt reached $1.5 billion, over fifty per cent of total assets. LTV reacted by firing chairman Jimmy Ling, replacing him with the chairman of the board of the First National Bank of Dallas. Then it started selling off corporate assets to meet external debt payments. And neither of these corporations is unique.

a better explanation of the present crisis. Their theory is inadequate because they have grafted a great deal of the conventional analysis onto their model of corporate power. For example, Paul Baran and Paul Sweezy accepted the liberal theorists' ideas of management control, and of internal finance. This made more difficult an understanding of the merger movement of the 1960s and its contribution to the present crisis.

Since its publication in 1966, Baran and Sweezy's *Monopoly Capital* has served as the Marxist alternative both to schematic Marxism and liberal managerialism. It has played this role not only in the United States, but also in Germany, France, Great Britain, and even in Czechoslovakia. With this in mind, let us examine the managerial model more closely, then turn to an examination of U.S. corporate behavior.

I. MANAGERIALISM: LEFT AND RIGHT

A. Origins of Managerialism

EVER SINCE THE APPEARANCE of Professor Gardner Means' and corporate attorney Adolph Berle, Jr.'s *The Modern Corporation and Private Property* in 1932, the idea of managerial control has been accepted in social science literature.[2] But a common understanding of what "management" means is not nearly as widespread.

Two contradictory meanings of management and managerial control have been generated from *The Modern Corporation*. The popular meaning runs something like this: "The modern giant corporation has outgrown the entrepreneur's capacity to provide supervision or capital. Consequently he has been supplanted by a professional manager. This new phenomenon in business history is sure to bring its share of surprises, but the end result is likely to be a corporation more socially responsible than before."

But to those who pursue its legal technicalities and its footnotes *The Modern Corporation* presents a grimmer portrait of a very different group of newcomers. It is composed not of professional managers but of a few hundred financial oligarchs who

---

2. See also Ralph Milliband, *The State in Capitalist Society*; Nicol Poulantzas, *Pouvoir Politique et Classes Sociales*; Charles Bettelheim, *La Transition vers l'Economic Socialiste*; Ernest Mandel, *Marxist Economic Theory*, vol. 2, pp. 411-12, 511-17.

have taken control of diverse corporations. Risking little of their own capital, they operate the corporations for their own benefit. Berle and Means fear that a widespread comprehension of this situation—which is indefensible in terms of traditional bourgeois law—will create a crisis of authority. To *prevent* such a crisis, control must be transferred to a "purely neutral technocracy, balancing a variety of claims by various groups in the community and assigning to each a portion of the income stream on the basis of public policy rather than private cupidity."[3] This technocracy is presented as a form of control that must be developed to preserve the corporate system. It is not intended as a description of reality.

The ambiguity between the popular and technical images of managerialism arises from the definition of "management" itself. Those relying on the popular image think that management is a "purely neutral technocracy" of high level corporate officers who are themselves employees of the corporation. Certainly those who base their theory of "managerial revolution" on Berle and Means have not realized that Dillon, Read and the House of Morgan are part of that "revolution." But the authors' definition of management clearly includes such participants. Management, according to Berle and Means, can include the employee-officers, but its scope is actually much broader: "Universally, under the American system of law, managers consist of a board of directors and the senior officers of the corporation."[4] This opens the ranks of management to outside directors representing banking and other financial interests.

The problem here is that 190 pages have intervened between the early use of "management" and this formal definition. Almost invariably, however, Berle and Means use management as a synonym for the board of directors. The two terms were practically synonymous both in legal terminology and in the business parlance of the pre-1929 period.[5] However, since James Burnham's *Managerial Revolution,* the first of the many books based

---

3. *The Modern Corporation* (New York, 1968), pp. 312–13.

4. Ibid., p. 196.

5. Management: "collect[ively] a government body, e.g. a board of directors, a board of governors, etc." Oxford Universal Dictionary (London, 1955).

WHO RULES THE CORPORATIONS?   79

on a misreading of Berle and Means, the term "management" has come to have a more restricted meaning, denoting professional executives who are employees of a particular corporation, and who may also be on the board of directors.

If we examine Berle and Means' categories of corporate control carefully, we see that the corporations that fall into the category of pure management control are precisely those most widely acknowledged then to be dominated by finance capital. Their pure management category—"management control—no single important stockholder interest"—is filled almost entirely by utilities and railroads. And no one familiar with the details of utility and railroad operation in the 1920s could deny that they were controlled—with disastrous consequences—by high finance. [6]

Berle and Means list only two *industrial* corporations in their category "management control—no single important stock holder interest": United States Steel and General Electric. The authors deal at length with U.S. Steel, arguing that "a self-perpetuating board of directors" exercises corporate control despite the fact that the directors own very little stock in the corporation. This point is repeated three times, italicized and illustrated with a table. The table shows that the directors own less than one and a half per cent of the common stock. Yet they are able to perpetuate themselves. Why?

In sworn testimony J. P. Morgan denied having selected the members of the first United States Steel board, but he did admit to having "passed" on each member. The organization of U.S. Steel was the most famous American example of the power of finance capital in the creation and control of monopoly. U.S. Steel was simply a merger of previously competing companies and iron ore interests. Morgan played the most important role in the merger because it depended upon his ability to raise enormous amounts of cash in order to buy out the individual capitalists at vastly inflated sale prices. Only the Morgan-First National syndicate could distribute the amount of bonds required to finance U.S. Steel.

---

6. See William O. Douglas, *Democracy and Finance* (New York, 1940), especially chapter 15. Douglas was chairman of the SEC and charged with the reorganization of the utility industry. Part 3 of his book is devoted to public utilities.

It was hardly an accident, as Berle and Means point out, that of the original twenty-four directors, fifteen were members of the Morgan-First National syndicate that floated the historic billion-dollar bond issue to found the new corporation in 1901. Over the years, the members preserved their directorships. By 1927, U.S. Steel's outside, non-employee directors accounted for twelve of fourteen seats. Of these the Morgan-First National group held five seats; Mather, a director of the Morgan-controlled Bankers Trust, had one seat; Kidder Peabody one; the Hanover Bank one; Continental Bank four. Finance capital had a clear majority. To suppose these financiers and capitalists, who were not only a majority on the board, but whose predecessors were affiliated with Steel from its creation, would have appointed two managers hostile to their interests requires a special kind of naiveté.

We can see now what the authors mean by United States Steel's self-perpetuating Board, although "hereditary" would be a more precise description. Not only do the representatives of financial institutions re-elect themselves each year, they are also able to pass on their director's seats to another representative of the same institution when the first representative dies or retires.

U.S. Steel was the largest and best known industrial corporation of the period. And A. A. Berle was a specialist in corporation finance, explicitly familiar with the litigation surrounding corporate control at U.S. Steel itself.[7] It is unlikely indeed that he would have chosen as his model managerial corporation in the industrial field a corporation that disproved his thesis, a corporation with only two managers by today's criteria. Berle's definition of "manager" however was broader; it meant simply the board of directors, who, like the Steel directors, held little stock, but ran the company anyhow. The main problem is that Berle never states *why* or *how* the directors of Steel were able to perpetuate themselves. But the answer would have been obvious for his fellow corporate attorneys.

Understanding of the technical meaning of management control has been confined largely to law school journals and to

7. Berle cites *U.S. Steel Corp. v. Hodge* (64 N.J. Eq. 807 [1903]), in which the plaintiff essentially charged conflict of interest on the part of the directors who voted themselves Steel's bond business. In the sixty-seven years since the case was adjudicated, the directors have never missed an opportunity to vote U.S. Steel's bond business.

businessmen who did not have to read Berle to know who was in charge. Academic social science predictably embraced the popular, apologetic meaning. Soon "empirical" studies began to appear, illustrating the further consolidation of managerial control.

B. The Nature of Corporate Control

BUT WHAT DO WE MEAN by "corporate control?" And what does it entail? This seems at first like an academic question: corporate control obviously means power to make the major corporate decisions. But what kind of power is meant? Power to initiate issues? To formulate proposals? To veto the proposals of others? And which are the major decisions, which the minor ones?

In 1966 the American Management Association sponsored the publication of what appears to be the definitive study of the distribution of power within the corporation.[8] The authors—two former corporation presidents who now hold numerous corporate directorships—interviewed hundreds of corporation presidents and directors to learn exactly how corporations of various sizes divided the tasks between directors and management.

The distribution of power among inside managers, stockholders, and outsiders on the board of directors, according to Juran and Louden, changes as a corporation grows.

In the small corporation, the head of the firm acts simultaneously as majority owner and chief executive officer (CEO). Yet corporate law requires that he create a board of directors. Typically the head merely complies with the letter of the law, e.g., naming relatives to the board. Here is how their duties are divided:[9]

What the Bylaws Say	What the Practical Situation Is
. . . All corporate powers shall be exercised by or under the authority of . . . the board of directors [which shall]	They sign whatever papers the owner and the lawyer say are needed "as a formality"
. . . select and remove all officers	They select the owner annually, and he does the rest

8. J. M. Juran and James Louden, *The Corporate Director* (New York, 1966). 9. See Louden and Juran, pp. 21-22.

. . . fix their compensation	They leave this to the owner
. . . conduct, manage, and control the affairs of the corporation . . . borrow money . . . and cause to be executed . . . in the corporate name . . . promissory notes, bonds, debentures	They sign whatever papers the owner and the lawyer say are needed "as a formality"

The small corporation finances its expansion, at least in part, by selling its shares. In its early growth this may involve selling shares primarily to relatives. But if the corporation is to develop to substantial size, ownership will spread beyond the family. Eventually the owners will have to formalize power relations through the board in order to establish a single chain of command. Without this chain of command, not only do the hired managers find it difficult to carry out their assignments, but they also find it easier to set up independent spheres of influence and accumulate their own power. "The growing number and power of the hired managers," say Juran and Louden, "can be better checked by a board of directors than by numerous owners acting without a board." In other words, the board functions as a legal weapon in the hands of capitalists to check the potential threat from the non-propertied, hired managers.

As corporate growth continues, the company generally finds public financing necessary. Public financing normally makes outside directors mandatory. At this point, the board of directors of the medium-sized corporation becomes a real arena of struggle. The owners seek membership in order to distinguish themselves from hired managers and solidify their control. The hired managers ask for board membership and equity in the corporation in order to bolster their positions.

In the very largest corporations, the enormous amount of outstanding stock makes it possible for only institutional investors or families originally associated with the corporation to have holdings sufficient to exercise power through equity. Hired managers are rarely significant equity holders in large corporations.[10]

Table X (Exhibit 10, p. 238) shows the evolution of board power beginning with the small family corporation and continuing through the medium-sized insider-dominated corporation. As the corporation reaches the $50-500 million range, however, out-

---

10. Mabel Newcomer, *The Big Business Executive* (New York, 1955).

WHO RULES THE CORPORATIONS?   83

sider domination develops. According to the Juran and Louden survey, tne very large corporation is almost always dominated by outsiders.

Their findings are confirmed by National Industrial Conference Board Studies beginning in 1953. At that time fifty-three per cent of the seats on the boards of large corporations were held by outside directors. The percentage increased to fifty-seven in 1958 and to sixty-three in 1967. And, according to the NICB, an even higher percentage of boards was dominated by outsiders than the formal majorities indicated.

As further confirmation of the trend, several previously "insider" dominated corporations have begun to open up their boards to outsiders. Standard Oil of New Jersey announced in 1966 that for the first time since 1887 it had added outsiders to the board. Mobil Oil recently nominated outsiders to its board for the first time in company history. And Bethlehem Steel nominated outsiders to its board for the first time in twenty years.

Outsider domination of company policy is promoted through a New York Stock Exchange requirement that each new listed company have at least two outside directors on its board. Even before the requirement, more than ninety-seven per cent of the companies listed on the Exchange had two or more outside directors.

As we will see in later sections, these New York Stock Exchange requirements, and the changes in board composition that emphasize outsider participation, merely formalize existing financial relations between industrial and financial capital.

LET US EXAMINE NOW how corporate power is distributed and exercised on the board of a typical giant corporation. The members of the President's Association interviewed by Juran and Louden agreed unanimously that in the giant corporation a strict separation could be made between board and management matters. Affairs can be run no other way if only because the typical outside director of perhaps a dozen corporations will not travel a thousand miles to listen to shop talk. Consequently the board retains some powers and delegates others to the Chief Executive Officer.

Pre-eminently, the board controls the money. The two boards cited by Juran and Louden as typical of the large corporation in action reflect this. A "large auto manufacturer" requires that the board of directors fix the amount of the company's working capital periodically, and set aside from net profits or surplus such amounts as are deemed necessary to safeguard adequate working capital. In keeping with this broad financial power, the board determines "the amount and manner of payment of any dividends paid by the company," as well as fixing the salaries of officers and executives and themselves as directors.

The by-laws of a "large pharmaceutical firm" are quite explicit in preserving the monopoly of outside directors in finance. The Finance Committee membership "is independent of operating management and consists solely of 'outside' directors, although company financial officers are invited to attend meetings regularly." This committee determines the distribution of profits, authorizes dividends and takes charge of capital investments, including the making of new capital investments, the sale and exchange of assets, etc. In addition to dominating financial affairs, the board also sets the overall policies and objectives for the company. They decide, for example, the rate and type of corporate growth to be pursued. The board may, for example, choose any of these four growth policies:

1. Avoid growth as an objective except as it is forced on us. Keep a taut ship and aim for this year's profits. Minimize research and development costs except as required to get current customer orders.

2. Grow with the economy, the objective being to hold the present share of market on our products. Keep modernizing the line and moving into added markets, all at a measured pace.

3. Grow at a rate substantially faster than the economy. Build research and development, both product and market, to a point which makes this possible. Develop executives at a rate well beyond that needed for replacement and slow growth. Go beyond our present product line, but do not leave [our field of] business.

4. Embark on a program of rapid building of a new economic empire. Go after acquisitions which are attractive financially whether in related fields or not. Strengthen legal and financial organization to permit discovery, acquisition, and exploitation of acquisitions.[11]

---

11. Juran and Louden, pp. 53-54.

While the board sets broad objectives, it doesn't give specific instructions. It may decide that the fourth policy, the empire-building strategy, best suits its objectives. But it doesn't tell the Chief Executive Officer what to say on the phone to the Chief Executive Officer of the target company.

While setting long-run objectives, the board also reserves certain powers in the area of short-range (one year or less) program development. It approves, in keeping with its long-run objectives, the annual profit plan, the annual capital appropriations plan, the financing program, the research and advertising budgets. The board decides whether or not to enter a new product line; whether to get out of a product line; it sets executive salaries and deals with "pressure groups."

All the directors and officers interviewed by Juran and Louden agreed that the most important act of the board was choosing the CEO. The CEO has the authority to carry out and execute the board's policies; he gives the "marching orders," in Juran and Louden's telling phrase, to the industrial army; he translates objectives into strategies. The CEO has enormous power, but it is power that has been delegated to him, power to execute the orders of others. Naturally the CEO acts as the corporation's chief spokesman; consequently he is popularly identified as the "top" person of the corporation. This popular confusion misconstrues the relations of power within the corporate structure and overlooks the continuity of institutional interests on the board that outlasts any specific CEO.

Finally, the directors interviewed stressed that "control subjects" were important to the board. "Control" here does not mean "direction" or "exercise of authority." Rather, it is akin to a Soviet "Control" Commission. That is, the "control subjects" permit the board to regulate management performance, to ensure that management meets the board's standards.

The "control subjects" most often mentioned by Juran and Louden's respondents are almost invariably expressed in monetary terms; the board translates all performance into dollar terms in order to control it. This translation overcomes one of the chief arguments raised against financial/outsider control of corporate decisions—their inability to control corporate activities when they know nothing about complex technologies or about the mechanics of everyday operations. "The country banker," writes Galbraith, "out of his experience and knowledge of the business, can readily interpose his judgment as against that of a farmer, on the prospects for feeder cattle—and does. Not even the most self-confident financier would wish to question the judgment of G.E. engineers, product planners, stylists, market researchers and sales executives" on the question of a new toaster.[12] What Galbraith fails to realize is that the technicians and the bankers simply deal with the toaster according to different standards. Galbraith's market researchers and engineers work according to the standards set by their spheres of production and distribution. Their language is shaped by the discourse of the laboratory, the factory, the district office: sales quotas, specifications, schedules, expense budgets. As Juran and Louden observe, their "units of measure are in things and deeds, more than in money: units booked this month, pounds per square inch, kilowatt hours per gallon distilled. [Their] standards are set from history or from engineering standards."[13]

"But," Juran and Louden continue, "his boss has the last word. In contrast, the board is faced with standards for the enterprise as a whole rather than for functional departments. The units of measure are strongly related to money because it is the only language in which all deeds are expressed. The board's standards are set not so much by engineering study or history as by 'the market.' "[14]

C. Marxist Managerialism

WHETHER BANKERS AND THEIR ALLIES or "inside" employee-managers control the giant corporations is an empirical question. But Sweezy and Baran chose to argue against simplistic managerialism—the theories of the beneficent corporation—by accepting its factual premises and debating its conclusions. And although they claimed there was abundant empirical proof to show that capitalists and bankers no longer were in control, they do not cite any.

---

12. *New Industrial State*, p. 82.

13. *The Corporate Director*, p. 145.

14. Loc. cit.

WHO RULES THE CORPORATIONS? 87

Having accepted the premise that inside "managers" ran the corporation, they argued specifically that these managers had to run the corporation just as the capitalists of the nineteenth century did—maximizing profits and trying to carry out the same accumulation policy. In their own words:

1. Control rests in the hands of management, that is to say, the board of directors plus the chief executive officers (*sic*). Outside interests are often (but not always) represented on the board to facilitate the harmonization of the interests and policies of the corporation with those of customers, suppliers, bankers, etc.; but real power is held by the insiders, those who devote full time to the corporation and whose interests and careers are tied to its fortunes.

2. Management is a self-perpetuating group. Responsibility to the body of stockholders is for all practical purposes a dead letter. . . .

3. Each corporation aims at and normally achieves financial independence through the internal generation of funds which remain at the disposal of management. The corporation may still, as a matter of policy, borrow from or through financial institutions, but it is not normally forced to do so and hence is able to avoid the kind of subjection to financial control which was so common in the world of Big Business fifty years ago.[15]

Baran and Sweezy go on to conclude that both the great financial institutions and the great capitalist families—the Rockefellers, Mellons, Fords, Morgans, and DuPonts—are no longer decisive in corporate affairs. Their former employees have taken over. To prove this assertion they provide a case study of Standard Oil. In 1911 the Standard Oil trust, then under control of the Rockefeller family, was broken up by the government. But Rockefeller interests sought to keep control of all the Standard Oil components: New Jersey, California, Indiana, Mobil, etc. Baran and Sweezy argue that if the various companies can be shown to have competed with each other rather than to have been united under Rockefeller control, this will demonstrate that outside control over corporations is no longer sufficiently important to be worthy of attention. The Rockefeller family was surely one of the strongest of capitalist families: if it has been vanquished, we can assume that the others have fallen too.

---

15. *Monopoly Capital* (New York, 1966), pp. 15-16.

But the example Baran and Sweezy select to illustrate conflict —the collision between Standard Oil of Indiana and Jersey Standard—actually affirms the continuing importance of outside control. They fail to point out that the conflict between Indiana Standard and Jersey Standard that broke out after World War II took place only after control of Standard of Indiana had passed to *another* outside controlling group: Jacob Blaustein (American Oil, Pan American Oil) and Chicago financial interests. Throughout the 1920s and 1930s Standard Oil of Indiana and Jersey Standard successfully worked together to prevent the Blaustein interests—American Oil Co.—from developing into another integrated oil producer. Blaustein, a Democrat, spent decades in courtroom and boardroom struggles that involved government officials and business figures at the very pinnacles of power. After World War II he emerged as the largest individual stockholder in Standard Oil of Indiana. Only then was Blaustein, together with Chicago financial interests, able to outvote the Rockefeller-Chase Manhattan bloc.[16]

The duration and intensity of the struggle indicate that Rockefeller forces can by no means be considered impotent. Their ultimate defeat proves only that Rockefeller-Chase Manhattan interests can be bested by other outside groups of stockholders. This is hardly a new development: even J. P. Morgan in his prime was unable to keep complete control of all the corporations in which he had an interest.[17]

Besides the Standard Oil case, Baran and Sweezy present little concrete evidence for their assertion of managerial control. There is, for example, no analysis of stockholdings, directorships, or credit relationships. But this lack of evidence cannot be blamed entirely on Sweezy and Baran. The great financial institutions have gone to great lengths to shield their control from the light of public inspection.[18] And until recently there was insufficient reliable evidence to challenge directly the strong point in the mana-

---

16. *Forbes*, 15 Sept. 1968, pp. 26-30. See also Patman.

17. Lewis Corey, *House of Morgan* (New York, 1933), pp. 293-304, provides an account of the battle in which Harriman wrested partial control of the Northern Pacific from Morgan.

18. *The New Republic*'s coverage of the Dixon-Yates scandal gives numerous examples of attempts to conceal control.

WHO RULES THE CORPORATIONS?   89

gerial facade—the doctrine of the separation of ownership from control. The publication of the Patman Report has changed all that.

II. STOCK OWNERSHIP AND CONTROL

A. *Stocks and Secrecy*

TO HIS FRIENDS AND NEIGHBORS, James Dowds Stietenroth was a Bible-reading native-born Mississippian, a life-long employee of the Mississippi Power and Light Company who had risen through the ranks to become secretary treasurer. But for twenty-six years with the company, Stietenroth told Senator Kefauver's Subcommittee on Monopoly investigating the Dixon-Yates conspiracy

> I was forced to live a life of deceit and hypocrisy when I pretended to be the principal financial and accounting officer of the company.... In truth the powers and pre-rogatives of my office had in large measure been usurped by others.[19]

Stietenroth had no access to the corporation's tax ledgers: these were kept in New York City. He had never been allowed to hire personnel to deal with tax questions. When he refused to sign documents authorizing new issues of Mississippi's shares, the SEC approved the certificates anyway. Control of Mississippi Power and Light was in the hands of New York-based Ebasco Services, Inc., supposedly an electrical repair service. Ebasco kept the books, prepared the tax returns, and handled the utility's financial problems.

Behind all the deception lay the 1935 Public Utility Holding Company Act, prompted by the utility empire building of the 1920s: financial speculators had skimmed the cash from utility company coffers, while leaving plant to decay. The 1935 Act had forced Electric Bond and Share, a Morgan-controlled utility complex, to divest itself of four operating utility companies—among them Mississippi Power and Light. To get around the law Electric Bond and Share created a wholly-owned subsidiary—Ebasco—to exercise control in the guise of electrical service repair. Meanwhile

---

19. Michael Straight, "New Light on Dixon-Yates," *New Republic*, 11 October 1954, p. 9.

Mississippi Power and Light bragged about its "local management"; controlled the local press through bribes; and cycled profits back to Wall Street. For twenty years concealment had enabled Wall Street to skimp on plant, equipment, and maintenance while reaping monopoly profits on practically no equity.

Such duplicity is hardly unique in the corporate world. Stietenroth provided just one illustration of the stratagems the great financial institutions use to keep their actions secret—of how the nexus of ownership is hidden by a complicated maze of street names, bank nominees, and dummy "managers." [20]

Much of the reform legislation of the 1930s—the creation of the Securities and Exchange Commission, the Public Utilities Holding Company Act, Glass-Steagall Act and that great blow to the insurance "industry," the Social Security Act—aimed at regulating finance capital. In this legal movement those who sought to check the power of finance capital were joined by those who merely wished to head off more restrictive legislation. The movement to check the power of finance capital failed because monopoly cannot operate without finance capital—it cannot carry out further concentration and centralization; it cannot coordinate inter-industrial relations. However, given the existing legal framework, modern finance capital has been forced to operate not merely in secret, but through deception and fraud.

IN THIS CONTEXT we can appreciate the political achievement of Wright Patman's House Subcommittee on Banking and Currency. Armed with the power of Congressional subpoena the Subcommittee secured reliable figures on bank trust department stockholdings. Prior to the publication of its report in July 1968 the size and nature of these holdings—approximately $275 billion—could only be guessed. And since this bloc contained the largest chunk of common stock in the country, our picture of corporate control was badly out of focus. One could make speculative extrapolations from the thirty-year-old data collected by

---

20. Under the nominee system an individual opens an account with a trust institution, but the shares are not listed in the name of the individual, but under one of several standard "nominees" of the bank. Such nominees have street names—Kane & Co., Sigler & Co., Carson & Co., etc.

the Temporary National Economic Committee (TNEC) [21] or try to work with the incomplete and often unreliable data produced by "independent" regulatory agencies such as the Securities and Exchange Commission and the Civil Aeronautics Board. [22] With these agencies, however, bribe-taking, swindling, and hotel room deals have attained the status of bureaucratic norms. Mere figure juggling and omission are standard operating procedure. For example, American Airlines reported to the CAB in 1967 that it had no stockholders with over five per cent of the capital stock. The CAB accepted the figure although anyone with the slightest knowledge of the company would have known it was fraudulent. The Patman Subcommittee investigation disclosed that Morgan Guaranty Trust did in fact hold 7.5 per cent of the American's stock. Similar secrecy and misrepresentation were revealed in the case of Eastern, TWA, and United Airlines. [23] More recently Ralph Nader's Center for the Study of Responsive Law has charged the CAB with failure to report the names of persons holding substantial blocs of stock in the case of sixteen airlines. The complaint names banks, stock brokerage houses, and holding companies. [24]

The motive for the falsification of official records by the airlines is very likely the same as in the case of the utility empires: financial institutions are holding stock in "competing" corporations in violation of the Clayton Act. In the case of the airlines they are also violating laws designed to split control of the airlines from the aircraft manufacturing corporations. [25]

---

21. This was Ferdinand Lundberg's method in *The Rich and the Super-Rich* (New York, 1968)—a book that represents a big step backward from his earlier and less pretentious study *America's Sixty Families* (New York, 1937). Far superior, but a bit dated, is Victor Perlo's *Empire of High Finance* (New York, 1957), which also relies on TNEC data.

22. Don Villarejo's "Stock Ownership and the Control of Corporations," *New University Thought*, August 1961/Winter 1962, is a model of this kind of study that often rises above the limitations of its sources.

23. Patman Report, p. 484.

24. *Wall Street Journal*, 14 August 1970.

25. For information on the activities of aircraft/airlines that led to their separation, see Elspeth Freudenthal, *The Aviation Business* (New York, 1940).

B. Finance and Control

ALTHOUGH IT STILL LEAVES great gaps in our knowledge of corporate stockholding in the United States, the data on stock-holding obtained by the Patman Committee is the most complete since the TNEC. The Committee carried out two surveys of bank trust departments. The first summarized the trust assets of the 3,125 insured banks with trust departments. The second study, far more significant, analyzed in depth precisely what these hold-ings were—but dealt only with forty-nine large banks. These banks were *not* the forty-nine largest, although they included most of the very largest. The banks surveyed were primarily the banks located in the Eastern financial capitals—New York City, Boston, Philadelphia, Pittsburgh, Hartford. No Texas banks and no California banks—Western Bankcorporation, Bank of America, Security Pacific, etc.—were included. And since it deals only with commercial banks, the Patman study lacks any analysis of the holdings of such key financial institutions as mutual funds, insur-ance companies, brokerage houses, and investment banks. Never-theless the Patman Committee has pieced together some key financial-industrial linkages involving the nation's largest financial institutions.

TABLE 1: 1966 ASSETS OF FINANCIAL INSTITUTIONS BY CATEGORY

Type	1966 assets ($ millions)	% of total
Banks and trust companies	476,071	46.3
Other credit agencies	188,388	18.3
Security and commodity brokers, dealers, exchanges, and services	9,716	0.9
Holding and other investment companies	55,847	5.4
Insurance carriers	219,342	21.3
Insurance agents, brokers, and services	3,262	0.3
Real estate	75,793	7.4

Source: U.S. Treasury, Internal Revenue Service, **Preliminary Statistics of Income, 1967: Corporate Income Tax Returns**, p. 20.

The sheer size of the commercial banks' assets is shown in Table 1: in 1966 they controlled 46.3 per cent of all assets held by U.S. financial institutions. The figure is even more impressive when we note that it does not include trust holdings. Nor does it take into account the functions of commercial banks in the econ-omy. Unlike other financial institutions they are deeply involved

WHO RULES THE CORPORATIONS? 93

in filling almost every external financial need of both financial
and non-financial corporations. Traditional sources of short-term
credit, commercial banks now provide "term" loans, i.e., medium
term loans; finance corporate take-overs; float state, municipal,
and federal securities; sell insurance; even lease jet planes and
industrial equipment of every sort. They demand to be let into
the Stock Exchange and into the mutual fund business. And as
the Wall Street banks increase their control over all financial
spheres, resembling more and more the Japanese Zaibatsu, Madison Avenue finds a new name for them: "financial super-
markets."

TABLE 2: THE GROWTH OF FINANCIAL INTERMEDIARIES
WITHIN THE AMERICAN ECONOMY, 1860-1965

	Total assets		Assets as % of			Increase in assets as % of net national capital formation
	Amount (bill.)	Rate of growth (% yr)	All fin. assets	National wealth	National product	
1860	1.2	7.0	16	8	27	—
1890	9	7.0	23	14	69	20
1912	34	6.1	26	30	130	70
1929	133	8.3	26	30	130	70
1939	167	2,2	36	42	185	—
1948	380	9,6	38	42	144	—
1965	1128	6.7	—	47	167	75

Source: Raymond W. Goldsmith, **Financial Institutions** (New York, 1968),
p. 157.

Combining the great Zaibatsu banks with other financial intermediaries—insurance companies, savings and loan associations,
credit unions, finance companies, mutual funds and pension
funds, we are able to trace the development of the financial sector as a whole in Table 2. Prior to the Civil War, financial institutions were modest middlemen—true intermediaries; this is reflected in the fact that their assets totaled less than ten per cent
of the *national* wealth.[26] Even at the dawn of the great corporate
consolidation movement thirty years later, the percentage had
climbed to only fourteen. But by 1965, total assets of financial
institutions amounted to nearly *half of all national wealth*. The
yearly rate of increase in these assets was greater than the rate of
increase in the national wealth as a whole, insuring, if the present
trend continues, that the assets of financial institutions will

26. *National* wealth defined as all land, structures, equipment and inven-
tories.

amount to over half some time in the seventies. Perhaps most striking of all, in 1965, the funds supplied by financial institutions to the non-financial sector—private households, governments, and non-financial corporations—equalled about two-thirds of the national net capital formation.

C. Trust Assets and the Socialization of Wealth

THE ASSETS HELD BY BANKS and insurance companies in the table amount to about two-thirds of the total held by financial institutions. But pension funds—about three-quarters controlled by banks—have been treated as an entirely separate category. To separate banks from the trust funds they manage would eliminate one of the most important bases of their economic power—one that only a few sophisticated observers fully understood prior to the publication of the Patman Committee Report.

As of 1967, the Committee reported, commercial banks held $607 billion, approximately sixty per cent of all assets held by United States financial institutions. Of this more than $250 billion was held by trust departments. A major portion—approximately two-thirds—was in stock. This approximately $180 billion dollars' worth of common stock generates forty per cent of all the trading carried out on the New York Stock Exchange.[27]

What are these trust accounts? Some are employee benefit or pension funds. These are growing rapidly: in 1955, pension funds totaled twenty-five billion dollars and at the end of 1967 one hundred billion dollars. Commercial banks administer approximately seventy per cent of these assets; $70 billion. Before 1980, it is estimated pension funds will amount to $285 billion, with banks controlling about $200 billion. Second are private trusts, a device used increasingly to avoid taxes and unify the assets of wealthy families. By placing disposal of the estate in the hands of bank trustees, income may be dispersed throughout the family while the concentrated voting power of the estate remains intact. In some cases this voting power is wielded in accordance with the

---

27. The ownership figures are from the Patman Report. The data on trading comes from the New York Stock Exchange *Annual Report*, 1969, p. 10.

families' wishes; more often it is not. In 81.9 per cent of the cases studied by the Committee, banks had discretionary authority over the investment of most of their trust accounts.

The institutionalization and socialization of family wealth through bank-controlled trust accounts is a variation on a favorite theme of the American bourgeoisie. As a rule the very great American fortunes—those that have lasted more than a generation—are those that wedded industrial capital to financial capital or vice versa. For example, the Rockefeller family capitalized two great Wall Street banks out of the profits of the Standard Oil Trust. And the Pittsburgh banker Judge Thomas Mellon used his credit power to purchase Gulf Oil Company from its founder and then went on to organize the aluminum trust (Alcoa). There are many other financial-industrial families.

By merging industrial into financial capital, through the trust department mechanism, the great capitalist families have been able to avoid dissipation of their estates. And at the same time they have gained a measure of social control over industrial capital by merging it with other trust department assets under their institutional control. This vastly increased the importance of their wealth in qualitative as well as quantitative terms.

Consider the concentration of these bank trust department assets. The ten largest commercial banks in terms of deposits hold less than twenty-four per cent of all United States deposits. Ranked in terms of trust deposits, the ten largest holders of these assets hold nearly thirty-seven per cent. The hundred largest commercial banks in terms of trust assets hold about eighty-two per cent of all the trust assets. The hundred largest commercial banks in terms of deposits hold less than fifty per cent of all United States deposits. Tables 3 and 4 show the pattern for the twenty-five largest commercial banks in each category.

D. *The Merger Movement on Wall Street*

NOT ONLY ARE TRUST ASSETS concentrated in a relatively few banks, but these banks are themselves becoming more and more closely linked. Between 1900 and 1965 the number of commercial banks in existence dropped by over one hundred per cent— from 30,000 in 1900 to 13,800 in 1965. This decline is a function of both failure and success, as manifested in an unprece-

96   FITCH & OPPENHEIMER

TABLE 3: TWENTY-FIVE LARGEST BANKS RANKED BY TOTAL TRUST ASSETS
November-December 1967

Rank	Bank name and city	Per cent of trust assets of all banks surveyed	Cumulative percentage
1	Morgan Guaranty Trust, NYC	6.73	6.73
2	Chase Manhattan Bank, NYC	5.46	12.19
3	Bankers Trust Co., NYC	4.44	16.63
4	First National City Bank, NYC	4.35	20.98
5	United States Trust, NYC	3.36	24.34
6	Mellon National Bank, Pittsburgh	3.05	27.39
7	Manufacturers Hanover Trust, NYC	2.94	30.33
8	Wilmington Trust, Wilmington	2.25	32.58
9	First National Bank of Chicago	2.18	34.76
10	Continental Illinois, Chicago	2.06	36.82
11	Chemical Bank, NYC	1.84	38.66
12	Northern Trust Co., Chicago	1.82	40.48
13	Old Colony Trust, Boston	1.69	42.17
14	Harris Trust, Chicago	1.55	43.72
15	Bank of America, San Francisco	1.48	45.20
16	Cleveland Trust Co.	1.45	46.65
17	National Bank of Detroit	1.38	48.03
18	Bank of New York, NYC	1.33	49.36
19	Girard Trust, Philadelphia	1.18	50.54
20	First Pennsylvania, Philadelphia	1.08	51.62
21	Mercantile-Safe Deposit, Baltimore	.93	52.55
22	Security First National, Los Angeles	.89	53.44
23	Crocker-Citizens, San Francisco	.84	54.28
24	Fidelity Bank, Philadelphia	.81	55.09
25	Wells Fargo, San Francisco	.76	55.85

Source: Patman Report, p. 78

dented merger movement. Between 1950 and 1955 the office of the Comptroller approved 376 consecutive bank mergers without a single disapproval. New banks are created, but do not offset the effects of mergers. Between 1953 and 1962, for example, there were 1,113 new commercial banks organized, but 1,669 mergers and absorptions.[28]

The most striking mergers have occurred at the very top of the commercial banking empire. In the mid-1950s a series of New York City bank mergers greatly concentrated the financial strength on Wall Street:

— The Chase National Bank merged with the Bank of Manhattan Company and the Bronx County Trust Company to establish the Chase Manhattan Bank, number two in deposits nationally;
— The National City Bank, based on the Stillman-Rockefeller

28. Baum and Stiles, *The Silent Partner* (New York, 1965), p. 108. See also Emmanuel Celler, "The Philadelphia National Bank Case: A Rejoinder," *National Banking Review* 226, 1963.

TABLE 4: TWENTY-FIVE LARGEST BANKS
RANKED BY TOTAL DEPOSITS
As of December 31, 1967

Rank	Bank	Percent of all bank deposits	Cumulative percentage
1	Bank of America, San Francisco	4.82	4.82
2	Chase Manhattan Bank, NYC	3.98	8.80
3	First National City Bank, NYC	3.84	12.64
4	Manufacturers Hanover, NYC	2.02	14.66
5	Morgan Guaranty Trust, NYC	1.84	16.50
6	Chemical Bank, NYC	1.79	18.29
7	Bankers Trust, NYC	1.52	19.81
8	Continental Illinois, Chicago	1.36	21.17
9	Security First National, Los Angeles	1.29	22.46
10	First National Bank, Chicago	1.29	23.75
11	Wells Fargo, San Francisco	1.02	24.77
12	Crocker-Citizens, San Francisco	.95	25.72
13	Irving Trust, NYC	.89	26.61
14	United California Bank, Los Angeles	.86	27.47
15	Mellon National Bank, Pittsburgh	.82	28.29
16	First National Bank of Detroit	.79	29.08
17	First National Bank, Boston	.73	29.81
18	Franklin National Bank, Mineola, NY	.54	30.35
19	Cleveland Trust Co.	.51	30.86
20	First Pennsylvania, Philadelphia	.47	31.33
21	Detroit Bank & Trust	.43	31.76
22	Manufacturers National Bank, Detroit	.42	32.18
23	Marine Midland Grace, NYC	.41	32.59
24	Seattle First National	.39	32.98
25	Harris Trust. Chicago	.39	33.37

Source: U.S. Congress, Committee on Banking and Currency, Sub-committee on Domestic Finance, Commercial Banks and their Trust Activities: Emerging Influence on the American Economy, Volume I. 90th Congress, 2d Session, 1968, p. 79.

Standard Oil fortune, merged with the First National City Bank, third in deposits;

— The Chemical Bank merged with the Corn Exchange Bank and then the New York Trust Company to become the Chemical Exchange Bank, sixth in deposits;

— The two Morgan banks, J. P. Morgan Company and the Guaranty Trust Company, merged to form Morgan Guaranty Trust, fifth in deposits;

— Finally, in 1961 Manufacturers Trust merged with the Hanover Bank, creating the Manufacturers Hanover Bank, fourth in deposits.[29]

As a result of this remarkable series of mergers the top five New York City banks by 1962 held fifteen per cent of all deposits in the country, seventy-five per cent of all deposits in New York City. This is more than double the concentration ratio of 1922, the heyday of unreconstructed financial power, when five banks controlled only thirty per cent of total New York City

29. See Baum and Stiles, p. 107.

TABLE 5: STOCKHOLDER LINKS AMONG SIX LARGEST NEW YORK CITY BANKS

Percent interest in

Stockholding bank	Chase Manhattan			First National			Manufacturers			Chemical			Morgan Guaranty			Bankers Trust		
	1962	1966	% incr.	1962	1966	% incr.	1962	1966	% incr.	1962	1966	% incr.	1962	1966	% incr.	1962	1966	% incr.
Chase Manhattan	2.04	2.30	12.7	1.90	1.62	-14.8	0.64	1.62	64.0	1.37	1.90	38.6	0.95	1.65	73.6	1.77	1.33	-33.0
First National	1.12	1.87	66.9	4.01	4.26	6.2	1.01	—	—	.96	1.76	83.3	0.99	1.32	33.3	1.79	2.30	28.4
Manufacturers Hanover	1.64	2.00	28.0	1.58	2.00	26.5	8.10	7.37	-9.9	1.17	2.25	92.3	1.69	1.95	15.3	1.85	2.48	34.0
Chemical Bank	—	1.37	—	.84	2.24	106.6	—	.46	—	3.99	5.79	4.76	—	1.09	—	1.63	2.02	23.9
Morgan Guaranty	3.03	3.18	1.6	2.72	3.89	43.0	1.32	2.20	66.6	1.30	4.13	217.6	6.61	7.75	17.2	5.34	4.63	-15.3
Bankers Trust	.71	1.70	139.4	.73	1.90	160.2	.99	1.33	34.3	.85	.47	-80.8	0.67	1.24	85.0	5.10	8.26	61.9
Total	8.54	12.42	45.4	11.76	15.91	35.3	12.07	12.41	2.8	9.64	16.30	69.1	8.54	15.00	37.6	17.47	21.02	20.3

Source: Patman Report, vol. 1, facing p. 876

deposits.[30] Today the five largest New York City banks control 21.32 per cent of the entire nation's trust assets.[31]

An analysis of the ownership structure of the top five New York City banks provides still more striking evidence of their concentration. Commercial banks are legally forbidden to display interlocking directorships, i.e., directors who sit on the boards of two or more commercial banks. But the banks are permitted to own each other's stock. And as Table 5 shows, the New York City banks, far from being discrete competitive institutions, actually own each other, and are accumulating each other's stock at a rapid rate. To a considerable extent the five banks actually constitute a single unified money cartel.

E. Trust Departments and Corporate Control

THE COMMERCIAL BANKING establishment, more concentrated than ever before, wields trust holdings whose magnitude overshadows the individual stockholdings of the past. In 1929 the Pennsylvania Railroad's largest single stockholder held a mere 0.34 per cent. Yet in 1967, with stockholding "dispersed," Morgan Guaranty Trust controlled 7.2 per cent, Chase Manhattan 5.6 per cent.

These large holdings in the Pennsylvania Railroad are not atypical. One hundred and forty-seven companies listed in the Fortune 500 had five per cent or more of their stock held by one of the forty-nine banks surveyed, including such giants as Gulf, DuPont, Boeing, and Firestone. There were twenty instances of five per cent control among the fifty largest merchandising companies, twenty-three among the fifty largest transportation companies. All told, the forty-nine banks reported holding at least five per cent of one or more classes of stock in 5,270 companies, an average of 108 companies per bank.[32]

30. U.S. Congress, Select Committee on Small Business, *Chain Banking: Stockholder and Loan Links of 200 Largest Member Banks*, 87th Congress, January 1963, p. 57.

31. See Tables 3 and 4. Although these New York City banks rank second to sixth in total deposits nationally, they are first to fifth in the city. The San Francisco-based Bank of America is the nation's largest in terms of deposits.

32. For those who argue that interlocks between banks and corporations could just as easily prove the corporations' control of the banks as vice versa, the bank stockholdings are something to consider. Does any corporation control five per cent or more stock in 108 banks?

Even this measure greatly understates the role of bank stock holdings in corporate control. A five per cent bloc is rarely in itself sufficient to gain corporate control, although such a holding is often sufficient to earn a say in matters vital to the interests of the holder. Where the bank-held five per cent bloc becomes significant is in those numerous cases in which the bloc is joined by holdings of only slightly lesser magnitude controlled by banks with convergent interests.[33]

But there is yet another way in which banks may attain influence over corporations: interlocking directorships. Stock ownership ~~that~~ gives substance to such interlocks: corporate officers—except for the president, or CEO—sit on the boards of financial institutions but lack the stock, the voting power, to play more than advisory roles. For bankers, however, the potential advantages of interlocks are multiple. They are a means of ensuring—or trying to ensure—that the corporation does not jeopardize the bank's investment.[34] The interlock may also ensure that the bank is allowed to service the corporation's financial needs. Or it may be used to shift corporate business to other firms in which the bank had a financial interest.

The Mellon complex illustrates the interlock's potential to orchestrate industrial holdings. In 1967, the Mellon National Bank had interlocking directorships with four railroads which might carry coal mined by Consolidation Coal (three interlocks) to four Eastern power companies.[35] The railroads could be equipped by Westinghouse Air Brake, Pullman, and Youngstown Steel Door (at least one interlock each), while the miners could be equipped by Mine Safety Appliance Co. (13.5 per cent of common stock, 24.6 per cent preferred, and two directors). The list could be extended practically indefinitely by considering the

---

33. See the Penn Central stockholding figures in Part IV.

34. For a discussion of conflict of interest between banker and corporate manager, see below.

35. The railroads were the Pennsylvania, Pittsburgh and Lake Erie, Cleveland & Pittsburgh, and Pittsburgh, Fort Wayne and Chicago. The power companies were Central Hudson Gas & Electric (8.3 per cent preferred), Pennsylvania Power & Light (one director), Duquesne Light Co. (two directors), and Monongahela Power Co. of Ohio (four directors). All data is from the Patman Report, vol. 1.

interlocks with corporations using coal, electricity, or transportation facilities provided by the above.[36]

And in the case of the largest trust departments, with director interlocks with two or more firms in a single industry, interlocks may provide a means of regulating competition. Take Cleveland Trust, which has director interlocks and stock holdings in three large iron producers, in both of Cleveland's major department stores, and in four of the top seven United States machine tool manufacturers.[37] The largest, Warner and Swasey, whose ads in trade journals feature the glories of free enterprise rather than machine tools, has 9.1 per cent of its common stock held by Cleveland Trust, as well as an interlocking directorship. The machine tool interlocks were too much for the Justice Department, which has filed a suit requiring the bank to divest itself of stock and directorships in all but one of the four firms.[38]

But Cleveland Trust's behavior, stock, and directorships simply reflect those of the better known New York banks.

The largest of all the commercial bank trust assets (16.8 billion dollars) are held by the Morgan Guaranty Trust, now the banking subsidiary of J. P. Morgan & Co. But perhaps as striking as the size of these assets is their extraordinary integration: between paper and publishing industries; chemical and cosmetics; metal mining, smelting and refining on the one hand and metal fabrication on the other; between electrical equipment manufacturers and electrical equipment users, etc. A great deal of effort seems to have been made, not simply to acquire large amounts of stock, but to acquire stock in large companies that do business with each other.

Like U.S. Steel, General Electric was an early Morgan creation. Together with Westinghouse it dominates the high cost electric

---

36. Recent data on the role of financial institutions in determining the purchasing patterns of corporations is contained in the FTC's "Mueller Report." This data is discussed in greater detail below.

37. The iron producers are Cleveland Cliffs (21.7 per cent common), Oglebay Norton (10.7 per cent common), and Pittsburgh and Lake Superior Iron (38.6 per cent common). The bank has a director interlock with each, as well as with iron-ore-producing Reserve Mining. The department stores are Halle's (40.5 per cent common, one director) and Higbee's (6.4 per cent common, one director).

38. *Wall Street Journal*, 27 March 1970, p. 11.

generator and transformer industry (British equipment sells for less than thirty per cent of the U.S. price—and is bought by West Coast controlled utilities, e.g., Southern California Edison). By having a dominant position in the nation's utility business—with five per cent or more of the stock in dozens of utilities—Morgan directors are able to help decide from whom the utility will buy its generators and transformers.

Not only is MGT in a position to create forward (selling) linkages with utility companies for G.E.—it is also able to effect backward (purchasing) linkages with the copper industry, which supplies the electrical equipment industry with its wire and cable. Here the bank is especially strong, with important holdings in four of the five largest copper producers. In addition, by holding 15.5 per cent of Asarco, MGT gets a say in the affairs of several other copper mining and fabricating companies in which Asarco has very large blocs of stock, including General Cable (36 per cent), Revere (33 per cent), and Southern Peru Copper (52 per cent), as well as lesser amounts in Phelps Dodge and Kennecott.

Holdings in the world's largest aluminum producer, Alcan, together with its position in Kaiser Aluminum and Chemical,[39] project MGT decisively into the affairs of the aluminum industry, a fact which takes on increased significance in the context of the bank's position in copper. Copper and aluminum can be used as substitutes, price fluctuations often determining the choice. Through its extensive holdings, MGT is in a position to moderate competitive pressures.

In the last of the three major non-ferrous metals, MGT also has a decisive role that is suggested by its three directors on the board of International Nickel, which produces most of the world's nickel. As also in the case of many of the companies cited, Morgan Stanley, the investment banking branch of the Morgan complex, takes care of Inco's long term financial needs.

Each of the metal companies cited operates in dozens of developed and underdeveloped countries and there is a tendency to speak of these companies as "integrated" and "multi-national"

---

39. Kaiser carries out joint land development activities with Aetna, a large insurance corporation which the bank is seeking to merge into its one-bank holding company.

WHO RULES THE CORPORATIONS?   103

because of the range of their industrial and geographic activities. But each company in these basic industries must sell to another in a market dominated by other giants. Giants sell to giants. Here the integration stops, at least formally speaking. And here begins the influence of great imperial banks like the MGT with its directorships and stockholdings throughout and across industrial and territorial lines. It is they who are the true integrationists and the true internationalists. This role helps explain how a man like Frederick E. Nolting can finish a tour of duty as United States Ambassador to Saigon (1961-63); then supervise the reorganization of United States intelligence activities (1964) and in the same year step naturally into the position of vice president for international affairs at the MGT.

Overall the forty-nine banks studied by the Patman Committee had 768 interlocking directorships with 286 of the Fortune 500. If smaller companies and non-industrial corporations are added, the total rises to 8,019 interlocks with 6,591 companies, an average of 164 interlocks with 135 companies per bank. Especially important are the links with insurance companies: the forty-nine banks had 146 interlocks with twenty-nine of the fifty largest life insurance companies, which compete directly with commercial banks for savings and the ability to provide external finance.

F. The Rise of the Financial Supermarket

INSURANCE COMPANY and commercial bank assets (including trust department assets) taken together amount to over three-quarters of the $1.1 trillion dollars in United States institutional investments. Aside from mutual funds, holding about one-twentieth of the total, the remaining assets are concentrated in real estate and personal loans. Consequently when we speak of finance capital in relation to the corporate sector, we are really talking about commercial banks and insurance companies: they are the only institutional lenders of real importance. [40]

Roughly speaking, commercial banks control short and

---

40. In December 1965 the total liabilities of the non-financial business sector in the Flow of Funds account were $461.9 billion. In turn the business sector held $20.3 billion on deposit in commercial banks. The great life insurance companies have only trivial liabilities to the corporate sector.

medium term lending, while insurance companies, along with pension funds, control long term lending. The *formal* merger of the
insurance industry to the commercial banking sector would thus
constitute a credit monopoly beyond anything in Louis Brandeis's nightmares. This is precisely what the commercial banks
now seek to achieve. A number of minor insurance companies
have been taken over, and in the last year there have been rumors
in the financial and business press of the following consolidations
between banks and insurance companies:

1. First National City Bank and Chubb
2. Chase Manhattan Bank and Traveller's Insurance Co.
3. Manufacturers Hanover Trust and Continental Insurance
   Company
4. Morgan Guaranty Trust and Aetna

As the Patman Committee's investigation of these mergers
pointed out, they involve four of the five largest commercial
banks in terms of deposits; four of the largest seven commercial
banks in terms of trust assets; two of the eight largest life insurance companies; and the third largest casualty company in the
United States. Altogether the four mergers would result in an
agglomeration holding over thirteen per cent of all financial assets
in the United States. But these mergers would only formalize
already existing interlocking relationships.[41]

The institutional framework through which commercial banks
hope to achieve monopoly control of corporate finance is the one
bank holding company. Arising out of a loophole in legislation
designed to restrict the increase of financial power, the one bank
holding company has become the dominant banking corporate
structure: nearly every large bank has declared itself a subsidiary

---

41. These interlocks are maintained chiefly to coordinate corporate investment policy between the insurance companies, investment bankers, commercial banks, and stock and bond exchanges. According to a consultant
on the staff of a large New York insurance brokerage firm, the select
policy-making body of the typical large insurance company is the finance
committee. It contains both members of the board of trustees and representatives of management, including the president. Whether officers or
directors, the members of this small body "are almost always themselves
key men in the outside financial community. This means that the company's connections with the money fraternity are guaranteed to be
superb." James Gollin, *Pay Now, Die Later* (Baltimore, 1969), p. 152. The
same insurance executive asserts that, taking senior specialists and active
finance committee members into account, only three or four men actually

WHO RULES THE CORPORATIONS?   105

of a recently created parent holding company. For example, Morgan Guaranty Trust is now the banking subsidiary of J. P. Morgan & Co.

The new structure enables banks to engage in a number of activities previously forbidden to them: control of insurance companies and mutual funds, operation of leasing companies in trucks and computers. Although strictly speaking "financial," such activities enable banks to intervene directly in corporate affairs. A holding company that leases aircraft to an airline—as Chase does to TWA—is able to shift aircraft purchases to its favorite aircraft and equipment producers, most probably those in which it holds stock (Boeing, in this case) or those to whom it has lent money. Insurance companies and mutual funds, like pension and trust accounts, are major purchasers of long-term securities. If the one bank holding company is permitted to control them, banks will have gained control over the entire money market—the market for short-term, medium-term and long-term funds. The single financial sphere closed to the banks would be the origination of corporate securities, from which they were banned by the Glass-Steagall Act passed in 1933.[42] The potential for financial dominance inherent in the one bank holding company has been recognized by A. A. Berle, who recently told the Patman Committee that:

> ... the one-bank holding company, left unlimited, can go in all directions, and there is no limit. It crystallizes around itself, first, a concentration of financial power, and second, a concentration of industrial power beyond belief in the United States. There is no question that a one-bank holding company, with the resources of its bank, with the stock-

direct the investment affairs of the typical multi-billion dollar insurance company. He further estimates the number of men controlling the investments of the top two hundred corporations to be about one thousand. Whatever the precise number may actually be, the number of financial institutions involved in the actual negotiations over, say, a hundred-million-dollar loan is probably no more than two or three. To speak of a money market in these circumstances is a bit misleading. A central planning board—one cut off from popular control and the interests of the people as a whole—one that fulfills and overfulfills the plan to the extent it enriches its own members—puts the matter more accurately.

42. This does not, of course, mean that banks have not engaged in "forbidden" activities since 1933, simply that they have been forced to do so indirectly.

TABLE 6A: COMMERCIAL BANKS
(Dollar amounts in millions)

Financial assets	Trust assets	Name of bank	Financial assets	Trust assets	Total assets	Percent of total financial and trust assets of all banks	Percent of total financial and trust assets of all banks and insurance companies
3	4	First National City Bank	$17,497	$10,872	$ 28,360	4.4	3.3
2	2	Chase Manhattan Bank	17,711	13,644	31,415	4.9	3.6
4	7	Manufacturers Hanover Trust	9,172	7,338	16,510	2.6	1.9
5	1	Morgan Guaranty Trust	9,168	16,825	25,993	4.0	3.0
		Total	53,608	48,679	102,287	15.9	11.8

TABLE 6B: INSURANCE COMPANIES
(Dollar amounts in millions)

Ranking by assets		Name of insurance company	Total assets	Percent of total assets of all insurance companies	Percent of total financial and trust assets of all banks and insurance companies
Life	Casualty				
—	3	The Continental Insurance Co.	$ 1,612	0.7	0.2
6	—	Aetna Life Insurance Co.	6,244	2.9	.7
—	(1)	Travelers Insurance Co.	4,148	1.9	.5
8	—	The Chubb Corp.	505	.2	.1
		Total	12,509	5.7	1.5

1. The Chubb Corp. controls the Federal Insurance Co. and the Pacific Indemnity Co., which control other insurance companies.

Source: Best's Insurance Reports and Rating Guides, Moody's Bank and Finance Manual, and Fortune.

TABLE 6C: RESULTING ASSETS FROM HYPOTHETICAL MERGER OF MAJOR COMMERCIAL BANKS AND INSURANCE COMPANIES
(Dollar amounts in millions)

	Total assets	Percent of total financial and trust assets
First National City Bank-Chubb Corp.	$ 28,874	3.4
Chase Manhattan Bank NA-Travelers Insurance Co.	35,563	4.1
Manufacturers Hanover Trust Co.-Continental Insurance Co.	18,122	2.1
Morgan Guaranty Trust Co.-Aetna Life Insurance Co.	32,237	3.7
Total	114,796	13.3

WHO RULES THE CORPORATIONS?   107

holding power in the bank's trust department, and especially if it also acquires control of mutual funds which have further stock interests, can probably attain control of any corporation in the country it really wants to get, aside from a few of the very large giants that are too large. This is already beginning to happen.[43]

But what does this control mean in practice? What influence do existing interlocking directorships and commercial bank trust assets have on the conduct of corporate affairs? Do bank directors actually play an active role on the boards of non-financial corporations? Or do they simply nod agreement to the proposals of the inside management? Are trust assets voted in opposition to management proposals? In sum, is the banks' potential for control exercised?

---

43. U.S. Congress House Banking and Currency Committee, *Hearings. One-Bank Holding Company.* 90th Congress, June 1969, p. 10.

WHO RULES THE CORPORATIONS?

PART 2

ROBERT FITCH AND
MARY OPPENHEIMER

III. DO FINANCIAL INSTITUTIONS
EXERCISE THEIR STOCK VOTING POWER?

"THE FIGURES FROM the Patman Report show an impressive
amount of commercial bank stockholding," a managerialist
might concede, "but they don't prove the point that banks
exercise decision-making power in corporate affairs." The
argument that banks hold stock but don't try to influence
management is exactly what bankers themselves used to claim,
especially before the very rapid growth of institutional stockholding in the late fifties and sixties. The "Wall Street Rule"
was "if you don't like management, sell."

But there have always been some on Wall Street who were

skeptical of the maxim's universality. David Rockefeller pointed out in 1958 that the growth of institutional investors might make the rule inapplicable:

> ... I suspect that such investors will become more demanding of management as time moves on—that as holdings expand, institutions, as well as individuals, will feel obliged to take more active interest in seeing that corporations do indeed have good management. That will be true especially if their holdings become so large that they cannot readily or quickly liquidate their investments, as is now their practice when they become dissatisfied with the management of a corporation in which they hold shares.[1]

Naturally Rockefeller did not mean that the Chase Manhattan Bank would never sell a large bloc of common stock, but that, if faced with a choice between changing portfolio or changing management, it might be cheaper to recruit new management.

Indeed, as institutional stock control rose from twelve per cent in 1949 to twenty-eight per cent in 1969, the Wall Street Rule became almost impossible to follow. Institutions were "locked in" to the corporations in which they had invested: the bank or mutual fund holding one million shares in a corporation found it difficult to locate buyers for the bloc without lowering the price greatly. The largest transaction ever handled on the New York Stock Exchange involved 1.18 million shares of Goodyear Tire and Rubber. The bloc traded at $24.25 a share, down $2 from the previous day's price. In other words, the sellers—several institutions—lost approximately eight per cent of the value of their stock.[2]

Even much smaller holdings cannot be liquidated without the loss of substantial sums. An institution that wanted to sell forty-nine thousand shares of Gillette recently lost ten per

---

1. "Business Enterprise and the Economy in the Next Ten Years," address to the Special Conference for Financial Executives held by the American Management Association at the Roosevelt Hotel, New York City, October 14, 1959 (mimeo), pp. 4-5. Quoted in Baum and Stiles, *The Silent Partner*, p. 80.

2. *Wall Street Journal*, 23 July 1970.

cent of its value on the trade, even though nearly thirty million shares were outstanding. Even Jersey Standard lost approximately twenty-five per cent of its value in a recent eight-week period on a relatively small volume of its 215 million shares. And the portfolio manager of a large mutual fund recently told the *Wall Street Journal* that sometimes he has had to wait as long as eight months to liquidate a supposedly marketable position without loss; closing out any position usually takes a week. "Of course," he told the interviewer, "if you want to sell out at *any* price, you are not illiquid. But I am not about to sell at any price."

Faced with such potential losses it is not surprising that the institutional investor may decide to intervene in corporate affairs. During the sixties, for example, financial institutions took an active role in the merger movement. The keys to merger success, as Texas conglomerator Jimmy Ling candidly admitted in a long interview before his ouster by the banks, were institutional credit and the right connections with financial institutions holding the stock of the target company.[3] In LTV's case partners in the New York investment banking house of Lehman Brothers had acted as go-betweens in the merger of Jones-Laughlin steel. And before the merger could proceed, Ling related, "we had to be sure that we had our flanks completely covered by the Bank of America, who would *reassure the Mellon man on the Jones and Laughlin board*, Frank Denton [chairman of the executive committee, Mellon National Bank & Trust Co.] that we had the wherewithal."[4]

Financial institutions were equally important in the merger of United Fruit into AMK. United Fruit's operations-minded management had a fairly low rate of return, but had piled up $100 million in cash that was being pursued by at least three conglomerators—AMK, Zapata Norness, and Dillingham. The final battle over who would dep o' United Fruit's assets pitted

---

3. "Some Candid Answers from James L. Ling," *Fortune*, August 1969, pp. 92ff.

4. Ibid., p. 95. Italics added.

representatives of Lehman Brothers, Lazard Frères, and Paine Webber Jackson and Curtiss—the management "ins"—against Morgan Guaranty Trust, Goldman Sachs, and Donaldson, Lufkin and Jenrette, all working for the victorious AMK. The key shares in the power switch came from investment funds— once viewed as loyal stockholders, not easily tempted by lucrative offers. The moral *Fortune* drew from their encounter could be a motto for the conglomerate age: "Don't trust your institutional shareholders unless you own more stock than they do, and don't sit on your assets." [5]

We may note, as a final example, that even smaller financial institutions can exercise their stockholdings aggressively. Edward A. Merckle, president of the relatively small closed-end Madison Fund (assets are $217 million), says he has aided in:

—the 1956 acquisition of Houston Oil by Atlantic Richfield;

—the 1964 merger of Champlin Oil and Refining into Celanese Corporation;

—the 1966 acquisitions of Wagner Electric by Tung-Sol and of Nopco Chemical by Diamond Alkali. [6]

But financial institutions do not invariably vote their holdings in *favor* of mergers and acquisitions. Philip Levin's 1967 struggle for control of MGM found mutual funds supporting both management and its challengers. [7] The *Wall Street Journal*'s Dan Dorfman recently cited charges by a Wall Street authority who accused the large institutions of killing proposed mergers through their stockholdings. "It's unwholesome," he declared, "for institutional holders to decide that a planned merger, which two corporations have decided upon, doesn't make any sense and therefore should be abandoned." "What chairman, or what president of a company," he added "will really have the moral courage to stand up to these people

---

5. Stanley E. Brown, "United Fruit's Shotgun Marriage," *Fortune*, April 1969, p. 191.

6. Many similar examples are contained in Arthur M. Louis, "The Mutual Funds Have the Votes," *Fortune*, May 1967, pp. 150–53.

7. Ibid., p. 150.

WHO RULES THE CORPORATIONS?   65

in the face of an onslaught of heavy selling of its stock?"[8] "Something," he concluded, "should be done about it by the Securities and Exchange Commission."[9]

Institutional investors also played a key role in deciding whether "in" management would be allowed to retain control of Collins Radio (1968 sales over $400 million). Collins was the object of a 1969 takeover attempt by E. Ross Perot, a frequent dinner guest of President Nixon and chairman of Texas-based Electronic Data Services (EDS) (1968 sales $8 million). After submitting a tender offer, Perot began to accumulate all the Collins shares he could. But he knew that the key to success was held by the ten institutional investors that together controlled about one-third of Collins' outstanding shares.

Meanwhile Collins Radio hired Sullivan and Cromwell to fight the merger. An emissary from this firm asked Nixon's Justice Department to disallow the merger, with no apparent success. Collins also tried unsuccessfully to find another merger partner, one less likely to cannibalize the firm for paper profits. But then, just when it seemed that Collins would be forcibly merged into EDS, Collins learned, as the *Wall Street Journal* puts it, that "it had a friend at the Chase Manhattan Bank."[10] Chase was reluctant to swap its 455,000 Collins shares (fifteen per cent of the total) for high-flying

---

8. *Wall Street Journal*, 7 August 1970. This partial liquidation of stockholdings in order to exert pressure on management must be distinguished from the selling out prescribed by the Wall Street Rule.

9. The present SEC is an unlikely ally for opponents of financial institutions. Its chairman, Hamer Budge, recently entered into salary negotiations for the presidency of one of the largest institutional investors—the eight billion dollar Investors Diversified Services complex of mutual funds—at the same time that he was drafting recommendations concerning IDS's most profitable subsidiary. President Nixon and George Mc-Kinnon, his appointee to the Washington, D.C., Circuit Court of Appeals, had served as director and vice president of IDS, respectively; both were intimately involved in the negotiations. Widespread publicity in Congress eventually forced Budge to decline the offer. See Bob Fitch, "Nixon and His Friends," *Ramparts*, March 1970.

10. "Tale of a Tender," 8 April 1970.

EDS.[11] Morgan Guaranty Trust was equally reluctant. The banks waited, hoping that EDS would increase its offer to $100 in stock for each Collins share tendered. This was expected to increase the value of Collins to about $85 per share. At this point Chase apparently intended simply to unload its own holdings at a profit.

But Perot wouldn't raise his offer so Chase and Morgan quashed theirs. Chase had no objection, however, to dumping Collins management even though it was headed by the firm's founder, Arthur Collins, and was highly regarded from a technological standpoint. Paper profits were their main consideration. Indeed, the *Journal* reported that Chase was actively looking for a more suitable merger partner for the firm, i.e., a partner willing to make a higher offer. It seems as if the old nineteenth-century values of entrepreneurship as well as the early twentieth-century values of management expertise have almost disappeared under finance capital's system of accounting.[12]

The voting power of financial institutions is not always exercised so dramatically as in the promotion and scuttling of mergers. Howard Stein, president of the Dreyfus Fund, pushed Polaroid—in which the Fund held six per cent of the common stock—to expand its long-range sales goal, its advertising budgets, and its hiring of trained personnel. The company complied.[13]

Even so mundane a topic as executive salaries is not beneath the notice of financial institutions. Baum and Stiles report that the institutional investors they interviewed had found that "a telephone call, followed by a visit with management . . . may

11. Their judgment has been confirmed by recent stock market developments. When EDS went public, the stock sold for a record 100 times earnings. Since then it has found a more modest base of support.

12. For other case studies see the role of financial institutions in takeovers described in the hearings before the Anti-Trust Subcommittee of the Committee on the Judiciary, House of Representatives, 91st Congress, Second Session; on Leasco Data Processing Corporation, 15, 16, 22 and 23 October 1969 (Logan, Berlind, Weill and Levitt, Inc.); on ITT (Lazard Frères); on Gulf and Western (Chase Manhattan Bank).

13. Louis, "The Mutual Funds Have the Votes," *Fortune*, May 1967, p. 205.

WHO RULES THE CORPORATIONS?   67

be enough to curb an inflated appetite. The calls may ask for
an explanation for the increases and, when one cannot be
given, may suggest that the compensation be 'adjusted.' "[14]
Baum and Stiles suggest that "While this sort of institutional
action is rare, doubtless the knowledge that it can happen has
a prophylactic effect."[15]

The exercise of the financial institutions' voting power has
implications that extend far beyond advertising budgets, concentration ratios, and stock market values: it has also demol-
ished the myth of management invincibility. Even by the late
fifties, proxy contests were showing that management could
be defeated about thirty per cent of the time.[16] And at the
height of the merger movement, managements were being
ejected so fast they seemed self-propelled rather than self-
perpetuating. As *Fortune*'s Gilbert Burck described the scene
in 1958:

> . . . the stockholder, relegated by Adolf Berle and other
> non-contemporary economists to a limbo of impotent
> ownership, has found himself inadvertently practicing
> Stockholder Power. . . . Proud old names have already
> been taken over, and dozens of veteran executives have
> been sacked. Foreboding, frustration, and even fear are
> epidemic in perhaps three out of five big corporate head-
> quarters. Anguished executives who should be minding
> the shop are instead behaving as if they were up to some
> underhanded adventure, spending long hours counseling
> with lawyers, management consultants, proxy specialists,
> and public-relations men skilled in the art of forfending
> take-overs.[17]

That financial institutions do not always exercise Stockholder Power is no proof of their indifference or impotence. It

---

14. *The Silent Partner*, p. 76.

15. Loc. cit.

16. Douglas V. Austin, *Proxy Contests and Corporate Reform*, Michigan
Business Reports Number 47, University of Michigan Bureau of Business
Research, Ann Arbor, Michigan.

17. "The Merger Movement Rides High," *Fortune*, February 1969, p.
80.

may mean that management is performing to their satisfaction. Alternatively, the financial institutions may already have restricted management's sphere effectively through loan covenants accompanying credit arrangements. It is to this second face of financial institutions—as purveyors of external finance as well as holders of large blocs of stock—that we now turn.

IV: EXTERNAL FINANCE

Introduction

THE DRAMATIC RISE in institutional shareholding during the 1960s broke down the effective separation of ownership and control on which the theory of managerialism rested. Once again ownership and control were united in the trust departments of the great Wall Street banks: Morgan Guaranty Trust, Chase Manhattan Bank, First National City Bank. It was a unity recalling the age of Morgan, when financial institutions had been able to control corporations through their lending power. The price of a loan was "a piece of the action," i.e., equity or common stock. And the increased equity in the corporation at the disposal of the banks consolidated their lending position. So the power of the financial institutions grew—loans were transformed into equity and equity created the basis for more loans. Only the Depression had stopped temporarily the growth of finance capital.

Liberal economists, however, have continued to deny that finance capital exercises power through its lending activities. On the contrary, they even deny that corporations rely significantly on external funds. Corporations, they say, get all the capital they need from retained earnings.

Galbraith's corporate ruling class, the "technostructure," is insulated from outside control because it has "a source of capital, derived from its own earnings, that is wholly under its own control." The financial self-sufficiency of the corporation leads in turn to operational autonomy. "No banker," says Galbraith, "can attach conditions as to how retained earnings are to be used. Nor can any other outsider. No one, the normally innocuous stockholder apart, has the right to ask about the investment from retained earnings that turns out badly." "It is

hard," Galbraith concludes, "to overestimate the importance
of the shift in power that is associated with availability of such
a source of capital. Few other developments can have more
fundamentally altered the character of capitalism." A failure
of earnings could indeed jeopardize this freedom, but "the
adaptation is, simply, that big corporations do not lose
money." [18]

Galbraith's emphasis on internal finance as the key to the
managerial liberation movement recalls its role in Sweezy and
Baran's corporate paradigm.[19] The only substantial difference
between their models is that Sweezy and Baran appear to include depreciation allowances in the category of internal funds
available for expansion, whereas Galbraith speaks only of retained earnings.[20]

But between these self-financing corporate monads and the
everyday reality reflected in the business and financial press
little correspondence exists. Though reliance on external
finance is by no means universal, corporate giants, including
GM and AT&T, do scramble for funds, pushing smaller firms
out of the market. Sufficient capital—despite its plenitude in
managerial theory—is simply not available. Even Standard Oil
of New Jersey, the model managerial corporation, has finally
been forced to turn to the capital market. The extent of this
growing reliance on external finance, its roots and consequences, are the topic of the following sections.

Standard Oil and External Finance

ROCKEFELLER-CONTROLLED STANDARD OIL of New Jersey,
flagship of the old trust "broken up" in 1913, serves as Baran
and Sweezy's model corporation. "It shows us," they say, "in

---

18. Galbraith, *New Industrial State* (Boston, 1967), pp. 81–82.

19. *Monopoly Capital* (New York, 1966), p. 16.

20. Economists frequently count depreciation as a source of funds for
expansion. This concept is erroneous. Depreciation is a cost of fixed
assets—a cost, not a gain. Depreciation can no more be used to finance
expansion than other deductions from revenues, provisions for bad debts,
fire loss, etc. The only internal funds that can be used for expansion are
retained earnings. See John A. Meyer, *Understanding Financial Statements* (New York, 1964), p. 102.

70   FITCH & OPPENHEIMER

the most developed form what the other giants are or are in the process of becoming."[21]

In recent decades Standard appeared to fit the managerial model fairly well.[22] Directors were chosen from within the company; outside directors were prohibited. No bankers dominated company affairs. And the company's borrowings were relatively insignificant in relation to total equity.

Standard's financial independence was based on its fantastic profitability: it may well have been the most profitable operation in capitalist history. John D. Rockefeller made it a matter of policy to keep profits in the company. "Take what you've got to have to live on," he told his partners, "Don't buy new clothes and fast horses; let your wife wear her last year's bonnet. You can't find any place where money will earn what it does here."[23] After the initial period of plowback, Standard began to pay dividends—$548,438,000 between 1882 and 1906. For ten of these years, dividends averaged forty per cent of net worth each year. But even at this rate, Standard retained most of its earnings. And still there was more capital. Thus the National City Bank (now the First National City Bank) was capitalized out of the company's profits.

But after decades of high profitability, Standard Oil is finally beginning to mature. Growth is slowing, and 1969 profits actually fell three per cent. Stock is slumping. "Most serious of all," according to *Fortune*'s Dan Corditz:

> while entering a period when it will have to invest almost $2.5 billion annually to meet anticipated demand, Jersey has seen its profitability decline to well below the average for all industry. Once able to generate its capital requirements almost wholly from its earnings, the company

21. *Monopoly Capital*, pp. 199-200.

22. The Rockefeller family is perhaps the most class conscious of the capitalist dynasties. It was they who first realized that the less the struggle for profits appears as a struggle for profits, the more profitable the struggle becomes. Hence the family emphasis on philanthropy, the public relations, and the elaborate managerial facade of the Rockefeller corporation.

23. *Masters of Capital* (New Haven, 1920), p. 53.

since 1965 has more than doubled its long-term debt—despite record interest rates—to $2,174,000,000. Yet early this year it found it necessary to raise $375 million by issuing new stock, and more equity financing is not ruled out in the near future.[24]

Standard's miserable performance and increasing reliance on external finance have caused "New York's primacy in Jersey affairs" to be re-asserted. In 1960 Jersey Standard had sixteen directors with functional specialties—marketing, refining, chemicals, accounting, finance. In 1966 outside directors were added for the first time, and the firm now has nine inside directors, six outsiders. Emilio G. Collado, member of the international council of Morgan Guaranty Trust, has been brought in to take over the duties of chief financial officer. And it was of course Morgan Stanley that handled Jersey Standard's stock offerings and bond issues.

All this is not to say that Standard executives run when Morgan partners whistle. It does indicate, however, that the model managerial corporation, the most financially independent in American history, has changed its basic financing pattern and restructured its board of directors. As the following section shows, the change in Jersey Standard is reflected throughout the entire corporate system.

The Scramble for External Funds

WHILE JERSEY STANDARD ENTERED the long-term capital market with the dignity that befitted a dowager among American corporations, other firms were less restrained. *Fortune*'s Business Round-Up speaks of a "frenzied rush to the long-term capital market."[25] Smaller firms, according to *Fortune*, are no longer able to compete for funds, and those who remain in the race have had to meet the "going market terms." "Going market terms" is *Fortune*'s euphemism for the usurious interest rates—in excess of eleven per cent—that banks have forced corporations to pay. And the stated interest charges do not include equity "kickers," compensating balances which must

---

24. "Jersey Standard on Troubled Waters," *Fortune*, July 1970, p. 79.
25. May 1970, p. 52.

be maintained at the lending bank, and the cost of shifting purchases to corporations in which the banks have an interest. When such devices are added in, the present cost of capital often approaches twenty per cent.[26]

Even at these rates many corporations fail to get loans sufficient for their needs. Some, like Penn Central, file for bankruptcy. Others, with less pressing obligations and better prospects of future profitability, sell pieces of themselves to raise the needed cash. Jersey Standard, as we have seen, recently offered 800,000 shares at $45 per share. Altogether corporations offered $8 billion in new stock issues in 1969, twice the 1968 total. 1970 promises to surpass the 1969 rate, indicating the shortfall between retained earnings and capital needs.[27]

So great has reliance on external funds become that insider newsletters in 1970 began to tout those new corporations that hadn't been forced into potentially ruinous indebtedness. The *Magazine of Wall Street* ran a computer survey of all corporations listed on the New York Stock Exchange and discovered that only six to seven per cent had no long-term debt. "The company able to get by without having to enter today's buyer's market for bonds, able to expand on internally generated capital," it concluded, "is something of a rarity."[28] Significantly, the profitable corporations without a high percentage of external debt were relatively small and closely held, e.g., Maytag, Andrew Jergens. Here's the way the Federal Reserve Bank of San Francisco summarized the trend in corporate financing during the 1960s:

> During the past several years . . . financial resources generated through internal cash flow have grown rather modestly, so that corporations have had to rely increasingly on external sources to finance their rapidly surging cash needs. Between 1960 and 1964, internal funds increased at an average annual rate of 10.1 per cent, and external funds advanced at a 4.9 per cent rate; between 1965 and 1969, in contrast, internal financing increased at only a 2.6 per cent rate while external financing

26. *San Francisco Examiner,* 15 February 1970.
27. *Fortune,* May 1970.
28. 18 July 1970. p. 9.

WHO RULES THE CORPORATIONS?   7 3

jumped to a 16.5 per cent average annual growth rate.
External funds thus have come to provide a growing proportion of all funds raised by nonfinancial corporate
businesses—one-third of the total during the 1965–1969
period (and 38 per cent in 1969 alone) as against less
than one-fourth of the total during the preceding five-
year period.[29]

CHART 1: CORPORATE RELIANCE ON EXTERNAL FUNDS

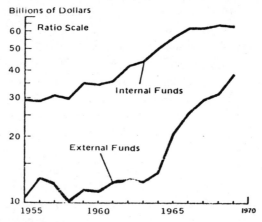

Source: Monthly Review Supplement, p. 4.

The sharp increase in reliance on external funds is illustrated
in CHART 1. The Federal Reserve Board figures are, however, somewhat misleading. "Internal finance" in the Board's
accounting scheme consists of both undistributed profits and
depreciation allowances. Yet only *profits* can be used to
finance *new* investment: depreciation allowances merely offset
wear and tear on fixed capital. Since corporations must grow
to survive, it is the undistributed profits that are the dynamic
variable. And here the trend is unmistakable: undistributed
profits supply a decreasing amount of total financial requirements (TABLE 1). Thus the Federal Reserve Board's chart actually overstates the role of internal financing relative to *net* new
investment.

29. Federal Reserve Board of San Francisco: "Wall Street Before the
Fall," *Monthly Review Supplement*, p. 4.

TABLE 1: SOURCES OF FUNDS
NONFARM, NONFINANCIAL CORPORATE BUSINESS, 1964-1968

Year	Profits	(Per cent of total funds) Depreciation	External Finance
1964	25.5	44.1	29.6
1965	24.9	37.8	39.2
1966	24.5	38.0	39.2
1967	22.5	43.7	35.0
1968	19.9	41.2	42.8

Source: Percentages calculated from **Economic Report of the President, February, 1970** (Washington, 1970), Table C-74.

From CHART 1 it might appear that up until the last turn of the business cycle (1965), those who thought giant corporations were self-financing had the better of the argument. But this is not so.

Both the Federal Reserve Board chart and the undistributed profits table are based on *all* corporations, not on *giant* corporations. When we analyze corporations by size—as is done in TABLE 2—we discover that it is indeed the giant firms with

TABLE 2: LONG-TERM DEBT
AS PERCENTAGE OF TOTAL LIABILITIES, 1960-1970

Corporation size* in million dollars	1960	1962	1964	1968	1970
1-5	7.4	9.3	10.4	11.7	12.6
5-10	8.2	9.1	10.5	12.3	12.9
10-25	9.0	10.1	11.6	14.8	14.3
25-50	10.9	12.1	12.8	14.4	16.2
50-100	12.9	14.1	14.0	19.3	19.6
100-250	13.9	14.0	14.1	17.3	18.7
250-1000	16.0	16.4	16.2	18.8	18.6

* 1,000 and over omitted owing to small size of sample.

Source: FTC-SEC, **Quarterly Financial Report for Manufacturing Companies.**

assets of $250 million and above that receive most of the long-term credit. Not only that, but they also use the most long-term credit in relation to their size. These figures should not be surprising, for it is the small corporation's lack of ties to financial institutions that makes it ill-equipped to compete with the giants in the scramble for external funds.

Having analyzed the role of undistributed profits and corrected our data for its small corporation bias, we can see that external finance has in fact played a major role in the net new investment of large corporations. But why has its role increased in recent years? One reason is the relatively more rapid growth of giant corporations in recent years. In 1959, corporations with assets of $1 billion and over comprised twenty-

WHO RULES THE CORPORATIONS?   75

seven per cent of total manufacturing assets. By 1969, their share had reached forty-six per cent. Since the larger corporations also rely more heavily on external financing, their rapid growth rates raise the role of external finance for corporations as a whole.

A second reason is that profits have fallen.

Of course, for managerialists, corporations never lose money. The surplus keeps rising, along with the real wages of the working class. This is the heart of the matter. The unarticulated premise of Sweezy and Baran's account of corporate finance is the *invulnerability of monopoly profits.* Internal funds are sufficient because the flow of profits grows ever wider and unchecked. But profits do fluctuate, and the business cycle does exist. The United States Department of Commerce can change the name of its publication from *Business Cycle Developments* to *Business Conditions Digest*, as it did in 1969, but the business cycle keeps on turning.

Beginning in 1965, managerialism notwithstanding, United States profits fell. The decline continued until late 1967, when the Vietnam buildup provided a temporary pickup. But by the first quarter of 1970 a very sharp drop had set in. Profit margins for manufacturing corporations fell to the lowest level since the 1961 recession. And while income fell, outgo—in the form of expansion and dividend payments—increased absolutely. Here's how *Fortune* described the resulting crunch:

> As the total flow of internally generated cash declined, cash flow and corporate investment (in inventory and plant) reached epic proportions—roundly $25 billion in the past year. This is nearly twice as big as the gap in 1968, and bigger even than the one in late 1966, just before a fantastic but temporary inventory build-up was cut back sharply. In the early sixties internal financing, on the average, fell only $2 billion short of investment. [30]

This shortfall stimulated the recent rush to the capital market. In this rush, not surprisingly, the larger corporations were more successful. The reason for their success is simple: these international corporations, with monopoly or near

---

30. May 1970, p. 52.

monopoly positions in several markets are, on the average, more profitable than small corporations. What better credit risk could a lender take?

Indeed, for these corporations the old reciprocal relationship prevails between external finance, stockholdings, and directorships. FTC figures show us that the very largest corporations get the largest share of credit. And a recent article by Peter Dooley shows that these corporations have the most interlocks with financial institutions: as interlocks rise so too does the size of the corporation.[31]

Dooley also indicates that the more interlocks between financial and non-financial corporations, the less solvent the non-financial corporation becomes. Supporting data for this surprising relationship can be found in a recent Dun and Bradstreet study of the top one thousand corporations. The financial reporting service points to a dangerous deterioration in working capital between fiscal 1968 and 1969. Although the minimum working capital position generally considered acceptable is a ratio of two dollars of assets to one dollar of liabilities, almost twenty-two per cent of these companies—the recipients of the greater share of external finance—have fallen below 1.75 to 1. Another thirteen per cent of the companies had ratios as low as 1.5 to 1. The report also notes that the ratio of cash on hand and marketable securities to current liabilities—the so-called "quick ratio" or "acid test"—has declined for the last four years. Between fiscal 1968 and 1969, the quick ratio declined from 27.4 to 22.2 per cent.[32]

The result of these two changes is a mammoth crisis in corporate liquidity, highlighted by the ailments of Lockheed, Chrysler, and the Penn Central. That the crisis has been stimulated by external financing may appear paradoxical: how can more funds mean less funds? Would not the corporations be in even worse shape had they not borrowed? These are valid questions and must be answered in order to have a full comprehension of the consequences of external finance. Basically,

---

31. *American Economic Review,* June 1969. Dooley analyzed the two hundred largest corporations and the fifty largest financial instutitions. FTC's billion dollar cut-off point would include 115 of the Fortune 500.

32. *Wall Street Journal,* 4 August 1970.

the problem lies in the assumption that funds are borrowed only when their investment will increase income by more than the cost of capital. The assumption is a reasonable one in terms of conventional micro-economic theory, but in the contemporary world it runs head on into the realities of the supply side of the external finance equation. It is to these that we now turn.

The Supply Side of the Equation

PERHAPS THE MOST NOVEL FEATURE of the present period of reliance on external finance is the role played by financial institutions. Between 1956 and 1965 financial institutions provided about two-thirds of the external funds used by non-financial corporations, considerably more than during the fifties. And even during the period 1900–1929, the age of frenzied finance, financial institutions supplied only one-third of total external funds.

The growing importance of financial institutions reflects the increasing socialization of finance capital noted above. Whereas prior to 1900 a private banker might lend his personal capital and that of his partners, the great fortunes have now been institutionalized and amalgamated with the rest of the social surplus produced by society as a whole. Deposited in banks by corporations and individuals, this surplus is then controlled by the great financial institutions. Morgan's grandson Henry Sturgis Morgan is still the world's key lender, even though he more than ever controls other people's money.

With loan capital socialized, why would it be difficult to obtain? Would not the financial institutions desire to lend be greater than the corporations' desire to borrow?[33] Galbraith, for example, argues that capital is no longer in short supply. No one would dispute the point, but the problem is one of access. How does one get to use capital?

The concentration of the banking community has operational consequences: the sources of very large blocs of long-term capital are fewer than might be supposed. One prime

---

33. Analagously, some managerial economists have maintained that corporations control the banks and not vice versa because the corporations, through their deposits, are net lenders to banks.

source is the investment banking fraternity, which maintains close relations with the commercial banks: First Boston with Mellon National Bank, Lazard Frères with Chase Mahattan, Morgan Stanley with Morgan Guaranty Trust. It would seem plausible that if a corporation was offered terms it disliked by one investment bank, it could always turn to another. But United States finance doesn't work this way.[34]

As in organized crime, the syndicate is the most common form of investment banking organization. The present syndicates were already established before World War I. Typically, each powerful investment banking firm has achieved a monopoly on the securities business of certain corporations, and its monopoly is respected by other investment bankers. The monopolist controlling the securities business of a particular corporation lowers his risks, however, by cutting in a few powerful "competitors" and several less important firms each time he floats a bond or stock issue. The exact number depends on the size of the flotation. Each of these participants buys a pre-arranged percentage of the shares or bonds, with the largest share going to the more powerful houses. The pecking order is very strict. Who is running the syndicate can generally be determined by reading "tombstones"–the advertisements announcing the sale of new securities. The order of

---

34. In 1953 the United States government charged seventeen investment bankers, including Morgan Stanley, Dillon Read, Lehman Brothers, Goldman Sachs, Kuhn Loeb, Glore Forgan, Kidder Peabody, Smith Barney and White Weld with having organized a conspiracy to monopolize the securities business of the United States. Investment bankers were alleged to have controlled the financial affairs of security issuers through such devices as interlocking directorates and syndicates. Judge Harold Medina, however, held the government to a much stricter standard of proof than he had in the Rosenberg case, arguing that interlocking directorates actually promoted competition and that the goverment case was without merit. (See U.S. v. Morgan et al 118F. Supp. 621 (1953).) In a sense Medina's dismissal was justified. The government presented a shamefully inept case, drawing primarily on old evidence and calling only one key witness. Nor did the government appeal the decision. The government case has been called by reform-minded Congressmen "a dismal episode in the history of the Anti-Trust Division." Committee of the Judiciary, House of Representatives, *Interlocks in Corporate Management*, Washington, 1965, p. 71.

WHO RULES THE CORPORATIONS?   79

precedence on the tombstone nearly always indicates who is managing the syndicate.

Once on top of the syndicate, it is highly unusual for a firm to come down, or for the corporation to choose another syndicate. To take just one example, five of the top ten industrial corporations are serviced by the investment banking house of Morgan Stanley and have never gone to the long-term capital market without its guidance. Between 1955 and 1969 General Motors' affiliate GMAC has floated thirteen bond issues worth over $1.8 billion dollars. Every one was managed by Morgan Stanley.[35]

The attitudes of chief executive officers of non-financial corporations reflect this limited competitiveness among investment bankers. While there is some disagreement, most agree that:

1. There are situations in which the corporations' bargaining position is not strong enough to permit a real choice of underwriters. The investment house makes it a condition of the sale of the securities that they have a place on the board.
2. Where there is a choice the qualifications of the man are as important as the situation.
3. Ideally the investment banker should sit on the board with the understanding that his house is to get more of the underwriting business. That is, he is an advisory director rather than a vendor-director.[36]

Given the monopoly conditions that govern the supply of long-term capital, a shortfall in internal finance leads to conditions of dependence, especially when the shortfall coincides with a capital goods boom like that of 1969. Even though many corporate executives—unlike economists—foresaw a downturn in 1970, the boom was financed almost entirely by credit. Rising inflation and the need for extra capacity to meet demand when the business cycle turned up once more, clearly presented the choices open to the executive: borrow or be left behind. So too with many owners and managers facing a liquidity crisis: bank control or bankruptcy.

35. *Moody's Bank and Finance Manual*, April 1970.
36. J. M. Juran and James Louden, *The Corporate Director* (New York, 1966), pp. 202–3.

Bankers: Capitalists or Technicians?

FACTS ABOUT INCREASING corporate credit reliance on financial institutions are hard to dispute—just like the facts about increasing Trust Department holdings. But though the facts are incontrovertible, their significance continues to be disputed. One Marxist managerialist, for example, has written:

> We never deny that corporations need banking services. Our point is that the need for these services doesn't force the corporation into dependency on the banks. Corporations need a variety of services—including legal and accounting services. One might as well say that since corporations need accountants that accountants control the corporation, except that this is too far-fetched to claim credence.[37]

This is in fact exactly what Galbraith claims in *The New Industrial State*. What seems far-fetched to the managerial Marxist is to him merely a matter of drawing logical conclusions from a shared premise: that a banking "service" functions in the sphere of production and exchange and in bourgeois law like an accounting service. Capital, Galbraith says, is no longer scarce. Business skills are. Therefore, power has passed from owners of capital (bankers, entrepreneurs) to "men of diverse technical knowledge, experience or other talent which modern industrial technology and planning require."[38]

But a banker lending his capital and an accountant lending his opinion on the nature of capital structure play quite different roles in the productive process. Let the Penn Central fiasco again serve as our example.

By the summer of 1969 the Penn Central had begun to experience a liquidity crisis. But Penn Central executives confronted it with the resourcefulness and ingenuity that have typified the great American rail moguls from Jay Gould to "Sell 'em" Ben Heineman. They fixed the books. With a little creative accounting the staggering losses could be turned into

---

37. Private communication.
38. See chapter 5, "Capital and Power," pp. 46–59.

WHO RULES THE CORPORATIONS?   81

tidy profits; Penn Central's woeful working capital position could be prettified. The virtuoso accounting partnership of Peat, Marwick, and Mitchell was brought in, and in a few weeks did a job on the Penn Central's books that would have made Mae West's make-up man jealous. The directors were so overjoyed by the brilliant turn-around in the company's paper performance that they declared another hefty dividend for the stockholders and paid out $700,000 to Peat, Marwick, and Mitchell.

The point of the example is this: Peat, Marwick, and Mitchell could create the illusion of a solid working capital position by some clever accounting. But the Penn Central's bankers, had they not already given up on the Penn Central's prospects, could have actually changed the corporation's working capital position by transferring real capital to its accounts. Glore Forgan Staats' "service" mobilizes labor machinery and material; Peat, Marwick, and Mitchell's does not.

Bourgeois law, which has rarely been accused of paying insufficient respect to the rights of capital, recognizes this distinction: it bestows upon the provider of long-term capital the right to attach conditions affecting the operation of the corporation in order to safeguard repayment of principle and interest. When a lawyer or an account offers his services to a corporation, there is no contract enabling him to limit managers' salaries, corporate dividends, or sale of corporate assets; to place restrictions on working capital or further borrowing. But when an investment banker or insurance company lends capital to a corporation, it may demand any of these. Here the legal system only reflects actual power relations operative in the market. As TABLE 3 shows, even the very largest corporations enter into agreements which limit the decision-making powers of the management.

This table by no means reflects all the restrictions that finance capital attaches to corporate operations, for it deals only with investment bankers. Similar agreements are negotiated with the commercial banks that provide medium term or simply "term" loans, and with the insurance companies with which corporate long-term securities are often privately placed.

TABLE 3: LONG-TERM LENDERS' CONDITIONS

Fortune's top 50 companies	Conditions
1. General Motors	limits sale of property, acquisitions
2. Standard Oil of New Jersey	no limitations
3. Ford	dividends restricted
4. Chrysler	limits sale, leaseback of co. property
5. Mobil	debt limitations
6. Gulf	dividends restricted
7. GE	limits on further debt creation
8. IBM	no long-term debt
9. Texaco	limits on debt
10. US Steel	sale of certain assets prohibited
11. ITT	limits dividends and acquisitions
12. Western Electric	(subsidiary of AT&T)
13. Standard Oil of California	limits sale of assets
14. McDonnel-Douglas	dividend restriction
15. DuPont	no limitations
16. Shell	limits debt creation
17. Westinghouse	dividends restricted
18. Boeing	dividends restricted
19. Standard Oil of Indiana	limitation on debt
20. RCA	dividends restricted
21. General Telephone	dividends restricted
22. Goodyear	dividends restricted
23. Bethlehem Steel	dividends restricted
24. Swift	debt limitation
25. LTV	dividends restricted
26. Union Carbide	debt limitation
27. General Dynamics	dividends, working capital restricted
28. Eastman Kodak	no long-term debt
29. North American Rockwell	dividends restricted
30. Procter & Gamble	dividends restricted
31. International Harvester	dividends restricted
32. National Dairy	dividends restricted
33. United Aircraft	dividends restricted
34. Continental Oil	limits sale, lease of co. property
35. Lockheed	dividends restricted
36. Firestone	dividends restricted
37. Phillips	no long-term debt
38. Armour	dividends restricted
39. Tenneco	dividends restricted
40. Litton	dividends restricted
41. Monsanto	dividends restricted
42. Sun Oil	limits asset sale
43. Singer	no long-term debt
44. General Foods	limits asset sale
45. Grace	dividends restricted
46. Caterpillar Tractor	dividends restricted
47. Textron	dividends restricted
48. Occidental	no limits
49. Borden	limits mortgage of property
50. Dow Chemical	debt limitation

A final reason for the fantastic increase in external debt is simply this: the suppliers of external finance—especially commercial and investment bankers—see the opportunity to create and profit from a speculative boom by financing take-overs. Corporate take-overs cannot be accomplished without financing or financiers. In the boom phase of the modern cycle, this financing takes on special characteristics that former SEC chairman William O. Douglas described quite well:

> If an investment banker did not have control over a company, he would not be able to load that company with the "cats and dogs" which he as an investment banker had acquired. . . . If a market operator were not in control of a company, he would not be able to use the funds of that company so that he could acquire another company and sell it to the first company at a profit.[39]

For now we will merely record the extent to which investment for take-overs increased relative to productive investment, especially in the post-1965 period, i.e., during that period when returns from productive investment also began to decline. (See CHART 2.)

Corporate Models

WHEN A CORPORATION comes under the control of finance capital, how are its basic operations changed? Superficially it is difficult to see why there would be any change at all. Management is interested in profits; so is finance capital. As long as management performs efficiently and profitably, why should finance capital intervene?

The answer to these questions requires that we break down the idea of a corporate model. Jersey Standard may be a good example of the giant corporation's world role, but it leaves out a good deal that we want to explore. Jersey Standard has completed its period of "heroic" growth: it is beginning to stagnate.[40] To take it as a model is to lose sight of the diversity of corporate goals and structures.

The American corporate landscape ranges from small, rapidly growing firms like Memorex and EDS through giants like Xerox and Avon to monopolists and price leaders like US Steel, GM, and Jersey Standard. With such diversity it would indeed be naive to expect one model of corporate behavior to apply universally, or to expect financial—or entrepreneurial or managerial—control to prevail through the corporate structure.

---

39. *Democracy and Finance* (New Haven, 1940), p. 11.

40. See above.

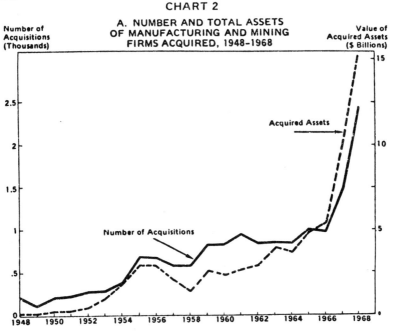

CHART 2

A. NUMBER AND TOTAL ASSETS
OF MANUFACTURING AND MINING
FIRMS ACQUIRED, 1948–1968

Number of
Acquisitions
(Thousands)

Value of
Acquired Assets
($ Billions)

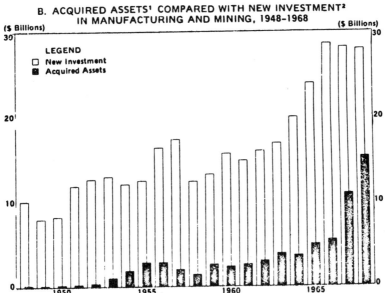

B. ACQUIRED ASSETS¹ COMPARED WITH NEW INVESTMENT²
IN MANUFACTURING AND MINING, 1948–1968

($ Billions)

($ Billions)

LEGEND
☐ New Investment
■ Acquired Assets

1. Acquisitions of mining and manufacturing firms with assets of $10 million or more.
2. Total new investment for plant and equipment by mining and manufacturing firms.

Source: **Economic Concentration: Hearings before the Subcommittee on Antitrust
and Monopoly of the Committee on the Judiciary, United States Senate, Ninety-
First Congress, First Session** (Washington, D.C., 1969), part 8A (appendix to part
8, State Report of the Federal Trade Commission, "Economic Report on Corporate
Mergers"), pp. 40–41.

Let us then try to give a sketch of the shadow cast by finance capital across the corporate landscape. Small corporations (i.e., with sales of $5 to $50 million), as Juran and Louden have shown, are managed by their owners. As the corporation grows, owners must delegate power to the managers and carry out public financing. In the case of stock offerings, their ownership is diluted; in the case of long-term financing, both owner and management are subjected to conditions demanded by finance capital. Either type of public financing makes outside directors *mandatory,* with a resulting formalization of the board. The trend toward outsider, i.e., finance capital, domination appears in corporations with sales between $50 million and $500 million. At this level of enterprise the issue of control is most sharply fought. Generally speaking, however, managers are not the principal figures in the struggle, although they are frequently the spokesmen for the competing stockholder and financial interests. As the corporation reaches sales of a billion dollars or more, the domination of the corporation by outsiders is generally complete.[41]

Conflict and Control

CONFLICT IS BUILT into the very nature of the relationship between finance capital and entrepreneurial or managerial capitalists. Bankers are like Christ's lilies of the field: they flourish, though they neither spin nor toil. Steel companies produce ingots; chemical companies produce plastic; auto companies make chassis; banks produce profits. What is their source?

Financial profits are simply a subtraction from industrial profits. The indentity of interests that has been asserted between bankers and entrepreneurs/managers breaks down when we examine the genesis of financial profits. The entrepreneur wants to make profits, and the bankers want to make profits, but the banker can make profits only at the expense of corporate profits. The famous struggle between Howard Hughes and the massed phalanx of finance capital in the early sixties illustrates the nature of this antagonism.

---

41. Juran and Louden, pp. 30, 38-39. See especially Exhibit 10, chart illustrating how the board of directors develops as the corporation grows.

Howard Hughes and TWA

EVEN BEFORE WORLD WAR II Howard Hughes had begun to pursue a grand industrial strategy of which control of TWA was an integral part. Having inherited Hughes Tool from his father, he pushed development into aircraft parts and electronics, which were purchased by General Dynamic's Convair through a reciprocal arrangement.[42] TWA in turn purchased its fleet from Convair. Hughes sold aircraft and electronic parts to Convair; TWA bought jets from Convair. And TWA's purchases were to be financed out of the profits of Hughes Tool. (See CHART 3.)

CHART 3: ENTREPRENEURIAL CAPITAL, 1957

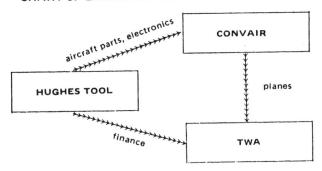

Hughes's independence brought down the wrath of the Wall Street lending syndicate that had been financing the major airlines since their founding in the late 1920s. Eastern, United, American, and Pan American all borrowed from the syndicate. Why not TWA? By remaining independent, Hughes cost the

---

42. The advance of corporate concentration means the decline of the market as a force in ordering the purchase and sale of commodities, especially between giant corporations. If, for example, the Chemical Bank has a dominant interest in both Texaco and Uniroyal, and Uniroyal needs to buy petrochemicals for tire manufacture, it will buy its petrochemicals from Texaco even though Gulf, in which Chemical Bank has no interest, might offer petrochemicals at a lower price. In turn, Texaco, in so far as it is possible, will equip its vehicles with Uniroyal tires, even though these may be relatively lousy. This relationship, known as reciprocity, has long existed in the aircraft/airline industry. See Elspeth Freudenthal, *The Aviation Business* (New York, 1940). A recent FTC report—the Mueller Report—details the prevalence of the practice today.

WHO RULES THE CORPORATIONS?   87

syndicate millions in interest payments. Hughes hoped to avoid paying this tribute by capitalizing Hughes Tool's surplus profits at TWA.

Had Hughes accomplished his objective, he would have brought off one of the most remarkable feats of vertical integration in modern industrial history. In the late fifties, when orders for jets began to be placed, the airlines were in an especially weak bargaining position in relation to financial institutions. Their total equity in relation to the cost of the new jet fleets was relatively low, putting the airlines under great pressure.

The result of this pressure was a system of financing in which the leading life insurance companies played the major role, protecting their investment through a system of restrictive agreements known as loan covenants. The restrictions they contained were, according to *Fortune,* severe enough "to raise the question of who really controls the key management decisions in the airlines in this era."[43] Agreements between Equitable, Prudential, and Metropolitan, on the one hand, and Eastern and American Airlines on the other, restricted such areas as future indebtedness, mergers and acquisitions, sale of assets, leasing of aircraft, rental of hangers, even leasing of office space. In addition Prudential in 1958 bought convertible debentures equivalent to eighteen per cent of Eastern's common stock if converted. Prudential and Equitable together own convertible notes from American equivalent to twelve per cent of its common stock in the case of conversion.

Howard Hughes battled against this kind of institutional control. He increased his equity in TWA; he poured Hughes Tool profits into purchases of Convair jets. Convair and Hughes explored the possibility of joint production of a dual purpose jet that would serve TWA's special need to fly both transcontinental and transatlantic flights. Still the cost of a sixty-jet fleet was greater than the tool company, TWA, and Hughes himself could finance. And the difficulties mounted as

---

43. "TWA: The Struggle for the Corporate Cockpit," May 1965. Other sources for this summary are the January and July 1959 and March 1961 *Fortunes.*

the economy moved into a recession that hit the airline industry especially hard. Hughes was forced to establish a $300 million line of credit in order to qualify for a $12 million credit to meet an imminent TWA payroll.[44]

Still searching for alternative credit sources, Hughes sold some of his jets. He invited plane manufacturers to participate in financing, broadening his orders to get a broader financial base. By early 1960, however, Hughes was practically defeated: the tool company had run out of cash; banks shut off credit for further jet purchases. At this point the commercial banks and insurance companies, together with the investment banking company of Dillon Read & Co., joined together to set up the credit plan that ultimately transferred control of TWA out of Hughes' hands.

In January 1961 Howard Hughes, Hollywood billionaire, aeronautical engineer, and owner of seventy-seven per cent of Trans World Airline's common stock, surrendered to the demands of a financial consortium led by the nation's largest financial institutions. For over fifteen years, Wall Street had sought to take control of TWA from Hughes. The device they used--the voting trust—had been perfected in the late nineteenth century by J. P. Morgan for use in railroad reorganization schemes. Hughes turned over the voting rights of his seventy-seven per cent controlling block to a group of trustees, a majority of whom were to be named by the financial institutions. Hughes kept the dividends and nominal "ownership" of his stock. But he gave up the prize—the right to determine corporate policy at TWA. In return the financial institutions agreed not to put the airline in receivership and advanced TWA a line of medium- and long-term credit.

Almost immediately after the agreement, the financial institutions—among them Equitable, Metropolitan, Prudential, Morgan Guaranty Trust, Chase Manhattan, First National City Bank, and Dillon, Read—sued Hughes, charging he tried to run TWA to service his own interests in violation of anti-trust laws,

---

44. A line of credit is the maximum amount of money a bank will advance to a customer. Banks usually require that the borrower maintain compensating balances. See H. G. Guthmann and H. E. Dougall, *Corporate Financial Policy* (Englewood Cliffs, New Jersey, 1962), p. 444.

particularly in providing aircraft and financing for the airline. Hughes countersued, charging that the financial institutions conspired to seize control of TWA in order to monopolize the lending—also in violation of anti-trust laws.

Both suits were probably correct. But the realization of the institutions' strategy can be seen in TWA's corporate and financial affiliates today. These affiliations are diagrammed in CHART 4. Chase Manhattan, which has five interlocks with Equitable, the leading TWA creditor, is now TWA's leading stockholder with 7.8 per cent. It is also the leading stockholder at Boeing with 8.7 per cent.[45] TWA buys its aircraft from Boeing and obtains financing from Equitable, Metropolitan, Prudential, and Morgan Guaranty. The latter two own .88 and 7.4 per cent of TWA stock respectively. Morgan maintains director interlocks with Boeing, as does First National City Bank, which participates in a Boeing leasing trust for TWA. All this reflects only a portion of the control that the great financial institutions have been able to achieve within the airline industry and, to a somewhat lesser extent, within the aircraft manufacturing industry. In the light of this scale of coordination, Hughes' ambitions seem rather modest.

The giant corporation is in fact forced to pursue a strategy of forward and backward integration. The great aircraft manufacturers—Boeing, McDonnell Douglas, Lockheed—cannot allow hundreds of millions of dollars in aircraft inventory to remain unsold simply because a rival happens to have built a better or a cheaper plane. Assured customers must be found; sales and purchases must be rationalized. Finance capital performs this function by abolishing the market and "socializing" industrial decision-making. Institutional stockholdings and loans, not market factors, become the basis on which purchasing decisions are made.[46]

But if anyone supposes that this "socialization" of decision-making, forced on finance capital by its own drive for profits, advances any social purpose other than its own, they need

---

45. That Chase is the leading outside influence at Equitable can probably be assumed from Chase's five interlocks with Equitable.

46. See further evidence below.

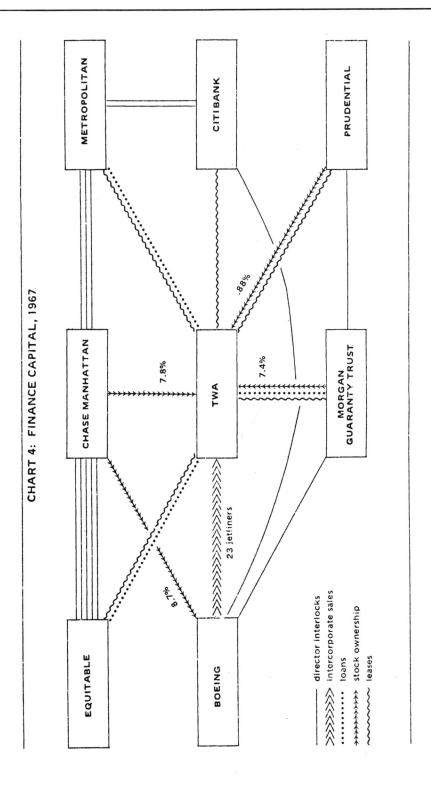

CHART 4: FINANCE CAPITAL, 1967

director interlocks
intercorporate sales
loans
stock ownership
leases

only check the unemployment figures in Seattle—which looked forward to twenty per cent unemployment in the fall of 1970; or the waste of technical and scientific talent produced by the massive aircraft company layoffs in California; or Lockheed's request for a government loan to stave off bankruptcy.

Conclusion

THE HUGHES CASE is a spectacular example of the dominant role external finance demands to play in the corporate world. Such cases are admittedly rare. These days the transition from industrial capital to finance capital is generally accomplished with less bloodletting and more legal legerdemain. There are, after all, very few entrepreneurial capitalists as rich and as independent as Howard Hughes; and perhaps even fewer willing to risk their capital in a battle against the entire United States financial oligarchy. Most are thoroughly conventional bourgeois who will simply seek the best terms finance capital has to offer. The independent arch-reactionary Henry Ford I, hater of Wall Street, gives way to the smoother, more liberal Henry Ford II who values Sidney Weinberg as his best friend and private financier.[47] And the most successful of the industrial bourgeoisie have integrated themselves into the financial establishment at the upper strata, as the Rockefellers once did. Similarly, the managerial strata of the bourgeoisie are integrated into finance capital, only on a lower and subordinate level.

Meanwhile, as our figures presented in CHART 1 indicate, the overall corporate dependence on external finance has increased rapidly since the mid-1960s. The failure of this extremely important trend to penetrate the literature of Marxist managerialism has stemmed from two misconceptions. The first was the inclusion of depreciation allowances as a source of internal funds for corporate expansion. With the composition and function of internal funds thus distorted, the basis was laid for minimizing the importance of external funds and financial institutions.

---

47. Former senior partner of Goldman Sachs, director of GM, and chairman of the finance committee of the Democratic Party.

92 FITCH & OPPENHEIMER

TABLE 4: STOCKHOLDER'S EQUITY IN RELATION TO CAPITALIZATION AND ASSETS, SELECTED INDUSTRIES, 1969

Fortune ranking (by sales)	Company	Stockholders' equity as % of capitalization	Equity (in millions)	Assets	Stockholders' equity as % of total assets
INDUSTRIALS (largest corporations in selected industries)					
Aerospace					
23	McDonnell-Douglas	79.5	573	1,508	38.0
26	Boeing	53.2	796	2,602	30.6
30	North American Rockwell	69.2	752	1,590	41.0
33	General Dynamics	67.7	328	1,066	30.8
36	United Aircraft	68.0	534	1,488	30.4
41	Lockheed	48.8	321	1,271	25.2
Auto					
1	General Motors	92.8*	10,227	14,820	69.0
3	Ford	90.0*	5,222	9,199	56.7
6	Chrysler	74.8*	2,100	4,688	44.5
Chemicals					
15	DuPont	82.9	2,684	3,452	77.7
24	Union Carbide	62.3	1,766	3,355	49.5
43	Monsanto	70.8	1,204	2,012	60.0
49	Dow	56.3	1,080	2,619	41.2
50	Grace (W. R.)	57.1	635	1,541	41.2
Conglomerates					
9	ITT	46.9	2,081	5,192	40.1
14	LTV	14.8	268	2,944	9.1
19	General Telephone & Elec.	36.1	1,947	6,909	28.0
34	Tenneco	30.5	1,371	4,054	31.6
39	Litton	62.5	704	1,580	44.4
48	Rapid American	17.4	175	1,827	9.5
Electrical Equipment					
4	General Electric	78.8	2,539	6,007	42.3
17	Westinghouse	76.7	1,389	2,477	56.1
21	RCA	54.0	1,023	2,634	39.9
Petroleum					
2	Standard Oil of N.J.	79.3	10,092	17,537	57.5
7	Mobil	82.4	4,309	7,162	60.1
8	Texaco	74.4	5,896	9,281	63.5
10	Gulf	75.2	5,039	8,104	62.1
13	Standard Oil of Calif.	87.4	4,428	6,145	72.1
TRANSPORTATION					
Railroads					
1	Penn Central	49.3	2,809	6,850	41.0
3	Southern Pacific	66.8	1,573	2,979	52.7
7	Norfolk & Western	50.6	1,136	2,633	42.7
8	Burlington Northern	68.9	1,768	2,875	61.5
9	Chesapeake & Ohio	48.9	1,125	2,671	42.1
Airlines					
2	United	35.3	588	1,946	30.1
4	TransWorld	29.8	361	1,422	25.4
5	Pan American	33.4	463	1,626	28.4
6	American	32.8	403	1,491	27.0
10	Eastern	23.9	224	1,031	21.7
UTILITIES					
Telephone					
1	AT&T	57.8	23,528	43,903	53.6
Power Companies					
2	Consolidated Edison	31.7	1,836	4,070	45.1
3	Pacific Gas & Electric	36.5	1,689	4,015	41.5
4	Southern California Edison	35.7	1,223	3,022	40.7
5	Commonwealth Edison	35.9	1,070	2,948	36.3
6	Southern Company	31.2	784	2,738	28.7

* Excluding auto finance subsidiary.
Source: Moody's industrial, transportation and public utilities manuals, 1969.

WHO RULES THE CORPORATIONS?   93

Just as fertile a source of error is the adoption of a static view of profit. An adequate account of corporate financing must include the role profit plays in linking the entire apparatus of credit and corporate control to the business cycle. As we have seen, when profits turned down in 1965, corporations began to rely increasingly on external finance.

This, of course, suggests a crucial proviso about external finance: it does not have the same importance for all corporations at all times. Overall its role is greatest in giant corporations and in periods of declining profits. But it also appears that giant corporations—especially in mining and manufacturing—increase their reliance on external funds during boom phases of the cycle as well as during declines.[48] That is, the ratio of external to internal funds peaks twice during each business cycle.

Other factors that appear to affect the need for external finance have their origin in the nature of the capital itself, i.e., in the particular sphere of industry. For example, TABLE 4 shows that utilities, which have a high percentage of fixed, "lumpy" capital, draw on outside capital for about two-thirds of their total capitalization. That is, only one-third belongs to the stockholders. In contrast retail food stores require relatively little investment in fixed capital; hence over ninety per cent of the capital belongs to the shareholders. Similarly, the high percentage of common equity in the food processing industry reflects the high percentage of circulating capital—food materials and labor—and the short circulation period.

Again, in the airline industry only one-quarter to one-third of the capital belongs to the stockholders. This is an industry with a high percentage of fixed capital (aircraft must be bought in fleets.) The auto industry, on the other hand, is mainly an assembly operation involving a high percentage of circulating capital, especially labor. Thus it requires relatively little outside capital in order to carry out production. But in addition each automobile manufacturer has a subsidiary (GMAC, Chrysler Finance, etc.) that finances auto sales. More specifically, they finance the dealer's automobile commodity

---

48. *Survey of Current Business*, November 1961, pp. 19ff.

capital. This capital, obtained almost completely from external sources, is not represented in our TABLE 4. But it is an enormous sum and is undoubtedly one of the chief reasons why fifteen men representing twenty-four financial institutions sat on GM's board in 1969.

In the conglomerate sector, we find the greatest dependence on outside capital. These corporations are highly leveraged.[49] LTV represents only $268 million controlling $3.75 billion in assets. Rapid-American stockholders control $1.7 billion in assets with only $175 million. These corporations are of course highly speculative vehicles totally dependent on financial institutions.[50] They often seem to operate more like mutual funds than like manufacturing corporations.

Notice finally the correlation between those industries that Berle and Means describe as "managerially controlled" and those having a low percentage of equity capital. These are corporations in which bank capital constitutes a majority of the capital employed. And the capital belongs to the banks, not the shareholders. It is social capital. Thus, as Hilferding pointed out, *"the dependence of industry on banks is a consequence of property relations."* An ever-growing portion of industrial capital does not belong to the industry that employs it. It has access to the capital only through the bank, which represents—in relation to industry—the real owners of the capital.[51]

The form of corporate control and the strategy of the controlling interests can also be decisive in determining dependence on external finance. A corporation can avoid collision with finance capital by electing to remain relatively small, maintaining narrow product lines, restricting borrowing, etc. Finally, some corporations may remain managerially or entrepreneurially controlled or revert back to these forms of control by default. This is especially true of corporations with low

---

49. Leverage is the capacity of equity to balance debt.

50. See *Forbes*, 15 August 1970, "L-T-V: unlike the formally bankrupt Penn Central, the bankers have a clear shot at L-T-V."

51. *Das Finanzkapital*, Marx Studien, Blätter zur Theorie und Politik des Wissenschaftlichen Sozialismus (Vienna, 1923), p. 283.

profit potential. Here finance capital is no longer interested: it cuts back its loans and sells out. We can see this phenomenon in the case of Cudahy Co., a large food processor. With 1969 sales of $354 million, it ranks 274th among the *Fortune* 500. But sales are stagnant. In 1959, Cudahy's sales were also $354 million. Worse still, from the standpoint of the investor, the company has failed to pay a single dividend during the ten year period and its operating profit margin has averaged only about one per cent. This unprofitable performance helps to explain why Cudahy has exactly two institutional investors among its 6,114 stockholders. The holdings of the two institutional investors amount to less than two thousand of Cudahy's 2.4 million shares—representing less than one-tenth of one per cent of the total. A large rapidly growing corporation like Polaroid, on the other hand, presents a very different picture. Polaroid has increased its sales since 1959 from $90 million to $466 million. Corporate profits after taxes have increased from $10.7 million in 1960 to $63 million in 1969. Polaroid's profit margin averages twenty-five per cent. During this period of growth it has naturally attracted a large institutional following: 239 of the company's 47,830 stockholders are institutions, and they hold over five million of its approximately thirty-three million shares, about fifteen per cent.

From the standpoint of the financial institutions there are different optimum control strategies for different types of corporation. If stock in a corporation is appreciating rapidly, it is most advantageous to exert control through large blocs of the rapidly appreciating stock. But if the corporation's stock is less desirable, the optimal strategy would require owning the smallest bloc of stock that would enable the financial institution to gain the corporation's loan business and to divert purchases and sales to favored corporations.

These differences mean that empirical analysis of each main industrial group must be carried out if United States finance capital is to be adequately understood. Such analysis would demonstrate that the conflict between industrial and financial capital helps shape domestic politics. The split in the Republican party, for example, pits the Eastern financial establishment led by the Rockefeller-Lodge-Scranton axis against their regional and entrepreneurial capitalist enemies like California's Henry Salvatori, South Carolina's Milliken family, and the scores of Texas and California oil millionaires without sizable foreign holdings. Similarly, the cliché "You can't trust Nixon"—heard even among Republicans in private—expresses the conflict between his personal business ties and ideological convictions which pull him to the Republican right and his recognition of the practical need to come to terms with the Republican "left" in order to govern. The former leads him to appoint ultra-rightists like Harry Dent, defense secretary Melvin Laird, the attorney general's top aide Kevin Phillips, and assistant to the secretary of defense William Baroody Jr.; the latter means positions for Rockefeller men like Secretary of Agriculture Clifford Hardin, chief foreign policy advisor Henry Kissinger, and treasury undersecretary Paul A. Volcker.[52]

In addition, the role of external finance makes clear how the bourgeoisie as a class has become obsolete by the criteria of its own historical mission. Increasingly, finance capital simply *administers* the social surplus represented by the savings accounts and insurance policies held by the middle and working classes. These funds are not allocated to various corporations and spheres of industry according to any democratically established priorities, but according to the possibility for profit. And this allocation has nothing to do with investment in the sense of risking one's own accumulated capital, i.e., capital earned in the market through exploitation of living labor.

Not only does the bourgeoisie not *invest* anything, it also *owns* much less than was previously the case. The $250 billion held in bank trust departments includes more than just the accumulated wealth of the bourgeoisie. The fastest-growing segment of the total consists of the pension trust funds, through which the financial oligarchy votes the shares that ultimately belong to the middle class and the workers. In other words, as finance capital matures, not only is the working class responsible for production, but also for financing and, increasingly, for ownership. All that is lacking is control.

---

52. Baroody's book, *A House Divided*, credited to Laird, is a forceful and well-reasoned plea for world nuclear destruction. (Melvin Laird, *A House Divided* (Chicago, 1962).)

V. FINANCE CAPITAL IN THE
MID-TWENTIETH CENTURY

Introduction

FORMALLY SPEAKING, finance capital involves a merger of industrial and financial capital so that the resulting agglomeration obeys a new and more complex economic discipline. As the Hughes case illustrates, the essence of this movement finds the accumulation of loan capital and speculative capital carried out alongside of and in contradiction to the accumulation of industrial capital.[53] The remainder of the present essay traces this relationship between financial and industrial capital in a more systematic manner. Having established that financial institutions control stock in non-financial corporations, sit on their boards, finance their activities, and take an active part in corporate affairs, we now turn to the capital accumulation strategies pursued by finance capital and the consequences of financial control for the economic system as a whole.

Our model of mid–twentieth-century finance capital resembles the pre–World War 1 model developed by Lenin and Hilferding in several respects. Perhaps most important is that both emphasize the merger of financial institutions with giant corporations as the basis of monopoly. In addition, both are characterized by high concentration and centralization of financial assets; interconnections between banks; interlocking directorates between banks and industrial and transportation companies; and banking "terrorism" as evidenced by foreclosure, calling of loans, and arbitrary denial of credit.

---

53. *Loan capital* has its origins in individual savings and corporate working capital. It is deposited in financial institutions which redirect it to the corporations, thereby assisting in the financing of industrial goods or the circulation of commodities.

Speculative capital has a similar origin. Instead of financing industrial goods or facilitating the circulation of commodities, speculative capital is invested in existing debt instruments in the hope that they will appreciate in value.

Industrial capital, of course, has its origin in retained profits that the corporation uses to maintain and expand plant in order to increase future profits.

But significant differences also exist. For historical reasons the United States developed a much more decentralized financial system than countries like Germany, Japan, Belgium, and Sweden. In Imperial Germany and great "D" banks—Deutsche, Dresdener, Discontogesellschaft—carried on all the financial roles that in the United States are played by an amalgam of commercial banks, insurance companies, investment bankers, and stockbrokers. German finance capital controlled German industry so thoroughly that it even outgrew the need for a stock market of the Wall Street type: no market existed for industrial shares because the banks had cornered so many. The time when United States financial institutions own so many shares that the stock market becomes a vestigial organ still seems years away.

Nevertheless, the Lenin-Hilferding model has its epigones, whose explanations of financial control and its consequences must be clearly distinguished from any serious analysis. There is a *simpliste* version which is especially remote from reality. It is, in part, an extrapolation from United States financial history during the age of Morgan and in part an uncritical counting of directors' noses—as if all directors carried equal weight in decision-making. Adherents of this theory conceive of the United States economic system as a great Monopoly board over which two players—Morgan and Rockefeller—contend. Sometimes Morgan moves ahead, sometimes Rockefeller. The cycle breaks only occasionally when a third player, Mellon, is given a chance to shake the dice.

This schema grew out of a more capable attempt to identify the leading power centers in the economy. This was the National Resources Committee's 1939 report on the American economy. Much of the report simply updated the 1913 Pujo Committee Report on the Money Trust: the major addition was the concept of "interest groups" that—robbed of all potential explanatory power—became the theoretical keystone of the Monopoly game theory of the economy.

The interest group, as originally presented, consists of a number of corporations linked by ownership by certain "interests": a commercial bank; an individual family like the Rockefellers; an investment banker like Kuhn, Loeb; or a city or

geographical region. The concept, however, lacks clear definition. No criteria exist for assigning a bank or corporation to
one interest group or another, resulting in a number of seemingly arbitrary classifications.

Some interest groups do hold together fairly well. The
Mellon group, for example, is linked by birth and marriage and
operationally through the Trust Department of the Mellon
National Bank. But then there is the Cleveland group, which
includes Hanna and Eaton interests. Not only are these interests often strongly opposed as carrier and shipper, but they
hardly see eye to eye politically. Cyrus Eaton won the Lenin
Peace Prize about the same time that George Humphrey,
spokesman for the Hanna interests and an unreconstructed
reactionary, served as Eisenhower's secretary of the treasury.
Living in the same city does not make Trotskyists and Com-
munists members of the same "interest group," even though
they may serve on the same United Front committees. Why
assume it is different with businessmen?

External Finance and the Rise of Union Oil

THE HISTORY OF UNION OIL of California provides one illustration of the role of external financing. It was external
finance that enabled Union's transformation from an insignificant California drilling operation to a major integrated firm
producing for national and international markets. But Union's
history also shows that external finance exacted a price for its
support—alterations in corporate control and in corporate
policy.

The Entrepreneurial Phase. Union was at first free of the influence of financial institutions. It was founded in 1883 as a
partnership between two Pennsylvanians, W.L. Hardison and
Lyman Stewart. Stewart was the company's leading figure. A
veteran of the Titusville oil strikes in Pennsylvania, this self-
taught geologist supervised drilling and sold fuel oil door-to-
door in Los Angeles commercial neighborhoods. Stewart
wanted to build Union into an integrated petroleum company
—drilling, transport, refining, distribution, and marketing. He

favored reinvestment of all the company's earnings—in oil lands, pipelines, refineries, and tankers.[54]

But ploughing back failed to provide financial resources needed to attain Stewart's corporate goal. In Union's early years Stewart's partner Hardison met the company's capital needs by raiding the vaults of his Pennsylvania bank.[55] When this proved insufficient, Stewart turned to I.W. Hillman, Los Angeles' leading banker. Hillman provided the funds for Union to build pipelines from oilwells to tidewater land, thus escaping the exorbitant freight charges levied by the Southern Pacific, Frank Norris' "Octopus." Hillman did demand some equity in the company as collateral for his loan. But he was still functioning basically as a modest though necessary middleman, receiving no voice in corporate affairs.

External Finance Increases. This was not the case as Union turned to progressively larger providers of external funds. The first of these was Thomas Bard, a wealthy Californian with diversified interests. Bard, who was brought in when the company was near bankruptcy after its only tanker burned, demanded that the partnership be reorganized as a corporation; that he be elected president; and that he be enabled to appoint a majority of the directors. Seeking an immediate return to his investment, Bard also wanted Union to begin paying dividends. Stewart and Hardison, however, still owned fifty-three per cent of the company's stock. Despite Bard's formal position, they might have been able to keep Union on its entrepreneurial track, reinvesting all its earnings.

But by now the earlier unity between Hardison and Stewart was breaking down. Hardison's interest in the oil business was

---

54. This section is based chiefly on Earl M. Welty and Frank J. Taylor, *The 76 Bonanza* (Menlo Park, California, 1966).

55. This must of course be distinguished from participation by financial institutions. That Hardison was diverting funds from a bank was purely coincidental. It might as well have been a utility, or a clothing store, or a factory. But Hardison came close to disaster as a result of his unconventional practices: a run by depositers developed when word leaked about Hardison's activities and he was saved from bankruptcy only by Stewart's timely success in bringing in the company's first gusher.

declining: he wanted to transfer his time and his funds to his expanding citrus operations. As fast as Stewart could raise the cash to buy them up, Hardison sold his shares in Union. And in the meantime Hardison combined with Bard to force the company away from its earlier ploughback policy. In May 1891, eight years after it began operations, the company paid its first dividends.

But at this time Union was growing so rapidly that even after paying out approximately one-third of its net income, considerable sums were left for reinvestment. Bank loans provided more capital—$12 million by 1914. And the issue of treasury stock provided still more capital, although it diluted the Stewart family's equity. By now the Stewarts held only one-eighth of the outstanding stock and relied on a complicated holding company structure to maintain control.

By 1914 Union was producing twenty million barrels per year—one-third of California's total oil production. Had prosperity continued, $12 million would have been a negligible external debt. Interest could be paid, principal retired, the lenders viewed as useful providers of corporate services. But prosperity did not continue. The depression of 1914 had sharp effects on Union's fortunes, forcing it to turn to more demanding sources of external finance.

The Los Angeles Syndicate. In order to pay interest on the company's debts and meet other pressing obligations the Stewarts turned to a Los Angeles financial group headed by W. L. Staats.[56] Los Angeles, before World War I, was primarily an oil town. The aircraft industry was non-existent; the munitions industry was still located on the East Coast. Consequently, local finance—in which the Staats group played the chief role—was based on oil, public utilities, and real estate. Grouped around Staats even then were such major corporations as Southern California Edison, Pacific Light and Power, Title Insurance and Trust, and Pacific Mutual Life.

The Staats syndicate was willing to help Union, but it

---

56. From this group developed today's Security Pacific and Western Bancorporation complexes.

wanted a high price for its services. They demanded first that Lyman Stewart resign from the board; second that the syndicate be able to name six of the company's eleven director's. Staats' bargaining power was all the greater because the syndicate had quietly been accumulating Union's stock.

Stewart finally agreed to the syndicate's demands. Although the Stewart family continued to play a leading role in corporate affairs, real power began to be distributed more widely— partly to managers, more substantially to the Los Angeles syndicate.

For the Staats syndicate, Union was the key to building a strong regional power base. The syndicate was powerful in utilities and in real estate, but local industry was almost entirely controlled from the East Coast. Union was, in fact, the largest California-controlled industrial corporation in the area. It could thus provide the syndicate with significant revenues. Even more important, Union could serve as a source of reciprocal arrangements with the other firms in the Staats complex.

In years to come Union's directors and their financial interests provided a better guide to the corporation's sales and purchases than any market factors. Pacific Power and Light provides power for Union's refineries; Union supplies Pacific Power and Light with natural gas. When Union discovered copper in Arizona while looking for oil, the mine was shared with United California Bank's director Harvey Mudd. (Union has three UCB directors, including Mudd.) Union's policy of reciprocity, favoring director's companies, has earned it distinction in the financial press. *Fortune* called its former president, Reese Taylor, "a Western chauvinist" for favoring California business. But, as *Fortune* points out, Union's policy was one key to its survival as a rapidly growing but strictly regional corporation.[57]

External finance was another key to Union's survival. As a rapidly growing corporation with high profits, Union was a favorite take-over target for Eastern interests, and only the Staats syndicate enabled it to maintain its independence. In

---

57. *Fortune*, April 1967.

1922 a Wall Street group led by Percy Rockefeller and Charles Sabin conducted the "Shell Grab"—an attempt to buy up Union Oil for Royal Dutch Shell. In response, Henry M. Robinson, head of Los Angeles' First National Bank, a Union director, and a member of the Los Angeles syndicate, adroitly combined financial aid with a campaign to arouse national chauvinism. In order to purchase the 314,000 Union shares (over sixty per cent of the total) held by Southern Californians, he organized "Union Oil Associates." The Associates vociferously urged Union Oil stockholders to unite against the foreigner, and for local control. In a last minute plea the Association asked the California bourgeoisie and petit-bourgeoisie, "If a foreign company wins control over you, whose ships will get the richest cargoes, whose pipe lines will run full? Who will make the profits, and who will pay the bills.[58]

Union Oil Associates won the proxy battle, then quickly set up a holding company that owned 57.5 per cent of the company's shares. Formal control of the corporation now rested with Robinson, Staats, and the Los Angeles syndicate. In the following decades this group had to help Union fend off still more Eastern take-over attempts. Union survived, partly through financial aid, partly through political connections in the Eisenhower administration. (Company director Herbert Hoover Jr. was number two man at the State Department after John Foster Dulles' death.)

And eventually, in 1965, California bankers achieved the merger to end all merger attempts. Throughout Union's history, its Eastern competitors had gained much of their power from the national scope of their operations. They had engaged in a number of extended price wars with Union in California, their local losses offset by profits generated elsewhere in the nation. Union, meanwhile, had to absorb its own losses. To escape the disadvantages of its regional base, Union decided to merge with Pure, a large integrated Midwestern producer. Thus it moved from a strictly regional corporation to a national one, too large to be merged without its own consent.

But the company's largest stockholder—shipping magnate

---

58. Welty and Taylor, p. 184.

D. K. Ludwig—objected to the merger and tried to stop it by selling his stock.[59] (As the merger was to be conducted through an exchange of shares, a precipitous drop in Union's stock could ruin the whole basis for the merger.) Union's $150 million working capital was too small to stop Ludwig's maneuver. Desperate, Union executives reached the Bank of America (two Union directors) which agreed to lead—with Security Pacific—a loan syndicate of seventeen banks providing $180 million to purchase Ludwig's stock. The loan, which enabled consummation of the Pure merger, increased Union's long-term debt by over three hundred per cent.

Enter Wall Street. Despite the size of the Bank of America-Security Pacific loan in the 1960s, California financial institutions have at times been unable to fulfill Union's long-term financial needs. During the Depression Union faced protracted price wars with major producers. Its plant stagnated; dividends had to be paid from reserves. Interest payments on its external debt were so high modernization was impossible. But the Los Angeles syndicate lacked the resources to help Union. The company turned for the first time to a Wall Street source—the investment banking house of Dillon Read. Through James Forrestal, the company floated $30 million in debentures. (Later, as secretary of the navy and of defense, Forrestal helped Union land some important military contracts.) When the company needed still more funds, Dillon Read came up with a novel expedient: Union could raise cash by selling its entire fleet to a Dillon Read subsidiary, then leasing the ships back. This provided a large chunk of ready cash, but may have cost Union some of its independence.[60]

Conclusions. The leasing arrangement Union concluded with

---

59. Perhaps he feared the merger would dilute his equity to the point where he would lose influence over such key decisions as tanker rentals.

60. The great integrated oil companies own most of the tankers they use and lease tankers mainly during emergencies. Leasing is too expensive (it is the most important industry in which great fortunes have recently been made—*vide* Onassis, Niarchos, Ludwig) and makes the lessee dependent on the lessor.

Dillon Read's subsidiary is one more instance of the reciprocity that has played so crucial a role in Union's development. In its larger outlines the reciprocity network of which Union is a part parallels the spheres of influence of the Los Angeles financial interests. The Los Angeles group's resources are limited: it can provide short- and medium-term credit, but for major long-term projects, Union has in the past had to turn East. But without the financial resources of the Los Angeles group there would be no Union Oil today. Its refineries, rigs, and pipelines would still exist, along with its shareholders' profits, but they would operate within the framework of a larger national or international concern.

Since the early twentieth century, the Los Angeles group's desire to build a strong regional power base has coincided with Union's wish to become an integrated oil producer. The convergence of their interests has muted conflict between financial, managerial, and entrepreneurial elements on the board. Appointing a majority of the directors, controlling a decisive bloc of stock, Union's financial allies have assured that strong internal opposition to their policies is unlikely to arise.

The exact role the Los Angeles financial institutions play in Union's affairs is impossible to describe: we lack the necessary access to board minutes. And because the Patman Committee studied neither investment banks nor California commercial banks we even lack detailed information on ownership of Union Oil stock. Nevertheless Union's history makes clear the indispensable role of external finance in the process of corporate development and illustrates the price financial institutions may exact for their services. At the same time Union's history indicates that non-financial elements—entrepreneurial and managerial—may co-exist with financial interests during the period of corporate maturity.

The Penn Central: Bankruptcy and Commercial Banks

THE PENN CENTRAL ILLUSTRATES yet another level of corporate development—the untrammeled dominance of finance capital in the stage of corporate senescence. Ironically, the Penn Central's predecessor, the Pennsylvania Railroad, was the corporation Berle and Means chose to illustrate the managerial thesis. It was the largest transportation company in the United States at the time, and reliable government figures on stock ownership were available.

The present behemoth is not only the largest transportation company in the Free World, it is the largest bankrupt transportation company in the entire world, including the Soviet Union. And once again reliable data on its stock ownership, financing, and internal operations are available. Now, however, they illustrate the complete inapplicability of the managerial model, especially in its more popular version.

In 1929 the Pennsy had nearly 11.5 million shares outstanding, of which the largest single stockholder—the Pennsylvania Railroad pension fund—held only .34 per cent. The second largest stockholder held .2 per cent of the shares, and the twenty largest shareholders together had only 2.7 per cent. The holdings of directors and officers were even less significant. Hence Berle and Means argued that the management—the directors and the officers appointed by them—exercised virtually unchecked power quite out of proportion to their equity in the corporation.[61]

Forty years later the Pennsy had grown, internally and through mergers, until its assets were nearly $7 billion. But the tendency towards dispersion of stockholdings had been reversed. Compared to the 2.7 per cent held by the twenty largest stockholders in 1929, in 1968 the twenty largest held 28.3 per cent.[62] The thirty-one largest held 31.8 per cent. Of these thirty-one, seventeen were commercial banks. Even more striking, nine of the ten largest owners were commercial banks, and they together held 22.1 per cent of the total—enough to exercise working control even according to Berle and Means' definition. The remaining twenty-two of the thirty-one largest shareholders included seven other commercial banks, five brokerage houses and investment companies, and one foreign bank—Credit Suisse. The largest single owner was Morgan

---

61. Berle and Means, p. 66.

62. Data for this section is drawn from Patman's entries in the *Congressional Record*, 2 July 1970, pp. E6167-74.

Guaranty with 849,275 shares, representing 3.4 per cent of the total. Thus while the total number of outstanding shares had doubled, the number held by the largest shareholder had in-creased forty times.

With this stockholding distribution, the heavy representa-tion of bank directors and officers on the Penn Central board becomes comprehensible. The Morgan holdings presumably accounted for their two directorships. A third director, the chairman of the First Pennsylvania Bank & Trust, was a Morgan son-in-law, and a former employee of Morgan Stanley. Overall, before the bankruptcy in April 1970, the fourteen board members included eleven men with fourteen interlocks with twelve commercial banks. The twenty-three member board of the Penn Central Transportation Co., which manages the railroad, had nineteen interlocks with fourteen commercial banks.[63]

The Penn Central's Creditors. The pre-bankruptcy directors had overseen a process of corporate "growth" that involved systematic neglect of rail facilities. The vice president in charge of operations, who had no links to financial institutions, was largely ignored by the board. Derailments became common; passengers on the "crack" Spirit of St. Louis had to wait hours while deteriorating track was repaired. Meanwhile revenues

---

63. There has been considerable change of directors since the bank-ruptcy and subsequent Patman revelations. It should be noted that out-sider domination at the Penn Central was only somewhat more pro-nounced than in other very large corporations recently surveyed by the National Industrial Conference Board.

This staff study shows that outside directors held sixty-three per cent of the board seats at manufacturing companies in 1967, up from fifty-seven per cent in 1958, fifty-four per cent in 1953. An earlier NICB study showed that in non-manufacuring corporations, approximately ninety per cent were considered to be dominated by outsiders, while the figure for manufacturing corporations was sixty per cent (*Wall Street Journal*, "The Outsider," August 1970, p. 1). The recent NICB survey parallels a similar survey carried out by the American Management Asso-ciation that placed the figure at ninety per cent outsider domination for "banks, public utilities, and other institutions with a strong public inter-est flavor" (cited in Juran and Louden, p. 235).

from rail operations were poured into other more profitable fields—real estate, amusement parks, leasing, etc.[64] When the years of neglect put the railroad's finances in a precarious position, the directors hired Peat, Marwick, and Mitchell to fix the books.[65] The outside directors also voted as a bloc to fire the inside directors, then brought in as president Western Electric's Paul Gorman, a man like themselves—with no railroad experience.[66]

The board's policies indicate a lack of the orientation toward operations and reinvestment of profits that would presumably characterize "company men" or managers. But in and of themselves such policies fail to prove that the directors were cannibalizing the Penn Central to feed their own financial interests. John Dorrance, after all, is not only a director of Morgan Guaranty Trust, but also serves as chairman of Campbell Soup. Perhaps his Morgan directorship had nothing to do with his decisions to pay dividends while the company was losing money, to invest in real estate rather than in railroads, and to oust the inside directors. Perhaps he was just a Campbell Soup executive appalled by Penn Central's sickly managerial stew.

But this interpretation of the board's interests cannot be sustained if we examine the minutes of the meeting at which the inside directors were fired. The minutes show, according to the *Wall Street Journal*, that Gorman reported to the board that in order to receive new credit of $200 million from certain "interested banks" the railroad would have to:

—reorganize its top management in a manner acceptable to the banks;
—use any cash received from the loans for the "essential needs of this company," rather than subsidiary companies;

---

64. "The Penn Central Bankruptcy Express," *Fortune*, August 1970.

65. See above.

66. He presumably had other acceptable credentials as the former president of Bankers Trust, long considered to be within the Morgan sphere of influence.

—grant the banks the right to dispose of part or all of any collateral backing the loans in the event of default.[67]

These demands could hardly have come as a surprise to the board, for the "interested banks" had several directors on the Penn Central Board. Further, of the ten banks providing the largest amounts of cash in the $200 million credit package, seven were also listed an o ig the top thirty-one stockholders: First National City Bank, Morgan Guaranty Trust, Chase Manhattan Bank, Irving Trust, Manufacturers Hanover Trust, Chemical Bank, and Continental Illinois. Citibank and Morgan, who agreed to lead the syndicate, were already the largest holders of the Penn Central's outstanding debt: Citibank was owed approximately $380 million, while Morgan was the largest broker for commercial paper. (See TABLE 5.)

When we consider these links between creditors, stockholders, directors, and policies we can see clearly how the relationship between a corporation and its bankers is unique, certainly quite different from its relationship with lawyers and accountants. The latter work on a fee basis: they almost never hold large blocs of stock. The bankers not only hold decisive positions on the board, but also have working control of the corporation through stockholdings. And the banks, unlike lawyers or accountants are major creditors of the corporation. Add together directorships, stockholdings, and creditor relations and they have an unassailable position.

The process through which the financial institutions attained their power over the Penn Central is too long and complex to recapitulate here. But consider the power the banks may derive from the credit needs of the giant corporations alone—especially when these credit needs are expanded by economic downturn, high dividend payments, and bad management. $200 million may seem like a small sum to those used to dealing with figures like the U.S. GNP ($900 billion) in freshman economics courses. But this is just another instance of how misleading academic economics can be. In fact, a credit package of this size can hardly be put together without the participation of the largest American banks—those on Wall

67. *Wall Street Journal*, 20 July 1970, p. 4.

110   FITCH & OPPENHEIMER

TABLE 5:
FINANCIAL INSTITUTIONS' INTERLOCKING RELATIONSHIPS
WITH PENN CENTRAL STOCK, DIRECTORSHIPS, AND DEBT

Name of financial institution holding stock (1)	Number of shares held and voted (2)	Percent of shares outstanding	Director interlock (3)	Debt held (4)
Morgan Guaranty Trust Co., New York (4 nominees)	849,275	3.4	(5)	$90,972,937
Chemical Bank New York Trust Co., New York (2 nominees)	721,119	3.0		19,531,303
Bank of New York, New York	522,632	2.2		
Bank of Delaware, Wilmington	500,000	2.1		
Merrill Lynch, Pierce, Fenner & Smith, New York	498,401	2.1		
Manufacturers Hanover Trust Co., New York	469,439	1.9		13,195,620
Chase Manhattan Bank, New York	436,669	1.8	(6)	7,832,500
Northwestern National Bank, Minneapolis	320,000	1.3		
Continental Illinois National Bank & Trust, Chicago	305,600	1.2		78,748
Butcher & Sherrard, Philadelphia	301,072	1.2		
Helene Fuld Health Foundation, Trenton, N.J.	282,300	1.1		
Bache & Co., New York	259,750	1.0		
State Street Bank & Trust Co., Boston	225,350	.9		
Thrift-Plan—Penn Central Co.	211,172	.8		
First National Bank, Minneapolis	200,000	.8		
Alleghany Corp., New York	196,195	.8	(7)	
Cyrus J. Lawrence & Sons, New York	186,898	.7		
Credit Suisse, New York	184,176	.7		
Loeb, Rhoades & Co., New York	163,988	.7		
National Shawmut Bank, Boston	141,100	.6		2,385,000
Paine, Webber, Jackson & Curtis, New York	135,682	.6		
Irving Trust Co., New York	134,499	.5		6,964,612
Boston Safe Deposit & Trust Co.,	128,500	.5		
Pittsburgh National Bank,	127,953	.5		
First National City Bank, New York	125,802	.5		386,611,095
United States Trust Co., New York	120,086	.5		
Brown Bros., Harriman Co., New York	109,508	.4		

1. The commercial banks held their shares of Penn Central stock through bank nominees. Below is a listing of the nominees and the banks controlling each:

    Morgan Guaranty Trust Co.—Carson & Co., Reing & Co., Kelly & Co., Genoy & Co.
    Chemical Bank—C. A. England & Co., J. C. Orr & Co.
    Bank of New York—Lerche & Co.
    Bank of Delaware—Carothers & Clark.
    Manufacturers Hanover Trust—Sigler & Co.
    Chase Manhattan Bank—Kane & Co.
    Northwestern National Bank—Perc & Co.
    Continental Illinois Bank & Trust Co., —Trude & Co.
    State Street Bank & Trust Co.—Harwood & Co.
    First National Bank, Minneapolis—Var & Co.
    National Shawmut Bank—Chetco.
    Irving Trust Co.—Pert & Co.
    Boston Safe Deposit & Trust Co.—Pratt & Co.
    Pittsburgh National Bank—Elm & Co.
    First National City Bank—King & Co.
    United States Trust Co.—Atwell & Co.

2. Railway Annual Report Form A 1968, as of Dec. 31, 1968, p. 108.
3. As of Dec. 31, 1969.
4. As of Dec. 31, 1969.
5. John T. Dorrance Jr. and Thomas L. Perkins.
6. Stuart T. Sanders
7. Fred M. Kirby.

Source: Congressional Record, July 2, 1970, p. E6170.

TABLE 6: THE PENN CENTRAL CONSORTIUM

Asset Rank	Name of Participating Bank	Asset Rank	Name of Participating Bank
1	Bank of America	8	Bankers Trust
2	Citibank	9	Continental Illinois
3	Chase Manhattan	10	First National, Chicago
4	Manufacturers Hanover	12	Marine Midland
5	Morgan Guaranty Trust	13	Irving Trust
6	United California Bank	15	Crocker-Citizens
	(Western Bancorporation)	16	Mellon
7	Chemical Exchange Bank		

Street. Consider how inclusive the "interested" banks in the Penn Central $200 million consortium were. As TABLE 6 indicates, only two of the top sixteen banks by asset size failed to participate. Unless a corporation is able to go through Wall Street channels—and meet their terms—it can't meet its financial requirements.[68] Their participation is critical to corporate survival—so critical that they have what amounts to a potential veto power over the decision-making process not only at the Penn Central but in the boardroom of almost every giant corporation in the country.

Conflict and Convergence of Interests. While the Patman Committee has emphasized the commercial bank conflict of interest in the Penn Central collapse, the Senate Commerce Committee has charged that the Penn Central's investment bankers, in collusion with top directors and officers, must also share in the responsibility. Glore Forgan Staats (now DuPont Glore Forgan), the Penn Central's investment banker, had several joint investments with vice chairman and chief financial officer David Bevan. Among them was a major share in Executive Jet Aviation, Inc. Bevan, who was in charge of the Penn Central's asset diversification program, had funneled $21 million of the railroad's assets—assets needed to keep rail operations from collapsing—into the Executive Jet venture. The $21 million was used to purchase Boeing 707s and 727s. But the company, according to Senator Vance Hartke, was not using the planes it had already bought. Still Penn Central officials pushed for more investment in 707s and 727s for Executive

---

68. Occasionally syndicates may be led by the Bank of America and another California bank. But the vast majority of term loans and revolving credit packages are assembled by the great Wall Street banks.

Jet. Even Bevan admitted, in testimony before the committee, that the venture was "one bad investment." In hindsight, he said, he wouldn't recommend doing it again.

But why did the Penn Central's directors approve the purchase of jets their subsidiary didn't need? This hardly seems like the rational maximizing behavior one reads about in textbooks, but it can be explained in terms of reciprocity and financial interests. At the time the Boeings were purchased, the chairman of the Penn Central was a director of the Chase Manhattan Bank, which, in turn, was Boeing's largest stockholder. Interlocks also existed between Morgan Guaranty Trust (two Penn Central directors) and Boeing. And several other Penn Central directorships were held by firms that had also participated in the syndicate that financed production of the Boeing planes. At the same time, sales of both planes had slumped disastrously, causing a steep decline in Boeing's stock. In these circumstances, it is possible—though not proven—that the Penn Central directors approved Bevan's plans because they feared for their investment at Boeing. In addition, Glore Forgan profited considerably from the commissions it earned from buying up corporations like Executive Jet.

However unfavorably this may reflect on the Penn Central directors' integrity, it has the ring of authenticity. Penn Central directors did recommend the purchase of Penn Central stock to securities analysts and subordinates while selling out their own holdings and those of the institutions with which they were affiliated.[69] Their behavior in both cases suggests that the Penn Central directors saw the railroad as a dying man whose vital organs could be transplanted to other, more promising patients. In the meantime these corporate surgeons collected their fees from the dying man's bank account and sold off his IOUs to the unwary.

Even if we ignore the Boeing–Executive Jet–Penn Central linkages and assume that only a bizarre coincidence is involved, Bevan's actions do expose the gray-flannel myth of the company man. According to legend today's top corporate officers bear no resemblance to the tycoons of the past who

---

69. *Wall Street Journal*, 25 September 1970, p. 5.

robbed their companies in order to promote their own interests. As Sweezy and Baran wrote in *Monopoly Capital*: "We
can say without qualification that the company man is dedicated to the advancement of his company: he is dedicated to
the advancement of his company precisely to the extent that
he is dedicated to advancing himself."[70] And this, they maintain, holds true no matter how high he rises in the managerial
ranks.

But the Penn Central example shows that at the very top
the managers, the "company men," are almost always inte-
grated into the financial bourgeoisie. When we consider
Bevan's outside interests and directorships the whole idea of
the company man becomes a contradiction in terms. For
Bevan was not just a director and financial officer of the Penn
Central, but held stock and served as director or officer of
many other corporations: Kaneb Pipe Line, Macco Realty Co.,
Philadelphia Surburban Water Co., Borden, Inc., Allegheny
Ludlum Steel, Trailer Tran Co., Lehigh Valley Railroad Co.,
Buckeye Pipe Line Co., Great South Western Corp., Arvida
Corp., Wabash Railroad, Provident National Bank, Western
Savings Bank. Many of these are Penn Central subsidiaries.
Others are not. Certainly Bevan was a company man. But
which company?

As an interlocking director and a member of upper management, it was up to Bevan to coordinate dealings between these
companies. But on whose terms? How, in fact, can one maximize the return on an inter-company sale for both corporations? Viewed from this perspective, it appears that in the gray
flannel suit, the Marxist managerialists have borrowed a
threadbare vestment from the liturgy of managerialism.

Conclusion

BOTH THE PENN CENTRAL and the Union Oil case studies
indicate that in order to live and survive within the framework
of contemporary capitalism, many corporations must turn to
financial institutions for aid. The latter, in turn, receive stock,
directorships, and consequently a voice in company policy-

---

70. *Monopoly Capital*, p. 38.

making. In both cases, the financial institutions are the key to the networks of reciprocity through which the corporation is linked to its suppliers and purchasers. In both, reciprocity is a mode of doing business rather than a matter of occasional convenience. Yet in the case of Union Oil, the financial bourgeoisie operated in a way that increased the stability of the corporation while their counterparts at Penn Central seemed anxious to make off with everything but the tracks themselves.

For the Marxist managerialists, this latter role is an anomaly. "The picture of a few finance capitalists manipulating stock," writes James O'Connor, "acquiring huge overnight profits, and frantically putting together and taking apart industrial empires with an eye to immediate financial gain is simply not consistent with what is known about managerial decision-making in the vast majority of large corporations today."[71] But "immediate financial gain" is exactly what the conglomerate "movement" was all about, and exactly what the railroad and utility "diversification" efforts are aimed at achieving.

This is not to say that the Penn Central's Bevan was particularly cynical, nor was Union's Reese Taylor a self-sacrificing company man. The subjective character of "managerial decision-making" had little to do with the policies their corporations pursued. The two merely represent giant corporations operating in industries at different stages of development. Should the rate of profit in the petroleum industry sink permanently to the two or three per cent level that has characterized the rail industry, it would not be surprising to see Union executives carrying out a "diversification" program similar to the one underway at the Penn Central. To understand the market forces and institutional pressures that compel a corporation to opt for a particular investment strategy, we must analyze the process of capital accumulation as it takes place in the giant corporation dominated by finance capital.

---

71. *Monthly Review,* December 1968, p. 32.

WHO RULES THE CORPORATIONS?
PART 3

ROBERT FITCH AND
MARY OPPENHEIMER

In Part One of this essay we presented an empirical analysis of corporate control. Relying chiefly on evidence provided by the recent investigations of the Patman committee, we located an important portion of corporate control in the trust departments of the large eastern commercial banks. Power had not been separated from property: its linkage with property had been concealed by its holders and confounded by academic science. Financial institutions—chiefly commercial banks but also insurance companies, mutual funds, investment and brokerage houses—were exercising an increasing sway over corporate activity through their securities holdings and their lending activities. Directors, officials, and trustees of large financial institutions were now the most influential stratum

33

within the bourgeoisie, more powerful than either the man agers or the individual capitalists who are being rapidly integrated into the corporate power structure on terms laid down by finance capital.

In Part Two, we analyzed how financial control is merely the outcome of the process of capitalist reproduction. On the one hand the gradual concentration and centralization of capital forces corporations to rely, over time, on the large pools of capital made available by financial institutions. On the other, the ups and downs of the business cycle force the corporation to rely on external capital at critical conjunctures in its development.

In this section we want to show what difference it makes. So what if banks or managers control corporations?

I. INTRODUCTION

IF MANAGERIALLY CONTROLLED corporations behaved like corporations dominated by finance capital, the question of who exercises corporate control could be left to academic sociologists. With nothing riding on the outcome, they could count up the proxies and let us know the score. But corporate control is intimately bound up with key aspects of corporate behavior. Managerially and financially controlled corporations behave differently. For example, under finance capital the rate and mode of corporate growth are no longer determined independently within the corporation. Rates of accumulation, dividend payout ratios, debt policy, relations with other corporations, and purchasing and sales relations differ, depending on who controls the corporation.

Further, the financially controlled corporation not only behaves differently from the managerially controlled corporation, but a *system* of corporations dominated by finance capital—and therefore indirectly by the stock market—operates differently from a system in which independent, self-financing corporations are the supreme economic decision-making units. These differences show up primarily in a declining rate of capital accumulation within the large corporations, in new modes of capital accumulation, and in the erosion of purely

market relations between giant corporations. This system of
finance capital represents a revolutionary advance over
nineteenth-century corporate organization. Finance capital is
far more centralized, far more socialized: it is able partially to
transcend market forces in order to shape economic activity to
a conscious social purpose.

II. THE RATE OF CAPITAL ACCUMULATION

CAPITAL ACCUMULATION is the fundamental dynamic of the
capitalist system: more than any other single factor, accumulation determines the rate and mode of economic growth. It
differs from profit-making: a corporation can make profits
without accumulating capital, but it can't accumulate capital
unless it makes profits. In the industrial sphere capital accumulation is the reinvestment of profits from the sale of commodities—what economic historians call "plough-back." [1]

By accumulation we mean the reinvestment process within
the individual firm. We are distinguishing it from capital
formation—by which we mean the rate of new investment for
the society as a whole. We are not arguing that the overall rate
of capital formation has slowed down, only that the rate of
capital accumulation in the mature monopoly corporations has
done so. What we are trying to show is that—to mix the terminology of Marxism with that of the accounting profession—the
source of surplus value remains the same: it is accumulated
from the workers, individual firm by individual firm. But the
uses of surplus value are increasingly determined socially by
finance capital. The giant corporation is the channel through
which surplus value is created, but new channels have been
developed that reallocate surplus value among the individual
firms.

---

1. Many economic historians are, however, unable to distinguish between the rate of capital accumulation and the rate of capital formation.
The latter shows how fast corporate assets are growing; the former, the
extent to which profits are recycled back into the business. A corporation could have a relatively high rate of accumulation, combined with a
low rate of capital formation; this would indicate a low capital/output
ratio, i.e., unproductive capital.

Marx and the classical economists who analyzed the origin of capitalist production naturally focused on capital accumulation. In particular they noticed the extraordinarily high *rates* of capital accumulation that characterized capitalism in its formative period, between 1600 and 1750. So impressed were they by the performance of the bourgeoisie that they made capital accumulation the *differentia specifica* between feudalism and capitalism—the key to economic growth and technological progress.

Under feudalism, the serfs produce a surplus, over and above the socially determined level of material survival. The surplus (tithes, taxes, etc.) goes to the landlords, the landed aristocracy who simply consume it. The aristocrats—landlords plus the church—spent the economic surplus on such feudal staples as tournaments, wars, castles, vestments, cathedrals. As a consequence, the rate of technological progress and the rate of economic development were relatively slow. Under capitalism, however, the economic surplus that the productive sector of the society, the proletariat, yields up to the ruling class, the bourgeoisie, is not simply consumed. Nor does the capitalist hoard this surplus like the miser. The capitalist invests the surplus productively, buying more raw material, human labor, machines. The capitalist saves to spend, to invest productively. The result is a much more rapid rate of technological progress.

But why does the capitalist invest his portion of the surplus, while the lord simply consumes his? The capitalist, facing a highly competitive market, cannot stay in operation without reinvesting his capital. Capital accumulates or it dies. If he fails to cut costs, to meet the competition of his rivals, other capitalists will drive his goods out of the market. And the chief methods of cutting costs involve expanding the scale of production. With the steady accumulation of capital and as the scale of operations increased it became possible for him to relax somewhat. Rather than continuing to save like a miser while producing like a capitalist, the mid–nineteenth-century capitalist, thanks to prior accumulation, could now continue producing on a competitive scale while emulating the consumption habits of his feudal forebears. Even if the mid-nineteenth-century capitalist maintained the same *rate* of accumulation as his father did, the *amount* of capital available for consumption would be substantially greater.[2]

That's where the balance between accumulation and consumption stood in Marx's day. But what would happen if all-out competition, which Marx thought was the driving force behind capital accumulation, were eliminated? Or at least sharply attenuated? What would happen to the *rate* of capital accumulation? What would happen to the technological progress characteristic of the bourgeois order? How would the stability of the system be affected?

According to Baran and Sweezy, the development of monopoly has no effect on capital accumulation at all. They state that there can be

> . . . no doubt that the making and accumulation of profits hold as dominant a position today as they ever did. Over the portals of the magnificent office building of today, as on the wall of the modest counting house of a century or two ago, it would be equally appropriate to find engraved the motto: "Accumulate! Accumulate! That is Moses and the Prophets."[3]

Whether or not the rate of accumulation has remained the same over the last two hundred years or not is a simple matter of fact. But as we go back two hundred years in capitalist development what facts we have about publicly held businesses are a function of the institutional investors' demand for hard information on which to base investment decisions.

---

2. Suppose capitalist A, in 1800, takes in £1000 net profit. He invests £900 back in the business and spends £100 on his family; rate of accumulation, ninety per cent. His son, however, B, has taken over a larger enterprise. Yearly profits of the business are now £10,000: £9000 is reinvested; he spends the £1000 remaining on himself, his family, mistresses, estates, etc. Rate of accumulation: still ninety per cent. Marx attributes growing prodigality of capitalism to the new "expenses of representation" and to the "Faustian conflict" growing "between the passion for accumulation and the desire for enjoyment" (*Capital* [Moscow, 1966], vol. 1, p. 594). But compound accumulation would seem to be a sufficient explanation.

3. Paul Baran and Paul Sweezy, *Monopoly Capital* (New York, 1966), pp. 43–44.

Eighteenth- and nineteenth-century figures about private business are, unfortunately, not nearly so widely available. But we are not completely in the dark.

The heroic anality of eighteenth- and nineteenth-century entrepreneurs, saving their profits and retaining them in the business, is a frequently told tale of economic history. Rates of accumulation were obviously very high. Just how high we are told less often. And aggregate figures for the various branches of industry are probably impossible to state with complete accuracy. The author of one widely used text cites as typical the records of one well-rooted British textile firm. They show that during the six-year period when the partners were bringing up-to-date the firm's power plants, machinery, and factory buildings, profits were ploughed back at a rate in excess of sixty per cent; that in 1830 the figure was eighty-five per cent; and that it rose to eighty-eight cent in 1831.[4] Other available records show that especially in the early stages of successful entrepreneurship, profit retention actually approached one hundred per cent. And some businesses were even more strenuous in their demands for profit retention.[5]

So despite gaps existing in historical records, it seems safe to conclude that early capitalist entrepreneurs accumulated at least half of their profits, and very likely considerably more. What about their modern counterparts? We can get a fairly precise idea of the present rate of accumulation by examining dividend payout ratios (the ratio of dividends to profits). Dividends are money that the corporation *cannot* plough back. The share of profits expended on dividends to stockholders is not available for productive reinvestment in the firm itself. Profits less dividends—retained earnings—represent the maximum portion of profits that can be devoted to capital accumulation. (In practice, not even the total of retained earnings is entirely reinvested.) Thus if the dividend payout ratio increases, the rate of capital accumulation must decline, for rela-

---

4. Herbert Heaton, *Economic History of Europe* (New York, 1948), p. 570.
5. Seymour Shapiro, *Capital and the Cotton Industry* (Ithaca, New York, 1967), pp. 179, 181. See also Victor S. Clark, *History of Manufacturers in the United States* (New York, 1949), p. 367.

WHO RULES THE CORPORATIONS?   39

tively less of the corporation's profit is available for reinvestment. What factors, then, influence the dividend payout ratio
and the rate of capital accumulation? There are two main
factors—both of which originate not in the sphere of production but in the financial sphere. First of all there is the pressure brought to bear by fluctuations in the secondary market
for the giant corporation's common stock, e.g., the New York
Stock Exchange. And second, there is the pressure exerted by
the lending activities of the financial institutions represented
on the corporate board. Thus a declining rate of capital accumulation can ultimately be traced to the growing influence
of financial factors in corporate decision-making.

TABLE 1: CORPORATE DIVIDEND PAYOUTS[1] BY ASSET SIZE: 1960–1970

Corporate assets ($000,000)	1960	1962	1964	1966	1968	1970
10-25	40.5	31.1	29.4	25.2	25.0	27.7
25-50	42.8	40.3	32.6	41.9	31.5	35.7
50-100	51.9	48.4	41.2	34.8	35.9	41.6
100-250	59.4	53.5	40.9	47.5	43.8	43.3
250-1,000	57.5	60.2	49.3	44.9	47.1	50.1
1,000-	70.8	64.0	56.4	56.5	53.5	55.5

1. Percentage of profits paid out as dividends.
Source: FTC-SEC, **Quarterly Financial Report for Manufacturing Corporations,
Third Quarter 1970.** (In part 2 of this article [SR I:5] corporations with assets over
one billion dollars were mistakenly eliminated.)

The bigger the corporation, the slower the rate of accumulation, and the higher the dividend payout ratio. This relation
emerges quite clearly from TABLE 1. For manufacturing corporations with assets ranging from under one million dollars to a
billion dollars and more, there is an almost perfect correlation
between the size of corporate assets and a high dividend payout ratio. In 1960, for example, corporations with assets
between one and five million dollars paid out a quarter of their
profits in dividends; corporations with assets between fifty and
one hundred million dollars paid out over fifty per cent; while
the rate for corporations with assets over one billion dollars
exceeded seventy per cent. Billion-dollar corporations not only
pay out a greater amount of their profits absolutely—accounting for over half of all manufacturing corporation dividends—
their dividend *rate* exceeds that of the smallest corporations
by anywhere from four hundred to six hundred per cent.

There are, it is true, wide differences between industries. Petroleum and utilities industries pay out a higher percentage of their profits than do manufacturers of transportation equipment. But as a general rule, the larger the corporation, the higher the dividend payout ratio, and the lower the rate of capital accumulation.

Why do the large corporations pay out so high a portion of their earnings? The answer requires that we examine what is unique to these giant corporations—the fact that a huge market exists for their stock, and that leaders of financial institutions sit on their corporate boards.

Stock Prices and Dividend Payout Ratios

CORPORATE DIRECTORS can use two sure-fire ways of raising the market price of their company's stock. The first is to increase profits. The second is to increase the amount of profits paid out to the stockholders, i.e., raise the dividend rate. And it is the bigger corporations that pay out the higher percentage of their profits in order to get the higher stock price. On the surface this seems paradoxical, since large corporations generally earn higher profits than small corporations. Stock values, however, are not determined by profitability alone. *Expectations of future profitability* also play a critical role. And the very large corporations—the ones whose stocks are most widely held and traded—have a built-in ceiling on the possibility for growth in their rate of profit. In contrast, for certain selected small corporations, the growth possibilities are less limited.[6]

We can see this point more easily if we compare the profit performances of Xerox and General Motors. (See TABLE 2.) Xerox is today a giant itself, but in 1960 it was one of the "elite" small corporations, with sales of $37 million and profits of $2.6 million. In comparison, General Motors had sales of $12.7 billion and profits of $892 million. Despite the disparity in their sizes, their rates of profit on assets for that

---

6. The big corporations have to compete only with these "elite" small corporations. The less profitable ones are unable to have their stocks listed on the main exchanges.

TABLE 2: GM AND XEROX COMPARED

Year	Gross revs. ($000,000)	Net income ($000)	Oper. profit Margin (%)	Earn. per sh. ($)	Div. per sh. ($)	Div. payout (%)	Price range	Price ÷ Earn.
			GENERAL MOTORS CORPORATION					
1960	12,736	959,042	15.0	3.35	2.00	60	55-40	14.3
1961	11,396	892,821	14.5	3.11	2.50	80	58-40	15.9
1962	14,640	1,384,000	18.6	4.83	3.00	62	59-44	10.8
1963	16,495	1,591,823	19.5	5.55	4.00	72	91-47	13.4
1964	16,997	1,734,782	18.4	6.04	4.45	74	102-77	14.9
1965	20,734	2,125,606	19.0	7.41	5.25	71	113-91	13.8
1966	20,209	1,793,392	16.0	6.24	4.55	73	108-65	13.9
1967	20,026	1,627,276	14.5	5.65	3.80	67	89-67	13.9
1968	22,755	1,731,915	14.9	6.01	4.30	72	89-72	13.5
1969	24,295	1,710,695	13.6	5.94	4.30	72	83-65	12.5
			XEROX CORPORATION					
1960	37.1	2,598	16.6	0.05	0.02	40	5-1	70.0
1961	59.5	5,323	22.5	0.09	0.02	18	11-4	88.9
1962	104.5	13,860	34.2	0.24	0.04	15	11-5	35.2
1963	176.0	23,001	33.8	0.38	0.07	18	29-9	51.4
1964	268.0	38,530	30.1	0.63	0.13	21	44-23	53.7
1965	392.6	58,648	29.0	0.93	0.18	20	71-31	55.7
1966	528.3	79,821	26.3	1.24	0.28	23	89-41	52.7
1967	701.4	97,281	24.4	1.48	0.37	25	104-65	57.7
1968	896.4	116,194	24.7	1.73	0.48	28	109-76	53.8
1969	1,482.9	161,368	27.5	2.07	0.57	28	115-80	47.2

year were fairly close. GM had a rate of profit of 15.0 per cent; for Xerox the figure was 16.6. The big difference was in the rate of future profitability: Xerox's profits increased much faster than GM's. By 1969 GM's profits had almost doubled, but Xerox's had increased thirty times—to $161 million. The stock market "knew" this would happen—a knowledge reflected in the premium the investor had to pay to buy Xerox stock. In 1961, for example, a GM stockholder paid about fifty dollars for a share of GM stock that earned a little over three dollars. At the same time, the Xerox stockholder had to pay about nine dollars to get less than a dime of earnings.[7] In this case the market's assessment of the future worth of the two companies was based on fundamentals: Xerox had a monopoly in the photocopying field; GM was the leader in the auto industry. But because the photocopying market was growing much faster than the auto market, Xerox grew much faster than GM.

The contrasting stock performances of Xerox and GM show the role that profit expectations have on stock valuations. For

7. The ratio of price to earnings was 88.9 compared to 16.7 in the case of GM.

a large corporation, vigorous capital accumulation won't pay off in terms of proportionately increased earnings and dividends. So it can't pay off in terms of a higher stock price either. But for a small dynamic corporation capital accumulation leads quite directly to a higher stock price. And the dividend rate can be kept quite low without creating stockholder dissatisfaction.

The stock of a giant corporation, however, does not compete in the market with that of the small corporations only, but with that of other giant corporations as well. And here too the corporate dividend rate has a decisive effect on comparative stock price. This role may be summarized very simply: if earnings are equal, the company with a higher dividend rate will have the higher stock price. Graham and Dodd give a striking example to illustrate this point. New Hampshire Fire paid *twice* the dividend of New Amsterdam Casualty and sold *twice* as high, although its earnings were just *half* as great. In 1948, according to the authors, after being prodded by its stockholders, New Amsterdam Casualty began to increase its dividend rate, which had been maintained at $1.00 for many years. By 1950 the dividend rate had reached $1.40 and the

**TABLE 3: STOCK PRICES
AND DIVIDEND PAYOUTS: 1938–1947 AVERAGE**

	New Amsterdam Casualty	New Hampshire Fire
Average earnings per share	4.04	2.04
Average dividends	.89	1.74
Average price	22.00	44.50

price of the shares had risen to 42, within a few points of New Hampshire [8] (see TABLE 3). Further evidence for the importance of dividends in common stock valuation comes from Cohen and Zinbarg, who cite the results of an unpublished study which indicates that between 1949 and 1963 dividend change was significantly related to price change in eleven of fifteen years, whereas earnings change was significant in only seven of the fifteen years.[9]

8. Benjamin A. Graham, David L. Dodd and Sidney Cottle, *Security Analysis* (New York, 1962), p. 482.

9. Jerome B. Cohan and Edward O. Zinbarg, *Investment Analysis and Portfolio Management* (Homewood, Illinois, 1967), p. 221.

Financial Institutions and the Payout Ratio

THE EVIDENCE presented so far indicates how high dividends and a low rate of capital accumulation may contribute to high stock prices. But the question of why the corporation is concerned with the price of its stock still remains unanswered. Why doesn't the corporation concentrate on profit-making and leave its stock price to be determined by impersonal market forces?

On one level, concern with stock prices simply reflects concern with corporate performance. The higher the price of company stock, the easier it is to carry out mergers and acquisitions, obtain credit, and hire top management talent. This partially explains the corporate preoccupation with stock prices—a preoccupation so profound that American corporations will actually deplete their working capital in order to support the price of their stock. Yet on another level the corporate obsession with stock prices reflects the interests of outsiders who, unlike the nineteenth-century entrepreneur, benefit only from common stock appreciation and from those portions of retained earnings that are translated into dividends. Large commercial banks, which own substantial blocs of corporate stock, obviously fall into this category: the higher the dividend payout ratio, the higher the dividend income flowing into their trust accounts.

Yet there is another way in which the pressure of the stock market for a high dividend payout ratio in large corporations suits the big financial institutions perfectly. The great Wall Street banks—Morgan Guaranty, Citibank, Manufacturers Hanover, Chase Manhattan, etc.—are wholesale banks. They base their earning power on lending to the giants of American industry. The greater tendency there is to pay out earnings as dividends, the greater the loan business which accrues to the wholesale banks.

The banks, therefore, have interests opposed to inside management. Left to follow their own self-interest, the officers seek growth—even relatively unprofitable growth—for its own sake. Unlike owners of capital, who will consider liquidating their investment when a particular line of business turns

44   FITCH & OPPENHEIMER

unprofitable, managers act as if "the show must go on" whatever the cost. "The officers," Graham and Dodd observe, "even though they may be inefficient, want to keep their jobs. Their bias is in the direction of large working capital, low dividends, maximum expansion, an all-common-stock capital structure, and the continuance of the business at all costs." [10]

Such an outlook conflicts with the objectives of a variety of financial institutions. Investment bankers must oppose an all-common-stock structure since they make much of their living selling corporate bonds. Commercial bankers will be unenthusiastic about corporations maintaining high levels of working capital, since this hurts their short-term loan business. And all financial institutions can unite around opposition to a low-dividend policy since they all seek profits from loans, not production. And a low-dividend policy decreases the need for loan capital and thus the size of banking and insurance company profits. In addition, of course, a low-dividend policy obstructs the accumulation of bank trust assets, insurance company reserves, and capital gains from security trading.

TABLE 4: CORPORATE WORKING CAPITAL BY ASSET SIZE: 1970

Asset size ($000,000)	Current ratio
10-25	2.27
25-50	2.23
50-100	2.28
100-250	2.25
250-1,000	2.14
1,000-	1.80

Source: FTC-SEC, **Quarterly Financial Report for Manufacturing Corporation, Third Quarter 1970.** Corporations with assets below $10 million have been eliminated from consideration since they are especially likely to be family-controlled. See J. M. Juran and James Louden, **The Corporate Director** (New York, 1966), p. 238.

Since the large corporations are most heavily dominated by outside directors, especially those representing financial institutions, we would expect the capital structure of these corporations to reflect the interests of the controlling financial groups. We would expect to find a high dividend payout ratio (see TABLE 1), a low level of working capital (TABLE 4), and a high level of external debt.[11] And this is what we find in fact.

---

10. *Security Analysis*, p. 665.
11. See part 2 (SR 1:5), p. 74, table 2.

The larger the corporation, the less the stress on maintaining working capital. And the bigger the corporation the more likely that a significant section of its capital structure is composed of bonds and other long-term debt provided by financial institutions.

The two factors making for a high payout ratio—the objective interests of the large financial institutions, which want to maximize their loan capital, and the pressure of the stock market, exerted on behalf of "optimum" dividend policy—complement each other. And as the assets of the giant corporations begin to make up an increasing portion of all manufacturing assets, we can expect the overall rate of capital accumulation to decline and the socialization of credit to intensify still further.

Financial Institutions and the Goal of Corporate Activity

OUTSIDE STOCKHOLDERS, unlike nineteenth-century entrepreneurs, benefit only from common stock appreciation and from that portion of retained earnings that is translated into dividends. As a result, the manner in which surplus is appropriated has undergone a significant change. This helps explain why and how the declining *rate* of capital accumulation described above has resulted in the new *modes* of capital accumulation detailed in the remainder of this section.

Prior to the development of a highly organized market for common stock, businessmen appropriated the profits of their firms directly. The nineteenth-century factory owner could simply go down to his office, open the safe, and take the boodle home. Few men own giant corporations in such a palpable way. And getting at the unaccumulated profits has become a much more complicated matter. The massive increase in the number of nominal "owners"—a change in the form of ownership—has changed its content. Rights to unaccumulated profits are divided into millions of shares. And holders of preferred stock, debenture holders, and other creditors without formal claims to legal corporate ownership have a right to corporate profits that takes precedence over the rights of the "owners." This means that the corporate bourgeoisie doesn't get its income from industrial profits, but from financial claims on industrial profits. This distinction helps us to bring the real goal of modern corporate activity into clearer focus.

Many popular writers on economics have argued that the goal of corporate activity is now production or sales, not profits. These formulations can't explain corporate behavior. One has only to observe what happens when commodities produced cannot be sold on the market or when the rate of profit declines as sales increase. The directors reshuffle managements, lay off the technostructure, close down unprofitable factories, strip their product lines. They show no interest in production for the sake of production—or even sales for the sake of sales.

Radicals, in turn, like to explain the manifold irrationalities of capitalism by observing that it is profits, not production, that turn the gears of modern industry. But this formulation too has now become inadequate. Just as production and sales are no longer ends in themselves, neither are industrial profits —at least for the stratum of the bourgeoisie that controls the giant corporation. Just as production must contribute to sales and sales to industrial profits, so too industrial profits must contribute to the appropriation of financial profits by the corporate oligarchs. Specifically they must contribute to the appreciation of common stock values; to increasing flows of dividends; to larger commissions for investment bankers; and to larger interest payments accruing to commercial bankers. The key point here is that the pursuit of financial profits can be partially dissociated from the pursuit of industrial profit. Dividends, for example, can be increased without a proportionate increase in industrial profits—even, perhaps, at the expense of future industrial profitability. Or a board of directors dominated by bondholders may decide upon a profit strategy designed chiefly to maximize the security of their bondholdings. Or such a board may decide that even though equity financing (common stock) is cheaper and will increase industrial profits more substantially, the corporation should pay for its expansion program by increasing its indebtedness to the interested bankers. Or the directors may decide to guide the corporation into an "unprofitable" sales agreement with another corporation because the directors have a financial interest in the other corporation. In this respect, the accumulation strategy of the modern corporation is made vastly more complex by the multiple interests of its directors and by the way they appropriate industrial profits, i.e., indirectly through the medium of securities. We must now examine these new strategies of accumulation.

III. THE MODE OF CAPITAL ACCUMULATION

HISTORICALLY, CHANGES in the *rate* of capital accumulation have had a profound effect on the *mode* of capital accumulation—the way in which profits are ploughed back and re-deployed. The shift from feudal to capitalist agriculture meant a shift by the European aristocracy from personal consumption of economic surplus to investment in fertilizers, breeding stock, etc. And in the process, the whole society was transformed. Relations between lords and serfs were changed into relations between agricultural laborers and agricultural capitalists. The same thing happened during the early manufacturing era. Acceleration of the rate of accumulation broke up guild production and changed relations between masters and journeymen into relations between capitalists and proletarians. The increase in the rate of the accumulation of the material forces of production created new social relations of production. This new social relationship crystallized in the form of *individual capital,* through which the accumulated wealth of the entrepreneur was employed reproductively through the continuous purchase of proletarian labor power and through the sale of commodities.

In the twentieth century the transformation of the joint stock company into the monopoly corporation has been accompanied by another change in the rate of accumulation. This time, however, the rate has slowed—at least for the giants operating in mature industries. As the rate of accumulation has gone down, new modes of accumulation have appeared, through which another form of capital is now evolving—*social capital.*

Defined by Marx as the "capital of directly associated individuals," social capital originates in the now familiar form of the joint stock company. It is the product of the pooling or the centralization of the individual capitals owned by the bourgeoisie. Nineteenth-century investors joined together to carry out massive undertakings—railroads, canals—enterprises whose capital requirements far exceeded the resources of any individual capitalist. If society had to wait for an individual capital to accumulate sufficiently to create the modern railroad, we might still be without them, wrote Marx.

Marx called this form of capitalist organization "the abolition of the capitalist mode of production itself." Today, as corporations like Standard Oil prepare to celebrate their hundredth anniversaries, Marx's prophecy may seem somewhat hollow. But Marx did not mean that capitalism would be destroyed by the joint stock company. He saw the joint stock company or corporation as an inherently contradictory form of organization that could only be a phase in the development of new forms of capitalist organization which would abolish competitive individual capitals. In an astonishingly prescient passage he argues that the joint stock company

> . . . establishes a *monopoly* in certain spheres and thereby requires *state interference*. It reproduces a *new financial aristocracy*, a new variety of parasites in the shape of promoters, speculators and simply nominal directors, a whole system of swindling and cheating by means of corporation promotion, stock issuance, and stock speculation. *It is private production without the control of private property.*[12] (Emphasis added.)

The socialization of capital goes hand in hand with the socialization of labor, leading inevitably to monopoly, increasing state intervention, and financial control of corporations. Eventually the processes of socialization "reach a point where they become incompatible with their capitalist integument. This integument is burst asunder. The knell of capitalist private property sounds. The expropriators are expropriated."[13]

The existence of social capital in this corporate form, along

---

12. *Capital,* vol. 3, p. 438.
13. Ibid., vol. 1, p. 763.

with the socialization of labor, provides the objective economic basis for a socialist society. But unless we recognize how social capital simultaneously supports and conflicts with the "free enterprise" capitalist system, we are unlikely to understand the tenacity with which the capitalist integument resists destruction. And until we comprehend the role social capital can play in unifying the political interests of the productive members of society, we are unlikely to make much progress in liberating social capital from its capitalist shell. For this reason it is all the more important to examine the new modes of capital accumulation through which social capital has evolved.

The Capital Transfer Process

IN THE CAPITAL TRANSFER process, a corporation operating in a low-profit industry takes its surplus value and recycles it into a corporation operating in another industry with a higher rate of profit. Capital is thus reconstituted. It serves a new social purpose, creating different commodities or services. Its potential for self-expansion is based on a different human need. This cross-industrial transfer distinguishes it from "classical" accumulation, in which surplus value was converted into capital by the entrepreneur, but the capital remained within the same firm.

This new mode of capital accumulation is typical of the mature monopolies. The railroads serve as our chief example. But the utilities industry, the largest single American industry, seems destined to follow the example set by the railroad industry. Both have monopolies or near-monopolies of given markets and are barred from overseas investment within the same industrial sphere. Further, both have comparatively low profits: in 1969 rail profits averaged between two and three per cent, those of electric power companies about eight per cent. For the *Fortune* 500, industrial profits averaged 11.3 per cent.

In the era of competition, low rates of profit could be raised by increased investment in labor-saving machinery, by taking over competitors, and by overseas investment. In the rail, telephone, and utility industries these methods are almost exhausted. Rail (freight) and telephone competition [14] are negligible; the utilities have no local competition whatsoever. Legal barriers impede territorial expansion through take-overs of neighboring utilities. Legal barriers—domestic and foreign—also hinder overseas investment. Finally, both railroads and utilities find it more difficult to raise their prices or lower their costs than do non-regulated industries. Price increases are subject to governmental regulation; cost reductions require massive investments in new technologies. These are prohibitively expensive in relation to their probable effect on profitability—especially since government regulation, weak as it is, limits spectacular increases in rates of profit. The result is that net profits cannot grow much faster than the national markets for rail, telephone and power services.

The least profitable and highly inefficient railroads are naturally most anxious to participate in the capital transfer process. While losing tens of millions of dollars yearly, Penn Central executives "diversified" into aircraft leasing services, pipelines, and real estate activities. The Missouri-Kansas-Texas, described as financially "weak" by the American Railroad Association, has invested in tugboat repair, cowhides, pumps, and packaging. The Chicago and Northwestern, another "weak" road, has sought a brighter future in whiskey, pesticides and fluorescent lights.[15]

But looking at the combined income statement and balance sheet for the seventy Class I railroads, we see that the trend away from railroading involves more than a few "badly managed" lines. Between 1963 and 1969 these companies' net

14. More and more rail companies are purchasing trucking companies, which compete only in the transport of non-bulk commodities. Telephone competition exists mainly in the production of switchboards, data sets and other terminal equipment.

15. *San Francisco Chronicle*, 15 February 1971. See also the discussion of the Chicago and Northwestern below. Presently bankrupt railroads include, in addition to the Penn Central, the Lehigh Valley, the Boston & Maine, and the Central Railroad of New Jersey. Nearly bankrupt lines include the Erie-Lackawanna, the Delaware and Hudson, the Rock Island, the Western Pacific, the Milwaukee, and Katy Industries.

WHO RULES THE CORPORATIONS?   51

TABLE 5: SOURCES AND USES OF RAIL FUNDS: 1963-1969

Year	Net railway income ($000)	Other Income ($000)	Total fixed charges ($000)	Fixed charges as percentage of total income
1963	805,658	336,079	367,970	32.3
1964	818,213	368,890	380,669	32.1
1965	961,515	365,402	400,665	30.2
1966	1,044,799	399,402	425,789	29.8
1967	676,433	457,545	460,922	31.8
1968	677,623	520,639	483,814	40.4
1969	654,669	505,267	521,345	45.0

Year	Roadway depreciation ($000)	Percentage of operating revenue	Equipment depreciation ($000)	Percentage of operating revenue
1963	161,104	1.7	507,758	5.3
1964	160,443	1.6	525,196	5.3
1965	159,516	1.6	547,063	5.4
1966	161,417	1.5	570,277	5.4
1967	160,427	1.5	595,874	5,7
1968	165,087	1.5	607,643	5.6
1969	165,445	1.4	600,358	5.2

Source: **Moody's Transportation Manual,** 1971.

profits from railroad operations decreased from $805 million to $654 million, but their net profits frᵒm non-rail operations increased nearly sixty per cent—from $336 million to $505 million. If the capital transfer movement out of railroading continues at the present rate, the "railroad" companies should be deriving most of their profits from non-rail activities by the end of 1971. (See TABLE 5).

Capital Transfers and Technological Obsolescence. Profits haven't fallen because rail transport is outmoded. Passenger trains may be empty, but forty-one per cent of all freight and by far the great mass of bulk commodities—steel, coal, petroleum—continues to be shipped by rail. New forms of transport—trucks and airplanes—have not even begun to compete for this vital segment of rail revenues. In fact, total rail revenues, as distinct from profits, have increased substantially since 1963.

Yet thanks to the capital transfer process, the railroads are starved for capital. Investment in actual road has remained almost constant since 1963, while roadway depreciation (allowances for wear and tear of capital) has actually declined as a percentage of total operating revenue. The industry averages yearly outlays of $1.2 billion for rail plant. To maintain an optimum level of efficiency, approximately $3 billion would be required. This total is unattainable due to the industry's low profitability, which puts limits on both internal and external generation of funds. The extra $1.8 billion can't be raised out of profits, for an investment of that size would wipe out the stockholders' dividends. Nor can the funds be raised externally; financial institutions won't lend for low-profit undertakings. To raise the extra $1.8 billion, one rail expert has estimated that "rails have to earn at least five per cent or $1.4 billion on their $28 billion investment." But in the years 1967–69, the railroads never earned more than $680 million. With such a low profit margin, loans are risky, and there are no opportunities for profitable "equity kickers" and other loan gimmicks beloved by financial institutions.[16]

Just how completely and irrationally the financing mechanism shapes the technology of railroading and forces capital out of the industry can be seen when we analyze the composition of the $1.2 billion yearly investment in rail plant: $900 million is spent for railroad cars, $300 million for everything else—tracks, yards, computers, etc. The $900 million is relatively easily financed through equipment trust certificates because the cars can be easily repossessed. But desperately needed computer systems cannot be repossessed so easily. Thus more and more railroad cars are purchased, but because the rails lack the proper data processing equipment, freight cars are now in profitable use only six per cent of the time. As freight car utilization goes down, so too does profit. It has been estimated that if the railroads could keep proper track of their freight cars, annual savings of $200 million could be achieved.[17]

The capital transfer movement arises, then, out of a kind of financial Catch 22. Capital isn't accumulated because of low profitability; and profits can't be raised because of low rates of accumulation. Financial institutions will lend money to railroads only to finance purchase of relatively superfluous equipment or to aid in the transfer of assets out of railroading.

This low profit potential and irrational investment policy,

16. *Fortune*, June 1969.   17. Ibid.

coming after decades of concentration and centralization of capital, is especially devastating to the system's claims to be technologically progressive. Capitalism's apologists often concede many of the system's weaknesses, only to remind their critics that "the system delivers the goods." The railroads no longer do. And the fault lies not in the technology of railroading, but in the financial control of the railroad industry.

On practical grounds, we would expect a managerially controlled railroad to respond to falling profits quite differently from the way American railroads respond. To shift capital out of railroading, into new industrial spheres, would conflict with the way in which the managers absorb surplus value: managerial income derives mainly from salaries; and salaries are not based on ownership of capital, but on business skills developed within a specific industrial sphere. Such specialties are not easily transferred across industrial lines. A top mining executive, for example, may transfer to another mining firm, but not into an unrelated industry such as retail sales. Consequently, a manager will try, as a matter of simple survival, to avoid capital transfers out of the industry in which he has developed his business skills. Similarly, instead of increasing dividends as a response to falling profits, a management-led team would be inclined to cut dividends, limit external debt, and maintain the railroad's working capital position. It would carry out these policies, not because they represent sound business practice, but to prevent control from shifting to outsiders.

Capital Transfer and Debt Transfer. The strategy of capital transfer has one drawback from the viewpoint of the financially oriented railroad director. No matter how successfully capital is transferred into new areas of industrial activity, the unprofitable husk of railroad operations remains.[18] And the railroad's debt, built up through decades of loans and equipment trust certificates, becomes more and more of a burden

18. There are of course *some* profitable railroads: these include Harriman's Union Pacific, the Southern Pacific, and the eastern coal roads.

on current rail revenues. How can the debt be transferred, along with the capital?

Northwest Industries, headed by Democratic Party financier "Sell-'em" Ben Heineman, is spearheading the move toward a solution. Heineman is held up by the liberal press as a model of the modern railroad man. His great public relations symbol is a gleaming suburban commuter train that whisks corporate executives through Chicago's old stockyards, bypassing the Chinese Wall of obscene public housing skyscrapers where inner-city blacks are imprisoned, and deposits them within walking distance of La Salle Street and Chicago's miracle mile.

The rest of Heineman's rolling stock is less impressive. Since 1964, when acquisition operations began in earnest, annual equipment maintenance expenditures have decreased from $38.7 million to $30.6 million. Freight damage along the Chicago and Northwestern's eleven thousand miles of track has risen sharply; the accident rate has doubled, along with the number of derailments. With the millions saved each year on maintenance, Heineman has been better able to take over several high-profit companies—including Velsicol Chemical, Fruit of the Loom, and the union-busting Lone Star Steel Company. Recently Northwest Industries bought a sizable percentage of the stock of B. F. Goodrich, the nation's ninetieth-largest industrial corporation. Nor have the stockholders been slighted. Despite profits of only $10.7 million since 1964, the company has paid out $51 million in dividends.

With his railroad assets picked clean and falling apart, Heineman would now like to get rid of his single bad investment—the Chicago and Northwestern Railroad—keeping only the new, high-profit operations. Consequently he has proposed selling Northwestern to its 14,500 workers. No more enthusiastic advocate of workers' control of dying industries can be found than this industrial statesman from Chicago—anything to get rid of a losing enterprise.

While the executives of the Penn Central and Northwest Industries may form the vanguard of the railroad destruction movement, the over-all level of deterioration of other railroads, especially in handling freight, is evident to shippers and government officials alike. The California produce and the food processing industries find it increasingly difficult to send goods to Eastern markets. The Corn Belt and Plains states experience similar problems moving grain eastward. These "bottlenecks" have led Secretary of Agriculture Clifford Hardin to speak of a "disastrous breakdown" in rail movement of farm products. [19] President Nixon's secretary of transportation, the ex-highway contractor John Volpe, speaks of the possibility of government take-over of some railroads. To credit Volpe with the initiative or the will to nationalize the railroads is to confuse the messenger boy with the author of the message. As syndicated Washington columnist Jack Anderson has reported, the railroads themselves are debating whether or not to ask for nationalization by the government. [20]

For decades, these same rail executives and their forebears have been arguing the superiority of the "free enterprise" American rail system over the government-owned rail systems in other capitalist countries. Now they want to present their systems to the taxpayers.

The total fixed charges accruing to banks and other financial institutions are increasing at a staggering rate. In 1966 fixed charges amounted to thirty per cent of total railway income; by 1969 fixed charges had reached forty-five per cent! A substantial amount of these charges represents the cost of simply transferring capital from one industry to another—a sort of tribute to finance capital for making possible the deterioration and shrinkage of the railway system. Finance capital, firmly in control of the United States railway system, fears that the railroads may be unable to keep up the payments on their debt. The Penn Central has gone bankrupt, making the process of debt recovery infinitely more tedious and risky; the bankers no longer have what *Forbes* magazine called a "clear shot" at the corporate treasury; [21] they are forced to work through court-appointed receivers and through a reorganization process that is sometimes difficult to control

---

19. *San Francisco Chronicle*, 1 July 1970.

20. See also "Will Big Brother Ride the Rails?," *Forbes*, 1 April 1971.

21. 15 August 1970

with precision. It is much easier simply to dump this carload of potentially bad debt on the taxpayers as a "gift" from American finance capital.

Capital Transfers and Capitalist Ideology. In the mature monopoly industries, finance capital is driven by the very logic of its self-interest towards bankruptcy and state intervention. Rail financiers like Ben Heineman naturally deny this. At an ICC hearing last year, Heineman was questioned about his willingness to keep investing in low-profit rail operations. He admitted that it was possible that a financially oriented board might starve a property, but said that doing so would be foolish: the railroad would wind up in bankruptcy and "one would lose one's total investment."[22] One could argue just as cogently against the possibility of drinking too much scotch whisky—a foolish act since the drinker ends up drunk, eventually with a hangover. Our analogy breaks down, however, since financiers like Heineman have discovered the secret of separating financial intoxication from its hangover through an ingenious process of political and legal distillation wherein Heineman gets intoxicated and the taxpayer gets the hangover.

For the first time in history, except during wartime or national emergency, industrial leaders are forced to admit that the profit motive is no longer sufficient impulse to guide the course of business in a key industry. This is a very dangerous admission. American capitalism has always sought to justify its existence on purely pragmatic grounds. "Leave us alone to make profits," the American capitalist credo says, "and we will make profits. With the profits we will hire more workers and raise wages, create newer and better commodities and services, and provide the basis of the welfare state through taxation of our profits." By admitting it is unable to accomplish its mission within the terms it defines—profitability—American finance capital raises ultimate questions about itself—questions which are sharpened when finance capital is forced to call in the state.

---

22. *Fortune*, June 1969.

When finance capital requests the state to take over rail operations, one form of social capital is being replaced by another. Finance capital is the capital belonging to corporations and individuals, employed by financial institutions according to priorities set by those institutions. State capital is the capital of the entire people, raised through taxation and employed through their representatives according to priorities that are formally subject to popular review. State capital employed in industry is in theory more democratic and a more highly developed form of social capital. But what class purpose does state capital serve?

At present, the mobilization of social capital in the form of state capital is a device to maintain the financiers' sinking fund payments. A socialist critique of the state's role in the transportation industry would question workers' taxes being used to subsidize capitalists whose private speculative investments have gone sour. A socialist critique of the railroads would involve looking at the entire transportation industry—airlines, trucking, automobile and mass transportation. It would show how the full mobilization of state capital, combined with the full participation of the working class in investment and policy planning, is the only alternative to the present prospect of ecological disaster—through the construction of more freeways, the abandonment of further sections of the railroad system, and the stagnation of mass transportation. And it would expose the major myth of capitalism, that final business decisions are made by industrial specialists, weighted with degrees and steeped in technological expertise.

Accumulation of Loan Capital

WHOLESALE DESTRUCTION of corporate capital, starvation of capital plants, and transfer and transformation of capital assets are not yet common industrial responses to falling profits. Utility companies may *wish* to diversify as the railroads have done, but legal and practical barriers prevent them from doing so. When possible, the utilities, like the railroads, prefer to take their monopoly profits and invest them elsewhere. One New Jersey basic utility company, for example, has set up a

TABLE 6: FINANCIAL DIRECTORSHIPS OF UTILITIES TRUSTEES AND DIRECTORS

CONSOLIDATED EDISON TRUSTEES

Outside directors:	Financial directorships:
E. V. Conway	chairman, Seaman's Bank for Savings National Securities and Research
John Door	none
Frederick M. Eaton	First National City Bank New York Life Insurance Co.
Grayson Kirk	Nation-wide Securities Corp. Dividend Shares Greenwich Savings Bank
Milton C. Mumford	Equitable Life Assurance Co.
J. Wilson Newman	Chemical Bank Mutual Life Insurance Company of New York Centennial Insurance Company Fidelity Union Trust
Richard S. Perkins	chairman, exec. committee, First National City Bank New York Life Insurance Co.
Richard K. Paynter	New York Life Insurance Co. Chemical Bank Seaman's Bank
William S. Renchard	chairman, Chemical Bank New York Life Insurance Co.
Lawrence A. Wien	none
James D. Wise	none
Inside directors:	
chairman and chief executive officer: Charles F. Luce	Metropolitan Life Insurance Co.
president: Louis H. Roddis Jr.	none

(continued on facing page)

holding company called National Utilities and Industries Corporation. Through the holding company, it has started a computer service subsidiary and taken control of a small airline. It is now trying to acquire companies in the fields of modular housing, vacation resorts, and appliance manufacturing. At the same time, National Utilities has begun turning away customers. The reason, according to the head of the company, interviewed in the *Wall Street Journal*,[23] is that there isn't enough natural gas available. Another reason is the difference in profit. National Utilites makes seven and a half per cent on its gas operations, but its computer business earns fifteen per cent. "For us," he said, "it was either get into some exciting new ventures or become a dull little company with no chance of keeping or attracting top people."

When they are forced to retain their industrial identities, the directors of most utility companies develop a second new strategy of capital accumulation. This new mode, typified by

23. 27 July 1970.

AMERICAN TELEPHONE AND TELEGRAPH CO. DIRECTORS

Outside directors:	Financial directorships:
William M. Batten	First National City Bank
Lloyd D. Brace	chairman, First National Bank of Boston
	John Hancock Mutual Life
Edward W. Carter	Pacific Mutual Life
	United California Bank
	Western Bancorporation
	Phoenix Insurance Co.
	Charter Oak Fire Insurance Co.
Archie K. Davis	chairman, Wachovia Bank and Trust
C. Douglas Dillon	chairman, U.S. and Foreign Securities
	partner, Dillon, Read
Edward B. Hanify	John Hancock Mutual Life Insurance Co.
	State Street Bank and Trust
	Provident Inst. for Savings
Henry T. Heald	none
J. Victor Herd	chairman, Continental Insurance Co.
	chairman, Diners Club
	Fidelity-Phoenix Insurance Co.
	Fidelity and Casualty Co., New York
	Glen Falls Insurance Co.
	American Title Insurance Co.
	Domminick Fund
	National–Ben Franklin Insurance Co.
	Commercial Insurance Co. of Newark
	Fireman's Insurance of Newark
	Boston Old Colony Insurance Co.
	Seaboard Fire and Marine Insurance Co.
	Franklin Life Insurance Co.
	Niagara Fire Insurance Co.
	Jersey Insurance Co. of New York
	Equitable Fire Insurance Co.
William A. Hewitt	Continental Illinois Bank
James R. Killian Jr.	none
J. Irwin Miller	Chemical Bank
William B. Murphy	none
Thomas F. Patton	Metropolitan Life
Monroe J. Rathbone	Prudential
Jay Taylor	First National Bank of Amarillo
Inside directorships:	
John D. de Butts	First National City Bank
Ben S. Gilmer	none
Frederick K. Kappel	Chase Manhattan Bank
	Metropolitan Life

the activities of such giants as AT&T and Consolidated Edison, involves the subordination of capital accumulation in the industrial sphere to the accumulation of finance capital, especially loan capital. The directors of these giant utilities, who are simultaneously representatives of the largest commercial banks, insurance companies and investment banking houses (see Table 6), have chosen consciously to limit expansion of telephone and power generating facilities. Since the mid-sixties, supply of these services has increasingly lagged behind demand. And in the meantime, these same directors have increased the rate of dividend payments and increased the rate of fixed (interest) charges paid out to suppliers of long-term capital, i.e., themselves. (See Table 7.)

TABLE 7: INTEREST CHARGE COVERAGE IN FORTY LARGEST UTILITIES

Company	Operating Revenues 1970 ($000,000)	Operating Income (1) 1970 ($000,000)	Interest Charges 1970 ($000,000)	Interest Charge Coverage 1970	Interest Charge Coverage 1965	Payout Ratio 1970	Payout Ratio 1965
Duke Power	386.1	68.3	51.6	1.32	3.49	.89	.60
General Public Utilities	416.8	110.1	72.2	1.52	3.12	.87	.70
El Paso Natural Gas	926.6	116.0	74.4	1.56	2.03	.66	.66
Transcontinental Gas Pipe Line	399.6	84.7	54.1	1.57	2.21	.61	.65
American Electric Power	665.7	176.6	107.2	1.65	3.40	.72	.71
Texas Eastern Transmission	652.5	119.6	70.9	1.69	2.16	.53	.59
General Tel. & Elec.	3439.2	450.9	265.4	1.70	3.29	.75	.55
Northeast Utilities	347.7	72.1	42.1	1.71	3.68	.81	.70
Tenneco	2524.7	243.7	136.9	1.78	2.21	.63	.60
American Natural Gas	565.1	100.9	55.0	1.83	2.64	.61	.60
Philadelphia Electric	504.4	107.6	58.0	1.86	3.45	.89	.75
New England Electric	323.8	60.4	32.1	1.88	2.72	.75	.75
Western Union	392.9	30.8	16.2	1.90	2.65	.61	.61
Panhandle Eastern Pipe Line	419.2	72.6	37.5	1.94	3.01	.54	.57
Public Service Elec. & Gas	741.3	144.1	73.5	1.96	2.98	.67	.62
United Utilities	496.2	81.2	41.0	1.98	2.62	.80	.68
Detroit Edison	529.3	91.0	45.8	1.99	4.72	.74	.65
Continental Telephone	372.7	82.3	41.4	1.99	2.09	.56	.37
Texas Gas Transmission	426.5	45.2	22.7	1.99	2.56	.53	.56
Commonwealth Edison	887.0	169.3	84.9	1.99	4.66	.75	.69
Consolidated Edison	1128.5	210.6	105.5	2.00	2.57	.78	.74
Niagara Mohawk Power	522.2	82.4	39.8	2.07	3.19	.74	.68
Virginia Electric Power	374.9	95.2	44.1	2.16	3.55	.62	.61
Southern Co.	738.1	171.8	79.4	2.16	2.77	.63	.66
Northern Natural Gas	516.2	94.8	42.8	2.21	2.87	.61	.64
Northern States Power	352.4	68.6	30.9	2.22	3.69	.68	.77
Columbia Gas System	822.8	128.8	57.5	2.24	2.89	.60	.62
Consumers Power	610.0	103.4	44.8	2.31	4.18	.68	.63
Middle South Utilities	450.5	100.2	43.1	2.32	3.12	.60	.56
Coastal States Gas	322.9	40.6	17.2	2.36	2.40	(2)	(2)

Southern Cal. Edison	720.7	184.8	77.6	2.38	3.13	.55	.58
Pacific Gas & Electric	1103.3	231.3	96.2	2.40	3.39	.61	.56
Peoples Gas	533.8	90.4	37.0	2.44	4.00	.56	.62
Consolidated Natural Gas	588.1	72.8	29.5	2.47	3.84	.69	.45
Florida Power & Light	416.1	97.5	38.4	2.54	3.89	.51	.50
Baltimore Gas & Electric	328.1	67.4	24.7	2.73	3.76	.65	.68
American Tel. & Tel.	16954.9	2821.7	1003.3	2.81	5.39	.65	.59
Pacific Lighting	683.5	59.8	20.8	2.88	4.07	.79	.62
Central & South West	358.4	85.0	25.5	3.33	4.47	.67	.67
Texas Utilities	453.0	120.5	35.4	3.40	4.60	.53	.58

1. Operating income is calculated after all taxes.
2. No dividends paid.

Source: **Forbes** magazine, 1 April 1971.

TABLE 8: CONSOLIDATED EDISON ACCOUNTS
AMOUNTS IN THOUSANDS

	1969	1968	1967	1966	1965	1964
Source of funds:						
Net income	127,189	128,519	122,917	110,307	111,777	100,957
Depreciation	95,915	92,459	89,792	88,259	83,561	76,835
Amortization of gas conversion costs	---	---	---	261	1,346	2,265
Sale of common stock	46,618	102,543	41,420	39,180	75,000	59,871
Sale of preferred stock	d 199	---	---	---	---	---
Sale of reacquired stock	82,400	63,748	77,734	46,785	100,000	125,000
Sale of bonds—net	67,500	d 37,000	22,000	5,000	d 47,000	52,000
Increase in short-term loans—net						
Total	419,423	350,269	353,863	289,792	324,684	416,928
Application of funds:						
Additions to plant	304,953	240,257	255,890	197,764	235,493	333,792
Common dividends	67,067	67,102	67,063	67,063	67,063	58,707
Preferred dividends	34,098	33,359	26,987	24,364	21,924	20,567
Other—net	12,405	3,551	3,923	601	204	3,862
Total	419,423	350,269	353,863	289,792	324,684	416,928

The practical impact of this mode of accumulation was felt by customers of Consolidated Edison during August 1970. As New York City temperatures reached the nineties, Con Ed announced that its generator in Queens had broken down. Power to the subways was cut; one-third of the trains were halted. The rest crawled through steaming tunnels at a top speed of eighteen miles per hour. Temperatures on the crowded platforms registered over one hundred degrees. Many commuters were overcome with heat prostration; a few suffered heart attacks and died. Of course, this was not the first nor the last breakdown during peak operating periods. About six weeks later, another heat wave found Con Ed again incapable of supplying power to New York City residents. Hundreds of thousands of people went without electricity in a failure that affected five other northeastern states as well. They were victims of what one company executive called "a fantastic coincidence."

Electrical power failures in New York City and other Eastern cities are the unintended consequences of long-range financial planning. A reading of Con Ed's income accounts (TABLE 8) will show that power failures are inevitable. Beginning in 1964, the year before the first epic blackout, Con Ed received about $100 million in net income. By 1969, net income had grown about twenty-seven per cent, to $127 million yearly. But while net income was growing at about five per cent a year, deductions from income were growing even faster. Dividend payments increased about twenty-eight per cent; payments to holders of Con Ed's long-term debt increased more than forty-five per cent—about nine per cent a year. The result is that while the amount paid to capital holders amounted to eighty-eight per cent of Con Ed's total income in 1964, by 1969 their share had reached ninety-three per cent. It is no wonder that the absolute amount spent on additions to plant *declined* nearly ten per cent between 1964 and 1969. Given increasing demand for service, and decreasing investment in facilities for producing it, New York City power failures are as natural an occurrence as the summer heat waves that precede them.

But why do the directors choose not to accumulate capital

in utility plant? The answer lies in Con Ed's rate of profit on invested capital. In the utility sphere, rising profits are greatly dependent on political institutions: on utility commissions granting rate increases, on tax assessors valuing utility property at bargain rates. In New York City the political climate has not been notably favorable. The result is that Con Ed's profits on invested capital are comparatively low and show no upward trend. This makes accumulation of capital in the industrial sphere relatively unprofitable; it makes credit harder to get and facilitates the withdrawal of industrial profits by the financing institutions whose representatives serve on the board of directors. The surplus value earned in the industrial sphere is channeled back to financial institutions where it is used as loan capital. Additional investment in utility capacity to take care of peak demand periods represents dangerous irresponsibility from the standpoint of finance capital.

Life under Con Ed, the nation's second largest public utility, is such a nightmare that many of its victims believe top management must be especially wicked or incompetent; even the business press refers to Con Ed's "management problems." But many of Con Ed's "problems" are mirrored in the performance of AT&T, the nation's largest utility. Both suffer from a seeming inability to forecast future demand and provide service during peak demand periods; both have capital structures dominated by loan capital which acts as a drag on profitability; both suffer from lack of investment in capital equipment. In New York City customers wait hours for dial tones, or are unable to get anything but busy signals when calling numbers that aren't actually busy; calls continually go astray; or are interrupted by calls coming in on the same line. The recently appointed head of New York Telephone (AT&T's largest subsidiary) acknowledges the company's lousy service, attributes the collapse to a gross underestimation of demand, and promises to "clean up" the mess.[24]

Like Con Ed, AT&T's top managers are beginning to draw

24. *Fortune*, May 1970. See the Federal Communications Commission chart rating the performance of AT&T subsidiaries, p. 266. In 1969, the FCC rated New York Telephone's performance as "poor" to "unsatisfactory" in the categories of switching, installation and maintenance.

criticism for bad management practices. "Managerial trainees are OK when they start out," charges one critic, "but after a while their heads become bell-shaped." But this is obviously too simple. Why do these top corporate officers, supposedly the best telephone heads capital can afford to hire, behave so inefficiently? The answer is that AT&T resembles Con Ed in two essential respects that help to explain its similar operational problems: its capital accumulation strategy and the composition of its board of directors. And the former is in important respects dependent on the latter. Not only are both boards heavily weighted by directors representing financial institutions, but several of the same banks and insurance companies send representatives to both boards: First National City Bank, Chemical Bank, and Metropolitan Life Insurance Company.[25] (See TABLE 6.)

---

25. Control of AT&T by financial groups was established as early as 1879. In that year, Boston financial interests led by William Saltonstall and William Forbes pushed aside inventor-president Alexander Graham Bell and demoted him to company electrician. Since then, control of the corporation passed through four stages: control by owners of a substantial majority of stock; control by the directors with a minority stock interest; control by investment bankers; and finally control by a consortium of commercial bankers, insurance executives and investment bankers. Despite the notorious history of AT&T as a corporate cockpit for competing financial interests and the continuity of tenure maintained by certain financial interests over almost the entire hundred-year history of the corporation, AT&T is often used by managerial ideologists as their prime example of managerial control and the impotence of finance capital. "At the time of his death," writes John Kenneth Galbraith, "the largest stockholder in AT&T was reportedly Billy Rose. It seems unlikely that this distinguished song writer and theatrical entrepreneur identified himself closely with the telecommunications industry or regarded himself as a force therein" (*New Industrial State* [Boston, 1967, p. 150). Galbraith would have us conclude that if the largest individual stockholder in the world's largest corporation is a trivial factor in the decision-making process, so too must the rest of the stockholders be. But speaking in terms of AT&T's largest *individual* stockholder simply shifts our attention away from the much larger AT&T stockholders who are not individuals, but financial institutions. In 1969 there were 646 of the latter. Together they held over 20 million of the corporation's 545 million shares, an amount valued by the market at approximately one billion dollars.

Another source of financial institutions' power comes from their bondholdings. Insurance companies are the major institutional holder of public utility bonds. Metropolitan, for example, in 1968 held about $250 million worth of AT&T bonds (including subsidiaries). Metropolitan is represented twice on AT&T's board, along with twenty other insurance companies.

It must be maddening for a mighty tycoon like AT&T director C. Douglas Dillon, whose words are carefully weighed in Washington, Johannesburg and Paris, to pick up his residence phone and find himself unable to speak to his Wall Street office. But it is also poetic justice. Consider how Dillon and his fellow directors have bled AT&T in the interests of capital. In 1969, AT&T earned about $2.2 billion net. Sixty per cent of this sum—$1.32 billion—was returned to the stockholders in the form of dividends. The company disbursed another billion to its creditors—chiefly insurance companies like Metropolitan, on whose board Dillon also sits. For its services, capital charged a rent of $2.32 billion, while AT&T's net income totaled "only" $2.2 billion. These staggering charges in themselves help to explain why Dillon and millions of less privileged New Yorkers keep getting busy signals when the phone on the other end isn't busy.

But the financial oligarchs who run AT&T are caught in deeper contradictions. To finance a $5.7 billion construction program, the company raised $2.5 billion in new capital from external sources—including many of the same financial institutions represented on the board. In 1970, Morgan, Stanley & Co. handled the company's $1.6 billion offering, including warrants, the largest single private bond offering in capitalist history. But even these gigantic sums seem inadequate measured against the five-year estimates of AT&T's investment needs: approximately $35 billion.

One seemingly attractive solution for a monopoly selling a vitally needed service is to raise its prices. This would increase income and provide more revenue with which to cover the investment program. But AT&T has been understandably reluctant to test the political climate by asking for really large rate increases. The worse service gets, the more consumer hostility grows and the harder it is for utility commissions to bend to Ma Bell's wishes.[26]

AT&T's directors *could* float enough bonds to take care of New York Telephone and all its other ailing subsidiaries. But it is highly unlikely that they will do so, for AT&T and its subsidiaries already account for about a quarter of *all* the corporate bonds sold in the United States. And AT&T's directors are the men who control the bond market at both ends. To let AT&T unleash all the bonds it needs on the American bond market would send prices down faster and farther than such market-makers as Morgan, Stanley; Dillon, Read; and First Boston would care to see. Nor would those AT&T directors who represent the largest *holders* of AT&T debt—insurance companies like Metropolitan, Prudential, and Equitable—care to see the prices of these bonds fall.[27] AT&T's directors have to make their decisions about the company's entry into the bond market not simply on the basis of AT&T's needs but on the basis of market conditions which affect their other flotations and the equity positions of their own financial institutions. Nor can they afford to make financial decisions based on short-term commissions for themselves. Thus, the socialized decision-making process precludes the largest corporations, by the very fact of their size, from acting independently in the financial sphere.

Accumulation of Speculative Capital

IN ANALYZING CAPITAL TRANSFER, the first new mode of accumulation, we saw how the process of reinvestment was bifurcated. Capital was not saved and reinvested in the same industry, as in the conventional mode, but was saved in the

26. Unlike the utility company's profits on its services, the financial institution's profit (interest) is not regulated by public utility commissions or other state agencies. It is simply passed along to the consumer as a necessary cost of doing business. Thus the representatives of financial institutions sitting on utility boards maximize their profits via a policy of high dividend payouts, combined with substantial external financing.

27. In 1969 life insurance companies held nearly $18 billion worth of public utility bonds and about $1.2 billion worth of utility stock (Institute of Life Insurance, *1970 Life Insurance Fact Book* [New York, n.d.]).

WHO RULES THE CORPORATIONS?   67

low-profit industry for reinvestment in the higher-profit industry. Financial institutions advance additional capital in
order to make the costly capital transfer process possible.
Essentially, they act as high-powered mediators in the conversion of industrial capital, often setting the terms of the acquisition, demanding and receiving a "piece of the action," and
winning other lucrative concessions, such as compensating
balances.[28] The capital itself, however, remains under the
formal control of the corporation that carries out the capital
transfer.

The second mode of accumulation—accumulation of loan
capital—again divides the accumulation process. Capital is
saved in the low-profit industry, then transferred to financial
institutions via dividends and finance charges. In this case, it is
the financial institution, not the corporation, that reinvests the
capital—in another industry, in government bonds, in real
estate, in other securities, or in the utility corporation itself.
These two strategies of capital accumulation are illustrated in
FIGURE 1, A and B (page 68).

In the case of accumulation of speculative capital, the final
mode we will analyze, productive reinvestment effectively
disappears from the picture. (See FIGURE 1C). The most
important source of capital is no longer the industrial corporation, but the financial institution. And the capital advanced by
financial institutions is advanced purely in order to earn financial profits, i.e., claims on profits in the form of stocks, bonds,
warrants, etc.

The typical vehicle for the accumulation of speculative
capital during the 1960s was the conglomerate corporation.
Corporate entities like Gulf and Western, LTV, AMK, and
National General are almost pure examples of this mode of
accumulation: with very little stockholder capital ten years
ago, they grew not because of productive reinvestment in
industrial capital, but because they purchased billions of dollars worth of the securities of other corporations. These purchases were made possible largely by capital advanced by
financial institutions. Conglomerate corporations maintain

28. See the Securities and Exchange Commission report released 10
March 1971.

FIG. 1: STRATEGIES OF CAPITAL ACCUMULATION

A. THE CAPITAL TRANSFER PROCESS

B. ACCUMULATION OF LOAN CAPITAL

C. ACCUMULATION OF SPECULATIVE CAPITAL

their existence only so long as they continue to generate financial profits through continued acquisitions. In many cases the conglomerator actually reverses the work of conventional accumulation. Instead of reinvesting to expand industrial capital, the conglomerator depletes industrial capital in order to create new paper values. If we examine the purpose of conglomerate acquisitions, as well as who derives profits from them, we can understand how and why the classical accumulation process is being turned inside out.

The largest of the pure conglomerates, Gulf and Western, was also the most active acquiring company of the 1960s. Between 1960 and 1968 it acquired ten corporations with assets of $50 million or more and three corporations with assets between $10 and $50 million. Gulf and Western's largest acquisition, Associates Investment Company, involved $1,582 million. If all its subsidiaries are considered, Gulf and Western has total assets amounting to $3.455 billion, making it the nation's seventeenth-largest corporation.

WHO RULES THE CORPORATIONS?   69

How did G&W accomplish such startlingly rapid growth? Testimony before the House Judiciary Committee has revealed that the Chase Manhattan Bank not only financed Gulf and Western's take-overs, but also helped choose the acquisition targets. G&W chairman Charles Bluhdorn admitted to the committee that Chase had worked closely with G&W and had "moved very quickly to make possible G&W's first major acquisition [New Jersey Zinc]." Chase officers introduced G&W to the companies seeking to be acquired, compiled fact sheets on companies or industries in which Gulf took an interest, and even sent G&W directives compelling G&W subsidiaries to throw their banking business to Chase. They also sent their vice president Roy T. Abbott to G&W, where he served as senior vice president, involved in acquisitions. At the same time, he continued to arrange Chase's financing of G&W's acquisitions. In many cases, the purpose of these acquisitions was to augment the value of securities already held in Chase's portfolio.

Despite his best efforts, Chairman Bluhdorn's testimony before the Judiciary Committee helps clarify the purpose of Gulf and Western's acquisitions:

> [Chief Committee Counsel Kenneth R. Harkins introduced a table (TABLE 9, page 70) listing G&W's abandoned transactions and the profits accruing to the company as a result.]
>
> *Mr. Harkins:* We have a table . . . entitled "Gulf & Western Abandoned Transactions. Profits."
>
> *Mr. Bluhdorn:* I have it.
>
> *Mr. Harkins:* This table sets forth profits in four of the transactions that Gulf & Western did not ultimately acquire, Armour Co., Allis-Chalmers, Pan American World Airways, and Sinclair Oil. The total profits in abandoned transactions from securities where you took a position amounts to $51,882,578 in the period between January 1, 1968, through April 17, 1969.
>
> Would you say that this indicates the profitability of taking a position in comapnies that are not acquired?
>
> *Mr. Bluhdorn:* Mr. Harkins, to begin with, these particular figures—I appreciate the committee making this up, and it certainly makes us look good from the point of

TABLE 9: GULF AND WESTERN
ABANDONED TRANSACTIONS AND PROFITS

Target company and date of transaction	Cost	Value received	Profit
Armour & Co. .... 16 Jan 1968 to 15 Oct 1968	$ 28,149,925 (1)	$ 44,400,000 (2)	$16,250,085 (3)
Allis-Chalmers Manufacturing Co. 7 May 1968 to 6 Dec 1968	117,074,000 (4)	122,080,000 (5)	5,006,000
Sinclair Oil Corp. .... 24 Oct 1968 to 4 Mar 1969	88,774,283 (6)	112,953,620 (7)	24,179,337
Pan American World Airways, Inc. January 1968 to 17 Apr 1969	10,802,844 (8)	17,250,000 (9)	6,447,156
Total profit			51,882,568

1. Cost of 77,000 Armour shares.
2. Cash received by G&W on sale of 750,000 Armour shares to General Host.
3. Plus General Host ten-year warrants to purchase 175,000 shares of General Host common at $30 per share. Profit figure does not include 20,000 Armour shares for which figures were not supplied.
4. Computed as follows: 3,000,000 shares acquired in tender offer for (1) $34,500,000 cash; (2) $25,875,000, market value on 26 July 1968 of $3,500,000 principal amount of G&W six per cent nonconvertible debentures; (3) $46,474,000, market value on 28 June 1968 of G&W warrants to purchase 2,700,000 G&W common shares. 248,000 shares acquired for (4) $7,874,000, market value on 30 Aug. 1968, of G&W warrants to purchase 496,000 shares of Gulf and Western common; (5) $2,250,000 broker fee; total, $117,074,000.
5. Computed as follows: $113,680,000 cash received on sale of 3,248,000 A–C shares to White Consolidated; plus $8,400,000, market value on 6 Dec. 1968 of 250,000 shares of White Consolidated common (discounted 20% since White shares were unregistered); total, $122,080,000.
6. Cost of 868,874 Sinclair shares. Figure includes listing costs and cost of tender offer amounting to $2,634,361.
7. Market value on 4 March 1969 of Atlantic-Richfield securities received by G&S on merger of Sinclair with Atlantic-Richfield. Figure does not include value of warrants G&W received to purchase 618,360 Atlantic-Richfield common shares at $125.
8. Cost of 450,000 Pan Am shares sold to Resorts International.
9. Value of securities received on sale of 450,000 Pan Am shares to Resorts International computed as follows: $8,000,000 cash; $9,250,000, market value on 17 April 1969 of 250,000 Resorts class A shares; total, $17,250,000. Does not include value of fifteen-year warrants received by G&W to purchase 450,000 Resorts class A shares.
Note: Number of companies in G&W's investment portfolio as of 30 April 1969—30; market value of portfolio as of 30 April 1969—$229,000,000.
Source: **Investigation of Conglomerate Corporations**, p. 110.

view of investors. I think, I must say, that perhaps it makes us look even better than we deserve to look.

If you look at Pan American World Airways, I should point out to the chairman and to the committee that while it shows this profit indicated, I would like to say that Gulf & Western still owns all of the Pan American World Airways shares that we bought, outside of the ones we sold some time back. I can tell you that if you would like to have them at our cost, without interest, I will be happy if any committee members will step forward after the session.

The Chairman [Representative Emanuel Celler]: The

sional security broker or whether you are in a general business of conducting all of these companies on a commercial, industrial basis. What is the primary purpose of your operation?

Mr. Bluhdorn: Mr. Chairman, may I say this to you, sir: Gulf & Western has assets of over $2 billion. We have said that we have 85,000 employees and sales of $1.6 billion.

Mr. Chairman, we have never said that we are a conventional company. We have said, and we believe, that what we have done all along the way has been for the purpose of building companies.

With respect to your specific question, yes, we have taken, at times, parts of our assets and have invested them in situations that we thought would be beneficial to the company and to our shareholders. We are not an investment trust. We are not a mutual fund. We have no apologies to make for the investments that we made.

In many of these cases, they were made purely for an investment point of view. We want to say here, and I want to say to you, Mr. Chairman, that our investment in Pan American, I believe, and I am glad to say in this room in Washington, D.C., we believe was made for the benefit of Pan American as well as this Nation, in which Pan American is an important entity.

The Chairman: You have a habit of being very expansive. May I have your attention, please.

Mr. Bluhdorn: I am sorry.

The Chairman: You have a habit of being very expansive on certain relations, which is all right. But I think it is not always necessary.

I would like to ask this question: You made a profit of $52 million on the acquisition of some four companies that you intended possibly to acquire and then did not acquire. In what way does that $52 million compare with the other profits that you may have made in your other operation during that period of time?

Mr. Bluhdorn: First of all, Mr. Chairman, these figures of the subcommittee are computed on a cumulative basis. But I would like to answer one other point, because you said I wander around.

May I please introduce into the record, Mr. Chairman,

the fact that companies like International Harvester, IBM, Sears, Roebuck, Procter & Gamble, Eastman Kodak, Shell Oil, General Motors, and I could go on and on, have assets of as much as 28.8 percent of their total assets invested in marketable securities.

The Chairman: That may be. I don't know whether it is wrong or right, I am just trying to get the facts; that is all.

Now, if you can answer my question, please do it. I am not condemning you for what you have done or what you have not done. I am formulating no judgment whatsoever. I want to get the facts, that is all.

Mr. Bluhdorn: I cannot answer this, Mr. Chairman, because we don't know what these figures are, per se. They are a number of transactions going over a period of time, as indicated here. So from a point of view of earnings, we have disclosed to the public very clearly what part of our earnings has come from operations and what part has come from securities. I made a speech in Boston long before anything was announced, stating that fact, Mr. Chairman.[29]

Throughout his testimony, Bluhdorn never effectively rebutted Committee Counsel Harkins' charge that Gulf and Western's corporate operations were more like those of a brokerage house than those of a productive corporation. Gulf and Western's subsidiaries may have produced some sugar, a bit of zinc, a few motion pictures, and some automotive parts. But the central Gulf and Western organization was tooled up to produce paper profits from trading in corporate securities. These financial profits accrued to Gulf and Western's stockholders and also to the stockholders in the companies G&W purchased for speculative purposes. With Chase vice president Roy Abbott installed as senior vice president at G&W, the flow of inside information furnished to Chase trust department officers afforded them excellent opportunities to augment the value of their portfolios through timely purchases of stocks on

29. *Investigation of Conglomerate Corporations: Hearings before Antitrust Subcommittee of the Committee on the Judiciary, House of Representatives, Ninety-first Congress* (Washington, 1970), part 1, pp. 105-7.

which tender offers would soon be made. A memo by Chase vice president Harold Young outlining the details of a phone conversation with Abbott shows how the process worked:

CHASE MANHATTAN MEMORANDUM TO CREDIT FILES
GULF & WESTERN INDUSTRIES, INC.[30]

Roy Abbott called to let us know that another proposed acquisition will be announced probably on Monday, April 25th. The company's name is Muntz Stereo Pak, Inc., which is in the cartridge tape business. This is the same company our Credit Company checked on recently for G&W. The acquisition, if consummated, will be for stock. The arrangement calls for a down payment of 10,000 shares of Gulf and Western Series B, preferred, and subsequent annual payments, equal to 30% of pre-tax earnings over a period of six years, aggregating 24,500 additional shares of Series B preferred. The latter shares will be priced at $175 per share. The company is presently being factored by James Talcott and has total debt of approximately $2,000,000. For its most current quarter it earned $245,000 after taxes. I suggested to Roy that he send us a brief outline of the company, including figures.

Also had a general conversation on the advisability of Gulf and Western keeping all of its banks up to date on acquisition plans. Roy, of course, fully appreciates the problems from our side of the desk at the bank and said this is certainly their objective. However he feels that this function is one which belongs to Herb Royland [senior vice president at G&W] and will discreetly cover the area with him at an early opportunity. Roy also fully appreciates the position we have taken on the proposed $15,000,000 line of credit and wants us to let him know if we do not get everything we want from Herb.

(signed)
Harold A. Young
Vice President (Chase Manhattan Bank)

A more spectacular example of the Chase-G&W credit and acquisition routine involved the attempt to take over Pan

30. Ibid., pp. 455–56.

American Airways. In the spring of 1969, with G&W playing a supporting role, Chase attempted to finance the take-over of Pan Am by a Mafia-run gambling casino known as Resorts International. The complex plan involved exchanges of various classes of common stock, cash, warrants (options on common stock) and the familiar price/earnings ratio gimmickry. Here is the story, greatly simplified: Resorts International began as Mary Carter Paint Company, a small manufacturer that had been severely penalized by the Federal Trade Commission for phony advertising ("Buy one, get one free"). Stung by this resistance to their marketing techniques, the owners decided to take their remaining cash and invest it in an enterprise untouched by the heavy hand of federal bureaucracy. They organized a gambling casino in the Bahamas and hired Mr. Eddie Allini to deal with dissatisfied customers and supervise collection of past due accounts. The casino–paint company, now known as Resorts International, prospered. As the take from the tables piled higher, the price of the former paint company's common stock rose correspondingly, from $3 to over $68 a share. Resorts International also developed a very high price/earnings ratio. And with revenues of less than $28 million Resorts International became a prize vehicle for a merger with a large company with a low p/e ratio. Pan American, which serves the Bahamas, seemed like an obvious partner.

Enter Chase Manhattan, which had been financing RI for some time. A plan was worked out to enable RI to acquire the 1.5 million shares of Pan American's stock held in Chase's trust department for various employee benefit trusts. In return, Chase received warrants to buy RI stock at an attractively low price. At about the same time, G&W, the other Chase protégé, sold its $1.8 million shares of Pan Am to Resorts International, making the casino the largest holder of Pan Am's common stock. In return G&W also received warrants to buy RI stock at bargain prices.

Chase's executives figured that the price of RI stock would probably double after the Pan Am take-over. By using their warrants to purchase RI stock, Chase stood to make approximately $150 million. Sizable profits would also accrue to RI and G&W stockholders. At the time of the transaction, Chase officials had no comment except to explain that the bank "simply made an investment decision for several fiduciary pension accounts."

The collapse of the great bull market, the extreme fall-off in Pan Am's shares, a congressional investigation of Chase's tie to G&W, together with other institutional pressures, prevented the bank from carrying out its self-imposed fiduciary assignment. But Chase's momentary willingness to hand over the main United States flag carrier to the Mafia in order to turn a paper profit encapsulates an entire historical period in the development of American finance capital.

Despite their advanced socialized form, the new modes of accumulation have a thoroughly decadent and destructive content. Unable to maintain itself profitably in the technologically mature monopoly industries, finance capital destroys them through cannibalization of their assets, disguised as "diversification." It cannot meet the financial needs of its largest utility monopoly without disorganizing its capital market, so it allows the capital plant to decay. Finally, its hunger for quick, speculative profits creates industrial monstrosities—the conglomerates—whose assets make no more pretense to industrial integration than those of a mutual fund. These debt-created, tax-propelled corporations are so weighted down with debt and so unprofitable that their collapse or at least their de-conglomeration can be confidently awaited.

The "conservative" bankers and insurance executives who supervise this new mode of capital accumulation destroy more private property through their everyday business activity than all the bomb-throwing anarchists in history. And they manage to accomplish it without even raising their voices.

Conclusion

TWO BASIC MECHANISMS underlie all three of the new modes of accumulation: the mobility of capital developed by financial institutions and the consequent emergence of an embryonic system of capitalistic planning within the nexus of financial institutions linked to the giant corporations. Given the capital hunger of a promising Xerox or Memorex, contrasted with the stodgy performance of corporations operating in mature industries, some mechanism is needed to distribute and redeploy capital according to profit potential. Out of this need has grown the socialization of the credit system throughout the United States: the credit system is massive; key branches of industry depend on it; and control over the allocation of credit is asserted by Wall Street, which regulates the rate of capital accumulation throughout the economy, retarding it in the mature industries—telephone, railroads, textiles, steel—and over-accelerating it in the newer industries—computer software, electronics, franchise foods.

Just as capitalism necessarily creates class differences and automatically polarizes wealth and poverty, finance capital extends the polarization to industry itself. At one pole—the negative pole—the credit system siphons off the assets of the mature industries, starving them for capital so that they stagnate technologically and can no longer carry out their proper functions. At the opposite pole, the newer industries, driven by the credit system into expansion beyond the limits of profitability, become "the main vehicles of crisis and swindle."[31] This polarization is not the consequence of the actions of myriad individual entrepreneurs; it is the outcome of an embryonic scheme of planning, generated by the socialization of the credit system.

The old mode of accumulation rested on the individual entrepreneur who husbanded his profits, capitalized them into productive assets, and exposed himself to risk in a competitive marketplace. In the new modes of accumulation, the individual entrepreneur has dropped out of the picture; the individual corporation itself no longer serves as the main vehicle for accumulation. The corporation—whose retained earnings provide only about one-fifth of investment needs—creates surplus value. But reallocation of surplus value—the selection of corporate investment targets—is increasingly socialized. Final investment decisions are no longer made by individual factory owners, but by finance committees composed of officers of the wholesale banks and insurance companies. And the funds

31. See *Capital*, vol. 3, chap. 27.

they commit are not their own, nor even those of their financial institutions; they are borrowed from corporations and individuals seeking an outlet for their savings.

The new modes of accumulation amount to a primitive and socially reactionary form of *planning* within capitalism itself. "Primitive" because planning is restricted to the largest corporations, because even these corporations retain considerable autonomy, and because many areas of the economy are still relatively untouched by planning—including the agricultural commodity market and the market for non-durable consumer goods. Planning under finance capital is "socially reactionary" because the objective of twentieth-century capitalist planning is in no way different from the ultimate objective of nineteenth-century capital accumulation—the enrichment of the bourgeoisie.

Nevertheless the investment decision—the key decision in a system of expanded reproduction—is no longer an individual one. Directly or indirectly, it now involves thousands of people. The active participants are the officers of commercial banks, partners in leading investment banks, insurance executives, mutual fund managers. Passive, but no less crucial, are the workers who not only provide industry with capital indirectly through their labor, but also provide it directly through their pension fund savings. Nor can the financial oligarchy itself allocate capital from the standpoint of what will benefit the individual corporation. From its monopoly position in control of society's long-term capital, it surveys the entire corporate scene in order to maximize return on its capital. The next step in the socialization of the investment system must be the transformation of its social relations: the elimination of the financial oligarchy and its replacement by committees of workers operating under the control of popular assemblies.

IV. FINANCIAL CONTROL AND THE RISE OF RECIPROCITY

THE MERGER OF FINANCE CAPITAL with industrial or "corporate" capital has retarded the rate of capital accumulation in the large mature corporations. These corporations have become more dependent for their capital on financial institutions, which increasingly dictate how capital is used. So far we have only indicated the effects of financial control on the capital accumulation process *within* large corporations. In this section, we shall analyze the consequences of financial control for relations *between* large corporations.

What kind of market behavior can we expect from these giant corporations? Their directors typically represent financial institutions and a number of their industrial allies. They may sit on the boards of a dozen or more corporations, all of which confront each other as buyers and sellers of products. How, then, will their behavior differ from that of the small nineteenth-century firm, headed by an entrepreneur with undivided interests?

Rather than making purchases and sales on the basis of traditional market factors (price, quality, and service), the giant corporation increasingly relies on reciprocity: it buys from its industrial consumers and sells to its industrial suppliers. Thus, in intercorporate relations, the forces of the market are weakening, giving way to human organization and intelligence—i.e., planning. At the same time, the networks of reciprocity in corporate America appear to parallel, and to be created by, networks of financial control. Finally, reciprocity provides the basis of yet another strategy of profit maximization—one in which the purchases and sales of a number of corporations are manipulated in order to maximize financial profits. The pursuit of this strategy feeds back into the system of production and exchange, rendering it even more chaotic and irrational. Consequently, it is in the relations between large corporations that the contradiction between the emerging social organization of production and the domination of finance capital is most clearcut.

*Intercorporate Relationships in
Traditional Economic Theory*

THE PURCHASE AND SALE of raw materials, and of capital goods, between giant corporations plays a role in the productive process as essential as the sale of finished products to their ultimate consumers. The value added by sales between corporations amounts to a *higher* percentage of GNP than does the value added by sales to households. Yet bourgeois economics has devoted little attention to these intercorporate relationships—especially the relationships between corporations within the capital goods industries. As consumers of economic surplus, rather than producers, professors and students have naturally tended to concentrate on the relationships between producers and consumers of finished products. The two-commodity, apple-and-banana illustrations so beloved by academic microeconomic theory reflect this one-sided, consumer-oriented view of the economy. So too does the typical textbook classification of intercorporate relationships as "anterior to the realm of economic analysis." [32]

To the extent that traditional microeconomics attempts to explain purchase and sales relationships between giant corporations it does so on the basis of the same assumptions that are applied to the behavior of individual consumers. It assumes (1) unambiguous maximizing behavior, and (2) the existence of a market. These assumptions are retained even by the Harvard economists who in the 1930s dropped the traditional premise of perfect competition and admitted the existence of monopoly and oligopoly. Yet to carry out traditional marginal analysis while admitting the existence of oligopoly required a further unstated assumption: that corporate directors are high-minded fellows who never act against the interests of their fellow stockholders. That is, marginalists deal with the issue of oligopoly by ignoring one simple fact of economic life: that a director who represents two corporations that buy from and sell to each other cannot possibly maximize profits for both corporations.

Take, for example, the case of Mr. John A. Mayer Jr., chairman of the board of the Mellon National Bank. Mayer sits on four boards of giant industrial corporations: General Motors, Heinz, Armco Steel and Alcoa. All four do business with each other. Alcoa sells aluminum to General Motors, Heinz and

32. C. E. Ferguson, *Microeconomic Theory* (Homewood, Illinois, 1966). p. 249.

FIG. 2: INDUSTRIAL DIRECTORSHIPS OF JOHN A. MAYER, JR.,
CHAIRMAN OF THE BOARD, MELLON NATIONAL BANK,
TOGETHER WITH BUYER-SELLER RELATIONS

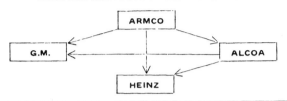

Armco; Armco sells steel to GM; Heinz buys aluminum and steel from Alcoa and Armco (see FIGURE 2). Even with the best possible intentions, how can Mayer simultaneously maximize profits for all the corporations he serves as a director? If he tries to get bargain steel for GM, he isn't maximizing for Armco, and vice versa.[33] Simultaneous maximization on intercorporate sales is an impossibility for a man who represents both companies. If this point is grasped, academic microeconomics becomes utterly untenable.

The traditional assumption of profit maximization is so out of touch with the reality of intercorporate behavior that the more worldly bourgeois economists have abandoned it alto-

33. The role of the Mellon Bank in steel pricing and industry reciprocity networks must be especially significant, given the bank's holdings and directorships in steel companies and major steel users:

Steel producers:
    United States Steel: 1 director
    Armco Steel: 1 director
    Allegheny Ludlum Steel: 3 directors, 5.1% common
    National Steel: 6.6% common
    Latrobe Steel: 2 directors
    Granite City Steel Co.: 1 director
    Jones & Laughlin Steel: 2 directors
Steel users:
    North American Rockwell: 2 directors
    TRW: 5.6% common, 1 director
    Westinghouse Airbrake: 2 directors
    General Electric: 1 director
    Mesta Machine Co.: 7.8% common
    Blaw-Knox Co.: 2 directors
    General Motors: 2 directors
    Youngstown Steel Door Co.: 1 director
    Pittsburgh Auto Equipment Co.: 15.1% common

gether. Berle and Means pointed out long ago the impossibility
of traditional maximization in intercorporate relations and
suggested that the inevitable "conflicts of interest" might be
resolved through reciprocity, i.e., through ignoring market
factors in intercorporate sales and purchases.

> The writers feel that the charge that directors are inter-
> ested on both sides of the transaction is entirely too
> loosely made in the financial community. A director,
> especially if he is an important man financially, will have
> a dozen or more interests all going at once. In many cases
> the action taken by him in one corporation is necessarily
> more or less adverse to the interests of other corporations
> in which he may be interested. Yet in a number of cases
> known to the writers, the directors have scrupulously
> ignored their own interests. The real problems arise where
> the director is an important factor in the "control" of
> two corporations at once. There, it would be almost
> beyond possibility for him not to consider the possibili-
> ties of both situations before casting a vote or inducing
> an action. Many directors are elected frankly because
> they have interests in other corporations whose activities
> may complement those of the corporation electing
> them. In other words, the corporations expect to trans-
> act business with each other or in the same field, to their
> mutual advantage, and the very duality of interest of the
> director is thus turned to the advantage of both.[34]

Baran and Sweezy, in contrast, deny that corporations move
in "communities of interest" and that outside directors with
multiple and conflicting interests control large corporations.
They argue instead that corporate interrelations are mediated
impersonally in the marketplace and that corporations are still
unambiguous maximizing units. All of this amounts to a defense of bourgeois micro-theory, which Baran and Sweezy do
not try to hide: "The appropriate general price theory for
an economy dominated by such [giant] corporations is,"
they argue, "the traditional monopoly price theory of classical
and neoclassical economics."[35] Elsewhere they assert quite

---

34. Adolph Berle and Gardner Means, *The Modern Corporation and Private Property* (New York, 1932; rev. ed. 1968), p. 205.
35. *Monopoly Capital*, p. 59.

emphatically the importance of profit maximizing to what
they consider "serious" economic theory, defining maximizing
as the firm's (whether individual or corporation makes no difference, they say) "search for the greatest *increase* in profits
which is possible in the given situation subject of course to the
elementary proviso that the exploitation of today's profit
opportunity must not ruin tomorrow's." This, they conclude,
is "all there is" to the profit maximization principle, "but it
also happens to be all that is necessary to validate the 'econo-
mizing' behavior patterns which have been the very backbone
of all serious economic theory for the last two centuries." [36]

Superficially, Baran and Sweezy's emphasis on profit maximization and the market determination of corporate relations
seems to be a defense of Marxism and an attack on the Pan-
glossian faction of managerialists who claim that since the firm
no longer maximizes profit, corporate behavior is guided by a
sense of social responsibility to its various "constituencies"—
workers, stockholders, consumers, the public as a whole, etc.

Baran and Sweezy appear to be defending Marxism because
in *Capital* Marx assumes the operation of the law of value and
maximizing behavior on the part of individual capitalism. But
such a defense of Marxism is actually tantamount to an admission of Marxism's irrelevance. Marx's contribution to political
economy did not lie simply in his discovery of the social determinism underlying what seemed to be natural market forces
determining relations between workers and capitalists. He also
argued that the system of competitive capitalism would inevitably give way to increasing concentration of the means of
production through the accumulation process. This concentration would transform capitalist private property into increasingly socialized production.[37] If after one hundred years of
concentration of production, the nineteenth-century marketplace still determined the relations between corporations, this
would be a convincing argument against Marxism, not a defense of it. And in fact the description of intercorporate relations developed by bourgeois microeconomists and reasserted

36. Ibid., p. 27.

37. *Capital*, vol. 3, p. 264; vol. 1, pp. 763–64.

by Baran and Sweezy omits almost everything we need to know about the socialization of intercorporate relationships.

Reciprocity and Market Relationships

TRADITIONAL OLIGOPOLY THEORISTS, along with Marxist managerialists, admit that the size of the market, and the extent of product differentiation, place certain constraints on the role of market forces in determining the level of prices. But they fail to acknowledge that other historical changes may have supplanted the market as the determinant of intercorporate relationships. They assert that the traditional market factors of price, quality, and service continue to determine which corporations buy and sell from each other, even though the level of prices at which they buy and sell has been influenced by corporate concentration. But consider what happens to the overall importance of the market if there is reciprocity: if corporations buy from those to whom they sell and sell to those from whom they buy. At the level of very small economic units, reciprocity would have little effect on the market. If a *Berkeley Barb* vendor buys dope from the dealer who buys his paper regularly, neither the price of underground papers nor the price of dope is likely to be very much affected. But if larger economic units are involved, the effects may be much more significant.

Consider, for example, the case of Anderson-Clayton, a large cotton export firm. It secretly bought the States-Marine steamship line and used its vessels to export cotton from the United States. Meanwhile, at the conferences that determine shipping rates, States-Marine was a firm advocate of higher rates. As charges rose throughout the steamship industry, most cotton exporters faced declining profit margins. Except, of course, for Anderson-Clayton: by relying exclusively on States-Marine for shipping service, Anderson-Clayton was able to maintain its profits, for the higher charges paid to the shipping firm were neatly recycled into the parent firm's coffers.

Not only did market forces disappear as the determinant of Anderson-Clayton's choice of a shipper, but the existence of reciprocity between Anderson-Clayton and States-Marine provided Anderson-Clayton with a new strategy for maximizing its profits at its competitors' expense. And like the strategies discussed above, reciprocity provides yet another technique through which planning can be used to divorce production from the pursuit of profit. Thus the extent and locus of reciprocal purchasing arrangements in the United States can provide an important indicator of the extent to which the role of traditional market factors has been supplanted by human organization and intelligence—the extent to which intercorporate relationships have been socialized.

Reciprocity in the United States

AS LONG AS CORPORATIONS sold only a limited number of products and as long as markets were relatively few, the opportunities for reciprocity were limited and unimportant. According to the Federal Trade Commission, systematic reciprocity existed even in the 1920s, but only with the increasing diversification and conglomerization of American industry has reciprocity become a "pervasive business practice." In a recent estimate of the extent of reciprocity in big business, a *Fortune* survey reported that sixty per cent of the five hundred largest manufacturing companies employed managers "whom they euphemistically call 'trades-relations men' and who adroitly, and more or less openly, conduct reciprocal affairs. In some industries—notably those that have long been dominated by big companies—reciprocity belongs to a traditional way of life." [38]

Another survey (TABLE 10, pages 54-55), from *Purchasing* magazine, identifies more precisely the location of reciprocity in American industry. Fifty-one per cent of the purchasing agents who responded to the survey acknowledged that reciprocity was a factor in their company's purchases and sales. But large companies were much more likely to use reciprocity than small ones. Seventy-eight per cent of all corporations with sales over $50 million acknowledged the use of reciprocity, compared to forty-six per cent of the companies with sales under $10 million. And corporations dealing with households (services and consumer goods) relied less on reciprocity

38. "A Customer Is a Company's Best Friend," *Fortune,* June 1965.

than did heavy industrial representatives. In the latter category, *all respondents* acknowledged that reciprocity was a sales factor in their firms.

Reciprocity, as memoranda from FTC dockets show, is not a simple matter of convenience. Reciprocal arrangements can and do prevail even when competitors offer better price and quality. General Tire, for example, bought enough Jones & Laughlin Steel products to demand that J&L buy General Tires, even though the quality of General's product left something to be desired. A series of memos between a Jones & Laughlin supervisor and the company's trade relations director illustrates the problem:

> Tony tells me Parrish won't give General any orders. The General tires do not hold up. He feels it would be throwing $10,000 out the window. What do we do now?

The trade relations man pushed for buying the tires anyway and received this reply:

> I talked to Tony today. The size involved at Minnesota Ore is 1800 x 25, 24 ply. The situation there is the same —they do not want General Tires. NY Ore Division doesn't want General Tires. Ontario uses them; but they get a $100 adjustment with each purchase, because the tires do not last. Aliquippa has used them, but none performed well and adjustments resulted.[39]

Finally, however, reciprocity appears to have won out over poor quality. A note to the J&L trade relations director read:

> RBC, Tony Szafranski checked today with Parrish at Minnesota Ore. In January, Minnesota Ore gave General a release for 6 tires, size 2100, approx. $13,000 value, for April delivery.[40]

39. Document no. 24 submitted in response to *subpoena duces tecum* in the matter of U.S. v. General Tire and Rubber Co., et. al., Civil No. 4-67-155 (Northern District of Ohio) (filed 1967), cited in *Economic Concentration: Hearings before the Subcommittee on Antitrust and Monopoly of the Committee on the Judiciary, United States Senate, Ninety-first Congress, First Session* (Washington, 1969), part 8A, p. 393.

40. Ibid., Document no. 22, p. 393.

The files of Cities Service provide a final example of the pervasiveness of reciprocity in the relationships between two highly concentrated industries—rubber and petroleum refining. In 1962 Cities Service made an extensive sales survey with a view toward entering the rubber-oil market. The firm found that the six largest petroleum refineries and the four leading

TABLE 10: 300 PURCHASING AGENTS

Survey

1. Is reciprocity (or trade relations) a factor in buyer-seller relations in your company?	yes no
2. In recent months, have you noticed any increase in trade relations problems because of excess capacity or declining sales?	yes no
*3. How does your company's purchasing agent assist you in soliciting business from suppliers? (a) Mention company products to suppliers (b) Provide lists of suppliers by dollar volume (c) Make calls on suppliers with company's salesmen (d) Other assistance (e) No assistance	 (a) (b) (c) (d) (e)
4. What percentage of your over-all dollar volume of sales comes from your company's suppliers?	Don't know under 1% 1 to 5% 5 to 10% 10 to 20% 20 to 30% over 30%
5. When both you and a competitor buy from a certain customer, do you think the customer's purchasing agent should divide the business he gives you in proportion to your importance as his company's customer?	yes no Don't sell to customers
6. Do you ever get involved in secondary trade relations problems (where a supplier requests business from you because he buys from one of your company's major customers)?	yes no
*7. Who handles trade relations in your company (please check the departments involved in making decisions)?	Purchasing Sales Top Management Trade Relations Dept. Others No one

* Replies add up to more than 100% because some respondents gave more than one answer.

tire manufacturers were linked by long-standing reciprocal relationships: B. F. Goodrich, for example, invariably bought its rubber oils from Gulf, not from Jersey Standard; Uniroyal bought from Texaco, not from Shell. The survey concluded that the reciprocal relationships were so tight that Cities Service—which in 1968 ranked as the nation's fifty-eighth

REPLY TO RECIPROCITY SURVEY

	By Industry								By Sales Volume			All P.A.s
Miscellaneous Non-Metallic Products	Chem., Petroleum, Other Process Industries	Iron & Steel	Services	Metal Fabricators	Construction Materials	Electrical	Consumer Goods	Less than $10 million	$10 to $50 million	Over $50 million	
%	%	%	%	%	%	%	%	%	%	%	%
68	100	100	45	56	55	44	36	46	62	78	51
32	0	0	55	44	45	56	64	54	38	22	49
50	63	69	28	37	31	41	15	20	37	52	35
50	37	31	72	63	69	59 ·	85	80	63	48	65
53	71	63	21	54	45	58	39	60	54	62	62
40	71	39	15	28	16	28	9	12	26	54	26
12	46	7.	12	22	12	6	4	14	24	11	11
15	31	15	12	10	16	2	6	2	18	20	11
28	0	23	57	33	28	24	58	38	30	14	25
17	16	7	27	9	6	6	27	8	6	30	8
22	0	8	15	36	55	28	40	32	34	4	36
33	16	0	12	26	22	40	21	30	18	18	28
5	16	15	15	17	6	10	9	6	16	6	10
10	36	15	19	3	11	8	3	8	18	18	9
3	5	15	0	4	0	4	0	2	4	4	3
10	11	40	12	5	0	4	0	4	4	20	6
70	84	76	46	58	39	52	33	56	52	58	57
20	16	22	33	27	50	40	46	24	36	34	34
10	0	0	21	15	11	8	21	20	12	8	9
40	64	38	17	22	24	16	9	20	28	41	24
60	36	62	83	78	76	84	91	80	72	59	76
48	95	70	57	54	32	58	60	56	64	72	59
40	75	62	27	38	16	40	33	30	40	50	38
58	56	62	33	66	55	60	69	72	56	38	64
12	11	15	0	3	6	2	3	2	2	8	4
7	5	7	9	1	0	0	0	0	4	10	2
28	0	0	15	4	0	6	6	4	4	2	1

Source: **Purchasing** magazine, 20 November 1961, pp. 76-77.

largest industrial corporation—would be unable to break into the market at any price:

> 1. Reciprocity dominates this market to a far greater extent than in our carbon black business.

> 2. Each of the large buyers has a favored supplier. In certain cases, this situation is so strong that it precludes entry into the market. The major market line-up follows:

CUSTOMER	SUPPLIER
B. F. Goodrich	Gulf
U.S. Rubber	Texaco
Firestone	Shell
Goodyear	Sun and Sinclair

> The Goodyear supplier line-up would appear to be the weakest of the group.

> 3. There exists general customer satisfaction with the supplier position. In no cases were we welcomed as a potential supplier with "open arms." In many interviews, we were told we would be measured on the basis of price, quality, and service.

Specifically, however, the Cities Service survey doubted this would be the case. It noted no reliance on "price, quality, and service." Instead it reported that "trade relations plays an all-important part" in the tire company purchasing program.[41]

Determinants of Reciprocity

IF SALES AND PURCHASES are governed by reciprocity, what determines reciprocity? Clearly, size and technology determine the players in the reciprocity game: only the giants generate enough sales to be allowed on the field. And the degree of industrial interdependence will determine which industries will participate most. But what determines the reciprocal pairings? Why does Goodrich buy from Gulf? Why does Uniroyal buy from Texaco?

The illegality of reciprocity makes this subject difficult to investigate. Required by anti-trust legislation to make purchasing decisions on the basis of market factors (price, service, and

---

41. Ibid., pp. 383–84.

WHO RULES THE CORPORATIONS?   89

quality), corporations are understandably reluctant to reveal exactly what reciprocal arrangements they have entered into. Their purchasing agents and trade relations men are willing to admit that reciprocity exists in principle—but refuse to divulge the specifics. Consequently, reciprocal links are typically revealed only after the fact—as the result of government indictments.

Such evidence is relatively scanty. But it does suggest that a considerable number of pairings are determined by the interrelations of finance capital itself. Frequently two corporations are reciprocity partners because they have common financial ties—especially stockholdings which are expressed through director and management interlocks and linked up ultimately to a control center in a bank or an institutionalized family fortune.

Consider the history of the relationships between DuPont, General Motors, and U.S. Rubber (now Uniroyal). Prior to 1962, when the United States Supreme Court ordered divestiture, the DuPont–Wilmington Trust group held approximately twenty-three per cent of General Motors stock. Individual DuPonts, together with family trusts, held perhaps five per cent more. In addition, there were substantial holdings in DuPont and in U.S. Rubber, neither of which were affected by the divestiture order.[42]

Sales and purchases among the three companies were coordinated so that GM bought its auto finishes and fabrics from DuPont and its tires from U.S. Rubber, while the latter purchased rayon, nylon, and synthetic rubber products from DuPont. Management interlocks were pervasive: DuPonts were board chairmen of DuPont and GM, while representatives of the Wilmington Trust sat on the boards of all three. U.S. Rubber's first president following the corporation's take-over by DuPont had begun his career at DuPont, transferred to GM, and then switched back to DuPont before being elevated to the top job at U.S. Rubber.

According to *Forbes,* U.S. Rubber functioned during this

---

42. The Temporary National Economic Committee estimated the holdings at about forty-four per cent and ten per cent respectively.

pre-1962 period as a "tradition-encrusted satrapy of the DuPonts which did little more than supply tires for what was then another DuPont preserve—General Motors." Uniroyal's president George Vila admits that prior to 1962, U.S. Rubber supplied tires to G.M. practically at cost.[43] But what interest would U.S. Rubber have in such a policy? If it were the independent profit-maximizing corporation of traditional academic theory, it would obviously follow no such course. But if we analyze pricing policy in the context of the stockholdings of the DuPont–Wilmington Trust group, we can see who profited from this non-profit transaction.

DuPont–Wilmington Trust and other family members held more than twenty-five per cent of GM's stock and ten per cent of U.S. Rubber's stock. Suppose that U.S. Rubber sells GM ten million tires a year. Each tire costs $9 to produce, and U.S. Rubber sells them to GM for $10. U.S. Rubber's total profits would amount to $10 million, the DuPont–Wilmington Trust share to $1 million. But suppose that U.S. Rubber cuts the price of the tires it sells to GM so that price just covers cost: $9. U.S. Rubber of course makes no profits, but GM saves $10 million. DuPont–Wilmington Trust holds twenty-five per cent of the GM common, so that its share of this $10 million is $2.5 million. By having U.S. Rubber lower its price and sell tires to GM at cost, the DuPont interests wind up $1.5 million ahead. Thus DuPont control of U.S. Rubber was valuable *not* because of the firm's inherent profitability but because of its contribution to DuPont's broader profit strategy. Similarly, leading DuPont family members themselves admitted that they had bought GM stock not for investment purposes but because they thought that control of GM stock would secure an important market for DuPont.

The DuPont example indicates clearly the role of outside control centers in planning contemporary intercorporate relations. Such outside intervention in purchases and sales is hardly surprising. How, in fact, could a system of giant corpo-

---

43. Since the divestiture Uniroyal's share in GM tire purchases has dropped to forty-two per cent. However, Vila says that the company now makes a profit on its GM tire sales.

WHO RULES THE CORPORATIONS?   91

rations operate any differently within a capitalist framework?
Would DuPont or any other giant corporation let its survival in
a key market be determined by competitive forces when a
simple exercise of stock power could eliminate the threat?

The answer, clearly, is no. The regularity with which giant
corporations are indicted for reciprocity is only one indication
of the pervasiveness of such relationships. Similar patterns
seem to exist in several of the industries we have examined
above: airlines and producers of aircraft, oil companies and
tanker lines, railroads and aircraft leasing companies. In all
these cases, the existence of enormous multiple corporate
holdings by financial institutions or individuals has made
nineteenth-century maximization obsolete. The new profit
strategy is far more complex, requiring coordination through
the boards of several corporations: it involves ownership of
large amounts of stock in the most profitable corporations and
small but controlling blocs in the relatively unprofitable corporations. The less profitable corporation is then induced to do a
large volume of business with the more profitable corporation.
This strategy results in higher profits than would be attained
by simply investing more and more capital in the highly profitable operation.

It may be objected that government litigation, such as that
carried out against DuPont, now prevents outside financial
interests from exercising control over sales and purchases. In
other words, reciprocity linkages aren't determined by stock
holdings, directorships, and ties to outside financial institutions. Such a possibility requires empirical investigation into
intercorporate relations, investigating whether the traditional
market factors of price, quality, and service do, in fact, determine market shares. But in the meantime, the pervasive influence of financial institutions and other outside groups on
intercorporate relations seems to provide a basis for further
investigation.

This is especially true since as giants increasingly sell to
other giants, the economic need for coordination of sales and
purchases has become manifest. The financial institutions cannot allow billion-dollar corporations to go bankrupt merely
because their product sells for a few cents more than that of

another giant. Inevitably the market becomes mere ideological grillework masking the engine of monopoly profit-making. By operating under the artificial and apologetic assumptions of bourgeois microeconomic theory, economists can only polish up the chrome a bit. The point is to rip it off.

V. FINANCE CAPITAL AND STATE CAPITAL

THE RELATIONS BETWEEN the three main forms of social capital we have been discussing—industrial capital, finance capital, and state capital—are illustrated in a beautifully compressed way by the fight for state subsidies to the supersonic transport (SST) program. Here we have the Boeing Company, representing industrial capital, struggling mightily behind its senatorial stalking-horses to fit its corporate snout in the public trough. Throughout the whole congressional debate, however, it never occurred to anyone to ask why Boeing, with its $2.6 billion assets, or General Electric Co. ($5.7 billion), the main subcontractor, didn't raise their own capital for the SST. And naturally not. Boeing and General Electric with their billions in total assets were obviously incapable of raising even the $300 million in *liquid* capital required to keep the project alive another year.[44]

The serious question conservative opponents raised was why, if the project was filled with such vast profit-making potential, wouldn't the banks touch the project? The question was posed rhetorically. Critics were familiar with Federal Aviation Agency studies showing that the SST would cost one-quarter to one-third more per seat-mile than subsonic jets. So even assuming the government could bludgeon the domestic airlines and foreign carriers into buying the high-cost monster —a doubtful proposition—the result would have been lower traffic volume across the Atlantic and higher fares, a combination that would have shrunk profits for the airline industry—an industry perilously close to bankruptcy, owing billions to big

---

44. In 1969, Boeing had $10 million in retained earnings; General Electric had $43 million.

New York banks and insurance companies. Predictably, the *Wall Street Journal* editorialized against the project.[45]

If the SST was beyond the means of industrial capital and unattractive to finance capital, one more form of social capital remained as a potential financier—state capital. Under a system dominated by finance capital, state capital performs as a kind of financial billygoat, feeding on the economic detritus whose profit potential has been eroded (rail transport) or is non-existent (SST). The power relations between the three forms emerge clearly. Industrial capital carries out few really substantial projects on its own. To undertake a big investment it must turn to finance capital or state capital. Finance capital surveys the industrial scene, supporting those corporations whose obligations offer the best potential profit. What's left is the financial province of state capital.

The rest of the congressional debate over state support to Boeing, GE, et al., centered on the issue of which was worse: the skin cancer and environmental pollution likely to be caused by the SST, or the thousands of aerospace layoffs required by cancellation of the project. This is typical of the kind of "trade-off" presented by our social order.

In this instance the trade unions lobbied for more jobs and more cancer. But it is a rare event when trade unions get a chance to participate in decisions about what is to be produced, how much and at what economic and social cost. The SST project arose as a public policy question only because banks and insurance companies decided to pass up the project.

How much longer will the American working class allow itself to be faced with similar horrendous choices? How much longer will it allow finance capital to govern the economic decision-making apparatus in civil society? How much longer will it allow its labor and savings to be used by finance capital as a weapon to beat down its standard of living, to prod its sons off to war, to destroy its homes and urban environment? To a great extent the answer depends upon how soon the working class sees a new set of alternatives. At present no concrete alternatives exist.

---

45. 22 March 1971; 16 April 1971.

Given the present mode of capital allocation, it will continue to be the case that jobs for machinists in aerospace will mean cancer for workers in the steel industry; higher wages in steel will mean higher prices for the rest of the working class; supernumerary jobs for railroad workers will mean higher prices for all goods transported by rail; truckers will be set against rail workers, aluminum workers against copper miners, etc. The American working class cannot begin to overcome these divisions without adopting a political and economic vision that transcends finance capitalism.

The New Left movement can contribute to the unification of the interests of the working class by extending its concern with the "right to make decisions that affect our lives" to include investment decisions about how economic surplus should be used. It can analyze who makes these decisions now, how they are arrived at, and whose interests are served.

In the vital theoretical work that must be carried out on these questions, we believe that the central importance of finance capital as an economic integrating mechanism, coordinating the interests of the bourgeoisie as a whole, will be clarified, along with finance capital's position as the chief political obstacle to human progress. We have faith that when the American working class has this knowledge it will begin to develop its own vision of America's socialist future and act to realize it. By seizing control of America's capital and the state, it will put them to use for the benefit of the whole world's humanity. There will be many who charge that such a seizure is tantamount to communism. If so we will have to make the most of it.

[14]

[CORRESPONDENCE]

III. "WHO RULES THE CORPORATIONS?"

James O'Connor : Robert Fitch

QUESTION: WHO RULES THE CORPORATIONS?
ANSWER: THE RULING CLASS

Introduction

BOB FITCH AND MARY OPPENHEIMER'S account of the relationship between financial and non-financial institutions in contemporary America is useful for two reasons: first, because it makes available a great deal of information previously accessible only to those willing and able to plow through recent staff reports of various congressional committees and subcommittees; second, the authors raise a number of questions about the economic significance of the relationship between banks and industrial corporations—questions that are slighted

117

or ignored in most recent Marxist economic works. Partly because of limitations of time and space and partly because only a handful of issues are really crucial to the authors' thesis, I will not try to review their entire account or take up every problem that they raise. Rather, I will consider four economic issues that might be of general interest to the American left: First, who controls the major American industrial and other non-financial corporations? Second, what are the goals of those who control the corporations? Third, what is the significance of control for investment, production, prices, and so on in any particular industry? Fourth, what is the significance of control for capital accumulation and the economy as a whole?

Who Controls the Corporations?

THE AUTHORS ARE NOT ABLE to supply a clear and unambiguous answer to the question raised in the title of their own work. The materials that they have assembled show that there exists an enormously complex set of interlocks within and between financial institutions and non-financial corporations. Their findings that financial institutions control an increasing share of the national wealth and that non-financial corporations increasingly rely on external sources of credit are indisputable. And their conclusion that "financial institutions control stock in non-financial corporations, sit on their boards, finance their activity, and take an active part in corporate affairs" is convincing.[1] But what their account fails to make clear is the actual locus of control of the great industrial corporations.

A good place to begin is to discuss the ways that Fitch and Oppenheimer use traditional Marxist theoretical categories. On the one hand, the authors refer to "bank control of corporations" and "bank influence over corporations" (1:76, 100). In other circumstances it would be nitpicking to point out that "control" and "influence" have different meanings, but in this case I believe that a basic theoretical confusion underlies the

1. Robert Fitch and Mary Oppenheimer, "Who Rules the Corporations?," part 2 (*SR* 1:5), p. 97. The three parts of this article (references to which appear in the text hereafter in the form "2:97") appeared in *Socialist Revolution*, vol. 1, numbers 4, 5, and 6.

inconsistency in language. Putting this aside for a moment, in the Marxist literature bank capital is defined as "capital invested in establishments which engage mainly in giving loans in the money form."[2] Thus, when the authors write that "banks control the corporations" it is reasonable to assume that they mean that the owners of bank capital control the corporations.

On the other hand, Fitch and Oppenheimer make a number of references to "finance capital" and "controlling financial groups." We are told that the "giant corporations [are] dominated by finance capital" and that the "social surplus . . . is controlled by the great financial institutions" (1:80; 3:44; 2:114, 77). The problem immediately arises that bank capital and finance capital have very different meanings: bank capital is owned by moneylenders who are *rentiers* pure and simple, while finance capital is owned by individuals who "are not merely rentier[s] but the head[s] of gigantic industrial-banking complexes."[3] Let us get around this problem by assuming that the authors mean "finance capital control" when they say "bank control": certainly, this assumption is consistent with their empirical studies which show the complex and interdependent nature of the relationships between financial and non-financial institutions.

Elsewhere in their work, Fitch and Oppenheimer write that "the very large corporation is almost always dominated by outsiders" (1:83). Presumably, these "outsiders" are the owners of finance capital, or at least their representatives. In still another place, we read that "the banks . . . represent—in relation to industry—the real owners of capital" (2:94). In this passage, unless "represent" is used to mean "own," the authors seem to be saying that the banks are merely the representatives of the "real owners"—that is, that the banks do not stand in an independent relation to industry. On the other hand, nowhere in their article do Fitch and Oppenheimer concede that the banks are also dominated by "outsiders." Nevertheless, they do acknowledge that the "great capitalist families" have

---

2. S. Menshikov, *Millionaires and Managers* (Moscow, 1969), p. 140. This book is an excellent empirical study of the financial and economic network of the American ruling class.

3. Menshikov, p. 15.

"merged industrial into financial capital through the trust department mechanism" and that "finance capital involves a merger of industrial and financial capital" (1:95; 2:97). Putting all of these passages together, it would seem reasonable to conclude that Fitch and Oppenheimer believe that "great capitalist families" are the "real owners" of *both* banks and industrial corporations. Put another way, the authors seem to believe that the American ruling class is composed primarily of finance or monopoly capitalists ("the heads of gigantic industrial-banking complexes"), not industrial capitalists on the one hand and bank capitalists ("merely rentiers") on the other. I am in full accord with this view.

Let us continue to explore the ways that Fitch and Oppenheimer use the categories of economic theory. In a discussion of a New York Stock Exchange rule that a company listed on the big board for the first time must have at least two "outside" directors, they write, "These requirements, and the changes in board composition that emphasize outsider participation, merely formalize existing financial relations between industrial and financial capital" (1:83). In Marxist theory, industrial capital is defined as capital in the form of raw materials, fuel, plant and equipment, labor power, etc., in industrial companies. Finance capital is a more sweeping category—it means money capital in banks and other financial institutions *plus* industrial capital. It is clear that raw materials, fuels, etc., do not have any "financial relations" with money in the bank, stocks, or bonds. The relationships between material objects are described by the laws of physics, not the laws of political economy. Consequently, when the authors say "industrial capital" they must mean "industrial capitalist" and when they say "financial capital" they must mean "financial capitalist." The question arises, why do they use the word "capital" in place of "capitalist"? The answer is that if they did not, they would be claiming that there are two kinds of capitalists, capitalists who own and/or control industrial capital, and capitalists who own and/or control financial capital. But, as we know, capitalists whose ownership is confined to money capital are not financial capitalists but bank capitalists. Bank capitalists have "financial relations" with "industrial capitalists" but it is impossible for finance capitalists to have financial or any other kind of relations with industrial capitalists precisely because they are the same people.

I want to cite one or two final examples of the author's confusing economic vocabulary. In a discussion of the rapid increase in external corporate debt during the past few years, Fitch and Oppenheimer write that "the suppliers of external finance—especially commercial and investment bankers—see the opportunity to create and profit from a speculative boom by financing takeovers" (2:82). To be consistent with the thesis that the "great capitalist families" have "merged industrial and financial capital," we would have to rewrite this passage and substitute "commercial and investment banks" for "commercial and investment bankers"—because finance capitalists cannot be described as "bankers" any more than they can be called "industrialists." In still another place, the authors claim that "conflict is built into the very nature of the relationship between financial capital and entrepreneurial or managerial capitalists" (2:85). This passage is curious because of its asymmetry: there is finance capital on the one side, and industrial and managerial capitalists on the other. Putting aside the question or what or who is a "managerial capitalist" (nowhere is the term defined and I have never run across it in either the bourgeois or Marxist economics literature), the passage is very confusing because finance capital means capital in the form of raw materials, fuel, etc., and money, while industrial capitalists are individuals who own industrial capital and who organize the production and realization of surplus value. Thus, the authors tell us that material objects (finance capital) oppose living individuals (industrial capitalists), a strange kind of conflict indeed.[4]

---

4. If Fitch and Oppenheimer fail to supply a clear answer to the question, "Who rules the corporations?" (as we have seen, at times they seem to say that bankers control industrial capital and at other times that finance capitalists control industry), they do succeed in explaining who *doesn't* control industrial corporations. In fact, they go to great lengths to dispute the managerial revolution thesis. Despite the fact that I am inaccurately described as a "Marxist managerialist," I wish to make only one or two comments on this subject (the *Monthly Review* article that Fitch and Oppenheimer cite was speculative in nature and designed more

122   JAMES O'CONNOR

AT THIS POINT, let us leave off our examination of Fitch and
Oppenheimer's economics vocabulary and reconsider the precise meaning of the word "capitalist." A capitalist is an individual who owns money capital (money over and above consumption needs) in sufficient quantities to buy labor power
plus the requisite raw materials, equipment, fuels, and so on.
Labor power is not purchased for any services rendered directly to the capitalist, but in order to produce tangible or in-
tangible objects for sale in the market. The capitalist makes a
profit if the exchange value of labor power (wages) is less than
the exchange value of the product of labor power (commodity
prices). In terms of the labor time expended in production in
relation to the labor time that the capitalist can command as a
result of the sale of the commodity, this is called surplus value.
In terms of money itself, it is called profit. Capitalists thus
depend for their material survival on their ability (*a*) to organize production in such a way that surplus value can be *produced* and *realized,* and (*b*) to organize the financing of pro-

---

to raise questions than provide hard answers—but far from accepting the
managerial revolution thesis, I refer to the "'corporate capitalist' who
necessarily combines and synthesizes the motives of the merchant, industrialist and banker"). The reason is that I believe that Fitch and Oppenheimer are attacking a straw man. To my knowledge, there are no Marxist economists who seriously believe that managers of industry have
wrested control from the large owners and exercise that control (for
more than a short time, anyway) in their own special interests. Although
Paul Sweezy can defend *Monopoly Capital* far better than I can, I cannot
help remarking that I think it is a pity that in their rush to "prove" some
new "thesis" Fitch and Oppenheimer have to lump Baran and Sweezy's
seminal work with the stupid and apologetic doctrines of the bourgeois
managerial revolution theorists. The heart of *Monopoly Capital* is the
theory of the generation and absorption of the "economic surplus." Nowhere do Fitch and Oppenheimer even begin to come to grips with this
theory. More, the authors claim that Baran and Sweezy "accept the factual premises of simplistic managerialism" (1:86)—by which they mean
the idea that there is a separation of ownership from management arising
from the wide dispersion of stock ownership, and hence an independent
managerial class that functions more or less autonomously. Without going
into the pros and cons of Baran and Sweezy's own thesis, I would like
to recall that these authors write of "the *combined* power of management and the *very rich:* the *two* are in fact *integrated* into a harmonious
interest group at the top of the economic pyramid" (*Monopoly Capital*
[New York, 1966], p. 37, emphasis added). This is hardly the "factual
premise of simplistic managerialism."

duction in such a way that they can *appropriate* the surplus value for themselves. For example, if an industrial capitalist organizes the production and realization of surplus value in some particular branch of the economy, but if all of the surplus value (in its money form, profits) is owed to a bank capitalist, then it is the banker who appropriates the surplus value, not the industrialist. In the event that the industrial capitalist is unable to win financial freedom from the banker, sooner or later he will be reduced to the status of hired manager. In this process, the bank capitalist is at first exclusively preoccupied with the problem of appropriating surplus value (that is, the problem of finance). At a certain point, however, the industry's loan/asset ratio reaches a level and the bank capitalist must concern himself more and more with the problem of producing and realizing surplus value (that is, the problem of production and sales). At this point, the owner of the bank ceases to be a bank capitalist ("merely a rentier") and transforms himself into a finance capitalist ("head of an industrial-banking complex ").

Workers can produce surplus value in two ways: Marx called these absolute surplus value and relative surplus value. Surplus value that is produced by cutting wages or keeping wages low or by forcing workers to work harder or longer at the same wage rate is called absolute surplus value. It is obvious that a capitalist cannot accumulate great wealth by appropriating absolute surplus alone. A wage cut, speed-up, or stretch-out enriches a capitalist only to the degree that the capitalist can sweat a few extra minutes of labor power out of the workers. Surplus value that is produced by equipping workers with more and better tools or by exploiting their scientific, technical and administrative know-how in production is called relative surplus value. The great capitalist wealth today (and the great wealth of advanced capitalist societies as a whole) has its roots in relative surplus value, or labor productivity.[5]

5. Although this formulation is sufficient for our immediate purposes, a number of other factors have to be taken into account in a full analysis of the contemporary capitalist class. For one thing, the production of relative surplus value and the development of monopoly production go hand in hand. Thus, profits are made up not only of relative surplus value

Let us consider next the ways in which surplus value is
appropriated. As Fitch and Oppenheimer write, the ruling class
draws its income not from industrial profits per se, but rather
from the financial claims on industrial profits (3:43). The
major financial instruments are bonds and stocks—these represent the chief claims on surplus value in the money form.
Owners of stocks and bonds appropriate surplus value *directly*
—that is, they acquire unpaid labor power directly from the
workers in the form of profits.[6] The question arises, who owns
the stocks and bonds? In the family-owned, family-managed
company the answer to this question is in principle simple. The
individuals who organize the production and realization of

---

in the money form but also of monopoly profit per se. To my knowledge,
there is no way of statistically breaking down capitalist income into these
two components. Secondly, the contemporary ruling class bases itself in
part on the production of absolute surplus value at home and abroad
(for example, sweatshops in the competitive sector of the home economy
controlled by monopoly capital, on the one hand, and branch plants of
the giant corporation located in foreign "cheap labor havens" on the
other). Again, I do not think that there is any way to separate empirically
capitalist income drawn from relative surplus value, from income drawn
from absolute surplus value. Finally, capitalists can organize the production of both absolute and relative surplus value *simultaneously.* For example, if worker productivity is measured by an index of 100, and if a
worker is forced to increase the intensity of his work by 10 per cent,
surplus value increases by 10. If his productivity is an index of 1000,
surplus value increases by 100. The point is, however, that in the long run
there are definite limits to the production of absolute surplus value, as
the monopoly capitalist class and capitalist governments have realized for
many decades. These and other issues related to the analysis of the contemporary capitalist class are taken up in detail in a work in progress pro-
visionally titled *Capitalism: An Introduction to Political Economy* (St.
Martin's Press).

6. The state also has financial claims on the corporation (and the working class) in the form of the corporate income tax (and the individual
income withholding tax). The state appropriates surplus value via taxation, and subsequently channels the surplus value to state contractors
and other capitalists who depend in whole or in part on particular state
budgetary expenditures, such as water investments, education and transportation facilities, and so on. State contractors and others thus appropriate surplus value *indirectly*—that is, their dependence on the working
class for their wealth and power is indirect. Put another way, they depend on the power elite (or political rulers) who mediate between the
working class and capitalist class. I will not explore this relationship at
this time (and mention it only in passing) because Fitch and Oppenheimer by an large skirt the whole problem of state capitalism.

surplus value are precisely the same individuals who own the financial claims on surplus value. Today, however, as Fitch and Oppenheimer demonstrate, financial claims on surplus value are owned not only by wealthy capitalists in their own name. These claims are also owned and/or controlled by owners of commercial banks holding corporate bonds and stocks (the latter in their trust departments), investment banks, insurance companies, mutual and pension funds, and other financial institutions. Why and how the financial institutions, especially non-commercial bank financial intermediaries, have attained such a commanding position is a complex story. In brief, there has been a tremendous increase in the demand for loans and money capital by consumers, business, and the state. At the same time, there has been a large increase in the supply of savings and money capital by both financial and non-financial companies and by the working class. Working-class savings increasingly have been mobilized by financial institutions, which are able to provide the liquidity and security sought by the typical small saver.

Finally, the question arises, if the financial claims on surplus value in the typical industrial corporation are no longer owned by the industrial capitalist per se, who does own these claims? That is, who owns and/or controls the financial institutions? At the turn of the century, most major industrial corporations were closely held by the financial giants of the day. The industrial corporation was a relatively new device and there was little or no widespread ownership of stock. John Moody in his classic study of the "masters of capital" estimated that the Rockefeller and Morgan groups shared ownership and control of corporate empires in excess of $20 billion, or about one-fifth of the national wealth at that time. Today, as we suggested above, these same groups of capitalists, together with a number of others, exercise control of the financial institutions. This is demonstrated beyond all shadow of a doubt by Menshikov in *Millionaires and Managers.*[7] Industrialists have become "bankers" in order to mobilize capital from the population as a whole and in order to insure that they participate fully in the

7. Chapter 6.

appropriation of surplus value. And bankers have become "in-dustrialists" because they realize that in the long run their financial claims are worthless unless surplus value is produced and realized in industry on a continuous basis. By and large, the same people organize the production and realization of surplus value and the appropriation of surplus value. Although financial and non-financial companies are formally separate, the American ruling class does not consist of "bankers" on the one hand and "industrialists" on the other. Rather, the domi-nant stratum of this class is made up of rich capitalists who own and/or control both kinds of institutions. This class puts a large share of its stockholdings in trust, and the managers of their banks represent these holdings in their role of fiduciaries. In turn, their industrial corporate managers deposit corporate funds in the same banks (Fitch and Oppenheimer neglect to point out that about seventy per cent of total demand deposits consist of roughly a hundred thousand corporate accounts amounting to over $100,000 each). To insure that their operat-ing companies have access to sufficient money capital, most large corporations are given preferential positions in the "capi-tal market." To insure that the broad experience of top bank managers is available to their operating companies (and to in-sure against "inside" managers feathering their own nests at the expense of financial capitalists), these managers serve as directors of non-financial corporations. And to insure maxi-mum coordination between industry and banking, the presi-dents and chairmen of the boards of directors of the industrial companies serve as directors of the big banks. The production and realization of surplus value requires that industrial com-panies are run efficiently and profitably; but the appropriation of surplus value requires that bank representatives stand at the beginning and the end of the classic process—M–C–M'.

The Goals of Monopoly Capitalists

WHAT GOALS WILL FINANCIAL INSTITUTIONS holding finan-cial claims on surplus value in the form of stocks and bonds adopt? In principle this question has a clear-cut answer in the event that there are two groups of people, one holding corpo-rate debt and the other holding corporate equities. For the group or institution holding equities, interest charges on loans (both working capital loans and bonds) add to costs. For the group holding corporate debt, interest charges add to income or revenues. It is obvious that the level of interest rates is a source of potential or real conflict between the two groups (just as interest rates divided the old-fashioned banker and industrialist years ago and continue to divide the small businessman and finance capitalist today). More, conflicts that reach well beyond the question of interest charges can arise (and have arisen) between debt holders and equity holders. For example, decades ago American bankers were preoccupied with the financial side of overseas economic expansion and actively sought the cooperation of other capitalist powers with the aim of expanding world trade as a whole. On the other hand, independent industrialists were interested mainly in expanding their own exports, not world trade.

Today, most conflict between financial and non-financial companies is confined to those sectors of the economy that are poorly integrated into the dominant monopoly capitalist empires. The integration of industrial and bank capital in most large-scale industry has muted or eliminated conflicts arising from interest charges. This special kind of vertical integration also has helped to create a more or less uniform view within the ruling class as a whole over the questions of foreign trade and investment, tariff policy, and related matters.[8] In short, the fact that every monopoly capitalist group and most of their financial institutions hold or control *both* corporate equities and debt instruments means that the "conflict" between "bankers" and "entrepreneurs" (or industrial capitalists) that dominates Fitch and Oppenheimer's world view is largely a figment of their imagination.[9]

What then are the motives of the monopoly capitalists or finance capitalists? What goals do they seek? How do they

8. It is true that the ruling class wants to exempt certain industries (e.g., steel) from its "free trade" programs and policies.

9. For example, see part 2, p. 85. The authors cite the split in the Republican Party as evidence of the "conflict" between "bankers" and "industrialists." They write that the split "pits the Eastern financial establishment led by the Rockefeller–Lodge–Scranton axis against their regional and entrepreneurial capitalist enemies like California's Henry

harmonize their short-term and long-term aims? How and why do they decide to appropriate surplus value in the particular ways that they do? What kind of trade-offs are they faced with? As these questions suggest, and as Fitch and Oppenheimer recognize' (3:46), the issue is enormously complex. Moreover, there is very little analysis of the subject in either the bourgeois or Marxist economic literature.

Unfortunately, Fitch and Oppenheimer's own thoughts on the subject are not very enlightening. They begin with the claim that "just as production and sales are no longer ends in themselves, neither are industrial profits—at least for the stratum of the bourgeoisie that controls the giant corporation" (3:46). But in no stage of capitalist development were "production and sales . . . ends in themselves." They have always been the means to the end of profits. The authors continue to say that "the key point . . . is that the pursuit of financial profits can be partially dissociated from the pursuit of industrial profit. Dividends, for example, can be increased without a proportionate increase in industrial profits—even, perhaps, at the expense of future industrial profitability." There is no question that dividends "*can* be increased" without an increase in industrial profits, but the authors do not tell us why or under what conditions finance capitalists will in fact increase dividends. More so-called examples of the dissociation of financial and industrial profits follow: "Or the board of directors dominated by bondholders may decide upon a profit strategy designed chiefly to maximize the security of their bondholdings. Or such a board may decide that even though equity

Salvatori, South Carolina's Milliken family, and the scores of Texas and California oil millionaires without sizable foreign holdings" (2:95–96). Although there is always some conflict between the main body of financial capitalists and new upstarts, Menshikov writes that "analysis of forty-nine of the new fortunes shows that only seven have served as a basis for creating new independent financial groups [and that] the prevailing tendency is the readiness of the new plutocracy to join the existing system of the financial oligarchy" (p. 68). In my view, the split is explicable mainly in terms of the conflicts between capitalists whose wealth depends mainly on the appropriation of surplus value *directly* (e.g., Rockefeller) on the one hand, and capitalists who appropriate surplus value *indirectly* via the state budget (e.g., "ultra-rightists" such as Melvin Laird, cited by Fitch and Oppenheimer as a leading member of the right-wing branch of the party) on the other.

financing (common stock) is cheaper and will increase industrial profits more substantially, the corporation should pay, for its expansion program by increasing its indebtedness to the interested bankers. Or the directors may decide to guide the corporation into an 'unprofitable' sales agreement with another corporation because the directors have a financial interest in the other corporation" (3:46).

Let us consider these three points in the order presented by the authors. In the first place, as Gabriel Kolko and other historians have shown, stability, predictability, and security always have figured importantly in corporate decision-making in America. And in economic theory, the standard "textbook entrepreneur" devotes considerable attention to the problem of minimizing risk and uncertainty. Clearly, if bondholders seek maximum security for their bondholdings, they will avoid any policy that might impair "future industrial profitability." On the contrary, they will strive for maximum security of *industrial* profits. Fitch and Oppenheimer's second example is not an example of *finance* capitalist control of industrial corporations, but rather of *bank* capitalist control. If bankers controlled the black pieces on the chessboard of American capitalism, and industrialists controlled the white pieces, under certain circumstances bankers might drive a corporation into increasing indebtedness "even though equity financing is cheaper." But, as we have seen, finance capitalists control both the black and white pieces. Finally, there is no question that directors who have financial interests in more than one corporation may "guide [one] corporation into an 'unprofitable' sales agreement with another corporation." In principle, this is hardly a novel situation: in every large corporation, the directors at one time or another "guide" one *branch* of the corporation into "'unprofitable'" agreements with other branches. But this does not prove that the directors are not interested in industrial profits. The example merely suggests that finance capitalists are less interested in industrial profits in any particular corporation making up part of their empire than in industrial profits in the empire as a whole.

The authors' attempt to contrast corporate decision-making in managerially controlled companies and finance capitalist-controlled companies is also a failure. "On practical grounds," they write, "we would expect a managerially controlled railroad to respond to falling profits quite differently from the way American railroads respond. To shift capital out of railroading, into new industrial spheres, would conflict with the way in which managers absorb surplus value: managerial income derives mainly from salaries; and salaries are not based on ownership of capital, but on business skills developed within a specific industrial sphere. . . . Consequently, a manager will try, as a matter of simple survival, to avoid capital transfers out of the industry in which he has developed his business skills" (3:53). True, top management receives income partly in the form of salaries, and the source of most of its income is surplus value produced by workers, technicians, and lower management at the operating level. It is clear that salaries in excess of, say, $50,000 annually far exceed the exchange value of managerial labor power. But few corporations today recruit top management exclusively from within the corporation, or even from other companies in the same industry. Modern business management is extremely flexible, and "management teams" move from company to company and industry to industry applying the same systems approaches to every aspect of corporate affairs from purchasing to marketing. It follows that modern management has every interest in expanding surplus value in *any* line of business that offers opportunities for maximum profits.

I DO NOT CLAIM TO HAVE a final answer to the question of the goals of the monopoly capitalists. The remarks that follow are thus meant to be suggestive, not definitive. In the first place, it is clear that as money lenders and bond holders, finance capitalists favor high interest rates. It is equally clear that as stockholders in industrial firms, finance capitalists must be devoted to maximum productivity consistent with maximum industrial profits. Further, as "industrialists" capitalists favor low interest rates—everything else being equal—because interest charges are a cost item. I believe that a case can be made that their industrial interests normally take precedence over their banking interests. As "industrial capitalists" they seek to organize the production and realization of maximum surplus value; as "bankers" they seek to appropriate as much surplus value as possible. But surplus value that is not produced cannot be appropriated.[10] Thus, although at first glance it appears that finance capitalists have conflicting interests, in fact they do not.

Next, let us return to the original distinction between absolute and relative surplus value. A century ago absolute surplus value was a relatively more important source of profit than it is today. When capital was predominantly in the form of unskilled labor power and primitive machinery, capitalists who organized the production of surplus value depended upon a sweated, low-paid work force.[11] At the time, the idea that high and increasing productivity was the secret of industrial wealth was comparatively novel: the prototype was the American steel industry before Carnegie rationalized the entire work process from beginning to end. In the absolute surplus value stage of capitalist development, there was one certain way to become very rich and powerful. The first step was to acquire as many financial claims on surplus value as possible; the second step was to drive up the price of these claims well beyond

10. It should be clear at this point that the Fitch-Oppenheimer analysis of the relationship between financial and non-financial institutions (and any similar analysis) complements, not substitutes for, Baran and Sweezy's analysis of the industrial economy in *Monopoly Capital*. Baran and Sweezy are concerned with the creation and absorption of the "economic surplus"—in other words, the production and realization of surplus value. Fitch and Oppenheimer are chiefly concerned with the appropriation of surplus value that already has been produced and realized. To be sure, Baran and Sweezy concentrate their fire on the ways that surplus value is realized (e.g., via the "sales effort"). But Fitch and Oppenheimer are silent on *both* the question of the work process (i.e., surplus value production) and the problem of marketing and sales (i.e., surplus value realization).

11. The American ruling class skillfully synthesizes the two modes of surplus value production. Domestic skilled labor was used to build up a highly productive industrial complex; immigrant labor was used to keep wages low and working conditions poor. The steel industry under Carnegie pushed unit costs so low that one European observer christened the industry "the eighth wonder of the world." The industry was so efficient because Carnegie simultaneously introduced the most modern plant and equipment and the most oppressive kind of labor relations, keeping labor productivity up and wages low.

the actual exchange value of existing plant and equipment. Put another way, getting wealthy meant promoting industrial mergers and acquisitions, watering the stock, speculating in stock, developing the fine points of "insider" trading, and so on. One consequence of all this activity was the frequent neglect of physical plant and equipment, administration and management within the industrial firm, and other productive features of the victimized company. But whether or not productivity was impaired by financial wheelings and dealings was a matter of relative indifference to the early speculator, in part because productivity and the total volume of surplus value was small in absolute terms and in part because the individual speculator had few if any *institutional* or *class* interests.

Today, the great mass of surplus value is relative surplus value. Modern industrial production is highly complex, machinery is very advanced, production techniques are scientific, and labor power is relatively skilled. In contemporary capitalism, not only is it possible to become very rich by organizing the production, realization, and appropriation of relative surplus value (without having to engage in potentially destructive speculation), but also no financial capitalist group in its right mind would engage in any activity that might have ruinous consequences for the productivity of its profitable enterprises. The volume of surplus value is too great and there is too much at stake. I hasten to say that it is still possible to become very wealthy by financial speculation—many if not most of the new oil, saving and loan, real estate, and other millionaires got where they are today by buying and selling real property and financial claims on this property.[12] I also hasten to add that I realize that stock prices have tended to rise considerably faster than the increase in total production (to a large degree because pension funds, mutual funds, insurance companies, etc., have mobilized masses of working-class savings and channeled these savings into the stock market, driving up prices).

12. I agree with Fitch and Oppenheimer when they write that "a final reason for the fantastic increase in external debt is this: the suppliers of external finance . . . see the opportunity to create and profit from a speculative boom by financing take-overs" (2:82). What I disagree with is the authors' claim that "suppliers of external finance" are so preoccupied with speculation that they neglect industrial productivity and profits.

My only point is that in the old days stock speculation was the only way to get really rich (putting aside traditional mercantile and real estate activity)—and a man got rich by riding the ups and downs in the stock market, ups and downs created by trading on inside information, watering stock, rumors, etc. Today, most stock trading consists of buying and selling *between* the large financial institutions—a very closed community, as Fitch and Oppenheimer imply throughout their work—institutions that have every reason in the world to keep speculation under control. Precisely because financial claims on surplus value are concentrated in a handful of giant financial institutions, it becomes more and more difficult to unload large amounts of stock at *any* price in a falling market. Thus, for example, during the stock exchange "crisis" of 1962, the mutual funds stayed out of the market and refrained from selling large amounts of stock, which buoyed up the market and helped to prevent a bust.

Fitch and Oppenheimer no doubt would be quick to reject the lines of analysis presented above, not to speak of my criticisms of their own analysis. Even in an epoch when productivity is the key to secure wealth and power, they believe that "finance capital" control is used to milk industrial profits—that is, to appropriate industrial profits at the expense of productive capacity and efficiency. In some passages, they express their views as certainties: "Unable to maintain itself profitably in the technologically mature monopoly industries, finance capital destroys them through cannibalization of their assets, disguised as 'diversification'" (2:72)[13] In other passages, they

---

13. See also the discussion of a takeover attempt of Collins Radio, pp. 65–66. "Technologically mature industries" is another curious economic category employed by the authors. If the expression means that technical progress has slowed down or come to a stop because of strictly scientific of technological limits to further progress (e.g., efficient steam engines were not possible until metal-working techniques reached a relatively advanced state), it is difficult to see why the authors label the railroads as "technologically mature." The reason is that they try to show that the backwardness of railroad plant and equipment is attributable to financial rip-offs of the railroads by the banks. If the expression means that technical progress has slowed down because market demand is stagnant or rises slowly, the authors would have to give their game up, precisely because they could not argue subsequently that the railroads do not really

hedge their bets: for example, they refer to corporations with external debt as being "forced into potentially ruinous indebtedness" (3:75). Whatever the degree of certainty with which the authors hold these views, they do try to support them with factual materials drawn from the transportation, communications, electrical power, and other industries. Thus, even though I have tried to explain why I reject most of their theoretical analysis, I still am obliged to consider their evidence and examples.

THE AUTHORS DEVOTE more attention to the Penn Central case than to any other firm or industry. Because it is impossible in a review to explore every important aspect of the relationship between the directors of Penn Central and the New York finance capitalists, I will confine my comments to one crucial question: as Fitch and Oppenheimer show, Penn Central has neglected to modernize its rail facilities and has engaged in a diversification program that itself has turned out to be quite unprofitable. The question is, did the directors of Penn Central neglect its productive facilities because the railroad could not *afford* a modernization program—that is, because the line was overextended financially as a result of heavy borrowing to finance the diversification program, as Fitch and Oppenheimer claim? Or can the neglect be attributed to the unprofitability of the railroad business *independent of the relationship between Penn Central and the financial institutions,* as I believe? The question is not whether or not the railroad was saddled with a big debt, but rather the underlying causes of the neglect. The first question that must be cleared up is the difference between "economic efficiency" and "technical efficiency." Neglect of physical facilities is not necessarily a sign of economic inefficiency: for example, New England is covered with abandoned textile mills that proved to be unprofitable from an economic point of view, even though they were efficient from an engineering point of view. The owners of

face a declining market, but rather are the victims of a group of predatory bankers seeking to milk the industry dry. Finally, if the expression means "fully automated," the railroad, utilities, and so on could hardly be called "technologically mature."

WHO RULES THE CORPORATIONS?   135

the mills abandoned them because labor costs were too high. Similarly, finance capitalists "abandoned" the railroads because labor costs and other operating expenses were too high in comparison with revenues. And to a large degree, the diversification programs of the railroads (and utilities) were the rational response of rational capitalists seeking the highest return on their capital.

At times, Fitch and Oppenheimer come close to recognizing this: at one place, they write that the Penn Central directors "saw the railroad as a dying man whose vital organs could be transplanted to other, more promising patients" (2:112). On the other hand, they insist that "profits haven't fallen because rail transport is outmoded. Passenger trains may be empty, but forty-one per cent of all freight and by far the great mass of bulk commodities—steel, coal, petroleum—continue to be shipped by rail. New forms of transport—trucks and airplanes—have not even begun to compete for this vital segment of rail revenues. In fact, total rail revenues, as distinct from profits, have increased substantially since 1963. Yet thanks to the [diversification program], the railroads are starved for capital" (3:51). This passage contains the sum and substance of Fitch and Oppenheimer's claim that the railroads remain a viable private investment—if only the banks would stop ripping them off. However, a close examination of their argument reveals that their claim is unfounded. In the first place, the authors neglect to mention that the volume of rail profits has gone down not only because interest charges have risen but also because wage and other operating costs have gone up. Second, they fail to discuss the relationship between the railroads and the Interstate Commerce Commission. In 1951, the ICC refused to relieve the railroads from umbrella rate-making practices designed to protect the traffic of rival carriers. In effect, the ICC told the railroads that they were forbidden to compete with water and other carriers. The Transportation Act of 1958 granted the roads a small measure of relief, and railroad rates subsequently declined. The average cost of shipping freight by rail fell by about fifteen per cent. Despite the relief, rail traffic declined in comparison with water, truck, and air traffic—stabilizing in 1962 at about forty-three per cent of total ton miles (down from more than seventy-five per cent in 1926). It is an open question whether or not rail traffic would rise significantly if the ICC permitted the roads to cut their rates even more. Third, although Fitch and Oppenheimer claim that "new forms of transport . . . have not even begun to compete for [the bulk commodity business]," the fact is that the railroads transport no natural gas, which to a large degree has replaced coal and other fuels that rails used to handle. To be sure, the railroads' share of total tonnage over years has declined less than railroad revenues, precisely because the roads retain *low value* bulk commodities. Finally, the *rate* of profit in railroading (in contrast to the volume of profits) actually *rose* during most of the 1960s—jumping from 1.97 per cent in 1961 to 3 per cent in 1967, chiefly as a result of the rate reductions. Nevertheless, finance capitalists believed (in most cases accurately) that higher rates of return were available elsewhere. In point of fact, the unprofitability of railroad investments explains why the roads have been nationalized in nearly every country in the world—a fact that the authors forgot to include in their account.[14]

Fitch and Oppenheimer subsequently turn their attention to the two great utilities—AT&T and Consolidated Edison. Nowhere do the authors suggest that the "bankers" actually have allowed the utilities' physical facilities to deteriorate. But they do write that "the directors of these giant utilities, who are simultaneously representatives of the largest commercial banks, insurance companies and investment banking houses, have chosen consciously to limit expansion of telephone and power generating facilities. Since the mid-sixties, supply of these services has increasingly lagged behind demand" (3:59). Immediately, we wonder what possible motive finance capitalists have for short-changing a corporation (AT&T) that pro-

---

14. In fairness, it should be pointed out that the Bureau of Accounts of the ICC has warned that potential abuses in railroad conglomerate mergers include under-investing in road maintenance and low capital spending for road facilities. But it should also be pointed out that the ICC is the (poorly managed) cartel of the railroad, water carrier, and interstate trucking industries, and its functionaries speak in the name of their special interests, not in the name of finance capitalists, capitalist economic rationality, or the "public interest."

vides vital services for other industrial corporations that are
integrated into what Victor Perls described as the "empire of
high finance." Nevertheless, we expect the authors to attribute
"limited expansion" to a shortage of funds created by the
greed and rapacity of the banks (and their shortsightedness?).
But the authors do not claim that there is a *general* shortage of
utilities services, only a shortage in New York City. This suggests that the banks are not responsible for the shortage, but
rather that there is an explanation rooted in local New York
conditions. And as it turns out, this is the explanation that the
authors supply: they claim, rightly, that the utilities face a
"hostile environment" in New York. They write that "one
seemingly attractive solution for a monopoly selling a vitally
needed service is to raise its prices. . . . But AT&T has been
understandably reluctant to test the political climate by asking
for really large rate increases" (3:65).[15] Thus, shortage of
funds at least in part can be put at the door of the regulatory
bodies and the "political climate"—not the bankers. Certainly,
the authors do not claim that AT&T starves its other major
operating companies, its manufacturing monopoly, Western
Electric, or its research and development arm, Bell Telephone
Laboratories. In fact, Bell Labs retains its reputation for being
the most advanced privately owned R&D center in the world.
Further, between 1960 and 1966, AT&T spending on plant
and equipment amounted to *seven per cent* of all corporate
investment. In 1965, the monopoly's capital budget soared
to nearly $4 billion. Accounting for seven per cent of the
country's spending on plant and equipment, but for only four
per cent of the country's productive facilities, AT&T in this
period was adding to productive capacity in comparison with
business as a whole. More, during this period about *forty per
cent* of all money raised in the United States through new
stock issues was raised by AT&T. If the supply of electrical
power and telephone communication services in New York
City is uncertain today, it is mainly because of a number of
other factors: the hostile political climate; slow-downs and
sabotage by Ma Bell and other utility workers; community-

15. See also p. 63.

and ecology-conscious citizens who have delayed the construction of atomic energy power plants; technical difficulties involved in hooking up Con Ed with the national power grid;
entrenched, inefficient management;[16] and high interest rates
created by government borrowing to finance the war.[17]

Although Fitch and Oppenheimer aim their big guns at the
relationship between financial institutions and the utilities
(which have had a symbiotic relationship for a long time), they
fire a few scattered shots at the ties between banks and manufacturing corporations. One of their main theses is that "Wall
Street . . . regulates the rate of capital accumulation throughout the economy, retarding it in the mature industries—telephone, railroads, textiles, steel—and over-accelerating it in
the new industries—computer software, electronics, franchise
foods" (3:75). Needless to say, this description of the allocation of capital resources is perfectly consistent with the conclusions of orthodox economic theory: capital moves from declining to expanding sectors of the economy in search of the
highest rate of return, and competition between industrial

---

16. Fitch and Oppenheimer dismiss too readily the "bad management"
explanation for AT&T's troubles. The telephone monopoly is one of the
few corporations that retain an old-fashioned promotion-from-within
policy. A number of years ago, I spent six weeks looking in and around
the telephone empire, and discovered that nearly every man in top management in Western Electric was a WASP, and that the atmosphere in top
management circles resembled that found in a posh club of retired capitalists, rather than an aggressive, efficiency-conscious business firm.

17. As the authors say, the 1935 Public Utility Holding Act was prompted by the fact that financial speculators were milking cash from many
utilities, at the expense of physical plant and equipment. Citing the
case of Mississippi Power and Light, the authors argue that Wall Street
continued to milk the utility, and concealed the fact that banks are the
real bosses of the firm. "For twenty years concealment had enabled Wall
Street to skimp on plant, equipment, and maintenance while reaping
monopoly profits on practically no equity" (1:90). They go on to say
that "such duplicity is hardly unique in the corporate world" and cite
the case of a major airline company trying to cover up the fact that some
of its stock was owned by finance capitalists. The reader is led to expect
that the authors use this example of corporate duplicity to show that the
banks control the airlines in order to rip them off financially. But they
fail to do so. Certainly, it would be difficult to find evidence that airline
productive capacity, maintenance, and so on are impaired by monopoly
capitalist control.

capitalists or financial groups frequently leads to over-investment in the expanding sectors. Putting this aside, the reader is surprised to learn that Fitch and Oppenheimer fail to mention even one example of a bank ripping off a manufacturing company at the expense of productive capacity and industrial profits. Early in their article, the authors imply that Chrysler has been so victimized. They write that "conventional corporate critics might counter that the Penn Central is an anomaly—a throwback to a vanished era. . . . Several corporations with assets larger than the Penn Central's have come close to playing out the same drama, with only a few of the lines changed" (1:76). In a footnote, they say, "Chrysler, the nation's sixth largest corporation, with four directors representing Manufacturers Hanover, has gone through a protracted crisis brought on by a profit decline. The various stages of the crisis have been marked by a purge of inside management by outside directors, a liquidity crisis, and a rescur operation led by Manufacturers Hanover." What the authors do not say is that the profit decline was not attributable to bank control but rather to the fact that in comparison with GM and Ford, Chrysler has small production runs and thus has been stuck with obsolete production capacity, owing to the Big Two's policy of introducing annual model changes. They also fail to tell the reader that the purge of inside management in 1960 was sparked by management's attempt to enrich itself at the expense of the corporation, thus abusing the trust of the company's monopoly capitalist owners.

In my view, the process of capital accumulation in American industry is far more complicated than Fitch and Oppenheimer allow. The steel industry can serve as an example. There is no question but that when steel passed into the hands of financial men in 1901, the industry ceased to be obsessed with the problem of lowering unit labor costs. However, the main reason was not that the monopoly capitalists were preoccupied with "financial profits" and ceased to take an interest in industrial production and industrial profits, but rather than the era of competition had ended, and U.S. Steel exercised a monopoly in product markets. So long as this monopoly position was secure, finance capitalists under normal conditions could count on a regular flow of industrial profits without being excessively preoccupied with productivity. For more than a decade after World War II, steel passed on wage increases in the form of higher prices without overly troubling itself with modernization. But with the revival of international competition, and with the danger of permanent inflation, steel entered into a vast capital construction and modernization program—with large help from the banks. At present, the steel industry has about $5 billion of outstanding debt (up more than one hundred per cent since 1960). Long-term loans have been used to finance the vast rebuilding program of the 1960s, suggesting that the banks are hardly indifferent to the problems of modernizing capacity, elevating productivity, and expanding industrial profits. In this connection, it should also be pointed out that even the most cursory glance at the productive capacity and level of productivity in the major industries—autos, rubber, glass, plastics, chemicals, aluminum, copper, electrical machinery, food processing, and so on—reveals that American capitalism is still a marvel of technological and engineering efficiency.

Monopoly Capitalism and Micro-Economics

ACCORDING TO FITCH AND OPPENHEIMER, the allocation of economic resources (composition of production and investment, price structure, and so on) in modern capitalism bears little resemblance in practice to the textbook theory of competition. I agree fully. All Marxist and most bourgeois economists agree that the competitive model is a highly inaccurate representation of the workings of modern capitalist markets. "In many a sphere of economic activity," Tsuru writes, "the market is no longer a place where buyers and sellers . . . gather and compete with each other. . . . It has come to partake more of the character of a sales department of a monopolist." [18] On the other hand, Fitch and Oppenheimer seem to think that the coordination and control of supplies, production, transportation, communication, prices, etc., within and/or between industries is a new historical phenomenon. I disagree. After all,

18. "A Road to Socialism," *Monthly Review,* February 1968, p. 13.

the principal example of "reciprocity" that the authors use in their debate with the "Marxist managerialists" was ended by a court decision more than a decade ago (at least, the presumption is that the practice was ended). In other words, their own example is out of date (the authors show how the DuPont interests used their financial power to force U.S. Rubber to sell tires to General Motors—in which DuPont had more stock than in U.S. Rubber—at prices little above costs in order to increase GM's—and thus DuPont's—profits).

Further, I don't think that coordination and control within and/or between industries can be attributed primarily to the "domination of finance capital." At times, monopoly capitalists use their banks to coordinate industry; at other times, coordination is exercised by the directors of industrial corporations (as in the electrical equipment industry price-fixing case). An important reason why the banks are needed to coordinate the plans of industrial corporations is that the Clayton Act forbids interlocking directorships between companies that compete in the same market. The monopoly capitalists have used the banks to escape this limitation: the Act does not forbid associates in a single banking house from serving as directors of competing corporations as long as each associate serves on the board of a different company.

Unfortunately, neither Marxist nor bourgeois economists have studied the economic effects of cross-industry planning in any detail, especially in the newer conglomerates.[19] Personally, I believe that such control is exercised primarily for

19. The staff of the Antitrust Subcommittee of the House Committee on the Judiciary wrote that "there is virtually no reliable current information available that will demonstrate either acceptable or undesirable effects that have resulted from the fact that common management personnel participated in, or influenced, particular business transactions. Without factual information concerning the actual operation of interlocks, 'commonsense' presupposition, reliance on past proof, and abstract reasoning have been predominant in the analysis of both the virtues and evils attributed to corporate interlocks" (*Interlocks in Corporate Management*, A Staff Report to the Antitrust Subcommittee of the Committee on the Judiciary, House of Representatives, March 12, 1965 [Washington, 1965], p. 229). Although this was written six years ago, we remain largely ignoratn of the "actual operation of interlocks" insofar as production, investment, industrial location, costs, and prices are concerned.

"financial" motives. In general, the importance of interlocks and reciprocity for economic planning, as opposed to financial planning, is twofold: first, to minimize the costs of selling in the capital goods sector of the economy; second, to coordinate investment plans with the aim of reducing or preventing over-investment in productive capacity. In specific, considering the authors' example of reciprocity, I think that a good case can be made that DuPont was less interested in a financial rip-off than in giving GM a head start in production and sales. After all, the auto giant's ability to buy cheap tires meant that GM could hold down costs and prices and hence make more sales and industrial profits. In point of fact, in Fitch and Oppenheimer's own discussion of the battle between finance capitalists and Howard Hughes, the authors admit that "the giant corporation is . . . forced to pursue a strategy of forward and backward integration. . . . Finance capital performs this function by abolishing the market and 'socializing' industrial decision-making" (2:89). According to the authors, Hughes the industrialist collided head on with the Eastern "syndicate" when Hughes attempted to win independence for himself and free TWA from "tribute" in the form of interest charges to the "syndicate." Although the other big airlines went to banks for financing, Hughes sought to bankroll TWA from profits generated by his own company, Hughes Tool. The struggle (which Hughes lost) is used by the authors as an example of the eternal conflict between industrialists and bankers. In Fitch and Oppenheimer's own words, "The entrepreneur wants to make profits, and the bankers want to make profits, but the banker can make profits only at the expense of corporate profits" (2:85). This statement is inaccurate in principle, and probably also inapplicable to the Hughes case. It is theoretically unsound for two reasons: first, banks coordinate economic activity as well as financial activity and thus help to produce surplus value, as well as appropriate surplus value; second, bank loans can and do stimulate production and sales, and thus indirectly activate the production and realization of surplus value. It is probably inapplicable to the Hughes case (I say probably because I do not have all of the facts) because the "syndicate" represents not bank capitalists but finance capitalists, who control capital in all of its forms, both money and industrial forms. Thus, it may be that Hughes was seen as a threat not because "bankers" wanted to milk profits from TWA, but mainly because Hughes threatened the finance capitalist monopoly on *industrial* capital and *industrial* profits. In other words, finance capitalists, not bank capitalists, entered the lists against Hughes, and it is reasonable to assume that strictly financial motives took second place to considerations of industrial monopoly and profits—that is, to the production and realization of surplus value.

Returning to the problem of reciprocity, it makes little difference whether a corporation forces one branch to sell cheaply to another branch, or whether finance capitalists compel one of their corporations to sell cheaply to another.[20] In both cases, it pays to increase efficiency consistent with profit maximization. Thus, it would have been in DuPont's long-run interests to improve efficiency in U.S. Rubber in order to buy tires even cheaper—just as it pays U.S. Steel or Alcoa to keep up productivity in their captive mines. Nor does it make much difference whether monopoly capitalists force their industrial enterprises to engage in price fixing, or whether corporations adopt a policy of price leadership on their own initiative. The forms of administered pricing are different in these two cases, but the economic effects are the same. Finally, it is hard to take Justice Brandeis's classic argument for opposing corporate interlocks seriously (as Fitch and Oppenheimer do)—namely, that "no man can serve two masters." The reason is that interlocked directors within and between financial and non-financial companies in fact serve *one* master—the monopoly capitalist interests.[21]

---

20. By way of contrast, Sloan of General Motors introduced organizational changes treating the various divisions as *separate* corporations in order to insure maximum efficiency in the allocation of capital. This strategy is commonplace today, whether employed by banks, newer conglomerates, or older multi-product firms like GM.

21. I also believe that the authors exaggerate the importance of interlocks for the monopoly power of the investment banks. They write that "sources of very large blocs of long-term capital are fewer than might be supposed. One prime source is the investment banking fraternity, which maintains close relations with the commercial banks. . . . It would seem

The existence of "one master" does not mean that industrial competition is outdated. Each corporation operates in a specific environment, some features of which are of the owners and managers of the corporations' own making, and other of which are not. Whatever the precise mixture of these features in any particular industry, the evidence is overwhelming that Chrysler, General Electric, and other companies that Fitch and Oppenheimer would claim are "dominated by finance capital" and which operate in oligopolistic industries producing consumer durable goods in fact place as much stress on new product development, model and style changes, advertising, forced obsolescence, and the "sales effort" in general as do their counterparts with relatively weak ties with the financial insti-

---

plausible that if a corporation was offered terms it disliked by one investment bank, it could always turn to another. But United States finance doesn't work this way. . . . Typically, each powerful investment banking firm has achieved a monopoly on the securities business of certain corporations, and its monopoly is respected by other investment bankers" (2:77-79). In the same section, the authors cite the *Investment Bankers* case: "In 1953 the United States government charged seventeen investment bankers . . . with having organized a conspiracy to monopolize the securities business. . . . Investment bankers were alleged to have controlled the financial affairs of securities issuers through such devices as interlocking directorates and syndicates. [The court argued] that interlocking directorates actually promoted competition and that the government's case was without merit. In a sense Medina's dismissal was justified. The government presented a shamefully inept case, drawing primarily on old evidence and calling only one key witness." The reader is left with the impression that Medina dismissed the case for negative reasons—that is, because the government failed to provide any solid proof of its allegations. In fact, the court itself prepared independent evidence of a positive kind, which Fitch and Oppenheimer fail to relate. What happened was that "the government contended that the directorship charts showed that when a security issue was made and a bank representative was on the issuer's board, the defendant who had a man on the board acted as wither manager or comanager in 86 per cent of the cases. The court, however, found that the Government's charts, and their use, were unsatisfactory because no attempt was made to relate the material to 'attendant circumstances' . . ." (*Interlocks in Corporate Management*, pp. 74-75). More, "as a result of his dissatisfaction with the Government's charts, the Court prepared one of his own. The Court's chart shows that [only] 12.5 per cent of the defendants' business in the management of new issues, during the 15-year period 1935-1949, was obtained from issuers upon whose boards there was any partner, officer, or employee of a defendant at the time of issue."

WHO RULES THE CORPORATIONS?   145

tutions (such as Ford Motor Company). As Baran and Sweezy showed, the "sales effort" is indispensable for maintaining and expanding aggregate demand. Further, the evidence is also overwhelming that corporations such as Alcoa, U.S. Steel, Uniroyal, and Anaconda Copper, operating in oligopolistic industries producing capital goods, place enormous stress on efficiency and productivity. These features of modern capitalism were described and analyzed by Baran and Sweezy in *Monopoly Capital*. In a nutshell, the behavior of the giant corporation largley is determined by the market structure—the degree of competition, type of competition, product produced, costs, government contracts if any, and so on, together with the condition of the economy as a whole. Two more recent empirical studies serve to drive this point home. One study demonstrates that "management-controlled companies" (that is, finance capitalist–controlled companies) and "owner-controlled corporations" earn the same rates of profit—and that total assets, total sales revenues, barriers to entry, and industrial growth rates "explain" nearly all variations in profit rates.[22] This study suggests that finance capitalists allow their corporations to make what they can, and to reinvest profits in accordance with market criteria of profitability. A second study shows that large corporations have higher profit rates than medium-sized and small corporations regardless of the degree of market concentration (that is, monopoly power in specific product markets).[23] As Fitch and Oppenheimer show, large corporations seek relatively more external financing than smaller companies—but far from draining industrial profits, as the authors imply, external financing appears to be the road to *greater* profits.

FINALLY, WE NEED TO SAY a few words about Fitch and Oppenheimer's discussion of the recent conglomerate movement—that is, the tendency of many corporations to diversify

22. David Kamershen, "The Influence of Ownership and Control on Profit Rates," *American Economic Review*, June 1968.
23. Courtesy of the author of the study, Professor Marshall Hall, Washington University.

into seemingly (and, at times, actually) unrelated product lines. The authors are dead certain that the conglomerates are motivated solely by the desire for a fast buck. In one place, they write that "'immediate financial gain' is exactly what the conglomerate merger 'movement' was all about, and exactly what the railroad and utility 'diversification' efforts are aimed at achieving" (2:114). In another passage, we read that "finance capital's . . . hunger for quick speculative profits creates industiral monstrosities—the conglomerates—whose assets make no more pretense to industrial integration than those of a mutual fund" (3:75). Unfortunately, space and time limitations do not permit a full discussion of the conglomerate merger movement at this time, but I would like to point out that these mergers have many purposes, of which speculation and "immediate financial gain" is but one. In no particular order of importance, some of these purposes are:

1. To create a pool of investment capital that can flow in any direction that promises a superior return. At any particular time, conglomerate funds are frozen in particular assets that seem profitable, but these assets will be liquidated when they lose their luster. Traditional one-product firms such as steel companies are diversifying with the aim of more rational financial planning (as opposed to immediate financial gain), which has been made possible by modern systems analysis. These companies are putting their money into industries in which the rate of return on capital is highest—which is precisely what the textbooks say that capitalists will do in a competitive capital market.

2. To create, consolidate, and capitalize on positions of control in marketing. During most of the 1960s, the single most frequent kind of merger was the "product extension" merger—that is, the combining of firms manufacturing products that are marketed in the same outlets. For example, the new chemical-drug-cosmetic conglomerates bring together production units that depend on the same marketing facilities. As the 1960s wore on, monopoly capitalists increasingly became preoccupied with marketing and sales. The reason is that they faced expanding product competition, not only from overseas trade and as a result of the new productive facilities added by

corporate expansion programs, but also as a consequence of the conglomerate movement itself. In fact, a good case can be made that conglomerate mergers increase competition in the high-profit industries that are the merger targets. In the words of one businessman, "In the good old days all the emphasis was on the product, rather than on the market and its needs. Production and finance told the sales department what they had to get for the product. Today and even more so in the future, marketing will tell finance and production the cost range in which they must operate to sell in the marketplace." [24]

3. To get tax write-offs. Under present tax laws, different tax rates are applied to different industries. An integrated corporation can purchase a firm in an industry that is taxed at a relatively low rate, charge the acquired firm high prices for supplies produced and sold by another branch of the corporation, and come out way ahead on the deal.

4. To get the benefits of cross-fertilization of technical-administrative know-how. The skills and abilities of systems experts, scientists, engineers, and administrators can be used to more advantage in multi-product companies. Principles of R&D, production planning and control, and scientific management in general, can be applied to many different lines of production.

5. To integrate production and distribution facilities horizontally and vertically. For example, many utilities are acquiring land for new home construction (and thus new utilities customers).[25] Bethlehem Steel is diversifying mineral exploitation and going into ocean shipping. These are forms of forward and backward integration. Further, there are a large number of "compatibility" mergers, which resemble horizontal integration. Magazine publishing companies have gone into the book business and have bought TV stations, can companies have merged with or acquired firms manufacturing paper containers, and so on.

6. To get a piece of low-risk, cost-plus government business by acquiring military contractors.

---

24. *Business Week*, 17 October 1970.
25. *Wall Street Journal*, 7 July 1970.

7. To diversify operations with the aim of spreading risks and reducing uncertainty. For example, modern R&D decreases the time lag between the invention and marketability of a new product. Possibilities of unforeseen discoveries in the lab motivate a company to go into a new field as a hedge against competing firms developing new products in their labs.

8. To keep up and accelerate corporate growth rates. The conglomerate merger is one way for a company to prevent its rate of expansion from slowing down, by getting into fast-growing fields.

9. To hedge against inflation. Inflation helps to finance mergers, which provide a new source of corporate earnings. Clearly, the big upsurge in mergers and acquisitions from 1966 to 1969 can be attributed largely to growing inflation.

Taking these and other considerations discussed above into account, it is difficult to take Fitch and Oppenheimer seriously when they write that "'immediate financial gain' is exactly what the conglomerate merger 'movement' was all about," and that "the conglomerator depletes industrial capital in order to create new paper values." A few years ago, I wrote that "the picture of a few finance capitalists mainpulating stock, acquiring huge overnight profits, and frantically putting together and taking apart industrial empires with an eye to immediate financial gain is simply not consistent with what is known about managerial decision-making in the vast majority of large corporations today."[26] Fitch and Oppenheimer quote this passage—disapprovingly. But despite the authors' best efforts, I see no reason at this time to rewrite the passage or to change its basic conclusion.

Monopoly Capitalism and Macro-Economics

ALTHOUGH FITCH AND OPPENHEIMER announce that they will examine "the consequences of financial control for the economic system as a whole" (3:97) they do not present any macro-economic analysis as such. As a matter of fact, in their discussion of "capital accumulation in the mature monopoly corporation," they assert that they "are not arguing that the

26. *Monthly Review*, December 1968, p. 32.

overall rate of capital formation has slowed down" (3:35). On the other hand, nowhere do they claim that the overall rate of capital formation has *not* slowed down—thus, on this crucial question we are left in the dark.

What they do assert is that "the rate of capital accumulation in the mature monopoly corporations has [slowed down]" (3:35). They define capital accumulation as "the reinvestment of profits from the sale of commodities—what economic historians call 'plough-back,'" which they distinguish from "capital formation—by which we mean the rate of new investment for the society as a whole." Subsequently, they argue that "profits less dividends—retained earnings—represent the maximum portion of profits that can be devoted to capital accumulation. . . . Thus if the dividend payout ratio increases, the rate of accumulation must decline, for relatively less of the corporation's profit is available for reinvestment" (3:38–39).

In the traditional bourgeois and Marxist economics literature, capital accumulation means the expansion of productive capacity, financed *either* by retained earnings *or* by borrowing. In Fitch and Oppenheimer's curious economics terminology, capital accumulation means the expansion of production capacity financed solely by reinvested profits. Now, if the authors define the "rate of capital accumulation" as the "dividend payout ratio" (which they seem to do), then their statement is strictly tautological, and lacks any significance for the real question of the growth of productive capacity. On the other hand, if they mean that "capital accumulation" (their definition) invariably declines when the dividend payout ratio rises, they are wrong. The reason is that *total* profits may be growing fast enough to finance *both* a rise in the payout ratio and an increase in the productive capacity. Further, if they mean that high payout ratios dry up the supply of funds for capital expansion, they are also wrong, precisely because borrowed money can be and is used for capital investment programs.

The central idea that the authors want to leave with the reader is that "finance capital" keeps payout ratios high in order to increase corporate indebtedness with the aim of "maximizing their loan capital" (3:45). According to Fitch and Oppenheimer, the result is a decline in the "overall rate of capital accumulation." As we have seen, if the "rate of capital accumulation" is defined as the payout ratio, their conclusion that the "overall rate of capital accumulation" declines is totally without meaning. On the other hand, if the expression means the "rate of investment" (or the rate at which productive capacity is added to the economy), the authors are totally wrong because new investment is often financed from borrowed funds, often with the participation of state capital. In either case, it is apparent that Fitch and Oppenheimer's discussion of the process of capital accumulation is very confused. Unfortunately, as I have tried to show, the careful reader is forced to draw the same conclusion about the authors' discussion of nearly every other theoretical issue taken up in the rest of their work.

—*James O'Connor*

[15]

R. Fitch (1971), 'Reply to James O'Connor', *Socialist Revolution*, 7, 150–70

REPLY

NEARLY THREE YEARS before writing this present article on corporate control, James O'Connor produced another, in some ways strikingly different, essay on the same subject. He called it "Finance Capital or Corporate Capital?" [1] In his first article, he argued that inside managers or "corporate capitalists" actually controlled the corporation. *Not finance capitalists.* The finance capital theorists, he charged, were "confused" over the issue of who controls the corporation. Now in the latest article, he has switched his position. Finance capitalists *do* control the corporation. But far from acknowledging the change, he now claims that we, his critics, are confused.

Apparently, O'Connor has been forced to shift his position on corporate control, now that the case for inside managerial control has been exposed as groundless. In addition, he has trimmed a few of his more inaccurate propositions about corporate behavior. e.g., that finance capitalists no longer manipulate stock, seek huge overnight profits, or rely on insider information, etc. But O'Connor has admitted none of this. In order

---

1. *Monthly Review*, December 1968.

to achieve consistency, he has misrepresented our arguments as well. Finally, he is compelled to substitute for the critical review of our articles he promises, a full-blown counter-theory of capitalism—a theory of corporate control for which he again provides no evidence; and a theory of corporate behavior which we think has a potentially soporific effect on the development of both socialist theory and political action: a piece of work whose title asks "Who Rules the Corporations?" only to respond with a tautology—"the ruling class."

Let us return to O'Connor's first article, however, to illustrate the original terms of the debate between the "finance capital" theorists and the theorists of inside managerial control.

There was, O'Connor wrote, "a split within the Marxist camp." On one side men like Victor Perlo and Sam Aaronovitch "continue to argue the classic 'Leninist' position." On the other were the authors of *Monopoly Capital,*[2] Paul A. Baran and Paul M. Sweezy—and O'Connor himself. The main issue was the nature and composition of the bourgeoisie. Specifically, who controls the largest agglomerations of capital—the corporations. The differences between the two schools emerged this way:

1. Baran and Sweezy held, in contrast to the Leninists, that "bankers and dominant stockholders" were losing power over the larger corporations to inside managers (i.e., men who devoted their full careers to managing a single corporation). Single, autonomous corporations, not financial groups, represented the key decision-making units.

2. The basis for the shift in corporate control lay, O'Connor said, in the ability of the modern corporation "to finance an increasing share of new investments, modernization investments, etc., *internally."* Far from depending on banks, nonfinancial corporations had reversed the power relation: banks were dependent on corporations.

3. Emphasis on marketing and sales rather than "financial influences and motivations" preoccupy "corporate decision-makers," according to O'Connor. Promotion of new industry,

2. New York, 1963.

mergers, speculation, quick overnight profits, profits based on "inside information" characterize the late nineteenth century and early twentieth century, not the present.

4. O'Connor implied that the old contradictions within the spheres of capitalist production and circulation seemed to be on the way out because of modern technology and state expenditures on infrastructure (roads, schools, etc.). Specifically he predicted that (*a*) "the modern decision-maker in the future may be able to lay his hands on any and all of the capital he wants or needs" (the Penn Central bankruptcy, which set off the corporate liquidity crisis of June 1970, upset the "corporate decision-makers" quite thoroughly), and (*b*) the "corporate decision-maker in the future may find that production literally 'takes care of itself' (as in the case of electric power industries for example) . . ." (the subsequent massive blackouts and brown-outs on the East Coast have dimmed the likelihood of this prospect).

5. Behavior of top management, according to the Marxist managerialists, is "structurally determined" by the market. "Even if 'outsiders' succeeded in establishing control, investment, production, pricing, and other major decisions would not change radically."

Theses 1 and 2 were matters of fact. Either inside managers controlled corporations, free of outside stockholder influence, or they did not; either the modern corporation financed "an increasing share of new investment internally" or it did not. It was the behavioral conclusions—theses 3, 4, and 5—that disturbed me most when I read the first O'Connor article. All three theses emphasized, at least implicitly, the increasing *rationality* and efficiency of the modern corporation; the identity between the interests of those who run the corporation and the smooth functioning of the corporation itself. This *"rationality"* implicit in O'Connor appeared quite explicitly in Baran and Sweezy. According to them, the corporation was a rational organization. It was the capitalist system *as a whole* and people's *perception* of the corporation that were irrational.[3]

---

3. *Monopoly Capital*, pp. 341, 338.

WHO RULES THE CORPORATIONS?   153

For socialists to admit that General Motors, Penn Central, Lockheed, et al. were somehow rational organizations, seemed like a considerable theoretical concession to the bourgeois order. Politically, the rational, market-determined behavior of the corporation seemed to foreclose the desirability of socialist struggles for workers' control of the corporations. Why should workers attempt to fight for control of corporations this side of the socialist revolution if their control would make no functional difference?

It seems to be more than coincidental that Baran and Sweezy, who have underplayed the possibility of workers' control of corporations in theory, in fact argue against the industrial class as an agency of revolutionary change,[4] and that O'Connor opposes the revolutionary possibilities of state employees—like himself—to the revolutionary potential of the industrial working class.

Of course if it were true that the corporation were rational and becoming more so, then we would be forced to look outside the corporation for agencies for revolutionary change. O'Connor does this when he emphasizes state employees. Baran and Sweezy do likewise when they argue that guerrilla struggle in Asia, Africa, and Latin America, together with the example of the socialist countries, will provide the needed spark to enable Americans "to question the necessity of what they now take for granted." Once that happens on a mass scale, they predict, "the most powerful supports of the present irrational system will crumble and the problem of creating anew will impose itself as a sheer necessity."[5] We might have to wait until the end of the present century for this—perhaps longer.

We interpreted the political message this way: the workers

4. "Industrial workers are a diminishing minority of the American working class, and their organized cores in the basic industries have to a large extent been integrated into the system as consumers and ideologically conditioned members of the society. They are not, as the industrial workers were in Marx's day, the system's special victims, though they suffer from its elementality and irrationality along with all other classes and strata—more than some, less than others." *Monopoly Capital*, p. 363.
5. *Monopoly Capital*, p. 367.

154   ROBERT FITCH

are hopelessly bought off with commodities; the capitalist class
had been restructured in such a way as to weed out the old
tycoons, leaving modern, efficient, rational profit-maximizing
managers in charge; the system had sloughed off many of the
old contradictions; revolution would have to be imported from
the "third world." This left the role of socialists undefined
and a bit redundant at least for a generation of so. I must
admit that we found the message depressing. And that we approached the question of corporate control, to see if there
weren't some flaw in an argument that led to such dismal
political prospects for workers' control and revolutionary
socialism.

The new corporate behavior was a product of alleged
changes in the capital market and in the nature of the ruling
class. We decided therefore to examine the empirical grounds
which underlay these doctrines.

NEITHER BARAN AND SWEEZY nor O'Connor presented any
evidence that corporations were controlled by inside managers
or that internal finance had increased, and they cited none.
With Galbraith the problem was more complex. He made use
of extensive citation. But chiefly he relied on Berle and Means,
The Modern Corporation and Private Property. Amazingly, it
turned out that the Berle and Means classic provides no support whatsoever for the theory of inside management control,
as we showed in "Who Rules the Corporations?" Liberal theorists had simply misread Berle and Means, attaching to the word
"management" their own interpretation rather than that of
the authors, who clearly included outside directors like J. P.
Morgan in their definition.

The best then that could be said in defense of the theory
of inside managerial control was that it was "not proved." But
on the other side an impressive amount of evidence had been
compiled by Wright Patman's House Banking and Currency
Committee. Patman's investigators gained full access, through
the use of their subpoena power, to the trust records of United
States commercial banks. After inventorying the huge agglomeration controlled by the banks—over $600 billion in 1967,
or three-fifths of all institutional investments in the country—

the Patman report described how banks gain leverage over corporations:

> Bank-managed investment services are of several types including private trusts, various kinds of employee benefit funds and plans, common trust funds, and agency accounts.
>
> These arrangements have enabled many major banking institutions to become by far the largest single holder and voter of stock in some of the largest industrial and commercial corporations in the United States. This situation has led in many cases to both direct and indirect representation on the boards of these corporations by banks. As pointed out above, companies which have previously been characterized as "management controlled" are probably controlled either by banks or by a combination of minority control through bank trust department stockholdings and management control.
>
> Although detailed data are not available in most cases, there is evidence that other factors used along with investment which increase the ability of commercial banks to gain influence and control over other corporations are found in the dealings between major corporations and commercial banks outside trust department operations. This would include the borrowing of large sums of money from the same commercial banks that also control large blocks of the corporation's stock and hold directorships as well as the use of deposit stock registration and transfer facilities, and other services of these same banks.[6]

This evidence together with subsequent reports of the Patman committee, including one that analyzed stock holdings in the Penn Central Co., convinced us that commercial banks— especially the large eastern commercial banks—form the chief locus of financial and economic power in the United States today. Bank control and influence is perhaps not as clear-cut as in Germany or Belgium, but it seems preponderant.

---

6. *Commercial Banks and Their Trust Activities: Emerging Influence on the American Economy*, Staff Report for the Subcommittee on Domestic Finance of the Committee on Banking and Currency, House of Representatives, 90th Congress, second session; vol. 1, July 8, 1968 (Washington), p. 18.

What about the second factual premise held by the managerialists—the doctrine of increasing corporate reliance on internal finance? As we showed, such reliance actually decreased between 1964 and 1968. Prior to that period, the Harvard Business School professor of corporate finance, John Lintner, had dismissed the theory as follows:

> If there were any major or continuing shifts in the relative reliance on internal financing, it would necessarily have to show up in the balance-sheet ratios just considered. This stability in the relative reliance on internal and external financing over substantial periods through the middle of the century is indeed what we find when we look to the data on the sources and uses of funds of corporations.[7]

Most recently, since our article appeared, figures made available by the Federal Reserve Bank of Cleveland in its "Economic Commentary" indicate that since the end of 1968 corporate non-financial businesses have placed even greater reliance on external financing.[8] This strong reliance on external financing, the FRB writes, "appears to have continued into 1971."

To give some life to this statistical picture, we made case studies of corporate reliance on external funds; we considered various kinds of corporations, including airlines, oil companies, railroads, the telephone company, and an electrical utility company. It seemed to us when we wrote "Who Rules the Corporations?," and it seems even clearer since the Lockheed debacle, that corporations cannot finance themselves through retained earnings and depreciation allowances, nor can they rely on state expenditures on infrastructure to keep them from the bankruptcy court. Besides, the real burden of proof always rested with the managerialists. No one disputes that financial institutions *used* to exercise influence over corporations. Man-

7. "Financing of Corporations" in Edward S. Mason, ed., *The Modern Corporation in Modern Society* (New York, 1966). pp. 179–80.
8. "The total net change in the volume of financing in the capital and credit markets was $40.6 billion during 1969 and $38.5 billion during 1970, compared with an average of only $23.6 billion during the five years previous to 1969."

WHO RULES THE CORPORATIONS?   **157**

agerialists argue that this situation has changed, and that the change has taken place because of the increase in reliance on internal funds. Naturally if reliance on internal funds hasn't changed over time their argument seems most insubstantial.

BEFORE WE DISCUSS O'Connor's specific criticisms and his attempt at a counter-theory, let us summarize the differences between us and the Marxist managerialists. These begin with answers to the empirical question "Who controls the corporations?" and extend to a behavioral question—What are the laws of development which govern corporate growth and interaction? Because we answer these questions differently, we differ on the answer to questions of fundamental political importance: Where should socialists look for the agency of revolutionary change? What class or classes will play that role in the United States?

Since we are at variance on so many other matters, it is not surprising that we differ as well on questions that seem to be methodological, but that actually involve a difference in theory. Baran and Sweezy, and O'Connor too, emphasize the market determination of all corporate behavior. The key to the understanding of corporations, they say, lies in the analysis of prices. Big corporations relate to each other through the market; they are all rational maximizers; there is no capitalist planning; corporations seek to maximize their own profits and the profits of their industry as a whole. Therefore Baran and Sweezy argue that "the appropriate general price theory for an economy dominated by such [giant] corporations is the traditional monopoly price theory of classical and neo-classical economics."[9] Baran and Sweezy seek to distinguish themselves from academic theorists by arguing that bourgeois theory, although it explains the behavior of individual corporations and industries, fails to explain the behavior of the corporate system as a whole. This belief parallels their conviction that while the corporation displays rational behavior, the corporate system is irrational.

We cannot here undertake a thorough critique of the Marx-

9. *Monopoly Capital,* p. 59.

ist managerialists' views on the suitability of orthodox economics—even re-integrated as Baran and Sweezy advocate—
as a basis for a radical critique of capitalism. Let us just suggest
in the way of a critique Sweezy's earlier indictment of the
Chamberlain-Robinson theory of monopoly price:

> Too many diverse factors enter into the determination of
> a given price to permit the construction of a precise
> theory with any but the most limited applicability. This
> is fully proved by the attempts of orthodox economic
> theory in recent years to establish objective laws of price
> under conditions of total or partial monopoly. Aside from
> a few empty propositions such as that price will be set
> where profit is maximized, monopolistic price theory
> rapidly turns into a catalogue of special cases, each with
> its own particular solution.[10]

Rather than try to build a theory on these "few empty
propositions" we seek to develop a Marxist theory of the
corporation. Marxism, we fell, has several advantages over
academic theory: (a) it recognizes the universality of contradiction; (b) it deals with social reality in terms of class; (c) it is
openly partisan, taking up theoretical questions chiefly to aid
in the building up of working-class power, preparatory to the
socialist transformation of society; (d) it is historically specific
to the era of capitalism and to its legal, political, and economic
institutions.

Baran and Sweezy and O'Connor look at the corporation
and see a unity. They see men, managers and machines all
moving towards a common end—the maximization of the
profits of a given industry.[11] In our view, the corporation is
divided by contradictions. The primary contradiction exists
between the proletariat—blue collar and white collar—and the
bourgeoisie: the corporate oligarchy as a whole. The secondary
contradictions exist between the various strata within the
bourgeois hierarchy. Essentially the extent, nature, and development of these secondary contradictions—between inside
managers, outside stockholders, commercial bankers, bond-

---

10. *Theory of Capitalist Development* (New York, 1942), pp. 270-71.
11. See *Monopoly Capital*, p. 48.

holders, etc.—are determined by the way each stratum derives its portion of the surplus value. The goal of analysis of these secondary contradictions is not to determine the exchange rate of the various forms of surplus value appropriated by these strata (i.e., prices), but to determine the conditions under which these strata come into conflict and their effect on the material circumstances of the working class and the other classes and strata in society; and to discover what are the objective economic forces within the corporation leading to disintegration and development. Baran and Sweezy and O'Connor do not share this approach. They seek to develop a radical critique of the corporation on the basis of traditional or neoclassical price theory and on the basis of empirical work that we feel is unsound. But we do not, as O'Connor charges, consider their work "stupid" or "apologetic." Far from lumping Baran and Sweezy with the managerial apologists, we criticized them for using ineffective means of attack: "Whether bankers and their allies or 'inside' employee-managers control the giant corporations is an empirical question. But Baran and Sweezy chose to argue against simplistic managerialism—the theories of the beneficent corporation—by accepting the factual premises and debating its conclusions. And although they claimed there was abundant proof to show that capitalists and bankers were no longer in control, they do not cite any." The purpose of *Monopoly Capital* is to provide a radical critique of the system, but we feel they failed to ascertain what the facts were concerning corporate control.

Unfortunately, this misrepresentation of our position is all too typical of O'Connor's method of "critical review." First he distorts our argument, then he punctures his rhetorical balloon with a great show of force. Here, for example, is O'Connor on our utility section, in which we analyzed the financial sources underlying the notorious operating problems of AT&T and Consolidated Edison: "The authors do not claim that there is a general shortage of utilities services, only a shortage in New York City."

We never said that the problem of utility shortage was confined to New York City, *we said the exact opposite*—that the problems of Con Ed and Ma Bell were typical of the utility industry as a whole: "Electrical power failures in New York City *and other Eastern cities* are the unintended consequences of long-range financial planning. . . . Hundreds of thousands of people went without electricity in a failure that affected *five other northeastern states as well*" (part 3, p. 62); "This new mode [of capital accumulation], typified *by the activities of such giants as AT&T and Consolidated Edison,* involves the subordination of capital accumulation in the industrial sphere to the accumulation of finance capital, especially loan capital" (3:58–59) (italics added).

We have made the same point three times to show that the situation in New York City wasn't atypical. We even provided a table which showed that AT&T and Con Ed weren't particularly debt-ridden, but that the utility industry as a whole had over-borrowed.

A great deal of criticism could be heaped on O'Connor's own analysis of the utilities industries' failures. One wonders how he could blame everyone for the industries' failures— utility workers, ecology activists, management inefficiencies, high interest rates, technology—everyone and everything except the bosses, the directors, who actually do decide how much to invest in capital equipment, and who are legally responsible.

Assuming, for the sake of argument, that the workers were really guilty of sabotaging electrical generating equipment, it's unlikely that such Luddite activity forced Con Ed to write off a sum as large as $200 million.[12] And this is how much was lost in potential outlays for capital equipment because of corporate dividend payments and interest charges—a sum large enough to buy several giant generators, or at least keep the biggest one Con Ed has in continuous operation. Why then blame the workers?

It seems to me that O'Connor attributes the blame as he does because of his emphasis on corporation rationality. He looks at Con Ed and sees that its performance doubly refutes his predictions for continued smooth functioning: it has both

---

12. I at least am unable to find any such entry on my copy of Con Ed's balance sheet.

operating problems and problems raising capital. Rather than take his corporate model back to the drawing board, O'Connor blames the opponents, not the wielders of corporate power. A rational corporation wouldn't have the kind of problems Con Ed has; so, O'Connor reasons, there must be some force outside the corporation preventing it from realizing its goals— if not recalcitrant workers, then a sticky regulatory atmosphere. Perhaps it is a personnel problem. We argue on the contrary that the misery caused by Con Ed is the product of corporate planning. Given the directors' decision to maximize dividends and to finance the corporation with bonds rather than equity (which would depress the stock's value), Con Ed's problems are entirely predictable. And where is the rationality from the standpoint of profit maximization of Con Ed borrowing money at eight or nine per cent when the company makes only five per cent on gross revenues? Loans like this could be defended, but chiefly from the standpoint of Morgan, Stanley and Co., which earns commissions by acting as Con Ed's investment banker. Their planning is rational only if one holds highly restrictive assumptions and values, i.e., the highest value must be placed on Morgan, Stanley and Co. being well compensated for its bond-selling efforts; and its institutional clients— the big insurance companies represented on the board—being rewarded for their "frugality." Three cheers for New York Life Insurance Company! Year after year it continues to put its money in Con Ed bonds.

But it seems pointless to debate the role of finance in the utilities industry with O'Connor, who predicted in December 1968 that "the corporate decision-maker in the future may find that production literally takes care of itself (as in the case of electric power industries, for example)," since his theory precludes consideration of the problems we're discussing. This is just as well because O'Connor's grasp of the elements of securities is unsure, as the following passage illustrates:

> Owners of stocks and bonds appropriate surplus value *directly*—that is, they acquire unpaid labor directly from the workers in the form of profits. The question arises, who owns the stocks and bonds? In the family-owned, family-managed company the answer to this question is

> in principle simple. The individuals who organize the pro-
> duction and realization of surplus value are precisely the
> same individuals who own the financial claims on surplus
> value. (pp. 124–25)

Obviously, corporations, including family-owned corporations,
don't hold their own debt. If they did they wouldn't be debt-
ors. Bonds are held by individuals and institutions other than
the corporation itself.

LIKE O'CONNOR· BARAN AND SWEEZY emphasize the corporation's market-determined rationality. They also insist on its
ever-widening profit margins,[13] and on the lack of class conflict within the corporation. All of this leads them, we feel, to
focus their attention outside the corporation when they begin
to compile a checklist of what's wrong with American society.
They cite alienation, waste, bad orgasms, status-seeking, unfair
IQ tests, racism, militarism—essentially the whole bag of social
criticism of the 1950s.

But Baran and Sweezy never talk about how workers are
exploited, how they are alienated as *workers* because of what
goes on inside the corporation. They never show how specific
corporations, in the course of their operations, make life un-
livable for ordinary Americans in the cities. "OK, Mr. and Mrs.
America," they seem to be saying, "you want monopoly capitalism? OK you'll get it, but you're also going to get . . . the
ill effects of the *system* of monopoly capitalism."

We have no desire at all to check criticism of the capitalist
system. But it seems that by focusing on the system as a whole
and acknowledging corporate rationality and ability to deliver
the goods, Baran and Sweezy provided a theoretical justifica-
tion for certain tendencies within the movement. The first was
the desire to shift prime responsibility for the socialist revolution in the United States to the peasants of the "third world,"
or to the blacks in the ghettoes. The second tendency sought
to shift socialist political focus from what goes on in the
primary institutions—banks, industry, transportation, public
utilities—in a word, the corporations; and displace it towards

13. See *Monopoly Capital*, pp. 71–72.

the secondary institutions—schools, universities, state bureaucracies, the cultural superstructure. These tendencies within the movement assumed that the rational corporation would go on making ever-higher profits, producing more "surplus," and that the industrial workers would continue to get their share.

So it seemed in 1966, right about the time the business cycle began to turn. Since then decreasing profit margins, decreased real wages, combined with rampant corporate speculation and the class need to maintain capital's exorbitant tribute in the form of *increased dividend payments and interest charges*—all these have begun to expose as a massive fraud the ability of the corporation to "deliver the goods." This situation however has another side to it. Consciousness is a product of social existence. If the corporations are rational and can guarantee indefinitely a decent standard of living, then the chances of big political changes occurring in the United States are not very great.

Our political purpose in "Who Rules the Corporations?" is not to deny that the secondary institutions in the United States are irrational and inhuman and produce real misery. We have simply tried to show that the rationality of the corporation, its ever-expanding profitability, and the unity of its class leadership are myths. Our work will be successful to the extent that it contributes to a reassessment of the political possibilities inherent in socialist struggles inside and against the primary institutions: the corporations.

O'Connor's new counter-theory of the corporation seems to lead in the opposite direction. Let us first, however, summarize his old position:

1. Corporations are controlled by inside managers.
2. Corporations finance themselves.
3. There has been a decline in corporate financial motivation and an increase in the preoccupation with marketing problems.
4. Intra- and inter-corporate conflict has been largely eliminated.
5. Corporations exemplify rationality and market predictability.

In the new theory, O'Connor has abandoned theses 1 and 2. But he still holds 3, 4, and 5. In other words, he has abandoned the empirical basis of his theory, which attempted to explain the basis of corporate behavior. And he has exchanged it for a new empirical infrastructure which is *seemingly* that of the "Leninists." Nevertheless he still tries to hold on to the old theories about corporate behavior.

Under the old theory, the independent, all-powerful corporation combined all the functions of the erstwhile competing strata of the old bourgeoisie. Internal finance made this possible. Now under the new theory, O'Connor says that it's the "finance capitalists" who control the corporation absolutely. Are the finance capitalists any different from the "corporate capitalists" who used to control the corporation? Apparently not, at least operationally. But before we go any further in the analysis of O'Connor's version of finance capital, we are compelled to point out that *he doesn't know what finance capital is.* O'Connor says finance capital "means capital in the form of raw materials, fuel, etc."

Actually, "finance capital is capital controlled by banks and employed by industrialists." [14] Unfortunately, we are compelled to go one step further and point out that O'Connor mystifies the meaning of "capital." This is the key to his theoretical plight with respect to the corporation and finance capital. O'Connor equates finance capital with material objects not only in his definition but in another passage where he says: "Thus the authors tell us that *material objects (finance capital)* oppose living individuals (industrial capitalists)—a strange kind of conflict indeed" (p. 121, italics added). [15]

O'Connor thinks that capital is a material object—a thing. It was to combat this notion that Marx wrote his great work. Chapter after chapter, he carries out the effort to disestablish capital as a thing. In the famous concluding chapter, entitled

14. V. I. Lenin, *Selected Works*, vol. 1 (New York, 1967), 711. This is a capsule definition which Lenin derived from Rudolf Hilferding, and then expanded upon.

15. We did no such thing, but this is again typical of the O'Connor methodology.

"The Theory of Modern Colonization," he concluded: "Capital is not a thing, but a social relation between persons established by the instrumentality of things." [16]

O'Connor's definition of capital is the typical "economists'" mistake that Marx fought against in "Wage Labor and Capital":

> Capital consists of raw materials, instruments of labor and means of subsistence of all kinds, which are utilized in order to produce new raw materials, new instruments of labor and new means of subsistence. All these component parts of capital are creations of labor, products of labor, accumulated labor. Accumulated labor which serves as a means of new production is capital.
> So say the economists.
> What is a Negro slave? A man of the black race. The one explanation is as good as the other.
> A Negro is a Negro. He only becomes a slave in certain relations. A cotton-spinning jenny is a machine for spinning cotton. It becomes *capital* only in certain relations. Torn from these relationships it is no more capital than gold in itself is *money* or sugar is the price of sugar.[17]

O'Connor, however, has the "economists'" view of capital; and he thinks that the corporation is also a thing—a kind of house under whose roof various productive activities take place. The big problem is getting the goods out of the door ("the sales effort"). Because O'Connor cannot conceive of the corporation as a social relationship, as a simple legal device structuring flows of capital, he cannot understand corporate conflicts. He thinks we are saying that bankers "rip off" the corporation. And this makes no sense to him. "Why would the banker come into the house and take the chairs from the table, since he has to sit down to eat too?" O'Connor reasons.

But the corporation is more than a collection of material objects; this is only one side of its nature. It is more than just

---

16. *Capital*, vol. 1 (Moscow, 1965), p. 766.
17. From the 1962 edition of the Foreign Languages Publishing House, Moscow.

a producer of commodities; *it is a commodity itself.* It has this
dual nature. And here is the key to what we are driving at with
respect to finance capital. To approach the modern corporation dialectically is to apprehend its dual commodity nature.
United States Steel not only produces commodities for which
there is a market; it *is* a commodity by virtue of the fact that
a market exists for the shares of its stock. Thus the modern
corporation has an exchange value as well as a use value. It is
a commodity as well as a producer of commodities. How does
this dual nature ramify throughout the corporate system?
How does the fact that a volatile market exists for the shares
of corporate stock affect the corporations' production and
sale of commodities? O'Connor ignores these critical questions
because for him the corporation is strictly a producer of commodities.

The essential fact however with respect to finance capital is
that the merger of bank capital with industrial capital creates a
new and more contradictory mode of circulation and accumulation. This is an inevitable outgrowth of the fact that bank
capital and industrial capital have their own independent laws
of motion. Here we come to the most serious and misleading
of all O'Connor's misconceptions. This is the idea that there is
one united, homogeneous ruling class. In the old theory there
were no finance capitalists; in this new one there are only
finance capitalists—it makes no difference from O'Connor's
standpoint, because he is simply trying to illustrate the homogeneity of the ruling class. And a rose is a rose. . . . But this is a
serious error that can prevent analysis of finance capital. When
Richard King Mellon served on the board of the Penn Central
he did not become a railroad man; he served to advance the
interests of the Mellon family which are chiefly controlled by
the Mellon National Bank; when Stuart Saunders served on the
board of the Chase Manhattan Bank, this did not make him a
banker; when Louis Cabot served on the Penn Central Board it
did not mean he had the interests of the railroad at heart. The
hitherto secret minutes of the last board meeting he attended
reveal this: "Another conflict of interest is my position as
chairman of a major shipper of carbon black and other products on the nation's railroads, where it is my obligation to

negotiate for lower, not higher, freight rates").[18] When Walter Wriston of the First National City Bank, the Penn Central's major creditor, decided as head of its banking consortium to dismiss the railroad's inside managers, he did so not as an industrialist or as a railroad man, but as a banker, safeguarding bank capital.

We never claimed, of course, as O'Connor charges, that conflicts between strata of the bourgeoisie are "eternal." We said the opposite. Naturally there are many convergences of interest between finance capital and industrial capital. But there are also areas of conflict. A dialectical understanding of the corporation perceives that conflict and convergence exist together. O'Connor, however, is able to see only the convergence of interest. Academic micro-economics is similar in this respect. It treats all capitals as the same, recognizing no distinctions between bank and industrial capital. This is what gives O'Connor's old and new theories of the corporation their unity: their insistence on the material nature of capital and its essential homogeneity.

We argue to the contrary that conflicts exist between strata of the bourgeoisie controlling capitals with different laws of motion. This conflict cannot be set aside merely because their interests also overlap. The analysis of inter-bourgeois conflict is needed to provide a socialist explanation of why the trains not only don't run on time but don't run at all; why utility companies can't provide power at peak periods; why Lockheed needs a federal bail-out; why the airlines are going bankrupt, etc. O'Connor's "unification" of the ruling class precludes such an analysis. This is why the phrase "Who Rules the Corporations?—The Ruling Class" is a tautological invitation to go back to sleep.

O'CONNOR FINDS HIMSELF TRAPPED in a clear contradiction by moving to his new position on the ruling class as a homogeneous collection of finance capitalists. He has not yet moved away from the old position that corporations behave according

18. Joseph Daughen and Peter H. Benzen, *The Wreck of the Penn Central* (Boston, 1971), p. 275.

to market criteria and can only be understood that way. This means, of course, that corporations as *individual units* maximize profits, i.e., that each corporation tries to make its own profits as large as possible over the long run. This view, which looks at the *firm* as the basic unit of the economy, contradicts the view that holds that financial groups are the key units and that these groups attempt to increase the holdings of their portfolios (bonds, stocks, warrants, etc.) independent of the profits of any one corporation in which they might have an interest.[19] In other words the outside controlling center might direct that two corporations which it controls do business with each other on terms favorable to only one of them. This contradicts the theory of profit maximization as held by academic micro-economists. According to their theory the "firm" would never enter into such a deal. If corporations don't maximize profits in this individual way, their entire theory is invalidated, a condition which they themselves realize.

---

19. The example we used involved U.S. Rubber, General Motors, and the DuPont–Wilmington Trust group. All three were controlled by the DuPont family, whose holdings were arrayed in such a way that it made sense to have U.S. Rubber sell tires to GM at cost. See part 3, pp. 89–90. O'Connor criticizes this example simultaneously as "nothing new" and as being old and outdated. Reciprocity, however, is "something new" according to the Federal Trade Commission's studies((see the Mueller report, cited in part 3, p. 85). If O'Connor has evidence not available to the commission with respect to reciprocity which would show that it began to develop earlier than students of the subject had thought, he should come forward with it. As it is, O'Connor dismisses an empirical finding without suggesting an opposing empirical base for his own views. As for our example of reciprocity being old and outdated, we merely chose a famous one that had been proved in court. For a more recent example there is the classic study carried out by the Patman committee: *The Penn Central Failure and the Role of Financial Institutions, Part III. Pennphil: The Misuse of Corporate Power.* Staff Report of the Committee on Banking and Currency, 92nd Congress, first session, February 15, 1971 (Washington, D.C.). The report shows how David Bevan of the Penn Central and Charles Hodge, the company's investment banker, engaged in a type of reciprocity which "maximized" the profits of the Pennphil Company (which they held closely) and drained off the assets of the Penn Central (whose investment program they controlled). Bevan and Hodge were Penn Central stockholders, but their holdings were comparatively small. They could carry out ventures profitable to Pennphil and unprofitable to the Penn Central and come out considerably ahead.

Baran and Sweezy realize it too. And they are consistent. They deny that financial groups or outside controlling interests are decisive in corporate control; and they assert that corporations maximize profits as individual firms. Our view is also consistent. We assert that financial groups and outside interests are decisive and that profit maximization is a dated concept. Between those two positions there is no more logical room. O'Connor's attempt to hold that individual corporations engage in profit maximization within the context of the domination of financial groups must be regarded as inherently contradictory.

It's impossible in the space available to straighten out all of O'Connor's other distortions and misrepresentations of our work. We will ignore them for now and respond to his challenge to produce evidence that bank control of airlines has lessened their effectiveness. Financial institutions not only control the major airlines through stock holdings and loans; they own most of the planes that airlines use. The First National City Bank's executive vice president announced recently that "after the Russian and American government we have the biggest air force in the world." Citibank, the leader in aircraft leasing, owns more than a hundred airplanes valued at over a billion dollars.

Bank control over the airlines is so heavy-handed that, even though airlines are suffering from considerable overcapacity, they continued to buy more giant planes. As Blaine Cooke, TWA's senior vice president, noted bitterly in 1969, "Economically there is no excuse for the airplane [the 747]. An industry that had a rational control over its own technology would not introduce the 747 at this time because there is no need for it. It is an airplane five or ten years ahead of its time in terms of growth of the market. The plane . . . in fact may result in bankruptcies or mergers." [20]

The reason why the bankers were willing to finance production and sale of the unneeded airbuses is that banks make an

20. Cited in "Citibank," a preliminary report by the Nader Task Force on the First National City Bank, David Leinsdorf, project director, Center for the Study of Responsive Law (Washington, D.C., 1971).

estimated fifty-six per cent profit on their aircraft leasing activity. And for that kind of profit, the risk of bankrupting an airline or two is quite sensible, especially since the amount of bank equity involved in the airlines is comparatively small. And in the event of bankruptcy, the banks take over all the rest of the planes anyway.

The airline industry provides an especially good example of how the pursuit of industrial and financial profits can conflict; and how a policy that is good for financial institutions is potentially ruinous for the corporation itself. Perhaps this exchange with O'Connor will draw attention to the dialectics of the corporation. For the first prerequisite in the revolutionary resolution of capitalism's contradictions is that they be recognized as such.

--Robert Fitch

[16]

THE RESURGENCE OF FINANCIAL CONTROL: FACT OR FANCY?

By Paul M. Sweezy

A long three-part article by Robert Fitch and Mary Oppenheimer on "Who Rules the Corporations?" in *Socialist Revolution* (vol. 1, nos. 4, 5, 6) purports to demonstrate that giant U.S. corporations are controlled by banks and other financial institutions. In order to support this thesis, Fitch and Oppenheimer (henceforth F&O) find it necessary to attack views expressed by Paul Baran and me in *Monopoly Capital*. We are labeled "Marxist managerialists" and are charged with many grave errors of omission and commission. How large this misguided group is supposed to be is not clear, since James O'Connor is the only other one specifically named as belonging to it; but it seems evident that F&O regard the three of us not as isolated cases but as representatives of a significant theoretical trend which can seriously mislead the American Left. Under the circumstances a detailed reply seems called for.

To begin with, F&O have misunderstood the theory put forth in *Monopoly Capital*. As a result, much of the evidence they present, to the extent that it is relevant at all, in no way refutes or contradicts the theory. This by itself would not be too serious, since putting down Baran and Sweezy is no more than incidental to their main purpose of vindicating the theory of financial control. But unfortunately in their earnest efforts to accomplish this purpose they have committed so many meth-odological, analytical, and even factual errors as to deprive their study of corporate behavior of whatever value it might otherwise possess.

Let me start with a passage from *Monopoly Capital* which is quoted by F&O. It purports to characterize the typical giant corporation:

(1) Control rests in the hands of management, that is to say, the board of directors plus the chief executive officers. Outside interests are often (but not always) represented on the board to facilitate the harmonization of the interests and policies of the corporation with those of customers, suppliers, bankers, etc.; but real power is held by the insiders, those who devote full time to the corporation and whose interests and careers are tied to its fortunes.

(2) Management is a self-perpetuating group. Responsibility to the body of stockholders is for all practical purposes a dead letter. . . .

(3) Each corporation aims at and normally achieves financial independence through the internal generation of funds which remain at the disposal of management. The corporation may still, as a matter of policy, borrow from or through financial institutions, but it is not normally forced to do so and hence is able to avoid the kind of subjection to financial control which was so common in the world of Big Business fifty years ago.*

It is perfectly obvious from this passage that Baran and I never had the slightest intention to deny the existence of either "outside" directors or corporate borrowing from financial institutions, from which it follows that all the evidence adduced by F&O on these points is entirely irrelevant. The question for F&O to answer is not whether bankers sit on corporate boards or whether corporations borrow from banks: of course they do. The question is whether these activities confer corporate control on banks and bankers. And here F&O have nothing to contribute but speculations, reiterated assertions, and an assortment of stories about individual cases which may or may not be relevant to the point at issue but which absolutely do not

---

* Part I, p. 87. The passage appears in *Monopoly Capital* on pp. 15-16. The omission in paragraph (2) is F&O's and has no bearing on what is here under discussion.

REVIEW OF THE MONTH   **3**

form a valid basis for any generalizations. I shall have to examine some of these case "studies" later on, but before we come to that, there are other questions to be considered.

The first relates to the holdings of corporate stock by bank trust departments. The Patman Committee, extensively cited by F&O, has shown that these holdings are large and highly concentrated in the hands of a few dozen of the largest big-city banks. Do they carry with them control over the corporations whose stock is held in trust in large amounts? F&O take it for granted that they do. Waxing lyrical, they declare:

> The dramatic rise in institutional shareholding during the 1960s broke down the effective separation of ownership and control on which the theory of managerialism rested. Once again ownership and control were united in the trust departments of the great Wall Street banks: Morgan Guaranty Trust, Chase Manhattan Bank, First National City Bank. It was a unity recalling the age of Morgan, when financial institutions had been able to control corporations through their lending power. (Part II, p. 8)

Such a momentous change, one would think, ought to be pretty carefully documented. But F&O offer *not one single case* of a demonstrated causal link between bank trust holdings and corporate control. In contrast, during the age of Morgan (roughly from the Civil War to the First World War) there were literally hundreds of fully documented cases of financial control over corporations. Bankers and particularly bank trust officers will of course explain this absence of evidence of control relations very simply: their business, they will tell you (and not only for the public record), is investing money for the benefit of the trust beneficiaries, a function for which trust officers are carefully trained. They not only do not control corporations; they do not even want any such responsibility which would bring all sorts of headaches and open them to expensive damage suits should losses be suffered by trust beneficiaries owing to improper actions by trustees.*

---

* In this field of trusts and fiduciaries, capitalist law defining the responsibilities of trustees to beneficiaries is both strict and on the whole strictly enforced. This is not surprising since the stratum of the population principally involved is what C. Wright Mills called the "very rich" who are well aware of their rights and never make a move without expert legal advice.

Naturally, I cannot prove that these disclaimers are sincere and reflect the actual state of affairs (the two things are by no means identical), any more than F&O can prove the opposite. Nevertheless, having informally interviewed a number of people in the trust business and taking account of the fact that they operate in huge bureaucracies under the watchful eye of customers' lawyers, courts, and bank examiners, I am inclined to discount the possibility that they are rationalizing or lying. Certainly, it is absurd in the extreme to compare the power over corporations which banks derive from their trust holdings to that of the financial tycoons of the age of Morgan. Such a comparison betrays not only a lack of knowledge of corporate history but, perhaps even more important, an absence of any feeling for what has been happening in the business world during the last century.*

Still, it must be conceded that there is one argument of a

---

* One small example will perhaps suggest what I have in mind. Everyone knows that the First National City Bank is a huge institution with scores of vice presidents, branches all over the metropolitan area, several major divisions (consumer, corporate, trust, real estate, international), and many thousands of employees. It is, in a word, a vast bureaucratic corporation in its own right, and its problems of structure, management, etc., are basically probably not too different from those of General Motors or Standard Oil. The contrast with one of its two predecessor corporations, the First National Bank, could not be more striking. Until his death in 1931, the First National was controlled in every sense by George F. Baker, Sr. who was nearly the equal of J. P. Morgan, Sr. during the latter's lifetime and inherited Morgan's mantle after his death in 1913. As late as the 1920s the First National had only five vice presidents who were also directors, occupied part of a small building at 2 Wall Street, would not accept deposits of less than a million dollars, and did no business at all with the general public. First National men sat on dozens of corporate boards, usually alongside Morgan men, and no one in Wall Street was in any doubt about their power. The changes in the business world which had taken place by the end of the Second World War, however rendered this kind of an elite corporation-oriented bank no longer viable, and the First National was in effect swallowed up by the National City Bank which had been one of the pioneers of the new style of banking which predominates today. That a change of this kind reflects a change in the nature of the relations between banks and corporations seems obvious enough. One of the most distressing—and for me depressing—aspects of the Fitch/Oppenheimer study is that they show no awareness, not to say understanding, of the qualitative changes which have characterized the history of monopoly capitalism and of which the First National story is only one example.

structural nature put forward by F&O in favor of the thesis of
financial control which makes sense. It does not suggest anything like comprehensive or permanent control, but it certainly
does leave open the possibility of decisive financial intervention
in cases where a corporation's management performs poorly.
The traditional Wall Street rule, F&O point out, has been "if
you don't like management, sell." But, they go on, the growth
of large institutional investments may make it practically impossible to apply the rule in some cases. And here they quote
David Rockefeller as follows:

> I suspect that such investors will become more demanding of
> management as time moves on—that as holdings expand, institu-
> tions, as well as individuals, will feel obliged to take more active
> interest in seeing that corporations do indeed have good manage-
> ment. That will be true especially if their holdings become so large
> that they cannot readily or quickly liquidate their investments, as
> is now their practice when they become dissatisfied with the man-
> agement of a corporation in which they hold shares. (Part II,
> p. 62)

Let us assume, for the sake of the argument, that this situation is on the way to becoming general, i.e., that in the typical
case institutional investors are, or soon will be, ready and able
to intervene in order to assure what David Rockefeller calls
"good management." The question is, what does he mean by
the term? F&O do not ask the question, perhaps because to do so
would raise serious doubts about the kind of implicit or explicit
assumptions concerning the motives of financial institutions that
are sprinkled throughout their essay. But whatever their answer
might be, I for one have no doubt that for David Rockefeller
and the vast majority of his financial colleagues, a "good management" is one which has a good record of earning profits and
expanding its company's profit-making base. This, it should be
noted, is typical *capitalist* behavior (as analyzed by Marx in
Capital), and it is what gives to capitalism its unique historical
character as a value-expansion process (*Verwertungsprozess*).

If I am right about this, the implications are interesting.
Financial control in this sense is certainly an argument against
bourgeois "managerialism," as exemplified for example by Galbraith, according to which present-day corporate managers are

no longer interested in maximizing profits. But for the kind of
"managerialism" which Baran and O'Connor and I are supposed to represent, what may be called the David Rockefeller
argument brings nothing but support, the stronger the more
seriously the argument is taken. For what we are saying is simply that in monopoly capitalism the giant corporation is the
basic unit of capital and that it operates according to the
classical/Marxian principles of profit maximization and capital
accumulation. Obviously, to the extent that financial watchdogs
oversee this process and hold managements to the straight-and-
narrow path of making and expanding profits for the corporation, and indirectly for its stockholders and creditors, our position is by that much strengthened.

I am not implying that the concentration of trust holdings
in a handful of huge banks raises no substantial questions. One
in particular—and it is an aspect of the problem about which
Representative Patman is specially exercised—is the question
of the availability to bank trust departments of confidential information on corporate affairs acquired by the same banks'
lending departments and representatives on corporate boards
of directors. There is no doubt, and the banks themselves do
not deny it, that the normal relations between banks and corporations provide the former with vastly more inside information than is available to the average investor. If this information is turned over to trust departments and used by them in
managing their clients' portfolios, it is obvious that the cards
are stacked in favor of one set of investors at the expense of
others. A case in point was provided by the Penn Central bankruptcy. According to a story in *Business Week* of July 24, 1971:

> A Patman committee aide, Benet D. Gellman, found that
> Chase Manhattan and several other large banks with loans out-
> standing to the corporation had unloaded huge amounts of stock
> just prior to its collapse. The Chase sold 436,000 Penn Central
> shares out of its trust accounts in one week.
> Patman was quick to note that Stuart Saunders, then Penn
> Central's board chairman, was also a director of the Chase. He
> charged further that the selling patterns of Penn Central stock
> strongly suggested that several banks, in selling portions of their
> stock, had acted in concert so as not to touch off too much down-
> ward price reaction.

The banks' answer to such charges is of course a pious denial. *Business Week* quotes David Rockefeller, chairman of Chase, as follows:

The trust and fiduciary investment functions of our bank are performed by departments that are wholly separate and distinct from our commercial lending activities, said Rockefeller. To assure the proper use and control of information received by the bank in its several capacities, there is no flow, or incidental communication of inside information, from commercial departments or divisions of the bank to the fiduciary investment department or to the pension or personal trust divisions of the trust departments.

Anyone familiar with the way business works will, of course, discount statements like this at very close to 100 percent. Here Patman wins hands down. But it is certainly no new discovery that the financial markets are stacked in favor of the big guy and against the little guy, nor is there any reason to believe that the particular twist given to this stacking process by the growth of bank trust holdings has had or will have any fundamental effects on the functioning of monopoly capitalism.

We shall return later to F&O's handling of the Penn Central bankruptcy.

II

Apart from basic questions of theory, I find it impossible to discuss "Who Rules the Corporations?" in a logical or systematic way. F&O jump about from subject to subject, from hypothesis to fact and vice versa, from assertion to case study, in a most bewildering way. For example, at the beginning of Part II they raise the question of the significance of trust holdings by banks and quote David Rockefeller as above. They next cite certain cases where financial institutions (not necessarily trust departments of banks) have had difficulty disposing of large blocks of stock. We now have the hypothesis to be tested or proved or at least illustrated: the trust holdings of banks are a source of corporate control. Here is the way F&O make the transition from hypothesis to "evidence":

Faced with such potential losses it is not surprising that the institutional investor may decide to intervene in corporate affairs. During the sixties, for example, financial institutions took an active role in the merger movement. (Part II, p. 63)

Off and running, F&O now proceed to treat us to several pages of anecdotes mostly culled from the pages of *Fortune* and the *Wall Street Journal* about how various types of financial institutions (banks, investment bankers, mutual funds) were involved in the merger movement of recent years, all of which add up to exactly nothing except that a large part of the business of financial institutions is dealing with corporations in one way or another. Hardly a surprising discovery, to be sure. And indeed as F&O conclude this section (entitled "Do Financial Institutions Exercise Their Stock Voting Power?"), they come pretty close to conceding that it is all much ado about nothing: "That financial institutions do not always exercise Stockholder Power [they have in fact not proved that they ever do] is no proof of their indifference or impotence. It may mean that management is performing to their satisfaction." Here again, as in the quotation from David Rockefeller, the question of "good management" is raised. What do financial institutions want from corporate managements? But once again F&O decline the implied invitation to provide an answer. Wisely, I think, for if they were to give the straightforward answer that financial institutions expect profitable performance from managements, they would be fatally undermining many of the arguments they so laboriously put together later in the essay.

This example of methodological muddle is by no means unique: on the contrary it is typical, as I think careful readers, once alerted, will have no difficulty convincing themselves. My aim in the rest of this critique is to dispose of various specific arguments and theories which might mislead a reader who has little prior acquaintance with the field of corporate behavior and finance, and approaches the Fitch/Oppenheimer study with the perfectly reasonable hope of gaining useful information and knowledge.

Dividend Payouts. F&O make much of a supposed interest of financial institutions in increasing the proportion of corporate profits paid out as dividends to stockholders. The alleged reasons are, first, that raising the payout rate is a "sure-fire" way of boosting the price of a company's stock; and, second, that the more profits are paid out as dividends the less money is left for investment, thus forcing the company to borrow more from the banks. Neither of these arguments, alone or in combination, has the slightest claim to general validity. There are circumstances in which raising the dividend rate will lead to a fall in stock price—for example, if investors and speculators judge that the effect will be to deplete a company's cash below foreseeable needs and thus to jeopardize its solvency. The problem is complicated and no simple formula can possibly cover all cases. And by the same token the main interest of banks is often to limit or reduce dividends rather than raise them, the purpose being to make sure that companies have enough money to service already existing loans. It is, I am sorry to say, all too characteristic of F&O's methods that elsewhere in their essay, when it serves their immediate purpose, they provide ample evidence for this concern of the banks. The discussion of dividend payout rates occurs in Part III, especially pp. 39-40, where the banks' interest in corporate liquidity is not even mentioned. On p. 82 of Part II, on the other hand, they present a table entitled "Long-term Lenders' Conditions" which lists conditions to which *Fortune's* top fifty companies have agreed in order to obtain long-term loans (these are called "restrictive covenants" and are a normal feature of loan agreements). In twenty-four of these fifty cases, the *only* condition noted is "dividends restricted," and in two others dividend limitation is listed as one of two conditions. The banks' enthusiasm for raising dividend payout rates seems, to put it mildly, less than overwhelming!

Even more peculiar is a piece of statistical "evidence" offered by F&O in connection with their argument that finance capital exercises pressure for higher payout rates. On p. 39 of Part III they present a table entitled "Corporate Dividend Payouts by Asset Size: 1960-1970." This shows that in every year there is a close correlation between asset size and payout rate: the larger the company the higher the payout rate. While the conclusion is not stated in so many words, it is clearly implied that this reflects the "fact" that the power of finance capital is similarly correlated with corporation size. Strangely enough, however, F&O fail to note—or, if that seems unlikely, at any rate fail to point out to the reader—that in every asset category there occurs a dramatic and continuous *decline* in the payout rate during the decade of the 1960s, presumably precisely the period when finance capital was moving from one triumph to another. For example, in the largest size category (assets over $1 billion) the payout rate in 1960 was 70.8 percent, and in 1970 it was 55.5 percent. Do the financiers lack the power attributed to them by F&O? Or the goals? Or both? The most plausible answer, I think, is both.

Before we leave this subject, let me cite one more example of how F&O handle "evidence." Because Baran and I maintain that "the making and accumulation of profits hold as dominant a position today as they ever did." F&O flatly assert: "According to Baran and Sweezy, the development of monopoly has no effect on capital accumulation at all." (Part III, p. 37) When I first read this, I rubbed my eyes in amazement. How could anyone really read *Monopoly Capital* without recognizing that the effect of monopoly on the accumulation of capital is what the book is all about?* But never mind, what Baran and Sweezy did in *Monopoly Capital* is one thing and what F&O are interested in demonstrating is something else. They want to show that the rate of capital accumulation has declined in the last hundred years or so and that this is due to the growing power of finance capital.

The first thing to note is that F&O *define* the rate of accumulation as the proportion of profits reinvested which, for a corporation, is simply the inverse of the dividend payout rate. One could of course set up a highly simplified model of capitalism in which the only form of accumulation is the reinvestment of profits by firms. But this is far from being the case in capitalist reality, where accumulation takes a number of other forms as well—savings by dividend-receivers and others with relatively high incomes, so-called forced savings due to price inflation, investment of speculative profits, etc. It is totally inappropriate, not to use a stronger term, to attempt to interpret,

---

* See, for example, pp. 81-88 and chapter 8.

as F&O here do, an actual historical process in terms of a concept which could have meaning only in the context of an abstract theoretical analysis. Let us ignore this, however, and see how good a case F&O can make with their own private definition of accumulation.

We have already seen (p. 9) that according to their own figures, the dividend payout rate has decreased sharply in the last decade, which means that in their sense the rate of accumulation has to the same extent *gone up*. But how about the last century? Here the problem would be to gather comparable figures for the nineteenth century. Of course no one has done it, and owing to lack of raw data no one could do it except in a highly speculative and impressionistic way. But this does not daunt our authors:

> The heroic quality of eighteenth- and nineteenth-century entrepreneurs, saving their profits and retaining them in the business, is a frequently told tale of economic history. Rates of accumulation were *obviously* very high. Just how high we are told less often. And aggregate figures for the various branches of industry are probably impossible to state with *complete* accuracy. (Part III, p. 38. Emphasis added.)

Next F&O cite what the author of a "widely used text" said about "one well-rooted British textile firm," to which they add that "other available records" show that "especially in the early stages of successful entrepreneurship, profit retention actually approached one hundred percent. And some businesses were even more strenuous in their demands for profit retention." Secure in the knowledge that these over-one-hundred-percenters must push the average up, F&O confidently continue: "So despite the gaps in existing historical records, *it seems safe to conclude* that early capitalist entrepreneurs accumulated at least half of their profits, and very likely considerably more." (Emphasis added.)

The reader, dazzled by this display of scientific economic history, is now ready for the clincher, which must obviously be proof that the "modern counterparts" of these early accumulators are indeed a different kettle of fish. But, alas, he is in for a sad disappointment. "We can get a fairly precise idea of the present rate of accumulation," we are informed, "by examining dividend payout ratios." (They have in fact *defined* the accumulation rate as the inverse of the payout ratio.) There follows the discussion of payout rates analyzed above. But what is carefully omitted is the "completely accurate" fact that, according to F&O's own figures, the unweighted average payout rate in 1970 was 42.3 percent. This corresponds to a Fitch/ Oppenheimer accumulation rate of 57.7 percent, which would seem to fit comfortably into the formula of "at least half of their profits, and very likely considerably more."

Faced with workmanship like this, one is hard put to know whether to laugh or weep.

Depreciation. Baran and I are accused of committing what F&O consider to be the egregious error of assuming that depreciation is a source of internal funds which has played a large part in liberating the managements of giant corporations from the kind of subservience to finance capital which characterized the age of Morgan. Not so, they say: "Depreciation is a cost of fixed assets—a cost, not a gain. Depreciation can no more be used to finance expansion than other deductions from reve-nues, provision for bad debts, fire loss, etc. The only internal funds that can be used for expansion are retained earnings." (Part II, p. 69n) All perfectly true in elementary accounting theory. But for better or worse we are talking about corporation finance, and in this realm matters stand very differently.

In the first place, no one knows even in theory what the "true" amount of depreciation is, so that in practice it is al-most always what the tax authorities allow.* And since tax authorities in a monopoly capitalist society are notoriously ser-vants of the leading echelons of the capitalist class, this means that characteristically a big hunk of what ought to be classified as profits and taxed accordingly is actually called depreciation and entirely escapes taxation. In practice, therefore, F&O's dictum that depreciation cannot be used to finance expansion is wrong: it often is used for precisely that purpose.

In the second place, and even more important, what is at

---

* The reasons for the theoretical indeterminacy of depreciation as a cost in a dynamic monopoly capitalist economy are explained in *Monopoly Capital*, pp. 99-104; but the subject, like much else in the real world of monopoly capitalism, is apparently not one that interests F&O.

issue here is not expansion as such but the availability of cash, the lack of which forces dependence on banks and in extreme cases means bankruptcy. And in this respect a dollar labeled depreciation has exactly the same significance as a dollar labeled after-tax profits: they both can be used for any corporate purpose and neither is in any way tied to replacing worn-out or obsolete assets. From the point of view of corporate managements, large and small, the key concept is not depreciation or retained earnings but *cash flow*. It is theoretically perfectly possible for a company with a relatively large amount of fixed assets, and hence a robust cash flow on depreciation account, to quit one line of business entirely and enter another more profitable line without ever retaining a penny of profits or borrowing a nickel from the banks. To be sure, this is not likely to happen in this extreme form, but it is important to understand how and why it could happen. The company with a strong cash-flow position is *never* forced to go hat-in-hand to the banks. The shoe is more likely to be on the other foot: such a company, whenever it wants to raise additional capital, say for a major acquisition or an ambitious foreign expansion program, can pick and choose among possible lenders, playing one off against the other and in the final analysis imposing its own terms on the financiers. And this is precisely the situation of General Motors, Jersey Standard, General Electric, IBM, and many of the other corporate giants which dominate the U.S. economy. Here we can see with crystal clarity how silly it is to equate, as F&O do, external financing with financial control. Logically, it could just as well be taken as an indication of corporate control over the banks and other financial institutions.

Who Controls Whom? I am not suggesting that control of the banks by the big corporations is the normal state of affairs. I do not know—any more than F&O do—enough about what goes on in the boardrooms and executive offices of the big business world to make such an assertion or even hypothesis, and the gentlemen directly involved are not likely to fill us in on the missing information. But it is interesting and salutary to note that a *prima facie* case for the theory of corporate control over the banks can be constructed on the same kind of data that F&O use to "prove" the opposite. Furthermore, F&O know it as well as I do, as shown by two little footnotes which they seem to have been anxious to make as unobtrusive as possible.

The first of these footnotes, on p. 99 of Part I, is addressed to unnamed persons "who argue that interlocks between banks and corporations could just as easily prove the corporations' control of the banks as vice versa." According to F&O, these people should consider bank stockholdings. Well, we have considered bank stockholdings (i.e., the holdings of the banks' trust departments) and have seen no reason to assume that they are used as instruments of control. What about the interlocks? Taken by themselves, it is certainly true that they could "just as easily prove the corporations' control of the banks as vice versa"—or rather, taken by themselves, they don't prove anything. Since F&O obviously know this, one cannot but wonder why they bother to put so much stress on interlocks.

The second footnote (Part II, p. 77) casually remarks that "some [again unnamed] managerial economists have maintained that corporations control the banks and not vice versa because the corporations, through their deposits are net lenders to banks." I am not one of the "managerial economists" referred to here since I must admit that I had not previously thought of this argument. Nor do I believe that, taken by itself, it carries much weight: global figures are frequently of little use in revealing relations of cause-and-effect or domination-and-subordination. What we would need to know is where the balance of power lies in the open or tacit bargaining between giant corporations and giant banks over who places deposits where and who borrows from whom, and there seems to be no way in which this question could be empirically decided. Perhaps the safest hypothesis is that both sides hold strong cards and that their mutual lending and borrowing operations provide no basis for assuming that either controls the other.

At the same time, however, one should not overlook that from the point of view of the slapstick methodology employed by F&O, the argument in question is a powerful one *against* their main thesis of financial control. That they have relegated it to a three-line footnote does not speak well for their sense of scientific integrity.

Reciprocity. F&O devote a lengthy section of their essay to what they call "Financial Control and the Rise of Reciprocity" (Part III, pp. 77-92). "Reciprocity" is the business term applied to the widespread practice of corporations' simultaneously buying from and selling to each other. General Motors needs business machines and IBM needs automobiles and trucks; their mutual requirements therefore lay the basis for mutually profitable deals. As suggested by their use of the expression "the *rise* of reciprocity," F&O are under the impression that there is something recent about the practice. They also believe, among other things, that reciprocity is tied to financial control, that it contradicts all theories which assume corporate maximizing behavior, and that "managerialists" like Baran and Sweezy—who are presumably unaware of the practice—are unable to take account of it in their theories and are hence refuted by its very existence.

Here, as in many other places, F&O reveal their ignorance of U.S. economic history. Reciprocity became notorious in this country during the nineteenth century when it was universally practiced by the railroads and their suppliers and customers. When it is remembered that during the second half of the nineteenth century, investment in railroads exceeded that of all other industries combined, it will be appreciated that nothing could be more out-of-focus than to view reciprocity as a recent development. Nor could it be argued that reciprocity declined during the early decades of the twentieth century, to experience a resurgence in the post-Second World War period. The Interstate Commerce Commission published a multi-volume report during the 1920s proving that reciprocity was as prevalent among the railroads then as it had been in the earlier period, and throughout its history the Federal Trade Commission (founded in 1914) has been more or less continuously engaged in a largely futile effort to curb the practice.

As for Baran and Sweezy's neglect of reciprocity, I must ask the reader to bear with me while I quote a passage from *Monopoly Capital* (p. 50):

The attitude of live-and-let-live which characterizes Big Business . . . derives from the magnitude of the corporation's investment and from the calculating rationality of its management. By and large, this attitude is reserved for other big corporations and does not extend to the smaller businessman. For example, the big three automobile companies behave toward one another in a way that Schumpeter appropriately called "corespective," while their behavior to the scores of thousands of dealers who sell their products to the public is notoriously overbearing and dictatorial. The reason, of course, is that each of the big ones recognizes the strength and retaliatory power of the other big ones and as a matter of deliberately calculated policy avoids provoking them. But corespective behavior is by no means limited to competitors. If one big corporation is not a competitor of another, it is quite likely to be either a customer or a supplier; *and in this realm of corporate relations the sovereign principle is reciprocity,* which enjoins corespective behavior as surely as competition does. (Emphasis added.)

It should perhaps be added, what is clear from the context in the book, that the "competition" referred to is monopolistic or oligopolistic competition, not the pure competition of traditional economic theory.

F&O might perhaps argue that Baran and Sweezy are inconsistent in admitting the ubiquity of reciprocity and at the same time insisting that corporations act to maximize profits. But this is only because they *assume* that corporations are typically controlled by financiers who also control other corporations and that there is no way these outside controllers can act to achieve simultaneous maximum profits for all of them. "That is," F&O explain, "marginalists deal with the issue of oligopoly by ignoring one simple fact of economic life: that a director who represents two corporations cannot possibly maximize profits for both corporations." (Part III, p. 79) They then go on to drive their point home in typical Fitch/Oppenheimer fashion:

Take, for example, the case of Mr. John A. Mayer, Jr., chairman of the board of the Mellon National Bank. Mayer sits on four boards of giant industrial corporations: General Motors, Heinz, Armco Steel, and Alcoa. All four do business with each other. . . . Even with the best possible intentions, how can Mayer simultaneously maximize profits for all the corporations he serves as a director? If he tries to get bargain steel for GM, he isn't maximizing for Armco, and vice versa. Simultaneous maximization on intercorporate sales is an impossibility for a man who represents both companies. If this point is grasped, academic microeconomics becomes entirely untenable.

The trouble with this argument is that it ignores a "simple fact of economic life," namely, that Mr. Mayer's primary responsibility is to maximize the profits of the Mellon National Bank, and there is no *a priori* reason why this should be incompatible with all four of the other companies' acting to maximize *their* profits.

This does not mean, of course, that GM, Alcoa, Armco, and Heinz may not indulge in all sorts of reciprocal deals with each other. It only means that if they do enter into such deals, each corporation is going to be doing the best it can for itself and not simply carrying out the orders of some financier who pulls the strings for all of them. On the other hand, the fact that Mr. Mayer sits on all four boards is by no means enough to assure that these corporations will select each other as reciprocity partners. GM, for example, might find it more profitable to do a deal with U.S. Steel than with Armco. It all depends on the specific circumstances, which may or may not include consideration of common banking ties.

It is interesting that what concrete evidence F&O introduce on actual, as distinct from possible, reciprocity relations fails to support their thesis that "the networks of reciprocity in corporate America appear to parallel, and to be created by, networks of financial control." (Part III, p. 78) They cite Congressional hearings to show that tight reciprocity relations exist between rubber and oil companies. From the point of view of a rival oil company which was anxious to break into this arrangement, the line-up was as follows:

CUSTOMER	SUPPLIER
B. F. Goodrich	Gulf
U.S. Rubber	Texaco
Firestone	Shell
Goodyear	Sun and Sinclair

I am writing this without access to corporate manuals, but I am quite willing to take it for granted that F&O carefully examined these pairs of companies for interlocks, banking ties, etc. And by the same token I conclude that the fact that they mention none reflects an absence of such relations rather than incompetence on the part of the authors.

On the next page, however, F&O finally come up with

their "proof," which is characteristically introduced by the sentence: "Consider the history of the relationships between Du-Pont, General Motors, and U.S. Rubber (now Uniroyal)." No one familiar with the subject doubts that these three companies were, and perhaps still are, under the common control of the DuPont family, or that they have engaged in extensive reciprocity dealings.* The focus of F&O's attention is the situation which existed prior to 1962 when, by U.S. Rubber's own admission, it was selling tires to GM practically at cost, thus in effect transferring profits from one corporation in which DuPont ownership was around 10 percent to another in which it was nearly 25 percent. The trouble is that this is part of the history, not the present status, of the relationships we are asked to consider. Since 1962, partly as a result of an antitrust suit forcing DuPont to divest itself of GM stock but probably also because of a change in DuPont managerial strategy, the situation has radically changed. Once again, F&O relegate to a three-line footnote (Part III, p. 90) facts which contradict their thesis: "Since the divestiture Uniroyal's share in GM tire purchases has dropped to 42 percent [which is less than GM's share of the automobile market]. However, Vila [president of Uniroyal] says that the company now makes a profit on its GM tire sales."

The upshot is that this bit of DuPont history brings support not for the Fitch/Oppenheimer thesis of outside/financial control but for the position adopted by Baran and Sweezy in *Monopoly Capital*. After sketching changes in the typical behavior of the various Standard Oil companies in the half century or so following the break-up under the Sherman Act of the original company in 1911, we wrote:

It is possible that the old Standard companies may still be subject to Rockefeller influence, perhaps even control: publicly available information is not conclusive one way or the other. But if they are, one can only infer that the Rockefellers have decided that the best way to promote their interests is to allow, or perhaps

---

* F&O's attempt to link DuPont control to banker control takes the form of designating the controlling power as "DuPont-Wilmington Trust." This is nothing but a cute trick: Wilmington Trust is in reality nothing but a DuPont house bank playing absolutely no independent role in the whole complex.

encourage, each of the companies to promote its interests. In these circumstances the issue of Rockefeller control becomes irrelevant to the behavior of the companies or the *modus operandi* of the system of which they form constituent parts. . . .

This does not of course mean that each giant corporation operates in isolation, that there are no alliances and alignments, no agreements and groupings. On the contrary, these forms of action—like their opposites, competition and struggle—are of the very essence of monopoly capitalism. All that we are asserting is that the relevant line-ups are determined not by ties to outside control centers but by the rational calculations of inside managements. In the oil industry, for example, Standard companies are as ready and willing to ally themselves with or fight against non-Standard companies as with or against other Standard companies. It all depends where the maximum profit lies. (*Monopoly Capital*, pp. 19-20)

The DuPont case could have been cited in support of precisely this position. Ironical that F&O, despite their opposite intentions, should make the point for us.

After they get done delivering themselves of sweeping generalizations and denouncing all existing brands of economics, F&O have an endearing way of coming down to earth and confessing, a little shamefacedly perhaps, that we needn't take them too seriously after all. The conclusion of their section on reciprocity is an excellent example. "It may be objected," they write, "that government litigation, such as that carried out against DuPont, now prevents outside financial interests from exercising control over sales and purchases." I wouldn't make this particular objection, since I doubt that—except in a few special cases—government litigation has played much of a role in this regard. But I can go along with the conclusion they draw from it: "In other words, reciprocity linkages aren't determined by stockholdings, directorships, and ties to outside financial institutions." The preceding fourteen pages were of course based on the assumption that this is indeed precisely the way reciprocity linkages are determined. Now, however, F&O in effect admit that all the seeming "evidence" they have offered has little or no bearing on the question:

Such a possibility [that reciprocity relations are determined in some other way] requires empirical investigation into intercorporate relations, investigating whether the traditional market factors of price, quality, and service do, in fact, determine market

shares. [Why assume that this is the only alternative possibility?]
But in the meantime, the pervasive influence of financial institutions and other outside groups on intercorporate relations seems
to provide a basis for further investigation. (Part III, p. 91)

So we end up with a plea for "further investigation."
Splendid! This is one of the few things in the whole Fitch/
Oppenheimer essay with which I can wholeheartedly agree.

The Mode of Capital Accumulation. F&O have a long
section (31 pages) entitled "The Mode of Capital Accumulation," defined as "the way in which profits are ploughed back
and redeployed." (Part III, p. 47) This is another one of those
private Fitch/Oppenheimer concepts—I do not remember ever
having run across it in the Marxian literature—which provides
the launching pad for what struck me, after several readings,
as a strange jumble of seemingly carefully researched facts
along with largely unrelated and sometimes quite nonsensical
speculations and pronouncements. In the very first paragraph
of the section, for example, we read: "Acceleration of the rate
of accumulation broke up guild production and changed relations between masters and journeymen into relations between
capitalists and proletarians. The increase in the rate of accumulation of the material forces of production created new relations
of production." We have already seen above (pp. 10-12) how
F&O define the rate of *capital* accumulation, to which they
now add the undefined notion of the "rate of accumulation of
the material forces of production." These rates, which in some
unexplained way must have existed in precapitalist as well as in
capitalist society and which are presumed to have been increasing, are now credited with bringing about a social transformation. This is sheer mystification of the real historical process in
which what Marx called primary accumulation played the decisive role. Only *after* the social transformation had taken place
does it make sense to speak of a rate of accumulation and even
then not in F&O's historically distorted sense.

There are many other passages which seem to me to be
similarly erroneous or confused, but analyzing them would
serve no useful purpose. I would, however, like to try to dis-
entangle what I take to be F&O's major theoretical argument.
If I have misunderstood them, I shall be glad to be corrected.

REVIEW OF THE MONTH   21

The key passage is the following:

In the capital transfer process, a corporation operating in a low-profit industry takes its surplus value and recycles it into a corporation operating in another industry with a higher rate of profit. Capital is thus reconstituted. It serves a new social purpose, creating different commodities or services. Its potential for self-expansion is based on a different human need. This cross-industrial transfer distinguishes it from "classical" accumulation, in which surplus value was converted into capital by the entrepreneur, but the capital remained within the same firm.

This new mode of capital accumulation is typical of the mature monopolies. . . . (Part III, p. 49)

According to this view, classical accumulation—which I suppose means accumulation in the period of competitive capitalism—took place entirely within firms each of which was committed to a particular line of production. Only later, in the period of monopoly capitalism, did a "new mode of capital accumulation" emerge which allows capital to be transferred from one line of production to another. This transfer process is presided over by financiers who manipulate it in various ways, frequently starving some lines of production (railroads, utilities), force-feeding others (computers, photocopiers, etc.), and of course taking the cream off the top for themselves. From the transfer process, which as we have seen is itself supposed to be a "new mode of accumulation," there thus emerge two other new modes of accumulation: the accumulation of loan capital and the accumulation of speculative capital. These new modes of accumulation have "an advanced socialized form" but "a thoroughly decadent and destructive content." (Part III, p. 75) They "amount to a primitive and socially reactionary form of *planning* within capitalism itself." (p. 77) According to F&O, "The next step in the socialization of the investment process must be the transformation of its social relations: the elimination of the financial oligarchy and its replacement by committees of workers operating under the control of popular assemblies." (*Ibid.*)

The programmatic hint in this last sentence raises interesting questions with which, however, I cannot attempt to deal in the present context. What I would like to call attention to

is F&O's peculiar conception of "classical accumulation." If
there is no transfer process, if every firm stays in the line of
business it happens to be in, and if all accumulation takes place
through ploughing back profits within firms, then the whole
competitive mechanism—which is central to classical, Marxian,
and neoclassical economics alike—goes by the board. For how
else than through capital flows from less to more profitable industries is an average rate of profit formed and supply adjusted to demand at prices equal to values or prices of production? Can F&O really be so ignorant of the history of economic thought that they are unaware of all this? Or, knowing
it, have they deliberately set up a straw man ("classical accumulation") as a point of departure which enables them to hail as
"new" (some of) the methods by which the transfer process is
carried out? To put it mildly, neither assumption is very flat-
tering.

     This is not the occasion to discuss historical changes in the
forms of capital accumulation and the role of banks and other
financial institutions therein. Suffice it to say that from the
earliest days of capitalism, accumulation has *always* encom-
passed many forms other than the direct ploughing back of
profits—which, incidentally, has acquired more, not less, importance in the era of giant corporations than it had in the
"classical" period—and that banks and other financial institutions have *always* played an indispensable role in mobilizing
capital and channeling it into the most profitable lines of activity. This role of the financiers has naturally carried with it
influence and sometimes control over industrial enterprises, but
only in the formative period of monopoly capitalism—roughly
the half century after 1870—was financial control the regular
and normal condition in the world of big business. Since the
Second World War the giant corporations have generally been
strong enough to stand on their own feet and relate to the financiers as at least equal, and often more than equal, partners.*

     Do any of the many real facts cited by F&O contradict this
theoretical perspective? I do not think so. As throughout their

---

     * Here, as throughout this critique, I am following F&O in confining
attention to the United States. Modifications would be necessary in the
case of other advanced capitalist countries.

essay, F&O in the section under examination *assume* financial control and then "explain" all sorts of things in terms of the presumed motives of the financiers. In the absence of proof of financial control and given F&O's lack of real knowledge of financiers' motives, such explanations are unfortunately worthless. I will cite only one of several possible examples. Discussing the way financial management allegedly prevents utilities like American Telephone and Consolidated Edison from foreseeing and meeting rising future demand for their services, F&O write:

AT&T's directors *could* float enough bonds to take care of New York Telephone and all its other ailing subsidiaries. But it is highly unlikely that they will do so, for AT&T and its subsidiaries already account for about a quarter of *all* the corporate bonds sold in the United States. And AT&T's directors are the men who control the bond market at both ends. To let AT&T unleash all the bonds it needs on the American bond market would send prices down faster and farther than such market-makers as Morgan, Stanley; Dillon, Read; and First Boston could care to see. Nor would those AT&T directors who represent the largest *holders* of AT&T debt—insurance companies like Metropolitan, Prudential, and Equitable—care to see the prices of these bonds fall. (Part III, p. 66)

This is simply a series of *non sequiturs*. The proportion that AT&T bonds constitute of all corporate bonds is irrelevant. If AT&T needs to sell bonds to raise capital, it can always do so on terms that are about as good as any other corporation can obtain. In this connection it is necessary to bear in mind something of which F&O are apparently ignorant, i.e., that regulatory agencies always permit utilities to charge prices which cover interest payments before the calculation of net profits: in the case of AT&T, which is the biggest of all regulated monopolies, this means that the corporation's bonds carry something very close to a government guarantee. Under these circumstances, banks and insurance companies would not want to sell (or buy) more AT&T bonds only if they were uninterested in selling (or buying) any more high-grade corporate bonds. But of course this is ridiculous, as F&O would have to agree, since one of their main contentions is that these financiers are always pushing the corporations to issue more bonds.

As to F&O's seeing in their alleged "new modes of accumulation" signs of "socialization" of the investment process and embryonic forms of "planning," I can only say that this strikes me as the most arrant nonsense. There is plenty of very real socialization of *production* (not investment) in the modern factory, and more than embryonic planning within the giant corporation itself and in the Pentagon; and these are of course harbingers of the socialized and planned economy to come.* But to find evidence of socialization and planning in the miserable speculative shenanigans which take place in parts of the financial superstructure of the corporate economy—and it is from this area that F&O derive most of their "evidence"— seems to me to betray a woeful lack of that sense of proportion and historical perspective which is so crucial to the fruitful practice of political economy.

The Typical and the Untypical. This brings me to what in the final analysis has to be one of the most damning criticisms of the whole Fitch/Oppenheimer performance. They do not understand the necessity, for scientific purposes, of grasping and focusing on what is typical and ignoring or relegating to a secondary position what is untypical. Instead, they seize upon any facts (or "facts") that lend support, or seem to lend support, to their preconceived ideas, without ever bothering to ask whether the phenomena they are dealing with are typical or untypical.

How else, for example, could one explain using the case of Howard Hughes (Part II, pp. 86-91) to illustrate *any* generalization about the U.S. economy? ("The Hughes case," F&O conclude, "is a spectacular example of the dominant role external finance demands to play in the corporate world.") Hughes, to put it crudely, is a billionaire nut who makes great copy for the popular magazines precisely because he operates outside all the norms of the system.

But even more revealing of F&O's failure to grasp even the first elements of scientific method is their answer to an absolutely correct observation by James O'Connor. "The picture

---

* This does not imply that socialist planning takes the same form as the planning of giant corporations and the Pentagon. Winter's harbingers of spring are by no means the same as spring.

of a few finance capitalists," O'Connor wrote (in MONTHLY REVIEW, December 1968, p. 32), "manipulating stock, acquiring huge overnight profits, and frantically putting together and taking apart industrial empires with an eye to immediate financial gain is simply not consistent with what is known about managerial decision-making in the vast majority of large corporations today."

To this F&O reply: "But 'immediate financial gain' is exactly what the conglomerate 'movement' was all about, and exactly what the railroad and utility 'diversification' efforts are aimed at achieving." (Part II, p. 114) In relation to railroad and utility diversification this is almost certainly not true: long-run rather than immediate gain is the only aim that makes sense. But this is not the point. O'Connor made a statement about "the vast majority of large corporations today," in other words, about *typical* corporate behavior. From F&O's answer one can only conclude that they either do not know what this means or do not understand its decisive importance for the subject under examination.

Penn Central. According to F&O, "The Penn Central illustrates . . . the untrammeled dominance of finance capital in the stage of corporate senescence." (Part II, p. 105) The evidence for this is at first sight rather impressive. "Overall, before the bankruptcy in April 1970 [actually it was in June 1970], the fourteen [Penn Central] board members included eleven men with fourteen interlocks with twelve commercial banks. The twenty-three-member board of the Penn Central Transportation Co., which manages the railroad, had nineteen interlocks with fourteen commercial banks." (p. 107) Furthermore, the big banks held large amounts of Penn Central debt: First National City Bank—$387 million, Morgan Guaranty—$91 million, Chemical Bank—$20 million, Chase Manhattan—$8 million. (table 5, p. 110) All in all, it would appear that here at any rate is a case in which F&O are justified in claiming that the banks had "an unassailable position." (p. 109) And the way they used this position indicates to F&O that "they seemed anxious to make off with everything but the tracks themselves." (p. 114)

And yet if we look at what actually happened at Penn

Central, we get quite a different picture. The banks, for all their apparent power, got not "everything but the tracks" but bad debts and huge financial losses. In a story on bank loan losses, *Business Week* (June 28, 1971) wrote:

> New York stock dealer M. A. Schapiro & Co. estimates that loan losses in 1970, mostly because of the Penn Central debacle, were the heaviest for any single year since the 1930s. The ten members of the New York Clearing House Assn. ran aggregate net loan charge-offs of $191.5 million. And the *New York Times* made an interesting document public this week: an internal message to senior officers from Chairman Walter Wriston of First National City Bank of New York. Citibank was the Penn Central's lead bank and, in the message, Wriston concedes that the bank last year had to revise "our net loss estimate upwards to $47.7 million, or more than four times as much as originally anticipated."

None of the possible advantages derived by the banks from their relationship to Penn Central—which, from F&O's account, were not very impressive anyway—could possibly have compensated for such enormous loan losses.

What is the explanation? That the banks, though firmly in control, were too stupid to protect their own interests? Perhaps there is an element of truth in this. But there is a much more plausible explanation, namely, that the banks were hoodwinked by a crooked management into approving and pouring money into what was dressed up as a profitable diversification program but was in fact a series of investment fiascos, from at least some of which top Penn Central management people personally profited. Let me quote again from *Business Week*'s report on bank loan losses:

> Looking back at Penn Central now, Woodruff [executive vice-president of Manufacturers Hanover Trust Co.] feels: "We were awed by its size. We should have had more information about the company. But I've heard that Penn Central financial people were adroit in avoiding giving information."
> Some government banking officials put it more bluntly: Penn Central's financial data were "fabricated, and bank credit groups just didn't pick it up until too late."
> Some bankers have a "there, but for the grace of God, go I" feeling about Penn Central. Says a senior executive of one of New York's six largest banks, "We had a less difficult time than others

did because a real smart young vice-president here spotted trouble. We gave them no unsecured loans, even though German"—Penn Central's last chairman—"was a member of our board."

Banks and other investors have of course been swindled and victimized in similar ways throughout capitalist history, and no doubt will continue to be in the future. For my part, I would not want to draw any heavy lessons from the episode. But if I were in F&O's shoes, I would be more than reluctant to cite it as an illustration of "untrammeled dominance of finance capital."

Baran and Sweezy on Profits. My purpose has been to criticize F&O's essay, not to defend Baran and Sweezy. But I cannot let them get away with blatant misrepresentation. On page 75 of Part II, they write:

Of course, for managerialists, corporations never lose money. The surplus keeps rising, along with the real wages of the working class. This is the heart of the matter. The unarticulated premise of Sweezy and Baran's account of corporate finance is the *invulnerability of monopoly profits.* Internal funds are sufficient because the flow of profits grows ever wider and unchecked. But profits do fluctuate, and the business cycle does exist. . . .

Beginning in 1965, managerialism notwithstanding, United States profits fell. . . . (Emphasis in original.)

The statement is absurd and shows either that F&O cannot understand a theoretical argument or, if they did understand it, that they have shamelessly distorted it. The thesis of *Monopoly Capital* is that there is a *tendency* for surplus to rise but that monopoly capitalism fails

to provide the consumption and investment outlets required for the absorption of a rising surplus and hence for the smooth working of the system. Since surplus which cannot be absorbed will not be produced, it follows that the *normal* state of the monopoly capitalist economy is stagnation. With a given stock of capital and a given cost and price structure, the system's operating rate cannot rise above the point at which the amount of surplus produced can find the necessary outlets. And this means chronic underutilization of available human and material resources. . . . Left to itself —that is to say, in the absence of counteracting forces which are no part of what may be called the "elementary logic" of the system—monopoly capitalism would sink deeper and deeper into a bog of chronic depression. (*Monopoly Capital,* p. 108.)

In various other parts of the book, especially chapter 8
("On the History of Monopoly Capitalism"), this theory is
applied to the analysis of all or parts of the last hundred years
or so of U.S. history, and nowhere is there anything which
could conceivably be interpreted to mean what F&O say in the
above-quoted passage. And, to cap it off, the statement that
beginning in 1965 U.S. profits fell is simply not true. Here
are the relevant official statistics (*Economic Report of the
President*, 1971, p. 282):

CORPORATE PROFITS (BEFORE TAXES) AND
INVENTORY VALUATION ADJUSTMENT
(billions of dollars)

	All Industries	Manufacturing
1960	49.9	24.4
1961	50.3	23.3
1962	55.7	26.6
1963	58.9	28.8
1964	66.3	32.7
1965	76.1	39.3
1966	82.4	42.6
1967	78.7	38.7
1968	85.4	42.4
1969	85.8	41.8
1970	77.4	34.1

It will be seen that total profits increased sharply in both
1965 and 1966, and for the whole period 1960-1970 went up
by 55 percent despite the cyclical decline of 1970. The other
decline of the decade, in 1967, was also of a cyclical nature.
And yet a few pages after the passage quoted above, F&O can
blandly assert: "As we have seen, when profits turned down in
1965, corporations began to rely increasingly on external finance."* (Part II, p. 93) It should not be necessary to remind
them that when one finds misstatements of "facts" about which
one has knowledge, one is not inclined to have much confidence in an author's reliability in other areas.

---

* This statement should also be evaluated in the light of F&O's own
figures (see p. 10 above) showing that the dividend payout rate sharply
declined during the 1960s. With profits rising and payout rates failing,
it is clear that corporations have never before been so amply provided with
internal funds.

III

In conclusion, I should like to return briefly to the question which F&O pose at the outset: Who *does* rule the corporations?

The best short answer, I think, is that *monopoly capital rules the corporations, including not only industrials and utilities but also banks and other profit-making financial institutions.* I do not mean this in any metaphysical sense: the corporations are of course run by people, not by abstractions. But the people are of no interest in themselves. As Marx said in the Preface to the first edition of Volume I of *Capital*, "Here individuals are dealt with only insofar as they are the personifications of economic categories, embodiments of particular class relations and class interests." The question is what economic categories, what class relations, what class interests do the people who run the corporations personify and embody?

F&O want us to believe that there is a basic split within the capitalist class between the industrial sector and the financial sector, that the two have different and conflicting interests, and that it is the financial sector which holds the upper hand and imposes its will on the industrial sector. This thesis is implicit throughout the whole essay and is stated explicitly in the following passage (Part III, p. 46):

> Radicals . . . like to explain the manifold irrationalities of capitalism by observing that it is profits, not production, that turn the gears of modern industry. But this formulation too has now become inadequate. Just as production and sales are no longer ends in themselves [who, beside bourgeois managerialists, ever said they were?], neither are industrial profits—at least for the stratum of the bourgeoisie that controls the giant corporation. Just as production must contribute to sales and sales to industrial profits, so too industrial profits must contribute to the appropriation of financial profits by the corporate oligarchs. Specifically they must contribute to the appreciation of common stock values; to increasing flows of dividends; to larger commissions for investment bankers; and to larger interest payments accruing to commercial bankers. The key point here is that the pursuit of financial profits can be partially dissociated from the pursuit of industrial profit.

Though they do not say it in so many words, it is clear from the examples they cite and the way they interpret them that F&O believe not only that the pursuit of financial profit is distinct from the pursuit of industrial profit—this indeed is self-evident—but that in pursuing their special interests the financiers regularly act in a way to reduce the long-run profit-making potential of the underlying industrial system. This amounts to saying that the rulers of the corporations do not personify the economic category of capital as such and do not embody the class interests and class relations of the bourgeoisie against the proletariat. Their primary concern is not to maximize the total pool of surplus value but, rather to maximize the amount of surplus value accruing to them even if this means reducing the total pool. In other words those who control the corporations, according to F&O, do not represent the capitalist class as a whole but a particular segment of the capitalist class which has its own special interests and acts as a debilitating parasite on the entire society. According to this theory, finance capital is not only the enemy of the proletariat. It is also, and in a more immediate sense, the enemy of industrial capital. This follows from the circumstance that finance capital is supposed to enlarge its take not by increasing the exploitation of the working class but by milking industrial capital. F&O are thus positing the existence of a basically antagonistic contradiction within the ruling class.

It is important to understand that what is at issue here is not merely struggles among contending groups and factions of the ruling class over the division of surplus value. Such struggles, many of which take place in the financial sphere, have always existed under capitalism and always will exist as long as the system survives. But Marxian theory has never treated them as a manifestation of antagonistic contradictions: as against the rest of society, the capitalists form a unified class which intuitively understands that its primary interest lies in maximum possible exploitation of the working class. Compared to this, the struggle over the division of the spoils is a secondary concern.

F&O, whether they recognize it or not, are proposing a fundamental revision of this central tenet of Marxian theory. If they were right—and this is at bottom a factual, not a theoretical, question—the implications not only for economic analysis but also, and perhaps even more important, for political strategy would be far-reaching indeed. But they are *not* right. The vast majority of large corporations, and this includes banks and insurance companies as well as industrials, are run by people whose primary aim is the maximization of the profits of the companies to which they are principally attached. This ensures that the policies they adopt will, apart from mistakes and miscalculations, operate to increase the pool of surplus value, which is precisely the common interest binding the capitalists, despite all their internecine quarrels and conflicts, together into a single and basically unified ruling class. This is what I mean when I say that monopoly capital rules the corporations: *monopoly capital is the economic category personified by the individuals who happen to sit in the executive suites and boardrooms of America's giant corporations.*

The question naturally arises as to whether this view contradicts the Leninist thesis of the dominance of finance capital in the imperialist stage of capitalism. I do not think so. The truth is that today's giant conglomerate-multinational corporations—and most of them have both characteristics—are essentially financial, not production, units. In the typical case, these financial units both own and control dozens or even scores of diverse producing subsidiaries, all operated in such a way as to maximize the profits of the group as a whole.

This constellation, I submit, corresponds perfectly to Lenin's concept of finance capital, by which he meant the *coalescence* of industrial and financial interests which emerges in the stage of monopoly capitalism. In the United States this coalescence reaches its apex precisely in the concentration of power in the hands of a few hundred giant corporations. It is this concentration of economic power which makes possible not only a more effective exploitation of labor but also the development and application of more advanced technology and a closer cooperation with the state in the profitable utilization of economic and social resources. It also makes possible the appropriation of a larger share of surplus value from other competitive or less-monopolized economic sectors: small competitors, other weaker industries, suppliers of machinery, retail and wholesale trade, etc. In addition, monopoly capital squeezes whatever it

can from the ever-fluctuating stock, bond, and real estate markets, and by utilizing the savings that accumulate throughout
the economic system via banks, insurance companies, and other
financial intermediaries. It follows that giant corporations in
manufacturing, extraction of natural resources, public utilities,
and provision of services are not, and cannot be, purely "industrial" in a world of mixed monopoly. They become, and are
able to operate as, monopolies only by exercising as much *control* as they can possibly muster in order to extract for themselves as much of the social surplus as is feasible. To possess
themselves of the necessary control, the giant corporations must
operate in a wide diversity of areas and through many chan-
nels- -in the capital and money markets as well as in industrial
markets. And it is this which provides the basis for the kind of
coalescence of industry and finance which is of the very essence
of monopoly capital.

Since such coalescence assumes concrete forms in the
course of struggles among greedy centers of power, each seeking greater control and maximum profits for itself, the particular forms of the coalescence vary over time, as between different
countries, and from one area of the economy to another. The
strategy of each power center must take full account of the
maintenance of the value of already-accumulated capital, the
avoidance or minimization of risk, and the probable counter-
measures of rival giants. The dividing lines between intensive
competition and various partnership arrangements among the
various capitalist units and groups are in no sense hard and fast.
Thus a General Motors will be lavish in spending for advertising
and promotion, thus sharing its surplus with TV, radio, and
the printed media. It will also willingly share some of its profits
with commercial and investment bankers, but at the same time
reserve for itself a huge financial plum in the form of a credit
company to finance installment sales of its products.*

---

* If F&O were right that GM and the other automobile companies
are under the control of banks, it would be completely incomprehensible
why they should be permitted to retain enormous (and enormously profitable) subsidiaries (General Motors Acceptance Corporation, etc.) to finance automobile purchases, a business in which they compete directly
with the banks.

What must never be lost sight of, in discussions of the various ways in which the giants share and struggle over the surplus, is that the source and size of what is being shared and struggled over lies in the labor-and-production process. Capitalists in all branches of the economy understand this well enough, even if their academic ideologists do not. And if by chance in their greed they ignore this first principle of capitalist existence, sagging commodity and financial markets soon bring them back to their senses. In the final analysis, it is this production and reproduction by daily life of an awareness of where the golden eggs come from which, willy nilly, welds the capitalists together into one great single interest group.

(October 15, 1971)

———

Since it is not for us to create a plan for the future that will hold for all time, all the more surely what we contemporaries have to do is the uncompromising critical evaluation of all that exists, uncompromising in the sense that our criticism fears neither its own results nor the conflict with the powers that be.

—Karl Marx

[17]

SWEEZY AND CORPORATE FETISHISM

Robert Fitch

Introduction

ISSUE NO. 8 OF *Socialist Revolution* contains a long essay by Paul Sweezy dealing with our articles, "Who Rules the Corporations?" The essay, entitled "The Resurgence of Finance Capital: Fact or Fancy?," appeared simultaneously as an editorial "Review of the Month" in *Monthly Review,* the magazine Sweezy co-edits. More recently, Sweezy inserted it in his latest anthology. The number of times Sweezy responded to our

---

"Who Rules the Corporations?," by Robert Fitch and Mary Oppenheimer, appeared in three parts in Socialist Revolution, *vol. 1, nos. 4, 5, and 6 (1970). A reply by Paul Sweezy was published in* SR 8 (vol. 2, no. 2, March–April 1972), *and also in* Monthly Review, *November 1971 Sweezy's reply has been included in* Modern Capitalism and Other Essays *(New York, 1972). This piece by Fitch is a rejoinder to Sweezy.*

criticism of his theory of corporate control is not extraordinary, given the broad range of issues that divide us, but the
tone Sweezy adopts, the charges he makes, and the lengths he
goes to to try to make the charges stick, are more than unusual. Sweezy does not acknowledge a single criticism we made
of the corporate model in *Monopoly Capital.* On the contrary,
he says we have "nothing to contribute" to the study of corporate control. We are so incompetent, it seems, we offer "not
one single case" to support our thesis of financial control of
corporations. Our discussion of the merger movement "adds
up to exactly nothing." We are, among other things, guilty of
peddling "arrant nonsense." We are "ignorant." We "lack scientific integrity" and use "slapdash methodology." At one
point in reading our essay, Sweezy finds himself "hard put to
know whether to laugh or weep." As a long-time reader of
Monthly Review, I cannot recall any Marxist or anti-Marxist
writer receiving such editorial treatment.

BEFORE DEALING with some of Sweezy's main criticisms, it
might be useful to restate the purpose of "Who Rules the
Corporations?" At the simplest and most obvious level, it
seemed useful to substitute for the unreal and ideologically
based model of the corporation reflected in academic economics and in managerial apologetics one that was based on
empirical research.

The model of the corporation we set out to criticize had
three chief features:

1. Ultimate control rested with inside managers—people
who make an entire career serving a single corporation.

2. As the power of these inside managers grows, the power
of the owners of capital dwindles. Big stockholders, financial
institutions and "interest groups"—Rockefellers, Mellons, Du-
Ponts, et al.—diminish in power too.

3. The transfer of control from capitalists to inside managers took place because corporations could finance themselves
from internal funds. Consequently, Wall Street and the rest of
the capital market were of decreasing importance.

Taken together these three points buttressed the ideology of
managerialism for several decades. In its pure bourgeois form,

managerialists tried to cushion the system from attack by arguing that capitalism has changed so much that the classic Marxist indictment was as irrelevant as a nineteenth-century leaflet.

According to managerial ideology, capitalists didn't run corporations anymore, managers did. With the shift in class power
came a transformation in principles that motivated corporate
behavior. The old compulsion to maximize profits disappeared.
Gone too, said the managerialists, was the class struggle. It no
longer made sense to speak about owners and workers, the
workers owning only their labor power, the capitalists owning
the means of production. The managers didn't own appreciable amounts of stock in the corporations they served. Besides,
managers were workers too, albeit high-paid workers. Meanwhile, the technological revolution was forcing corporations to
upgrade everyone's skills. Soon, they said, everyone in the
work force would be a manager or a scientist or some kind of
paper-shuffling factotum. For the overwhelming majority of
people, working for a corporation would no longer be a curse,
but a high-paid and exciting career.[1]

The second conclusion managerialists draw is that the corporation has become a bureaucratic *meritocracy*, in which the
individual gets ahead in the corporation because he uses his
brains and energy inside it, not because he has accumulated
capital outside or through it.

There was of course *some* truth in the managerial view.
Since the turn of the century, corporations had added several
layers of bureaucracy. Bureaucracies do tend to promote on
the basis of merit. But the bureaucracy inside the corporation
had not been created to serve itself. The capitalists who created it guaranteed that it would continue to serve the interests
of the controlling persons within the corporations, i.e., themselves—the big rich, partners in investment banking houses,
directors of commercial banks, etc. And for these people, the
object of the game was still to increase their *capital*.

What *had* changed was the complexity of the game: especially the incredibly various and ingenious ways the capitalist

1. John Kenneth Galbraith, *The New Industrial State* (Boston, 1967),
pp. 262-81.

class had devised to tap the savings of the masses and mortgage them to their purpose. Variable annuities, mutual funds, and the private pension fund are all essentially creations of the post–World War II period. These devices enabled the financial bourgeoisie to convert the workers' savings into financial and industrial capital which served to provide financial leverage for the bourgeoisie's own capital. In the case of pension funds, the most important source of corporate control in our system, all the workers got out of the deal was the illusion of a happy retirement, followed by bitter disillusionment and a pinched and humiliating old age. On these developments, the managerialists were notably silent.

BECAUSE BARAN AND SWEEZY grafted a good deal of the managerialist model to their own in *Monopoly Capital*, they accept the notion that (1) the corporation is essentially a bureaucratic meritocracy in which the ownership of capital plays only a residual role in determining power relationships; (2) the corporation is essentially "rational" in its operations—i.e., what's good for the managers is good for the corporation as a profit-making entity; so (3) there are no internal contradictions within the capitalist class.

Our first goal, in "Who Rules the Corporations?," was to rectify empirical errors made by the managerial school that enabled them to reach conservative conclusions about society. The second goal was to re-explain this data through new categories, such as the existence of classes and strata whose conflicts help to structure the behavior of the corporation. Neither Sweezy nor the managerialists take account of the varying ways the different strata of the capitalist class derive surplus value—how this determines their attitudes, the way they act inside of the corporation, and how these actions affect the economy as a whole.

Along with class conflict, we wanted to build into our model another decisive feature of corporate reality that is largely ignored in academic economics: the fact that the corporation is not just a producer of commodities but a commodity itself. The practical outcome of this omission is that the operations of the New York Stock Exchange—with its yearly turnover well in excess of a trillion dollars—are treated as if they have no effect whatsoever on corporate behavior. Of course movements of stock prices do profoundly affect corporate behavior, as even a few of the more worldly economics professors realize; it's just that this realization never finds its way into academic writing.[2]

The question remains: "Very interesting, but what difference does it make?" By far the most important result of our work is that it enables us to show that corporations are not, as Sweezy says, "the decisive units of the economy." *Capital* is the decisive unit. It's not corporations who are maximizing profits. It's capitalists who are trying to maximize returns on their wealth—stock, warrants, loan capital, etc. This distinction is crucial not only in any attempt to understand why corporations behave as they do; it also provides an escape from the fetishistic thinking that dominates contemporary academic thinking.

I. CORPORATE FETISHISM

THE CORPORATE FIRM has become the great fetish of modern economics. In the world of modern economics, and most notably in Sweezy's work, the giant corporation controls men and bends their work to its purpose. Instead of capitalists maximizing profits on their capital, we have the *corporation* maximizing profits for itself. The economists, like Sweezy, forget that the corporation is not a person, it is simply a legal device for structuring the flow of surplus value to various classes of investors under conditions that limit individual liability; a device whereby through many contributions, capital can be concentrated ever more tightly in the hands of a few. Like capital, it is a relationship between people. With the economists, however, the relationship is concealed, power is reified, and the actual work of a class of men united by their common

---

2. John F. Childs, senior officer of the Irving Trust, has written an excellent monograph on the subject: *Earnings per Share and Management Decisions* (Englewood Cliffs, N.J. 1971).

ownership of the means of production is hidden. Sweezy puts it perfectly when he says, "In the United States this coalescence [of financial and industrial interests] reaches its apex precisely in the concentration of power *in the hands* of a few giant corporations" (emphasis added). Corporations don't have hands. People do. And in the United States a specific class of people has power, not a group of corporations.

This is neither a quibble on our part nor a slip on Sweezy's part. He believes that "the real capitalist today is not the individual businessman, but the corporation."[3] According to his fetishistic account, even top managers carry out corporate dictates according to a set of rules entirely independent of their will. If managers want to get to the top of the corporation they have no choice but to carry out corporate policy. What is this strange god "corporate policy" that Sweezy has created?

In fact, of course, managers often maximize their self-interest in ways that *reduce* corporate profitability, most spectacularly in the case of the Penn Central.[4] These conflict-of-interest cases are part of the everyday workings of capitalism which Sweezy cannot absorb into his theoretical model.

In addition, as we shall see, Sweezy is forced to distort the nature of corporate reciprocity, a major form of *non-market* corporate interaction whose study is absolutely essential for anyone concerned with the inner tendencies of the system, from economic coercion to a "live and let live" practice that binds businessmen together by mutual interest. This is because Sweezy has eliminated the living capitalists and substituted an abstract "corporate policy" that requires corporations to maximize profits even when such "maximizing" would *reduce* the

3. *Monopoly Capital* (New York, 1966), p. 43.
4. See especially U.S. Congress, House of Representatives, Committee on Banking and Currency, "The Penn Central Failure and the Role of Financial Institutions" (staff report), 3 January 1972, chapter 4, the sections entitled "Taking Care of Yourself and Your Friends" and "CBK Industries: Bevan and Hodge Do It Again." Bevan was the Penn Central's chief financial officer, chosen by senior director Richard King Mellon. Hodge was the railroad's investment banker and the leading figure after Mellon died. See also U.S. Congress, House of Representatives, Special Subcommittee on Investigations, "The Financial Collapse of the Penn Central Company," Staff Report of the Securities and Exchange Commission, August 1972.

profits of the controlling capitalists.[5] In the real world, corporations can and do constantly violate market criteria when buying and selling to each other. By showing who rules the corporation and how ownership mediates intercorporate relations, we have established that the corporation remains a reflection of specific ownership interests with no separate goals of its own.

This is why it is so important to reply to Sweezy's charges. Given the tone Sweezy adopts and the sweep of his charges, one would think that he has already established a solid empirical basis for his theories, and that we have tried to set up a new model without empirical evidence. Actually the cases are reversed. We invite the reader to make the comparison with us.

SWEEZY'S "CORPORATE PARADIGM" has three features. The first is *insider control.* "Real power," Baran and Sweezy say, "is held by the insiders, those who devote full time to the corporation and whose interests and careers are tied to its fortunes."[6] Sweezy cites neither a single case study nor a single survey to substantiate this point.

In contrast, we cited the study sponsored by the American Management Association, which found that the larger the corporation, the more likely it was to be dominated by *outside* directors. We cited studies by the National Industrial Conference Board, now the Conference Board, showing an increasing tendency towards domination by outside directors. We mentioned the cases of Standard Oil of New Jersey, Mobil Oil and Bethlehem Steel—corporations that once prohibited outsiders, but which are now increasingly open to outsider influence. Finally we cited the results of the New York Stock Exchange Survey.

The second point of Sweezy's "paradigm": "Management is a self-perpetuating group. Responsibility to the body of stockholders is for all practical purposes a dead letter." This statement echoes the Berle and Means thesis of 1929—but Baran

---

5. To take a simple example, a purchase by the corporation of its own stock at inflated values designed to benefit insiders, when real maximization would dictate a sale.

6. *Monopoly Capital,* p. 16.

and Sweezy give us no evidence to support it, only a further assertion purporting to describe why the capitalists lost control: "At the same time, the domineering founders of family fortunes were dying off, leaving their stockholding to numerous heirs, foundations, charities, trust funds, and the like so that the ownership unit which once exercised absolute control over many enterprises became increasingly amorphous and leaderless." [7]

Now it's not just that recent events such as the firing of president Semon "Bunky" Knudsen by Henry Ford III make this statement seem dubious on its face. There is a whole literature on the operations of foundations and bank trusts that, if it indicates any one thing, shows that these devices were set up to avoid taxes and to concentrate corporate control in the hands of the great capitalist families, not to diffuse it. [8] Sweezy ignores it, of course, both in *Monopoly Capital* and in his reply.

In contrast, we cited the extensive studies of the Committee on Banking and Currency, especially the report on "Commercial Banks and Their Trust Activities: Emerging Influence on the American Economy." [9] These studies show that bank trust departments have accumulated enough stock to control the largest American corporations. They show, in addition, a systematic effort on the part of the banks to *conceal* their trust department holdings from public scrutiny, a point whose significance we shall expand on later. To show the further concentration of stockholdings by financial institutions, which are in turn controlled by key capitalist families—a point we failed to emphasize sufficiently—we cited United States Treasury statistics, congressional hearings, New York Stock Ex-

---

7. Ibid., p. 18.

8. But in 1941, when Sweezy appeared to be closer to his sources, he wrote the opposite: "Family control is frequently *buttressed* by such relatively new devices as trust funds and endowed institutions for educational, scientific or charitable purposes" ("The Decline of the Investment Banker," *Antioch Review*, Spring 1941; reprinted in *The Present as History* [New York, 1953]). See also the Patman Committee "Report on Charitable Trusts" for sources and contemporary data on "charitable" trusts. For a popular account see Joseph C. Goulden, *The Money Givers* (New York, 1971).

9. U.S. Congress, House of Representatives, Committee on Banking and Currency, 90th Congress, second session, 8 July 1968.

change annual reports, the House Select Committee on Small Business's study on chain banking, and numerous secondary sources.

This brings us to the third point in Sweezy's corporate paradigm and our third data comparison. Baran and Sweezy say, "Each corporation aims at, and normally achieves financial independence." At one time, they say, corporations were dependent on outside sources of financing. But now the need for outside financing has "declined in importance or disappeared altogether as the giants, reaping a rich harvest of monopoly profits, found themselves increasingly able to take care of their financial needs from internally generated funds." In other words, internal funds, and profits especially, have increased as a percentage of the total sources of funds available to corporations. The percentage of internal funds has gone up and the percentage of external funds has gone down. Well, has it or not? This is not a question of opinion. It's an easily substantiated matter of fact. But Baran and Sweezy do not substantiate their argument about increasing internal funds over time. Nor could they since the facts undermine it. These facts were available to Sweezy. John Lintner's definitive article on corporate finance appears in E. S. E. Mason's widely sold paperback anthology. Lintner, who is a professor of business administration at the Harvard Business School, is cited by Sweezy as an authority on corporate finance in *Monopoly Capital.* First Lintner cites the study done for the National Bureau of Economic Research by Raymond Goldsmith, which shows that the ratio between internal and external funds "for all nonfinancial corporations was remarkably stable at a level of 40 to 42 percent in each benchmark year during the first quarter of the century." Then he reviews Brill's findings which show a moderate decline (41 to 37 per cent) in the late twenties, with subsequent fluctuations during the Depression period. For the postwar period the ratio has held at the highest levels (44 per cent in the three decades covered.) Lintner observes: "This stability in the relative reliance on internal and external financing over substantial periods through the middle of the century is indeed what we find when we look to the data on the sources and uses of funds of corporations." He continues: "This finding is directly contrary to the broad Berle and Means thesis and to Berle's more recent position, and to widespread impressions not only among the lay public but among economists and professionals." After analyzing the figures on retained earnings, Sweezy's "rich harvest of monopoly profits," Lintner adds that "the conclusions seem inescapable that there has been no secular net change in the relative dependence on internal funds to expand assets among all nonfinancial corporations over this broad sweep of time." [10]

The Lintner data stopped in the mid-fifties. We brought the evidence up to date. Concentrating on the period since the 1966 turn in the business cycle we found that a trend had indeed been established—but it was *away* from the use of internal funds. Citing the study of the Federal Reserve Bank of San Francisco, we noted that between 1965 and 1969 "internal financing increased at only a 2.6 per cent rate while external financing jumped to a 16.5 per cent average annual growth rate." [11]

The reason for reviewing this evidence is that the weight of Sweezy's theory of the "giant corporation" turns on the question of internal finance, the third point of his corporate paradigm. From Sweezy's point of view it was because internal funds increased that the managers were able to take over. [12] But internal funds have not increased. So not only is *each* of the empirical bases for Sweezy's model bare of any factual support, the real facts about internal finance strip it of its logical connective tissue as well.

Taken all together, the entire basis of support for Sweezy's theory of the giant corporation laid out in chapter 2 of *Monopoly Capital* lies in a few quotes from the novel *Cash McCall*, a brace of self-serving quotes from big businessmen like Henry Ford II, and Crawford Greenewalt taken at face

---

10. *The Corporation in Modern Society* (New York, 1966), pp. 177–80.
11. *Socialist Revolution* 5, pp. 72–73.
12. *Monopoly Capital*, p. 16. "The corporation may still, as a matter of policy, borrow from or through financial institutions, but it is not normally forced to do so and hence is able to avoid the kind of subjection to financial control which was so common in the world of Big Business fifty years ago."

value. And, finally, a three-page verbatim quote from a University of Wisconsin professor which reveals only that successful corporations try to cut costs. Aside from an "informal interview" with a bank trust department officer, which we will examine later, his reply adds no factual supporting material.

Given the paucity of data Sweezy is able to mobilize in support of his argument, it becomes clear now why Sweezy has throughout his critique chosen to fight on the grounds of *methodology*, i.e., the systematic organization and presentation of scientific data. Being, as we shall show, relatively unfamiliar with data and literature concerning corporate organization, Sweezy has no choice but to restrict himself to a criticism of the way such data should be organized. Such a self-protective restriction, however, leads Sweezy into serious errors.

II. RECIPROCITY

NONE OF SWEEZY'S ATTACKS raises more fundamental issues than his criticism of our reciprocity section. It is here we discover most concretely what difference it makes "Who Rules the Corporations." The analysis of reciprocity shows that we are not dealing with a simple empirical question with mere sociological implications—managers vs. bankers. Or to put it another way, it's not just that in Sweezy's model, corporations are controlled by managers while in our model they're controlled by the very rich, but that in both models the corporations behave the same way and interact with each other similarly. The difference goes deeper. And it reflects different ways of approaching economic analysis. Very schematically, the differences between the two models break down as follows:

Managerial model	*Finance capital model*
Corporations are the decisive unit in the economy.	Capital is the decisive unit.
Managers control the corporation.	Owners of capital control corporations.
Corporate policy aims to	Corporate policy aims to

increase the "strength, rate of growth and size" of the *corporation* through profit maximization.

maximize returns on individual capitals.

Reciprocity as "mutual benefit" between stockholders.

Reciprocity as exercise of coercive financial power.

Conflict of interest impossible.

Conflict of interest between stockholders unavoidable.

Corporations relate to each other on the basis of price, quality, and service, i.e., market criteria.

Corporations relate to each other increasingly not on the basis of market criteria but on the basis of financial factors, extra-market power.

The patterns of corporate reciprocity can help us test the predictions of the two models. If the Sweezy model is correct, corporations won't engage in intercorporate transfers that violate market criteria of price, quality and service. In other words, corporation A will not buy from corporation B if corporation C sells at a lower price. The finance capital model predicts that this type of non-market behavior will take place if a large stockholder—individual or institutional—owns decisive amounts of stock in corporations A and B, but not in C.

Admittedly much of Sweezy's criticism has a surface plausibility. Conclusions follow premises, etc. But Sweezy's major problem is that he defines and re-defines "reciprocity" to suit his purpose and comes up with contradictory definitions. First he defines "reciprocity" as "the business term applied to the widespread practice of corporations simultaneously buying from and selling to each other." Here is the example we get: "General Motors needs business machines and IBM needs automobiles and trucks; their mutual requirements therefore lay the basis for *mutually profitable deals*" (emphasis added). The other usage enters when he is arguing against the fact that reciprocity is more pervasive today than in the early period of United States corporate development: "Reciprocity became notorious in this country during the nineteenth century when it was universally practiced by the railroads and their suppliers and customers." In this denotation of "reciprocity," the practice is *coercive*, not *mutually profitable*.

Sweezy uses the coercive definition to show that reciprocity has not become more important over time. He uses the non-coercive, "live and let live" definition when he wants to argue against our contention that he has ignored reciprocity in *Monopoly Capital.* [13]

The only meaningful definition of reciprocity, however, is the one based on coercion. If coercion or the implicit threat of coercion were not inherent in reciprocity, then it would not be illegal, cr even very interesting. As Willard Mueller, chief economist of the Federal Trade Commission, observes, "a firm has an incentive to engage in reciprocity when doing so permits it to make a sale that it *could not otherwise make* or could make only at greater cost" [14] (emphasis added). Thus Sweezy's IBM-GM example is inappropriate. Reciprocity would exist only if, say, GM bought IBM computers although there were computers available from another corporation offering better price, quality, and service.

Has Reciprocity Grown More Pervasive?

SWEEZY CHARGES that in our reciprocity section we reveal our "ignorance of U.S. economic history" by claiming that

13. "The attitude of live-and-let-live which characterizes Big Business . . . derives from the magnitude of the corporations' investment and from the calculating rationality of its management. By and large, this attitude is reserved for other big corporations and does not extend to the smaller businessmen. For example, the big three automobile companies behave toward one another in a way that Schumpeter appropriately called 'co-respective,' while their behavior to the scores of thousands of dealers who sell their products to the public is notoriously overbearing and dictatorial. The reason, of course, is that each of the big ones recognizes the strength and retaliatory power of the other big ones and as a matter of deliberately calculated policy avoids provoking them. But co-respective behavior is by no means limited to competitors. If one big corporation is not a competitor of another, it is quite likely to be either a customer or a supplier; and in this realm of corporate relations the sovereign principle is reciprocity, which enjoins co-respective behavior as surely as competition does." This is the only mention Baran and Sweezy make of "reciprocity" in *Monopoly Capital* (p. 50). And they misconstrue its meaning.

14. U.S. Congress, Senate, Committee on the Judiciary, Subcommittee on Anti-trust and Monopoly, Staff Report of the Federal Trade Commission, "Economic Report on Corporate Mergers," Hearings on Economic Concentration. 91st Congress, first session, Part 8A, Appendix to Part 8, pp. 323–24.

reciprocity is more pervasive today than in the 1920s or previously. This charge shows that in addition to being unable to give a consistent definition of "reciprocity," Sweezy is unfamiliar with the literature on the subject, found in business magazines, court records, legal publications, and government reports. If there is anything that all authorities on reciprocity agree on, it is that reciprocity is increasing as American industry becomes more concentrated.[15]

Sweezy claims support from the Interstate Commerce Commission which he says "published a multi-volume report during the 1920s proving that reciprocity was as prevalent among the railroads then as it had been in the earlier period." Sweezy does not footnote this multi-volume report and I have been unable to find it in any California law library. I *have* found a short article published by the ICC in 1932 entitled "Reciprocity in Purchasing and Routing" (188 ICC 417). But it fails to establish the claims Sweezy makes. Sweezy also refers obliquely to the Federal Trade Commission as an authority (once again giving no specific reference) for his view that the importance of reciprocity has not increased. But here is what the FTC said as recently as 1969: "Although business firms practiced reciprocity on a systematic basis as early as the 1920s there is mounting evidence that, as firms have become larger and more diversified they have resorted more frequently to its use."[16] Further evidence for the view Sweezy equates with "ignorance of U.S. economic history" comes from the private correspondence of the DuPont family. It shows that as late as 1924 the practice of reciprocity was novel to Pierre S.

---

15. See, for example, *Fortune*, June 1965, "A Customer Is a Company's Best Friend," p. 180. "Especially interesting is the way that reciprocal relationships are multiplying all through U.S. business these days, and being pursued with new techniques and formal organization. There are a number of reasons for the increase. Estopped from vertical growth, big companies have branched out horizontally into other industries, becoming more and more diversified until they have found themselves with a long list of suppliers in one hand and a long list of products for sale in the other. That conglomerates should move to make the most of the possibilities they perceive in such a situation seems only natural and practical."

16. Staff Report of the Federal Trade Commission, p. 332.

DuPont, then chairman of both DuPont and General Motors.[17] As chairman DuPont became aware of it, he ordered that it be employed systematically.

Reciprocity and Conflict of Interest

BY DENYING THAT reciprocity is becoming more pervasive, Sweezy precludes an understanding of the sources of its development in the increasing conglomeratization of the United States economy. To be unable to link conglomerates with reciprocity casts a shadow over one of the most important trends in corporate interaction. This is the use of non-market and frequently coercive means to move products. Reciprocity is the exercise of raw economic power by giant conglomerate corporations, especially against smaller rivals and suppliers. It is not "mutual benefit," as Sweezy calls it. In *Monopoly Capital*, Sweezy seeks to draw distinctions between the cut-throat methods of the past and the present big business ethic "which calls for solidarity and mutual benefit."

There is no way Sweezy can get around the contradiction although he tries several times. First he says that although we might argue that reciprocity and profit maximization are inconsistent, this is so only because we "assume financial control over corporations." We assume nothing of the kind. Reciprocity involves buying and selling goods on the basis of considerations other than price, quality, and service. Why would a corporation enter into a purchase agreement of this kind—i.e., why would it not maximize profits? One possible reason is of course financial control. An outside financial institution may control stock in both corporations and choose to regulate the purchases and sales according to its stock interest in both.

But there is another explanation. One corporation may simply compel the other corporation to buy its commodities by the exercise of extra-market power, e.g., a steel corporation says to its coal supplier, "Use our steel in the construction

17. Letter from G. H. Kerr to O. S. DuPont, 31 March 1924, Government Exhibition 530, p. in U.S. vs. E. I. du Pont de Nemours & Co., 6 F. Supp., 235 (N.D. Ill., 1954), cited in George F. Stocking and Willard F. Mueller, "Business Reciprocity and the Size of Firms," *Journal of Business*, April 1957, p. 81.

of your new corporate headquarters or we'll stop buying coal from you."

The second way Sweezy tries to avoid the obvious contradiction between conventional profit maximization and reciprocity is even less satisfactory. In "Who Rules the Corporations?" we cited the case of John Mayer, chairman of the board of the Mellon National Bank, who sits on the boards of four other corporations—all of which do extensive business with each other: Alcoa, General Motors, Armco Steel and Heinz. And we point out how convenient it is to have Mayer sitting on the board of both Heinz (four Mellon directors, thirty-one per cent of the common stock) and Alcoa (twenty-five per cent of the common stock, three directors). Our hypothesis is that Alcoa must sell aluminum cans more cheaply to Heinz than it would to Campbell, Inc., and that it would make sense for the Mellon National Bank to have Alcoa sell its aluminum cans to Heinz at cost. But in any case, Mayer, the Mellon Bank chief who sits on both boards, cannot maximize profits for the two corporations simultaneously. If he maximizes the aluminum price for Alcoa, he is not minimizing the cost for Heinz, and vice versa. This is self-evident, and in response to this obvious demonstration all Sweezy can muster is a simple denial: "The trouble with this argument," says Sweezy, "is that it ignores 'a simple fact of economic life,' namely that Mr. Mayer's primary responsibility is to maximize the profits of the Mellon National Bank and there is no a priori reason why this should be incompatible with all four of the other companies acting to *maximize* their profits" (emphasis added). We can see how incompatible profit maximization for the Mellon Bank is with profit maximization for the other corporations if we take a simple numerical example. Let's say Alcoa charges its ordinary customers fifty cents per pound for aluminum sheets, and that it makes ten cents profit or twenty per cent on each pound sold. Let's postulate further that the Mellon Bank controls twenty-five and thirty per cent of Alcoa and Heinz shares respectively. On a ton of aluminum at fifty cents per pound, the Mellon Bank will earn fifty dollars. If Alcoa sells the aluminum at cost, however—forty cents per

SWEEZY AND CORPORATE FETISHISM   109

pound—the amount of income added to Mellon's stake by virtue of the savings to Heinz would be sixty dollars. Clearly if Mellon Bank maximizes profits, than Alcoa cannot maximize its profit.

In this real world conflicts of interest abound. With key commercial banks controlling huge blocs of stock in competing corporations, with corporations seeking control over corporate suppliers and corporate customers, with an ever-growing number of interlocking directorates, how could it be any other way? The mystery is how Sweezy can close his eyes to the daily operation of a corporate America in which indictments, judicial consent orders, and regulatory decisions of the FTC, FCC, FPC, CAB et al. show that conflict of interest, far from being impossible, is routine. The most famous recent case is the Penn Central fiasco, in which the railroad's investment banker, in league with the chief financial officer, carried out a series of stock acquisitions that benefited their own private portfolios and bankrupted the railroad. There is no way that Sweezy could have taken Penn Central into account in 1966, when *Monopoly Capital* was written. But what about the notorious case of the Chrysler Corporation, in which corporate officers set up accessory subsidiaries and forced Chrysler to buy exclusively from them; or the Texas Gulf Sulphur case, in which Morgan partners on the board concealed knowledge of a valuable mine discovery from the other stockholders in order to exploit it for themselves; or the American Can case, in which directors of American Can, controlling twenty per cent of Metal and Thermite Corporation and sitting on its board, forced the company to buy scrap metal from American Can at above market prices? These are textbook cases, and there are literally hundreds of others that have been litigated in court and thousands that never get to court or even FTC dockets. Corporate directors engage in conflict of interest so systematically that they fully expect to be sued and lose a fair percentage of the suits. Routinely, therefore, they take out conflict-of-interest insurance—for which the company pays.

The results of our counter-critique are the following:

—Reciprocity is coercion, not mutually profitable deals

between corporations who operate on a live-and-let-live basis.

—The practice of reciprocity is on the increase because of increasing corporate size and conglomeration.

—Most important, we see that the notion that all corporations maximize profits is only apparent. The exceptions, those corporations who relate to each other on the basis of financial reciprocity, show that there are underlying forces regulating corporate interaction that are determined by specific ownership interests. Marginalism tells us that the general law of corporate behavior is profit maximization by the firm. Actually this turns out to be a special case of a more general law: the law that capitalists seek to expand their capital and do so regardless of what form it takes or whether the capitalists meet each other in the marketplace as formal competitors. Such "exceptions" cannot be dismissed as "untypical" any more than physicists could dismiss cases of apples falling "up" as mere exceptions to the law of gravity. Essentially, this is the methodology underlying Sweezy's critique in the next section on "the typical vs. the untypical."

III. TYPICAL VS. UNTYPICAL

WE ARE COMING NOW to what Sweezy calls "one of the most damning criticisms" of our whole "performance." Allegedly, we focus on the "untypical" instead of what Sweezy calls "the typical." In Sweezy's words, we "seize upon any fact (or facts) that lend support, or seem to lend support to [our] preconceived ideas without ever bothering to ask whether the phenomena [we] are dealing with are typical or untypical."

Sweezy has two examples of this penchant of ours. One is our case study of the struggle for control of TWA between Howard Hughes and Wall Street. The other is our handling of the merger movement. But before we examine these instances to see if Sweezy's strictures are justified, let us consider his premise. He says, "They do not understand the necessity for scientific purposes of grasping what is typical and ignoring or relegating to a secondary position what is untypical." Is it, really, good scientific methodology to exclude the untypical from scientific focus? It certainly seems that Sweezy's metho-

dological guidelines would put a halt to many lines of contemporary investigation and preclude many successful experi-
ments from ever taking place. Eclipses, for example, are far
from typical solar events, yet their analysis tells us a great deal
about the everyday operation of the solar system. Similarly,
the ordinary human cell is not cancerous, yet the study of
such cells can reveal much that physiologists want to know
about typical human metabolism. In the same spirit, geologists
study earthquakes, economists analyze depressions.

Thus, while it would seem that study of the atypical has
strong claim to scientific attention, Sweezy would forbid use
of our Howard Hughes–TWA case study. The reason, Sweezy
says, for discounting our evidence in the TWA struggle is that
Hughes is "a billionaire nut who makes great copy for the
popular magazines *precisely* because he operates outside all the
norms of the system."

Now, in "Who Rules the Corporations?" we made the point
that Howard Hughes was not a typical American businessman.
First because he is possible the richest; second because he held
seventy-five per cent of the stock of a giant American corporation, an extremely high percentage; and third because he was
audacious—attempting to integrate the operations of his airline into those of his aircraft company, contrary to the wishes
of the financial institutions that sought to operate the airline
industry as a unified cartel.

What would be the result, we asked, if Howard Hughes
entered into a test of strength with finance capital over control
of TWA? Certainly it would tell us a great deal about where
the power lies in the United States economy, if a man with
seventy-five per cent of the stock in a corporation, backed by
the world's largest personal fortune, has control of his corporation wrested from him by outsiders. This, of course, is exactly what happened. The big banks and insurance companies—
Chase Manhattan, Morgan Guaranty Trust, Equitable and Prudential—seized control of Hughes's stock through a series of
legal battles and took over the airline. The outcome of the
power struggle seemed to bear out dramatically what the Patman committee's study showed statistically: that the big financial institutions had controlling power in the airline industry.

We should point out here that our conclusion is hardly idio-syncratic. *Fortune* magazine concluded a six-year investigation of the case by noting that the terms imposed by the financial institutions were severe enough "to raise the question of who really controls the key management decisions in the airlines in this era."

Our evidence was based on events of the early 1960s and on records of institutional stockholdings as of 1967. Since then the Institutional Investor Study has enabled us to draw an even clearer picture of where control lies in the airline industry:

—six financial institutions control thirty per cent of TWA's stock;

—five financial institutions control fifteen per cent of East-ern's stock;

—eight financial institutions control twenty-five per cent of United's stock;

—seven financial institutions control thirty per cent of North West's stock;

—five financial institutions control twenty per cent of Del-ta's stock.

These figures show that the financial institutions have more than enough stock even by Berle and Means's conservative standards to exercise control. The Hughes case study shows that the banks and insurance companies zealously exercise their voting rights in support of their objectives, in this case monopoly of airline loan business.

It is easy to brush aside our evidence and the evidence that others have compiled as somehow undefinitive, or "atypical." It's true of course that there will very likely never be another Howard Hughes–type struggle over control of an airline. By now the financial institutions have accumulated so much vot-ing stock in the airlines that no single capitalist could possibly challenge them.

Unfortunately, Sweezy has no new facts, or old ones for that matter. What he offers instead is "an even more revealing example" of our "failure to grasp even the first elements of scientific method." We were wrong, says Sweezy, to criticize the notion that today's finance capitalists, unlike those of yesterday, no longer try to take apart and put together industrial empires with an eye to immediate financial gain.[18] But it seems to us that today's business leaders are just as financially oriented and just as merger-minded as ever. There is a great deal of evidence to back up this contention, from the statements of big business leaders like Jimmy Ling, ex-chairman of LTV,[19] and the congressional testimony of investment bankers like Felix Rohatyn,[20] to the actual figures available about today's merger movement versus the merger movements of the past. These latter figures show that the recent merger movement (1965–1969) is the largest in American industrial history, not only in terms of the number of firms acquired and the dollar size of assets acquired, but also in terms of the acquired assets expressed as a *percentage* of total corporate manufacturing and mining assets.[21]

What's Sweezy's criticism then? He doesn't dispute any of this, really. In fact, in his own article on mergers[22] he describes

18. See *Socialist Revolution* 5, p. 114.

19. "Some Candid Answers from James Ling," *Fortune*, August 1969, p. 92 and passim. Ling admitted that as chairman of LTV all he was interested in achieving was as large and fast an increase in earnings per share as possible. To a certain extent earnings per share can be bought or more specifically borrowed rather than earned. For several years the investment banking houses of Goldman, Sachs and Lehman Brothers financed Ling's policy. They profited considerably on the upswing of the stock. They sold when it peaked and got rid of Ling when it hit bottom. LTV is now controlled by a committee headed by the chairman of the First National Bank in Dallas. See also House of Representatives, Committee on the Judiciary, Hearings before Anti-trust Subcommittee on Ling-Temco-Vought, "Investigation of Conglomerate Corporations," 92nd Congress, second session, 15, 16, 22 and 23 April 1970.

20. House of Representatives, Committee on the Judiciary, Hearings before the Anti-trust Subcommittee on International Telephone and Telegraph Company, "Investigation of Conglomerate Corporations," 92nd Congress, second session, 20, 21, and 26 November and 3 December 1969.

21. U.S. Congress, Senate, 91st Congress, second session, Committee on the Judiciary, Staff Report of the Federal Trade Commission, "Economic Report on Corporate Mergers," Part 8A, pp. 30–45. "The current movement," says the FTC report prepared by Willard F. Mueller, "is unique in its duration, magnitude and conglomerate nature."

22. "The Merger Movement: A Study in Power," *Monthly Review*, June 1969. This article consists chiefly of a stitching together of quotes from contemporary business magazines. It seriously misconceived the character of the merger movement. Incredibly, Sweezy thought the leaders of the merger movement were upstart capitalists, potential supporters of

the financial motives that he calls "the secret" of the "burgeoning of the latter-day conglomerates." So where *do* we
disagree? In this: Sweezy has decided that the merger movement is not *typical* of current business behavior. As far as I am
concerned the notion that the merger movement is "atypical"
of capitalism seems a bit far-fetched. But even if not, there is
no way to resolve it in the context of this debate. Because for
all his emphasis on methodology, Sweezy has ignored the most
elementary methodological rule—the necessity to define one's
terms. Nowhere does Sweezy ever tell us what "typical"
means! Such vagueness has its advantages. A phenomenon like
the merger movement, which at its height in 1968 accounted
for one-third of all corporate investment, can be slipped into
the infinitely expandable category of "atypical" and dismissed.
But as methodology, such efforts bear a striking resemblance
to the dictum of Lewis Carroll's Humpty Dumpty, who said,
"When *I* use a word, it means what I choose it to mean."

IV. BANK TRUST DEPARTMENTS:
THE HEADACHE OF PROFITS

SWEEZY'S CRITICISM of our section on bank trust departments goes right to the heart of our argument. The question
Sweezy raises is whether the banks through their enormous,
but only recently publicized trust holdings, influence decision-
making in the corporations in which their stock holdings are
especially large. Sweezy says banks don't really control this
stock. We say they do. As we shall see, we are joined in our
assessment by the Securities and Exchange Commission and
the Anti-trust Division of the Department of Justice, to say
nothing of knowledgeable corporate critics like House Banking
and Currency Committee chairman Wright Patman and consumer advocate Ralph Nader. More important perhaps, everyone in the real world acts as if bank trust departments can
control corporate stocks, i.e., congressional bills to regulate
the powers of bank trust departments are opposed by the
banks with the biggest trust departments.

"fascist-type movements." Actually they were, for the most part, Democrats with backing from old-line Wall Street investment banking houses
like Goldman, Sachs; Lehman Brothers; and Loeb, Rhodes.

Even Sweezy admits banks *could* control corporations. But they'd rather not. The huge bank holdings "raise questions," Sweezy says. But the banks "not only do not control corporations, they do not even want any such responsibility." Why not? Because, according to Sweezy, such control "could bring all sorts of headaches and open them to expensive damage suits should losses be suffered by trust beneficiaries."

We have to follow Sweezy's argument to his footnote,[23] because it's here he reveals the source of the many misconceptions he has about bank trust assets, their composition and function in the financial system:

"In this field of trusts and fiduciaries, capitalist law defining the responsibilities of trustees to beneficiaries is both strict and on the whole strictly enforced. This is not surprising since the stratum of the population involved is what C. Wright Mills called the 'very rich' who are well aware of their rights and never make a move without expert legal advice."

Evidently Sweezy has failed to keep up with the huge changes that have overtaken the bank trust business in the last thirty years. True enough, in the 1930s, when Sweezy carried out his research for the National Resources Committee, the biggest chunk of bank trust assets was formed by the assets of the very rich. Nowadays, the picture has changed. *Employee pension funds* occupy that position, a change brought about by the introduction of pension benefits as a negotiable item in collective bargaining during World War II.

Restrictive labor legislation prevented unions themselves from controlling pension assets. The corporation and the union were compelled by Taft-Hartley to nominate a trustee; the banks stepped forward and the pension fund bonanza was on. By 1945 the total pension fund assets had reached $5.4 billion. By 1950 they had reached $12 billion and the almost geometric progression continued so that by 1970 the total had reached $130 billion, just about half of the entire $270 billion pension fund industry.[24]

In the last year especially, however, the burgeoning pension

---

23. *Socialist Revolution* 8, p. 160, fn. 2.

24. Agency accounts and personal trusts constitute the remaining $140 billion.

fund industry has come under attack both from Nader and from congressional critics like Martha Griffiths and Senator William Proxmire. These liberals—curiously, socialists seem to have ignored the issue—have taken up the complaints of rank-and-file workers. The main "beef" of the workers is that only one out of three of them will ever get a private pension under the present bank-controlled system. And even these relatively lucky finishers in the pension sweepstakes get benefits amounting to less than $1,100 a year. Meanwhile the banks and their battalions of middlemen—accountants, lawyers, actuaries, etc.—reap a giant $4 billion for "managing" the workers' pension money.

Since Sweezy misunderstood the composition of bank trust assets it is not surprising that he was also wrong about the degree of accountability the banks have to their putative beneficiaries for trust department money. Far from being strict, this accountability is exceedingly lax. But not criminally so, because the law reads differently from the way Sweezy thinks it does. As Charles Leinenweber explains in a perceptive article in *Ramparts:*

> The growth in pension assets, combined with the shift in their deployment, turned them into a solid-gold tool for corporate control.
>
> The tool was shaped in the muffled workshops of Wall Street law firms. There, bank lawyers silently hammered out sets of agreements that would deliver to banks absolute authority over the funds they handled. Chase Manhattan, whose law firm is the famed Millbank, Tweed, Hadly & McCloy, and which alone accounts for nine per cent of the banks' pension share, recently showed a masterful sample contract to the House Judiciary Committee. The contract contains sixteen primary articles, including provisions to exempt the bank from any responsibility toward pensioners.
>
> But its heart lies in an elaborately worded Fourth article, which contains, strung throughout in incredible but air-tight legalese, all the necessities for corporate control. The bank, the contract says, shall have the power and authority "to oppose or consent to the reorganization, consolidation, merger or readjustment of the fi-

nances of any corporation, company or association, or to the sale, mortgage, pledge or lease of the property of any corporation, company or association any of the securities of which may at any time be held by it . . ." What this means is that the bank, as trustee, enjoys unlimited authority to utilize the stocks and bonds it buys with pension funds, as an entry into the decision-making processes oftthe corporations it has a stake in. Indeed, the bank can exercise "any right, including the right to vote, appurtenart to any securities or other property held by it at any time."

All this is wrapped up in the shortest article of all, the Fifth, which states: "The powers listed in the Article Fourth of this Agreement shall be exercised by the Trustee in its uncontrolled discretion." Uncontrolled discretion—the poetry of the ruling class.[25]

Banks handle pension fund assets belonging to workers very differently from the way they handle the trust assets belonging to the very rich. According to the survey carried out by the Securities and Exchange Commission, the bank has *sole* investment authority in the case of 88.8 per cent of its pension fund assets. By contrast, in the case of its personal trust assets, the bank has sole authority over only 22 per cent. And there is an inverse correlation between the size of the personal trust assets and the amount of authority the bank holds. Interestingly, the correlation works in the opposite direction in the case of pension fund assets: the larger they are, the greater the tendency for the bank to exercise full authority.

Having disposed of Sweezy's objection that the bank trust assets are legally beyond bank authority, we are back to our original question: banks can control corporations, but do they? Sweezy says that banks "do not only not control corporations, they do not even want any such responsibility, which would bring all sorts of headaches." What evidence does Sweezy have that the banks eschew responsibility for control? It seems, on the face of it, that the bankers try quite hard to get complete authority over the assets and succeed 88.8 per cent of the time in the case of pension fund money, the largest single bloc of

25. July 1972.

trust assets. Why try so hard to obtain "uncontrolled discretion" if you're not going to use it?

Sweezy's belief that banks try to avoid the headaches of control is based solely on the statements of bank trust officers he has "informally interviewed." Such "informal interviews" raise, from the standpoint of methodology, some serious questions. Who are these officers? What questions did Sweezy ask them? What did they reply? And most important of all, why rely on informal interviews when we have the systematic interviews with bank trust officers carried out by the SEC Institutional Investor Study available? Is Sweezy even aware they exist?

Investigators from the Institutional Investor Study contacted officers from 215 institutional investors including the largest bank trust departments. These officials were asked specifically whether or not their institutions "participated" in the corporate management of portfolio companies.[26] Most officers refused to answer, citing as grounds possible self-incrimination.[27] Nevertheless, some submitted anonymous responses that constituted valuable admissions: one officer argued strongly against the idea that banks remain aloof from participation in management:

> If . . . an institutional investor finds himself locked into a position, for whatever reason, where he considers the management is failing to meet its responsibilities, then he has a duty, as both a shareholder and a fiduciary, to do

---

26. "Institutional 'participation' is defined to include any contacts between representatives of the institution and the portfolio company, regardless of by whom initiated, in which the institution expresses its views as to what corporate management should do. It does not include ordinary contacts between securities analysts and companies or contacts by common directors." The term also excludes views expressed in the institution's capacity as a creditor or in any other non-shareholder role. Securities and Exchange Commission, *Institutional Investor Study*, vol. 2, ch. 15, p. 2755.

27. The study says, "Institutions are particularly sensitive to questions concerning joint participation by a group of institutions with common objectives. Existing antitrust laws and the 1968 tender offer provisions in the Exchange Act appear to have the effect of impeding frank discussion of concerted action by institutions, if not of precluding such actions." Ibid., p. 2760.

whatever he can properly to induce the management to improve its handling of the company.

It is believed that most involvements in portfolio company affairs should be limited to the voting of shares. However this is the point of view of a relatively small holder of shares in a given situation. From the standpoint of the public interest, generally there seems to us to be no reason why there should not be "participation" in corporate affairs, wholly aside from the voting of shares, where the interest is substantial or where the issues at stake seem to call for action. . . .

If we found ourselves in a position with respect to a substantial interest in a portfolio company's stock where a management decision would unquestionably diminish the value of our stock, we would make our voice heard and take whatever action seemed appropriate to protect our trust.[28]

Another officer went even further. He not only admitted involvement, but admitted that such involvement could lead to conflicts of interests similar to the ones we described in "Who Rules the Corporations?":

We believe that some of the more difficult problems arising from institutional ownership of common stocks arise when there are relationships between the institution and the portfolio company other than the ownership of the common stock itself. For example where a bank is also a lender, a depository and an investor in the common stock of a portfolio company, involvement in management decisions of the portfolio company is, on the one hand, *almost inevitable* (arising from the bank's lending relationship) but questions can arise as to whether such involvement reflects the viewpoint of the lender or the common stockholder. Another example is where an investment banking firm having a relationship with a company finds itself in the role of a large common stock investor in the company, whether as a conduit for others or for its own account. We do not suggest that the answer lies in disenfranchising the commercial bank or the investment

---

28. Ibid., pp. 2758-59.

banker. We simply identify the situation of dual relationships as one deserving of primary attention.

Another area of concern is the possible use of institutional assets as a resource of investment banking firms interested in the promotion of mergers and other acquisitions. We do not allege that this is happening but the possibility of abuse seems clearly to be there.[29]

The Institutional Investor Study did not, however, limit its investigation to an analysis of what the big institutional investors say about themselves. It made a study of bank involvement in corporate transfers involving 109 companies. Many of the cases were identical to ones we cited in "Who Rules the Corporations?" In the 1960s, as the study shows, there were substantial amounts of money to be made by the banks in arranging corporate transfers of control. Such a transfer, of course, constitutes the highest exercise of corporate control. And well-documented cases would seem to constitute proof of corporate control of a reasonably high order. We cited case studies of this type and got this reply from Sweezy:

> The question for F&O to answer is not whether bankers sit on corporate boards or whether corporations borrow from banks: of course they do. The question is whether these activities confer corporate control on banks and bankers. And here F&O contribute speculations, reiterated assertions, and an assortment of stories about individual cases which may or may not be relevant to the point at issue but which absolutely do not form a valid basis for any generalizations.

According to Sweezy, we offer "not a single case of a demonstrated causal link between bank trust holdings and corporate control." What about the case we cited involving the Cleveland Trust? In that case, let us recall, the Justice Department charged the Cleveland Trust with violating Sections 7 and 8 of the Clayton Act by its holding and voting of stock in four major tool manufacturers: Acme-Cleveland, Pneumo-Dynamics Corp., Warner-Swasey Co., and White Consolidated Industries, Inc.[30] Cleveland Trust holdings were the following: Warner-

29. Ibid., p. 2758. Emphasis added.
30. U.S. v. Cleveland Trust, 3/31/70 (ATRR) #455, A-13.

SWEEZY AND CORPORATE FETISHISM   121

Swasey, the largest manufacturer of automatic screw machinery, 11 per cent; Acme-Cleveland, third largest, 27 per cent; Pneumo-Dynamics, fourth largest, 14 per cent; White Consolidated, seventh largest, 5 per cent. The Justice Department denied the Cleveland Trust's contention that it held the stock "solely for investment." (The Clayton Act expressly permits corporations to hold stock in other corporations if they do so "solely for investment.") According to the Justice Department, *"the Cleveland Trust consistently exercises the voting rights to these shares of stock to elect directors, and to influence important management and policy decisions."* In addition, the complaint avers, Cleveland Trust *"does substantial business with each of the four toolmakers"* (emphasis added).

Aside from the case of Cleveland Trust, one of the best case studies on bank trust department control of portfolio companies' stock comes from Sweezy himself. Quoting *Business Week*'s account of Leasco Data's attempt to take over the Chemical Bank, a *Monthly Review* "Review of the Month" reads: "Wall Street's choicest gossip for weeks has dealt with what happened during those fifteen days (in February 1969) or what it thinks happened. . . . One thing that did happen was that Leasco's stock plunged from 140 to 106 in two weeks— driven down, many on Wall Street believe, as bank trust departments sold what Leasco shares they held." Leasco's customers threatened to take their business elsewhere. "Investment banker Lehman Bros.," the article continues, "admits that it was pressured by commercial banks not to help Leasco—a ticklish situation since Lehman is a heavy borrower of bank money."

The nation's big banks, rocked by the thought of one of their number being taken over, did cluster to create what one banker calls "a massive groundswell of opposition that was felt in Washington and Albany. The whole industry was aghast." [31]

It's strange indeed that Sweezy overlooks not only our case studies, but those in his own magazine. Yet he insists that "any well-trained social scientist must recognize as flimsy and sophistical" the evidence we present. But on the basis of much

31. *Monthly Review*, June 1969, p. 17.

122   ROBERT FITCH

the same evidence involving the same case studies, the SEC Institutional Investor Study concludes as follows:

"Institutions with large holdings or the economic power to
acquire such holdings could be and often were major forces in
the determination of the outcome of such [transfer] efforts.
While, as noted in prior sections of this chapter, institutions
are disposed to be somewhat passive in ordinary management
decisions, their participation in contested take-overs was often
active and crucial. This appears to result from the fact that
unlike ordinary questions of corporate policy, participation in
corporate take-overs afforded to the institutions involved opportunities for immediate profit from the effects upon the
market of such efforts." [32]

The team that produced this study included nine SEC
economists, three consultants, twelve financial analysts, six
lawyers, and twenty computer specialists. The commission
was headed by men such as William C. Freund, chief economist of the New York Stock Exchange; Charles Buek, president of the U.S. Trust Co.; John C. Whitehead, a partner in
Goldman, Sachs & Co.; Alfred P. Johnson, economist of the
Investment Company Institute; and Robert M. Loeffler, senior
vice president of Investors Diversified Services, the world's
largest mutual fund complex.

There are several reasons that explain why these conservative bankers, economists and lawyers arrived at many of the
same conclusions we did about the role of financial institutions in corporate control. The best reason, however, is that
financial institutions really do make big profits from controlling corporate shares. These profits, as one can easily imagine,
will buy sufficient amounts of aspirin to relieve the throbbing
headaches suffered by Sweezy's bashful bankers. [33]

32. *Institutional Investor Study*, vol. 2, ch. 15, p. 2847.
33. Speaking of bankers, Sweezy makes this aside regarding our comparison of bank stock holdings and bank power to the Age of Morgan. "One
of the most distressing—and for me depressing—aspects of the Fitch/
Oppenheimer study is that they show no awareness, not to say understanding, of the qualitative changes which have characterized the history
of monopoly capitalism and of which the First National story is only one
example." The story Sweezy tells of the First National—one of the First
National City Bank's predecessors—is accurate enough when he sticks

V. BARAN AND SWEEZY ON PROFITS

I HAVE NO INTENTION of "refuting" every one of Sweezy's
criticisms or of maintaining that no mistakes exist in our work.
Certainly in his section on profits, Sweezy has made two valid
points. First he points out that we were mistaken in claiming
that the business cycle turned in 1965. He is absolutely correct. The business cycle really turned in 1966: a mistake we
also noticed and rectified in a subsequent issue of *Socialist
Revolution.*[34]

Second, and more seriously, Sweezy maintains that we have
distorted his position on the tendency for profits to rise. It
was our guess that the source of his view that the percentage
of internal funds available to corporations had increased over
time, lay in a belief that the rate of profits had increased in a
linear way. We said that the "unarticulated premise of Sweezy
and Baran's account of corporate finance is the invulnerability
of monopoly profits."

It is clear to me now after re-reading *Monopoly Capital* that
this is a one-sided interpretation. Sweezy does think profits
can fall. Our mistake was not malicious, however. Why label it,
as Sweezy does, a "shameless distortion"? The statement in
Monopoly Capital that served as the basis of our mistake reads
as follows:

> The whole motivation of cost reduction is to increase
> profits, and the monopolistic structure of markets en-
> ables the corporations to appropriate the lion's share of

to the period he is familiar with—the 1930s and before. He says about
the First National that its directors "sat on dozens of corporate boards,
usually alongside Morgan men, and no one in Wall Street was in any
doubt about their power." Now there is, according to Sweezy, a "new
style of banking which predominates today." Undoubtedly so; the banking world is, as Sweezy says, more bureaucratized and relies more on the
savings of workers and middle-class people. But this has altered the
power relationships between the banks and the corporations less than
Sweezy seems to think. Citibank still sits on dozens of boards—one
hundred and five to be exact—and holds five per cent or more of the
stock of eighty-eight corporations. And still has Morgan directors sitting
next to it on the boards of giant corporations. To take a few examples:
AT&T, General Motors, Ford Motor Company, Standard Oil of New
Jersey, General Electric, U.S. Steel.
34. No. 7, p. 163.

the fruits of increasing productivity directly in the form of higher profits. This means that under monopoly capitalism, declining costs imply aggregate profits which rise not only absolutely but as a share of national product. (p. 71.)

Needless to say, however, this admission on our part does nothing to strengthen Sweezy's theory of internal finance, for which no empirical evidence exists whatsoever, or his theory of corporate control, for which he has produced none.

VI. SWEEZY'S CONCLUSIONS

SWEEZY SAVES FOR LAST his own answer to the question, "Who Rules the Corporations?" Here's how he attempts to deal with it:

"In conclusion, I should like to return briefly to the question which Fitch and Oppenheimer pose at the outset: Who *does* rule the corporation? The best short answer, I think, is that *monopoly capital* rules the corporations, including not only industrials and utilities but also banks and other profit-making financial institutions."

Now if this seems a bit abstract, Sweezy does have a definition of monopoly capital. "This is what I mean," says Sweezy, "when I say that monopoly capital rules the corporations: monopoly capital is the economic category personified by the individuals who happen to sit in the executive suites and boardrooms of America's giant corporations."

The broad sweep of this generalization cannot hide its painful circularity. Here is the chain of Sweezy's reasoning:

Q. Who rules the corporation?

A. Monopoly capital rules the corporation.

Q. What is monopoly capital?

A. The individuals who rule the corporation.

Evidently the people who rule the corporation, rule the corporation. This much was never really in dispute. But we might hope for a more substantial answer.

But so much for Sweezy's positive contribution to the debate. He returns to his methodological criticism by observing that we are revisionists of Marx. He arrives at this charge by imputing to us the views that:

1. the pursuit of financial profit is distinct from the pursuit of industrial profit;

2. there exists a split between financial and industrial capitalists in which the finance capitalists have the advantage; and

3. the financial bourgeoisie tries to win financial profits even if this results in a reduction of the total pool of surplus value available for the capitalist class as a whole.

From these observations Sweezy draws the conclusion that we believe the contradictions between the various strata of the bourgeoisie are deeper than those between the workers and the bourgeoisie.

We don't hold the premise, which is silly enough: we never argued that the pursuit of financial profit is *distinct* from the pursuit of industrial profit, but that it can be "partially dissociated," a claim that is established every time the stock market turns down, or gyrates wildly upward.[35]

As for the notion that we believe that conflict between workers and bosses is less profound than conflict between the strata of the bourgeoisie, Sweezy has simply invented it.

Perhaps most ironic of all, though, is that Sweezy thinks the idea "revisionist" that the financial bourgeoisie maximizes its profits even if this reduces surplus value as a whole. "Talk about centralization!" wrote Marx in volume 3 of *Capital*, "The credit system which has its focus in the so-called national banks and the big money lenders and usurers surrounding them constitutes enormous centralization, and gives to this

---

35. In fact we specifically repudiate the premise Sweezy attributes to us: "Just as production must contribute to sales and sales to industrial profits, so too industrial profits must contribute to the appropriation of financial profits by the corporate oligarchs. Specifically they must contribute to the appreciation of common stock values; to increasing flows of dividends; to larger commissions for investment bankers; and to larger interest payments accruing to commercial bankers. The key point here is that the pursuit of financial profits can be partially dissociated from the pursuit of industrial profit. Dividends, for example, can be increased without a proportionate increase in industrial profits—even, perhaps, at the expense of future industrial profitability." *Socialist Revolution* 6, p. 42.

class of parasites the fabulous power not only to despoil industrial capitalists periodically, but also to interfere in actual production in a most dangerous manner—and this gang knows
nothing about production and has nothing to do with it."

Whether this passage makes a "revisionist" of Marx, we will
leave to the judgment of those who specialize in such matters.

VII. CONCLUSION

WE HAVE ESTABLISHED that corporations are controlled by
capitalists working through financial institutions. And it is not
these corporations that constitute the basic units of the system, but individual units of capital. To see the corporation as
in any way independent of the interests of the owners of
capital—who nearly always constitute a small cohesive group
however large their share of the common stock may be—is to
be victimized by a form of fetishism. Overcoming this fetishism is the beginning of understanding modern business organization.

One of the most important inferences that we have been
able to draw from the recognition of the primacy of individual
capitals over the corporation as the decisive unit in the economy is that individual corporations do not necessarily maximize profits. What is really being maximized is the return on
various forms of capital by capitalists. Realizing gain on one
type of capital frequently results in a loss for another type
within the same corporate framework. And the final result
may be a net capital loss. All corporate actions, e.g., sales and
purchases of assets, dividend policy, decisions about capital
structure, have to be analyzed in terms of the controlling persons to find out who benefits and who loses. And it's time
socialists and workers began to take these issues out of the
boardroom and into the community. How a utility company
decides, for example, to finance its expansion will affect not
only the company's profits, but also the air we breathe, the
rates we pay and the kind of service we get. If it can be shown,
for example, that the company's recourse to the bond market
has benefited its investment bankers at the expense of its balance sheet, this can constitute powerful anti-capitalist propa-

ganda. It shows that the bourgeoisie breaks its own rules and can't be trusted with the property it controls. And unlike protests for higher wages for particular groups, which can never transcend the system, criticism of this type points to another system, socialism, which alone can meet the needs of the community without exploiting its members. It points to control of society's assets by the only class that is capable of managing them without exploitation—the working class.

Our analysis of reciprocity exposes another area in which corporations violate their own criteria of efficiency. A significant number of corporations are compelled to buy and sell at prices that do not maximize their profits. This means that capitalism is far less efficient than its ideologists have allowed. The charge leveled at socialism by Von Mises and others, that there is no rational basis for prices, turns out to be true not of socialism, but of modern capitalism itself! In place of rational prices that allocate resources efficiently and democratically, we are left with a price system that constitutes nothing more than a rudimentary and regressive planning mechanism by and for the financial bourgeoisie.

As a whole, I do not consider "Who Rules the Corporations?" to be definitive, nor do I make any claim to infallibility. Some of the generalizations, especially those on accumulation and the broader tendencies of the system, are already being modified by myself and others. But an empirical foundation has been created that can help socialists and workers to see beyond the wooden abstractions and flickering shadows of the corporation and the capitalist class that have prevailed for too long on the American left. Consequently I have undertaken to reply to Sweezy at such length to ensure that this is not obscured.

Index